...DISCOVER...
NOVA SCOTIA
THE ULTIMATE NATURE GUIDE

GARY L SAUNDERS

Co-published by
The Nova Scotia Museum
and Nimbus Publishing Limited

Produced as part of the Tourism Nova Scotia and Nova Scotia Museum programs of the Department of Tourism and Culture, Province of Nova Scotia.

Minister: Honourable Rodney MacDonald
Deputy Minister: Michele McKenzie

Co-published by the Nova Scotia Museum and Nimbus Publishing

A product of the Nova Scotia Government co-publishing program.

Nimbus Publishing Limited
PO Box 9166
Halifax, NS   B3K 5M8
(902) 455-4286

Printed and bound in Canada

CANADIAN CATALOGUING
IN PUBLICATION DATA

Saunders, Gary
Discover Nova Scotia: the ultimate nature guide

Co-published by the province of Nova Scotia.
Includes bibliographical references and index.
ISBN 1-55109-242-5

1. Automobile travel-Nova Scotia-Guidebooks. 2. Natural history-Nova Scotia-Guidebooks. 3. Nova Scotia-Guidebooks. I. Nova Scotia. II. Title.

FC2307.S38 2001   917.1604'4   C2001-900347-1
F1037.7.S38 2001

Canadä   The Canada Council | Le Conseil des Arts
            for the Arts | du Canada

We acknowledge the financial support of the Government of Canada through the Book Publishing Industry Development Program (BPIDP) and the Canada Council for our publishing activities.

Contents

Acknowledgements

A book like this is like a solo stage performance with many helpers in the wings. Let me single out a few:

Sue Browne, who conducted research and fieldwork of her own and enhanced my text with insightful commentary.

The Nova Scotia Museum's Debra Burleson and John Hennigar-Shuh, who let me tap the expertise of Marion Zinck, Scott Robson and digital mapmaker Kevin McGrath.

Etta Moffatt, designer par excellence.

Photographers Paul Shields, Richard Plander and Roger Lloyd. Thanks to them, my book is handsomer than it might have been.

Howard Donohoe of the Department of Natural Resources, who checked the geological content.

For valued input from their diverse disciplines: Myrna Blenkhorn, David L. Carter, Anne Chapman, Les Corkum, A.W. Davidson, John Elliott, Wally Ellison, Tonia Endres, the late Ron Harper, Patricia Haylock, Eric Georgeson, Merritt Gibson, Bob Guscott, Brian Kinsman, Dirk Van Loon, Sheena Masson, Paul McCulloch, Dianne Nickerson, Neil Van Nostrand, Jean and Ed Raymond, Max Spicer, Robert Utaro and Bert Vissers.

Eric Robeson, a friend indeed in any computer crisis.

For writerly support during medical interruptions: Jane Buss, Susan Atkinson-Keen, Eric Facey, Jeff Joudrey, Susan Kerslake, Allison Mitcham, David Quinton and David Taylor.

Finally, the Nova Scotia Department of Tourism and Culture for their vote of confidence in awarding me the grant that paid my first year's gas and oil.

And any I've forgotten. Thank you all.

Before You Begin

HOW TO USE THIS BOOK

Most highway travel guides tell us what to look at, where to eat and shop, and where to sleep. Few tell us how Nova Scotia came to look the way it does and how we may read its thousand landscapes. This book tries to do that. Its theme is the roadside landscape, backdrop to our travels, the tapestry of rocks, rivers, lakes, trees, wildlife, clouds, and human activity that is the warp and weft of scenery.

Trillium

The first part of the guide starts you off with an overview of the natural landscape of Nova Scotia and the plants and animals you may encounter. There is also a glossary of terms that may be unfamiliar. The margins of these sections are shaded so you can refer back to them easily. The main part of the guide is an interpretive narrative for the Trans Canada Highway, Highway 102 from Truro to Halifax, the 10 tourist travelways, four scenic drives, and numerous side roads. The text is salted with local history, natural oddities, quotations, and things to do and see; cross-references help readers compare examples of similar geology, flora, or fauna from route to route. And, because car travel can be wearisome, there are suggestions for stops and walks.

A guidebook is meant to be carried in your glove compartment, your windbreaker pocket, your knapsack—to be used. That said, it is a good idea to preview the text of your intended route. If you have passengers, appoint a narrator-navigator to read and interpret for you. It's also a good idea to keep dated notes of what you discover, preferably in a journal. And remember, this book is only an appetizer. Before heading out, arm yourself for the topics that interest you most. Good, inexpensive field guides exist for everything from sea slugs to galaxies.

FINDING YOUR WAY

Standard road maps are okay for highway travel, but contour maps show actual landforms. Buy a current copy of *A Map of the Province of Nova Scotia,* or obtain National Topographic maps for areas of particular interest.

Don't hesitate to ask for directions. Most Nova Scotians enjoy talking to interested travellers. It's a courtesy from our rural past, when co-operation meant survival. While you're at it, ask older residents about local history, natural and unnatural. They know things too numerous for a book such as this.

THE KEY
to the maps in this book:

	Trans Canada Highway
	Nova Scotia 100 – Series highways
	Secondary road
+++++++	Railway line
	Ocean, lakes and ponds
	Rivers and streams
⊓⊓⊓⊓	Dykes
	Park
🚶	Hiking
🛶	Canoeing
⌂	Camping
	Picnic area
	Point of interest
•	Town or village
	Urban area
	Conservation area
⊛	True North

DRESSING FOR THE WEATHER

Springtime in Nova Scotia tends to be cloudy, cool, and moist. July and August can occasionally bring 30°C temperatures, but sea breezes temper most afternoons, and the temperature can be 5° cooler where winds blow onshore. Coastal fog is common along the Atlantic and Fundy shores, moving in at night and off by noon on sunny days. Autumn offers crisp sunny afternoons and frosty nights.

The only constant of the weather here is its changeability. The best advice is to be prepared for change. Bring sturdy footgear (preferably waterproof), a change of socks, a sweater, and a poncho or rain suit. And UV rays are a danger even in our moderate climes. Don't forget your sunscreen, hat, and sunglasses.

LAND ETIQUETTE

Nova Scotia has the highest percentage of freehold (private) land in mainland Canada—about 75 per cent. Most of this is in small farms and woodlots, which means that every time you travel any distance from a public road, stream, or beach, you could be trespassing. Most landowners are lenient, but ask permission anyway.

Never block side roads. Leave gates as you find them—open or shut. If a woods road looks muddy or rutted, don't drive in and have to be towed out. Respect owners' rights, and they'll return the favour.

OUTDOOR ETHICS

"Take in, take out, leave only footprints." Today everyone knows this rule, but of course there's much more to it than tidiness.

Camping

Most forest fires are caused by people. Forego the pleasure of an open campfire unless you're in a camping park with proper grills or it's a matter of survival (e.g., hypothermia, signal fires; even then, douse the coals afterward with plenty of water if you're in a wooded area). Cook with propane or naphtha.

Buy and use only environmentally-friendly products and discard any residues safely. At the beach, never leave six-pack rings or plastic bags where gulls or seals can swallow them.

Don't cut brush to sleep on, except in an emergency; carry an air mattress instead.

Wildlife

See that no one in your group harasses or harms wildlife, whether gulls, eagles, or ladybird beetles. Refrain from handling or "rescuing" baby animals that seem lost or abandoned; mother moose and sow bears in particular resent this. Nine times out of ten the babies are okay, and in any case, it's against the law. Give a wide berth to bull moose and buck deer during the September/October mating season.

Obey all signs protecting nesting sites (e.g., eagles, piping plovers), fragile dunes, and rare plants or animals. Don't feed wild or caged animals. And of course, don't store food where you sleep unless it's in a covered container, at least.

Collecting
Flowers are a plant's way of reproducing. It's okay to pluck a few leaves for identification, but picking or digging up flowers is wrong, unless they're obviously abundant. With fossils, you're free to gather any lying on the shore, but those embedded in cliffs are out of bounds without a special permit.

SAFETY
Nothing ruins a hiking or camping trip faster than people or pets getting lost or injured or soaked or stranded or stung or otherwise incapacitated. A full-scale rescue can cost thousands of dollars, hundreds of volunteer hours—and sometimes other lives. A few precautions can usually avert such happenings.

Fundy mud

Woods Survival
Nova Scotia law requires that anyone travelling in the woods carry (a) matches (waterproofed or in a waterproof container), (b) a compass (know how to use it), and (c) an axe or strong sheath knife.

Include a sheet of light plastic for emergency shelter and some hard candy or chocolate for quick energy. (Hardware stores sell pocket kits for a few dollars.)

TIP: In dry weather shiny (moist) shoreline mud means the tide has recently fallen; dull (dry) mud means it has been out for some hours and may return soon.

First Aid Kit
Despite the best precautions, accidents will happen. Carry at least a basic kit (bandages and tape, aspirin, disinfectant, antibiotic salve, a first aid manual), and know how to use them.

Waves
Nearly every year someone is washed off a cliff in Nova Scotia. Remember that ocean surf comes in rhythmic patterns of smaller and larger waves. The big ones reach much farther up the beach, collapse with more force, and draw back with a more powerful undertow. Standing at the small-wave limit makes you a prime target for the next big one.

Tides
Fundy tides can be deceptive and dangerous, especially at new and full moon. They have trapped many unwary clammers, beachcombers, hikers, and rockhounds. A few have spent six uncomfortable hours stranded on some cliff face; a few have drowned.

Low tide

Before venturing out on the flats, check local tide times with a newspaper, radio station, or tourist bureau, or ask a knowledgeable

7

resident. Going out on a falling tide allows you six full hours before it returns. If you don't know the tide schedule or how long the tide has been out, expect it back sooner than you think.

Cliffs

Keep away from cliff edges, especially in windy weather. Avoid walking under crumbling rock faces or directly under other climbers. They may accidentally dislodge rockfalls. If working under cliffs, wear a hard hat. If breaking rocks with a hammer, wear safety goggles. Don't rock-climb unless properly equipped—and never climb alone.

Wildlife

Heed those deer and moose crossing signs. From dawn to dusk drive 10–20 km/hr slower in those areas. As poachers know, bright lights daze these animals. Even a 100-kg (220-lb) white-tail can wreck a car. Should a deer or moose stop in the middle of the road, pull over, douse your headlights (but leave flashers on), and wait a while. The animal will usually make up its mind and amble off.

Poison ivy

Poison Ivy

For poison ivy lesions, old-timers got relief by scrubbing them with the crushed leaves of white ash.

"Leaves three, let it be," runs the folk rhyme. It's a good rule to follow in poison ivy country, for this small, three-leafed vine or shrub (*Rhus* spp) contains an oil that's intensely irritating to one in every two humans. Some are so allergic they get a nasty rash from its airborne pollen, or just from standing in the smoke of its burning leaves (which incidentally turn red in autumn). Pets can brush the irritant onto humans.

Fortunately poison ivy is not abundant here. Still, be watchful around thickets, open woods, roadsides, sand dunes, and damp areas. If you or someone in your party touches the plant, *immediately wash the affected skin with laundry soap and warm water.* If this is impossible contact a doctor.

Insects

Pretty tourist pictures never show the mosquitoes, black flies, no-see-ums, deer flies, and moose flies that assail people from May to August. None of these two-winged insects is dangerous (unless one is severely allergic), but they will take a blood meal if you give them a chance.

Tansy is an old-time insect repellent that will keep flies away for 10 minutes or so. If you prefer not to use a commercial product, try rubbing all exposed skin with crushed tansy leaves. This aromatic plant was likely brought to Nova Scotia by Acadian settlers.

All are attracted by the smell of CO_2 (in our breath) and by normal sweat. Perfume, cologne, after-shave lotion, and fragrant bath soaps seem to draw them too. By avoiding these, and not wearing bright clothing, you may escape some bites. One can wear protective netting, but it's cumbersome, hard to see through, and easy to rip. The only effective deterrent is fly dope. Choose a reputable brand and keep it in your purse or pack whenever you leave the vehicle in fly season. Be sure to follow directions.

Finally, *always* tell someone where you're going and when you expect to return.

The Nature of Nova Scotia

OVERVIEW

Nova Scotia is like a great ship docked off eastern
North America, its low rounded stern sheltering
southern New Brunswick, its high rugged prow
aimed at Newfoundland. The frigid North Atlantic
pounds its eastern coast, westward lies the tide-
churned Fundy, northward the sheltered Northumberland Strait. This ship looks vastly old and battle-
scarred. Its deck tilts south and east, and along its
starboard side the sea has invaded the valleys. Long
curving cracks score the surface, as if the plates had
been buckled by ancient collisions, then welded back
together. In places the naked framework shows
through. Rusty waters wash the Fundy side.

Cliffs at Cape d'Or

Geologically Nova Scotia is almost an island. Only
the slim Isthmus of Chignecto keeps it from being so.
Yet it is big enough to contain a diversity of landscape
and a diversity of weather, flora, and fauna. Moreover,
it has had an exciting past. When ancestral North
America and North Africa collided 400 million years
ago during the formation of the supercontinent Pangaea, Nova Scotia
was trapped in the middle. It became part of the Appalachian chain,
the system of lofty mountains born of that collision.

In the aftermath, molten rock welled up from the Earth's mantle,
baking the older Meguma formations, flooring the province's southern half with hard crystalline rock. Other fireworks had already
welded Cape Breton together. Then for ages the future province
broiled under a tropical sun that evaporated its inland seas, leaving
deep deposits of salt and gypsum. For ages it had steaming jungles of
giant ferns, mosses, and horsetails, which in time turned to coal.
Meanwhile, erosion reduced the mountains to sand, silt, and mud,
filling the lowlands with softer sedimentary rock.

Some 200 million years ago, Pangaea rifted apart and the North
Atlantic began to form; cracks and rift valleys developed. Lava poured
out, creating features still visible today. In the last 80 million years of
relative calm, weather and water have reduced the softer lowlands
nearly to sea level and left the flinty uplands standing like hard knots
in a worn old schoolhouse floor.

Then, starting 75,000 years ago—only yesterday in Earth time—
the latest in a series of ice sheets bevelled the hills, gouged the valleys,
and scattered gravel and boulders everywhere, creating the landscape
we see today.

9

An Accident of Sea Level

Nova Scotia's shape on a map is not a permanent feature. Should the sea fall 100 metres (328 ft), that shape would change dramatically, and its area would more than double. This is because the province sits on a submerged platform or continental shelf. The shelf has an underwater landscape consisting of hills and valleys. The higher ridges have names like Banquereau, Western, LaHave, and Baccaro—the fishing banks. The water over them is seldom deeper than 200 m/650 ft. The outermost of these ridges is Sable Island. Beyond it the shelf plunges to depths beyond 4 km/2.5 mi. During the last Ice Age, much of the continental shelf was dry land. We know it was because draggers have hauled up pine stumps with soil still attached.

Today the land is pretty stable. But the sea, helped perhaps by global warming, is still inching up, undermining Mahone Bay's gravel islands, eroding Atlantic Shore headlands, and forcing owners of Fundy and North Shore cottages to shift them landward.

Vital Stats

The smallest mainland province at 55 490 km²/21,425 sq mi, Nova Scotia is twice the size of Vancouver Island and half the size of Tennessee. It is centred on the 45th parallel of latitude, which puts Yarmouth on a level with Toronto and upstate New York.

The province is nearly as long as Florida (roughly 550 km/340 mi) and so narrow that one is never more than 56 km/35 mi from the ocean. A kayaker who followed every curve of its coast would paddle some 7 450 kilometres (4,625 miles). A motorist who drove every road would log over 25 000 km (15,000 mi).

The human population hovers near 900,000. This means that each resident has about 6 hectares (15 acres) to roam in. New Jersey's eight million citizens have 1/25 that much.

Between the mid-1600s and the 1960s about 80 per cent of Nova Scotia's wetlands were drained for agriculture. Since the 1970s, government and private agencies have restored many of these, notably around Amherst.

A Wealth of Wet

Fully 5 per cent of Nova Scotia's surface—an area nearly as big as Rhode Island—is fresh water. The province boasts 1,500 lakes of 25 ha/62 ac or larger. Except for Lake Rossignol, Shubenacadie Grand Lake, and Lake Ainslie, most are small. On the granitic Southern Upland many are naturally acidic, a condition worsened by acid precipitation from New England. As a result, fish cannot live in some of them.

Many of our streams follow ancient faults or Earth cracks. Since these run mostly at right angles to the coast and the peninsula is narrow, our rivers are short. This, together with a shortage of large headwater lakes, causes many to run low in summer. Our biggest watersheds are the St Marys, Shubenacadie–Grand Lake, and Annapolis-Cornwallis systems.

Apart from abundant lakes and streams, we are

Salt marsh

blessed with lots of wetland, both tidal and fresh. The major tidal marshes occur south of Amherst and around the Annapolis and Minas basins. Others lie along Northumberland Strait and, on the Atlantic shore, around Yarmouth, Petpeswick, Cole Harbour, and Boylston.

The biggest freshwater wetlands are on Cape Breton Island. Other bogs occur east of Amherst, south of the Noel Shore, near Aylesford in the Annapolis Valley, and throughout the western interior.

These days people have more respect for bogs and marshes. We now know that they regulate surface runoff, reduce erosion, stabilize water tables, and filter pollutants from groundwater. They also provide vital habitat for everything from minute crustaceans to huge moose. Tidal marshes also serve as nurseries for marine fish too tiny to survive in the open ocean.

Nova Scotia Weather: A Forecaster's Nightmare

Situated halfway between the Equator and the North Pole and squeezed between a vast continent and a vast ocean, Nova Scotia gets weather from four worlds. Ocean air is moist; continental air dry. Ocean air is mild; continental air can be bitterly cold. This is a recipe for unsettled weather.

But because the province is nearly an island, most of its weather bears an ocean imprint. The chilly Labrador Current bathes its north-eastern parts, sometimes filling Sydney Harbour and vicinity with drift ice—hence the name Glace Bay. Occasionally it conveys drift ice as far south as Halifax, as it did in 1943 and 1987. Conversely, the Gulf Stream comes within 50 km/30 mi of the South Shore, bringing balmy air from Mexico and Florida and sometimes tropical turtles and fish. The mingling of these cold and warm air masses brews fog offshore and wind, snow, and rain inland. Also helping to stir the weather pot are temperature differences between the tide-churned Bay of Fundy and the protected and warmish Northumberland Strait.

Late Springs, Late Autumns

Water is by nature slow to heat and slow to cool. In spring our coastal waters are at their chilliest; it takes all summer to warm them. Once heated, however, they hold the warmth for several months. This explains why Midsummer's Day (June 21) still finds our weather cool, and why our coldest weather comes well after Christmas. Many a garden is blackened by hard frost in June, while November can smile with "Indian Summer".

For the same reason, our winters are generally mild with several thaws and ice storms. Lowland snowfall accumulations tend to be moderate, but snow in the Cape Breton Highlands can reach depths of 3 m/10 ft.

Each autumn one or more tropical storms may lash our shores. Having spent their fury farther south, however, most do little damage. Notable exceptions were Hurricanes Carol and Edna (1953 and 1954), which flattened large tracts of old forest, especially south-

Sometimes out on the Bay of Fundy when the fog comes in thick, you can sit on the boat's rail and lean your back up agin' it. So that's pretty thick fog out there. But you gotta be careful 'cause if the fog lifts quick, you'll fall overboard.
—Nova Scotia sailor quoted in **Scotia/Fundy Marine Weather Guide**

The frost-free growing season of Yarmouth and the Annapolis Valley is a month longer than northern Cape Breton's.

11

facing slopes. Tree-ring analysis shows that such gales tend to follow a cyclic pattern. Naturalist Titus Smith, Jr and others noted big blows in 1650, 1700–10, 1790, 1820, and 1870–80 (including the Saxby Gale of 1869—see **Glooscap Trail** at Nappan, **Evangeline Trail** at Grand Pré).

THE DYNAMICS OF LANDSCAPE
Landscapes don't just happen. Every scene is the result of geological processes spun out over unimaginable spans of time. Understanding those processes helps explain why landscapes (and seascapes) look the way they do.

Bones of the Earth
Just as bone structure helps make a friend's face unique, so bedrock shapes most of the landforms around us. This is obvious along the seacoast, not so obvious inland. Yet under every square metre of Nova Scotia, including its lakes, there is bedrock, bulging up in hills, dipping down in valleys, holding water and bogs in its hollows. And from this foundation comes the basic material for soil.

Soil: The Earth's Skin
All life on dry land depends on a fragile film of loose earth averaging only 25 cm/10 in thick. Soil sustains our forests, crops, livestock, and the teeming life of our marshes and mud flats—even of our offshore fishing grounds. The very water we drink is stored in bedrock and soil. Fortunately, most of Nova Scotia is mantled by this life-giving substance. In places it is deep and fertile (e.g., Stewiacke and Annapolis valleys). In other places there's hardly enough to hide a worm (e.g., Shelburne and Canso Barrens).

Yellow Fungi

Brown lichen

Soil starts with rock. When bedrock is exposed to weathering and/or glaciation and to the activity of bacteria, algae and lichens, rock dust is produced. Mulched by their dead bodies, colonized by mosses and liverworts and finally seed plants, then further mulched by fallen leaves and animal droppings, it becomes true soil. As fungi and other bacteria break down the humus, they are joined by invertebrates such as earthworms, millipedes, and springtails. Slowly the blended minerals and humus develop a layered profile. This profile differs under forest, field, and swamp; but certain elements are fairly constant.

Texture

Soils can be fine or coarse, well drained or swampy. The kind of bedrock or parent material they are derived from is important. Granitic soils are by nature less fertile than shale-derived (clay) soils. In addition, too much sand makes a soil arid, and too much clay makes it sticky and ill-drained.

Fertility

Some soils won't grow anything but lichens (e.g., roadside gravels, Cape Breton Highlands). Others are fertile enough to grow wild blueberries (e.g., glacial gravels near Parrsboro), but won't grow vegetables. Deep outwash deposits (e.g., Truro, Antigonish) can support pastures, gardens, and good mixedwood forest. The fertile loams of river intervales (e.g., Stewiacke Valley) can support lofty elms and lush garden crops.

The most important factor is the presence of humus—plant and animal material in various stages of decay—in the upper horizons. Humus holds moisture, reduces erosion, and fosters "good" bacteria and fungi and invertebrates. Mixed with rock dust (clay, silt, sand), it produces that magical substance called topsoil. If you've ever tried to start a lawn on new landfill, you know how important topsoil is.

To build 2.5 cm (1 in) of good topsoil, nature takes on average 500 years. To destroy it takes only one deep-burning forest fire, one poor road-building job, or a few years of careless farming. Soil conservation is the most basic form of earthkeeping.

pH

Old-time farmers, lacking litmus paper, tasted soil to see if it was sweet or sour. Sour meant acidic (low pH), sweet meant slightly alkaline (medium pH). The cure for sour soil was and is to add lime (calcium), which releases essential soil nutrients. For this reason farmers quarried and burned lime (e.g., Lime Rock, Pictou County). Some plants tolerate highly alkaline conditions (e.g., gypsum outcrops), but too much calcium or potash can also stunt growth.

Erratics near Peggy' Cove

THE TRACKS OF A MONSTER

Nobody knows why, but every so often the Earth goes into deep refrigeration, which lasts for many thousands of years. Four times in the last 1.6 million years, Canada has looked like today's Greenland—a white, whistling wilderness with a few mountains poking through. The latest or Wisconsinan ice sheet overran Nova Scotia four times between 75,000 and 12,000 years ago, retreating during three warm interludes. We are in the fourth interlude now.

The glaciers scraped ancient soils down to bare rock and dumped them across the lowlands or out to sea. They shattered granite bedrock like crockery and dragged the broken pieces across soft lowland sandstones and shales. They bulldozed uplands and spread gravel across the lowlands, moulding it into graceful drifts and mounds (Lunenburg County). They widened old valleys (Parrsboro,

Until the 1840s, people believed that the giant boulders perched atop hills were left by Noah's flood or by floating icebergs. Swiss naturalist and lecturer Louis Agassiz proved they were the work of periodic continental glaciers.

13

Salmon, and James rivers) and lined them with great ramps and aprons of outwash. They deepened old valleys, converted others into bogs and swamps, and created Lake Ainslie. They polished bedrock and scored it with straight lines, peppered every farmer's field with rocks, left trails of pink and grey boulders at Peggys Cove. At its maximum the latest ice sheet reached nearly to Sable Island (itself an artifact of that sheet), where it floated on the sea, spawning icebergs that drifted south past future Florida.

At last warm weather came and held. For thousands of summers a million streams poured meltwater into the sea. Small local icecaps clung for centuries to upland ravines, but finally they too melted, leaving Folly Lake in the Wentworth Valley and wide peatlands like Aylesford Bog. The land, relieved of its burden of ice, slowly resumed its normal level. The sea, lowered as much as 120 m/400 ft by so much water being locked up in ice, rose in stages, carving new shorelines at each new level.

Life Returns

For centuries after the ice sheets retreated, Nova Scotia resembled a giant, soggy gravel pit sprinkled with lakes. Perhaps deep in the soil and bedrock some bacteria and fungi survived. But every higher form of life had died or left. Where then did today's plants and animals come from? The answer is that they're all immigrants. All of them descended from ancestors that waited out the onslaught farther south.

The latest return migration began about 12,000 years ago. After wind-borne spores of bacteria and primitive plants had rebuilt a living soil, sedges and grasses arrived, followed by the invertebrates that lived off them. Centuries later, clumps of dwarf birch, willow, fir, and larch appeared, bringing in turn the wildlife that depended on them.

For a time after the last glaciation, one might have travelled on foot from the future Chignecto Isthmus across Prince Edward Island to the Gaspé, and back along the south bank of the proto-St Lawrence River to the Magdalen Islands and Antigonish.

Slowly the green tide advanced north and east. By the time humans arrived about 11,000 years ago, salamanders again mated in shallow pools, frogs sang from springtime ponds, turtles and snakes sunned themselves in the brief arctic summers, birds and spiders caught insects among the trees, mastodons and caribou browsed in the valleys. Once again salmon, shad, and gaspereau thronged swollen rivers, and the marshes echoed to the cries of waterfowl. Mussels, lobster, sticklebacks, and flounder moved back to our coastal waters.

About 4,000 years ago the rising postglacial ocean began to flood the coastal plain that stretched east and south of Nova Scotia. After that, it became harder to get here. Finally only the Chignecto land bridge remained. Some species that had crossed the earlier plain got stranded, for instance Gaspé shrew in Cape Breton and Blandings turtle in southwest Nova Scotia.

While the glaciers were melting, freshwater species found it easier to migrate up the meltwater streams. When the ice was all gone, most of these streams dried up. That's why freshwater fish and mussels grow scarcer the farther one moves into Nova Scotia. For example, one finds brook sticklebacks in the Shinimicas River and River Philip, but none farther east. Another barrier to freshwater species was the return of high Fundy tides as sea levels stabilized.

New organisms still trickle in, sometimes with human help. Tuna appeared in our waters in the 1960s, coyotes in the early 1970s, black rats (again) in the mid-1990s. Recently a Mediterranean seaweed turned up along the South Shore.

HUMAN IMPACTS

No other species has had so dramatic an impact on Nova Scotia's landscapes as humans—especially Old World settlers since the early 1600s. Dyking of marshes, land clearing, mining, highway construction, and clearcutting of forests are obvious examples. Less obvious are the effects of air pollution, the introduction of Old World species (including the accidental releases of genetically altered hatchery fish), and possible genetic downgrading caused by the practices of trophy hunting and forest high grading. The pros and cons of these human disturbances fuel many debates about nature and our place in it.

Topographical

The most obvious human impact, apart from land clearing, has been from mining. Gypsum was quarried in a small way in central Nova Scotia in the late 1700s, and since then the province has become the world's largest supplier (e.g., Windsor, Milford, Little Narrows). This has left large holes in the land and spoil heaps of discarded rock, which in some cases have been smoothed and revegetated. In the 19th century there was copper mining at Cape d'Or, iron mining at Nictaux and Londonderry, and coal mining in Inverness County, around Glace Bay, and at Joggins, Stellarton, and Springhill. Most of these mines were underground, but heaps of slag remain above ground at Londonderry. Nineteenth-century gold mining along the spine of the province also left small spoil heaps. Since the early 1990s strip mining for coal has been practised at Stellarton, followed by land reclamation. Salt mining, as at Malagash, Nappan, and Pugwash, is all underground.

A four-lane paved highway permanently removes from natural productivity approximately 6.5 ha/15 ac of land per 1 km/0.6 mi.

Road building has also left scars. It requires thousands of tonnes of crushed rock for underlay and surfacing. Rock quarries and gravel pits were often highly visible, and seeding of steep banks a hit-or-miss proposition. Moreover, construction and stream crossings went ahead with little regard for fish and other wildlife. Today attempts are made to prevent erosion and to contain silty runoff.

Other major geological disturbances include the construction of the Canso and Windsor causeways, the Wreck Cove hydroelectric project with its massive water diversions and flooding, and, to a small extent, the Annapolis tidal power project.

Flora

After nearly four centuries of European settlement, three-fourths of Nova Scotia's land surface is still forested. That forest contains the same species; but the mixtures are far different, and big old trees are rare.

When we think of the forest primeval, it's tempting to imagine every tree as huge. This is a fallacy. Coastal trees were small and stunted then as now. Lightning fires, hurricanes, and insect outbreaks destroyed old forests then too, and young trees took their places. But the coming of Old World settlers vastly accelerated those processes.

Before Europeans arrived, native people routinely burned patches of woods in spring to increase food for game and to make it easier to hunt. Such regular burning prevented dangerous buildups of dry debris, which allow flames to "crown" and leap from tree to tree. Smokey Bear didn't know that.

Likely there were more broad-leaved trees than now. It was the practice of settlers to clear the deep-soiled lowlands first, which meant mostly mixed deciduous and coniferous forest. After abandonment, those lands restocked mainly to spruce and fir.

As land clearing, shipbuilding, and lumbering accelerated, the ratio of long-lived trees like white pine, yellow birch, hemlock, beech, and sugar maple declined in favour of shorter-lived, light-demanding pioneer species like white birch, spruce, fir, and aspen.

Acadian settlers relied mostly on dyking to gain new farmland, clearing only nearby slopes. But the Planters, and Loyalists who followed, were veteran land clearers. Their standard procedure was to cut and pile the unsalable wood and to burn it. The ashes were spread over the ground as fertilizer, made into potash for soap, or sold. Later most of the early farms were abandoned. The eastern mainland has 600 000 ha/1,000,000 ac of abandoned farmland now growing white (pasture) spruce that sprang up between the late 1800s and the mid-1930s.

Forest fires became a regular feature of summer in the settled areas. After the 1850s, steam-powered portable sawmills and locomotives spread fires into the interior. Today hardly a hectare of woodland has not known fire.

Imported pests and diseases have had a less obvious but equally powerful impact. In 50 years, a European bark fungus accidentally introduced to Point Pleasant Park in 1897 decimated beech throughout the province and beyond. Beech was our most abundant broad-leaved tree, comprising 60 per cent of the deciduous forest.

In the mid-1990s a Mediterranean seaweed called green fleece or devil's finger (Codium fragile) appeared in our waters via the Eastern Seaboard.

Around the same time, an Asian fungus played havoc with our white pine. Dutch elm disease has wiped out many of our white elms since 1970 and is still killing them. Other destructive imports are balsam fir adelgid (an aphid-like sap sucker), gypsy moth, and winter moth. (Spruce budworm is a native insect.)

The change in plant life around early clearings and roads was often dramatic. Nearly a third of our seed plants—for example dandelion, Scotch broom, Queen Anne's lace, yarrow, tansy, and tall buttercup— were introduced from Britain and Europe after the 17th century. They came in bedding and clothing, in garden seeds, in fodder. Despite plant quarantines, new species are arriving in Western grain.

Such exotics rarely invade woodland or do much harm to native species. Purple loosestrife (*Lythrum salicaria*), introduced from Europe early in the century and now colonizing wetlands, is an exception.

Fauna

For wildlife the greatest ongoing impact of three centuries of European settlement has been habitat change. Early logging, land clearing, and fires opened large tracts of woodland to the sun. The increased light and warmth attracted light-loving plants, which in turn encouraged species such as butterflies, garter snakes, crows, meadow voles, red fox, white-tailed deer (a newcomer via New Brunswick), squirrel, and grouse. At the same time, the increased sunlight discouraged deep-woods species like salamander, thrush, pine marten, and lynx.

By the late 1700s, the government had passed laws and fines to protect desirable "fish and game," but policing was sporadic and ineffective. Meanwhile animals considered dangerous, such as cougars, bears, and wolves, as well as "vermin" such as skunks, hawks, eagles, and owls, were shot on sight. Unregulated trapping decimated marten, lynx, beaver, otter, and fisher.

White-tailed deer carry a brain worm harmless to deer but deadly to caribou and moose, which pick up the cysts from deer via snails while browsing.

These combined effects of habitat change, hunting, and trapping eliminated several species, among them walrus, woodland caribou, wolf, sea mink, and Atlantic grey whale. The cougar seems to be making a comeback by slow migration from farther west.

Ocean fish that spawn in fresh water, such as salmon, sea trout, alewives, shad, and eels, often found their way blocked by mill dams. Often streambeds were buried in sawdust and tree bark from river drives.

In the 1920s and 1930s wildlife refuges became popular. The idea was that if humans were kept out, wild animals would thrive. The government set up the Tobeatic, Waverley, Liscomb, and Chignecto sanctuaries. Another popular remedy was that of transplanting wildlife. Beaver were planted in western watersheds, and woodland caribou were introduced to Liscomb and Cape Smokey. The beaver transplant succeeded, but caribou could not co-exist with white-tailed deer in a human-dominated landscape, and so died out.

Beaver dam

A CATALOGUE OF LANDFORMS

1. basalt flow
2. cuesta
3. drumlin
4. dune system
5. dyke
6. erratic boulder field
7. estuary
8. fault line
9. kame
10. kettle lake
11. meander
12. outwash plain
13. plateau
14. river terrace
15. salt marsh
16. sand spit
17. sea stacks
18. tombolos

1. basalt flow—*cooled and hardened basalt that flowed out from fissures in Earth's crust.*

2. cuesta—*gently sloping plains bounded on one edge by an steep slope.*

3. drumlin—*a glacial landform that is dome-shaped. The long axis of the drumlin indicates the direction of glacier flow.*

4. dune system—*mounds or ridges of sand piled by wind, usually vegetated.*

5. dyke—*an embankment built to protect lowlands from flooding.*

6. erratic boulder field—*large rocks deposited by a glacier, usually in an area far removed from their source.*

7. estuary—*the mouth of a river where fresh water mixes with seawater as a result of rising sea level.*

8. fault line—*the surface expression of a fault (a fault is the surface of rock rupture along which movement has occurred).*

9. kame—*a ridge-like or hilly glacial deposit of coarse sand and gravel formed at the front of a glacier by meltwater streams.*

10. kettle lake—*a water-filled depression originally formed by a large chunk of ice broken off a glacier and that over time was completely or partially buried by glacial outwash or till.*

11. meander—*a turn or sharp bend in a river's course.*

12. outwash plain—*a broad, gently sloping surface of sediment constructed by rivers flowing from an ice sheet or glacier.*

13. plateau—*an elevated tract of flat ground.*

14. river terrace—*a narrow, nearly-level surface of land that borders a river.*

15. salt marsh—*marshland periodically flooded by saline tidal water.*

16. sand spit—*a sandy bar built by currents into a bay.*

17. sea stack—*small island that stands as an isolated, steep-sided rock mass. They have been isolated from the mainland by weathering and erosion.*

18. tombolo—*a sand bar connecting an island to mainland or joining two islands.*

Reading the Land:
Principles & Processes

READING THE LANDSCAPE

Anyone who lives near an ocean beach or a river knows that nature is constantly remodelling. One big storm can reshape a sand spit; one big flood can rearrange a river. However, most changes are too slow to see. It may take a thousand years for wind, water, and frost to lower the Cape Breton plateau by two centimetres. Yet such remodelling is eventually visible in every landscape.

Amherst Marshes

Unless you know a geologist with time to spare, learn to "look" beneath. Ignore surface details of forest, pasture, soil, and lake, and concentrate on the contour of the land beneath. In other words, think landforms. Cape Blomidon is a landform. So are Amherst's level marshes and Halifax's Citadel Hill. To a geologist, Cape Blomidon's familiar face is a tilted block of red sandstone capped with basaltic lava that overflowed during the early age of dinosaurs. Likewise, Amherst's marshes are an ancient seabed, now dyked and drained to grow hay. Citadel Hill is a hump of gravel, sculpted by a glacier over 12,000 years ago and later reshaped by humans.

Landscape Symphonies
Seen from a moving vehicle, landscapes unfold to the eye much as music does to the ear. There's a kind of rhythm, an interweaving of large and small features; of mountain, woodland, and seashore, of field, ravine, and sandbar. Like musical motifs these elements appear, blend, and reappear. Scattered through the composition are grace notes: a spray of white Indian pear blossoms, a night heron mirrored in a sunset pool, a windblown pine on a rocky ridge.

Seen this way, the Atlantic shore becomes a repetition of cove and headland, grey sea and white beach, tan bog and burgundy barren, serene pasture and snug village. The Annapolis Valley becomes a pattern of orderly fruit orchards, fenced fields, tall pine groves, well-

Annapolis Valley
from North Mountain Lookoff

to-do towns. Cape Breton is a Wagnerian epic of plunging cliffs, misty mountains, brooding ocean, sheltered lochs.

To a jaded or hurried motorist such panoramas are visual Muzak. To the attuned eye they are a symphony played with colour, shape, and texture on the face of the ancient Earth.

Upland, Lowland

In general, uplands in Nova Scotia mean hard rock, and lowlands mean soft rock. In the millennia since the youngest rocks were laid down, erosion has worn away most of the soft rock, leaving nearby harder formations standing higher (e.g., Cobequid Mountains, Cape Breton Highlands). The softer the rock, the faster the erosion. Think

Shubenacadie River tributaries at low tide

of a wooden floor subjected for decades to heavy foot traffic. Eventually, only the harder knots and denser wood will be left. These bumps and ridges correspond to uplands and lowlands.

Given enough years, even harder rocks wear away. Some rocks in northwest Cape Breton are a thousand million years old. In this vast time, they have lost several metres of elevation to rain, wind, and frost. The process has been accelerated in the last 1.6 million years by glaciation. But for periodic uplift, these hills would be lower than they are.

Weathering and erosion are still going on. It is especially evident around our coasts, where powerful storm waves have gouged out coves and bays in zones of soft rock or of fractured hard rock. Inland, lakes and river valleys also demonstrate the erosive power of moving water and ice. Minas Basin's soft red sandstones are eroding so fast that its waters are continually muddy.

Hills come in three basic types. Small ones

Erosion removes, on average, roughly 2.5 cm/1 in of rock from Nova Scotia's bedrock surface every thousand years.

are usually mounds of gravel left by ice or running water. Medium-sized ridges are usually gentle folds in sandstone or shale bedrock, often with a deep coating of gravel. The biggest hills are extruded or uplifted rock of a resistant nature.

Rock Signatures

The textures and colours and heft of rocks provide clues to how they came to be. The best way to learn the different rocks is to befriend a geologist or a rockhound. They will show you how to test rocks for hardness, density, streak (powdered pigment left on an unglazed tile), graininess, and so on. The next best way is to buy a good pocket guide and take it on every hike.

Most rocks that break apart in layers were laid down under water —hence sedimentary. Sandstone, limestone, shale, and siltstone are of this type. Look closely at a photo of the Rockies, and often you'll see lines running slantwise across their face. These tilted and folded layers or strata represent thousands of years of sedimentation. Each layer represents a variation in deposition—a storm, a season, a year. Sedimentary rocks tend to be soft.

Rocks that cool from molten magma are called igneous (Latin for "fire"). So are rocks of any type that have been remelted and cooled. Igneous rocks are grainy (hence "granite"), either coarse-grained, meaning they cooled slowly deep in the Earth, or fine-grained, meaning they cooled quickly at or near the surface or under water.

When sedimentary or igneous rocks are heated or compressed enough, the layering and graininess may disappear. Such rocks are called metamorphic (Greek for "changed"+"body"). Some are faintly layered, others show swirling patterns and a fine glistening grain. Often they show veins of white quartz or other minerals that precipitated out of superheated water or steam or were squirted in while molten.

In calculating the ages of strata, geologists assume that "under is (usually) older." A March snowbank contains the record of that each snowfall and thaw in hard and soft layers, dust, and soot. Rock layers build up in the same way. Road cuts and ocean waves let us see those strata. (Colorado's Grand Canyon is a famous example.) Occasionally older rocks are pushed over younger, but geologists can tell this. Veins of other rocks or minerals that cut *across* layers are more recent additions.

Large crystals in igneous rocks mean slow cooling within the crust (which gives them time to grow); small crystals mean fast cooling in water or air.

The Sea as Sculptor
Ever since land first emerged from the global ocean, the sea has been actively undermining cliffs, shaving off gravel headlands, conveying sand and pebbles alongshore, creating marshes, and drowning entire forests.

Storm waves and ice, by pounding and grinding coastal cliffs, continually chip away flakes of rock. Sedimentary rock erodes faster than igneous or metamorphic. Also, formations that lie edge-on to the waves break down faster than those that lie flat or slope seaward. Cliff erosion may take a lifetime to become visible, especially in harder formations.

Beaches are built from sand and pebbles found nearby or brought down by rivers carrying loose gravel left by glaciers or eroded from solid rock. These materials are transported by longshore currents and ocean waves and are dropped where currents slacken. Lightweight sand and clay move farthest; heavier boulders, stones, and pebbles

As the land rebounded in stages from its load of ice, the sea carved new beaches below the old ones. Today the latter can be seen as wave-cut terraces (e.g., Kentville's main street, Parrsboro, Arisaig Provincial Park).

remain close to the source. Sandbars and barrier beaches, by joining headlands and islands, can change a rugged coast to a gentle one in a few centuries. Mostly this happens during winter storms, which strip away all but the heavier material. One big storm can cut a drumlin headland in two or completely remove a sandbar.

Rivers Are Forever

Water runs downhill, seeking the easiest and most direct route to the sea. The steeper the grade, the swifter the stream and the greater its erosive power and sediment load. Though rivers run downhill, their valleys move headwards. Like cracks spreading upward in masonry, they erode uphill until they reach the height of land. Given time, the upstream parts of adjoining watersheds meet, carve up the land between them, and reduce it to sea level. A contour map of the Cape Breton Highlands shows this process clearly.

You can tell the age or stage of a stream by its profile. New streams tend to be short and steep with V-shaped valleys and little or no delta at the mouth. Mature rivers typically have wide valleys (often with one or more terraces and numerous sandbars and islands), tend to meander, and usually have a broad marshy delta. As one moves upstream, younger features appear until one reaches the place where a tiny new valley is being started.

The streams of Nova Scotia... tend to be noisy and tumultuous in freshet, gently musical in summer, and some of them go almost dry in September.... Only two or three of them are more impressive than sizable brooks, and whenever they look like a true river—the Lahave below Bridgewater, for example— they are invariably narrow inlets of the sea.
—Hugh MacLennan

Normally rivers branch and rebranch like the limbs of a deciduous tree. Straight-flowing rivers do so because they follow zones of fractured rock caused by faults or stress cracks in the Earth (e.g., the south slope of North Mountain in the Annapolis Valley).

As river valleys deepen and widen, the resulting steady flow of sediment migrates seaward and settles offshore. Thus, every mountain and hill is eventually reduced to powder and deposited at the bottom of the sea, to be lifted high in some future era. In the words of H. H. Swinnerton in *The Earth Beneath Us*, "It is the streams and not the hills that are everlasting."

Flat Land Is Waterworked Land

The marshes of Grand Pré and Amherst are flat because they were built up millimetre by millimetre under water, like coffee grounds settling in a cup. Thus, Canada's vast prairies were once the bottom of a shallow sea. The sediment layers vary in colour, density, and thickness, much like tree rings. Once they turn to rock, they may be tilted or folded. But at the start each bed of shale, sandstone, salt, gypsum, and limestone was as level as a gym floor.

Glacial Diaries
Gravel: whether it's a thin smear over bald bedrock or a thick bed under farmland or forest, few parts of Nova Scotia are without it. This blanket of ground-up rock is the work of weathering, stream erosion, and glaciation. Gravel pits are rich with clues. For instance, angular rocks in a mass of unsorted pebbles and sand point to a ground moraine left at the front or sides of a retreating glacier. Rocks with one or more bevelled faces were likely dragged over bedrock by a glacier. Sharp-edged ones suggest shattering by frost or crushing by the weight of ice or by faulting. Sharp-edged grains of sand point to wind abrasion in post-glacial sand dunes. Rounded pebbles and sand point to tumbling in a meltwater stream.

Downstream from a melting glacier a fan of pebbles, sand, and silt spreads out. Larger boulders and rocks are dumped nearest the ice, then come pebbles of decreasing size. Finer materials like silt and clay settle farthest away in quiet ponds and lakes. As in streams today, these materials came to rest in uneven layers and lenses. Alternations of coarse and fine materials suggest changing rates of flow (e.g., from spring through summer).

Drumlins (from Gaelic, *druim*) are rounded hills 15 to 30 m (50 to 100 ft) high shaped by moving glaciers. They are common in Lunenburg County, Yarmouth County, and southeast Cape Breton. A typical specimen is shaped like a hard-boiled egg cut lengthwise and laid flat side down. Most drumlins, like fish, are tapered toward the tail and face "upstream" to the direction of ice flow. Because ground-up slate makes slippery clay and clay acts as a lubricant to carry the moving ice smoothly over obstructions, slate areas have more true drumlins. (Citadel Hill is underlain by slate.) Sandstone areas (e.g., west of Truro) tend to have drumlin-like formations (drumlinoids, of course).

Like other glacial deposits, drumlins contain rocks of all sizes in a matrix of sand and rock dust composed of older soils and bedrock scrapings. The boulders were plucked from fractured bedrock.

Eskers are rare in northern Nova Scotia (though there's a fine one near Parrsboro). They're far more common along the Sable, Jordan, and Clyde rivers in southwest Nova Scotia, and around certain inland lakes. Kentville has one along its Main Street. These sinuous gravel ridges are the beds of vanished meltwater streams that ran under or within glacial ice.

Kames These are heaps of gravel deposited as the glacier melted. They appear along the sides of valleys and as conical heaps where gravel-laden water funnelled down through holes in the ice.

The reddish colour of many Lunenburg County drumlins came from red Triassic sandstone, which the south-moving glacier over-rode while crossing the future Bay of Fundy.

23

READING FLORA

Some plants tolerate dry soil, some tolerate wet, most like something in between. Some demand full sunlight, others tolerate shade, a few can handle either. Some withstand salt spray, others turn brown at the merest hint of salt. Some shoot up each spring from perennial roots, others die each autumn, relying on seed for survival.

As different as plants are, they all share certain traits and behave in certain ways. They must have light, water, carbon dioxide, and nitrogen, plus a growing medium that supplies essential minerals such as potassium, phosphorus, magnesium, and iron. They accurately reflect local climate and soil conditions and respond so definitely to disturbance (e.g., land-clearing, fire) that for decades afterward the signs are obvious.

Trout Lily

To Do: Walk in summer through (a) dense softwoods into (b) a clearing to (c) a roadside. Note the increasing abundance of plants, insects, and other life, from very few in (a) (except in the treetops), to more in (b), to most in (c).

Nature Hates a Vacuum

Scrape away a patch of lawn in summer and watch what happens. Within a week seedlings will appear. In a month the bare soil will be on its way to being green again. Or take a garden. Every gardener must compete with what are called weeds and pests. If it's possible to live there, some form of plant life will occupy it. Bacteria live in boiling hot springs, lichens cling to bare boulders and raw gravel, rockweed survives on wave-battered cliffs.

Light and Shade

Some plants must have full sunlight (cinquefoil, timothy hay, crowberry, Canada goldenrod, aspen). Others thrive in the dim light (mosses, certain ferns, wood anemone, young beech and sugar maple, and hemlock). So you can expect to find certain plants in certain places and not in others.

Wet versus Dry

Plants also have definite moisture needs. Some prefer wet feet (e.g., pond-lily, arrowhead, cattail, leatherleaf, pitcher plant, marsh marigold, pondweed, rushes, reeds, sphagnum, cord grass). Others prefer dry conditions (lichens, dune grass, sweetfern, beach pea, coltsfoot). Most favour neither wet nor dry. A few, unable to compete elsewhere, endure extreme wet (black spruce, larch) or very dry (jack pine).

Exposure and Elevation
Extremes of heat and cold, wind, and salt spray are hard on plants.
Some can't grow on the seashore or on high hills at all. Some that can
are crowberry, green alder, sea-rocket, cord grass, beach pea, white
and black spruce, and balsam fir.

Aspect
Sometimes hikers are surprised to see beech and maple on a south-
facing slope and spruce and fir on the other side of the hill. Aspect,
or direction of slope, is important to plants. The south side of a hill
receives more sunlight, has less snow cover in winter, warms up
sooner in spring, and stays warm longer in the fall. In effect, it has a
more southerly climate. The north side is just the reverse. Plants
respond to these differences. (So do animals. For instance, in winter
deer choose south-facing hillsides during the coldest months.)

Slope
The steeper the slope, the harder it is for plants to grow. Gravity itself
becomes a challenge. Soil tends to wash away, and rock slides are
frequent. Only the hardiest seed plants can survive clinging to ledges
and crevices. Those that do, grow very slowly.

Edge Effect
Look for the greatest variety of plants (and animals) where ecosystems meet. A field edge contains more plant species than the forest or
meadow on either side; mixed woods more than coniferous woods.

Succession
Succession is like a parade of life in slow motion. When an established
community of plants is cut, burned, or otherwise disturbed, a sequence
of renewal is set in motion. This sequence usually follows a more or less
predictable order. Suppose a summer fire runs through a spruce-fir
forest. Within weeks the forest floor will green up with ferns arising from
underground rhizomes, which the heat did not kill. In the years that
follow, lichens will appear on bare mineral soil. Deciduous trees will send
up stump shoots and root suckers, and many seed plants will germinate
from dormant seeds or from seeds brought in by wind, water, or animals.
   A decade or so later, young fir and spruce from nearby survivors
will germinate in the shade of these plants. This succession of plants
is echoed by changes in the area's animal life, from amoebae to
mosquitoes to moose.

Dispersal
Every plant has some means to spread itself. Primitive plants do so by
producing billions of spores and letting the wind carry them. Seed
plants use the wind as well (fireweed, dandelion, poplar). More
reliable, specialized, and energy-efficient seed-dispersal strategies

*Recently tiny white-
cedars over 700 years
old have been
discovered growing in
the crevices of vertical
limestone cliffs along
the Niagara
Escarpment.*

include the catapult (witchhazel, touch-me-not), hitchhiking (bur, beggars tick), animal digestive systems (cherry, blueberry), water transport (elm), and helicoptering (conifers, maple, ash). Observing seed dispersal can add greatly to your enjoyment of plant life.

A Calendar of Roadside Wildflowers

One of the easiest ways for motorists to get acquainted with our seed plants is by watching them bloom along the highways. Many flower en masse at fairly set times of the year, lighting up entire roadsides with washes of pink, yellow, and white. Here's a spring-through-autumn guide to these natural displays, grouped by landscape types.

Aster

One of our earliest roadside wildflowers—sometimes as early as late March—is the lemon-coloured, dandelion-like coltsfoot. Look for masses of its horseshoe-shaped leaves on the sunny side of ditches and gravel slopes.

Shadbush (serviceberry) is a May-flowering shrub of the rose family. Its long-petalled white blossoms brighten forest edges and usually coincide with the start of the shad run. Another name for it is Indian pear. Red-berried elder is another early blooming shrub, but the flowers are cream-coloured and less obvious. This is also the season for mayflower, or trailing arbutus, Nova Scotia's provincial flower. But you won't see it from a car.

In April–May look under sugar maple, beech, and yellow birch for spring beauty, trout-lily, bloodroot, trillium, and lady's-slipper orchids. They bloom early to catch the sun before the unfolding leaves of the trees darken the forest floor.

Less conspicuous but quite lovely are the pure white blooms of hobblebush, whose flat umbels mature from outside in. The plant is named for its habit of rooting its branches in the soil, which creates loops that can trip a person or a horse.

Another name for wild raisin is witherod (Old English for withe, akin to L vi(ere) to weave). Old-timers plaited its tough pliable shoots into rope rings to secure oars to a boat's rowing pins. Its clustered pink and blue berries wither to resemble raisins.

By late spring, roadsides are commonly awash in the pale pink of wild rhododendron (rhodora), which blooms even before its jade green leaves are fully flushed. In rocky barrens such as those around Canso and Shelburne, the tiny pink cups of the evergreen mountain laurel, or lambkill, are also seen.

By mid-June you'll see the frothy blooms of pin or fire cherry and mountain-ash along hedgerows and cutover areas. Wild raisin also comes into bloom around this time. Its pink and red berries later shrivel in purple-blue clusters. Disturbed sites often feature pale green sprays of wild sarsaparilla.

Early June is the time to watch for dandelion (*dent de lion,* French for "tooth of a lion," referring to the jagged leaf margin). For a few weeks this relative of chrysanthemum spangles whole roadside meadows with gold.

Individual dandelion blossoms last only a few days before turning into the familiar grey fluff-balls. They consist of scores of parachute-equipped seeds, which ride the lightest zephyr for great distances. After dandelions come the less spectacular but equally golden buttercup, which lasts into fall.

Two mid-season, white-blooming shrubs of forest edges are blue-berried elder and highbush cranberry, a viburnum. Both put out masses of creamy-white blooms, which rival mock orange and snowball in exuberance. Lowbush cranberry favours stream banks and is not usually seen from the road. The viburnums are great favourites with birds.

Here and there on dry roadsides in midsummer you'll see clumps of chalky white plants. These are pearly everlasting. You may also spot dusky gold black-eyed susan or white or lavender yarrow.

Highbush Cranberry

In late July and early August there are spectacular pink fields of fireweed on cutover and burnt areas. August is also the time of Queen Anne's Lace, a tall, fine-leaved European perennial closely related to the garden carrot. Its circular white doilies, each with a dark purple floret surrounded by hundreds of white ones, wave above the hay. On maturing they fold into a bird-nest shape ringed with brown seeds.

In the central counties, away from the coast, roadside ponds exhibit the golden globes and shiny oval leaves of yellow pond-lilies. Along the Atlantic coast the lovely, jasmine-scented white water lily is a common sight.

Late July is also the time for native wild roses, of which there are at several species, most of them fragrant. All are pink, and all but one are single-petalled. Occasionally you may spot an escaped garden rugosa type.

From mid-August to late September the brilliant yellow Canada goldenrod and its allies hold the stage. Along the coast, look for seaside goldenrod at the high-water mark of tidal marshes. At this time the pale mauve and purple asters contrast vividly with the goldenrods.

By now the roadside grasses have faded from springtime green to ochre, tan, and gold. Part of the golden tint comes from the small flowers of hawkweed, a cousin of dandelion that prefers dry places. One strain with scarlet blooms is called devil's paintbrush.

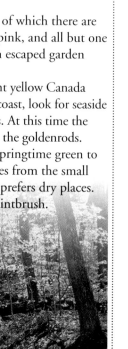

READING FAUNA

Unlike plants, most wild animals roam freely all their lives. Even mussels and barnacles travel a bit before they root themselves to one spot. Some creatures, like the Arctic tern and the great whales, roam the globe.

Yet all wild animals have certain habits, obey certain rules. They must eat and drink, which means going regularly to certain places. For example, otters and white-tail deer make their rounds of good hunting and fishing territory. Likewise, animals must rest and sleep, and each species has its preferences. Successful hunters and trappers make it their business to learn such behaviours and how they change with the seasons. You can use the same skills.

The newest definition of "wildlife" includes plants; but for our purposes the word refers broadly to animals, which live by eating plants or other animals: invertebrates, fish, amphibians, reptiles, birds, and mammals.

Living Space

Every organism needs a certain type of living space or niche. That niche must provide food, water, and shelter within a reasonable distance. This holds true from the smallest to the largest creatures. Amoebae need oxygenated water teeming with the microscopic organisms on which they feed. Polychaete worms need soft sea-bottom mud with suitable prey. Barnacles need seashore cliffs flooded by the ocean twice every 24 hours. Slugs require damp vegetation, which they eat with raspy tongues. Orb spiders frequent places with plenty of flying insects. Spotted salamanders seek forest glades not far from shallow freshwater ponds or ditches in which to breed. Bald eagles need shallow water with fish to eat and tall living trees to nest in and spot prey from. A field mouse needs grassy cover and seed-bearing plants. Otters need undisturbed woodland lakes and streams with trout and other fish. White-tailed deer need forest and farmland with green foliage in summer and deciduous twigs and lichens in winter, plus nearby conifer thickets for shelter and hiding. The special places that provide these niches are called habitats.

Range

How much space an animal needs is dictated by its size and living habits. In general, plant-eaters find their food nearby, while predators must travel for it. Studies show that the average common meadow vole lives out its short life on 0.24 ha/0.6 ac of land. Hummingbirds, whirring from flower to flower, are content with 0.1 ha/0.25 ac apiece. Robins need four times that much. Spotted salamanders may travel up to 182 m/600 ft to breed. White-tailed deer occupy 5–8 km²/2–3 sq mi apiece. A pair of barred owls occupies an average of

229 ha/565 ac. Otters travel 24 km/15 lineal miles or more on their continual fishing circuits.

Territory

Many creatures defend their living space for all or part of the year. Ants from neighbouring hills will fight when they meet. This instinct is strongest during breeding season. Male songbirds advertise their territory by sound (singing, winnowing, drumming, etc.), by colour (brightly hued plumage), and by fighting. A common springtime spectacle is that of small birds ganging up on crows to chase them away from their nests. Black bears claw trees to warn off rivals, reaching as high as they can, thus signalling size. White-tailed bucks scrape and urinate on special places to advertise readiness to mate.

Carrying Capacity

The capacity to support wild creatures varies with their demands. At optimum population levels, they and their environment will stay healthy indefinitely. Billions of bacteria can co-exist comfortably in a test tube. Hundreds of ladybird beetles may share a small garden. Scores of mice may inhabit a granary. A half-dozen deer may thrive on a 25-ha/40-ac woodlot.

When a range is not fully occupied, surplus animals from nearby habitats tend to move in. When the number of animals exceeds a certain limit, natural controls are triggered and adjustments made. These include lowered birth rates and fewer offspring (e.g., one fawn a year instead of three). If these fail, stress-related diseases, fighting, and eventual starvation will prune the surplus. This applies to every creature, including humans. To maintain a steady population over time, only two offspring need survive during the life span of their parents.

Observing Invertebrates

For such a large and diverse group, only guidelines can be offered. It's a good idea to survey the various groups in a handbook and then zero in on a particular phylum (e.g., *Mollusca*) or class (e.g., *Insecta*), or even a family (such as *Coleoptera*, the beetles).

Carpet Trick. One of the best ways to get a sense of the invertebrates— and of the Coal Age world—is to lay a piece of carpet or heavy cardboard on moist bare earth (not compacted gravel) in a shady spot in spring or summer. After a couple of weeks, carefully peel it back and observe.

You should see millipedes, sowbugs, centipedes, mites, and beetles scurrying for cover. (They'll stay longer in dim light, such as at dusk.)

Millipedes or "wireworms" are lustrous black, from 1 to 3 cm (0.4– 1.2 in) long, and glide like miniature trains over the lumpy soil. Most are harmless plant composters that help keep soil fertile and aerated.

As a rule you should release, alive and undamaged, any insects you catch. But if you choose to keep them, learn to kill them humanely and to mount and store them properly. Any good insect handbook will tell you how.

Swifter than the more primitive millipedes, centipedes run down smaller invertebrates. Their many legs resemble the paddles of a racing scull, but move in waves rather than in unison. Adults reach 5 cm/2 in+ and are shiny copper red. Juveniles are paler and barely 1 cm/0.4 in long. They have a painful bite.

Sowbugs are grey and slow-moving, easy targets for birds and rodents. If unable to escape down some crevice, they roll armadillo-like into a ball (hence "pillbug"). Their Carboniferous relatives grew to the size of hogs.

You may see a tiny spider mite or two, slow-moving predators with scarlet bodies.

Usually there are earthworms, perhaps with clumps of earthworm eggs, which look like tiny beads of clear plastic.

As anglers know, fish can see things on shore—but not below a certain angle. When approaching a pond or stream, crouch low or keep a screen of foliage between you and the water. Fish can also feel vibrations, so tread softly.

Observing Fish

There are fish that never leave salt water, fish that never leave fresh water, a few saltwater fish that breed in fresh water, and one freshwater species (the American eel) that breeds in salt water.

Freshwater fish are active all year but hidden by ice for four or five months a year. Saltwater fish are also active all year, but inconspicuous (except to divers) in winter. In summer the easiest ones to observe are inshore species like sticklebacks in tidal pools, sculpin and flounder in shallow water, and ocean perch (cunner) around wharves. Capelin, a smelt-like fish, spawn on beaches at high tide in June in eastern Cape Breton, and smelt and tomcod enter our estuaries from mid-winter onward to spawn. Except for an occasional dead shark, mackerel, or billfish washed up by a storm, landlubbers rarely see the fish of the open sea.

Among the easiest freshwater fishes to find are the little lake and creek chub, which sometimes migrates in swarms, and the golden shiner, banded killifish, and dace. The bottom-feeding white sucker is also easy to spot, while yellow perch, a fish of shallow weedy lakes, is more elusive.

Shad migrate about when serviceberry blooms—hence "shadbush."

The best time to see alewife (also called gaspereau or kiyak) and shad is in early May, when they migrate upstream to spawn. Sea trout and Atlantic salmon also migrate upstream at various times from spring through fall. Normally these anadromous (Greek for "running upward") fish live in the ocean.(Fish that stay in fresh water are called landlocked e.g., landlocked salmon in Shubenacadie Grand Lake).

If you're very lucky you may see eels wriggling across wet fields and swamps at night, heading for salt water and the distant Sargasso Sea off Florida, where all Atlantic eels breed.

Observing Amphibians and Reptiles

You won't see any in the coldest months. Both groups, being "cold-blooded" or exothermic, are paralyzed by cold weather and must hibernate.

Salamanders. With their colourful markings, long tails, and froggy faces, they look like wet-suited lizards. Their usual home is in or under rotting logs or forest leaf mould, where they also hibernate. One good time to see these amphibians is on a rainy night in April. With ice still in the ponds and snow lingering under the trees, they set out for shallow ponds and ditches to mate. Anyone with patience, rain gear, and a good flashlight is apt to see them then.

Frogs and Toads. These amphibians hibernate in the mud of ponds and ditches and announce the coming of spring with a variety of songs, of which the tiny tree frog's is the best known. Frog and toad eggs appear in early May as clear, jelly-like masses attached to submerged plants and rocks, incubated by the warming sun. Later you'll see gilled tadpoles of various sizes and types wriggling about the shallows, hunting insect larvae and other food. Gradually these "polliwogs" absorb their gills and tails and sprout legs. The adults live in moist habitats such as deep ponds (American bullfrog), forests (wood frog), wet meadows (leopard frog), and pondside bushes (spring peeper or grey tree frog). Though toads resist drying out better than frogs, none strays far from water.

Green Frog

Reptiles. Our commonest reptile is the green and yellow, matchbox-sized eastern painted turtle—the kind pet shops used to sell. Look for it sunning itself on a half-submerged rock or log by a sluggish stream in summer. A much larger streamside dweller is the wood turtle, sometimes seen trundling across a road. Our largest reptile is the snapping turtle (top shell to 25 cm/10 in). It spends most of its time lurking in the mud of woodland ponds, waiting for an unwary fish, frog, or duckling to pass. Although capable of inflicting a nasty bite, snappers avoid humans unless provoked.

All three sea turtles (Atlantic Ridley's, Atlantic loggerhead, and Atlantic leatherback) feed along our coast in summer, but migrate to tropical beaches to breed.

Maritime Garter Snake

Snakes. None of our snakes is poisonous. They may "strike" when handled, but their tiny teeth barely nick the skin. Turning over boards and rocks in autumn is a good way to find snakes. Of our five native species, the one most often seen is the eastern garter snake, which is also our largest (up to 90 cm/36 in). Two of the best places to look for it are sunny rock piles and paths through broadleaf forest. (Rocks stay warm overnight, and the forest floor gives good camouflage.) Our smallest snake is the beautiful northern red-belly (up to 30 cm/12 in). It feeds on slugs and earthworms and likes moist woods, bogs, and abandoned farm buildings.

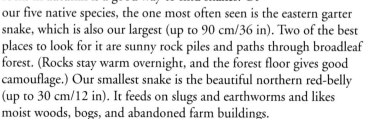

Bird-watching

Bird watchers probably have more fun than any other sort of naturalist. Even on a short hike they usually spot a jay or a chickadee. But the hobby can be confusing for beginners. Nova Scotia sits on a busy flyway. Many regulars wear different costumes coming and going. Besides the regulars, which number in the hundreds of species, numerous transients touch down here.

Barred Owl

While veteran bird watchers rightly pride themselves on being able to identify large numbers of birds, beginners often content themselves with knowing the birds that visit window feeders, such as sparrows, juncos, and jays, plus the odd crow, robin, ruffed grouse, starling, blackbird, and a hawk or two.

The best approach is to use a good eastern bird guidebook and to seek birds by habitat— e.g., wetland, meadow, upland, shoreline. An important aid to telling species apart is to observe their beaks, wings, and feet. These tell much about the owner's lifestyle.

Observing Land Mammals

Of all creatures, they are the most like us. This should make observing them easier. In fact it doesn't help much, because wild mammals are also the shyest and most intelligent of creatures. Not only do they possess exquisitely tuned senses, but on their own turf they are masters of camouflage and evasion.

Red Fox

Most of us feel lucky to glimpse a deer or a fox beside the highway, but the thrill of seeing mammals in the wild is well worth the extra effort. Humans do have a couple of advantages. Superior reasoning power isn't one of them; but human eyesight about equals theirs and, unlike them, we see in full colour. They apparently see in greys or grey-greens.

Generally speaking, herbivores are easier to spot than carnivores. This is because there are far more plant-eaters, and they must devote much of each 24-hour period to grazing. Here are some hints.

Imitate an Expert. If you know any skilful hunters or trappers, go out in the woods with them and observe. They keep a sharp eye out for droppings or scat (feces) and can tell what animal voided them. They watch for browsing of foliage or twigs and can tell whether the browser was a mouse, hare, deer, porcupine, or moose. They are alert for paths worn in moss or grass and tracks in wet mud or snow. They watch for otter slides, beaver cuttings, and kills of any kind. While such skills can't be developed overnight, a keen amateur can learn much by watching such a person at work.

Dusk and Dawn. Many of Nova Scotia's mammals wake at sunset and go to sleep soon after sunrise, or vice versa. Search at those times, where you have seen recent tracks or scats.

Move Upwind. The nose of a red fox or a deer (or of a pet dog) is perhaps 400 times more sensitive than a human's, so every mammal for hundreds of metres downwind knows you're there.

Walk Both Ways. Have you noticed how often one sees something on the return trip that was missed going the other way? Reversing direction gives you a new angle and a second chance.

Keep Quiet. Wild animals almost always smell, hear, or see us before we're aware of them. One exception is in windy weather, when foliage is swishing and branches creaking. If you're a patient person, the best way to see woodland mammals is to find a comfortable, concealed place and just wait alertly. If you are not so patient and prefer to keep moving, be sure to pause often. Each time, take 15 to 20 minutes to survey your surroundings and to listen. If that stump looks like a deer's chest, it may well be. A peculiar clump of brown and white saplings may be a buck's legs. Here binoculars are a great advantage. By changing our depth perception, they reveal things we might otherwise overlook. Sometimes, a low whistle or grunt will halt a moving animal for a moment.

A Miscellany of Land Mammals

Anyone can observe a porcupine. In summer porcupines graze on meadow greens as well as the foliage of aspen and birch. In winter they climb to the tops of conifers like larch, pine, or spruce to feed on the tender upper bark.

Skunks are also easy to spot (and smell). Braver folk will walk up to a skunk to count its stripes. Among less hazardous but equally interesting creatures, probably the easiest to observe are fox squirrels and chipmunks. Like porkies and skunks, they're so confident of escape they hardly bother to hide. These rodents live on foliage, seeds, and fruit in summer and mostly on stored nuts in winter.

The groundhog, a sort of Eastern prairie dog, can be seen near rock piles on sunny spring days, munching on greens after its long winter snooze.

Beavers are also easy to find, thanks to their dams and lodges. Find a dam in good repair, with signs of fresh cuttings nearby. Come at dusk to such a place when there's a full moon under clear skies. Pick a comfortable spot under cover and downwind, wait for an hour or so, and you may see the beavers at work. Be prepared for a barrage of noisy tail-slapping when you rise to go.

From spring to fall, white-tailed deer haunt the edges of fields and cutovers at dawn and dusk. As winter comes on they retreat to south-facing slopes where deciduous twigs are more plentiful and conifer thickets offer shelter from storms. Moose prefer swampy woods and cutovers, and may assemble in small herds in hardwood groves when snow is deep. Sometimes people are startled to see one in their headlights, especially in western Nova Scotia, in Guysborough County, and on Cape Breton Island.

Predators like bobcat, coyote, and weasel are naturally scarcer than their prey, but much more secretive. People have hiked the woods for years without seeing one. Perhaps the easiest to spot is the red fox, which patrols the margins of tidal marshes and pastures hunting mice and voles.

Winter is the best time to look for these mammals, for their tracks tell the story of their movements. Look for bobcat signs where snowshoe hare abound, such as on the edges of cutovers, along streams, and in swamps. Mink and otter frequent streams and lakes. A good tracking guide can be helpful.

OBSERVING SEA MAMMALS

Whales and Porpoises. Although whales can show up almost anywhere around our coast, including estuaries, some places yield more sightings because food is more plentiful. Like bears on the berry barrens in late summer, they gather in those places to fatten up before heading south to calve and raise their young.

One such feeding place is the mouth of the Bay of Fundy near Brier Island. Another lies off Cheticamp, a third is near Cape North in Cape Breton. Unless you own a sea-going vessel or fish for a living, or you have marine connections, your best bet is to book a whale-watching tour at one of those locations. For listings see the current *Nova Scotia: Complete Doer's and Dreamer's Guide.*

Seals. Although grey seals come ashore to whelp and breed each fall, they are reclusive, seeking out remote beaches along Northumberland Strait and on Sable Island.

Harbour seals, on the other hand, are amiable creatures, that tolerate a fair amount of human disturbance. You can see them from spring through fall almost anywhere along our long coastline. The trail section of this book gives directions to likely sites.

Reading the Seashore
Ever notice how any rocky seashore has different zones from the high tide mark down to deeper water, wider zones on gently sloping shores and narrower where cliffs are steep? Flora and fauna living in

Activity: At low tide find a rock pool with submerged barnacles and quietly observe them. After a few minutes each will open briefly and rhythmically sweep microscopic organisms into its mouth with pinkish feathery tentacles.

the upper zones must cope with an environment that shifts every six hours from wet to dry and back again. Those living farther down must cope with crashing waves. The outermost live in a cold, dimly lit world much like the deep ocean.

On most shores there are six main zones:

The Black Zone lies above the highest tides, but ocean spray wets it in storms—enough to support blue-green algae, which are grazed during low tide by periwinkles. Between storms these microscopic plants shelter under a gelatinous varnish.

The Periwinkle Zone is submerged only during full and new moon. In between, it gets enough spray and rain to enable tiny rough-shelled periwinkles to venture from clefts and graze on algae with rough, ribbon-like tongues. Once a month they may ascend to the Black Zone. These molluscs bear live young.

The Barnacle Zone, being exposed for several hours twice daily and often pounded by strong waves, is a tough place to live. The survivors are fastened strongly and protected by either great flexibility or strong shells. Here barnacles pepper the rocks like miniature white and grey tents. Each cone contains a living shrimp-like crustacean lying on its back inside a double-walled, self-secreted calcium house. Each house is tightly shut at low tide but opens when the tide returns. Barnacles are preyed on by dog whelks, roving snails that pry open the shells and suck out the contents.

The Rockweed Zone lies farther out. At high tide the algae float upright, looking like a golden forest swept by breezes. They are buoyed up by air bladders, which pop underfoot as one walks the upper fringe at low tide. This exposed mass of slippery brown growth is called "bladder wrack." The zone is home to blue mussels, common and smooth periwinkles, rock crabs, and limpets.

The Irish Moss Zone is the opposite of the Periwinkle Zone, being exposed only during the highest monthly tides. Crabs, sea urchins, and starfish, which cannot risk drying out, live here. Sea lettuce appears as vivid patches of green among the mossy reds of other marine algae.

The Laminarian Zone resembles the ocean proper. Named for the wide-bladed *Laminaria* or kelp group, these large organisms are attached by ropy holdfasts to the rocks below. This colder and dimmer zone supports not only creatures from the previous zone, but ocean species such as sponges, marine worms, anemones, and jellyfish. Sometimes in winter white-tailed deer roam the beaches to feed on kelp and sea lettuce at low tide. Sheep on the Mud Islands off Cape Sable do the same.

Brown algae grew in the oceans eons before green plants appeared on land. They are thought to date back to a time when heavy mists and clouds continually darkened the sky.

Laminaria

Nova Scotia Trails Map

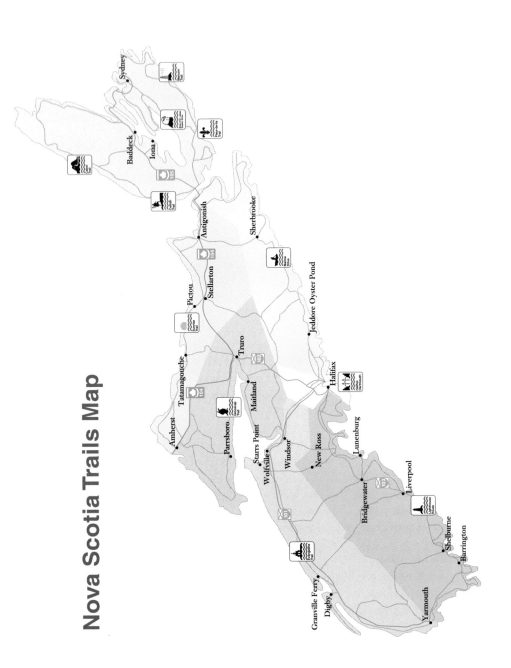

The Nature Tours

OVERVIEW

Below we present a guided nature tour of each of the province's principal routes. We start with the Trans Canada Highway (west to east) and Highway 102, which connects Halifax and Truro; then we proceed alphabetically through the travelways, and finish with the Bras d'Or, Digby Neck, Flintstone (Shelburne-Carleton on Route 203), and Kejimkujik Scenic Nature Drives.

Each route starts with an overview and a map. Then we take you from one end to the other, highlighting geology, flora, fauna, and relevant human history as we go. There are periodic halts for views, side trips, hikes, and water trips by canoe, kayak, or motor boat.

Origins of Nova Scotia's Roads
Before Old World settlers arrived in the 1600s, the Mi'kmaq had elaborate travelways based on lakes, streams, and woodland portages and paths. In the earliest years of settlement, most long-distance travel was still by sea, with shorter journeys on foot or, for the well-to-do, on horseback. It used to take Richard John Uniacke four hours to ride from his Mount Uniacke estate to Halifax, a distance of about 40 km/ 25 mi. Mail was carried by post riders who met packet boats at various ports and carried letters and parcels in saddlebags.

Good roads were slow in coming. Often they followed earlier footpaths and wagon trails. The first such roads were Acadian cart tracks around Port Royal, Grand Pré, Halifax, Lunenburg, Beaubassin, Tatamagouche, Louisbourg, and Cobequid Bay. The Acadians had an oxcart path along a Mi'kmaq portage from Cobequid Bay to Tatamagouche around 1700.

After the mid-1830s the busier routes were widened and corduroyed (i.e., logs were laid crossways in wet spots) for coaches. The coach's body was mounted fore and aft on two broad leather belts, and swung to and fro. Inside, it had two to three seats placed cross-wise, and it carried 6 to 12 passengers. Leather window flaps kept out rain and wind, and four corner lamps lit the interior.

By 1837 three coach roads were operating. One of these ran from Truro to Windsor and on to Annapolis Royal. Passengers were moved by stages (hence "stage coach") from inn to inn, where fresh horses were waiting. The roads were rough at best, and in spring and fall were often impassable. At such times coaches sank to their axles, and passengers had to get out and push. Coach owners were expected to maintain the roads they used.

Gradually, surfaced (gravelled) roads replaced these muddy tracks. At one point soldiers started to build a military road from Halifax up the spine of the province to Guysborough—the Old Guysborough Road—but it was never finished. After the 1870s railroads replaced some roads, but it was the advent of Henry Ford's "Tin Lizzie," the 1920s motor car, that provided the greatest impetus to road building in the province. One by one, today's travelways were completed. The last major coastal highway to be constructed was Rte 7 between Dartmouth and the Canso Causeway, now called the Marine Drive.

Although Nova Scotia's highways weren't designed for nature study, they are convenient corridors for the student of nature.

A road was begun between Lunenburg and Halifax in 1767, and much effort was devoted to constructing a cross-peninsula road from Halifax to the Bay of Fundy–a badly needed connection. By 1815 two main roads, called "Great Roads," crossed central Nova Scotia. One connected Halifax to Windsor and Hantsport; the other connected Halifax to Truro with an extension to Pictou. In 1816 stages began to operate on these roads; from Halifax it took nine hours to travel the 45 mi /72 km to Windsor, and about two days to Pictou.
– R. C. Harris & J. Warkertin
Canada Before Confederation, *1974*

Theme Regions

In the 1980s land managers and parks planners used satellite imagery, aerial photos, and ground data to classify Nova Scotia's land surface into areas of kindred geology, topography, soils, flora, fauna, and climate. These they called Theme Regions. In relation to the routes they are as follows:

The Trans Canada Trail Foundation is creating a coast-to-coast-to-coast hiking trail linking sections of old railway roadbeds and other corridors. Parts of the Nova Scotia portion include a corridor linking Inverness and Port Hood via the Canso Causeway to Guysborough Harbour; thence to Cross Roads Country Harbour, and northwest via Aspen and East River St Marys to Pictou; thence along the Gulf Shore via River John, Tatamagouche, and Wallace Bridge, dipping south to Oxford and exiting at the Nova Scotia–New Brunswick border midway between Tidnish and Fort Lawrence.

Plateau-Taiga   Carboniferous Lowlands
Highlands   Triassic Lowlands
Avalon Uplands   Fundy Coast
Atlantic Interior   Atlantic Coast

Trans Canada Highway Nature Tour

Amherst to North Sydney, 418 km/260 mi

OVERVIEW

Imagine yourself flying above this route on a clear October morning. Sun-up finds you high above the Amherst and Minudie marshes, heading southeast. Below, the Missaguash and Nappan rivers are brown squiggles on watered green silk, Amherst is a toy town, and the Trans Canada Highway is a grey ribbon curving across the Northumberland Lowland.

This softly rumpled green and ochre plain looks old, and it is. It dates back to the Carboniferous period, that time of calamites and giant dragonflies, of the beginnings of salt and gypsum and coal. Three hundred million years of erosion have so abraded its soft sandstones and shales that hardly a lake remains. But it is rich in rivers: Shinimicas, River Philip, Pugwash, French, Waughs, and River John. Down its gentle incline from the blue Cobequids to the Northumberland Strait they glide, bright in the sun.

Now the flat-roofed Cobequid Mountains angle in from Cape Chignecto like a low garden wall, their slopes brocaded in scarlet and orange and dusky gold. Through skeins of morning mist on the top you glimpse moss-green conifers, a few lakes, a swath of new highway.

The raking golden light picks out ravine after purple ravine where waterfalls tumble over diorite that was old when the Rockies were born. In these hills nestle Southampton and Mapleton, heartland of Nova Scotia's maple industry.

At Wentworth the highway, as if changing its mind, veers sharply south through the only gap in the Cobequids east of Parrsboro. Our aircraft roars down the mountain pass, skims Folly Lake with its necklace of cottages—and suddenly you're out over Minas Basin. Is the water really that pink?

Now your pilot banks east over the Cobequid Lowlands, with the mountains on your left. Evergreen woodlots, sloping pastures, U-pick gardens scroll by. For a time the plane's shadow tracks down the Cobequid Bay. The farther east you go, the browner the water becomes.

Folly Lake

Now there are satiny mud flats flecked with tiny birds that wheel and dip as one. An incoming tide weaves herringbones of light and dark as it curls around crumbling red headlands and noses into creeks shaped like winter silhouettes of maple trees.

Up the narrowing estuary you go, across the Salmon River's great apron of glacial gravel gridded with Truro's streets and rail lines, over

St Anns Bay

the Cobequids again, and down the West River to Pictou's bird's-foot harbour on the Gulf Shore.

The Pictou-Antigonish Highlands seem more round-shouldered than the Cobequids, but they wear the same rich brocade. St Georges Bay yawns between Cape George and western Cape Breton. The church spires of Antigonish swim by, then Canso Strait with its S-shaped causeway half in shadow, then many-fingered Bras d'Or Lake in its saucer of hills. Near Iona we see chalky scuffs—the marks of gypsum quarries.

Toward Whycocomagh the Big Ridge looms over our left wing, its massive tableland falling away in plush folds to steep ravines and pastures dotted with tiny houses. There are white sails on the purple lake. Then you're out over St Anns Bay with its sandspit and the needle-thin Bird Islands.

Circling to land at Sydney Airport, you glimpse the Trans Canada Highway doing its hairpin turn down Kellys Mountain to leap Big Bras d'Or Channel on a spidery green bridge. Then you lose sight of it in the web of roads and suburbs that a century of coal mining and steelmaking has spun here on the shores of Cabot Strait.

At Thomson Station our nature tour follows the old Trans Canada Highway, now called Trunk 4, through the beautiful Wentworth Valley. In December 1996 the province opened the 45-km/28-m Cobequid Pass or Western Alignment Highway from here to Masstown. This toll road, which exits at the Thomson Station overpass, runs through some good sugar bush country and crosses the Cobequids at a slightly higher elevation.

THE TOUR BEGINS

It seems only right that we should enter Canada's Ocean Playground over an ancient sea bottom, for as we cross the muddy Missaguash River into Nova Scotia, there are beneath us 25 m/80 feet of mud, silt, drowned forest, and driftwood. That's what road builders found when they probed for bedrock here.

STOP: *Time and Tides*

Pause on the hill by the Tourist Information Centre to take this in. Clearly the 22-km/14-mi Isthmus of Chignecto, which joins Nova Scotia to the rest of Canada, has its secrets. Not all of them have to do with human history—though there is plenty of that too. The knoll where you stand overlooked Beaubassin, site of the first Acadian farms in the area. Later the British built Fort Lawrence here. Its cannon pointed across the Missaguash (then called the Marguerite) to France's Fort Beauséjour on the far rise. Shots were fired, homes were burned, sword and musket drew blood on both sides.

To the casual eye today, it's a peaceful landscape of gentle ridges grading into grasslands that stretch level to the horizon.

Look again. Along the horizon and along the Missaguash and every other creek, earthen dykes are holding back the highest tides in the world. Take away those dykes, and these maritime prairies would flood once more. Fundy built them in the first place.

For thousands of years its muddy waters brought in layer on layer of brown sediment scoured from Cumberland Basin's soft sandstone floor. Millimetre by millimetre, the inmost layers crept above the reach of all but the highest tides. As erosion and glaciation altered the basin's form, the waters reached even higher.

Tantramar marshes

The process was slow, with many backward steps. After each Ice Age there was no new sediment for a time, because this was dry land. The glaciers had drunk down the sea a hundred metres or more. That's when trees moved in. But each time the ice melted, the sea rose faster than the sagging land. It drowned the trees and washed their bones up on new beaches. Land and sea played tag like this for centuries. But the marsh kept growing.

In this the tides were helped by an amazing salt-tolerant land plant called cord grass or *Spartina*. Cord grass traps silt the way a snow fence traps snow. By so doing it sets the stage for other plants like goldenrod and goose-tongue. Once rain and snow have desalted the fertile muck, freshwater sedges and rushes can start to build soil, turning the mud flat into land.

The Dyke-Builders

The first Acadian settlers on the Isthmus arrived from Grand Pré near Windsor in the late 1670s. They brought sheep and cows, neither of which thrive on salt-marsh hay. But the people knew what to do. From their Breton ancestors they had learned how to drain tidal marshes in the manner of the Dutch. In fact they preferred draining marshes to clearing upland; the yields were better. It takes a lot of good hay to keep a herd of cows healthy all winter.

So the Acadians laboriously built earth-and-brush embankments along the creeks and across the estuaries. This arrested the mud-building process, trapped the tidal nutrients, and created new land from the sea bottom. They solved the problem of freshwater flooding by channelling creeks under the dykes via aboiteaux ("water boxes") hollowed out of big logs. In each log they hung a hinged vertical clapper. Like a valve, it opened to let fresh water out but shut against incoming tides. To prevent washouts, all dykes were carefully sodded.

The Acadians let new dykeland lie fallow for three to five years before sowing it in hay. This was to flush out the salt. When yields began to decline, they opened the aboiteaux and let Fundy silt rejuvenate the land.

Dykes vs. Waterfowl

(Below) "Dyke Lands" (detail) by Fred B. Schell, **Picturesque Canada** *(1884)*

Until the Acadians came, these marshes were alive with ducks and geese. Unfortunately, dyking destroys waterfowl habitat. Only a few decades later, local Mi'kmaq were complaining of a decline in birds. This decline worsened with time.

Today the only large natural tidal wetland left is the John Lusby Marsh in the Chignecto National Wildlife Area (south of Hwy 104 between Exits 1 and 2). Meanwhile, wild geese have adapted to grazing dykeland.

After the Acadians were deported in 1755, their dykes fell into disrepair. Then Yorkshire people came and settled Amherst. As demand for hay rose, the dykes were repaired and extended. Until the 1970s, great hay barns with red side doors dotted the landscape; a few still stand. Ditching after World War II has eked more hay out of the tired soil.

Tantramar derives from tintamarre *(Old French for hubbub or racket), a reference to noisy flocks of geese and ducks that once darkened the skies here in spring and fall.*

Before you leave the border, tour the Information Centre and talk with staff. The exhibits will give you an eagle's-eye view of the province, and the staff can recommend maps and brochures to help you plan your nature tours. We especially recommend the book of contour maps called *A Map of the Province of Nova Scotia* (Province of Nova Scotia and Formac Publishing, 1992).

Locals call dyked lands "marshes"; Minas Basin folk call them "dykes."

Ask too about the Chignecto Ship Railway. Its broad trackway lay just east of the centre and led to Amherst Dock on the Minas Basin. This was an 1880s scheme to transport ships across the isthmus by train to Northumberland Strait, thereby reducing the voyage be-tween Saint John and Québec by 800 kilometres (500 miles). The scheme wasn't quite realized, but it shows the Victorian urge to conquer nature. [See also the **Sunrise Trail** at Tidnish.] Ask too about the Amherst Point Bird Sanctuary.

Crossing the Amherst Marsh, watch in summer for marsh hawks

(northern harriers) hunting meadow voles to feed their nestlings and mates hidden in the tall grass. Winter bird watchers sometimes sight rough-legged hawks, snowy owls (when lemmings are scarce up north), snow buntings, and Lapland longspurs.

SIDE TRIP: *Bird Sanctuary*
One of Nova Scotia's greatest waterfowl areas is Amherst Point Bird Sanctuary, less than 10 minutes south of town from Exit 3. Staff at the border chalet can provide detailed directions. Once there, follow the signs to parking.

Amherst Point Bird Sanctuary

In recent decades Ducks Unlimited (Canada) and government have been restoring idle wetlands all along the eastern seaboard. Dams are built to raise water levels, and potholes are blasted to make ponds. Ducks and geese are increasing—to the point where farmers are complaining, and airport officials worry about collisions with planes. Here the Missaguash Marsh was developed first, then the Tintamarre Complex in New Brunswick, then the East Amherst and Amherst Point wetlands. As a result, the area has experienced a similar upsurge in waterfowl. Uncommon species like black tern, teal, grebe, wigeon, coot, and moorhen have returned as well.

To access the Sunrise Trail to Pictou along the Northumberland Strait shoreline, take Exit 3 to Amherst and follow Victoria Street north to Rte 366.

BACK ON THE HIGHWAY
Once you leave the Amherst flats, the road climbs a gentle incline through glades of young aspen, red maple, and birch broken by spruce groves, pastures, and blueberry fields. This is a landscape of broad ridges and gentle swales underlain by tightly folded layers of sedimentary rocks, including salt and gypsum.

In fact, at nearby Nappan a tidal arm of ocean once broiled under a tropical sun for so long that it left a thick bed of glittering rock salt. Later, sand and silt buried the salt. [See also the **Sunrise Trail** at Pugwash.] By injecting hot water some 30 m/100 ft down, pumping the brine to the surface, and boiling the water away, Domtar Chemical's Sifto Salt Division extracts 65 000 tonnes of table salt a year.

The **Glooscap Trail** leaves the Trans Canada Highway at Exit 4 to join Rte 302 at Upper Nappan.

The woodland through here is mostly red maple, spruce, trembling aspen, and white birch—and all second growth. Cumberland County once had magnificent forests of spruce, hemlock, and pine,

A local history states that the maple leaf in Canada's flag was modelled after some leaves picked by Amherst Mayor Tom Park Lowther at his farm in Fenwick. A local Member of Parliament in Prime Minister Lester Pearson's government had asked him to "find some perfect maple leaves."

some more than 300 years old. In the 19th century these were heavily cut for masting, ship timber, and lumber.

These forests also saw great fires, especially after the Intercolonial Railway came through from Montreal to Halifax in 1876. Coal-burning locomotives had a habit of scattering live coals right and left from their fireboxes. Sawmills at Shulie and Apple River also started forest fires by burning sawdust. Serious fires continued well into the 1960s, when a network of forest roads, radio-linked lookout towers, and mobile fire crews got them under control. Nature is still healing these scars.

Then there was farming. From the early 1800s on, large tracts were cleared, only to be abandoned in the 1880s as people sought easier lives in town and city. The Great Depression saw a further exodus. Most of the cleared land soon reverted to forest. Willow, alder, and larch invaded the wetter clay soils; birch, white spruce, and balsam fir restocked the sandy soils.

Three young Loyalist soldiers found a well-wooded sandstone ridge in 1790 and liked it. John and Charles Boss and David Herrett had trekked here from Sackville, NB, after serving with George III's army at Harper's Ferry in the American War of Independence. There were abundant springs, so they named it Springhill.

Thirty-seven years later, someone discovered coal. For a while people just heated their homes with it and sold a few loads to local blacksmiths. In 1870 the Springhill Mining Company was formed. A spur line was built to Springhill Junction, and mining commenced. For many years coal was shipped from Parrsboro.

Springhill made world headlines in 1891 and again in 1956 when gas explosions killed dozens of men and boys. There was another hazard. Once a coal face is mined, the supports are removed, and the roof is supposed to collapse gently. At Springhill the sandstone between the seams is unstable. Sometimes it exploded into the excavations. In 1958 such a rock burst trapped scores of men far underground, killing 75. The last two collieries were closed for good.

Forest Plantation

Amid so much mixed forest, the sudden appearance of a human-made block of softwoods, 1.4 km/0.9 mi east of the Fenwick Road, is eye-catching. The trees are black spruce, planted in 1986 by the pulp interests of K. C. Irving of Saint John after a stand of old-field white spruce was harvested. In 1996 some were 6 m/20 ft tall and just entering the rapid-growth pole stage. At this stage, conifers shoot up 0.5 m/1.5 ft or more a year. Here they have outstripped the speckled alder, willow, and red maple that survived early herbicide treatment. All of these will be shaded out, except where openings exist.

As any carpenter can tell you, black spruce makes poor, twisty lumber. But its long fibres and dense wood are ideal for papermaking. This plantation is destined for pulp. By the year 2020—barring fire, blowdown, or pests (budworm prefers white spruce or balsam fir)—it will be ready to harvest.

Beyond Fenwick Road we enter a terrain of broad ridges and wide valleys resembling ocean swells. Here and there a remnant white pine towers above the canopy of younger spruce, maple, aspen, and birch. Coming down the long ridge to Springhill's Exit 5, we see many paper birches. So many in one place are unusual; normally this tree is sprinkled among spruce and fir. A grove of white birch is a sign of major disturbance.

In fact, the Shulie-Oxford forest fire roared through here in 1921, killing the conifers and baring the mineral soil. Scorched and dying, a few old birches peppered the blackened earth with seed. Some red maple seeds also germinated. Thus this grove was born.

Birch and maple that grow from seeds typically have single stems; sprouted trees grow in clumps.

What happens next? These birch are close to the age limit for the species. Already some have dead tops, and high winds have toppled a few. Fir and spruce have infiltrated, biding their time. As more birch fall, the fir will shade out all but the most vigorous birch, setting the stage for another cycle—if Smokey Bear will permit it.

Another sign of the 1921 fire is the tall crowded grove of black spruce on the right near the foot of the ridge. The cones of this tree are glued shut with resin and need high heat to open them and release the winged seed.

SIDE TRIP: *Coal Town*
About 4 km/2.5 mi south of Exit 5 on Rte 142 is the famous coal town of Springhill, birthplace of singer Anne Murray. Mining began here in 1870 and lasted a century.

For a firsthand look, tour the Springhill Miners' Museum on Black River Road off Rte 2 (open May–Oct., admission charged). For a detailed history read R. D. Brown's *Blood on the Coal: The Story of the Springhill Mining Disasters* (Lancelot Press, Hantsport, NS, 1976).

Springhill is near the heart of Nova Scotia's small but enterprising maple industry. Many of the operations are less than two kilometres from a main road, so if you happen by in March–April, try to arrange a tour.

BACK ON THE HIGHWAY
As the highway swings east and climbs another long ridge toward Oxford, pockets of a smallish pine appear among the aspen, birch, and maple. Jack pine is a native cousin of white and red pine, and it thrives on burnt land.

The two chief fire species hereabouts are jack pine and trembling aspen. Jack pine is known to degrade forest soils by excreting chemicals that inhibit other plants. Aspen, on the other hand, enriches the ground for other plants. Naturalist J. Fraser Darling, touring North America in the 1950s for the United Nations, called aspen a calcium pump. Its roots delve deeper than any conifer's, retrieving valuable minerals leached down by rain and snow and placing them back on the surface in its leaf fall. The leaves of aspen contain more calcium than those of any other eastern deciduous tree. (Which is why they turn yellow in autumn. Acidic leaves turn red.)

Oxford is the authentic blueberry capital of Canada. You don't see many fields around the town, but berries from all over Cumberland County are shipped from here. Oxford is proud of its tractor-drawn

Some pines seem to court fire. They favour sandy soils that dry out quickly after rain. They drop gummy needles that burn like dry shavings. They often restock burned areas. Could it be? It could. The ground under an older pine forest is often so deep in needles and so cool that its seeds cannot germinate. Other seeds can, and they become rivals for light and space. A fire solves both problems by clearing the thick duff and killing the competition. It also kills some of the old pines; but some survive and, stimulated by stress, produce bumper crops of cones. This virtually guarantees a new pine forest on the same ground. Of course the new forest is equally prone to fire.

45

Blueberry fields in the fall

blueberry rake called The Blue Machine, its frozen vegetables, and its greenhouse roses. And River Philip next door has a salmon run.

The Oxford Lowlands are low because the bedrock is soft. It is so soft, in fact, that the surrounding woods are pocked with ponds, sinkholes, and caverns. Percolating rainwater dissolves the calcium out of calcium sulphate, alias gypsum, leaving a lumpy landscape called karst topography. [See also the **Evangeline Trail** near Windsor and the **Cabot Trail** near Aspy Bay.]

If you've time, pull off at Exit 6 and drive 0.5 km/0. 3 mi north to the Lion's Parkland. Its shallow, dammed lake tastes salty-sulphurous. Half a kilometre north, on your left past the greenhouses, is the Department of Natural Resources (DNR) Cumberland East office. For years it has hosted a colony of purple martins. The birds nest in four two-storey, 12-room houses out back. In 1995, 18 nests produced only three eggs, none of which hatched. In 1996 the same thing happened, but an electric heater in House #4 helped three nestlings to hatch. Nearby Collingwood has also hosted a colony.

While at the DNR office, ask for directions to the River Philip Demonstration Forest, and check on the status of Wentworth Provincial Park.

SIDE TRIP: *Beaver Village*

Seven kilometres (4.3 mi) east of Oxford, visible to the right of the Thomson Station/Birchwood overpass and toll road exit, note the two small beaver dams on a branch of the Pugwash River. This is beaver country. A 1991 census showed that Cumberland County had an estimated 3,891 beavers, with Oxford district averaging one colony per 4 km²—twice the county average.

If you'd like a close-up view of an active beaver pond, return to Oxford's DNR office and get directions to the River Philip Demonstration Forest. RPDF offers a 0.7-km/0.4-mi interpretive trail with extensive beaver works. There are also cavity trees (important for wood ducks, woodpeckers, raccoons) and old pines from the glory days of lumbering. Wear waterproof boots.

STOP: *River Philip Demonstration Forest*
Nova Scotia has more than 30,000 woodlot owners—the highest number in mainland Canada. Most owners can't afford to do expensive silviculture or road building on their own, but linked with other owners they can.

Approximately 200 owners hereabouts have done just that, pooling 45 000 ha/111,195 ac for joint management. Because they view public support as crucial to successful forest management, some have opened their woods to the public. They offer self-guided interpretive trails and forestry demonstration sites. They also allow the Cumberland Snowmobile Club to use their trails as part of a countywide network. This Wyvern-based group holds races, rallies, and other events, which draw thousands.

For more information about the demonstration forest, ask at local tourist centres for a brochure. As with any private lands, get permission before entering, and observe the take-in, take-out rule.

Though beavers are our largest native rodent (up to 27 kg/ 60 lb), they seem insecure until their front door is at least a metre under water, with a cache of fresh saplings submerged nearby. The deep water deters most predators, and the saplings ensure ample winter food. Actually, water doesn't deter mink or otter, but a beaver's razor-sharp teeth and bulldog courage do.

BACK ON THE HIGHWAY
Our tour now takes Exit 7 at Thomson Station and follows the more leisurely route of the former **Trans Canada Highway** (now Trunk 4). Transport trucks (except for local traffic) are prohibited from using this two-lane highway and must continue along the Western Alignment of Hwy 104, a four-lane toll road.

VIEW: *Wind Gap*
Near Mahoneys Corner there's a good view of the Wentworth Valley about 10 km/6 mi south.

(Park at the Wilson Gas Stop—2.2 km/1.4 mi east of Exit 7.) In clear weather the notch is striking. It was carved during or before the last glaciation by the Wallace River or a predecessor that flowed across the lowlands. On the soft lowlands its bed has long been erased, but the more resistant Cobequids have preserved it. So this ancient dry stream bed sits about 100 m/ 330 ft above the plain—a measure of the amount of erosion since. Such a raised dry river valley is called a wind gap.

Being the only break in the Cobequids for 50 km/30 mi either way, in 1876 the Wentworth gap was chosen as the route for the Intercolonial Railway between Montreal and Halifax. The valley is named after Loyalist Sir John Wentworth, Nova Scotia's lieutenant governor from 1792 to 1807.

Notice how flat and eroded the tops of the Cobequids are. Glaciers didn't do all that. Rain, frost, ice, wind, lichens, bacteria, and plants were also at work. In the last 80 million years erosion has reduced the once-alpine Cobequids to today's modest peneplain.

The process continues. Each year the headwaters of the Wallace and its sister streams creep higher, forever nibbling sand and pebbles from the hillsides, forever tumbling them downhill and across the lowlands to the strait. In a million years the Cobequids could be 30 m/100 ft lower.

As you near the pass, notice the valley's U-shaped profile, one sure sign of a glacier. The moving ice ground off overlapping spurs of rock like a bulldozer straightening a crooked road.

Motorists have dubbed this stretch of highway "Death Valley." Near the summit high winds and sudden chilling of moist Fundy air can quickly create winter driving conditions from October through May. This, plus heavy truck traffic, has caused several deaths each year. The alternative route is intended to ease the situation.

Cave near Wentworth

STOP: *Wentworth Provincial Park*

This park on the Wallace River is a nice place to lunch or nap. (The camping portion may be closed.) It's also a good place to view spring wildflowers or to cross-country ski. For downhillers, Wentworth Ski Hill, a few kilometres south, offers good facilities for intermediate and expert skiers.

SIDE TRIP: *Climax Forest*

If you'd like to actually get up *into* the Cobequids rather than just pass through, take Valley Road on the west side just south of Exit 9. Drive 1 km/0.6 mi west to Station Road and turn left. This gravel road climbs steeply for 0.8 km/0.5 mi though lovely deciduous forest to the Wentworth Youth Hostel, a former railroad station. The ridge you're on runs right across northern Nova Scotia from Apple River in the west to Balmoral Mills in the east. It's an even better place to view spring flowers, which include trillium, lady's-slipper, trout-lily, and three kinds of violets. The fall foliage is superb, and there are hawks, pileated woodpecker, and great horned owl.

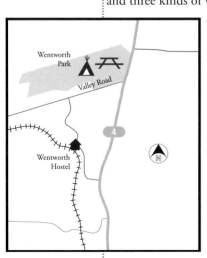

Here you see Nova Scotia's typical upland broadleaf forest: sugar maple, beech, and yellow birch. Stop and savour the spicy air and the milky green light. These three species tolerate shade when young—hence the term "tolerant hardwoods." It means they can reproduce in each other's shade indefinitely if undisturbed. The result is called climax forest. Hobblebush, striped maple, and ironwood hobnob with them. The gnarled look of trees up here is due to winter gales.

About 25 minutes south along the railway tracks is Smith Brook. (WARNING: Listen/watch for trains!) A trail here descends (left) to a waterfall and a human-made tunnel.

BACK ON THE TRUNK 4

Half a kilometre (0.3 mi) beyond the Valley Inn Motel, opposite a blueberry field, there's a lovely waterfall. Watch on the right for a road barred by iron posts. Pedestrians are welcome, so park and walk. A five-minute stroll along a trail through young birch and maple brings you to where Higgins Brook bursts through a notch and cascades down several ledges into a pretty reflecting pool. The murmur of waters and the cool breeze off the falls are refreshing.

These VIA Rail tracks belonged to the Intercolonial Railway. Notable Scottish engineer Sir Sandford Fleming supervised the construction. Worried perhaps about the weight of boxcars full of pig iron from nearby Londonderry, he browbeat the penny pinchers into building a steel, rather than a wooden, bridge over Folly River.

In his day Fleming was famous for inventing time zones and standard railway time, devices for rationalizing train schedules across Canada's vast breadth.

VIEW: *Folly Lake*

Perched 180 m/590 ft above sea level like a turquoise brooch on the bosom of Wentworth Pass, this lake feeds Wallace River to the north and Folly River to the south. Where it sits, an ice cap once lingered after the lowland ice had melted. In melting it plugged both ends of the lake with sand and gravel. If these dams were removed, much of the lake would drain. It's surprisingly deep—60 m/ 200 ft in places—and a mecca for trout anglers and cottagers.

In 1995–96 Lafarge supplied 500,000 tonnes of crushed aggregate from here to build the Confederation Bridge between New Brunswick and Prince Edward Island.

At the south end, gravel and sand have been dug for highway construction since 1960. At the north end, Lafarge Construction Materials quarries diorite, a hard crystalline rock used in concrete.

It's said the lake got its name from an ill-conceived 19th-century farming venture nicknamed "Flemming's Folly." One James Flemming, perhaps sensing a ready market for farm produce at nearby Londonderry, tried to farm here. The early and late frosts defeated him.

Up here blueberries grow much better than potatoes. At the top of the rise south of the lake there are fields of them. This native member of the heath family often follows wildfire. Copying nature, owners torch the fields with tractor-drawn oil burners every two years to discourage weeds and to promote bud formation.

From the berry fields one can see, toward Truro, a series of 1970s Scott Paper clearcuts in various stages of regrowth. Coming down the hill, there are views of Cobequid Bay with Noel Shore beyond. The waters have an odd russet tint. From here to Glenholme the highway follows Folly River, whose narrow gorge you'll glimpse to the east. It's narrow because the Precambrian bedrock is so hard.

Just south of Folly Lake you cross the Cobequid Fault, an earth fracture that runs from Cape Chignecto to Cape Canso and up through western Newfoundland. It occurred about the time that North Africa rammed North America.

Between Folly Mountain Cemetery and the railway bridge, you travel 80 million years a minute! The bedrock under the cemetery was formed 600 million years ago, while the bedrock by the railway bridge was new when dinosaurs appeared nearly 200 million years ago. And in that short space Folly River changes from a limpid mountain stream to a silty lowland river.

SIDE TRIP: *Nova Scotia's First Boom Town*

High on the south slope of the Cobequids, where the Great Village River crosses the Cobequid Fault, lies the sleepy village of

49

Londonderry started out Acadian, but was resettled in 1839 by 20 families of farmers and weavers from Londonderry in Northern Ireland. They raised sheep for wool and flax for linen. Their pastoral life was shattered after 1848, when prospector George Duncan found rusty rock along the Great Village and Folly rivers.

The next year, C. D. Archibald formed the Acadian Charcoal Company to smelt the ore. Later the Acadia Mining Company set up four blast furnaces and built homes for 200 workers and their families.

To extract the iron, raw ore was mixed with crushed limestone and fed down tall stacks superheated by charcoal. As the blast furnace melted the ore, impurities bonded with the limestone to form slag, which was removed.

It took 56 m³/160 bu of charcoal and 70 m³/200 bu of limestone to smelt one tonne of pig iron out of four tonnes of raw ore. Moulding the pig iron into bars required another 13 m³/3.5 cords of dry hardwood per tonne. Whole hillsides were stripped to feed the beehive charcoal kilns. The acrid smell of woodsmoke became a fact of life.

In 1874 Sir William Siemens, inventor of the open-hearth steel process, formed the Steel Company of Canada and bought the operation. He successfully lobbied the Intercolonial for a loop of track (satirized as the "Grecian Bend") to service the mines. For years the settlement around the station was called "The Curve."

At their maximum the Londonderry operations stretched from east of Folly River (East Mines) to the Portapique River, with 37 km/23 mi of underground shafts and tunnels. Ore from Nictaux in the Annapolis Valley was also smelted. [See the Evangeline Trail.]

By 1908, cheap Sydney coal and plentiful Bell Island Newfoundland ore were hurting the operation. Different companies came and went. According to the Colchester Sun, everything was sold for scrap in 1913.

Londonderry, population under 250. Driving through, you might never guess that it has known the throb and clank of heavy industry, the bustle of 5,000 people, the tramp of striking workers, the heartbreak of plant closure, the devastation of a great fire. All because a geological event millions of years ago (i.e., the collision noted above) riddled these hills with iron ore.

Today few of its inhabitants give a second thought to its silent slag heaps and rusting metal. Trueman Matheson of the village likes to talk about Londonderry's glory days when roaring blast furnaces smelted thousands of tonnes of pig iron from high-grade local ore and shipped it around the world. Many Nova Scotian towns still use water pipes cast at Londonderry.

Trueman set up the modest but informative outdoor display beside the road as you enter from the Minas side. It features a map of the former town, a monster flywheel from the mill, and a boiler. In 1996 he had to close his labour-of-love museum when a government grant was cut.

To reach Londonderry you can exit either south of Folly Lake (dirt road west, about 6 km/ 3.7 mi) or west past the railway bridge (a bit longer, but paved).

Ask locally, or at the Book Nook or Coles in Truro, for Trueman Matheson's A History of Londonderry, N.S. (1983, 150 pages). For information on iron mining in Nova Scotia generally, visit the Nova Scotia Museum of Industry in Stellarton.

STOP: *Acadia Mines Bridge*
Until December 1996, the steel Bailey bridge spanning the Great Village River gorge between Londonderry and Acadia Mines was mainland Nova Scotia's highest single-span steel structure. Here one can look *down* from 27.4 m/90 ft on the tops of tall spruce. For safety reasons the bridge was replaced in 1996 with a structure nearly as high. The gorge alone is well worth a short detour west. Ask for directions locally.

BACK ON TRUNK 4
At Glenholme, for the first time since Minudie, we're at back at sea level. The Cobequid Low-

This engraving, "Acadia Mines" by Schell & Hogan appeared in **Picturesque Canada** *in 1884 and shows Londonderry in the background.*

lands surrounding the eastern end of Minas Basin consist of tilted and eroded brick-red sandstone sediments from the Triassic Period. [See the **Glooscap Trail**.] The same formation extends through the Annapolis Valley and out under St Marys Bay. [See the **Evangeline Trail**.]

In the age of dinosaurs this landscape looked much like today's Grand Canyon, with arid, piny uplands and green river valleys. Dry winds blew sand around for millennia. Then monsoon rains soaked for millennia more. Later the whole Fundy trough subsided. Lava flowed along the North Mountain and elsewhere. Later still, the Atlantic breached Fundy's shallow outer end, setting its famous tides in motion.

Since then, fierce tidal scouring has been filling the inner bay with pinkish mud. At Economy the ebb tide goes out so far that no salt water can be seen for hours. [See the **Glooscap Trail**.] The muck is full of invertebrate life, which in turn supports a diversity of fish and birds. Recently scientists have discovered that the top few centimetres of this mud act as a solar collector for a simmering broth of algae that fuels the whole food chain.

Like Tantramar and Grand Pré, this is a land of Acadian dykes. Wide reclaimed pastures line both sides of the bay. The first of these can be seen just east of the Rte 2 intersection, in a bend of the Folly River.

STOP: *Little Dyke*

Less than a kilometre from the Glenholme intersection you can visit the site of an original Acadian dyke. Exit right at Glenholme onto Rte 2, drive south 0.6 km/0.4 mi past Erskine United Church, turn left onto Little Dyke Road, and park beyond the last house (where you should ask permission). A short downhill hike takes you to the dyked estuary of the Folly and Debert rivers.

The original dyke is gone, absorbed into longer ones built later. But you can get a sense of the work the Acadians did. With no

One of the world's biggest concentrations of shorebirds descends on the upper Bay of Fundy each August to fuel up on tiny mud shrimp before migrating to South America.

backhoes or dump trucks to lighten the labour, they usually enclosed a single creek. The whole community would turn out during low tide to build the dyke, leaving those who lived nearest to tend it. With some cleared upland for vegetables and dykeland for pasture, one creek would support several families.

The Folly Village cemetery beside the church was established in 1770 and contains legible stones dating to Napoleon Bonaparte's time.

On the sandy roadsides between Glenholme and the Debert exit, all three native pines grow together. (The darker, more crowded, ramrod-straight trees are black spruce, which sprang up after a fire over 50 years ago.)

ALTERNATIVE ROUTE: "COBEQUID PASS"

Opened in November 1997, this four-lane highway is a westerly alternative to the two-lane Wentworth Valley route. The government built it in the face of numerous traffic deaths there (52 between 1987 and 1997). Built partly with private funds, it was the first tolled section of **Trans Canada Highway** in Canada.

Strictly speaking, Cobequid Pass is a geological term long used to identify the natural gap in the Cobequids at Folly Lake. During construction the highway was called the "Western Alignment"; Cobequid Bypass is a more accurate (though medically unpleasant) term for this route.

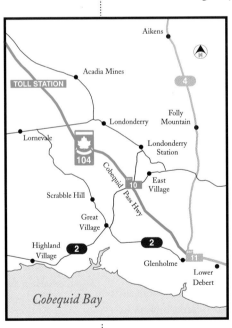

The new highway runs from near Thomson Station in Cumberland County to Masstown in Colchester County, a distance of approximately 41 km/25 mi. It's a little shorter than the Wentworth route but not as scenic. However, because it angles across an unpopulated area of the Cobequids, it gives motorists a superior view of that upland. You should see more wildlife—moose in particular—since old clearcuts have regenerated in choice winter foods like balsam fir, birch, and maple. The road builders, worried about car/wildlife collisions, have installed five special tunnels for animals wanting to cross the highway.

For the first 6 km/3.7 mi the highway passes through a broadly rolling landscape of farm and woodlot. After climbing steadily for a few kilometres, it levels off into hardwood country, picks up the headwaters of the Great Village River, and follows its valley down to the Cobequid coastal plain.

VIEW: *Jack Pine*

As you leave Hwy 104 at Exit 7, the most striking sight is a grove of slender pines with yellow-green foliage lining the road on both sides. These are jack pine, the smallest of our three native pines. [See also the **Trans Canada Highway** just east of Exit 5.] After 3.5 km/2 mi it is joined by a few red pine, more robust and open-looking with darker, tufted needles and reddish bark. Both are here for a reason. Fire passed through this area over 50 years ago, killing the spruce and fir. The heat stimulated existing red pines to produce more seed (most trees respond to stress this way). It also opened the dormant, resin-sealed cones of jack pine.

Of the two species, jack pine tolerates poorer soils and more exposed sites. This makes it an important post-fire colonizer of places such as the Canso and Halifax barrens [see also the **Cabot Trail** near Neils Harbour], but it doesn't like wet feet. This is demonstrated in the next 3 km/1.9 mi, where dry knolls alternate with wet hollows. The knolls feature pines and red spruce, but the hollows are occupied by black spruce, often called "swamp spruce."

After 1.5 km/0.9 mi the pines fade out, and we're in spruce country. This is announced by a huge mid-1990s clearcut to the south, followed by red spruce stands near the Collingwood exit (Exit 8).

Old fields on Mt Thom reverting to forest

VIEW: *Forest Take-Over*

Another 1.4 km/0.8 mi and we pass, to the south, an old pasture grown up in aster, goldenrod, and alder. (The alder indicates wet or clayey soil.) By 2010 balsam fir, red maple, and white spruce will have invaded the drier parts, converting this century-old clearing back to young forest.

At 13 km/8 mi beyond Exit 7 we begin to climb the north slope of the Cobequid Range, a slope that extends, intercut by streams, from westernmost Nova Scotia nearly to Pictou. As we climb, the landscape in spring and summer does a quick change from mixedwood forest to almost pure broadleaf forest, from sombre olive and moss greens to cheery lettuce greens. The three main species are sugar maple, yellow birch, and beech.

Not far west of here, around Westchester and Southampton, is the province's premier maple syrup country. From late March through mid-April many camps offer guided tours and sugaring-off events, while nearby churches sponsor pancake suppers.

The same mix of forest covers most of Nova Scotia's uplands and accounts for their brilliant autumn colours. These hardwoods are pretty far north here. By growing on upland slopes they avoid both the frost-prone lowlands (cold drains downhill) and the fierce winds and ice storms of the highest hills. They do best on south slopes with deep loamy soil. The hardier spruce and fir usually occupy north slopes and areas of thin soil.

Be prepared for untimely snow and ice up here in late fall and early spring. A mild day on the lowlands can be wintry up here.

VIEW: *Gravel Pit*
Soon we pass a large gravel pit to the south. This gaping landscape scar is one of the prices we pay for modern transport. Such pits are more noticeable in mountainous terrain, where side hills and valleys must be crossed. Provided glacial drift is abundant (as here), it's cheaper to use gravel than to blast roadbeds out of flinty Cobequid rock. The pit was dug into a deposit called a kame, created by silt-laden meltwater travelling along the edge of a glacier.

Immediately after the pit we see a big spruce plantation backed by long vistas of older clearcuts from the 1980s and earlier. A few minutes later, Sugarloaf Mountain looms to the east. It is named for the resemblance of its massive rounded dome to the glass-encased, moulded sugar "loaves" that rural stores used to display. [See also the **Cabot Trail** at Aspy Bay and Margaree Forks.]

After Westchester Road we pass more sugar maple ridges and, just before the toll plaza, a big clearcut spruce ridge to the north. Roadsides now tend to be rocky, whereas before they were smooth and green. A few minutes south of the toll plaza we enter the Great Village River's watershed, and the landscape becomes more lush. Ten kilometres/6 mi farther, we glimpse the river bed itself to the west, dramatically carved into deep glacial drift and resistant rock.

Coming down off the Cobequids, we re-enter rolling foothills much like those we left near Exit 8. There are glimpses of the silt-brown waters of Cobequid Bay with Hants County beyond. Cliffy road cuts give way to seeded and manicured gravel aprons cut from soft brown sandstone. Red maple, fir, and white birch once again become common, mixed with spruce, fir, and larch, signs of a long history of land clearing, logging, and wildfire. Typically the forest cover is broken into several age-classes, reflecting harvests going back to the 1960s and beyond.

Minutes east of Glenholme, just beyond the dyked tidal mouth of Folly River at Masstown, we rejoin Hwy 104. At nearby Glenholme you may access the **Glooscap Trail** (Hwy 236).

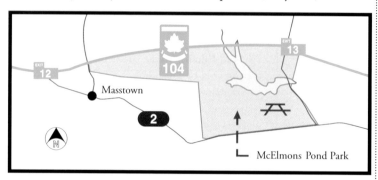

STOP: *McElmons Pond Wildlife Sanctuary*
Lakes are scarce in sandstone country, so waterfowl flock to this artificial one to nest and rest. Migrating Canada geese come here between expeditions to nearby stubble fields and mud flats. Wigeons, pintails, and teal come for the introduced pondweed. Wood ducks sometimes use the nesting boxes that provincial biologists have nailed to dead trees in the secluded far cove.

The dam is important. It keeps the water from rising too high (which drowns nestlings) or dropping too low (which exposes them to hungry foxes). A fish ladder lets trout pass over the dam.

For hot and weary human travellers, the picnic park at McElmons Pond offers cold spring water, cool breezes off the pond, and a short woodland trail with lady's-slipper and trillium in season. (Please don't pick the flowers; and don't wade or swim in the pond unless you want to study leeches.) The floating rope barrier in mid-pond protects the woodies from unwanted boaters. Take Exit 13 south, drive 1 km/0.6 mi, and watch for the pond.

By continuing south 1 km/0.6 mi to Rte 2 and then heading east, you'll soon come to a cairn beside the Chiganois River. It marks the ancient Mi'kmaq canoe route and Acadian oxcart trail over the Cobequids from Minas Basin to Tatamagouche and then to Île St Jean (Prince Edward Island). In the early 1700s, cabbages, potatoes, cheese, and beef were hauled over this route and shipped to Fortress Louisbourg. [See also the **Sunrise Trail**.]

The squat, gnarled deciduous trees along the marsh are native northern red oak, apparently self-sown.

From the cairn you may backtrack to the **Trans Canada Highway**, or pick it up either at Exit 15 (in Truro's west end) or at Exit 17 (in east Bible Hill).

As early as 1866 there were proposals for fishways to help fish to get to the spawning grounds; but it was not until 1870 that James King in Nova Scotia developed the ... King Fish Ladder.
— M. H. Scargill, **A Short History of Canadian English**, 1977

Had you lived at Debert Village in 1885, you might have seen carpenters finishing a stilt-legged wooden chute near the Intercolonial Railway station. Made of tongue-and-groove lumber, it was 33 cm/13 in wide and 23 cm/9 in deep and ran from Belmont up Debert Mountain, 11 km/7 mi in all.

The chute belonged to local lumber baron Thomas Gotobed McMullen, who operated portable sawmills here in the 1880s. Portable mills were convenient, because all bulky slabs, edgings, and sawdust could be left in the woods. In that time of few roads, the easiest way to bring out the lumber was by flume or sluice. (River drives were reserved for logs.) Just enough water was diverted from a mountain stream to float the boards single file at a walking pace. To prevent pile-ups, they were tacked together with lightweight chain. Each evening the hardware was collected in a bucket and toted back up the mountain.

At one point McMullen and his brother Archibald operated 34 km/21 mi of long-distance sluiceways. T. G. is also noted for two fine wooden buildings in Truro, namely his Queen Street home and the former Immanuel Baptist Church on Prince.

According to forest historian Ralph Johnson, "In 1893 [Thomas McMullen] loaded 40 barks with more than 22 million board feet [of lumber] at $10 per thousand and shipped it to Liverpool, England."

VIEW: *Debert Neolithic Site*

Stone Age hunters and Canadian troops have both camped on these sand plains north of Exit 13. In 1963–64 archaeologists found quartz-like skinning knives, spear points, and hand-worked stone chips here. Carbon dating placed them at 10,600 years ago—Canada's earliest evidence of human occupation next to the Yukon's 20,000-year-old Bluefish Cave site. The unmarked site is protected by law.

Scientists attribute the artifacts to Partridge Island and Cape d'Or, where flint-knapping workshops have been found. Stones unique to Labrador were also found.

These nomadic hunters depended on caribou for winter food and clothing. In winter, woodland caribou eat mainly lichens that grow on windy bogs and barrens. To get at them the animals dig with their shovel-shaped hoofs. With the first snows of autumn, the herds would have left the Cobequids and filed along well-worn trails, probably along the Folly and Debert river valleys, crossed the bay, and headed for the Southern Uplands. Caribou are excellent swimmers.

Somewhere near here the hunters would have waylaid them. Perhaps, like the later Beothuk of Newfoundland, they built makeshift fences of half-felled conifers to channel their prey to favoured killing sites. Or they might have fired the marsh grasses. Our caribou went extinct in the 1920s.

During World War II, Camp Debert trained thousands of soldiers and aviators for the war in Europe. Residents of nearby Masstown, Belmont, and Onslow heard the thunder of artillery practice, the roar of aircraft landing and taking off, and the crackle of rifle fire as mock battles were fought in the woods. Today the camp stands silent. There are aspens in the cement bunkers, and dandelions wave in the cracked tarmac.

The original meaning of Truro was "true road".

VIEW: *"Hub of Nova Scotia"*

Near Exit 15 to Truro and Halifax there are views of Truro and its agricultural hinterland. Between 1759 and 1784, people from New Hampshire and Northern Ireland took over the lands of the Acadians expelled in 1755. This area milled the first oatmeal in Nova Scotia and had the first model farm in Canada at Truro, 1857. (The Agricultural College's weed garden and herbarium alone are worth a visit.)

Truro occupies a valley paved with glacial outwash eroded from the surrounding hills by the Salmon and North rivers when the coast was below sea level. As the land rose after the last Ice Age, the rivers carved terraces and channels in the outwash and built wide mud flats and marshes out in the bay. These marshes, since dyked and drained, help make Truro, Onslow, and Old Barns a leading dairy district. Heavy rains and sudden winter thaws regularly inundate the floodplain.

Unlike its namesakes in Cape Cod and England, Truro is useless as a seaport. Its estuary is silty and the channel variable. But Truro benefits from two facts of geography. It lies almost exactly midway between Sydney and Yarmouth and the nearby Cobequid Mountains squeeze all eastbound road and rail traffic past its front door.

SIDE TRIP: *Bores and Birds*

For a relaxing break, pause at Truro to watch the tidal bore, to bird-watch, and perhaps to visit the museum.

One of the province's best bore lookoffs is within sight of Exit 14. Take Exit 15 toward Halifax and go 1 km/0.6 mi; after crossing the Salmon River take Exit 14 (the first ramp) and turn left onto Hwy 236 (the **Glooscap Trail**). Tidal Bore Road is just beyond the Hwy 102 overpass on the right. Drive 0.5 km/0.3 mi and you'll have a ringside seat. The best bores occur during full and new moon (i.e., twice a month), especially in June and October.

Ask at the nearby Palliser Restaurant (incidentally a fine dining place) for a folder listing times. Be on hand 10 minutes beforehand; weather affects bore schedules. The interpretive centre at the lookoff offers a six-minute continuous videotape telling the geological story of Minas Basin.

If there's a substantial wait, walk the nearby dyke and look for birds. The air along the dykes is bracing—spicy with hay and salty with mud.

Cowbird

One of the commonest summer birds here is the bobolink (the one Wordsworth wrote about). This small, yellow-headed blackbird has a habit of springing from the tall hay, burbling a few notes, and dropping out of sight. Two other common blackbirds are the red-winged (fond of cattail swamps and ditches) and the cowbird (which lays eggs in other birds' nests).

Eagles cruise the mud flats from here to the Shubenacadie River, summer and winter. Ring-necked pheasant, Hungarian partridge, and northern harrier live here too. Along back roads in young forest there are yellow-shafted flickers, a ground-feeding woodpecker that eats enormous quantities of ants. Its piercing staccato cry, white rump patch, and yellow-striped

Eagle

57

underwings identify it. In winter you could see a flock of mourning doves. In April you might hear the eerie winnowing of snipe overhead.

Truro's Victoria Park (Park Street off Brunswick) is another good bird-watching site. Expert birders have tallied up to four dozen species here on a single summer stroll along its many woodland and streamside paths. Even novices usually spot warblers, thrushes, and flycatchers in season and woodpeckers, chickadees, and jays in winter.

Victoria Park

The Colchester Historical Society Museum at 29 Young Street is well worth any time you can spare. Volunteer workers will be happy to tell you about the area's natural history.

The Cobequid Trail Foundation is developing a pathway leading from the Bible Hill Recreation Site past the Agricultural College and out through Lower Truro along the abandoned Dominion Atlantic Railway line. The trail offers walkers, cyclists, equestrians, and wheelchair users a way to explore without the noise of traffic. Eventually the trail may link up with the Trans Canada Trail. [See the **Marine Drive** near Boylston and Musquodoboit Harbour and the **Sunrise Trail** at Tatamagouche.]

From the park or museum you can access the **Trans Canada Highway** via Prince and Walker streets across the Salmon River bridge to Pictou Road and out through Bible Hill to Exit 17. After passing an old manganese mining area, it climbs the eastern end of the Cobequids.

The flooding of the Salmon River cannot be prevented by engineering methods.
—C. E. 'Ted' Henry, Department of Agriculture engineer, 1952 (Quoted in Truro's **Daily News,** March 1, 1997)

BACK ON THE HIGHWAY

NOTE: If you choose to bypass Truro you'll see where, not far east of Exit 15, the North River has been bulldozed straight. "Stream improvement" is done to prevent flooding and ice damage to homes built on river floodplains. Besides marring the scenery, this procedure ruins a stream for trout and salmon. It removes their hiding and spawning places, and it kills the invertebrates they feed on.

About 16 km/10 mi east, the highway slices through hillside thickets of spindly spruce and fir "as thick as hair on a dog's back." These trees germinated together after logging or fire in the 1950s. Stands like this often start with 150,000 seedlings per hectare (60,000/ac). In old age roughly 1/30 this number will remain. At every stage the surplus is culled by competition for light and space. (The equivalent in animals would be predation and fighting.)

The surviving trees have small and shallow root systems. Unlike open-grown trees, which seldom blow down, they depend on each other to resist wind. If a few are uprooted or cut, those nearby will topple. Being even-aged, they will all grow old together. Selective cutting will not work here. Past land use or abuse dictates clearcutting plus planting.

Going up the long hill there's a good rear view of the Truro basin.

After Riversdale Road the highway levels off, with views of distant deciduous hills, conifer clearcuts, and marching hydro towers. Then we begin a long curving descent to Kemptown on the upper Salmon River. Years ago, people dug coal from the folded shales here. In the 1970s a house settled into an old shaft overnight.

Parts of this interval are a botanist's delight. One can find Jack-in-the-pulpit, trillium, bloodroot, wild columbine, violets (blue and white), Solomon's seal, and dogbane here, not to mention beds of wild leek. Such floral abundance is rare in Nova Scotia. It's thought to represent a pocket of Alleghanian flora from the now-submerged coastal plain. Kemptown's interval was the nearest thing to a rich Virginia forest these plants could find in Nova Scotia.

During the climb up the Salmon River's east slope, note the 1980s clearcut on the right. The previous forest was mostly spruce, but it regenerated to almost pure fir. This is common on Nova Scotia clearcuts. Fir seedlings have deeper taproots than spruce seedlings and so survive the critical first few summers when the moss dries out. In recent decades balsam fir has overtaken spruce as our most common conifer.

Per capita, we Canadians discard more solid waste than any other people.

STOP: *Balefill Facility*

Near Kemptown is a facility that Colchester County calls the most comprehensive solid waste management strategy in the province. Since the 1980s, tighter environmental standards for garbage disposal have made it harder for towns to find suitable disposal sites. Further legislative pressure, this time to reduce the need for landfill sites themselves, has created a crisis for many municipalities.

In August 1995, the Municipality of Colchester opened its Regional Balefill Facility, the first such facility in the province. At the same time they organized a collection system relying on blue-bagging of paper, glass, metals, and plastic and, since May 1996, 8,400 curbside county compost bins for spoilables. The latter was a first for North America.

Contractors collect and haul these products to the facility, which handles final sorting and recycling. Scrap metal and wood are salvaged. A batch composter shreds and heats all spoilables and in two weeks produces garden compost for sale.

In its first year, the program reduced the county's landfill needs substantially. For example, in August of 1995, 2388.6 metric tonnes of garbage were brought to Kemptown, of which only 300 tonnes were recycled. In August of 1996, 2356.6 tonnes were brought, of which 625 tonnes were recycled.

East of Kemptown we go through a grove of sugar maple, yellow birch, and beech. The elevation is lower than at Wentworth, and the trees look healthier. The usual upland shrubs like hobblebush and striped maple are here, and there are trillium and trout-lily in springtime. Scattered through the open woods are huge glacial erratics overgrown with polypody fern, lichens, and moss.

VIEW: *Mount Thom*

From this 480-m/800-ft hill of folded Carboniferous siltstone and sandstone you can see the Northumberland Strait, Pictou Island, and some of the Pictou–New Glasgow lowland.

To your left going down to Salt Springs, note the line of old willows following a rivulet. Crack or brittle willow often shows up around Scottish home sites hereabouts. Like French willow, these may well have come from France, with whom 19th-century Scottish nationalists had strong ties.

The tree is named for the brittleness of its new twigs, which shed freely in strong winds or ice storms. Where live winter twigs fall into moist mud, new willows often grow.

East of Truro red pine is rare today. The grove surrounding Exit 22 is an Ice Age relic. But it seems red pine was common east of here when the continental shelf was mostly dry land. Grand Banks fishermen have dredged up fully rooted red pine stumps. This grove germinated around 1900, probably after fire. Unless there's another fire, it should prosper; there are enough young pine coming along.

STOP: *Picnic Park*

If you've time, pull off to a table under the cool canopy of evergreens at Salt Springs Provincial Park. In 1813 men sank a 61-m/200-ft shaft here to extract brine, but the venture failed.

The West River intervale is pleasantly pastoral, with hay barns and rolling pastures. In 1817 one of Canada's first agricultural societies was established here. Its manifesto read in part:

> *Let this be held the farmers' creed;*
> *For stock seek out the finest breed,*
> *In peace and plenty let them feed.*
> *Your lands sow with the best of seed,*
> *Let it not dung nor dressing want,*
> *And then provisions won't be scant.*

Members of the West River Farming Society manured their fields and sweetened them with natural calcium from nearby Lime Rock. The society offered prizes for best cattle and best wheat, and in 1818 staged Nova Scotia's first ploughing match. It also fined members for cussing.

For a spectacular view of five counties, detour 3 km/2 mi between Greenhill and Alma to Green Hill Provincial Park (watch for signs). Legend has it that in the summer of 1398—almost a hundred years before John Cabot's voyage—Prince Henry Sinclair, Lord of the Orkneys, stood on this very hill and watched smoke rising from a natural coal fire near Pictou. It is said that he travelled via Baie Verte overland to Cape d'Or and wintered there.

In autumn, the New Glasgow/Stellarton/Trenton basin glows with the golds of aspen and birch, the crimsons of pin cherry and moun-

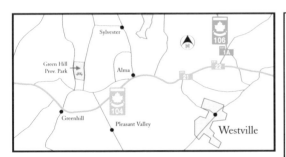

tain-ash. But it's mostly a stunted forest. In the early 1800s shipbuilding and lumbering led to rapid land clearing. The discovery of coal accelerated the process. In such a setting, forest fires were common, and little could be done to stop them. Even in the 1940s there were frequent brush fires here.

This scrub deciduous forest is a direct result of those fires. The soil is damaged, so it can no longer grow large trees. Native conifers are scarce because, unlike deciduous trees, they can't sprout from the stump or sucker from roots. So when the original conifers were cut or burned, the remaining broad-leaved species took their place. Fortunately, Carboniferous soils are fertile. Given a few decades of leaf fall and no fire, this land will heal.

VIEW: Pithead

To many older residents of Stellarton, the stone structure near the East River bridge on the north side evokes bittersweet memories of coal mining long ago. Every morning in the late 1800s, their grandfathers entered that pithead and were whisked nearly 250 m/800 ft down to work the 12-m/39-ft Foord Seam, one of the world's thickest coal deposits. You are driving over shale and sandstone honeycombed with galleries and drifts where sweating men with begrimed faces toiled and died long ago.

Three hundred million years ago, this basin was a tropical jungle watered by broad, slow rivers. Millipedes and sowbugs the size of sheep grazed among the giant horsetails and tree ferns. The dim green glades hummed with insects, including dragonflies the size of gulls. Web-footed salamanders of all sizes slithered through the ooze. Then monsoon floods buried the jungle in sand and clay. For thousands of centuries the sediments built up, squeezing out

Thomas Troop, for whom the hill is named, likely had no time to enjoy the view. He and his family came here from Scotland with 700 other Highlanders in 1801. Wealthy lairds had confiscated their lands to raise sheep for English woollen mills.

In 1801, after enduring a nightmarish 13-week voyage aboard the Sarah, *they landed at Pictou. On the way they lost 47 to smallpox and nearly lost 25 young men to a British Navy press gang. After weeks of quarantine, several pioneers took up land hereabouts. There followed months of cutting trees and building log cabins. Alexander Stewart and his neighbours kindled the first fire in a proper hearth here on December 31, 1801.*

That winter they might have starved if local Mi'kmaq hadn't shown them how to hunt and trap. In the spring the settlers tramped an axe-blazed trail 20 km/12 mi to Truro to attend divine worship.

Clearing and ploughing these hilly fields by hand was backbreaking toil. By the 1880s the younger generation was leaving in droves for industrial centres like New Glasgow and Sydney, Toronto and Boston. Goldenrod, alder, white spruce, and balsam fir gradually invaded the fields.

Ironically, those hard-won fields helped bring on Nova Scotia's worst spruce budworm epidemic. Budworm larvae relish white spruce and fir. In the mid-1970s clouds of the small brownish moths drifted in from New Brunswick on prevailing westerlies and settled on the older trees like dirty snow. They laid eggs, multiplied, and soon the epidemic spread to Cape Breton.

Geologists say that before the 1800s natural asphalt seeps sometimes burned until snow came, and that coal seams might burn for years.

61

On May 9, 1992, 26 coal miners died in a massive explosion at the new Westray Mine in nearby Plymouth. The mine was closed forthwith, and an investigation commenced. In 1993 the miners' families erected a monument nearby. In addition a memorial tree has been planted above the spot where each miner died. From Exit 25 head north on Rte 348 for 0.7 km/0.4 mi, turn right at St Gregory's Church and drive 0.9 km/0.6 mi.

the moisture and transforming the matted foliage, bark, and trunks into black, glistening carbon. Imagine how many pressed giant ferns and horsetails it took to create the Foord Seam.

Although coal was "discovered" near Pictou in 1798 (the Mi'kmaq knew about it long before), little was dug before 1866. Until then New Glasgow was known as a builder of wooden sailing ships. Then, like its namesake across the ocean, New Glasgow became a builder of steel steamships. Nova Scotia's first, the *Richard Smith*, was built here. New Glasgow also had the first working steam locomotive in what was to be Canada, and its first all-metal railroad. By thus embracing "the high tech of the 19th century," it broadened its industrial base. The mournful whistles and clanging bells of locomotives became a part of life. So did coal smoke, which tainted the air and sullied clean linen. Soon more blast furnaces lit up the night sky. Factories turned out steel rails, rolling stock, and marine supplies, brick and tile and water pipes. There were machine shops, and in later years a factory making prefabricated buildings.

But Pictou basin coal is "gassy"—high in methane and sulphur. From time to time there were explosions, and lives were lost. After World War II, coal mining in Nova Scotia went into decline. Cheap Middle East oil gradually took its place as the fuel of choice. Today Nova Scotia Power is Stellarton's chief market. Out along Stellarton's Fowler Street the Pioneer Coal Company has strip-mined coal to feed the Trenton power plant. Until 1994 it did the same in Westville, which now has a new ball field where the mine used to be.

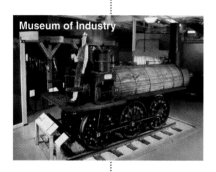
Museum of Industry

For the whole story of these coal and steel towns, visit the Nova Scotia Museum of Industry in Stellarton (south from Exit 24). Model railway buffs will love the train display.

SIDE TRIP: *Electricity and Waterfowl*

Waterfowl and bird watchers alike flock to Trenton's coal-fired electrical generation plant in winter, and for good reason. Its hot-water emissions keep the river from freezing. Stand on the bridge any day from December to March, and you're likely to spot mergansers (all three species), goldeneyes (two species), greater scaup, bufflehead, wigeon (American and European), mallards, black ducks, and Canada geese. Not to mention gulls: herring, black-backed, Iceland, and glaucous. [See also the **Sunrise Trail**.]

To get there, take Exit 25 onto Rte 348. Drive 3 km/2 mi through New Glasgow and past Frasers Mountain to the brown brick building with the sign. In summer, visit Trenton's 81-ha/200-ac Steeltown Centennial Park, which recounts the town's long steelmaking history.

If the weather is fine, drive up Frasers Mountain for a view. Joseph Howe, our famous 19th-century journalist and a discerning traveller, called it "the finest in Nova Scotia." The panorama —five towns plus Pictou Island, Prince Edward Island, and Cape St George—is remarkable.

BACK ON THE HIGHWAY

Across the bridge, as the road swings northeast to briefly follow McLellans Brook, note the dark blue-grey shales exposed along its channel. Originally deposited as level layers of clay in still water, they've been folded like the pages of telephone book. The "wet look" of the right-hand cliffs is from natural coal oil seepage.

SIDE TRIP: *Park Falls*

Waterfalls are restful places any time of year. There is a pretty one not far south of Exit 27, at the bridge where McLean Brook tumbles off the upland on its way to Sutherlands River. The surviving wall of an old concrete dam reminds us that a mill once stood nearby. Perhaps you can find an old-timer to tell its story.

Drive 1.5 km/0.9 from the exit, bear left, and soon you'll come to the bridge. (If you meet Rte 347 to Thorburn, you've gone too far.)

BACK ON THE HIGHWAY

VIEW: *Telford Burn*

Three km/1.9 mi east of Exit 27, the highway crosses an old forest fire site. Except for charcoal inside old stumps, it's hard to believe a fire raged through here in 1967.

About 9 km/5.6 mi east of Telford there's a place dear to our national rodent. Whatever the attraction, at least three generations of beavers have braved the rumble and stink of traffic to live here. The site was occupied in the late 1960s, in the late 1980s, and again in 1995. Look on the north side for a dam, a pond, and a lodge.

The reason for these comings and goings is unclear. Perhaps wildlife officers wrecked the dam for safety's sake. More likely—since beavers can repair most dams in a few nights—the animals ate all the nearby aspen, maple, and willow bark and moved to another brook.

The work of beavers can annoy humans, but

June 7, 1967 was a hot dry breezy day. The fire started south of the highway around noon. Around 2:00 pm, powerful south winds fanned it into a roaring wall of flame that flung burning bark and twigs downwind and sent rabbits and deer racing for safety. By nightfall it had blackened 1943 ha/4801 ac of mixed woodland and razed several homes.

Telford Burn greened up quickly because the fire burned fast, and a down-pour doused it before the humus layer got burnt too badly. While the earth was still steaming, plumes of ostrich and bracken ferns shot up from underground rhizomes. Next spring, islands of green appeared as charred willow, aspen, red maple, and white birch sent up shoots and suckers. Millions of tiny aspen seeds parachuted in on silken threads. By June the dormant seeds of cherry, elder, and wild sarsaparilla began to germinate. Some seeds of fir and spruce also survived the heat and sent out leaves.

Drawn by the surge of insects and berries, jays and crows came to feed, bringing sumac, mountain-ash, and shadbush seeds from meals eaten elsewhere. Plantain, goldenrod, and sedge attracted deer mice, voles, sparrows, and juncos. Hawks and owls hunted them from tall snags, and foxes stalked them through the bushes. Woodpeckers hammered the rotting wood for beetle larvae.

As wind and gravity brought the snags to earth, springtails, earthworms, milli-pedes, and beetles multiplied in the sun-warmed, rotting wood. Salamanders, shrews, and snakes appeared. Since then, bacteria and fungi have converted most of the fallen logs to soil. The new Telford forest is well on its way.

other organisms prosper from it. Cattails, pond-lilies, protozoa, invertebrates, trout, frogs, ducks, redwings, muskrats, mink, and even moose partake of it. When a big rainstorm ruptures the dam and drains the pond, its fertile muck spawns a new explosion of life—until the next family of beavers arrives. [See also the **Glooscap Trail** near Beaverbrook.]

One hundred and fifty years ago, these Antigonish Highlands were as Scottish as Cape Breton's. Watch along the north side of Barneys River (about 5 km/3 mi east of Exit 29) for the checkerboard patterns of settlers' hillside pastures, long since grown up in forest.

Beaver dam near Telford

The name "budworm" refers to the larva's habit of feeding inside the buds of leaves and flowers as they open. As for "spruce," in Nova Scotia the insect prefers balsam fir, with white spruce as its second choice.

The oldest fields have of course been logged more than once. In recent years the spruce budworm has hastened this process; trees over 40 years old are apt to be defoliated and killed. Landowners send the bigger logs to local sawmills and the small wood to Stora Forest Industry's newsprint mill on Canso Strait. You can recognize budworm damage by the scorched look of older trees, caused by increasing numbers of larvae feeding on needles.

Just over 6 km/4 mi east of Barneys River Station is the village of Marshy Hope, population 47 in 1997. When local pioneer James Mappel's neighbours urged him to abandon his swampy, frost-prone farm, he demurred, saying he hoped things might improve. "A marshy hope," they quipped. Beside the white Presbyterian church on Rte 4

Marshy Hope

*Illusion? Some people swear Hartshorn Brook runs uphill for a short distance. "Here," says journalist Parker Barss Donham, "where the highway begins its long ascent into Barney's River, a 200-foot stretch is plainly visible—and plainly defying gravity." [**The Weekly Record**, April 15, 1997]*

lies the grave of Gaelic bard John MacLean. MacLean came to Barneys River from Scotland in 1819. His "Oran do dh'America" ("Song of America") expresses the pioneer's cordial hatred for the forest:

Piling tree trunks on top of each other in bonfires has strained every muscle in my back and every part of me is so black that I'm just like a chimney-sweep. It's no wonder that I'm gloomy, living here back of the mountains in the middle of the wilderness at Barneys River with nothing better than plain potatoes. Before I ... tear the tyrannous forest up from its roots by the strength of my arms I'll be worn out, and almost spent before my children have grown up.

64

To visit the bard's grave, take Exit 31A near James River to Rte 4 and turn left. Not far west you'll see the white church and cemetery on the right.

Between Exits 29 and 30 is Glen Bard, named for the embittered Scot. It's a spectacular drive in early October, as sugar maple, beech, and birch prepare for winter. The hillsides fairly throb with red, orange, and gold. A winter drive can be memorable too, especially in late afternoon as the westering sun floods the upper slopes with amber light and etches the snow with blue shadows.

Believe it or not, Hartshorn Brook (the little stream on the right) carved this winding gorge. It had help from glaciers, but still it must have been a powerful torrent when in flood. Hillside gravel terraces give some idea of its Ice Age dimensions. At its east end, Glen Bard opens on an expanse of deep gravels dumped by the James, Ohio, and other streams around 12,000 years ago. Such outwash plains occur where large volumes of meltwater funnel between steep hills. Truro and Parrsboro have similar deposits. [See the **Glooscap Trail**.]

STOP: *Glacial Diary*
Spend a few moments at the first gravel pit to read, layer by layer, the story of this plain. Rounded pebbles denote water fast enough to tumble stones along. Layered sand means slower water—perhaps in late summer when less ice was melting. Fine silt and clay mean water at rest, as in a shallow sea or lake. The sea lapped these hillsides then.

Glacial runoff varied from spring to fall, during sudden rainstorms, and between cool and hot weather. Sometimes a temporary pond burst its gravel dam. The layers were rippled and uneven as in stream beds today, only thicker. Today's streams don't have a glacier up there grinding gravel for them day and night.

For a broader view of that postglacial world of vast rivers and roaming mastodons, take Exit 30, turn right, and drive to Beaver Mountain Provincial Park. There's a 6-km/3.7-mi hiking trail leading through broad-leaved woodland to a lookoff. (The sign is in the southwest part of the loop.) Allow two hours.

Beyond Beaver Mountain the valley broadens into the Antigonish Lowland. This basin has a lot going for it. High hills shelter it from wintry west winds, and warmish Gulf waters temper ocean breezes. Fertile soils make for profitable farming and forestry, and Christmas trees are an important hinterland product.

The bedrock here is a bit older than that of the Pictou basin, yet softer. Limestone, salt, and gypsum rim the north side hills, pocking the lowland with sinkholes, salt springs, small ponds, and disappear-

> Christmas Tree Pioneers
> *It was from Goshen south of here in the mid-1930s that two brothers, Seward and Merritt Feltmate, reputedly trucked Nova Scotia's first load of Christmas trees to Boston. Today the province leads Canada in the export of natural balsam fir Christmas trees. [See also the **Lighthouse Route** and the **Evangeline Trail**.]*

ing streams—typical karst topography. [See also the Windsor area of the **Glooscap Trail**.] Three rivers—James, South, and West—are doing their best to bring everything to sea level.

With so much sediment pouring in, Antigonish Harbour is convoluted, marshy, and sand-barred, a headache for sailors but ideal for waterfowl. So many ducks and geese visit its marshes spring and fall, it's been designated a Natural Heritage Area.

VIEW: *Peppermint Cliff*
At Crystal Cliffs on the road to Cape George there's a 20-storey wall of sparkling pink gypsum striped with white limestone.

Cattails

STOP: *Superplant!*
If there was a prize for Canada's most versatile wild plant, cattail would likely win. It's been called "Supermarket of the Wilderness," and for good reason.

As you near Antigonish (3 km/1.9 mi west), watch for a roadside cattail marsh on the south side. The plants are tall with sword-shaped leaves that swish in the breeze. In July the sturdy central stalk develops a velvety, chocolate-brown flower head. Toward autumn, these fluff up and release thousands of cottony seeds that sail on the wind to germinate in faraway ponds and ditches. These plants are broad-leafed cattail; a narrow-leafed species is also found occasionally.

Every part of the cattail can be eaten. Pull out its central shoots (they come out clean even in muddy water) and eat them raw. They have a nutty flavour. Steamed and buttered green flower heads taste like asparagus. The male pollen (found in early summer on a spike atop the female flower) makes a high-protein flour. The dried roots yield about 5 tonnes/ha (2 tons/ac) of an excellent starchy flour.

Cattails near busy highways may contain heavy metal residues from vehicle exhaust. It is better to pick from more isolated areas.

Apart from its culinary aspects, the cattail is prized for dried flower arrangements (especially the narrow-leaved variety) and is an icon of duck-hunting magazines. First Nations peoples across Canada plaited mats from cattail leaves and used the oily flower heads as torches while spearing eels and sturgeon at night. Cattail marshes are wildlife havens. Red-winged blackbirds choose the weathered old canes for building their nests, which they line with

In the early 1980s a forest scientist at Petawawa, Ontario, insulated a jacket with dried cattail fluff. She found it quite warm, but in May was chagrined to find numerous small flies hatching from eggs laid in the flower heads the previous summer.

last year's fluff. Bitterns and rails stalk frogs and snakes through the mazes. Muskrats nibble the green leaves and heap dead stalks into mud-plastered "push-ups" to winter inside.

Cape Breton is justly famous for its rugged terrain. Yet your first glimpse of it, as you descend the long hill past Aulds Cove to the causeway, may be disappointing. It looks oddly flat. That's because you're looking across its ancient and eroded upland surface, called a peneplain. It would be lower still, but parts of it have been lifted and tilted during movements of the Earth's crust.

Canso Causeway

VIEW: *Canso Causeway*

Until 1955, going to Cape Breton meant a ferry ride across the 0.8-km/0.5-mi Strait of Canso from Aulds Cove (if travelling by car) or from Mulgrave (if travelling by train). Either way, you left the mainland behind. Cape Breton really was an island then.

At one stroke the causeway and bridge broke the island's proud isolation, created a deepwater superport, and triggered an industrial boom. It also added two new wildlife species to the island's fauna.

This is the world's deepest causeway—66 m/217 ft. At mid-span a 20-storey building would sink out of sight. Powerful tides and ice floes used to sweep back and forth. For over a century, sceptics had claimed nothing could withstand them. In 1952 construction crews began blasting Porcupine Mountain's eastern face to supply rock and fill. Month after month, relays of roaring yellow 40-tonne trucks dumped their loads into the abyss and returned for more. With glacial slowness the causeway nosed toward Port Hastings. Three years and 9100 tonnes later, the causeway opened its toll gate (since removed). The quarry is still active behind the mountain, which today is largely hollow on that side. Another name for the hill is King Solomon's Mountain.

The causeway is vital to Stora Enso's big paper mill at Point Tupper—the only major plant left from the 1960s boom. The mill depends on a steady flow of pulpwood from eastern mainland woodlot owners—particularly since budworm has killed half the fir on its highland Crown leases. Paper mills also have a tremendous thirst for fresh water. In Stora's case it is piped under the strait from a lake back of Mulgrave.

Canadian writer Alistair MacLeod, who lived in Inverness as a youth, explores that mystique in his short story "The Return." A boy of 10 observes his father's emotion at coming home with his Montreal-born wife: "There it is," shouts my father triumphantly. "Look, Alex, there's Cape Breton!" He takes his left hand down from the baggage rack and points across to the blueness that is the Strait of Canso, with the gulls hanging almost stationary above the tiny fishing boats and the dark green of the spruce and fir mountains rising out of the water and trailing white wisps of mist about them like discarded ribbons hanging about a newly opened package. "Yes, there it is," says my mother without much enthusiasm, "now you can sit down like everybody else."
– **The Lost Salt Gift of Blood,** 1976

67

The two new additions to Cape Breton's fauna were bobcat and coyote. Both crossed on the ice bridge that has formed on the Gulf side most winters since 1955. Bobcats arrived in the late 1950s, coyotes in the mid-1980s. Their arrival had ecological consequences. Bobcat and lynx live mostly on mice and snowshoe hare. The aggressive bobcat, a southern animal, soon starved its northern cousin off the Bras d'Or lowlands. In the snowy Highlands, however, the lynx's great

Cape Porcupine

padded feet and thick coat are strong advantages—so this is where it is now found.

Cape Breton's white-tailed deer now have two new predators, and sheep farmers complain of losing stock to coyotes. As of 1996, however, porcupine and skunk were still absent from the island.

On the island side you may have to wait for a ship or yacht to pass through the swing bridge over the lock. Afterward, pull into Port Hastings' Tourist Information Centre for a good view of the gouge in Cape Porcupine's Precambrian face. The quarry is still active.

At Port Hastings the **Trans Canada Highway** becomes Hwy 105.

After the initial climb out of Port Hastings, we enter a region of gently rolling Carboniferous lowlands cradled between North Mountain (Bras d'Or Lake side) and the Creignish Hills to the north. By the time we reach Queensville these Avalon Uplands will dominate the landscape. From there to St Patricks Channel, the Big Ridge—McIntyres Mountain, Camerons Mountain, and River Denys Mountain—keeps us company. Then Whycocomagh Mountain, Salt Mountain, and North Side Mountain see us to Baddeck. Like the uplands across the lake, they were islands in a Coal Age sea that preceded the Atlantic Ocean.

VIEW: *Shapeshifter Bog*
About 15 km/9 mi east of the causeway, on the west side of the road, a peat bog that was once a pond is being transformed into woodland. Like most level peat bogs, this one started out as a shallow glacial pond thousands of years ago. (Sloping bogs are usually draped over bedrock.) Century after century, water-loving sphagnum mosses crept out from the shallow edges. As the plants aged and died, the cold, tannin-rich waters preserved their remains. Slowly a ring of peat accumulated, shrinking the pond. A thousand years are nothing in the life of a bog.

As the peat spread and deeped, cranberries, sedges, and rushes took root, followed by woody shrubs like bog rosemary, bog-laurel, leatherleaf, and mountain alder. Sometimes insect-trapping species like pitcher plant, sundew and bladderwort appeared, plus small orchids such as arethusa and rose pogonia.

Pitcher plant flower

Today, with drier hummocks developing, larch and black spruce seed in from the tall trees behind. Neither species minds wet feet, but cold soggy moss makes a poor seedbed. Bog spruce solves this problem by rooting its lower branches in wet moss—a trick called layering. (Sometimes when the parent tree dies it leaves a "fairy ring" of clones.)

In 1996 a botanist tracked a single black spruce clone for over 20 km/12 mi along the coast of Labrador.

These pioneer trees grow very slowly. Often a tree the size of one's finger can be a century old—half its life-span. But it is another gain for the forest. This boreal habitat is home to spruce grouse, grey jay, snowshoe hare, and voles.

A dismal sight meets us east of Exit 3 to River Denys—the bleached skeletons of dead and dying elms on the floodplain of River Inhabitants. They are victims of Dutch elm disease, a fungus of Asian origin (not Dutch—the Dutch merely identified it) that entered North America in the 1930s and reached Nova Scotia in the 1960s.

The spores of *Ceratostomella ulmi* enter healthy trees in May on infested elm bark beetles. These little insects (one species native, one introduced) normally hatch from eggs laid in dead and dying trees within a flight radius of about 300 m/1,000 ft. As they munch on green inner bark, spores from their bodies are whisked away in the tree's sap stream. Soon white fungal filaments proliferate, plugging the tree's plumbing. Like a blood clot in humans, this starves the affected parts. Within weeks, whole branches suddenly turn yellow, wilt, and die. Over half of all infected trees succumb within three years.

The first Dutch elm disease reported in the province was from two Liverpool elms in 1969. The next year it showed up in Kentville. In each case a funeral parlour was nearby. Infected beetles probably arrived in rough-sawn (i.e., bark left on) elm coffin crates from Québec or Ontario. Despite vigorous urban control measures, Dutch elm disease has since invaded every county. [See also the **Evangeline Trail** at Wolfville, the **Glooscap Trail** at Truro, and the **Lighthouse Route** at Liverpool.]

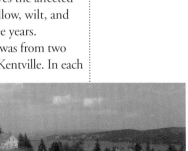

Bras d'Or Lake

VIEWS: *Cape Breton's Inland Sea*
Between Whycocomagh and Baddeck, the Trans Canada Highway hugs Bras d'Or Lake, an inland sea covering 260 km²/100 sq mi. Some think the name was originally "Bras de l'Eau" ("arm of water"). The lake's long narrow bays are folds of bedrock deepened by glaciers. The southeastern part is fairly shallow; elsewhere it's commonly 180 m/590 ft deep. In St Andrews Channel a depth of 260 m/853 ft has been recorded.

Ever since the publication in 1879 of C. Dudley Warner's *Baddeck and That Sort of Thing*, Bras d'Or Lake has been a mecca for cottagers and sailors. Alexander Graham Bell spent his summers near Baddeck, as did the editor of *National Geographic Magazine*.

The natural history of the lake is unusual. Cores taken from the lake bottom showed it to be coated with preglacial muds and glacial sands and gravels. Microscopic bottom fossils suggest the water was fresh between 4,500 and 9,000 years ago. Even today, its waters are fresher and warmer than the Atlantic's. Plants from both freshwater and saltwater ecosystems mingle in its tidal marshes.

Double-crested Cormorant

The marine life is a blend of southern and northern fauna. There are polychaete worms from southern and northern waters, American oysters, blue-blade herring, black-spotted stickleback, and a race of Greenland cod. This rich fauna supports a thriving population of great blue heron, double-crested cormorant, and bald eagles. The marine algae resemble Gulf Shore seaweed, but ice floes confine it to deeper water here.

Coming into Whycocomagh from the west, one used to see floating metal cages offshore. They housed young salmon and trout. The Eskasoni Mi'kmaq band practised aquaculture here from 1990 until 1996. It was a good site because Indian Island sheltered it from northerly storms and drifting ice, which can drag anchors and wreck equipment. Unfortunately, human poaching became a serious problem, and the site was abandoned.

In an aquaculture operation, natural salt water circulates freely through the pens. Fish are fed daily on fish meal (capelin or herring), with binders and vitamins and any medication needed. Food is sprinkled on the water; in winter submerged pumps maintain holes in the ice. During the bitter winter of 1993–94, chain saws were needed. Fish are marketed when they reach about 3 kg/7lb.

A typical salmonid aquaculture operation consists of linked cages, each 15 m/50 ft square, with different mesh sizes. A setup with 22 cages gives a total capacity of 30 000 m³ and a potential harvest of 450 metric tonnes.

Aquaculture must cope with temperature extremes, bacterial diseases, spring runoff, predators, and boaters. To curb disease the cages are moved every three years. Overhead netting deters ospreys, herons, and cormorants. Boaters are asked not to walk on the cages nor to tie up to them. Disposing of dead fish is no problem, thanks to the lake's resident eagle population. One winter the guard saw more than a hundred eagles feeding on the ice at one time. In 1995 Eskasoni Fisheries Limited also operated at Seal Island Bridge, Lingan, and Nyanza.

Geologically, Whycocomagh Bay (from Mi'kmaq for "Head of the Waters") lies in a saucer of soft rock hemmed in by 300-m/1,000-ft Skye Mountain to the southwest and Whycocomagh Mountain to the north and east. Both consist of flinty Precambrian gneiss and schist, which is three times older than the lowland rock. The bay was hollowed out by glaciers and by millennia of scouring by the Skye and Indian rivers. In the early 1600s French traders like Nicolas Denys sailed the lake in search of furs. For uncounted centuries before Europeans arrived, hundreds of Mi'kmaq people called this home. Many still do, living on the Whycocomagh Reserve, where they operate craft shops selling ash baskets, quillwork, beaded leather, snowshoes, and other fine goods. Mi'kmaq poet Rita Joe was born here to Annie and Joseph Bernard on March 15, 1932.

> *The winding old road is all that remains*
> *The church and grounds*
> *Where my forefathers lay*
> *Whycocomagh, We'kopa'q*
> *The end of water,*
> *and I, Rita Joe, am one of the children.*
> — **"Whycocomagh"**
> **Songs of Rita Joe,** *1996*

Leaving the reserve, we cross the Skye River in its deep-cut channel of glacial outwash. Whycocomagh North was settled in the early 1800s by displaced Highland Scots. For a time it housed nearly 2,000 people. An 1868 census listed a shipwright, carriage-maker, wheelwright, tanner, two millers, two blacksmiths, two tailors, and a dyer. The Scots held outdoor Sabbath services in Gaelic with simultaneous English translation.

Rounding the bay and climbing partway up the flank of Salt Mountain, we catch vistas of water with matchbox houses beyond, of Indian Island at the bay's mouth, and of St Patricks Channel beyond. Outcrops along the mountain reveal a pebbly brown pudding-stone made from cemented beach rocks and gravel as the Devonian seas receded.

LEG STRETCHER: *Salt Mountain Trail*
For an exhilarating walk and a grand view, hike this 1.8-km/1.1-mi loop in Whycocomagh Provincial Park. The trail leaves a south-facing upland pasture with apple trees, and passes from deciduous forest to mixedwood to conifers in less than 200 m/650 ft of elevation.

Named for nearby salt springs, the hill itself is a cemented mass of pebbles and mud called conglomerate. The trail is part of a memorial to Hugh McLennan, a local boy killed in the second Battle of Ypres, April 1915.

The park's main entrance is just east of the Trans Canada Highway/Rte 252 junction, marked by a large routed pine sign. A short drive under pleasant trees brings you to a parking area near the DNR office. Ask for a trail brochure and directions.

The Cabot Trail joins Rte 105 between Exits 7 and 11.

SIDE TRIP: *Gypsum Quarry*
Most people know that interior walls in North American homes are usually sheathed in "gyproc"—powdered gypsum pressed between two layers of thick kraft paper. Fewer know that Nova Scotia has long been the world's largest supplier of raw gypsum. Like rock salt it

is an evaporite from our time in the tropics inside Pangaea. [See also the **Glooscap Trail** near Windsor.]

In a typical open-pit gypsum mining operation, the soft rock is drilled and dynamited and carried in giant off-road trucks to a conveyer. There the rock is elevated and tumbles down through crushers and screens to emerge as a coarse white powder.

The old quarry at Little Narrows on St Patricks Channel would hold several football fields. The finished gypsum is conveyed over the highway to a warehouse and wharf. For years the unwanted rock dust was dumped on massive spoil heaps to the east. Rain and frost gullied them badly, but seeding with grass and legumes helped to counter erosion. Today all rock debris is returned to the quarry.

Take Exit 6 to the ferry, cross over, turn left, and drive 3.5 km/2.2 mi on Rte 223 to the Little Narrows Gypsum Company operation. For a panoramic view, follow the public road under the conveyor and park at the top of the next hill. To explore further, ask permission at the quarry office. [See also the **Bras d'Or Scenic Drive**.]

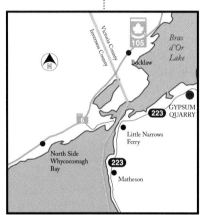

BACK ON THE HIGHWAY

At Little Narrows Exit 6 links up with **Bras d'Or Scenic Drive**.

After Bucklaw and Wagmatcook the road loops up around Nyanza Bay. The broad, flat brushland extending into the lake is a fan or delta of gravel and silt that Middle River has washed from the Highlands and deposited here.

Middle River's utmost tributaries nearly meet those of the Northeast Margaree on the Gulf of St Lawrence side. [See the **Cabot Trail**.] When they meet, the intervening bedrock will slowly disappear.

Cape Breton Island has the highest concentration of nesting bald eagles east of Alaska, and most of them live around Bras d'Or Lake. They haunt these shores from nesting time in late February until autumn. They come for the good fishing, the unsullied water, the plentiful big green trees for nesting, the tall dead trees for perching, and the comparative lack of human disturbance.

In summer eagles eat mostly "rough fish": eels, sculpin, and flounder. These they pick up dead on the beaches or snatch from shallow water on the wing. Come fall, the big birds drift south and west. Some linger near the mouth of the Shubenacadie to pick up stranded tomcods in December and January; most winter in the sheltered Annapolis Valley where they scavenge offal from poultry farms. [See the **Evangeline Trail** near Kentville.]

At Exit 7 you have the option of heading north on the inland section of the **Cabot Trail**.

"Only two of Nova Scotia's streams have any kind of delta. They are the Baddeck and the Middle River of Cape Breton .... If they discharged into the ocean, the tides and storms would have carried the silt off .... But these two streams discharge into the salt water of the tideless upper Bras d'Or Lake."
— Hugh MacLennan, *Rivers of Canada*, 1974

Continuing east on Hwy 105, we round the long curve of Nyanza Bay to the Baddeck River's marshy delta. From spring to autumn, scan the sky here for ospreys. Locals call them "fish hawks," and this is apt, for these big hawk-like, black-and-white birds consume nothing else. If you see one soaring, park and watch. With luck you'll see it pause, flutter, fold its wings, and plummet. When it emerges, shaking the water

Middle River delta at Nyanza

from its long wings, you may see a wriggling fish in its talons. The talons, which are long, wickedly curved, and backed by rough scales, keep the prey from escaping.

Novice canoeists can easily ascend 6 km/3.7 mi up this braided river. Its numerous channels and islands teem with waterfowl, notably blue-winged teal and American wigeon. Wood pewee and various warblers abound.

After Inlet Baddeck there are splendid views of St Patricks Channel to the right. As the highway climbs a slight rise behind Baddeck (Mi'kmaq for *abadak*, "place with an island near"), we see the headland of Beinn Bhreagh (Scottish Gaelic, "beautiful mountain") across Baddeck Bay, with Boularderie Island beyond. A mastodon thighbone was found near here in 1833.

SIDE TRIP: *Harbour Cruise*

A short ferry ride from the Baddeck wharf takes you to Kidston Island, where there's a cormorant colony. For years the birds nested across the channel on Spectacle Island. The island has no suitable cliffs, so they roosted in a sparse grove of conifers. After a few years, accumulated guano (dung) killed the trees. If the wind is toward you, you'll know that these birds live on fish—mainly sculpin, eel, and flounder.

Between Kidston Island and the wharf are underwater conical heaps of stone ballast dumped by ships before loading pulpwood for overseas. Nowadays ships use water for ballast, pumping it in or out as needed. Ballast, dry or wet, can be a source of unwanted organisms from far away. [See also **Sunrise Trail** at Fox Harbour; **Marine Drive** at Eddy Point.]

SIDE TRIP: *Uisge Ban Falls*

One of Cape Breton's more spectacular waterfalls tumbles off hard-rock uplands north of Baddeck. It's on the North Branch Baddeck River, on Falls Brook not far from New Glen. To reach it, take Exit 9 at Baddeck and follow the sign for Forks Baddeck. Go past the golf course until you've crossed two single-lane bridges. Keep right after the second bridge until you see a sign for MacPhee's Cross Road. After going 1 km/0.6 mi, turn left, and drive a short distance to a parking lot with a picnic park and toilets nearby.

Before winging off to feed its young or itself in a suitable tree, the osprey arranges the fish head-forward to reduce air resistance.

You walk up a narrow mountain forest trail with the little stream purling near you ... brush blackflies out of your ears, and see the occasional track of a moose or a deer in the soft earth. You smell the moss and find yourself in a kind of tunnel among the spruce and birch, the light filtering through as it does in the paintings of Emily Carr. Then you find yourself at the foot of a mountain and hear the noise of a cataract ....You ... work your way around a corner, and there, very close, very white, the spray-moistened air fragrant, is a narrow waterfall....
— Hugh MacLennan
Rivers of Canada, 1974

From here a well-kept, 3.5-km/2.2-mi (distance one way) trail takes you up to the falls. There are footbridges, handrails, and lookoffs, with no hard climbs. *Uisge Ban* (pronounced "ooshka ban") is Gaelic for "white water." The falls form two cascades, plunging between 150 m/500 ft cliffs of Precambrian diorite and gabbro more than a billion years old.

Nearing the exit to South Gut St Anns, the highway skirts sinkhole ponds and chalky cliffs—sure signs of gypsum country.

To reach North River Park via Hwy 105, exit west to the **Cabot Trail** at the Lobster Galley Restaurant and proceed past St Anns to North River Bridge.

SIDE TRIP: *Gaelic College*

St Anns Bay is so steeped in French and Scottish history, it deserves a stop. Turn west at Exit 11, proceed over the bridge at South Haven (purists call it by its fine old Saxon name, South Gut St Anns) and drive a short distance to the Gaelic College of Celtic Arts and Culture. Here you'll find exhibits and knowledgeable guides to recount stirring tales like that of fiery Presbyterian preacher Norman McLeod, who built a ship and sailed his flock to New Zealand; of the gentle strongman Giant MacAskill; and of doomed Fort Dauphin.

If you see Canada geese, they could be the descendants of a small flock that provincial wildlife biologists raised and released near St Anns in the 1980s.

BACK ON THE HIGHWAY

After the Englishtown turn-off to the Cabot Trail, Hwy 105 ascends the west flank of 244-m/800-ft-high Kellys Mountain. Like the Highlands to the west and Skye Mountain to the south, this oblong mass of gneiss and granite is nearly 800 million years old.

The mountain offers two fine views, one toward St Anns Bay and one toward Great Bras d'Or Channel and the Sydney lowlands. The former overlooks the magnificent Englishtown sandbar and the site of Captain Daniel's ill-fated fort. As you ascend the St Anns side, see how the lush lowland mixed forest gives place to sparse balsam fir and white birch, looking almost boreal.

VIEW: *Nature and History at Englishtown*

Fresh water freezes before salt water does. But for this fact of physics, France's fortunes in Acadia might have rested here instead of at Louisbourg. Here in 1629 the dashing Capt. Charles Daniel of Dieppe, having torched Lord Ochiltree's rival premises at Baleine to the east, brought his Scottish prisoners and forced them to build a stockade for him. Soon the great sandbar boasted a chapel, village, gardens, and one of North America's first apple orchards. The Jesuit priests he brought with him named the place Fort Sainte Anne. Later

Storm waves and longshore currents created Englishtown's unusual 2-km/1-mi-long spit. The sand came from nearby Barachois Brook and from a fringe of soft Coal Age rock south of Wreck Cove Point. The suspended particles, meeting North River's outflow of fresh water, settled like snowflakes behind a wall. Currents have carved the end into a double hook that changes shape from time to time.

Nicolas and Simon Denys each ran trading posts and a farm here. [See the **Fleur-de-lis Trail**.]

When the Treaty of Utrecht of 1713 evicted France from Placentia in Newfoundland, Louis XIV chose Fort Sainte Anne to safeguard his country's fishing and fur-trading interests in the eastern St Lawrence River. He fortified it with earthworks and cannon and renamed it Fort Dauphin.

Three flukes of nature undid Fort Dauphin. First, the sandbar's strong currents and shifting shoals made it tricky to sail through. Second, North River pours so much fresh water into the inner harbour that it froze in winter, immobilizing the fleet. Third, drift ice plugged the outer bay for weeks each spring. For these and other reasons, the Sun King abandoned Port Dauphin.

During Cape Breton's birth, continental plate movements tilted up the eastern rim of Kellys Mountain. Motorists and truckers respect the resulting hills with its hairpin turn down to Seal Island Bridge, especially in winter. The wall of shattered pink granite in the quarry west of the bridge tells of violent faulting in the distant past.

To a geologist, diminutive Hertford and Ciboux islands are two eroding slivers of late Carboniferous rock situated 3 and 5 km (1.9 and 3.1 mi), respectively, off Cape Dauphin. To a seabird they are ideal nesting sites: isolated and cliffy. Each summer they are thronged by nesting Atlantic puffins, razor-billed auk (a small cousin of the extinct great auk), black guillemot, kittiwakes, gulls, and cormorants. For several weeks it's a very noisy and smelly place. Eagles sometimes cruise the cliffs looking for dead or careless chicks.

Bird Island

Kellys Mountain, long a favourite native berry-picking ground, was sacred to the ancient Mi'kmaq people, who named it Kukmijnawe'nuk, *"place of my grandmother". Legend says their man-god Glooscap retired to a cave near its northern tip with his grandmother. Since the 1980s the cave has been desecrated with spray paint, beer cans, and other mementoes of our culture.*

Mi'kmaq legend says Glooscap created the Bird Islands in a fit of pique while trying to impress two maidens. As he leaped ashore from his canoe, it broke, landing him in the drink. The maidens laughed, and Glooscap zapped them into stone—one pillar for each side of his cave. His broken canoe became the two islands.

Englishtown Sandbar

75

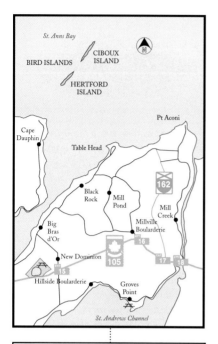

In 1895 the New Glasgow Iron, Steel and Railway Company joined forces with the Nova Scotia Steel Company of Trenton to become the Nova Scotia Steel Company. They then bought Newfoundland's Bell Island, which offered an estimated six million tonnes of high-grade iron ore only 100 km/60 mi by water from Port aux Basques. Limestone and most other minerals needed for the blast furnaces lay within 40 km/25 mi of Sydney. When capitalists realized Sydney was the closest place to Great Britain on mainland North America, a giant steel mill was almost inevitable. Soon the town had Canada's biggest steel plant.

Sydney's steel plant

SIDE TRIP: *Seabird Safari*

You may visit the island by booking a tour. Demand is brisk, so call ahead. If possible do so before mid-August, when many of the birds leave. (Reservations are, of course, weather permitting.) After a 45-minute boat trip, your guide cuts the throttle and coasts in close enough for pictures—but not near enough to bother the birds. You could spot grey seals basking on the lower ledges. A trip to remember.

About 3 km/2 mi past the bridge, turn right at Exit 14 and drive about 5 km/ 3 mi to Big Bras d'Or.

BACK ON THE HIGHWAY

Great Bras d'Or Channel is Bras d'Or Lake's only natural outlet big enough for ocean-going vessels. Because of the lake's small tides and convoluted shoreline, its waters are out of sync with Atlantic tides. This creates currents exceeding 11 km/hr (7 mph). The automated light on the sandspit has saved many a vessel.

Crossing Seal Island Bridge onto Boularderie Island, we leave the hard-rock zone behind. A sure sign of softer rock is the spit enclosing a pond on the right at the east end of the bridge. Like the Englishtown spit, it was shaped by opposing currents. This one is tooth-shaped (cuspidate).

After Kellys Mountain, Boularderie's pastoral face seems tame. We are coming into the ultimate Carboniferous landscape. It is underlain by nearly horizontal layers of eroded sandstone, shale, and siltstone, which dip under Cabot Strait with hardly a headland worth the name.

Coal underlies the whole 1300-km^2/500-mi^2 region from Sydney River to Mira Bay to a depth of nearly 2000 m/6,500 ft. A single sandstone outcrop near Cranberry Point has 34 separate seams, each one a buried forest. These deposits contain an estimated one billion tonnes of recoverable coal.

Between Exits 17 and 18 we cross Little Bras d'Or, Cape Breton's second natural saltwater inlet. Nearly 10 km/6 mi long, it opens on the Atlantic near Point Aconi. It's too narrow and shallow for any but small vessels.

Cranberry Point

SIDE TRIP: *Fossil Trove*
North of Sydney Mines at Point Aconi the sea has exposed coal
seams up to 1 m/3 ft thick. And about 5 km/3 mi down on the
Great Bras d'Or side there are fossil tree trunks rivalling those of
Joggins. [See the **Glooscap Trail**.] The delicate fossil ferns imprinted
on blue shale are particularly fine.

Take Rte 162 at Exit 17, drive just over 6 km/3.7 mi on pavement
to the McCreadyville intersection, then go right almost 2 km/1.2 mi
to the Point Aconi/Mill Creek Road. Ask at a local gas station for
directions to the point, about 3 km/1.9 mi to the north. The tall
smokestack is that of Nova Scotia Power's coal-fired electrical generating plant at Point Aconi.

BACK ON THE HIGHWAY
As we swing south again toward North Sydney, woods and farms give
way to suburbs and signs of commerce. The trees show signs of
exposure to salty northeasters and to chilly air from drift ice that
sometimes lingers offshore till May. (Glace Bay got its name from
this fact.) Long exposure to smoke and fumes from the steel mill
across the harbour hasn't helped either. The harbour is a drowned
estuary like Pictou's, only with two valleys, not three.

Before we know it, there are the signs for the Newfoundland ferry.
The tour is over.

SIDE TRIP: *Petersfield Provincial Park*
While in the vicinity, look in on a pleasantly run-down estate where
footpaths wander woods and shorelines, and clumps of half-wild
exotic perennials and shrubs mingle with native plants. This attracts
a variety of birds. There's parking, picnic tables, and drinking water.

You'll find the park across the harbour from Sydney on Rte 239. Cross Sydney River bridge at the lights and drive north along the harbour toward Westmount. The gate is just before the Coast Guard College.

Highway 102
Nature Tour

Truro to Halifax, approximately 100 km/62 mi

OVERVIEW

This route connects Truro and Halifax across the narrow waist of the peninsula. In doing so it crosses four major geographical regions, namely the Triassic Lowlands around Cobequid Bay, the Carboniferous Lowlands of the Stewiacke/Shubenacadie watersheds, the Atlantic Interior, and a slice of Atlantic Coast.

Shubenacadie tributaries

On the way it passes—but you won't see it—mainland Nova Scotia's largest body of fresh water, Shubenacadie Grand Lake. An older route, Highway 2, runs beside 102 as far as Bedford Basin, and once or twice we slip over onto it. You can drive either route in an hour (if you don't stop); plan on two hours.

After 200 years of settlement, this well-populated corridor has long since lost its original Acadian forest of yellow birch, sugar maple, red spruce, and hemlock. Instead you'll see mostly shorter-lived, light-tolerant species such as white spruce, red maple, balsam fir, white birch, and aspen. Drive the back roads, however, and you'll meet pockets of original forest in family woodlots and remote ravines.

Nonetheless, this route offers some of the best forest and farmland in the province. From 1760 on, New England planters and Loyalists travelled up the larger streams from the Minas Basin, harvesting timber to build ships and carving out wilderness farms. Road builders later followed the same easy routes. Some woodlands were never cleared. Many farms reverted to forest. Wildfires were frequent. Those forces created the land mosaic we see today.

From Truro to Enfield the highway traverses a broadly rolling landscape broken by alluvial (water-laid) flatlands around Brookfield, Stewiacke, Shubenacadie, and Lower Sackville. The bedrock, never severely folded or compressed, is fairly soft, so you won't see many outcrops or, for that matter, lakes. (Where water can cut through rock it does not back up to form lakes; lakes are frustrated streams.) After Enfield, we enter a rugged landscape of low rocky ridges and valleys characteristic of the Atlantic Interior. Finally, the Atlantic Shore is announced by a mostly evergreen forest of spruce and fir stunted by high winds and salt-laden mist.

THE TOUR BEGINS

Truro calls itself "The Hub of Nova Scotia," and with good reason: it lies almost dead centre between Sydney and Yarmouth, Halifax and

79

Amherst. Prevented from being a seaport by its massive Fundy tides and vast mud flats, it capitalized on geography. Because the town is hemmed in by the Cobequid Mountains and Minas Basin, early roads were forced to converge here. After Confederation in 1867, it became a railway centre. By the mid-1800s it was exporting carriages, furniture, stoves, textiles, and other goods.

Built on the site of an Acadian village, the town is probably named for Truro on Cape Cod, via Truro the capital of the west England county of

Flood plain panorama

Cornwall. The name is said to derive from "True Road." The town is laid out in military grid fashion on the floodplain of the Salmon and North rivers. (Low-lying streets like Willow and Park get inundated almost every spring.) Both rivers have their channels in an ancient outwash plain deposited under salt water when sea level was much higher some 10,000 years ago. A good place to view Truro and its hinterland is from the top of Wood Street near Victoria Park. Ask for directions locally, or obtain a street map from the town office (opposite St James Presbyterian Church on Prince).

VIEW: *Truro*

From the top of Wood Street, near the microwave tower, there's a splendid floodplain panorama of Truro, Bible Hill, Lower Onslow, Brookside, and North River. The ridge to the north is Penny Mountain, an outlier of the Cobequids.

It's hard to believe, but for millennia the valley below was full of water. Seawater lapped the lower slopes, and glacial meltwaters at times reached to where you stand. As the ice melted and the land rose, the river dwindled by stages. These stages appear as distinct step-like terraces (visible) as you climb Wood, Forrester, and Pleasant streets. They are matched by less obvious terraces across the river.

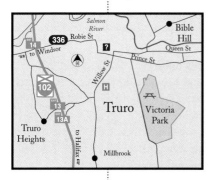

LEG STRETCHER: *Truro's Jewel*

Victoria Park embraces 162 ha/400 ac of forest centred on a rugged ravine near the centre of town. It offers two waterfalls, nature walks through old forest, rustic stairs, and a Participark. Near the entrance are ample parking, picnic tables and shelters, a barbecue, playground, a swimming and wading pool, and toilets.

Geologists point out that the park's Lepper Brook runs through an ancient valley whose upper part was carved out of 300-million-year-old Coal Age sediments (greyish) and whose lower part (below the swimming pool) cuts through a fringe of younger (reddish) Triassic formations. The park was conceived on Queen Victoria's Golden Jubilee in 1887 and established a year later when Susan Waddell

Stevens (hence Waddell Falls) donated property around the gorge. Sir Adams G. Archibald, Truro's Father of Confederation, chaired the first committee, and local lawyer James Ross devoted years to its development.

You can enter or exit Victoria Park in two ways: off Brunswick (via Park or Palmer streets), or from the top of Wood Street (six streets east).

From Park or Palmer streets you can cross Lepper Brook near the swimming pool and stroll up the paved ravine road under big hemlock and spruce past Jacob's Ladder. This consists of more than 100 wooden steps linking the upper and lower levels and will test your knees and stamina. Once down, you can continue past the Holy Well (replica of an Acadian well once used in nearby Bible Hill), and on to Joe Howe Falls and Waddell Falls. On the way, you'll move from the floodplain of Lepper Brook into its gorge, cut through tilted Coal Age shale.

A favourite walks begins behind the swimming pool, where a much shorter wooden stair leads uphill through old hemlock/pine/red spruce woods along Flemming Road and comes out above the inner waterfall. From there you can descend steep railed stairs to return along Lepper Brook to your vehicle.

The clearing just above Brandy Spring was the site of a Catholic glebe, home to Irish priest Father Cummaine in 1885–86. Fragments of the garden remain, notably two honey-locust trees. Rare this far north, this southern member of the pea family is related to laburnum and acacia. It bears sweet-scented white blossoms, sugary seedpods longer than a large banana, and lovely fine-leaved foliage. Apparently to discourage browsing bears and other wildlife, the tree's trunk and twigs are armed with very sharp three-tined thorns. Since 1995 these trees have succumbed to old age.

Victoria Park

Watch too for English or European hawthorn, with small, deeply cut leaves. ("Haw" is Old English for the scarlet, apple-like fruit.) Along the east side, red pine have been planted.

From here the trail runs uphill. True old-growth hemlock, said to be 300 years old, clothe the whole slope, grading into red spruce near the top. On such an ideal site, moist and cool and sloping, the hemlock can reach great age (350+ years) and size (up to 122 cm/48 in diameter and over 30 m/100 ft tall).

The grove is slowly dying of old age. One by one the ancient trees are being invaded by wood fungi, which enter through broken branches and tops. The red spruce are under threat from native eastern spruce beetles, which tunnel under the bark of aging trees to feed and lay eggs. In the 1980s several hectares

Brandy Spring got its name when British soldiers on local manoeuvres during the Fenian troubles of the late 1860s used it to cool their flasks .

81

south of the brook had to be clearcut to save the remaining healthy trees.

Pruned elms

Prince Street in Truro

TO SEE: *Rescue Operation*

If you drive along Truro's older streets, especially Prince and Queen, you'll observe recently cut stumps and pruned elms. Since the mid-1970s, Truro has lost 200+ elms to the insect-borne Asian fungus called Dutch elm disease. The Tree Commission, prodded in the early 1980s by the late Dick Bulmer, a Department of Natural Resources (DNR) forester, has greatly slowed the spread of the disease by sanitation cutting. This means removing dead branches and dying trees before the elm bark beetles have a chance to breed there. The beetles hide under loose bark and spread the spores to healthy trees they visit while feeding. [See also the **Evangeline Trail** at Windsor and Kentville, the **Trans Canada Highway** near River Denys, and the **Lighthouse Route** at Liverpool.] Watch for elm stumps carved by local sculptors.

White elm is a superb urban shade and ornamental tree. Many Maritime towns planted it widely from the late 1700s on, especially during Queen Victoria's Golden Jubilee in 1887 (hence so many "Prince," "Queen," and "Victoria" streets).

The Maritimes' largest agricultural college is located across the Salmon River from Truro in Bible Hill (follow Queen Street east to the Walker Street lights, turn left across the bridge, and right at the first lights up College Road). It's worth a visit, if only for the many fine horticultural displays (in season), the variety of native and exotic trees on campus, its greenhouses, its experimental gardens, and its collection of provincial weeds. Call ahead to find out what to see and when.

Tidal Bore, Salmon River

TO SEE: *Truro's Tidal Bore*

Thanks to Fundy's monster tides, all streams hereabouts are invaded twice daily by muddy salt water. A series of low waves called a bore rolls upstream, as if the river had suddenly reversed its flow.

One of Nova Scotia's best examples occurs at the mouth of the Salmon River. [See also the **Glooscap Trail** near Maccan and Windsor.] The optimum viewing site is just west of Exit 14A. Take Tidal Bore Road, the first right just past the Robie Street overpass on Hwy

236. After a few minutes you'll see ahead the red-roofed Palliser Restaurant. Park behind it and stroll out to the spacious viewing lawn.

From here you can watch the bore come charging round the bend, foaming upstream between the dykes, pushing a cool moist breeze. After the bore passes, stay to watch the channel rapidly fill. Bore times are posted during the tourist season; they are also available in brochures inside the restaurant, in the local *Daily News*, and on CKCL (AM 60). High tides occur twice every 24 hours, with the highest bores (approximately 1 metre/3 feet) occurring at new and full moon in spring and fall.

While waiting, visit the Fundy Eco-Region interpretation centre west of the restaurant and watch the video presentation on Fundy's tides and their origins.

TO SEE: *Historic Bridge Site*
Just upstream from the bore site you'll see some old bridge abutments where Hwy 2 used to cross. The span was called the Board Landing Bridge because it was here in 1760 that some two dozen Planters (settlers) disembarked, carrying the rafters and planks from their barns and houses back in Massachusetts. The pieces were all numbered for easy reassembly. The Planters occupied lands depopulated during the expulsion of the Acadians in 1755. (Contrary to popular wisdom, American colonists largely engineered this deportation, not British soldiers.)

LEG-STRETCHER: *Birding around Truro*
On both sides of the Salmon River west of Truro there are wide expanses of hay meadow enclosed between 4–5-m (12–15-ft) dykes originally built by Acadians. In June/July one can see a small black-white-yellow bird rise from the tall hay, sing a few notes, and disappear farther on. This is the bobolink, a blackbird that nests abundantly here. Other blackbirds to listen and watch for are the red-winged (where cattail swamps abut the roads) and the brownish cowbird.

Robins and sparrows are abundant throughout the region, and flickers may been seen along back road fields and second-growth forest, flashing white rump patches as they loop from one good anting site to the next. Other birds commonly seen hereabouts are pheasant, Hungarian partridge (introduced), Wilson's snipe, northern harrier, and bald eagle. The woodland and streamside paths of Truro's Victoria Park provide great opportunities for seeing and hearing warblers, thrushes, woodpeckers, flycatchers, etc. Experts have tallied some four dozen species on one stroll.

Leaving Truro along west Robie Street, we take Hwy 102 at the Hwy 236 (Exit 14) interchange opposite the mouth of the Salmon River. Before we pass under the Truro Heights overpass, the bedrock

I wrote this book on a desk made from one such pine board, a 71-cm (28-in) wide white pine plank used for wainscoting in a pioneer home at Mingos Corner on the Onslow side.

under us has changed from the shoreline's rusty Triassic to older dark grey shales and sandstones. The shift is hidden, however, under deep drifts of glacial sand and gravel that have been carefully bulldozed and sown to swards of timothy, bluegrass, and clover. If we could peek far below the sod and gravel, we'd see a rock floor warped into broad folds and cut here and there by ancient streams.

For 2 km/1.2 mi we climb a gentle slope of mixed farmland and mostly broadleaf forest. To the east, in the valley of McClure Brook, we glimpse Hwy 2 running almost parallel through the native community of Millbrook and a ribbon of suburb. Larch or tamarack becomes more plentiful, its jade green spires (gold in October, bare in winter) shooting up above other trees. Five minutes later we see in a field to the west the triple-gabled natural wood structure housing the Nova Scotia Forestry Association offices. This is the Nova Scotia home of Smokey Bear and various forest conservation efforts.

LaFarge
Brookfield Plant

Brookfield, a dairy and lumbering centre, lies amid lush farmland and hardwood hills on a northern branch of the Stewiacke River. For a closer look, take Exit 12. If you drive 1 km/0.6 mi west along the Pleasant Valley road, you'll see a towering, fenced grey and green concrete structure on the left with a big aluminum conduit curving up one side and a high red and white stack. This is the LaFarge Brookfield Plant of LaFarge Canada Incorporated, which makes cement from local gypsum deposits.

The first mining of gypsum in North America was in Nova Scotia about the year 1770 ... [Nova Scotia's] gypsum and anhydrite deposits are among the largest workable deposits in Canada. Nova Scotia is the most productive gypsum mining region in the world.
– G. C. Adams,
Gypsum and Anhydrite in Nova Scotia, Nova Scotia Department of Natural Resources

Gypsum (Greek from *gypsos,* meaning chalk) is an evaporite that comes in stony, chalky, and fibrous forms, commonly interbedded with limestone, dolomite, and shale. Most gypsum is *calcined* (dried) before use. Besides being made into cement, it is used in plaster casts (dental and surgical), fertilizer, crayons, asbestos gaskets, coal mine packs, drilling muds, plaster of Paris, and alabaster sculptures.

About 330 million years ago the Brookfield area was an inland sea shimmering under a tropical sun. Repeated evaporation and flooding left thick deposits of gypsum (calcium sulphate), which were later buried under glacial till and river silt. [See also the **Trans Canada Highway** near Little Narrows and the **Glooscap Trail** near Windsor.]

VIEW: *Shortts Lake*

From the highway we catch only a glimpse of the east shore of the lake, about 4 km/2. 5 mi south of Brookfield. As one of the few sizeable lakes in Colchester County, it has long been popular with cottagers and boaters. It occupies a shallow basin carved in sedimentary rock and fed by three brooks from the west and north. Its popularity, and the presence of gypsum, have led to two problems. One problem is that water vegetation like pondweed, encouraged by phosphates from wash water and by nitrates from raw sewage, are overrunning shallow

84

caves in summer. A related factor may be 30 years of dumping limestone dust; yet a 1990s environmental assessment did not prove this. (In fact, it's common practice to add calcium in moderate amounts to lakes to counter the effects of acid precipitation.) The second problem is chain pickerel, a voracious predatory fish. Since it was illegally introduced from central Canada around 1990, this smaller version of northern pike has been gobbling native brook trout, yellow perch, minnows, and suckers. Whether it will invade the Shubenacadie watershed remains to be seen.

To tour the lake shore with its numerous cottages, follow the Pleasant Valley Road a short distance beyond the LaFarge plant and turn left onto Shortts Lake West Road.

Nova Scotia had around 100,000 licensed anglers in 1994. Besides creating 29,000 jobs, they contributed $81 million to the economy.

On the way back, note the "Old Halifax Road" sign (1.5 km/0.9 mi west of Exit 12). This was a 19th-century coach road that ran roughly parallel to today's Hwy 2, passing through what is now the Provincial Wildlife Park and Middle Musquodoboit.

SIDE TRIP: *Canoe Trip*

The Stewiacke is ideal for novice canoeists. For a pleasant 6- to 7-hour family trip, take Exit 12 at Brookfield and drive approximately 30 km/18 mi along Rte 289 to its intersection with Rte 336 at Upper Stewiacke, where the bridge offers a good spot to embark. Pick-up can be arranged at Stewiacke River Park, located a few minutes down a marked dirt road just south of Alton on Hwy 2.

There are no rapids, only riffles. Head winds on the broad meanders can become side winds in five minutes and be at your back five minutes later. These meanders shift from time to time, slicing great crescents of sod and soil out of pastures; here and there farmers have tried to stabilize the banks by dumping rocks.

You'll pass groves of tall maple and spruce and an occasional white birch too big to wrap your arms around. From such trees the Mi'kmaq fashioned birchbark canoes. Kingfishers will pace you downstream, scolding you from perch to perch with their rattling cry. Muskrats cruise the banks with only nose and tail showing, darting into dens or diving if you steer too close. Often woodland is broken by pastures from which curious black-and-white Holstein dairy cattle gaze sleepily

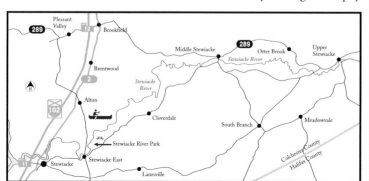

In 1994 large numbers of a tall (1–2 m/ 3–5 ft), steeple-shaped dark green plant appeared along the highway median north and south of Exit 11. It was a mugwort or wormwood (there are many kinds) of the Artemisia genus, an aromatic relative of ragwort and daisy. It undoubtedly arrived as seed, perhaps on craft material imported by the Farmer Clem market nearby. For two years it thrived, then all but disappeared.

A check revealed that the plants weren't herbicided. They may have succumbed to a series of freeze/thaw episodes during the winter of 1996–97 (the seed is tiny) or died from road salt or mowing. They could well return (watch for them), but probably won't become a problem. Most introductions, including farm grains and vegetables, can't out-compete local plants. [A notable recent exception is purple loosestrife, a wetlands species. See the Glooscap Trail (Truro side trip) and the Evangeline Trail at Belleisle Marsh.] Farm species survive year after year by being sown or planted, weeded, fertilized, watered, and generally babied until harvest.

Nonetheless, the arrival of any new plant upsets farmers, because it can choke out fodder crops (a problem with dandelion, tall buttercup, cadlock) and even poison cattle (e.g., jimsonweed). So weed inspectors from the provincial Department of Agriculture and Marketing keep a close eye. If they suspect one to be troublesome, they will take steps to get rid of it. Spraying herbicides, a common practice until the late 1980s, is deemed a last resort.

Most new weeds now arrive here as seeds mixed with Western feed grain. [See also the Trans Canada Highway near New Glasgow, the Evangeline Trail near Hebron, and the Lighthouse Route near Jordan Falls.]

down at you. In fact, curious cows are about the only hazard; if you land beside a pasture, they may swarm you.

On April nights along the lower stretches it's not unusual to see a group of people out with flashlights and pails, dip-netting smelt as the tide comes in. Salmon, shad, and gaspereau also come up this river to spawn, the salmon seeking smaller brooks, the others heading for shallow parts of Shubenacadie Grand Lake. There can be trout near the mouths of incoming brooks and in the deep pools along the outside of bends. By August you'll startle broods of black ducks in moulting plumage, all quacking and paddling furiously around the next bend because they can't fly.

Unfortunately, you won't see many live elms. This immense broad-leaved tree, which looks at a distance like a feather duster, thrives in the rich earth of river valleys, floating its flat seeds on spring freshets to colonize new sites. Since the 1970s, Dutch elm disease has killed over half the elms here.

For information on Stewiacke Valley history and resources, visit the Stewiacke Valley Museum at Upper Stewiacke on Rte 289, open afternoons from Canada Day to Labour Day. For details check the latest Nova Scotia Travel Guide.

After passing Shortts Lake on Hwy 102 we travel through denser woodland, a rich summer-time brocade of lettuce-green hardwoods and moss-green conifers, some old and deformed, some young and steeple-shaped. The broad-leaved species are mainly trembling aspen and red maple; the evergreens are red spruce, black spruce, and balsam fir. An occasional white pine towers above the surrounding forest, its tasselled dark boughs flaring toward the prevailing summer southwesterlies.

VIEW: *Power Pylons*

Some 7 km/4 mi south of Brookfield there's a good view of huge metal pylons marching along the east side of the highway like *Star Wars* giants. As we all know, but tend to forget, they carry high-voltage electricity from place to place, so that factories like LaFarge can hum, and coffee can be brewed without building a fire.

What many of us don't consider is that power lines, like roads, must be kept clear of invading alders, willows, and other shrubs, as well as trees. In Nova Scotia's moist maritime climate, this is a continual chore. Power line rights-of-way are essentially clearcuts, and as such they are artificial habitats which favour insects, birds, and mammals that thrive in full light, among them butterflies, warblers, white-tailed deer, and coyotes.

A weed is any plant in the wrong place.
– Anonymous

Observe, too, along this stretch of highway the dense roadside growth of young spruce and fir that has seeded in from nearby trees. This natural (i.e., not planted) regeneration typifies clearcut woodland in most of Nova Scotia. Note, too, that the growth tends to be lusher along the south side. Here seedlings are shaded all day by the tall trees behind, while the north bank is exposed to direct sun.

Much of this woodland has been harvested several times. Thus, as we approach the Shubenacadie River we see a new clearcut on the right and an older one, well grown in, on the left.

Old dyke near Truro

Nearing Exit 11 to Stewiacke, we cross the river's floodplain. Note the low dyke protecting the fields to the north, and how the flats have been ditched and formed into low hills to offset spring flooding and to improve hay production.

LEG STRETCHER: *Mastodon Ridge*

As you near the Stewiacke exit (#11) on Hwy 102, watch for a life-size replica of an Ice Age mastodon to the east. In 1991 nearly complete skeletons from two real mastodons were unearthed at East Milford, just over 10 km/6 mi due south of here. Brainchild of local businessman Bill Hay, the model is an accurate depiction, in fibreglass and steel, of the long-haired brown beast that roamed this valley and most of upper North America 70,000 years ago.

To get close to the model mastodon, take Exit 11 at Stewiacke, go east under the 102, turn left, park in the Kentucky Fried Chicken/Tim Horton's lot, and walk up the hill.

Mastodon Ridge

SIDE TRIP WEST: *Eagle Watch*

One of mainland Nova Scotia's prime eagle viewing areas is the lower Shubenacadie River. There's even an Eagle's Nest Point near its mouth. [See also the **Trans Canada Highway** at Bras d'Or Lake, the **Evangeline Trail** near Kentville, and the **Glooscap Trail** at South Maitland and near Avonport.]

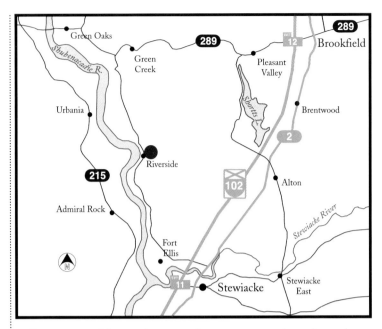

For opportunities to observe eagles summer or winter, leave the 102 at Exit 11, cross eastward to Hwy 2, and drive north, watching for a gravel road to the west just beyond the bridge. If on Hwy 2, watch for the river and a sign saying "Riverside Scenic Route" and turn west. In three places, notably near Fort Ellis (appproximately 4 km/2. 5 mi) and Riverside (approximately 9 km/5.6 mi), the road swings close to the river's east bank, giving the motorist a good view upstream and down. If no eagles are flying, scan the banks with binoculars for tall trees where eagles perch to watch for prey. They can spot a minnow from a kilometre or more.

The lower Shubenacadie is one of the few places in Nova Scotia where bald eagles overwinter. [See also the **Glooscap Trail** near Maitland.] For a bird this large to do so, there must be a reliable food supply. The attraction here is fish, namely tomcod, a small saltwater species that arrives at the river mouth in December and January to spawn.

Bald eagles are fully capable of catching live fish while flying; they have been photographed carrying a wriggling eel or flounder. Unlike the osprey, however, they seldom dive for a meal, preferring to snatch it from shallow water with taloned feet. Still more to their liking—no wild creature wastes precious energy if it can avoid it— is to scavenge dead fish. Hundreds of tomcod are crushed by ice pans churning in the fierce tides near the river mouth and end up on the mud flats at low tide, a banquet spread by Nature.

TO SEE: *Tidal Spectacle*
Also worth watching, if you happen to arrive at the right time (i.e., within about two hours of high tide at the river mouth), is the influx of a Fundy tide over the mud flats.

Seeing this spectacle from high above dramatically illustrates how easily one could get trapped on those mud flats. The swirling wash is chocolate-coloured from the silt disturbed by the powerful currents. As the waters rise, they seek the lowest channel. The bore of vanguard waves runs first up one channel and then another, until the various streams meet and merge into herring-bone patterns that disappear one by one until the highest flats go under. As the salty brown water erases the flats, the colours change in shifting mackerel patterns from satiny pastels to mirror-bright sky reflections. In half an hour the stream bed is full from shore to shore, and the bore is surging on its way toward tidehead.

Tide floods mud flat

Fundy tides reach inland up the Shubenacadie for some 25 km/15 mi.

SIDE TRIP: *Tidal Bore Rafting*

The Shubenacadie River's mouth at rising tide is a cauldron of whirlpools up to 10 m/33 ft across, swirling among fierce tide rips created by opposing currents squeezed between high cliffs. Standing waves over 2 m/7 ft high are common. While these have drowned unwary or heedless boaters, large rubber rafts with powerful outboard motors can safely navigate the maelstrom.

For a really close look, sign up for a summer rafting cruise with one of the local companies. They catch the bore at the mouth, follow it upstream, and bring you back. Consult the current *Complete Guide for Doers and Dreamers* for times, prices, and directions. Life jackets are supplied; bring waterproof clothing.

BACK ON THE HIGHWAY

SIDE TRIP: *Shubenacadie Wildlife Park*

Exit 11 is the turnoff to the largest of Nova Scotia's three wildlife parks. Bear right, turn left under the 102 overpass, drive approximately 1 km/0.6 mi, turn south on Hwy 2, and after 7 km/4. 3 mi watch for the sign.

The only wild creatures most of us ever see are crows and robins, an occasional skunk or porcupine, and maybe a deer in the headlights. Here you can meet more wild animals in a day than you might in 10 years of back-country hiking. And, to help parents answer the questions children ask, there are interpretive signs.

Among the mammals on display are black bear, moose, lynx, bobcat, otter, mink, weasel, porcupine, and harbour seal. The park also boasts the rare once native eastern cougar and pine marten and a resident pack of timber wolves. (The latter are being closely studied and are not on public display.)

Waterfowl are a specialty of this park, which has extensive wetlands in the rear. For years former supervisor Eldon Pace was a noted breeder of rare waterfowl, which mingled with native species that either nested or visited during migration. Other birds on display include bald eagle and great horned owl, as well as African cranes. Beautiful peacocks roam free, their cries echoing over the wooded paths.

Before leaving, be sure to visit the interpretive displays in the Creighton Forest Environment Centre at the entrance. They depict the native species in their various habitats.

The buildings on your way to the park are those of the DNR's forest fire control service, set up here in 1948. A rapid-strike team of highly trained helicopter crews is on call from spring through autumn. State-of-the-art electronic communications link department fire depots, patrol aircraft, and lookout towers across the province. The same network is used for game law enforcement and lost-person emergencies.

Just across the river from the park, an ancient Mi'kmaq village existed down into historic times. The word *shubenacadie* is said to mean "place where wild potatoes grow. "

We tend to think of Stewiacke and Shubenacadie as highway towns, but they were settled in the age of sail, before railways or even good roads. Most goods came upriver by boat from Minas Basin, borne on the great Fundy tides. So both towns are located at tidewater—the farthest upriver a small vessel could navigate—near where the Stewiacke joins its parent stream.

Meander on Stewiacke River

BACK ON THE HIGHWAY

VIEW: *Meander*

Just south of Exit 11 on Hwy 102, where the Stewiacke enters the Shubenacadie, there's a superb meander sweeping across the whole valley. Despite its size, on the inside this loop is so tight that the river almost intersects itself. If and when it ever does, the outer loop will be cut off and form an oxbow lake. [See also the **Lighthouse Route** near Darling Lake.]

Meanders in a river are a sign of old age. They are caused by the build-up of sediment wherever current is slack. With too little slope to create much current (except during spring breakup or after heavy rains, when it floods), it swerves from side to side in its channel, seeking a lower route. Because the current is strongest on the outside of a curve, these banks get undermined. The surplus sand and silt settles in the slower water along the inner curves downstream, building new land. As a result, over time each meander moves like the body of a snake, gradually migrating downstream.

The water's muddy colour comes from the brownish siltstone that underlies this district. Farther upstream (e.g., at Upper Stewiacke, or at Enfield on the Shubenacadie), where the streams flow over harder sandstones, the waters are clear except after heavy rains.

After leaving the Stewiacke's floodplain, we cruise over a mixed-wood ridge and come down into a duplicate plain, that of the Shubenacadie.

TO SEE: *Wild Cucumber*

Approaching the bridge, watch on your right for a pale green (in summer) plant twining over roadside alders and chokecherries. This is wild cucumber, a (possibly) native vine once planted along stone walls and fences, especially farther west. Its spiny seed pods, about the size of a large walnut, persist into late fall.

After the bridge, look on the left for the big shade tree standing in the pasture. It's a fine specimen of red oak, a native hardwood common in western Nova Scotia and along this river. Like most oaks grown in the open, it has a rounded, sturdy look with branches twisting every which way. Such trees were prized for the curved timbers and knees used in building wooden ships along the Minas shore a century ago.

Now begins a long sweeping climb that takes us 4 km/2.5 mi past the exit to Maitland (at the river's mouth), past tall groves of aspen with dark evergreens pushing up underneath, onto a high cleared ridge topped by a farmstead on the far right. In summer, when cattle corn is grown here, the farmstead looks like a tiny island in a waving sea of green and gold. There is a voluptuous quality to the land here, all great rounded hills with farms on their flanks and dirt roads disappearing into woodlots.

VIEW: *Shubenacadie Valley*

As we top the next rise we get a fine panorama of the cleared land hereabouts, both the flatlands and the hills. Being inland, it is protected from Fundy and Atlantic fogs, and the water-laid flatlands are free of the glacial boulders that so plague upland farmers from here to New York State. One serious drawback, however, is spring flooding. It is nothing to see the whole valley floor under water for a week in late March, which means soggy soil well into May, especially if there's much rain.

But in summer the fields are dotted with black-and-white Holstein cattle, a high milk producer originating in northern Germany. Silos—tall concrete towers capped by aluminum or steel domes—dominate the bigger farms. For access to the silo interior, a tube runs down the side, and an electric auger at the base extracts the

There are few finer agricultural tracts than those which compose the settlements of the Stewiack [sic].
– Thomas C. Haliburton
History of Nova Scotia, 1829

mush of fermented corn or hay as needed through the winter.

Silage reduces the need to make sun-dried hay, always a chancy business in our damp climate. Now the grass is harvested quickly and baled on-site, at the peak of freshness, in plastic pods or tubes that are left outside all winter and opened as needed.

Meander on Shubenacadie tributary

At Shubenacadie the clays are covered with only a few feet of gravelly drift; in fact, in J. E. Ettor's field, near the railway, there is less than one foot of gravel on top of them.
– J. W. Goldthwait
Physiography of Nova Scotia,
1924

Coming down the hill toward Exit 9, we see a small white spruce plantation on the west side. The yellowing foliage of many of these trees points to poor drainage. The soil is likely high in clay, and spruce don't like wet feet. The only way to cure the problem is to dig ditches or install tile drains—an expensive proposition for a crop that won't be harvested until 2030 or so. Better not to plant them here in the first place.

Important Mastodon Find
A few kilometres south of Exit 9, near East Milford in the Shubenacadie valley, is the western world's largest gypsum operation, that of National Gypsum (Canada) Ltd. Here in 1991 Nova Scotia's most important mastodon find was made. Mastodon bones had been found in the province three times before—a thigh bone at Lower Middle River in Cape Breton in 1833, a tooth near Baddeck in 1895, and a complete tusk near Windsor in 1989—but nothing like this.

That October day, Stanley McMullin was excavating for the Milford Gypsum Company when he noticed something. It was embedded in dark grey clay under 30 m/98 ft of overburden and looked like bone. It proved to be a yellowing shard of tusk. Later he unearthed some pinkish molars the size of coffee mugs. Quarry superintendent Jim McCubbin immediately telephoned the Nova Scotia Museum of Natural History in Halifax. That same day, the museum dispatched geologist Bob Grantham and assistant Kelley Kozera to the site.

That winter, working with propane heaters under plastic, museum crews carefully removed about 60 per cent—all they could find—of the skeleton of a 22-year-old mastodon bull. Nearby they found some bones of a 6-year-old calf—the first such find for Canada, the sixth for the world. The fragile bones were quickly sealed and taken to the museum for a four-year process of cleaning, drying, analysis, and replication.

Scattered throughout the clay were scores of other intriguing items too numerous to tally. Someone had the idea of boxing hundreds of soil samples and sending them to public schools to analyse. As a result, some 10,000 school children found such things as the skin of a garter snake; a turtle shell; teeth of beaver, caribou, and mole; bones of muskrat, birds, frogs, and fish; and thousands of pine cones.

The pinkness of the mastodon teeth suggested suffocation or drowning as the likely cause of death. Perhaps the animals were attracted by salt licks and fell into natural sinkholes where they drowned. Sinkholes and caves, caused by acidic rainwater dissolving the soft alkaline subterranean rock, are a common feature of gypsum areas. [See also the **Evangeline Trail** near Windsor and the **Trans Canada Highway** near Antigonish and St Anns.]

Between Exits 9 and 8 we run through older and taller woods that developed after extensive logging and forest fires around the 1900s.

TO SEE: *Two Clearcuts*
Between Exits 9 and 8, about 5 km/3 mi north of Elmsdale on the west side, is a recent clearcut of the bad old kind, the kind done without thought for the future. This kind is known by its heaps of brush amid torn-up ground and muddy ruts, by the lack of a green belt to screen its ugliness from motorists, by the ragged look of the many trees left standing. Deformed fir, spindly white birch, clumps of red maple, and diseased aspen have been left exposed to every wind so that in time they will splinter or blow down. The only good thing one can say about this cut is that it was small. Yet it represents thousands of hectares of fertile Nova Scotia woodland logged in this way for lumber and pulpwood since 1900.

A kilometre/0.6 mi farther on, on the same side, is a kinder sort of harvest, carried out around 1985. It was clearcut and not logged

Mastodons (from Greek mastos *meaning breast and* odous *meaning tooth, from the nipplelike points on the molars) and woolly mammoths were close kin to today's elephants, but with smaller ears and long thick coats to withstand severe cold. Mammoths differed from mastodons by having a domed head and straightish tusks. Their coarse, reddish hair, up to 2 m (6 ft) long, hung nearly to the ground like a musk-ox's.*

Roaming in herds, these mammals inhabited forested areas of North America and parts of the then-dry continental shelf during and between the Ice Ages. Their main food was conifer foliage, shrubs, and grasses, with mastodons preferring forest edges and river valleys (like moose) and mammoths roaming open tundra (like caribou).

It is amazing to think that our Ice Age ancestors faced and killed these tough-skinned monsters with nothing but wooden spears. Mammoth hides are tough, so they may have used throwing sticks for added thrust. We know they killed them, because mastodon and mammoth bones have been found scratched by stone butchering tools. For easier killing, hunters likely used fire to stampede these animals into cul-de-sacs or bogs. They may also have stampeded them over cliffs to their death, as Plains Indians did with bison, often on a large scale, into historic times.

piecemeal, because all the trees were of one advanced age, and anything left standing would have invited windthrow and loss of valuable wood. A roadside screen was left. The contractor spread the debris of tops and branches over the site to mulch the humus and shelter any seedlings. He left some existing tall white pine uncut in hopes of getting a crop of pine. When he saw this wasn't happening, he cut them and planted fast-growing spruce a few years later. Today the site is a flourishing evergreen forest that will provide wood for children now in school.

Until the 1920s no reforestation was done in Nova Scotia. Even then it was very small scale. Large-scale tree planting did not start until the late 1970s. All our other forests have seeded in naturally, and still do.

Five kilometres/3 mi farther on, we cross Nine Mile River, flowing in from the northwest to join the Shubenacadie above Elmsdale. (The Shubenacadie keeps us company a few kilometres to the east, from Milford, down past Enfield, and into Shubenacadie Grand Lake.) Several dead elms, victims of Dutch elm disease, stand like skeletons on the floodplain. Such trees, while bark remains, continue to breed elm bark beetles, thus spreading the disease to healthy trees.

In dry summers Nine Mile River, like most Nova Scotia streams, runs nearly dry. This is partly due to lack of upstream lakes—common in soft-rock areas—and to land clearing and logging on the watershed.

TO SEE: *Pine Grove*
Clearly visible east of the Elmsdale exit there's a fine grove of tall white pines. Typically, such groves arise on sandy soils after a light ground fire has killed enough competing trees to give the seedlings, which need shade for a time, a start. (Such fires seldom kill the thick-barked parent trees.)

A walk through this grove shows that almost no white pine seedlings have appeared to replace the overstorey trees when they die or are cut. Instead the ground is covered with young fir, spruce, aspen, and maple. Pine seed are produced almost yearly, but fail to survive the dense, cool shade. The way to have ensured a future stand of white pine here was to fell about half the old pines and let some light and warmth in. Now, short of using fire, it is too late. [See also the **Halifax-Dartmouth Tour** at Point Pleasant Park and the **Evangeline Trail** at Berwick.]

SIDE TRIP: *Clay Capital of Maritimes*
For an interesting detour, leave Hwy 102 at Exit 8, drive south to Elmsdale, and backtrack north on Rte 2 to Lantz. As you approach the village you'll be struck by the increasing number of red brick structures: first the gates of the Christ Church cemetery, then, in the village itself, after which you'll see a large school, a sports arena, and an Anglican church, all of brick. The explanation is a layer of excellent brown clay that underlies this part of the Shubenacadie River valley. In places it is up to 12 m/40 ft thick. Near Shubenacadie there is also grey clay within a metre of the surface.

Lantz has been making bricks since the late 19th century. Until 1905 the Miller Brickyard operated here; they were succeeded by the L. E. Shaw Group, the current owners.

Brickmakers prefer brown clays because the iron in them oxidizes during baking and turns a handsome "brick red." Shubenacadie clay is grey and fires white; some of it is flecked with pits of lignite or soft coal the size of a pencil. Shaw mixes a Milford shale with brown clay for their Lantz products, and with Shubenacadie clay for buff or grey products.

Where there's good clay, you're likely to find potters. Indeed, Lantz has been noted for pottery since 1949. But not all clays are equal. Alma Lorenzen of Lorenzen Pottery has tried samples from different parts of Nova Scotia and New Brunswick and prefers the local product. So do the Deichmanns of New Brunswick and the Morrises of Yarmouth.

Lorenzen mushrooms

Aside from normal screening and reworking, Lantz clay is so pure it requires only slight additives to improve its firing range. In the early 1950s the Lorenzen studio began making its famous ceramic replicas of Nova Scotia mushrooms, now found in collections worldwide. To date they have done over 200 species. To give you some idea of the heat required, these ceramic mushrooms are first fired at 920°C/1,600°F, then glazed at 1145°C/2,005°F.

BACK ON THE HIGHWAY

A few more kilometres of rolling woodland and farms, and we see on the right a sign saying "Historic Shubenacadie Canal."

From here a vessel travelling up from Minas Basin would have had only a few kilometres to go to reach Shubenacadie Grand Lake, and another 35 km/22 mi or so until it reached Halifax Harbour.

As we come down past the truck weighing station (an important legal measure for keeping vehicle loads below a weight that would damage the highway), we see the Enfield overpass and, beyond that, a large quarry in the side of a rocky hill. You'll see a lot more rock cuts between here and Halifax, as well as more pines. This is no coincidence. We are entering a zone of harder and older rock called the Atlantic Interior. Pines do best on acidic, sandy soils, here supplied by quartzite (a hardened form of sandstone) and by greywacke (a cement-like rock).

After so many kilometres of gentle topography and lawn-like roadsides, these hard-rock uplands are startling. Enfield marks the local boundary between the Carboniferous lowlands and the Atlantic Interior, which is part of the Southern Upland that makes up all of southern Nova Scotia from Cape Canso to Cape St Marys. The grey

Lantz clay is far superior to all others, wonderful to work with.
– Alma Lorenzon (Personal correspondence)

cliffs walling us in are slates (compressed shale) thrust up into lofty mountains when the continents collided 400 million years ago. Later they were worn down. Most of the resulting soil was scraped away by the ice sheet and dumped offshore.

When the continents pulled apart to form the Atlantic Ocean 200 million years ago, a slab of the African plate stuck to the North American plate. Thus, the southern half of the province was once part of North Africa. Geologists use the Mi'kmaq name *Meguma* for this rock. The rocks of Morocco look very similar and have fossils in common.

For 6 km/3.7 mi we drive beside a chain-link fence guarding the western runways of Halifax International Airport, then level off on a high windblown site. This site was chosen not only for its flatness and its elevation—nearly 800 m/500 ft above sea level—but because it was fairly fog-free. Unfortunately, after the tree cover was removed, fog increased. Halifax is Canada's second-foggiest airport after Torbay, Nfld.

The stunted tree growth up here is due mainly to removal of soil by retreating glaciers over 10,000 years ago. Where dense bedrock lies near the surface, or where clay has waterproofed the cracks, spruce bogs occur. The racetrack just beyond the airport overpass sits atop one such bog.

Under the airport itself are slate formations containing pyrites or fool's gold (iron sulphide, FeS_2). Once exposed to air and rain by bulldozing, they produced sulphuric acid runoff. With other toxins, this leached into the Shubenacadie River, causing fish kills downstream.

A Puzzling Stone
Less than 2 km/1 mi from the airport to the southeast is a 15-tonne stone perched atop three other stones as if put there by human hands. Some think British soldiers building the Old Guysborough Road in the 1800s lifted it there. Others believe it's one of many mysterious dolmen-like megaliths that Celtic peoples erected as grave markers and observatories all over northern Europe thousands of years ago, and which appear to occur in New England as well. If they are right, Celtic traders were here, perhaps 2000 years before Cabot and Cartier.

After another rise we pass the industrial park at Exit 5A and are in a country of rock outcrops and sparse mixedwood forest of black spruce, white birch, pin cherry, and occasional white or red pine.

TO SEE: *Washboard Strata*
A kilometre or so south of Exit 5A, the roadside rock cuts undulate like ocean swells. Most sedimentary rocks begin as more or less level layers of clay, silt, or sand under water. During mountain building, however, immense pressures can buckle these layers or **strata** like a rug.

Here they are tilted nearly on edge. Pull over, look closer, and you'll see delicate ripple marks on some of the cuts. They were shaped by gentle waves in shallow water when the mud was horizontal. The undulating surface was probably caused by immensely long periods of weathering and by glaciers planing alternating layers of softer rock along the folds. Ice also smoothed the profiles of the cuts, leaving straight scratches or striae along its line of travel.

Coming down the long curve toward the valley of the Dartmouth Lakes, you'll see a forest of full-grown maples on your right and, thriving in their shade, a dense undergrowth of juvenile spruce and fir. In two or three decades these conifers will overtop and shade out all but the tallest maple, unless they are cut first. Then for a few decades the conifers will reign, until the hardwoods again dominate.

Miller Lake to the southeast, with its treed islands and rocky shoreline, typifies the lakes of the Atlantic Interior. It marks the western boundary of the Waverley Game Sanctuary, established in 1929 as the Waverley Crown Land Reserve. Since September 1974 this 5698-ha/14,075-ac tract has been designated a Boy Scout Wilderness Activity area. (The camp at the south end of Miller Lake belongs to the Boy Scouts Association of Nova Scotia.)

Extending more than 10 km/6 mi southeast to upper Lake Major [see also the **Marine Drive**] and east to Lookout Hill, it offers pristine lakes, undisturbed forest, and rocky barrens.

Opposite Miller Lake there are deep ridges of glacial drift, probably scraped off the upland around Halifax International Airport, which is nearly bare of soil.

TO SEE: *Lake Monster*

Near the south end of Miller Lake, just before the Hwy 118 exit, there's a half-sunken log not far from shore. For years it wore a green Loch Ness monster head. When that version vanished mysteriously, a replacement was erected. Spring ice removed that in 1996. Today, a smaller monster is best seen from the north-bound lanes.

Exit 5 provides access to communities along the Dartmouth Lakes. On Lake William, about 5 km/3 mi south of here, DNR maintains a float plane base for use in fire spotting and wildlife work.

Waverley was one of Nova Scotia's first gold districts, becoming a major producer in the 1860s and 1870s and again in the 1890s.

While little evidence of mining activity appears in today's local landscape of the Waverley residential area, in the 1980s people felt the impact. Groundwater, seeping through old mine workings, carried arsenic-bearing minerals typical of these gold-bearing Meguma rocks. Health problems in the area were put down to arsenic in well water. Water testing and treatment have

> *One of the earliest mines, at Waverley near Halifax, produced 13,103 ounces [371 470 g] of gold in 1865 and employed 270 men with an annual income per man of $895, which fell to $584 the following year.*
> – Albert E. Roland,
> **Geological Background and Physiography of Nova Scotia**, 1982

eased the problem, which could show up in Meguma rocks elsewhere in the province.

SIDE TRIP: *Lily Pond*

From late July to early August a 6-km/4-mi round-trip detour onto Hwy 118 toward Dartmouth is worth taking just to see and smell the white water lilies. They grow in profusion in a shallow roadside lake (the second pond, not the first, which is too shallow in summer). This water lily is one of four species native to the province, all remarkable for being able to root in muddy bottoms under two or more metres (6+ ft) of water and to float their leaves and flowers on the surface. They do this by sending up long, air-filled, flexible stems trailing a few dark green, nearly circular, leathery leaves.

Lily

The blossoms are white to pinkish with a spicy perfume that resembles roses or jasmine. It is a night-blooming plant and depends on moths for pollination. The flowers last only a few days when picked; better let them be. Our other native pond-lilies consist of two species with butter-yellow flowers and one with small white flowers.

Our white waterlily (Nymphaea odorata) is closely related to the famed lotus of Greek and Egyptian mythology.

Frogs use the larger leaves as rafts from which to sing and to catch insects. Moose eat water lily leaves and stems, sometimes completely submerging themselves to reach them. Beavers relish the long, thick rhizomes, often called "beaver root".

BACK ON THE HIGHWAY

Hwy 102 continues down the hill, crossing Lake Thomas on a causeway and climbing the opposite side of the valley through dramatic rock cuts. Lake Thomas is on the Shubenacadie Canal. It is one of five sizeable lakes strung out along this ancient river valley linking the Atlantic Coast with Minas Basin. The others are Lake Fletcher and Shubenacadie Grand Lake to the west, and Lake William, Lake Charles, Lake MicMac, and Lake Banook to the east.

Thousands of years before Europeans arrived, the waterway was a Mi'kmaq canoe route. [See also the **Trans Canada Highway** near Debert and the **Sunrise Trail** near Tatamagouche.] A Mi'kmaq family from Chebucto (Dartmouth) wishing to visit relatives in Tatamagouche would paddle and portage up the Dartmouth Lakes, cross Shubenacadie Grand Lake, and run down the Shubenacadie on a falling tide to Cobequid Bay. Waiting for the next high tide, they would cross to the opposite shore, paddle up the Chiganois as far as possible, tote everything a few kilometres across the Cobequid Mountains, and come down the French River to Tatamagouche Bay. The trip might take three or four days, depending on the weather. A couple of hours more would take them across the strait to the future Prince Edward Island to trade with kindred tribes.

Dead Pines

As we get into more piny country, watch for trees with dead or dying tops. This is caused by a wind-borne fungus called white pine blister rust, accidentally imported from Asia via New York on nursery stock around 1890. The fungus attacks the pines' inner bark, choking off sap flow. The upper foliage turns rusty and dies. The disease has a two-host life cycle, switching from pine to wild gooseberry and currants (*Ribes*) and back.

Legacy of Wildfire

Observe how many uplands hereabouts are clothed in a stunted deciduous forest of pin cherry, aspen, white birch, and red oak, with scattered white pine. While looking healthy, the trees are only one-half to one-third normal size for their age.

Sometimes this is the result of a recent major forest fire, such as the one that ravaged the country south of Shubenacadie Grand Lake in the 1950s. More often it is caused by repeated small wildfires.

How could that be, since broad-leaved trees burn poorly? The answer is that it took decades to develop this forest. Most of our forests are naturally two-thirds coniferous (pine, spruce, fir, etc.) and one-third broad-leaved (maple, birch, aspen, etc.). Coniferous species are highly flammable in summer and, indeed, can benefit from an occasional fire to remove competing vegetation. [See the **Trans Canada Highway** near Springhill.] Once burnt two or three times, however, the forest runs out of seed trees. Meanwhile, broad-leaved species rush in to occupy the vacant ground. In doing so, they rely not only on seeds carried by wind, rain, and animals, but by their ability to sprout from stumps or roots, an ability that our conifers lack.

So, decade by decade, the forest becomes more deciduous. This solves the problem of forest fires. Unfortunately, the repeated destruction of organic matter, and subsequent leaching of nutrients from bare soil, has robbed the soil of its capital.

The white pine here survive thanks to thick, fire-resistant bark and deep roots.

As we near the Atlantic Shore, the terrain becomes more rugged, and white pine and red oak become more plentiful. Hikers need to watch their footing in this jumbled landscape of mossy grey boulders, ponds, and bogs. Near Exit 4C, to the west, there is a small rocky lake, part of the

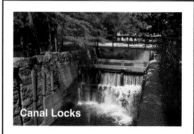

Canal Locks

The Shubenacadie Canal was the white man's way of improving the waterway. This ambitious early 19th-century project was designed to move small cargo ships overland between the Atlantic Ocean and the Bay of Fundy. This would save Halifax merchants the long sea voyage around western Nova Scotia, thereby allowing them to compete with the burgeoning Loyalist port of Saint John, NB. They hired 40 Scottish stonemasons to build a series of locks to lift and lower vessels from lake to lake. For various reasons the project was never finished. [For a fuller account see the **Halifax-Dartmouth Area Nature Tour**, *Shubenacadie Canal.]*

It takes about 500 years for nature to build 2.5 cm/1 in of good topsoil. After bacteria, lichens, and blue-green algae, trees are the greatest soil builders.

Until the advent of spotter aircraft and water bombers, the (then) Department of Lands and Forests had no quick way to control wildfires. After lookout towers gave the approximate location, crews were trucked as near as possible and left to hike in with back tanks and shovels, hoping there was a lake or brook nearby for refills. Spotter planes meant earlier detection, and water bombers meant they could pounce on a fire while it was still small.

Kinsac chain. The 19th-century Japanese print-maker Hiroshige could not have designed a more Oriental landscape than this lake with its islets, dark pines, and hillside cottages. Under snow, the effect is even more pronounced.

On the hill overlooking Exit 4B to Lower Sackville, two of our three species of pine, white and red, are found growing side by side. You can tell them apart by the foliage—that of red pine tends to look more bunchy or tufted—and by the bark, which is cinnamon red in red pine and grey in white pine.

Note also, against the far hill opposite Exit 4A, a step-like structure looking like a rumpled football field. It is a military rifle range, with a step-like series of gravel berms to absorb bullets. (The provincial government maintains smaller firearms ranges in each county, where DNR officers test the marksmanship of would-be hunters.) Glaciers had a hand in deciding where to put this range. For convenience it had to be close to the city, but for safety it was crucial there be no cliffs or boulders to cause bullets to bounce or ricochet. Halifax has a very rocky hinterland, but thanks to the presence of drumlins this place meets the criteria.

Drumlins are hills of gravel that moving glaciers produce as they scrape across bedrock—but with a difference. Drumlins have sculptured whaleback profiles, the result of having shale and slate "upstream." Being made of clay, shale and slate break down into clay when pulverized in the presence of water. Clay being slippery, it allowed the ice to slide up and over the gravel, shaping it instead of bulldozing it along. [See also the **Lighthouse Route** near Mahone Bay.]

After we cross the flats along the Sackville River (which is notorious for flooding) and ascend the ridge toward Halifax, pine and oak gradually give way to scrubby spruce and fir. Though many are scarcely 3 m/10 ft tall, they may be 50 or more years old; thin acidic soils, little sunshine, and salt air stunt their growth.

Observe how the top surfaces of the rock cuts have been polished by glacial ice as it retreated seaward.

Less than 5 per cent of Nova Scotia's forest fires are caused by lightning (a common cause in drier central and Western Canada); the rest are people-caused. The main culprits are spring debris burning, garbage dumps, and arson.

Ironstone road cut near Halifax

The exits immediately north of Halifax display excellent examples of road cuts in Halifax slate. The reddish ones are called ironstone, because iron pyrite or fool's gold has oxidized (rusted) in contact with air. Pyrites are plentiful here because in Devonian times red hot magma welled up, cooking the slate and causing iron sulphate to crystallize. At the exit toward Halifax, along the ramp, you can see where Devonian granite and Precambrian slate make contact.

Near Exit 1 you get a good view of Halifax Harbour with its islands and the North Atlantic beyond. In summer there could be a fog bank lying offshore. The three tall stacks to the northeast are part of the Tufts Cove oil-fired generator, which supplies much of the twin cities' electricity. By 2002 natural gas from Sable Island will have replaced oil here. [See **Marine Drive** at Country Harbour.]

Now the road cuts have changed to mostly greyish quartzite. The thin film of soils on the profiles tells why farming would fail here. But good soil has accumulated in some of the sheltered valleys—witness the scattered tall white pine.

Prince's Lodge

SIDE TRIP: *Hemlock Ravine*
For a dramatic example of how shelter improves tree growth, follow the Kearney Lake exit 1 km/0.6 mi down to the Bedford Highway, turn left at the lights, and drive north a few minutes to Prince's Lodge, the domed structure beside Bedford Basin. Opposite the lodge is Kent Road, which leads to the south end of the ravine. The road is potholed and steep, but don't worry; only 0.3 km/1,000 ft takes you up the hill and down to the parking lot beside Julie's Pond. From there a winding footpath leads uphill through towering hemlock trees that were saplings when Halifax was founded in 1749.

For more information on the ravine, see the **Halifax-Dartmouth Area Nature Tour.**

BACK ON THE HIGHWAY

We're in the suburbs of north Halifax, and the tour is over. For numerous interesting natural history excursions, see the **Halifax-Dartmouth Area Nature Tour**. From the city you can also access the **Lighthouse Route** and the **Evangeline Trail**. To reach the **Marine Drive**, cross to Dartmouth and follow the signs to Hwy 107.

Cabot Trail
Nature Tour

Baddeck to Baddeck
296-km/184-mi loop

OVERVIEW

Magazine and television advertisements extol this trail as one of North America's most scenic, and so it is. Snaking around the entire northern peninsula and across the highlands, it offers unforgettable vistas of hill and ocean, forest and farm. Its plant life covers the gamut from tidal marsh to coastal forest to upland deciduous forest to boreal taiga and peatland.

Geologically, the lowlands along this route are areas of softer sedimentary bedrock, worn down by erosion and glaciation. The oldest (say 350 million years) typically contain limestone, gypsum, and salt; the youngest (say 285 million) contain coal.

Lone Shieling at Grand Anse Valley

The highlands, though two to three times older than the lowlands, have resisted erosion because they are made of much harder rock. They are remnants of the ancient tableland that forms the highest land in Maine, New Brunswick, Newfoundland, and Labrador. These faulted and folded crystalline rocks erode much more slowly than the softer sedimentary formations of the valleys.

The highest part of this ancient plateau or peneplain reaches 532 m/1745 ft—high enough, at this latitude, for subarctic weather and vegetation. Most of the plateau lies inside Cape Breton Highlands National Park. Our route touches it only at French Mountain.

For those interested in more geological detail, the park offers interpretative exhibits at several lookoffs and at the entrance and exit pavilions.

From sea level to the Highlands you'll see tidal marshes, run-down pastures reverting to white spruce, ravines lush with sugar maple, yellow birch, and beech, seas of young balsam fir and white birch studded with tree skeletons standing from the 1980s spruce

103

budworm epidemic, and, on the top, sphagnum bogs sparsely treed with dwarf black spruce.

Cape Breton's fauna lacks a few mainland species (e.g., skunk and porcupine), but otherwise resembles the mainland's. Moose are common in the remoter parts. Along its eastern cliffs there are rare Gaspé shrews. The Highlands are the only known Nova Scotia nesting place of the greater yellowlegs, a large sandpiper.

If you hike or ski the various coastal and back-country trails you'll see starkly beautiful rock barrens, prairie-like bogs studded with tea-coloured ponds and dwarf trees, clearcuts waist-deep in raspberry and elder, thickly wooded talus (broken rock) ravines. An interesting form of vegetation here is the krummholtz—coniferous trees, some more than a century old, pruned by windblown ice crystals and flattened by heavy snows.

THE TOUR BEGINS

Leaving Highway 105 at Exit 7 west of Baddeck, we follow the Middle River and Northeast Margaree systems north to the Gulf of St Lawrence coast, travel thence up along the western Highlands, eastward across the upper boundary of Cape Breton Highlands

White spruce field

National Park, and thence south to join the Trans Canada Highway near Englishtown. One can also connect from the Ceilidh Trail at Margaree Forks. From South Gut St Anns to Nyanza Bay the trail overlaps the Trans Canada Highway.

If you plan to visit the plateau, drop in at the Department of Natural Resources (DNR) office just west of Baddeck and obtain a road map. We'll note six access points en route.

Leaving Nyanza Bay on St Patricks Channel of Bras d'Or Lake, we strike north over the east flank of Hunters Mountain. Looking back as we climb this 213-m/700-ft knob of early Carbon-iferous rock, we glimpse the lake's shining bays behind Marble Mountain and Sporting Moun-tain. We pass farm after old farm being colo-nized by white spruce and alders—a reminder that a century ago 90 per cent of the people here lived on the land.

SIDE TRIP: *Plateau*

About 2.5 km/1.5 mi south of Lower Middle River, a gravel road exits northeast to the plateau. After ascending Crowdis Mountain it continues north to the Big Barren. This is a tawny peatland land-scape with vistas of grey granite and islands of dark spruce, watered by sluggish streams. Those same streams become mountain torrents upon reaching the plateau's edge. The dense thickets of black spruce and tamarack make ideal lynx and moose habitat. The lynx are scarce and reclusive, so your chances of sighting this ghostly hunter of snowshoe hare are slim.

Despite glaciation, forest soils up here are surprisingly deep. Geologists think these soils pre-date the glaciers, reasoning that the 10,000 years or so since the ice melted is too short a time for weathering to have built such thicknesses at this altitude. They speculate that for a time the plateau had its own ice cap, a cap too thin to flow under its own weight. At this elevation there would have been little water to lubricate its flow. These factors, combined with the flattish terrain, would have kept it motionless and prevented the usual scraping away of soil.

From Big Barren, the road wends north another 80+ km/50 mi through a maze of forestry roads to Cheticamp Lake. Consult a DNR map.

BACK ON THE HIGHWAY

Middle River's expansive pastoral valley plain comes as a pleasant surprise in so rugged a region. The explanation is that: (a) the basin is floored with easily eroded Coal Age sediments, producing lots of sand and silt; (b) ancient faults on either side have dropped the valley floor; (c) glaciers and mountain streams have dumped vast amounts of drift (unsorted rock debris), filling any hollows in the valley floor; and (e) geological uplift has allowed the river to cut ever deeper into those sediments, reworking them and spreading them evenly across the plain.

Today this once-powerful glacial torrent meanders peacefully through farmland, woodlot, and marsh.

Middle River's uppermost stream, Fiona Brook, reaches within 3 km/1.9 mi of the Northeast Margaree's uppermost stream, Nile Brook. When they and other tributaries meet, Middle and Margaree rivers will begin in earnest to reduce the adjoining Highlands to sea level.

STOP: *Lakes O'Law*

Beyond Upper Middle River the valley narrows to enclose an odd string of lakes, notably Second and First Lake O'Law and Harvard Lake. Interestingly, the valley lines up with that of the Margaree. Could the Margaree have flowed through here to Bras d'Or Lake? Some geologists think so. They say a gentle northward tilting of the land reversed its flow. Then glaciers plugged the river with gravel, forming these lakes, which drain feebly northward through Lake O'Law Brook.

Margaree's loss is our gain. Today these lakes are like jewels. In autumn they mirror the gorgeous colours of sugar maple, birch, and beech that mantle the surrounding hills. Three Sisters Mountain is especially lovely. At First Lake O'Law (the northernmost) the province has a picnic park in a reclaimed pasture under towering hills.

Lake O'Law

105

STOP: *Salmon Museum*
This museum in Northeast Margaree is devoted to the Atlantic salmon and to the anglers who come from all over the world to try their luck. Exhibits explain the salmon's life cycle, recount the names of famous personalities who have fished the river, and stress conservation. You'll find the museum open from June 15 to October 15, 9 am–5pm.

SIDE TRIP: *Fish Hatchery & Plateau*
For a very scenic excursion with an educational bonus, drive up the Northeast Margaree intervale. (Watch for signs at Lake O'Law Brook and in the village of Northeast Margaree.) Proceed north toward Portree about 10 km/6 mi, loop across the river, and return down the other bank.

The valley here is flat and wide, with steep-sided highlands looming all around. Frasers Mountain to the east rises to over 427 m/1400 ft. You'll have perfect views of the famous river. Observe how the main stream has migrated to and fro across the floodplain, creating a braided pattern of islets and channels—and more than 30 named salmon pools.

Margaree River

Drop in to the salmon hatchery between Margaree Valley and Portree to learn how baby salmon are hatched and raised from tiny organisms with yolk sacs to fingerlings to parr to smolt big enough to release. It's open 9 am–4 pm any day.

You might also visit the Margaree Salmon Association's interpretation centre here. It describes the interface between land use, fish habitat, and angling success. The centre's observation deck overlooks one of the river's best pools. If the salmon are running, you can watch up to 100 of these silvery fish in their natural habitat at the same time.

Local people care a lot about their river and its fish and want visitors to understand how to keep the ecosystem healthy. The angling season is June 1–October 15, subject to water conditions; several local stores sell licences.

Botanists prize this area for its unusual vascular plants. In spring watch for bloodroot, a white-flowered member of the poppy family. It prefers moist rich soil in shady places, such as above the high-water mark along brooks, where it may form carpets.

VIEW: *Plateau Access*
From the village of Margaree Valley (5 km/3 mi north of Northeast Margaree), Fielding Road runs east past Frasers Mountain to the plateau. Cape Clear, a stunning 460-m/1500+-ft lookoff on Second Forks Brook Road, takes in a vast sweep of valley upstream and down. The autumn view toward Margaree Forks is exceptionally fine. For precise directions, consult a DNR map and inquire locally.

VIEW: *Sugarloaf Mountain*
This highland remnant overlooking Portree has been cut off from the main upland by the naturally eroding valleys of two or more streams. Since then, glacial action and weathering have been rounding its

Sugarloaf Mountain

Officially Nova Scotia has three mountains, two hills, one village, one brook, and one set of lakes called "Sugarloaf." The name derives from the moulded dome of sugar that old-time general stores displayed before bagged or pre-packaged sugar came into use.

contours. The process is being hastened by a fault or crack, along which the river runs for 15 km/9 mi. You can see this fault as a nearly straight scarp or cliff west of the mountain.

BACK ON THE HIGHWAY

Continuing along the valley, the road veers sharply north at Margaree Forks, where the southeast and northeast branches join in a wide floodplain before flowing out through the drowned estuary of Margaree Harbour into the Gulf of St Lawrence.

Between Margaree Harbour and Cheticamp, the trail snakes along a low coastal plain that seldom exceeds 30 m/100 ft above sea level. The plain is made of mostly Coal Age sandstone and is rapidly eroding. The waves here have a much longer fetch than at, say, Cape Mabou, which is sheltered by Prince Edward Island. The farther a wave travels, the taller and more destructive it can be.

At Belle Côte you can access the plateau via a dirt road that climbs east some 15 km/9 mi into the country behind Pembroke Lake (see also below).

The name Cap Le Moine (French for "Friar's Head") comes from big shoreline boulders that reminded Acadian settlers of cowled heads. The coast here has a harsh look. Over-harvesting of trees and clearing of pastures have long ago denuded the land of forest, and severe exposure has done the rest. Strong west winds, moist with salt spray, prevent all but hardy grasses, tamarack, and white spruce from growing here. Mountain alder huddles in protected hollows.

Marsh marigold, a native plant of the buttercup family, is virtually confined to isolated spots along the Inverness shore. Roland's Flora of Nova Scotia lists it from a beach near Mabou, a wet meadow at Northeast Margaree, Margaree Harbour, St Joseph du Moine, Cheticamp, and from the mouth of Grand Anse Brook, Pleasant Bay.

Margaree Valley

VIEW: *Plateau Access*

A dirt road exits the trail about 1 km/0.6 mi north of the village, climbs steeply past Squirrel Mountain, Angus Lake, and Pembroke

Lake, and branches into woods roads about 15 km/9 mi inland. Refer to a DNR map or ask at a local store or service station.

Now the trail wends over and around great heaps of brown glacial till, a sure sign that we've entered a zone of softer rock. Along the shore, steeply tilted soft grey sandstone is exposed. Some layers show pronounced ripple marks—fossil wave patterns. The lowest layers consist of limestone and gypsum from the ancient Windsor Sea. In a few decades, at current rates of erosion along this stormy shore, people will have to shift the road and outermost houses inland.

Grand Étang

At Grand Étang (French for "big pond") note the sinkhole pond east of the road. It connects to the sea along a fault line. (Petit Étang just beyond Cheticamp is a smaller version.) In such alkaline environments eutrophic marshes with uncommon plants often develop. [See also the **Ceilidh Trail** near Lake Ainslie.]

Have you noticed something odd about the houses? A lot of the roofs slope southeast. This is to present a lower profile to the vicious *suete* (Acadian French for *sud est*), a southeast gale that howls off the Highlands and out to sea. Local fishers routinely double the wind velocity of any Maritime forecast involving southeasterlies. Not doing so could mean not making it back to shore.

VIEW: *Cheticamp Island*

Cheticamp Island

Like Port Hood Island to the south, this is a fragment of eroding Coal Age sedimentary rock. Acadians looking for new land after the Expulsion at first settled inland to farm, but then took to fishing mackerel and cod. The island gave some protection, there was plenty of wood, and the soft red sandstones and conglomerates made good soil for potatoes, cabbage, and turnips. In the 19th century many Newfoundlanders also came here to find work in the coal mines along this coast.

Cheticamp

You can reach the island north of Point Cross, where the sign says "Plage St-Pierre." The road follows a bar built by longshore currents bringing sediment up the shore. As the current slows, the suspended particles settle to the bottom like snow behind a hedge. But the continual stripping of sand has left a bouldery beach behind. At the island's south end a tombolo, likely encouraged by highway construction, joins the island to the coastal plain and helps moderate the waves.

STOP: *Ferry Wharf*

Besides being the western gateway to the Cape Breton Highlands National Park, Cheticamp is the northernmost ferry terminus for Îles-de-la-Madeleine. Boats leave from Le Quai Mathieu in mid-town. In addition, whale-watching cruises are available spring through fall, with excellent prospects for sighting most of the major species.

As the white streaks of limy excrement on nearby green asphalt roofs suggest, the ferry wharf is a good place to observe gulls and cormorants. A favourite roost is the old pier just offshore. Look for black-backed and herring gulls on shoreward perches, and cormorants on the outer ones, drying themselves in the breeze.

STOP: *Visitor Centre/Bird Walk*

You'll need a permit to travel or camp in the national park. Check in at the visitor centre a few hundred metres past the Cheticamp River bridge, on the right. There are excellent photographs, maps, and interpretive texts describing the park and its many attractions. While you're there, pick up information on trails, bird-watching, and camping.

Behind the centre there's a pleasant walking trail near the river. Summer bird watchers have been rewarded by sightings of northern waterthrush, yellow-bellied flycatchers, and Blackburnian and blackpoll warblers.

The Trail between the park entrance and Le Buttereau follows the dry channel of the ancestral Cheticamp River as it carved its way along a trough of softer rock. The channel was abandoned when glacial debris blocked the northern outlet. [See also the **Evangeline Trail** at White Rock and the **Trans Canada Highway** at Folly Lake.]

Cheticamp River

Cormorants often stand with wings outstretched. They do this to dry their feathers after fishing expeditions. Unlike most birds, these underwater speedsters lack oil glands. Without waterproofing, the feathers cling to their bodies, giving them enough speed to outswim some fish.

On another occasion my companion, accompanied by a big Norwegian, spent a number of days in the interior of the park. One evening they reached a prominence affording a view of the wide sweep of forest-clad hills and valleys, an expanse of muskeg, and ... a distant glimpse of the sea. As they stood in silence enjoying the beauty, the Norwegian said softly to himself, "God doesn't want this country to be logged; He intended it for a park."

– Wilfrid Creighton, **Forestkeeping,** *1988*

Cheticamp River

STOP: *Eroding Cliff*

At Buttereau Picnic Park (4 km/2.5 mi north of the park entrance) the vertical pink face of Grande Falaise (French for "big cliff"), part of Jerome Mountain, vividly demonstrates how weathering breaks

Le Buttereau

down the hardest rock. Great blocks and slabs of rock, some larger than an auto, lie heaped at its base. Most of them were pried loose by the power of freezing water. Freezing water expands, exerting a powerful outward force. In addition, daily heating and cooling of the south-facing cliff causes continual flaking.

As the heavy blocks cartwheeled down the slope, they collided with others, breaking each into smaller pieces. Weathering and frost action reduced these to pebbles, to sand, and to rock dust, which rain then washed to the bottom of the heap. Eventually the smaller particles found their way into Jerome Brook, which deposited them offshore. If this process continues long enough, the whole mountain will be washed into the sea.

These cliffs are underlain by dark grey basalt, a hard volcanic rock. [See also the **Fleur-de-lis Trail** and the **Marconi Trail**.]

Do *not* climb the slope. The rock face is unstable and can collapse on climbers without warning. All varieties of rock are present near the picnic site.

LEG-STRETCHER

Directly across the highway is Le Buttereau Trail. This self-guided path (folders are provided at the start) gives some idea of how Acadian settlers fared here in the 1760s. In 1755 they had been taken from their lush dykelands [see also the **Sunrise, Glooscap**, and **Evangeline trails**] and scattered to the four winds. Some trekked back up the Eastern Seaboard and, finding their lands taken, moved to the Cheticamp area.

One group chose the little harbour that Jerome Brook had scooped out of the cliff. A long sandbar, unusual on this rocky coast, provided shelter for boats. Along the brook valley they found good soil for crops. The ridge where the trail now runs became a cattle pasture.

This 1.9-km/1.2-mi trail starts at sea level opposite the picnic park, climbs through alders up a ridge clothed in gnarled white spruce, and descends to abandoned farmland on the Gulf side. You can see the Gulf of St Lawrence and the coastal plain stretching toward Cheticamp.

Farther up the shore there are "sea stacks"—Pillar Rock, for example. Sea stacks are formed when lava squirts under and into existing rock and

Sea Stacks at Pillar Rock

cools slowly enough to form a mass of polygonal columns. Here the overlying rock eroded away, allowing ocean waves to undermine the basalt. Weaker parts broke along vertical lines, leaving the harder parts standing free. [See also the **Glooscap Trail** near Apple River and Parrsboro and the **Digby Neck Scenic Route** at Brier Island.]

Presqu'ile (French for "almost an island") is an eroded sliver of Coal Age rock joined to the shore by a double sandspit or tombolo.

From Buttereau north to Pleasant Bay the landscape changes dramatically. We are leaving the soft-rock zone behind and entering a region of flinty igneous rocks that predate the Carboniferous. Being harder, they form steeper cliffs.

> *In the first years many settlers suffered from scurvy, caused by lack of vitamin C (ascorbic acid), which resulted in bleeding gums, blotchy skin, and ennui. The Mi'kmaq taught them that a beer brewed from fermented spruce foliage would cure it. (The trail brochure gives a recipe for this refreshing drink.)*

STOP: *Cap Rouge*

This Parks Canada roadside loop, 7 km/4.3 mi north of the park entrance, provides an excellent interpretation of local geology. Looking south we see the great walls of pink and black stone around Le Buttereau, with the Cheticamp barachois beyond. Coloured roadside illustrations of the scene allow one to "read" the rocks.

From here the road curves inland to follow Jumping Brook up into the Highlands. Since it climbs slantwise up the contour, the steepness is less obvious than farther north at Grand Anse. Likewise, the transition from deciduous to coniferous forest is less abrupt. As at Le Buttereau, erosion along these slopes is intense. One has only to hike a short distance off the road to find the forest floor heaped with angular rock fragments called talus.

If we could see down through the forest canopy and the fallen leaves and humus, we would see conical fans of loose rock lying against the hillsides like road fill from a rock crusher. The surface of such a fan grades from great angular blocks downslope—their greater mass carries them farther—to fine material near the top. (This is the reverse of the pattern on beaches, where the waves must work against gravity.) Rockfalls happen more often in the upper zone than lower down. Sand and rock dust continually filter downward through the pile and out the bottom.

Where trees can find enough soil, they take root. As they grow, they stabilize the lower slopes. However, every so often rain and frost pry loose another block. With muffled thunder it comes tumbling down the slope, smashing and splintering trees until it finally comes to rest. Then silence returns.

Our first taste of Highland comes near French Lake, about 6 km/ 3.7 mi east of Cap Rouge, near the south branch of Fishing Cove River. Long rolling vistas of bog and barren and purplish conifers appear. The subtle tans, greens, and pinks, the greys and purples, have an austere loveliness seldom seen outside the Arctic.

> *[Soil] would come from ... high terrain ... by rain and frost slowly reducing mountains, which in stages would be ground down from boulders to cobbles to pebbles to sand to silt to mud by a ridge-to-ocean system of dendritic streams. Rivers would carry their burdens to the sea, but along the way they would set it down, as fertile plains. The Amazon had brought off the Andes half a continent of plains.*
> – John McPhee, **Basin and Range**, 1981

It's surprisingly flat. [See also the **Trans Canada Highway** at Canso Causeway and the **Sunrise Trail** at Cape George.] The flatness is the result of 80 million years of erosion since the Cretaceous uplift. The better-drained gravelly slopes grow balsam fir, pointy as steeples and fragrant with resin. Most of the trees are less than 30 years old, having germinated after the 1980s spruce budworm epidemic. On poorly drained flats and clay soils, the usual vegetation is sphagnum bog ribboned with islands of slow-growing black spruce.

At this elevation (about 430 m/1400+ ft above sea level) the weather is fickle, with sunshine one minute and chilly rain squalls the next. Streamers of grey cloud often swirl through the forest, beading the needles and old man's beard with moisture.

Signs warn of moose on the highway, and one needn't stray far off the road to see their 20-cm/8-in hoof-prints and grape-sized olive green dung along the paths. Keep track of your movements; sudden fog can swiftly blot out landmarks. Near the highway you'll find soft green and pink blankets of sphagnum moss whitened with reindeer lichens, which look like miniature trees. (Hobby stores spray-paint them and sell them to model railroad buffs; but picking here is illegal.) Low shrubs include blueberry, mountain and bog laurel, Labrador tea, and rhodora. Larger ones are wild pear, wild raisin, and leatherleaf. Canada burnet (whose flower looks like a bottlebrush) grows here as well. The only trees are stunted black spruce and larch.

This isn't true plateau. The plateau looks much more boreal. Bogs there are bigger, and the trees are smaller and sparser. The Russians call it taiga, a useful word that North American plant scientists have borrowed. To see real taiga, take one of the access roads noted.

V-shaped valleys are generally postglacial. Glaciated valleys are normally U-shaped in cross-section, not V-shaped, and tend to have waterfalls (in hanging valleys) spilling over their rims where brooks have been cut through.

Plateau Valley in the fall

LEG-STRETCHERS

In this area there are several hiking trails of varying lengths (e.g., Bengies Lake, 3.2 km/2 mi; Fishing Cove, 16 km/10 mi). For maps and details refer to Cape Breton Highlands National Park literature; David Lawley's *Nature and Hiking Guide to Cape Breton's Cabot Trail*; Michael Haynes's *Hiking Trails of Nova Scotia*; or Pat O'Neil's *Explore Cape Breton*.

Between here and Pleasant Bay the trail crosses part of the ancient, much-eroded Atlantic Upland (of which northern New Brunswick and western Newfoundland form part). Geologists call it the Cretaceous planation surface, because most of the erosion occurred during the latter part of that period, in the 80-million-year span leading up to the most recent ice ages.

In Cape Breton the eons of erosion left a slightly domed plateau near the centre. With streams impeded by the many bogs and lakes, erosion slows down. The most active erosion happens along the edge, where numerous short, swift rivers busily carve V-shaped ravines into the hills, gradually working farther upstream. A general uplift of the region during the Cretaceous Period accelerated this process.

Mackenzies River

As we descend toward Pleasant Bay, where Mackenzies River cuts deeply into the peneplain, we get a good sense of the erosive power of a mountain stream. Seen from the air, or on a large-scale topographic map, the river system resembles a many-branched deciduous tree (hence dendritic, via Greek *dendron* meaning "tree"), with its crown facing east.

When two streams close in on each other, they whittle the intervening rock to a narrow ridge, locally called a boar's-back. In time the ridge disappears into a wide river valley. Where a stream enters the sea over hard-rock formations, coves are small (e.g., Fishing Cove).

Along this stretch there are several lookoffs with interpretive displays.

LEG-STRETCHER: *Slope Bog*

A few kilometres east of French Lake you can walk through a slope bog. [For a description of bog types, see the **Marine Drive** near Tor Bay.] A 0.6-km/0.4-mi year-round boardwalk loop trail explains its origin, flora, and fauna. Notable plants include bog buckbean, Canada burnet, and a tufted rush.

The tangy tea smell is mostly tannic acid, released when foliage decays under acidic conditions. Tannin also accounts for the tea-like colour of the water. [See also the **Fleur-de-lis Trail** near Framboise, the **Marine Drive** near Tor Bay, and the **Sunrise Trail** near Tatamagouche.] If you stop here for more than a few minutes between May and August, you'll need fly repellent.

Vanished Caribou

About 10 km/6 mi south of here, near the headwaters of the Aspy River, herds of woodland caribou once roamed the high, open tundra of the Plateau. In summer they grazed the brook valleys and lake shores, sometimes coming to the coast for kelp. At first snow they

Ever since the 1850s, there have been tantalizing but unconfirmed reports that the rare northern hawk-owl (Sernia ulula) resides in the province. Finally, in the summer of 1996, a team of naturalists and biologists surveying Highland flora and fauna confirmed that it does indeed nest there. The preferred habitat of this daytime hunter is a balsam fir thicket. Such thickets sprang up abundantly on the Highlands after the 1980s budworm epidemic. Sure enough, that's where the Nova Scotia Museum–funded team found them— only a few, but enough to add another bird to our checklists.

migrated to high open country like these barrens. Here high winds swept away the snow, allowing them to paw through the crust with their shovel-shaped hooves to reach their staple food, reindeer lichen. During storms they sheltered in dense fir and black spruce thickets where they fed on old man's beard lichen. [See also the **Sunrise Trail**, the **Marine Drive**, the **Trans Canada Highway**, and the **Evangeline Trail** near Caribou, Liscomb, Debert, and Aylesford, respectively.]

Caribou declined sharply in mainland Nova Scotia in the late 1800s and in Cape Breton Island after 1900. The causes of extinction were several. Human-made forest fires destroyed many of the old coniferous forests that sheltered and fed them in winter. Logging cut into their winter habitat. (Between 1919 and 1931, the Oxford Lumber Company logged the interior of Inverness and Victoria counties heavily.) Illegal hunting decimated the herds; some logging camp foremen hired full-time hunters to keep meat on the table. Returning World War I veterans, hungry for meat after years of rationing, added to the illegal kill.

Caribou are herding animals. Once their numbers drop below a certain level, the remnant population declines more rapidly. After 1920 it was a rare thing to see a caribou in Cape Breton. In the winter of 1934, Provincial Forester Wilfrid Creighton was sent to the Highlands to investigate rumours of sightings. He saw none; by then the herds were probably no more.

The final straw may have been a hair-like brain worm found in white-tailed deer. White-tails were naturally invading the province in the late 1800s (as coyotes did in the 1980s). In this they were helped by several introductions. The brain worm is harmless to deer but sickens moose and caribou.

Lookoff

As Creighton describes in his history of the Nova Scotia Department of Lands and Forests, *Forestkeeping,* the province tried in vain three times to reintroduce woodland caribou—in 1939 (seven Newfoundland animals to Liscomb Sanctuary), in 1968 (19 Québec animals to Cape Breton Highlands National Park), and in 1969 (40 more Québec animals to the national park).

VIEW: *Pleasant Bay Lookoff*

You might not guess it now, but for 15 days in August 1947 a forest fire raged across these hills. As the map at the lookoff shows, it ran from here along the coast to Red River and north on both sides of the park boundary in two tongues, one reaching beyond the Lone Shieling. Headlines in provincial newspapers told of buildings burnt, of timber losses, of 225 people evacuated by sea. More than 2 000 km²/772 sq mi of woodland was razed.

As you can see, the mountain regenerated. First came birch and aspen, then an understorey of fir and spruce. Thanks to a pocket of

Eroding drumlin at Polletts Cove

Polletts Cove

sandy soils and the sheltering hills, this area has always had an isolated population of native red oak.

LEG-STRETCHER

Dedicated hikers who don't mind wading the odd brook might wish to tackle the 19-km/11.8-mi Red River/Polletts Cove coastal trail, which begins on the north slope of Bald Mountain. (See national park brochures for directions.) The Trail alternates between vistas of headland and ocean framed in coastal white spruce, and woodland stretches through large sugar maple and yellow birch.

The rare pine marten may inhabit pockets of older conifers here. Once fairly common across the province, this tree-going native weasel is swift enough to run down a squirrel—but easily trapped. Its silky chestnut-coloured fur, identical to Russian sable, fetched too high a price for it to be left in peace. By the 1900s, logging plus uncontrolled trapping had all but eliminated the marten from Nova Scotia. Reintroductions have had some success.

Again we ascend into the Highlands, this time by the Grand Anse River valley. The route is much steeper than at Jumping Brook—over 300 m/1000 ft in a few kilometres. So the shift from deciduous to coniferous forest is more dramatic. One moment we are gliding through aisles of big sugar maple, beech, and yellow birch; the next we're in a wind-blasted fir forest.

Fir and spruce are specially adapted to boreal conditions. Shallow roots allow them to tolerate thin rocky soils with high water tables. Waxy evergreen foliage with superb moisture retention allows them to cope with dry winter air. (Conifers evolved during a time of widespread desert conditions.) The ability to respire and photosynthesize almost year-round lets them make the most of acidic, infertile soils. Flexible, drooping branches and an A-frame shape shed snow and ice before they cause much damage.

Lone Shieling

Broad-leaved trees, on the other hand, close down in winter, damage easily in ice storms, and demand deep, well-drained soils. They favour slopes, lowering the risk of damage from early or late frost, because cold air drains to valley bottoms.

STOP: *Lone Shieling/Climax Forest*

Halfway up the Grand Anse Valley, about 10 km/6 mi east of the Pleasant Bay lookoff, watch on the south side for a thatch-roofed stone structure. It sits amid 40 ha/100 ac of deciduous forest donated by Prof. Donald MacLeod. It's part of the largest undisturbed old-growth deciduous forest in the Maritimes, 1600 ha/ 4000 ac in all. Sugar maple dominates the lower slopes, yellow birch the upper ones, with beech and red spruce sprinkled through.

Professor MacLeod had the shieling built to honour Highland Scots ancestors who settled hereabouts in the early 19th century. The shieling had one side for sheep, the other for the shepherds, protecting both from weather and marauders.

Meandering from a small parking lot down through the trees is a 0.8-km/0.5-mi self-guided trail. Almost 20 species of woodland fern have been tallied here. And if you come before leaf-out in April/May you'll be treated to the sight of Dutchman's breeches, green spleenwort (*Asplenium viride*), and trout-lily in flower. By blooming early they catch the sunlight while the trees are leafless.

This path [across the plateau] which is used by the mail carrier twice a week, in going from coast to coast, is the only trail across the plateau. Where it passes over the peat bogs on the tableland, corduroy roads [small logs laid crossways] alone prevent the traveller or his horse from sinking knee deep.
– J. W. Goldthwait,
Physiography of Nova Scotia, *1924*

In places there's an almost unbroken carpet of sugar maple seedlings. Like yellow birch and beech, they have the ability to persist in their parents' shade until a fallen tree creates an opening in the forest canopy. Then they put on a spurt of growth to reach the sky. Beech and yellow birch require slightly more light than sugar maple but can maintain their place in this so-called climax (i.e., self-perpetuating) forest.

VIEW: *Highland Fir Forest*

A few more kilometres and the road enters high and rolling terrain clothed in a typical highland forest of young balsam fir and white birch. The numerous standing dead trees were victims of the 1974–81 budworm outbreak. As their bark and smaller branches fall, they help nourish the young seedlings of the future forest. Insects and fungi invade the standing snags, providing food for chickadees, nuthatches, and woodpeckers. When the tops break off in winter storms, the process of decay accelerates. Finally the trunk collapses, providing shelter and nourishment for myriad soil

Highland Valley

creatures. The whole process can take decades.

As the new forest develops, most of the birch dies out, leaving a natural balsam fir monoculture. It fosters a variety of other creatures. Crossbills nip the fir buds, voles and snowshoe hare nibble on twigs and bark, and moose browse on the young shoots. (So far, the Strait of Canso has kept porcupines out of these woods.) At about age 35 the young forest pokes through the older canopy—an enticing banquet for the budworm caterpillar the next time weather conditions are right. Tree-ring analysis reveals at least five major outbreaks since the early 1700s. Budworm manages this forest.

Those patches of grey and pink along the shoulders and ditches are reindeer lichen, of which there at least three species here. They are colonizing bare gravel and rock, as their postglacial ancestors did thousands of years ago. Without the work of bacteria, lichens, and algae there would be too little soil here to support tree growth. The scattered yellow roadside flower seen in late summer here is hawkweed, a hardy relative of dandelion.

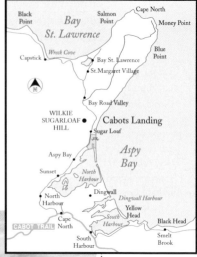

Aspy Valley Fault

Geologists consider the wedge of mostly Precambrian rock between Pleasant Bay and the Aspy Fault a fragment of the original North American continental plate. At nearly one billion years old, it is the most ancient formation in the province.

STOP: *Aspy Bay Escarpment North*

Aspy River in its upper reaches runs unusually straight for about 10 km/6 mi and fairly straight for the remaining 30 km/19 mi to Aspy Bay. It follows the Aspy Fault, a major crack in the Earth's surface. The crack happened during the formation of Cape Breton, when two masses of bedrock slid past each other along a zone of weakness. Money Point is the out-thrust northwest end of this formation.

At MacGregor Brook the trail suddenly veers south. We follow its steep gorge (a smaller fault) across the Aspy Fault and down into the valley. Halfway down, watch for a pull-off with a good view of the escarpment running northwest and southeast. Interpretive graphics explain the geology. The valley of the North Aspy is mostly climax beech forest.

117

As we leave the beech forest behind, more conifers appear, and the odd farm. Once in the valley, the road hugs the fault line for a time, then crosses to the Aspy's east bank—where we leave the park for a while—and follows it down to the village of Cape North. This is the northernmost point on the Cabot Trail.

At Cape North you can see some of Nova Scotia's finest examples of beach formation, dune succession, and sandbar development. Outcrops of whitish gypsum gleam like old snow from the hillsides.

Aspy Bay (Old English word *aespe* for aps or aspen) was likely named for the many aspen groves that followed early forest fires. The place is rich in geology, history, and coldwater beaches. The bay itself is a Carboniferous basin scoured out by streams and glaciation. This has supplied plenty of sand and gravel to create the river's triple-branched, complex floodplain and a delta that extends far out into the bay.

Fronting Aspy Bay are two curving bars of yellowish sand that enclose North and South harbours. The bars were built by longshore currents and together stretch over 7 km/4 mi. The Aspy River maintains an opening in each through which boats can pass.

Cape Breton, originally called Isle Royale, was first discovered by John Cabot, a British navigator. The early 'voyageurs' to it were from Bretagne, in France: hence ... its present name.
– Abraham Gesner,
The Industrial Resources of Nova Scotia, 1849

Light at Black Rock

Bay St Lawrence

SIDE TRIP: *Cabot Landing*

Aspy Bay is an excellent place to see shorebirds and waterfowl, many of which use nearby Money Point as a stepping stone when crossing Cabot Strait from Newfoundland. Various sparrows (fox, white-crowned, tree), as well as northern shrike, are reported. Sometimes one can watch gannets, great white birds more than twice the size of herring gulls, plummeting from the sky into schools of herring.

While in the area, take a drive up around North Harbour to Cabot Landing Picnic Park. Turn west at the village of Cape North toward Bay St Lawrence. Drive 18 km/11.2 mi, crossing North Aspy River and veering northeast along the fault past North Harbour and Sunset. After the village of Aspy Bay, watch for the sign.

The first transatlantic cable was landed at Money Point in 1867, and the point boasted a rare cast-iron lighthouse.

East of the park is the 328-m/1,076-ft Wilkie Sugarloaf, an upland remnant isolated by erosion. To really see Aspy Bay (and perhaps some gannets), ask about the 15-km/9-mi dirt road that starts just before Bay Road Valley and ends on the cliff near Money Point.

Cabot Beach

About 2.5 km/1.5 mi up the beach, a cairn marks the supposed landfall of Venetian explorer John Cabot. Legend has it that Cabot and his son Sebastian landed here in June 1497 after sighting Cape North and Sugarloaf. Newfoundland, on the other hand, claims Cape Bonavista as the landfall. Whichever is true, both provinces celebrated the 500th anniversary in June 1997.

Aspy Bay is the nearest sheltered harbour to Newfoundland, 96 km/ 60 mi away. As such it was a convenient assembly point for Mi'kmaq crossing Cabot Strait to Cape Ray. (Beothuk scholar Ingeborg Marshall and others believe the Mi'kmaq routinely visited New-foundland before 1600.) Before embarking in their special ocean-going birchbark canoes, however, they sent scouts to St Paul Island. When the scouts deemed conditions favourable, they lit fires to signal their companions to join them.

By leaving at dawn in clear weather and keeping Cape North's 427-m/1400-ft headland in view as long as possible, then sighting ahead to southwest Newfoundland's 518-m/1700-ft coastal moun-tains, the Mi'kmaq could keep on course during 10–12 hours of steady paddling. The attraction was plentiful moose and furbearers. According to Marshall, Nicolas Denys stated around 1650 that "the Cape Breton Indians have destroyed the moose population and 'abandoned the island'."

The surveyor J. B. Jukes was told in 1839 that Micmac used to cross in these frail vessels from Cape Breton Island to Cape Ray. Speck recorded that Micmac who formerly travelled this route would stop over at St Paul's Island, which was [then] therefore called Tuywe gan moniguk, or "temporary goal island."
– Ingeborg Marshall, **A History and Ethnography of the Beothuk**, 1996

TO DO: *Whale-watching*

Northern Cape Breton is one of the province's two best places for observing whales. [See also the **Digby Neck Scenic Drive,** Briar Island.] These large mammals migrate from tropical waters to fatten on plankton and fish. Likely summer sightings are humpback, fin, and minke, which are joined in July by pilot whales. With luck you might spot a sperm whale, or even the rare Atlantic right whale. Porpoises and dolphins are present all summer. Whale/ seabird cruises are available from Bay St Law-rence, about 10 km/6 mi north of the park.

Meat Cove got its name from an immense slaughter of moose in the early days. Historian Thomas Haliburton wrote in 1829: "At the period of the first ... English rule in the Island, [moose] become the object of most destructive pursuit, merely for the sake of their hides. Their carcasses were left by hundreds along the coast, from St Anne's to Cape North; and to such an extent [was] the butchery ... that as vessels passed by, the stench wafted from the shore was insuffer-able. Ever since ... that indiscriminate massacre, the numbers of the moose have been comparatively scanty. The Cariboo, however ... is still plentiful."

BACK ON THE HIGHWAY

After Aspy Bay our route trends southward. It follows the park boundary from near South

River village to Broad Cove, leaving it for good at Ingonish Beach.

Near Dingwall the terrain has a lumpy look, like a lawn worked over by moles. There are numerous small hills, mounds, and hollows and occasional odd pinnacles tufted with spruce at the top. There are snowy cliffs, and driveways are surfaced with crushed white rock.

All these signs point to gypsum. Gypsum is a soft compound of calcium and sulphur that underlies large areas of central and eastern Nova Scotia. [See the **Halifax-Dartmouth Tour**, also the **Trans Canada Highway** at Oxford, Antigonish, and Little Narrows; the **Glooscap Trail** at South Maitland and Walton; and the **Evangeline Trail** near Windsor.] These deposits were laid down during the drying-up of tropical seas over 300 million years ago. They have made Nova Scotia the world's largest supplier of gypsum, the major component in gyproc wallboard. Calcium dissolves in weak acids— including normal rain—so gypsum country is riddled with sinkholes, caverns, and pinnacles—what geologists call karst topography.

Dingwall had a major gypsum quarry from 1933 to 1955, when the operation was moved to East Milford, Hants County.

From South Harbour to Ingonish we ascend the Highlands one last time. Again the bedrock is igneous and resistant to erosion. Barren ridges, peat bogs, and slopes of balsam fir pass in monotonous repetition. Because of rough terrain, a lack of harbours, and poor commercial forest, settlement lagged here.

Neils Harbour

LEG-STRETCHERS

The Neils Harbour area has a number of fine hiking trails ranging from 3 to 26 km/2 to 16 mi in length. Besides the Coastal Trail (just south of the harbour), there are trails at Ingonish, Broad Cove Mountain, Warren Lake, Lake of Islands, Clyburn Valley, and Middle Head. The Clyburn Valley is noted for warblers in spring, and Middle Head is a good place to watch Arctic and common terns.

For a winter experience of Highland forest with glimpses of Plateau taiga, a 6-km/3.7-mi cross-country ski trail starts at the Black

Brook Cove campground and links up with the Coastal Trail. Near the cove is a stand of jack pine—rare in Cape Breton.

For trail details consult Cape Breton Highlands National Park literature, Michael Haynes's *Hiking Trails of Nova Scotia*, Pat O'Neil's *Explore Cape Breton*, and/or David Lawley's *Nature and Hiking Guide to Cape Breton's Cabot Trail.*

VIEW: *Igneous Showcase*
Between Black Brook Cove and Broad Cove the road follows a narrow belt of gneiss and schist nearly a billion years old. Constant undermining by North Atlantic breakers has heaped the shore with fragments of rock, which the sea has tumbled smooth. Near Green Cove the beach is cobbled with these close-fitting rounded pink boulders.

Looking across the marsh towards Ingonish

The narrow finger of land at Ingonish is Middle Head. It's a granite spur that welled up as molten magma flowed across a soft-rock basin of younger age. The spur acted as a breakwater, trapping sand from north/south longshore currents to build the long spit enclosing South Bay. Ingonish Beach consists of quartz feldspar crystals derived from granite and is backed by granite boulders tossed up by storms.

Just before arriving at Ingonish Marsh

Ingonish Beach

The Ingonish River estuary teems with shorebirds during migration. Waterfowl nest and feed here all summer, and great blue heron are common.

As we climb the north side of Cape Smokey, notice the whitened skeletons of softwood trees rising above new green growth. In May 1968 a fire started on Cape Smokey and raced up this 366-m/1200-ft ridge; it took several days to put out.

Tradition says the Portuguese had a fishing station here as early as 1521.

LEG-STRETCHER: *Fire Aftermath*
To see how long it takes a fire scar to heal on the Highlands, hike a short way into the burn. Park in the gravel pit near the summit (just north of the entrance to Cape Smokey Provincial Park) and walk up the dirt road to the left. After about 225 m/750 ft, next to the culvert and ditch, leave the path and walk south into the burnt area for 0.5 km/0.3 mi.

Dig just below the soil surface and you'll find a gritty black layer: charcoal from the fire. There's also charcoal on the protected under-

Ingonish flats with Cape Smokey in the distance

sides of roots where weathering couldn't remove it.

The greening of Smokey is still far from complete. Exposed bedrock is being colonized by bacteria, algae, and map lichens. Lichens produce acid secretions that crumble rock into sand. In the cracks grow taller lichens, chiefly reindeer, British soldier (scarlet tops), and splash cup lichens. Where enough soil has collected, we find bracken fern, sheep laurel, Labrador tea, and lowbush blueberry. In the sheltered hollows there is bunchberry, a remnant from the previous mixed forest.

On the deepest soils, black spruce and balsam fir seedlings are poking through the charred tree trunks. They are protected from wind and drought by white birch saplings (from wind-borne seed) and by pin cherry and mountain-ash seedlings (planted by birds). They should do well if moose and snowshoe hare don't browse them too heavily. The exposed granite knolls will stay treeless for decades.

In this sparse post-fire woodland a number of songbirds and small mammals thrive on foliage, seeds, berries, and insects. For 5 to 10 years after the fire, Smokey was a popular place to pick blueberries.

STOP: *Cape Smokey Provincial Park*
This provincial park, 10 minutes south of Ingonish Beach, offers a chance to rest up for the hairpin turns as we descend the mountain. Sit and, weather permitting, enjoy the views of sheer cliff and the wrinkled vastness of Cabot Strait. The low headland to the southeast is Point Aconi, with the Sydney lowlands beyond. St Anns Bay lies to the south. Note the large area of burn inland.

From the park there's an 8-km/5-mi (return distance) trail that runs along the rim of the tableland. The coastal views are spectacular. With any luck you'll see an eagle riding updrafts along the 275-m/ 900-ft cliffs.

In the heaps of rubble at the foot of the cliffs live the rare rock vole, the Gaspé shrew, and other small mammals.

Wreck Cove Power Project

A few kilometres north of here, in the belly of a mountain, there is a cathedral-sized, human-made cavern where two giant turbines spin day and night to generate over 200 megawatts of electricity for the provincial grid. The generators are powered by water from four artificial lakes high on the Plateau, called the Cheticamp, Gisborne, McMillan, and Wreck Cove Brook flowages. It took a dozen dams, four canals, and three tunnels to funnel the water from elevations exceeding 400 m/1400 ft down to the station.

The resulting electricity helps to power industry and to make our toast and coffee. It is "clean" power; but a large area of "waste" land had to be drowned to make it possible.

For tour information write Nova Scotia Power at PO Box 910, Halifax, NS B3J 2W5. [See also the **Evangeline Trail** at Annapolis Royal.]

STOP: *Barachois Brook*

This typical Cape Breton mountain stream gets its name from the three sandbars at its mouth, which all but enclose MacDonalds Big Pond. Longshore currents carved them from water borne mountain dust.

During hot summers the stream nearly dries up. It's intriguing to stroll this pavement of close-packed, multi-coloured cobbles, not only to muse on their long, tumbling journey from the mountains, but to observe the various plant species that take advantage of the temporary low water to colonize. Some have been here for a few years, others are temporary. An example of the former is shining willow. Commonly seen on river flats, it has stout roots and flexible stems that withstand the tug of strong currents and the bulldozing of spring ice. Seedlings of white birch, red maple, and white ash exemplify the latter. Pearly everlasting, New England aster, and coltsfoot are annual visitors as well.

A few hundred metres downstream, twined around an old yellow birch, there used to grow a wild clematis called virgin's bower. In late summer its pods split lengthwise to release wisps of creamy silk full of seeds. The plant may still be there.

Indian Brook, which crosses the trail about 3 km/2 mi north of Barachois Brook, has a fine waterfall some 2.5 km/1.5 mi upstream. Inquire locally about a trail, or hike up the gorge itself (summer only). [See also the **Bras d'Or Scenic Drive** at MacIntosh Brook.]

At Barachois Brook you can link up with the Trans Canada via Route 312, which takes you along Englishtown's massive curving beach to a ferry. France had a small fort on this spit as early as 1629; the Gaelic College of Celtic Arts and Culture (Exit 11 on the **Trans Canada**

Englishtown Light

123

Highway) has information on this and other points of local history.

If you take Rte 312, notice near the south end of the beach a series of half-buried sand and gravel ridges, unusual "fossil" beaches marking various stages in the bar's southward march. Like the present beach, each had a hooked (recurved) tip, shaped by strong currents swirling through the narrow passage. As the passage narrowed over the centuries, currents increased until a balance between erosion and deposition was achieved. Every so often a big winter storm removes a whole section of the beach, restarting the process.

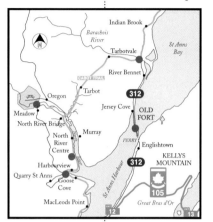

The trail continues west up Tarbot Vale, a ravine that Barachois Brook is carving in hard granite. A few minutes later the ravine opens on a sheltered valley cleared by pioneer Scots over a century ago. The vale curves eastward around Murray Mountain toward the drowned estuary of North River. Today most of the farms are abandoned.

North River Bridge and St Anns brings you out just beyond South Gut St Anns at Exit 11.

SIDE TRIP: *North River Falls*

For a good sample of ravine and lower plateau vegetation and topography, go to North River Provincial Picnic Park and take either the short or the long trail. The trail to the right of the sign leads downstream past several salmon pools to Little Falls—a 15-minute walk each way. (The angler's path to the left also leads to the falls, but is hazardous.) The water is so clear, you'll be able to see any fish in the river.

It's also a great place to spot warblers and flycatchers. These little songsters are attracted by the abundance of insects, which include blackflies, mayflies, and caddis flies in the spring and dragonflies, moths, and butterflies all summer. (Sparrows and finches also feed their young on a high-protein insect diet; but prefer open places with plenty of seed-bearing plants.)

LEG-STRETCHER: *Waterfall Hike*

If you're up to a day hike to Nova Scotia's premier waterfall, take the 18-km/11.1-mi (return) trail that starts at the sign. (This trail lacks designated campsites; allow seven to eight hours in and back and tote enough food.) An option is to walk only the outer section, a 19th-century wagon road that once rambled by. There was also a schoolhouse and a tannery.

The inner section runs for several kilometres through deciduous forest along the river to a plateau of old pastures overgrown with white spruce and carpeted in thick moss. Some of the oldest trees display large, half-round shelves trimmed with orange. These are the spore-bearing organs of bracket fungi, which are decomposing the dead wood. To the west, if the weather is clear, you may glimpse a conical peak of the Highlands. Farther on you'll see overgrown stone walls and crumbling house foundations. Until the 1880s a community of Highland Scots— MacLeans, MacLeods, MacAskills, and MacKenzies—worked the land here.

Beyond the pastures you'll come to a fork in the trail and a wooden sign pointing right, toward the falls. Another hour of steady hiking and stream crossings will bring you to the east branch of the North River. Now the trail goes upward in the dim and cool light of the canyon gorge. The going is fairly easy until the gorge steepens and narrows, making handrails and rest stops necessary. Soon you'll hear the roar of the falls. At 32 m/105 ft, they are the highest in Nova Scotia. [See also Rainbow Falls, **Glooscap Trail** at Moose River.]

Beulach Ban Falls

For more detail see Haynes's *Hiking Trails of Nova Scotia*. To get to the falls, exit the Cabot Trail just north of the bridge. Follow the Oregon Road 3 km/1.9 mi—keep left—to North River Provincial Park.

A forest access road branches north at Oregon to the Plateau, passing Timber and Sieferts lakes to link up with the Middle River road system. Consult DNR maps before going; ask too about the fire tower road on the headwaters of Barachois Brook.

BACK ON THE HIGHWAY

STOP: *Pioneer Cemetery*
Just over 2 km/1 mi south of North River Bridge, watch along the water side for tiny North River Bridge Pioneer Cemetery. Surrounded by wild hazelnut, shadbush, red maple, and white birch, it is a lovingly tended memorial to the men and women who first farmed this valley.

There are few stones, suggesting that most of the graves had wooden markers. Those that remain hint at the hard lives of these men and women.

VIEW: *Pioneer Land Clearing*
For clues to past land clearing hereabouts, look at 300-m/1000-ft Murray Mountain across the river. The summit, clothed in maple, beech, and birch, was never cleared. A third of the way down, however, note an undulating horizontal line that separates the deciduous woodland above from the evergreens below. It marks the upper limit of pasture, since invaded by white spruce. In one place a

125

wedge of deciduous forest divides the dark softwoods—a brook valley too steep to clear.

VIEW: *Goose Cove Beaver Project*

Just beyond the mouth of North River, where the trail makes a broad hairpin turn around Goose Cove, notice the freshwater marsh on the left. Created by silt from two brooks that tumble off the Highlands and meet above the bridge, it has attracted several generations of beavers.

For many years the rodents have being trying to dam the flow here. As each dam washes away, the brook carves new channels and spreads fertile mud and silt over the marsh. On the west side of the cove, there's a stand of young balsam poplar that sprouted from stumps they cut at least 30 years ago. In 1995 there were freshly felled aspen in the stream above the bridge. As you round the cove, notice several washed-out dams amid the grass.

These are "bank beavers." The ponds they make are too shallow to protect a lodge, so they imitate muskrats and burrow into the bank.

Goose Cove marsh teems with life. There are beds of rushes and clumps of speckled alder. Drier slopes support broadleaf goldenrod, nightshade, sensitive fern, and dewberry, as well as chokecherry. On warm afternoons dragonflies dart after mosquitoes, and water striders run after aquatic insects. A grove of cattails attracts muskrats and red-winged blackbirds. Robins feed on chokecherries, kingfishers hunt minnows from a dead spruce, and leopard frogs converse.

Upstream 5 km/3 mi on the west side of the stream, an old road leads to Quarry St Anns, where gypsum was once mined. Ask locally for directions.

At South Gut St Anns the Cabot Trail merges with the **Trans Canada Highway,** ending at Baddeck on Bras d'Or Lake.

The deposit of gypsum at Goose Cove ... is exceedingly interesting and of great extent. It is about one mile back from tide water, rises four hundred feet ... and contains millions of tons ... of superior quality.
– Robert R. McLeod, **Markland, or Nova Scotia,** 1903

Ceilidh Trail Nature Tour

Canso Causeway to Margaree Harbour
120 km/75 mi

OVERVIEW

Ceilidh (*kail*-ee) is Scots Gaelic for a festive gathering, and this trail
is certainly Scottish. Probably it boasts more Scottish place names
per kilometre than any other in the province.

Margaree Harbour

Between Creignish and Long Point, and again
from Chimney Corner to Margaree Harbour, the
land lies open to strong westerlies off Northumberland Strait. Gales, salt spray, and the abrasion
of drifting snow have dwarfed even the hardy
alders and white spruce. Coastal erosion of the
soft sandstones, conglomerates, and limestone is
active and unremitting.

Geologically the trail runs over the soft rock
sedimentary formations that underlie (and account
for) St Georges Bay and the Bras d'Or Lowlands.
Into the latter the Mabou and Margaree rivers have
carved their valleys. The uppermost (youngest)
layers are coal-bearing, and the coast has a history
of coal mining at Port Hood, Mabou, Inverness,
and St Rose-Chimney Corner.

Because softer Carboniferous rocks underlie
this whole coast, the terrain is only rugged where
mountain streams have cut into it. In fact, the Ceilidh Trail seldom
climbs above 90 m/300 ft. Even so, its vistas can be breath-taking,
for they are framed in majestic backdrops of resistant igneous rock:
first the Creignish Hills to the east, then the Mabou hills to the west,
and finally the lofty Cape Breton Highlands and the drowned glacial
valley of Margaree Harbour.

This trail, though short, offers various opportunities for side trips,
loops, and link-ups with other trails. For example, from Margaree
Harbour you can follow the Cabot Trail up the coast. Or you can
trace the Southwest Margaree up to Lake Ainslie and across to
Whycocomagh, returning to the causeway via Highway 105.

THE TOUR BEGINS

From the old coal port of Port Hastings to Creignish, Route 19 runs
through a low rolling landscape of farm and forest. Occasionally,
beyond the long sandspit sheltering the shore, we glimpse Canso
Strait. To our right, not far inland, rise the domed Creignish Hills,
far older and harder than the coastal bedrock. [See also the **Trans
Canada Highway** near Kingsville.] Its lower slopes are mantled in
dark spiky spruce and fir, the middle zone in mixed forest, and its

upper slopes in billowy groves of sugar maple, yellow birch, and beech. It is these that glow orange and scarlet in autumn.

Much of the level land here was once sheep pasture. Since the 1890s most of it has been colonized by white spruce on the sandier soils and alders on the wetter clays. Exposure is a fact of life for every living thing here, especially in winter.

The history of 19th-century and earlier Scottish immigration can be traced all along this coast in names like Creignish, Craigmore, Glencoe, Dunmore, Mabou, North Cape Highlands, Port Ban, Strathlorne, Kenlock, Inverside, Inverness. Its capes, coves, and valleys echo with surnames like Campbell, McIntyre, Cameron, Graham, Mackay, MacDonald. Did homesickness entirely account for this? Or did the landscape itself, with its patent similarity to Scotland's, move the expatriates to label it so? If it did, then geology vindicates them. Bedrock and fossils prove that nearly 200 million years ago ancestral Nova Scotia and Scotland were neighbours inside the super-continent Pangaea.

... we went through Port Hastings and then saw nothing but Scottish names for sixty miles. First there was Craigmore and then Campbell, and soon the Judique—a number of them, said by the Scots to be a French word, and by the French called a mongrel Gaelic.
– Will R. Bird,
This Is Nova Scotia,
1950

SIDE TRIP: *Lookoff*
Less than 1 km/0.5 mi south of Creignish, a narrow road (though paved for a kilometre) climbs the steep western slope of the Creignish Hills toward Queensville and Rhodena. Along this road various points offer dramatic views of the shore below and of Cape St George, Antigonish Harbour, and Northumberland Strait. Notice how much the coastal lowland on this side resembles that around Antigonish.

BACK ON THE HIGHWAY

LEG-STRETCHER: *Long Point Provincial Park*
Before heading on, stop at this picnic park near the mouth of Chisholm Brook. It will give you a better feel for this landscape. Take a quiet stroll in the shade of pasture spruce. Inhale the bracing sea air. You're now halfway up the east side of St Georges Bay, with Cape George between you and Northumberland Strait. On a clear day you should be able to make out the thin blue line of Prince Edward Island along the horizon.

From Long Point to Judique, the road continues across rumpled lowland checkered with pastures and softwoods. Gradually the Creignish Hills fall away to the east. So much black spruce and tamarack (larch) indicates wet ground. That's because shale underlies much of this land. Shale is made of compressed clay, whose particles overlap like the pages of a book, forming a nearly watertight seal. Another sign of wet soil is the abundance of alder.

The Judique district was noted for its brawling Highlanders. It is said that on arriving at a dance they would challenge all comers with, "Judique on the floor! Who'll put him off?"

STOP: *Barachois Pond*

At Judique North the trail crosses a pond created when a sandbar sealed off the entrance to the cove behind Indian Point. Along this shore, wind-driven waves meet the shore on a slant, creating longshore currents. These currents act as a conveyor belt for suspended particles of sand and silt eroded from the soft cliffs. As the particles meet the quieter waters of the cove, they settle to the bottom like drifting snow behind a fence. The resulting underwater ridge eventually became the exposed bar you see today, and the water it enclosed became Indian Point Pond. Such a bar and pond are called a *barachois* in French.

Barachois Pond

Should such a cove be completely cut off, it becomes a freshwater pond (except for salt water percolating through the gravel at high tide). But where a sizeable stream enters the pond, the outflow maintains a gap through the bar, as Judique Interval Brook does here. [See also the **Glooscap Trail** at Advocate Harbour, the **Marine Drive** at Milford Haven, etc.] Despite rain and snow and a constant flow of fresh water, such a pond will never become truly fresh, but will remain brackish (salty). So its flora and fauna must cope with both worlds.

Indian Point Pond is a special case because the road with its culvert acts as a two-way bottleneck. Thus, the inner pond supports freshwater grasses and aquatic animal life, while the outer supports a salt-marsh ecosystem. In time, the inner part may become a meadow.

The first marine worms and crusta-ceans to colonize the continents in the Devonian Period had to cope with both saltwater and freshwater environ-ments.

VIEW: *Coal Age Islands*

For a bird's-eye view of this coast, exit west at Harbourview and drive 3 km/2 mi past Port Hood Mines and Port Hood Station to Port Hood proper. Take the **No Exit** road to Marble Hill and drive about 2.5 km/1.5 mi. Park at the foot of the hill and walk the rest of the way. You'll see spectacular views of Port Hood Island (Henry Island is hidden behind it), of Cape Susan toward Canso Strait, and of the rugged Mabou Hills toward Inverness. On a clear day you may be able to make out Cape George on the mainland.

At one time the old rail bridge to the west was busy with coal trains running to and from Port Hastings. It also carried thousands of Cape Bretoners away to look for work in Upper Canada, the Canadian Prairies, and in the "Boston States".

Henry Island and most of Port Hood Island share the same bedrock as the Pictou coalfields and Pictou Island. Are there coal measures under Northumberland Strait as well? Probably. It would be nice for once to have a good look at the sea floor but it would take a tidal wave to uncover it!

See how fast the coast is eroding. One reason—apart from the softness of its bedrock—is that the rock layers are steeply tilted, like a book lying on its spine. As rain and seawater enter the seams and freeze, the resulting ice expands and pries the cliff apart, slab by slab. In addition, tilted layers make a better target for ocean waves than level layers.

Exposed to Northumberland Strait's long fetch of open water, this shore takes a continual pounding. Coves are gouged from zones of weaker rock, leaving harder rock jutting out as headlands. Cape Linzee is one of those, and behind it rises Marble Hill. Actually the latter started out as limestone, a hardened form of chalk, which in turn consists of the pressed shells of microscopic marine life. And limestone that is compressed and heated in the Earth becomes marble, a very hard rock indeed.

In the late 1800s, tiny Port Hood was home to a thousand people, many of them coal miners. But its collieries kept flooding and had to be closed. Port Hood Island was earlier called Smith's Island after its first settler, Capt. David Smith of Cape Cod, Massachusetts, who came in 1786. Decades earlier, the French quarried freestone from its southwest side to build Fortress Louisbourg.

Though many people summer in the island's abandoned houses, in recent years its only permanent residents were Bertie and Shirley Smith. From spring to fall, for a small fee, he or someone from Port Hood will generally ferry you out (15 minutes one way).

The Ceilidh Trail bypasses the village, but near the Harbourview exit the Chestico Historical Society runs a museum recounting local history. The final descent to Mabou Harbour runs along a trough of faulted rock deepened by the Southwest Mabou River system and is exhilarating.

Now you can see the 300-m/1,000-ft Mabou Highlands to the north. Their flanks are patterned with the pale greens and tans of sheep pastures, the jades of maple and beech, and the dark olive greens of spruce and fir. At their base, behind Hughes Point, the Northeast Mabou River emerges. The main branch meanders across a wide floodplain cut into the hills and richly checkered with farms and woodlots and tidal marshes. These marshes are not dyked because the tides do not warrant it.

Dotting the floodplain are the fountain-shaped skeletons of dead and dying elms. Dutch elm disease, an Asian fungus introduced to Ontario and Québec in the 1930s and 1940s, reached Nova Scotia in the 1960s. It is carried by native and introduced elm bark beetles and can kill a big tree in one summer. The disease has now reached almost every nook of Nova Scotia. [See also the **Glooscap Trail** at Truro, the **Evangeline Trail** through the Annapolis Valley, the **Lighthouse Route** at Liverpool, and the **Trans Canada Highway** at River Denys.]

The floodplain's irregular outline is due to postglacial ocean flooding of uneven terrain. [See also the **Sunrise Trail** along the Northumberland Plain.] Land clearing, followed by farm abandonment on this side of the river, has resulted in colonization by light-loving trees like white birch, white spruce, and aspen.

VIEW: *River vs. Mountain*

Just north of the "Welcome to Mabou" sign, watch for a road to the left. The view it offers provides a lesson in how the resistant Mabou Highlands forced the Southwest Mabou River to jog 90° west through softer rock to reach the sea.

Inverness coast

STOP: *Harbour Panorama*

A kilometre/0.6 mi north of the village on Rte 19 is Mabou Provincial Park. It lies on a hillside snuggled against a block of Mabou Highland cut off from the main upland by the Northeast Mabou River. Here you'll find not only white birch, maple, white spruce, and aspen, but hawthorns and apple trees. The latter suggest the site was once a farm. If so, its occupants had a splendid view and wonderful sunsets.

About 3 km/2 mi east of Mabou at Glendyer Station, take some time to hike an abandoned Canadian National Railway line. Less than 0.5 km/0.3 mi south the railbed crosses the Mabou River on a trestle bridge and runs west along its estuary. The marshes are great for spotting kingbirds, kingfishers, wading birds, and waterfowl.

To explore the upper Mabou valley, exit to Rte 252 about 200 m/0.1 mi south of the picnic park. Far up the valley, the main branch nearly meets the upper Skye River, which wends southeast into Whycocomagh Bay. This route gave Mi'kmaq paddlers from the Northumberland Shore and Prince Edward Island ready access to Bras D'Or Lake.

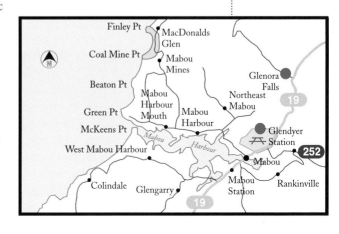

Mabou Harbour

Mabou Mines

To get a better sense of the Mabou Highland landscape, drive west from Mabou Village about 5 km/3 mi, cross the Northeast Mabou River, and turn right at the "Mabou Coal Mines Road" sign. This winding gravel road takes you 6 km/3.7 mi through darkly wooded ravines and under high sheep pastures to the coast. It's a very Scottish landscape, not unlike the southern Highlands today. However, these spruce and larch weren't planted.

One last dip near Mabou Mines, and you climb a steep hill and find yourself in front of an immensity of sky and sea—the Gulf of St Lawrence. Here hillside pastures slope down to gravel banks that fall away to steep cliffs above a crescent beach where white waves play far below. To the south, the capes named Coal Mine, Beaton, Green, and Linzee jut out like headlands in a Chinese painting. Northward, Finley Point shelters a wharf with fishing boats. Beyond lie Cape Mabou, Sight Point, and the hills of Margaree. Bald eagles commonly coast on the updrafts from the beach.

These pastures clothe coarse glacial gravels more fit for blueberries than hay. The grasses are not only raked by gales and salt spray, but have to compete with aggressive ground juniper, lambkill, wild rose, and vetch. A few years ago someone fought back with herbicide, but the native shrubs seem to be winning.

From here to Mabou Harbour the bedrock is all early Carboniferous, a mosaic of hard red sandstone, siltstone, conglomerate (pebbles cemented in sand, sometimes called pudding stone), and limestone. The cove below is being carved from a coastal strip of reddish sandstone marbled with gypsum and salt deposits.

The highland itself, though far older, is also far harder and therefore has not worn away. It's a faulted block of volcanic and other igneous rocks going back to the dawn of shelled sea creatures and beyond.

From 1875 to 1993 Inverness County had four coastal collieries that produced nearly 9.9 million tonnes of coal. The one in Inverness opened in 1865; by 1993 only the St Rose Colliery still operated.

LEG-STRETCHER: *Shore Walk*
Park at the wharf beside Finley Point and explore fossil cliffs, sea caves, coal seams, and a stream that disappears into a gypsum sinkhole. The road from here to MacDonalds Glen peters out after a kilometre/0.6 mi or so and is rough. For those who care to hike it, Mill Brook is supposed to have an immense beaver dam. The Mabou Highlands offer several hiking trails developed from old logging roads. The easiest is the 3.5-km/2.1-mi (one way)

MacKinnon Brook Trail, an extension of the old coastal road from Mabou to Sight Point (see below).

BACK ON THE HIGHWAY

Between Mabou and Inverness, Rte 19 skirts the eastern slopes of the Mabou Highlands. You'll see many steep gorges where mountain streams cross the road.

Falls at Second Fork Brook

LEG-STRETCHER: *Glenora Falls*

One such gorge 6 km/3.7 mi north of Mabou leads to Glenora Falls at the foot of a 295-m/970-ft hill. Exit west off Rte 19 just beyond the sign, and follow a dirt road 0.5 km/ 0.3 mi to a small bridge. Just beyond, to the left, a footpath soon brings you to a pretty 8-m/ 26-ft cascade.

Continuing north, the trail wends among eroded soft-rock hills to the Strathlorne lowlands. (*Strath* is Scottish Gaelic for "broad valley"; "lorne" honours a former governor general of Canada, the Marquis of Lorne.)

Mabou farm near Glenora Falls

Strathlorne Nursery

In the 1980s and early 1990s this provincial forest nursery raised millions of carefully selected spruce seedlings to replenish the budworm-devastated Highlands farther north. The seedlings included many thousand clones of budworm-resistant native highland black spruce, produced from scions (shoots).

The nursery site itself was chosen for its flatness and for fertile, rock-free alluvial sands, which allow machines to lift delicate baby trees without damaging their roots.

Three interpretive trails totalling 5.7 km/3.5 mi have been developed. The main trail is chipped for easy walking and has a self-

133

guiding brochure. Different forest management practices are demonstrated, and there's an active beaver dam.

Lake Ainslie

*Freshwater rushes fringe the west shore of Lake Ainslie. This is our largest natural body of fresh water. Lake Rossignol in western Nova Scotia is bigger, but much of Rossignol is flowage created after 1930 by dams to power the Bowater-Mersey paper mill in Liverpool. [See also the **Cabot Trail** at Wreck Cove.]*

SIDE TRIP: *Lake Ainslie*

With minor adjustments—replace modern frame homes with thatched stone cottages, mask October's flaming colour—Lake Ainslie would make a good movie location for Scotland. Set in its bowl of brooding hills, with Mason Mountain to the north and Gairloch Mountain to the east, bordered by a patchwork of farms and woodlots, it is the picture of rural peace. Take an hour or two to cruise its pleasant shores. Better yet, stay overnight. There are cottages near Mason Point (west side), a hostel in Twin Rock Valley (one-third down the east side), and RV camping (with permission) along the shore.

Exit at Kenlock to Strathlorne Station and swing southeast (counter-clockwise) around the lake. One can also do this tour from the **Trans Canada Highway** via Exit 5.

Sheep farm on Creignish Hills

Origin of Lake Ainslie

A lake happens when stream water is prevented from reaching the sea and instead fills a natural basin. Nova Scotia's largest natural lake was created around 10,000 years ago by a rapidly melting local ice cap.

For a time the brimming lake likely emptied through Hays River into Mabou Harbour. Later it probably flowed down the steep valley into what is now Inverness Harbour, a distance of only 6 km/3.7 mi. But melting glaciers dump immense quantities of sand and pebbles. Enough sand built up west of Loch Ban to dam that outlet. Seeking a new one, the rising lake breached its rim at the next lowest point—and the Southwest Margaree River was born.

If the sand hills between Kenlock and Strathlorne Station were to be removed, Lake Ainslie would again flow out at Inverness. But it would end up considerably lower.

STOP: *Alkaline Bog*

Near McCormick Corner at the west end of the lake, where the road crosses sluggish Black River, there's an unconventional bog. Instead of being acidic, it's alkaline (i.e., high pH). The sweetening effect of underlying gypsum gives uncommon species such as spike-rush, lobelia, and sedge a chance to mingle with more typical plants such as meadowsweet ("hardhack"), pussy willow, green or downy alder, sweet gale, and Canada burnet. Red osier dogwood is plentiful, and there are blue flag iris, sensitive and royal ferns, and swamp milkweed. In short, a very diverse flora.

LEG-STRETCHER: *Ainslie Lakeshore*

Summer campers and cottagers along this secluded shore often wake to the yodelling of loons. Several pairs of these primitive diving fish-eaters usually nest here. Unlike loons in the naturally acidic lakes of western Nova Scotia, they seem to be in good health.

The pinkish beach sand south of Mason Point is strewn with pebbles in pastel hues of blue, green, ochre, and rust. You'll find beach potentilla (also called silver weed), coltsfoot, knapweed, and nightshade. In shallow coves with boggy seepage, look for tall reed-like plants growing in ankle-deep rich muck. There are three types: knee-high spike-rushes in shallow water, hip-high rushes farther out, and 3-m/10-ft-tall plants offshore.

Beyond the rushes the silty bottom is rippled with wind and wave marks that are almost rock-hard underfoot. The ripples look identical to fossil wave marks preserved in 300-million-year-old slates. [See also the **Glooscap Trail** near Parrsboro and the **Lighthouse Route** at Cape LaHave.]

After we pass the sandstone hump of Mason Point, the landscape is gentler. Now the road winds through a rolling pastoral landscape of glacier-rounded hills graced by farms, woodlots, and glimpses of lake. Beyond Claverhouse, high hills of resistant Devonian granite close in until the lake is less than a kilometre wide.

After South Lake Ainslie, we turn north onto Rte 395 for Scotsville. The south end of Lake Ainslie is less than 10 km/6 mi from Exit 5 on Hwy 105 at Whycocomagh.

Going up the east shore on Rte 395, you'll experience a mild roller coaster ride over broadly folded bedrock. You'll climb steep knolls,

Lake Ainslie is named for Governor Ainslie, who administered that office when the Island of Cape Breton was a separate province. "This sheet of water is twelve miles long and six broad, and ... was first settled in 1820 by Scotch Highlanders. [Those on] the eastern and northern sides ... were from Mull, Tiree, Coll, Isle of Muck, and a few from the Isle of Skye."
—Alexander Campbell of Strathlorne quoted in R. R. MacLeod, **Markland or Nova Scotia**, 1903

snake across glacier-smoothed uplands, and dip into a dozen valleys carved by brooks tumbling off Gairloch Mountain. From the high ground you'll see stunning lake vistas opening to the west behind forests of maple and spruce.

STOP: *Trout Brook Provincial Park*

Here's a pretty picnic park with an exhilarating brook walk for a bonus. Trout Brook is tame in its lower reaches, but only 4 km/2.5 mi upstream it becomes a torrent, especially in spring or fall. Farther up, the steep, winding gorge is densely forested with sugar maple, yellow birch, and beech. [See also **Bras d'Or Scenic Drive** at MacIntosh Brook.] And of course there are trout.

If you're a non-hiker, this park offers a white sand beach to loll on. At Trout Brook Bridge you can observe how wind-driven waves and ice are gnawing into the bedrock, and how storms have piled windrows of sand. The large chunks of driftwood were bulldozed into place by rafting ice. Observe, too, how the beach pebbles grade from coarse to small upslope, and how the sand also grades from coarse to fine.

As you near Scotsville from the south, farms become more common on the slopes. Sequestered in Twin Rock Valley is the Glenmore International Hostel. Watch for the Twin Rock Valley road sign about 4 km/2.5 mi north of East Lake Ainslie.

STOP: *Freshwater Marsh*

Near Scotsville at Lake Ainslie's northeast corner, there's a shallow cove funnelling into the Southwest Margaree River. It's a waterfowl haven.

Park just east of the country store where Rte 395 meets the road to Strathlorne Station. Don rubber boots and pick your way down the rocky bank through a thicket of speckled alder. When you see cattails ahead, slow down and walk softly. Mergansers, black ducks, and other waterfowl often come here to nest and feed. With care, you may be able approach through the cattails and watch them unobserved.

Once they catch sight of you, watch how different water birds take wing in different ways. Mergansers, being fish-eating divers, have sacrificed wingspread for underwater speed and so must run over the water into the wind to get aloft. In contrast, bitterns and great blue herons have plenty of lift. They simply leap upward, tuck up their long legs, and beat the air powerfully.

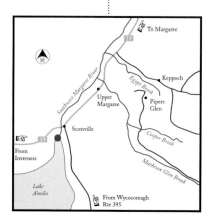

Part of the attraction of this lake are the swarms of gaspereau (alewives) that come up the Southwest Margaree to spawn in shallow coves and brooks each spring. Schools of these silvery herring-like fish can be seen from the nearby bridge between late April and early May.

LEG-STRETCHER: *Egypt Falls*

Pipers Glen

Hidden in lush deciduous forest just north of
Scotsville on Matheson Glen Brook is a beautiful
15-m/50-ft cascade. The trail isn't recommended
for the young, elderly, or ailing. (It's so steep near
the end that a rope railing has been installed.)

To reach the falls, drive past Upper Margaree on
Rte 395 for 0.5 km/0.3 mi and watch the east side
for a sign to "Piper Glen and Egypt Falls." That's
the easy part. Pat O'Neil (*Explore Cape Breton*) says to follow this dirt
road about 2 km/1.2 mi until it branches; take the one on the right,
and go another 2 km/1.2 mi until you see a small house on the left,
opposite a road with a small white bridge. Drive exactly 0.9 km/.56 mi
on this road, eyes peeled on the right for a small white sign, half-
hidden by foliage, marked "Egypt Road." That's the start of the trail.

*Egypt Falls was once
called Appin Falls,
after the Scottish
birthplace of the
Stewarts who settled
Pipers Glen in the
1800s.*

SIDE TRIP: *Canoe Trip*

For a superlative day trip, paddle the Southwest Margaree from
Scotsville (or from nearby Upper Margaree) to Margaree Forks and
on down to tidewater. The upper reaches curve through glens clothed
in sugar maple, yellow birch, and beech. Then the valley widens to
vistas of meadow dotted with huge elms. At Margaree Forks the
larger Northeast branch comes in to form the main river, whose
original name was Margré or Margeurite.

Except between Fordview and East Margaree,
where harder rocks hem in the lowlands, the
valley is expansive and pastoral with many rushy
islands. The drowned estuary has tidal marshes
where waterfowl congregate during migration.

Wind can be a problem on the lower reaches.
And if there are salmon anglers about, do them
the courtesy of giving their lines a wide, noiseless
berth.

Margaree River

The Margaree has been a renowned salmon
river since the 1800s. It offers the fish a reliable flow of clean cold
water, and it's deep enough all summer for them to slip safely in from
the sea. There are no dams or major waterfalls. Siltation and industrial
pollution are minimal. Numerous tributaries offer spawning beds of
fine gravel and sand. Young fish can find ample food. Angling is
strictly regulated to ensure there are enough fish to offset both the
annual catch and natural predation by ospreys, eagles, and otters.
Poaching is not allowed.

These features make the river a natural nursery for Atlantic
salmon. Add to this a diversity of pools, riffles, and wadeable depths
with easy access, and you have a salmon angler's paradise.

While the Southwest Margaree is easy paddling from spring
through fall, during the spring and early summer beware of sub-

137

merged steel barriers in the middle and lower section. Part of a commercial fishery, these fence-like steel contraptions may block more than half the channel and can puncture canoes and unwary paddlers. Generally they are flagged, but in bad weather or poor light they may be hard to spot.

From Margaree Forks to Margaree Harbour, Rte 395 merges with the Cabot Trail.

BACK ON THE HIGHWAY

Unless you opted to join the Trans Canada Highway at Margaree Forks, proceed west from Scotsville past North Ainslie, Strathlorne Station, and Kenlock to Rte 19 and thence north toward Margaree Harbour. (For more information about the river, see the **Cabot Trail.**)

In March–April there are maple syrup operations in the valley. Some operators welcome visitors with weekend pancake suppers and sugaring-off, by appointment.

Less than 5 km/3 mi north of Kenlock is the old coal-mining town of Inverness. The famed writings of Alistair MacLeod centre on Inverness and nearby Dunvegan, where he lived as a child. The area was first settled by MacIsaacs and MacLeans from the islands of Skye and Rhun in Scotland, followed by MacLeods from Dunvegan. The first land grants extended 2.4 km/1.5 mi in from the shore. Some residents also trace their ancestry to Inverness in Scotland.

Margaree Harbour

STOP: *Inverness Miners' Museum*

Housed in a CN railway station built in 1901, this museum is worth a stop to explore the town's colourful mining history through exhibits and audiotapes. Inverness once had 2,000 people, but coal mining here was difficult because the rocks were so severely folded. Since most seams stood nearly on edge instead of nearly level, much less coal was exposed from floor to ceiling. [See also the **Trans Canada Highway** and the **Marconi Trail** near Sydney, which has nearly horizontal coal beds.]

The town overlooks a barachois pond (McIsaac Pond), and there's a private campground offering both woodland and beach sites. As noted above, the dry river bed running inland from McIsaac Pond probably drained meltwater from a local ice cap until sand hummocks dammed the exit and created Lake Ainslie and the Southwest Margaree.

To access the McKinnon Brook Trail toward Mabou from the Inverness end, drive south from the town about 3 km/2 mi to the war monument just west of the village of Broad Cove Banks. If you plan on hiking the whole way, ask for directions as there are rock slides to navigate.

If you're not going far, simply park near the monument and enjoy the coast road with its sheer cliffs and vistas of ocean. From this road the Sight Point Trail climbs 7.5 km/4.6 mi (one way) up a stream valley to the plateau. For details of these and other trails, contact the Nova Scotia Trails Federation (see References).

From Inverness to Margaree Harbour, Rte 19 stitches together wee communities with lovely Scottish names like Inverside, Campbellton Road, Dunvegan (after the castle on Skye), and Scotch Hill.

Just south of Dunvegan, Rte 19 turns east, while the trail continues on Rte 219 to Margaree Harbour.

The last place before that is tiny Chimney Corner. Calling it this is a fine bit of nautical whimsy. Except for Mabou and Margaree, the whole coast has not a single harbour worth the name. This tiny cove, a mere nick in an otherwise inhospitable shore, was carved by a small brook trickling through a half-moon barrier beach. In a bad storm on a lee shore, even a Chimney Corner is welcome.

The cove has one remarkable feature. Part-way up the cliff is a bench-like marine terrace cut by ocean waves when the land was still depressed from the crushing weight of glacial ice. When the land rebounded, the beach was left high and dry. [See also the **Sunrise Trail** at Arisaig and the **Glooscap Trail** near Parrsboro.]

Rounding Grey Cape, we dip into a small hollow and cross a tiny brook with a tiny pond and sandbar, and the long inlet of Margaree Harbour opens before us. This estuary is a wide, flooded valley half full of glacial gravels over which the river winds in many marshy channels to the Gulf of St Lawrence. Back from the river, a gently rolling landscape of light green farms and dark green woodlots slopes up through high pastures to deciduous uplands that glow with orange and scarlet in autumn.

In late April or early May, when the shadbush or Indian pear is in bloom, an ancient biological drama is replayed on the Margaree. Two silvery members of the herring tribe come in from the sea to spawn— the gaspereau (alewife to scientists, kiyak to western Nova Scotians), and its larger relative the shad. Like salmon and sea trout, they are anadromous sea-dwellers that spawn in fresh water. Relying on some internal compass, perhaps activated by lines of electromagnetic force, they home in on their birth stream. Once near it, they rely on taste and smell to guide them to the place where they were born.

Alewives that hatched in Lake Ainslie home in on Margaree Harbour. According to old-timers, the fish generally wait for a warm southwest wind before heading upstream on their 50-km/30-mi journey. After fertilizing and laying their eggs in shallow coves and streams along Ainslie's northern shore, they return to sea. The hatchlings follow soon after.

Each spring licensed commercial fishermen from Nova Scotia and New Brunswick string nets along the lower river, harvesting many tonnes of the bony but succulent fish. Ospreys and eagles, with

"Look," he said excitedly, "the blackfish, the pilot whales." Out of the stillness of the calm, blue ocean, they rose and rolled in glistening elegance...sending geysers of white water before them as they shattered the glass-like surface...
–Alistair MacLeod, **No Great Mischief**, 1999

139

hungry nestlings to feed, also patrol the stream and lake.

TO DO: *Alewife Watch*
From mid-April to early May, alewives pass under the bridges at East Margaree, Margaree Forks, and Upper Margaree. Ask for directions to the best observation sites. The fish come in bunches, so be patient.

To protect the stocks, individuals are permitted only a small number for personal use; check local regulations. Alewives are delicious barbecued in foil or baked with seasonings.

At Margaree Harbour the **Ceilidh Trail** links up with the **Cabot Trail.**

Evangeline Trail Nature Tour

Bedford to Yarmouth via Annapolis Valley
325 km/202 mi

Tides of Fundy, Tides of Fundy
What is this you bring to me?
News from nowhere—vague and haunting,
As the white fog from the sea.
– Bliss Carman (1861–1929)

Cape Split

OVERVIEW

The trail properly begins near South Uniacke, just outside the **Halifax-Dartmouth Area Nature Tour** area. So it starts on the eastern rim of the great pavement of grey and pink granite that dominates most of the western interior. That accounts for the rocky ridges, stunted spruce, and boggy hollows that greet us as soon as we leave the softer rocks south of Pockwock Lake. Near Newport Corner, however, the basement rocks are again softer, ridges have a skin of soil, trees are taller, farms become frequent. Then we are near the Fundy shore, with its chocolate-brown rivers, dyked marshes, and white gypsum cliffs.

Swinging west after Windsor, we enter the broad trough of the Annapolis Valley, drained by the Cornwallis (east) and Annapolis rivers (west). Shielded from cold Fundy and Atlantic fogs by the North and South mountains, with a growing season weeks longer than the provincial average, the Valley is Nova Scotia's premier orchard and farming district. From end to end it is floored with reddish sandstone, the source of its deep sandy loams, on which forests of great white and red pine once flourished.

At the western end is the beautiful land-locked Annapolis Basin, site of North America's oldest European settlement north of Florida. Beyond Digby, pastoral scenes give way to the windswept capes, stunted softwoods, and bluish cobble beaches of St Marys Bay and the French Shore. [See also the **Lighthouse Route** and the **Marine Drive**.] The trail ends at Yarmouth, where it links up with the **Lighthouse Route**.

THE TOUR BEGINS

The Evangeline Trail starts at Exit 3 on Hwy 1 just north of Pockwock Lake. You can also access it at Exit 2, 3A, or from Exit 3 off Hwy 101.

Pockwock Lake, the main Halifax reservoir, lies about 2 km/1 mi south of here. Damming its southern outlet has deepened and enlarged it to about half the size of Bedford Basin. At 107 m/351 ft above sea level, it feeds water at ample pressure downhill to city mains and faucets. Thanks to the lake's relative isolation, hard-rock basin, and carefully tended woodland, Halifax water is rated among the best in Canada.

Geologically, this lake straddles two rock formations 150 million years apart. The western shore faces the Southern Upland, which formed during the Devonian Period some 370 million years ago; its eastern shore consists of older, softer Meguma quartzites and slates of late Cambrian age.

Uniacke Estate Museum Park

STOP: *Uniacke Museum*

In 1995 this estate, long a part of the Nova Scotia Museum complex, was renamed Uniacke Estate Museum Park. The 931 ha/2,300 ac of landscaped grounds, mostly woodland, were rejuvenated and opened for the public's year-round enjoyment. (The pre-Victorian house, which retains its original form and furnishings, is open June through October.)

Richard John Uniacke

Richard John Uniacke, the estate's first owner, was an Irish aristocrat-adventurer who was attorney general of Nova Scotia from 1797 to 1830. Travelling the so-called Great Road from Halifax to Windsor, he fell in love with the landscape hereabouts. Some say the drumlins and lakes reminded him of home. The location, halfway between the two towns on the province's main road, was ideal. In those pre-railroad days, it took Sir Richard only four hours on horseback to reach his duties in Halifax, and the ride home was often pleasant.

The Great Road developed from a Mi'kmaq foot path into an Acadian drove road along which cattle were driven to market. Cattle on long treks need fresh water every few hours, so the builders made sure the road crossed watering places regularly.

Sir Richard bought up more than 4452 ha/ 11,000 ac. Between 1813 and 1815 he cleared 40 ha/100 ac, built and furnished his colonial mansion, dug a pond, and began to lay out English-style gardens.

The estate boasts six pleasant walking trails featuring cultivated grounds, Atlantic Interior woodlands, two lakes, a brook, a beaver dam, drumlins, and huge glacial boulders. The nearer trails offer comfortable benches and interpretive panels explaining the estate's history. Ask about the white oaks, grown from acorns which owner Richard Uniacke brought from his native Ireland, and about the rare American chestnut trees (*Castanea dentata*). The parent trees originated in the eastern United States before an Asian chestnut blight destroyed the native stock in the early 1900s.

Most of the trails can be walked in shoes, but you'll need boots for the 5.7-km/3.5-mi Wetlands Trail. The Hothouse Hill Trail has a 1-km/0.6-mi extension that includes some of the old Halifax–Windsor Road.

To find the estate from Hwy 1, after crossing the Hants County line, watch for the Nova Scotia Museum's blue-and-white "key" sign.

In 1904 the chestnut blight, a fungus, entered New York on Chinese chestnut seedlings. By the 1940s it had killed most of the trees in the native chestnut's range in eastern and central US. Long before that, however, Loyalist settlers had brought nuts and seedlings to Canada. Ontario's trees were later infected, but those in the Maritimes seem to have escaped.

*In the 1960s George Swain, horticulturist at the Kentville agricultural research station, cross-bred Nova Scotia's specimens and produced a few dozen offspring. Some of these survive. Imported Chinese and Japanese chestnut varieties can infect healthy North American chestnuts. [See also the **Halifax-Dartmouth Area Nature Tour**, Halifax Public Gardens.]*

West of Mount Uniacke Hwy 1 verges on the massive granite batholith that arches from here almost to Yarmouth. (On Hwy 101 it forms the upland between Exit 3 and Stillwater.) This mass of lighter rock welled up like hot wax from the Earth's mantle after the African and American continents collided 400 million years ago. Cooling slowly, it infiltrated and baked the overlying quartzite and slate.

Later, weathering and glaciation bared the higher domes, revealing crystalline bedrock speckled with white quartz, pink feldspar, and darker minerals. Then came the glaciers, bulldozing the fertile ancient soil into the ocean, gouging out hollows along old fault lines and rivers, heaping windrows of gravel. They left a landscape of ragged ridges, scattered boulders, numerous bogs, and thin gravels and clays. No wonder trees grow poorly here.

The bedrock here is hard and continuous like a floor, cupping water in its hollows to create many bogs. The blocking of ancient streams and valleys gave rise to a dozen or more small lakes between Pockwock and Mount Uniacke, as well as lakes like Big Indian, Five Mile, and Panuke to the west.

As you pass the village of Lakelands between Lily and Pigott lakes on Hwy 1, notice the rumpled Rawdon Hills to the north. They are upended layers of slate running between upper Panuke Lake and East Gore. Being softer and more worn down, with well-developed streams, they have fewer lakes. This is typical of the older Meguma rocks, which are mostly quartzite (hardened sandstone), slate (compressed shale), and greywacke (rock fragments in a matrix of silica).

Here Hwy 1 turns west and descends to the Windsor Lowlands.

Ellershouse, a few kilometres west of Hwy 1, grew up around the Dominion Atlantic Railway line and is named after German-born Francis von Ellershausen, a mining engineer who arrived in 1862. Disappointed with gold mining at Mooseland and Waverley in Halifax County, von Ellershausen turned to lumbering in Hants County. With European backing he acquired 24 300 ha/60,000 ac of timber around the St Croix, Indian, and Ingram rivers.

He built a large steam sawmill at Stillwater Lake, and on the St Croix he had three water-powered mills and the province's first groundwood pulp mill (1875). He also had a mill extracting tannin from hemlock bark, then used to prepare leather.

To operate his mills he imported 70 German workers and housed them in 30 tenement homes. He built a non-denominational church (St Louisa Union, now United Church of Canada) and his family mansion in Ellershouse. (The house still stands.) In later life he planned to develop a large lake like the one at Uniacke House. But fearing flooded tracks, the railway refused permission. Von Ellershausen later went bankrupt mining copper in Newfoundland; he died in Berlin in 1914.

Near Ellershouse is Panuke Lake. This glacially gouged valley cuts the province nearly in two between Windsor and East River on the Atlantic. Along the lakeshore the Nova Scotia Museum of Natural History administers a 160-ha/395-ac forest preserve recently handed over by the Bowater Mersey Paper Company of Liverpool.

As we approach the community of St Croix on Hwy 1 or Hwy 101, we descend into a broad valley bordered to the north by white cliffs, some over 30 m/100 ft high. See how the St Croix and its meandering tributary, Thumbhill Creek, have cut down through the soft gypsum. Downstream, level green dykelands that date to the 1670s fringe the Avon estuary.

This is an area of deep alluvial soils made from local limestone, sandstone, and shale. These sedimentary rocks were laid down under a shallow inland sea (geologists call it the Windsor Sea), which spread across the lowlands of central and eastern Nova Scotia in a tropical climate 300 million years ago. Prolonged evaporation of seawater left deep deposits of calcium sulphate or gypsum (Latin for chalk).

LEG-STRETCHER: *St Croix*

To get the feel of this landscape, park north of where Hwy 101 passes

---

The crests of slate ridges running up the spine of Nova Scotia often contain gold-bearing quartz. A century ago small towns sprang up around these outcrops. There were gold mines near West and East Gore, Rawdon, and Newport Corner. At Renfrew, on the eastern edge of these slates (north of Shubenacadie Grand Lake), there was a gold rush in 1862. Renfrew soon had 10 active mines with 700 resident miners and their families. Among them was Edmund Horne, who later founded Québec's great Noranda mine. In four decades Renfrew's gold ran out—but not before yielding the equivalent of $20,000,000 at today's prices.

Today Renfrew is a ghost town. In the late 1990s Edgar Horne, grand-nephew of Edmund Horne, worked his "Double Nugget" seam with Shawn "Klondike" Sullivan, still hoping to strike the mother lode.

The hills make way for grainfields and grassy marshes encompassed by the St. Croix and Avon Rivers, which unite below the ancient town of Windsor.
–Ruth Kedzie Wood, *The Tourist's Maritime Provinces,* 1915

over Hwy 1 and follow the easy footpath to various viewing points. Since you're at tidehead here, you may see a small tidal bore coming upstream, mingling Fundy's cocoa-coloured waters with the St Croix's clear water. A side path takes you to Thumbhill Creek and close-up views of gypsum cliffs. You may spot brownish marsh hawks hunting meadow voles, and kingfishers and eagles fishing from nearby trees.

If you're interested in seeing a dam and hydroelectric plant, continue on Hwy 1 to the village of St Croix and ask for directions to the Salmon Hole Reservoir.

VIEW: *Gypsum Quarry*

Millions of people live in rooms sheathed in evaporated salts. Plasterboard, trade-named "gyproc," is powdered gypsum pressed be-tween sheets of heavy kraft paper. Nova Scotia supplies about half the gypsum mined in North America, averaging 1.5 million tonnes a year, making it the world's largest supplier. The industry began in the 1700s when local farmers began carting the whitish rock to wharves for sale as fertilizer in the US. Later, gypsum was found near Milford in the Shubenacadie valley and on Bras d'Or Lake.

Gypsum Quarry

The local quarries operate at Gypsum Mines (Rte 14) and at Wentworth Creek and Miller Creek, north and south of the St Croix, respectively. [See also the **Halifax-Dartmouth Area Nature Tour** at Milford and the **Bras d'Or Scenic Drive** at Little Narrows.]

SIDE TRIP: *Gypsum Quarry*

To reach the Fundy Gypsum Mine quarry, exit north at Five Mile Plains to Sweets Corner on Rte 14 (about 3 km/2 mi), turn left, and drive 1.5 km/0.9 mi. You can rejoin Hwy 101 (or the **Glooscap Trail**) at Garlands Crossing (an old quarry) or link up with Hwy 1 at Three Mile Plains.

Either way, you'll meander through a curiously rumpled landscape made of discarded piles of rock debris overgrown with grass or planted in spruce. The area is riddled with sinkhole ponds and caves where rainwater seepage has dissolved gypsum from harder rocks. Geologists call this karst topography. To see a sinkhole up close, exit into Windsor and ask about King's-Edgehill School's "Devil's Punchbowl."

BACK ON THE HIGHWAY

VIEW: *Noble Headland*

If it's a clear day as you approach Windsor on Hwy 1, leave it at Exit 4 just to see the view toward Cape Blomidon. It embraces the Avon and

... Blomidon, noblest of American headlands, nearly six hundred feet above the waters; its steep base of bright red sandstone partially covered by bright green bushes, and surmounted by two hundred feet of perpendicular basaltic cliffs, crowned by 'forests old', upon which the eyes of Evangeline once looked ...

– Thomas Cross, **On the basin of Minas**, 1880

St Croix estuaries with their patchwork of farms and woods, the pinkish Minas Basin, and Cape Blomidon looming like a World War I battleship against the Parrsboro Shore.

Thomas Chandler Haliburton

Cape Blomidon

Haliburton ... suggested that few towns existed in Nova Scotia because local farmers had eliminated the need for local merchants by sending their produce to market from their own landings.
– R. C. Harris & J. Warkentin, **Canada Before Confederation,** 1974

As we continue along Hwy 101, the landscape levels into the Avon River dykelands. On the left are the grounds and buildings of Canada's longest-running farm show, the Hants County Exhibition. Held each September since 1765, it earned a Royal Charter in 1766 and renewed it in 1815.

Just east of the Windsor overpass there was until 1997 a stocky red brick chimney on the right. It leaned so precariously over an old factory, it had to be removed. The factory recalls Nova Scotia's short-lived manufacturing boom after joining Confederation in 1867. Windsor was the home of Thomas Chandler Haliburton (1796–1865), a judge and political gadfly who is sometimes called the father of American humour. His witty newspaper columns, written under the pen name of "Sam Slick, Yankee clockmaker," agitated Halifax politicians and painted a charming (though sexist and racist, say modern critics) portrait of rural life in the 1820s. "Clifton," the judge's home in Windsor, is open to visitors as Haliburton House, part of the Nova Scotia Museum Complex.

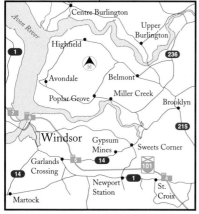

VIEW: *Mud Miracle*

Where the Windsor/Falmouth Causeway crosses the Avon estuary, a tidal marsh is evolving before your eyes. The causeway was built in 1970 and immediately changed the estuary. Strong currents that had scoured the river bed twice daily for millennia abruptly ceased, dumping their loads of sediment. Mud flats began to build downstream. When they grew thick enough, salt-tolerant cord grasses appeared on the highest parts, first the erect type, then the spreading type, called marsh hay.

More than once, ice floes scraped them away, but new seeds germinated. Once the cord grass was established, spike grass appeared, plus the reed called "black grass." Under the matrix of living roots tunnelled worms, molluscs, and crustaceans. Flying insects munched on the foliage and laid eggs. By 1993 sandpipers showed up, feeding on the invertebrates. Since then waterfowl have been moving in, and great blue herons have been seen hunting minnows on the newly risen flats.

In the 19th century, gypsum and timber boats docked at Windsor at high tide, and a ferry took passengers across the Avon to Falmouth. In 1837 a wooden bridge was built, followed by a steel railway bridge 30 years later. The present causeway was constructed in 1970. Considering the massive tides, it was a major engineering feat.

As cord grasses continue to trap silt with each high tide, the mud flats will continue to rise until deposition equals erosion. This stable environment will attract less salt-hardy plants such as sea lavender and seaside goldenrod. In time the mud flats will become a permanent tidal marsh like those in Cobequid Bay and around Grand Pré.

For a good look at the mud flats and river, pull off Hwy 101 at the downtown Windsor exit and go to the Windsor Tourist Centre where the Avon and St Croix rivers meet. A ridge, part of the dyke system that protects local lowlands, separates the centre from the estuary. Stairs ascend the dyke. There's a trail and benches with views of waving marsh grass, salty mud flats, and the rivers. Binoculars are useful. WARNING: Don't walk on the mud flats; they're sticky, deep, and treacherous.

After crossing the causeway, leave Hwy 101 at Exit 7 (Falmouth) and rejoin Hwy 1. It takes us along the Avon estuary, a broadly rolling landscape of field, orchard, and woodlot. We pass Hantsport, the fifth largest shipbuilding centre in the world in the 1850s. The shipyards of E. Churchill & Sons and J.B. North alone produced 142 wooden vessels (one of them 1897 tonnes) between 1852 and 1903. Imagine the number of prime pine, spruce, yellow birch, and larch cut to make this possible. [See also **Glooscap Trail** at Maitland.]

The artificial lake above the causeway has been named Pizaquid, the Mi'kmaq name for this area.

Since 1929 Hantsport has been headquarters to Minas Basin Pulp & Power. Long before recycling became popular, the mill made egg cartons and fruit containers from discarded paper. The port is also an important gypsum shipping point.

In late June it's common to see washes of lavender, blue, and purple along the roads from here to Grand Pré. These are wild lupins, an accidental import from western Canada. [See also the entry for Hebron on this tour, the **Lighthouse Route** at Sand Hills Beach Provincial Park, and the **Marine Drive** at Lawrencetown.]

Upper Gaspereau

In the 1870s the shipyard of Ezra Churchill & Sons of Hantsport was among the world's largest.

As we cross ridge after broad ridge, a pattern emerges. Each contains a short stream running at right angles to the Avon—and these match streams across the river. For instance, Halfway Brook on this side faces Cogmagun River on that side. The secret is that between Mount Denson and Wolfville we are riding over early Carboniferous formations that were gently folded when North America and the African plate collided nearly 400 million years ago. The sediments they came from were brought down from now-vanished mountain ranges by ancient rivers. They form a broad band from Gaspereau nearly to Chedabucto Bay and crop up in western and northern Cape Breton. Being older and harder than the gypsum formations, these "Horton Group" rocks are less eroded and therefore higher.

After the Gaspereau dykelands, we cross a spur of Southern Upland between Greenwich and Kentville, then enter the Annapolis Valley.

Near here, Canadian realist painter and long-time Wolfville resident Alex Colville painted his famous early work, Elm Tree at Horton Landing.

From 1926 to the outbreak of World War II, the MV Kipawo ferried passengers and freight across Minas Basin between Kingsport, Parrsboro, and Wolfville. The Mi'kmaq people called the Partridge Island area Owokum for "crossing over."

SIDE TRIP: *Another View of Blomidon*
Leaving Hwy 101 at Exit 9, drive northeast just over 1 km/0.6 mi past Avonport Station for this spectacular view. Blomidon owes its distinctive profile to two distinct rock types. The lower slope consists of soft red Triassic siltstone and sandstone. The steeper upper part is dark basaltic lava that welled up through a crack when the Fundy rift valley was taking shape in the early Jurassic. Directly behind the cape is Partridge Island, with Parrsboro and the Cobequid Mountains beyond. [See also the **Glooscap Trail.**]

Even though the Cobequids look fairly rugged from nearby, from this distance they seem remarkably level. [See also the **Trans Canada Highway** near Streets Ridge and Canso Causeway.] What you're seeing are the planed-off roots of lofty ancient mountains eroded by 80 million years of weathering and glaciation since the Cretaceous Period. The resulting planation surface or peneplain embraces the resistant uplands of Gaspé, northern New Brunswick, and western Newfoundland, as well as Nova Scotia's Southern Upland, Aspotogan Mountain in Lunenburg County, and the Pictou/Antigonish and Cape Breton Highlands.

The great Horton dyke at Grand Pré, which had withstood the tide for two centuries, was also broken. The History of Kings County states, "The 'Saxby Tide' in the autumn of 1869 made a clean sweep of [the Horton Dyke], carrying masses of it out bodily. The whole 3,000 acres were flooded, cattle were drowned, and 'Long Island' became an island in reality. The salt left on the land destroyed the crop of grass for three years."
– Albert Roland,
Geological Background and Physiography of Nova Scotia, *1982*

BACK ON THE HIGHWAY
Grand Pré National Historic Site (north off Hwy 1 at the sign or Exit 10 off Hwy 101) is famous because of a poem. In 1847 the American Henry Wadsworth Longfellow published his long narrative poem *Evangeline*, about two imaginary Acadian lovers tragically separated here in the deportation of 1755.

Today the site, settled in 1680 by Acadians from Port Royal farther west, breathes pure peace. Around the restored stone Church of Saint-Charles, ancient French willows sweep a broadloom of velvety lawns inset with curving ponds and flower beds. The original village well is still here, and beyond the church a huddle of apple trees whisper about bygone days.

Biologists and bird watchers prize Grand Pré for another reason.

Its extensive tidal marshes and offshore mud flats are among the province's most productive bird habitats. This is because in summer they teem with invertebrate life.

At the base of all this productivity is a recently discovered phenomenon. It seems the translucent upper layers of rich muck act as a solar collector, a kind of greenhouse in which bacteria and blue-green algae thrive. These feed microscopic animals, which become food for mussels, clams, minnows, bloodworms, and millions of shrimp-like crustaceans called amphipods (Latin for "equal-footed").

Thanks mainly to these mud shrimp, the upper Bay of Fundy is a protein supermarket for millions of shorebirds heading south in the fall. On average, one to two million birds stop over each autumn. It's one of the few places along the Atlantic Flyway where they can get the right mix of food and safe rest. On any given day, Minas Basin may host most of the sandpipers in eastern North America.

Among the most common visitors are semipalmated sandpipers and plovers arriving from their Hudson Bay breeding grounds. Settling on the flats at low tide, they follow the receding waters out, rapidly stabbing their long beaks into the wet mud after prey. Every so often they rise in a twittering mass like dry leaves in an autumn gust. Banking, they dip and wheel as one, then settle and feed some more. As the tide returns, they reverse the process, eventually swarming on nearby beaches and fields to rest and digest their meal.

The chief attraction is the tiny mud shrimp *Corophium volutator*. It lives in tubes in the moist muck, as many as 40,000 to a single square metre. This organism breeds twice a year.

> *Longfellow never visited Nova Scotia. But Canadian poet Charles G. D. Roberts (1860–1944) taught literature at King's College in Windsor from 1885 to 1896, and he had this to say in his* **A Sister to Evangeline**:
>
> *There was one long street, thick set with its wide-eaved gables ... [Nearby] rose the spar of the church, glittering like gold in the clear flood of sunset. And everywhere the dear apple blossoms— for it was spring when I came home. Beyond the village and its one black wharf, my eyes ranged the green, wind-fuggled marshes, sate beyond the sodded circumvallations of their dykes. Past the dykes ... stretched the glowing miles of the flats; for the tides of Minas were at ebb. How red in the sunset, molten copper threaded with fire, those naked reaches gleamed ...*
>
> – Sir Charles G. D. Roberts, **A Sister to Evangeline**, 1898

A major oil spill in the upper Bay of Fundy in autumn could wipe out most of the semipalmated sandpipers in the world.

Semipalmated sandpipers

With exquisite precision the sandpipers arrive in time for the fall hatch. The birds come famished from their long flight, but in 10 days they double their weight. This is enough protein to carry them 8 000 km/5,000 mi to Surinam, South America.

One of the bird's favourite local resting places is along the east side of Evangeline Beach, beyond Grand Pré. For obvious reasons it is protected; but smaller congregations of shorebirds sometimes grace nearby beaches and marshes. To find the beach, ask directions in the gift shop.

NOTE: For a good article on the shorebirds of upper Fundy, see the summer 1988 issue of *NS Conservation* (Vol. 12, No 2), published by the Nova Scotia Department of Natural Resources (DNR).

Fertile marshes like these also act as a hatcheries and nurseries for dozens of commercial fish species that need such sheltered, nutrient-rich waters before they can live in the open ocean.

Walking the flats at low tide, look for clamshells with little counter-sunk holes, the work of moon snails. These small predators plough through the mud until they find a suitable clam. Extending and firmly attaching its "foot," the snail drills a hole with its raspy mouth and sucks out the contents. The local species is called spotted moon snail. Little raised "sand collars" indicate where females have laid eggs.

Bloodworms—one of the earthworm's many marine cousins—operate in a different food chain. These many-legged hunters rear up from the bottom and snatch small fish from the incoming tide. Many are in turn eaten by sandworms and larger fish—both of which are eaten by ospreys. But commercial harvesting of bloodworms may be endangering the mud-flat ecology.

Just west of Grand Pré, Hwy 1 forks to take an alternative route for a kilometre or so. Take the older shore road for yet another vista of Blomidon and the Minas Basin marshlands.

Annapolis Valley from North Mountain lookoff

The Annapolis Valley

This fertile 135-km/85-mi corridor of orchards, woodlots, farms, and tidy towns, home of the Apple Blossom Festival, blessed with more sunshine than anywhere else in the province, deserves its own introduction.

Exactly why is it so fruitful? One reason is that Minas Basin acts as a heat sink, slowly releasing stored summer heat to take the chill out of spring. Moreover, the North and South mountains warm incoming cool air by forcing it to descend and expand. Spring or fall fogs coming in from east or west are usually dissipated by the time they reach the central part. For these reasons the Valley has the province's longest growing season and is one of Canada's prime fruit-growing regions.

The Annapolis Valley vividly illustrates how geology shapes our lives. North Mountain would not exist without its crust of 200-million-year-old lava. Without the mountain, the Valley would be just as exposed as any other Minas farming district. Yet until the late Triassic, neither Fundy nor the Valley existed. The landscape was much like today's Grand Canyon without the Colorado River—a reddish sandstone plain with spiky conifers and a climate that alternated between drought and monsoon.

All this gradually changed when the North American and African plates began to pull apart 200 million years ago. Very slowly, a few centimetres a year, fractures appeared along the Eastern Seaboard. Between the cracks, parts of the crust subsided, forming rift valleys like those in the American Midwest, in Africa, and in Israel today. One valley became the Fundy trough, another the North Atlantic.

Through the weakened crust came pulses of lava that glowed fiery red at night and smoked and steamed by day. Oozing like black porridge, it covered the floor of future Fundy several times. Up to 17 flows occurred along the future Digby Neck, and lesser amounts spilled out at Five Islands, Cape d'Or, Cape Chignecto, Isle Haute, Grand Manan Island, and along New Jersey's Palisades. Cooling, the Nova Scotia lava became the layered greyish "trap" rock we see from Blomidon to Briar Island. And, like urethane varnish on a wooden floor, it slowed the wearing down of the softer rock below. Meanwhile, most streams ran north to the Fundy depression.

On the South Mountain side, molten rock from the Pangaea collision came up against the valley sandstones to form the South Mountain's scarp. From there it slopes gently away to the Atlantic Shore. Being nearly twice as old as North Mountain, its surface layers have mostly weathered away, leaving only the resistant granite basement rocks. So it is slightly lower. Between them, the two ridges

Every summer until the 1940s men set out on the flats outside the dykes to harvest the salt-rich cord grass— "marsh hay"—to augment their winter fodder. To cure the hay while keeping it above the tides, they pounded a circle of posts into the mud, floored it, and piled the hay on top. Traces of these staddles *may still be seen along the basin.*

Many driveways along North Mountain's crest are paved with dark basalt chips. [See also the **Cabot Trail** *near Aspy Bay, where driveways are paved with white gypsum chips.]*

Barn on North Mountain

formed a natural trough for water to flow along.

The softer valley rocks eroded faster than either. The forces of erosion had about 150 million years to work in. Today the Valley is 150 m/500 ft deep—one metre every million years—and 3–11 km/ 2–7 mi wide. The process is being continued by the Cornwallis and Annapolis rivers and their tributaries. Both rivers rise in a postglacial bog near Aylesford.

The process was accelerated when one or more larger east–west rivers developed and "stole" the flow of the slower-cutting north–south streams. The older streams then turned to follow the main valley, leaving dry beds or "wind gaps" across North Mountain (e.g., at Karsdale, Delaps Cove and Parkers Cove). Later, southbound glaciers deepened and widened them.

Prescott House Museum at Starrs Point

VIEWS: *Apple Orchards*

One doesn't go far into the Valley without seeing orchards. From Wolfville to Berwick they march by row over the rolling fields, apple and pear, cherry and peach, squat old grey trees gnarled by decades of pruning and picking, vigorous saplings newly planted with circles of brown manure at their base. North America's first apple orchards were planted by the French near the Annapolis Basin soon after 1605. But it was in the east end of the Valley, suitably cold in winter but tempered by the Minas Basin, that the industry flourished.

Two things put Valley apples on the map: the advent of steam power in the 1860s and the discovery that Britons loved apples. By the 1900s, shipload after shipload left the Canning wharf for overseas. Names like Gravenstein, Macintosh, Delicious, and Russet became household words in Britain too. By the 1930s, Britain was buying half the crop. Then came World War II and the U-boat menace. The export market

Valley-born author Ernest Buckler in his 1952 novel The Mountain and the Valley *evokes the two mountains vividly: "On the north side, the fields and orchards ran down to the big bend of the river, cut wide by the Fundy tides ... .The North Mountain rose sharply beyond the river. It was solid blue in the afternoon light of December that was pale and sharp as starlight, except for the milky ways of choppings where traces of the first snow never quite disappeared. On the south side of the highway, beyond the barn and the pastures, the South Mountain rose. Solid blue too at the bottom where the dark spruces huddled close, but snow-grey higher up where the sudden steepness and the leafless hardwood began."*

*How often already you've had to be told,
Keep cold, young orchard.
Good-bye and keep cold.
Dread fifty above more than
fifty below.*
– Robert Frost,
Good-Bye and Keep Cold

never recovered. In the 1950s and '60s many orchards were cut down. Today multinational corporations buy most of the crop for processing.

From mid-May to early June—if late frost hasn't killed the blossoms—the orchards are awash in pink and white. The Apple Blossom Festival celebrates this event with parades and bands and a queen. In autumn the trees droop with scarlet and pink fruit: Cortland and Ida Red apples, Bartlett and Clapp pears, Italian plums, sour and sweet cherries, apricots. Roadside stands in New Minas and elsewhere overflow. Pickers toil late into the night. Truckloads of blemished fruit are juiced, bottled, and canned.

Apple orchard looking down over the dykes

In late February and early March you'll see workers pruning the trees. Removing surplus shoots and limbs increases sap flow to remaining branches, stimulates the growth of flower buds, allows sunlight to ripen more fruit, and simplifies picking.

In summer you may spot little cardboard houses swinging like Chinese lanterns from the branches. These are insect traps used to monitor cyclic orchard pests like apple maggot, codling moth, and red spider mite. Thanks to the pioneering work of Dr Pickett of the Kentville agricultural research station in the 1920s, fruit growers now spray only when natural controls fail—a gain for both environment and pocketbook. Fungi such as apple scab also damage fruit. Growers are turning away from costly and perhaps harmful fungicidal sprays in favour of resistant apple strains and better sanitation. Ebyse Peill's farm at Starrs Point has several hectares devoted to such strains.

America has only two native crab apples, a western and an eastern species, and the latter isn't native to Nova Scotia. The New World's first domesticated apple trees were cuttings brought by Acadian settlers to Port-Royal in 1605. Europe already had many varieties. Among French favourites were L'Épice (Spicy Apple), Fameuse (Family Apple), and Pomme Grise (Grey Apple—a russeted variety). At Grand Pré a few Pomme Grise trees still persisted in the 1980s. [See also the **Trans Canada Highway** at Englishtown.]

The Acadians also had orchards at Port La Tour, Grand Pré, Gaspereau, Canard, and Cobequid (Truro), and among their customers were the English.

Like the Acadians, British settlers had different apples for pies, cider, and sauce and for eating. Because few of these varieties shipped well, few of them remain. Cox's Orange Pippin, Gravenstein, and Macintosh are still with us, and the winter-keeping Russet. Cortland and Ida Red are among the varieties bred since World War II at the Kentville station and elsewhere. For the freshest fruit, visit one of the Valley's many U-pick operations or buy at a roadside market.

Entering Wolfville from the east is like returning to a more civilized era, a time of fine mansions, broad lawns, and great trees.

The familiar juicy domestic apple probably never existed in nature. It was bred from small-fruited wild European ancestors that may have originated in uplands around the Black Sea.

A French census of 1698 [lists] some 1584 apple trees growing in the gardens of fifty-four families at Port Royal alone. At Beaubassin [Chignecto Isthmus] another thirty-two acres could be found.
– Anne Hutten,
Valley Gold: The Story of the Apple Industry in Nova Scotia, 1991

Most Valley fruit tree species belong to the rose family, Rosaceae. What a nice family!

Especially trees. For over two centuries the New Englanders who settled here have planted and tended fine maples, Colorado blue spruce, linden, black locust (a pea relative rare elsewhere in the province), and horse-chestnut. Because the town relied less on native elm than Kentville did, Dutch elm disease did little damage here. [See also the **Lighthouse Route** at Liverpool, the **Glooscap Trail** at Truro, and the **Trans Canada Highway** at River Inhabitants.]

STOP: *Wolfville's Chimney Show*

The oversized brick tower dominating the Robie Tufts Nature Centre on Front Street is literally for the birds—chimney swifts to be precise. Like the chimney of Acadia's University Hall, it's a favourite roost for these swallow-like birds. As dusk falls, twittering flocks gather above the chimneys and, as if on cue, suddenly dive inside for the night.

Notice the shrubs around the centre. They've been planted for beauty, but also with hungry birds in mind: highbush cranberry, dogwood, blue-berried elder, sumac, pin oak, shrubby cinquefoil.

Like swallows, swifts catch insects on the wing, but are even more adept. They belong to the hummingbird tribe. From daylight to dusk they eat and drink on the wing. They even mate while in flight. They walk with difficulty because their feet have atrophied. Besides frequenting unused chimneys, swifts roost and nest on vertical surfaces like cliff faces, silos, barns, and mine shafts. Stiff tail feathers allow them to hitch up and down like woodpeckers. To fasten their nests they secrete a glue in their saliva.

Wolfville's Main and Acadia streets were once lapped by Fundy waves. Both streets are built on postglacial marine terraces. (Walk north toward the basin and you'll notice the definite drop in elevation.)

Like a loose stair tread that rises when we step off, parts of eastern Canada have rebounded as much as 20 m/65 ft since the last ice cap melted 12,000 years ago. Even though the sea has meanwhile risen too, some sea beaches have been left high and dry, often in a series of steps marking stages of uplift. [See also the **Glooscap Trail** at Parrsboro and Truro and the **Sunrise Trail** at Arisaig.]

Other ancient seashores in this region occur along the road at Woodside, at Black Rock, and at Harbourville, Moody Brook, and Turner Brook. Some even have ancient sea cliffs and wave-cut benches mantled in shingle. Ask locally for directions.

To arrange a walking tour of local natural history, talk to staff at the Tourist Centre or the Robie Tufts Nature Centre. They can name local members of the Blomidon Naturalists Society who lead nature walks. See also the Society's *A Natural History of Kings County*, available at Box of Delights on Main Street and at other bookstores in the Valley.

At this time [1755] there were about five thousand descendants of the original [Acadian] settlers of Nova Scotia on the bends of the numerous rivers which flowed through flat and abundant valleys to the basin. In August the marshlands, reclaimed after the methods of their ancestors ... who in their own Brittany had known how to thwart the invading sea, were yellow with ripening grain.
– Ruth Kedzie Wood, **The Tourist's Maritime Provinces,** 1915

Blomidon is sailor talk for "Blow-Me-Down," a place of fickle wind and tide. Its fierce downdrafts could capsize a sailing ship. The Mi'kmaq called the cape "Owbogegechk," which meant "abounding in dogwood." In fact, plenty of round-leafed dogwood (Cornus rugosa) still grows here.

SIDE TRIP: *Dyke, Lookoff, Blomidon, Cape Split, Eagles*
Leaving Hwy 101 at Exit 11 (or Hwy 1 just east of Exit 11) proceed
north to Port Williams. As you cross the Cornwallis River bridge, note
how this tidal stream swings in broad loops across its floodplain. Such
meandering is typical of slow-moving rivers as they near the sea. [See
also the **Glooscap Trail** at Minudie, Highway 102 at Stewiacke.]

STOP: *Wellington Dyke*
This 1.5-km-long/0.9-mi embankment took seven arduous years to
build (1817–25), but it eliminated the cost of maintaining several
smaller dykes.

Building the Wellington Dyke

A journalist writing in the *Nova Scotian* in 1825 said the job
required about 300 men, 100 teams of oxen totalling 500 animals,
and consumed "9,788 logs of birch, 18,036 loads of poles 12 ft. long,
71,756 pickets from 8 to 16 feet long, 15,141 loads of stone ...."
A stroll along it affords not only soothing scenery but glimpses of
tidal life. The seaward side offers 200 ha/490 ac of natural tidal
marsh. In spring and fall there are sandpipers, yellowlegs, geese,
sharp-tailed sparrows, short-eared owls, and northern harriers ("marsh
hawks"). Occasionally white-sided dolphins (of which the Bay of
Fundy has a large population) and harbour porpoises are sighted.

Typical plants include cord grass, glasswort, sea lavender, and
sweet-grass (*Hierachloe odorata*), an aromatic plant the Mi'kmaq and
other native peoples use in religious ceremonies.

To reach the dyke, take Rte 358 north through Port Williams to a
white church about 3 km/2 mi beyond town. Turn east toward Starrs
Point on Lower Church Street and proceed about 3 km/2 mi until
you see the Wellington Dyke sign. This road takes you to the outermost (and most recent) of five dykes built across the Canard River.
In all, dykes enclose some 1215 ha/3,000 ac of hayfields, grain, and
pasture in the Canning/Starrs Point area.

While you're on the dyke, check out an aboiteau (Acadian for
"water-box"). This is a gated square culvert that lets fresh water out

without letting seawater in. There's one where the road meets the dyke. [See also the **Glooscap Trail** at Old Barns.]

Lookoff

STOP: *The Lookoff*

For a superb panorama embracing five counties and the Parrsboro shore, drive to The Lookoff north of Pereau. From this 150-m/500-ft elevation on a clear day you can see the Avon and Cornwallis estuaries, the dykelands around Wolfville, New Minas, and Kentville, and the towns of Waterville and Berwick to the southwest. Farther on you can see far up the Minas Basin toward Truro, and the scarp of South Mountain behind Wolfville Ridge. At your feet you'll see Pereau with its rectangles of pasture, orchard, and woodlot.

Six rivers flow into the great estuary opposite, and four of them bear Acadian names: Pereau, Habitant, Canard, and Gaspereau, the latter two separated by the "Great Meadow" (Grand Pré).

Now imagine that scene with the dykes between Canard and Grand Pré breached by high tides. This happened during the Saxby Gale of 1869, when parts of the Wellington Dyke collapsed, and much of the land was flooded. [For more detail on this storm see the **Glooscap Trail** near Minudie and Parrsboro.]

To reach The Lookoff, proceed to Canning and watch along Main Street for the Rte 358 sign. Turn left and drive about 5 km/3 mi across Pereau Creek and up the steep side of Blomidon to a railed parking area on the right. The historic Acadian Dyke Drive parallels Rte 358 through Starrs Point and Lower Canard to Blomidon Provincial Park.

SIDE TRIP: *Blomidon Provincial Park*

For spectacular views, good hiking trails, camping, picnicking, and rock-hounding, visit this park. From Canning, follow Rte 358 and watch for signs.

There are two large picnic/camping areas, one at the base of the headland and one on top. You can get to the beach from the entrance

In Mi'kmaq mythology Cape Blomidon was the home of man-god Glooscap. From its height he supposedly flung five great rocks or clods across the basin at his enemy Beaver, thus creating Five Islands. The legend says that Beaver built a great dam between Cape Split and the Parrsboro Shore, a dam that Glooscap destroyed. Perhaps this legend echoes a geological event, an earthquake perhaps, that let the sea flood Minas Basin between Cape Split and Cape d'Or.

parking lot. Be sure to check tide times first. Tides rise with surprising rapidity; people have been stranded on the cliffs for hours. The cape's massive slope of tilted rust-red Triassic siltstone and sandstone is marbled with salt and gypsum and capped by nearly vertical cliffs of charcoal grey basalt.

From the lower parking lot you can access 16 km/10 mi of all-season walking trails. These include the Borden Brook Trail and the longer Woodland Trail (which parallels the main road). The "Coniferous" and "Deciduous" interpretive mini-loops just north of the inner camping area are well worth exploring for insights into central Nova Scotia's forest ecology. An oddity to look for in summer is the purple trillium, whose flower mimics rotten meat to attract the flies that pollinate it.

South of the road, the shorter Jodrey Trail skirts fields and cliffs, offering glimpses of Minas Basin (through a protective chain-link fence) before emerging at a monument to the late businessman Roy Jodrey of Hantsport, who donated this land. Watch for blue lobelia, rare elsewhere in Nova Scotia, which grows profusely in places here.

If you've come this far and you like to hike, visit famous Cape Split. To reach it, continue on Hwy 358 over the top of Blomidon and down into the broad curve of Scots Bay. Pause at the government wharf on the far side of the bay to see the pillow lava. Pillow lava forms when molten rock is chilled by cold water while being forced up from below. Cape Split experienced two main lava flows, totalling 75 m/ 245 ft. Other lines of hardened lava show up as dark, ragged rocks in the mud flats at low tide. [See also the **Glooscap Trail** at Advocate Harbour and Economy.]

In the 1980s, Massachusetts and Connecticut asked the province to help reinstate their national symbol. For several years DNR biologists captured surplus eaglets (in good years a nest may have three live young, one or two of which often die from sibling rivalry) and shipped them south.

The birds were taken to remote areas of the two states and fed and raised in open-ended treetop boxes with minimal human disturbance. This is called hacking [see also the **Glooscap Trail** at Cape d'Or]. Now bald eagles are making a comeback in the northeast. Peter Austin-Smith's book Bald Eagles in the Maritimes recounts this success story.

The cape itself is over 7 km/4 mi beyond the federal wharf, and the road takes you only half-way. From the parking lot at road's end, a 6.5-km/4-mi hike of moderate difficulty will take you there. After threading spruce woods it climbs through mixed and deciduous forest to a high, windy, grassy lookoff. The broadleaf forest in late May (it's cool up here and spring comes later) is spangled with spring beauties and Dutchman's breeches. You'll also see lady's-slipper, violets, and trillium. Spring flowers hasten to bloom and set seed before the forest canopy cuts off their sunlight.

From the lookoff you can see the curving basalt cusp of Cape Split plunging under the Bay of Fundy in a snaggle of dark eroded columns [See also **Glooscap Trail** at Five Islands]. Fierce 13-knot tides and swirling ice floes have gnawed this cape ever since the sea broke through the Cape d'Or–Cape Split barrier millennia ago. At full and new moon you can hear the hollow roar of the incoming tide as the trail nears the cliffs. It's estimated that the flow equals the combined volume of all the streams on Earth. Currents exceed 4m/13ft/second. Look for—but don't pick!—rare arctic-alpine species such as roseroot, saxifrage, Arctic birch, and curly grass fern.

On your way back, pause in Canning, formerly Apple Tree Landing, chief port for Valley apples going overseas. Until the 1930s its air was scented each autumn with the fragrance of warehouses full of new softwood barrels stuffed with ripe apples. With luck you might find an old stevedore to talk about those days.

Canning is close to Sheffield Mills, the winter bald eagle capital of Nova Scotia. DNR tallies reveal that overwintering local eagles increased from a few dozen in 1980 to more than 400 in the 1990s. Why? The answer is increased poultry refuse from local chicken farms. Like many predators, bald eagles will scavenge free meals.

Sheffield Mills is on the Sleepy Hollow River, about 5 km/3 mi west of Canning. Organized winter eagle-watching tours are available. Ask locally at the gift shop and interpretive centre or contact DNR's wildlife office in Kentville. November to early March is the best time.

When the wind is hitting against the tide it causes rips and whirlpools that assault a ship from all four directions. The swirling, surging water is like it was on springs dancing over the bow, stem, port and starboard all at the same time. Cape Split Gut is approximately three and a half miles wide and with thousands of tons of water surging down through the narrow channel in only six hours it does not take a heavy breeze of wind to cause it to get dangerously rough. If an open boat got caught in the Gut at half tide and it was a bit rough it would be engulfed in a matter of minutes.
– Ted Simpson,
By the Sea in Nova Scotia

BACK ON THE HIGHWAY

Have you noticed, travelling west from Wolfville, that pine groves get more common? Pines thrive on sandy loams, and sandstone is the dominant rock under this landscape. After the glaciers melted, they left mounds of sand. Ages later, white and red pine migrated into the province from farther south and west and colonized the sandy bottom. So did northern red oak. All three species seed in after lightning fires kill competing vegetation, especially if the fire doesn't destroy the humus. Sandy soils dry out faster than clay soils in spring, making their plant cover more prone to forest fires.

This natural cycle was disrupted in the 1780s when thousands of New England Planters flooded in. Land clearing, shipbuilding, lumbering, and human-caused fires soon depleted the great trees. Their place was taken by white spruce, aspen, and other short-lived species.

Today only isolated groves, second-and third-generation offspring of those original trees, remain near Wolfville, up the Kentville Ravine, at Berwick, and a few other places on the Valley floor. Even so, they dwarf the occasional stand of planted Scots and jack pine (e.g., near Lawrencetown). If all human activity halted for a century, pine and oak would gradually reclaim the Valley floor.

STOP: *Pine Grove*

Near the exit to Port Williams, an imposing island of tall, grey-barked conifers soars above the Wandlyn Motor Inn. Their flaring silvery green crowns and grey bark mark them as white pines. Park beside the Wandlyn Inn and ask permission to walk into one of these white pine groves. See if you can spot any white pine seedlings. Except along the well-lit edges they will be rare, for they need more sunlight than such dim groves afford. Instead you'll find lots of fir seedlings. [See also the **Halifax-Dartmouth Area Nature Tour** at Point Pleasant Park.] Unless some pines are cut or die, the next grove will be chiefly balsam fir. Another natural grove, this one of pole-sized young red pine, occurs on a sand ridge between Hwy 101 and the Cornwallis River, 2.5 km/1.5 mi west of Kentville. Again, so little light falls on the forest floor, and the carpet of dead needles is so deep, that few other plants can grow there. [See also the **Trans Canada Highway** near the Springhill Exit.]

SIDE TRIP: *Stolen River*

Long ago, near Hwy 1 between Greenwich and New Minas, one river "captured" another. How could that be? Picture a small boy scratching a groove in the mud below a melting snowbank. The meltwater immediately fills the groove and runs downhill. Suppose a bigger boy then draws a deeper groove across the first. The water will forsake the first channel and follow the second. The small boy's stream will go dry below that point.

This is essentially what happened at White Rock. Long before the

Nova Scotia has the highest resident bald eagle population east of Alaska.

For centuries a few overwintering eagles survived by eating stranded marine life on nearby mud flats, especially tomcod, which arrive after mid-December to spawn. However, such natural food sources could not support today's overwintering population. But as long as local chicken farming continues, that population should remain high.

Gaspereau River developed, the ancestor of Black River flowed off the Southern Upland down to the Cornwallis River. On the way, it had to cut through a ridge of hard white quartzite (hence White Rock) and slate, which slowed its progress. But the young Gaspereau River, working its way upstream through the soft bedrock between Wolfville Ridge and South Mountain, finally cut across the Black River. The Gaspereau "stole" its waters, thereby augmenting its own flow and accelerating its erosion. Deep Hollow Road runs along lower Black River's dry bed. The road stands 30 m/90 ft higher than the Gaspereau's bed here.

"Gaspereau" is an anglicized form of the old Acadian word for alewife, *gasparots*. The alewife is a kind of herring that spawns in certain freshwater lakes across the province. [See also the **Lighthouse Route** near Burlington and the **Ceilidh Trail** at Lake Ainslie.]

To reach Deep Hollow Road, turn south off Hwy 1 (or off Hwy 101 at Exit 11) and follow the winding ravine toward White Rock. The sensation of driving up a river bed is heightened by the steep-banked outer curves. On the way back, notice that the former Horton District High School stands on Black River's old delta. [See also the **Glooscap Trail** at Parrsboro and the **Cabot Trail** north of Cheticamp.]

LEG-STRETCHER: *Nature Trail*

Hell's Gate Generating Station, one of three on the upper Black River, takes advantage of the drop from here to the Gaspereau River. The Blomidon Naturalists Society has developed a local footpath into a 0.5-km/0.3-mi trail. The trail runs from a parking lot at White Rock Pond and up along the Gaspereau nearly to the station. There are steep slopes, a nice waterfall, quiet pools, and pleasant broadleaf glades of maple and birch where, in summer, salamanders hide, and dragonflies flit after mosquitoes and deer flies. On the way look for various minerals and, in summer, wood warblers and flycatchers.

BACK ON THE EVANGELINE TRAIL

Approaching Kentville on the trail, we dip into a ravine and see a sign on the left marked Kentville Agricultural Centre. (If on Hwy 101, take Exit 12 and drive west.) This 162-ha/400-ac federal research station was set up in 1905 at the request of Valley fruit growers.

STOP: *"Rhodos," Azaleas, Mushrooms*

The grounds near the buildings and Blair House Museum are open to the public year-round, with guided tours in summer. Here you can enjoy a pleasant stroll among labelled exotic trees and shrubs under a natural pine and hemlock forest. There are beds of annuals in summer, and in late May and early June the station's rhododen-drons and azaleas light up the ravine with reds, pinks, mauves, and dusky gold. These robust evergreen shrubs, which grow wild in the Appalachians, Europe, and southeast Asia, are cultivated cousins of

The rare American chestnut trees on the centre's grounds were bred by cross-pollinating a tree in Bridgewater (since cut) with one at Mount Uniacke Estate Park. North America lost its native chestnuts to an Asian blight in the 1930s, but Loyalists had already brought clean seedlings and nuts to Nova Scotia.

wild blueberry and sheep laurel.

The centre's 3-km/2-mi hiking trail is considered the best place in Atlantic Canada to observe forest fungi. It goes up the ravine under old pines, hemlocks, and red spruce and past rock outcrops and waterfalls. Thanks to the late Ken Harrison, more species have been described here than for anywhere else in North America. They include such conifer-loving species as Grevell's boletus and chanterelle; mixedwood forest species like russula, birch polypore, and honey mushroom; and deciduous associates like horn-of-plenty, fly agaric, and destroying angel. September through October are the best months to see mushrooms, especially after rain.

The research centre is open year-round; Blair House is open from May to Labour Day, Monday–Friday. Tours of study plots require a staff person and are by appointment only.

VIEW: *Downtown Esker*
The north side of Kentville's west Main Street is a winding gravel ridge built by water running under a glacier. As the brook enlarged its ice tunnel—its bed of sand and pebbles—also rose. When the glacier melted, the stream dried up, leaving this raised bed. [See the **Glooscap Trail** south of River Hebert.]

Crow Condo
At times between 1990 and 1995, Kentville and West Brooklyn residents were besieged by thousands of crows, which converged at dusk on a grove of elms south of town. Crows are communal, talkative, and sociable. The racket was deafening.

People weren't used to this. Before 1990, most of the birds had roosted on Boot Island near Grand Pré. Why they switched is a mystery. In 1996, after trying exterminators, noisemakers, stuffed owls, hot lead, and other strategies, the citizens seem to have succeeded in evicting their unwelcome guests— or the crows found a quieter roost.

Crows have prospered around humans for eons. Like the herring gull, they are intelligent and opportunistic scavengers who will eat almost anything. They are also year-round residents. However, to prosper as they do requires more than wits and versatility. When any wild animal population explodes like this, it means that food is plentiful and enemies scarce.

What do the crows eat every day? Let's see. The east end of the Valley is densely peopled (which means many garbage dumps), and it has many grain fields (which means earthworms and grubs during ploughing and harrowing, grain stubble after harvest, mice all year, and dead animals beyond the back fence), orchards (which means insects and fallen fruit), dairy, poultry, and pig farms (which means spilled feed, manure, and insects), woodland (which means birds' eggs and nestlings in the spring), and finally, slow tidal rivers (which means mud flats, which means worms, crustaceans, and stranded fish).

Biologists have studied crow vocalizations and come up with a basic language: Assembly call (loud, long notes); scolding call (staccato, continuous, used to warn of predators); contact call (usually four notes); announcement call (like scolding but shorter). There are also calls and notes for feeding, courting, panic, and imitating other creatures.

As for enemies, they have few. They're too big for hawks to tackle and too wily for foxes and coyotes to catch unless sick or wounded. Few farmers bother to shoot, trap, or poison them, since the birds do eat many noxious pests.

No wonder, then, that crows have always converged on the Valley in autumn. And when the various flocks further convene in March to mate and seek nesting areas, their numbers can become enormous, even frightening. At times in 1995 an estimated 35,000 birds darkened the sky.

From Kentville to Berwick the Valley gradually narrows. The once-broad Cornwallis River dwindles to a brook, and the North and South mountains, with their fluted ravines and lush deciduous forests of maple, yellow birch, and beech, seem to close in. Minas fogs seldom penetrate this far. A mini-continental climate prevails— hot and dry in summer, cold and dry in winter. If you're not used to it, the summer heat can be oppressive.

SIDE TRIP: *Harbourville*

If you're feeling over-heated some sultry August afternoon here, drive north over the mountain to any spot on the Fundy shore. In a few minutes the air temperature can drop by 10° to 15° C (18° to 27° F). It's a different world.

Harbourville, north of Berwick, is a good choice in any weather. Turn north onto Rte 360 (or take Exit 15 off Hwy 101) and drive 19 km/11.8 mi (about 15 km/9.3 mi from the 101). From Welsford to Somerset you ascend a gentle sandstone slope; from there to Garland the road steepens as it zigzags up the resistant lava scarp; then you cross the mountain's crest, going with the tilt of the bedrock down to the salt water. Beachcombing is good here.

After the Valley's heat, Fundy's cool salt air is like a tonic. Slow tree growth here reflects the shift to cooler climate, and the stronger winds. Tough balsam fir, spruce, and birch dominate.

LEG-STRETCHER

If the tide is low, walk down to the beach and dawdle by the wharf. Examine the various kinds of rockweed, green algae, and barnacles. Talk to someone about the tides, local history, and the fishery.

The small fortress-like island in the middle of the bay is Isle Haute, a reminder of the area's volcanic past. [See also the **Glooscap Trail** at Advocate Harbour.]

Before returning to Hwy 1, take a 2-km/1.2-mi detour east toward Black Rock (named for basalt lava) to see a colony of giant Japanese knotweed. Watch on the south side for a tall bush with stout, pinkish, bamboo-like stems and heart-shaped leaves the size of pie plates. This colony likely sprang up from discarded rootstocks in a load of garden soil someone dumped.

Knotweed or false bamboo is related to rhubarb and buckwheat. Once established, it sends up vigorous suckers each May. The shoots, which resemble pink asparagus when they emerge, grow 2–3 m (6–10 ft) in a few months. This plant and its smaller relative were popular ornamentals in old-time gardens. The young shoots are edible cooked— but too sour raw. [See also **Bras d'Or Scenic Drive** at Eskasoni.]

BACK ON THE HIGHWAY

Now both mountains keep you company, sometimes visible, sometimes hidden behind a ridge or a grove of trees. North Mountain is more noticeable because its scarp is steeper and more uniform. It is like that from here to Digby Gut, rising to over 225 m/738 ft north of Annapolis Basin. Digby Neck is part of the same formation. [See also the **Digby Neck Scenic Drive.**]

Antique postcard image from The Apple Capital Interpretive Centre

VIEW: *Old Forest*

Berwick, the "Apple Capital of Nova Scotia," is worth a 1.5-km/0.9-mi detour north just to view this fine grove of ancient white pine and hemlock. Many of the trees pre-date the Acadian Expulsion of 1755. One hemlock stump at Berwick, cut around 1980 had 360 annual rings. Allowing 10 years for the seedling to grow to stump height, this places its germination at around 1600. Some may be even older. Thanks to the United Church of Canada and previous owners, they have been preserved. Berwick Camp is private property, but the gate is usually open in summer, and someone will probably let you stroll around if you park outside and ask.

A striking and unfortunate feature of this grove is that young pine and hemlock are virtually absent. Heavy foot traffic has eliminated them. The only way to ensure that the grove continues is to fence off less-travelled areas and let natural regeneration seed them in, or to plant white pine and hemlock in fenced-off areas.

AVPM Company shipped its first 2,000 bales of peat to New England in 1949. By 1971 it had 200 ha/500 ac in production and had opened two US plants. Now a major world supplier, it comonly ships close to one million bales a year from plants in Nova Scotia and Prince Edward Island.

Peat is used for growing everything from roses to mushrooms and is good for mopping up oil spills. For centuries the rural Irish and Scots have burned dry peat to heat their homes and cook their meals. Russia and Finland operated large hydroelectric plants (up to 600 megawatts) on peat fuel. North American natives used dried sphagnum moss for diapers, sanitary napkins, and for dressing wounds. In commercial production, a bog is ditched using a big balloon-tired excavator on crawler treads. Once it's dry, the green layer of moss and sedge is skinned off, leaving raw peat. When the surface is dry enough, cottage-sized, tractor-drawn vacuum cleaners trundle back and forth, sucking off the top few centimetres. This is repeated until the water table or permanently wet zone is reached. Then no more peat can be harvested unless the ditches are deepened.

After more drying, the cocoa-coloured humus is sifted for twigs and debris, compressed, and bagged for shipment. Once a section of a bog is harvested, operations are moved to another part. Harvested areas eventually green up; cabbage, carrots, and onions can also be grown.

VIEW: *Aylesford's Brown Gold*

When you buy Nova Scotia peat for your greenhouse or garden, chances are it came from Caribou Bog near Aylesford, a product of the Annapolis Valley Peat Moss Company. Potting soil is mostly peat, the dark brown fibrous substance left when plants decompose in a cool, acidic, oxygen-poor environment. (Peat that gets deeply buried under sediment and subjected to prolonged pressure becomes soft coal or lignite.)

Most peat derives from sphagnum. Peat holds moisture like a sponge, absorbing up to 90 per cent of its weight as water.

In the old days peat was dug by hand with special spades and piled to dry. Later, machines were developed to cut and stack it in blocks. Now the peat is vacuumed.

Cranberries

Nova Scotia pioneered cranberry cultivation in Canada. One of the pioneers was Annapolis County's William MacNeil, who planted a small area on the edge of a peat bog here in 1870.

For a light-hearted look at this Thanksgiving fruit, read Beatrice R. Buszek's The Cranberry Connection (1977). It recounts her adventures with a bog near her home at Granville Centre on the Annapolis River.

Aylesford: Cranberry Capital

Besides peat, Aylesford supplies much of Atlantic Canada's fresh cranberries.

Cranberries have been eaten since ancient times. A Bronze Age tomb near Egtved, Denmark, yielded a clay mug containing a brown sediment from a drink made out of wheat, cranberries, bog myrtle, and honey. Canada's native people kneaded cranberries and dried meat into cakes to form the nutritious trail food called pemmican. Settlers and their descendants have picked and eaten cranberries ever since.

The wild cranberry or "crane berry" (*Vaccinium macrocarpon*) is a low-growing, evergreen vine and the largest of our three common native species, all of which grow in bogs. All belong to the heath family (*Ericaceae*) and are related to blueberry, foxberry, crowberry, laurel, and wild rhododendron. Plant breeders have produced several cultivars or varieties.

Preparing a cranberry bog for commercial production entails bulldozing (unless already harvested for peat), ditching, spreading 15 cm/6 in of sand (to promote rooting and discourage weeds), irrigating in summer and flooding in winter, fertilizing, protecting from frost, weeding, and pollinating (with honey bees). Even so, weeds, insects, and disease are an ongoing threat, and frost can damage buds, flowers, and fruit.

SIDE TRIP: *Caribou Bog*
One of Nova Scotia's biggest raised peat bogs lies south of Hwy 1 between Aylesford and Millville. It was created by the melting of a tongue of glacial ice that lingered here, depressing the land to form a shallow lake. Over the millennia, sphagnum moss and heath plants colonized the lake, filling all but the central part with peat. [See also the **Cabot Trail** near Fishing Cove; **Trans Canada Highway** near Port Hawkesbury.]

To the ancient Mi'kmaq this area was *Kobetek,* "home of the beaver." [See also **Glooscap Trail** at Beaverbrook near Truro.] It's the highest point on the Valley floor and feeds both the Annapolis and Cornwallis rivers. Ask locally for directions to the bog.

If you need to cool off, exit at Brickton and drive to Cottage Cove Provincial Park on the Fundy Shore, about 3 km/2 mi past Mount Hanley.

Here in mid-Valley we still see the familiar mosaic of small towns, open country, farmsteads, aspen groves, and piny woodlots. But the valley floor is noticeably flatter and drier. A glacial lake once existed just west of here, and when it evaporated it left fields of sand, making for dry soils. In addition, it's too far from the Minas Basin and St Marys Bay to receive much fog.

So you'll see more barley, wheat, and rye, grains that need prolonged dry weather to ripen properly. Level fields make for easy harvesting with machinery. Sometimes too the autumn fields are polka-dotted with pumpkins, another heat-loving plant. They are destined for the oil seed market.

Sometimes in summer, wells run dry here and fields turn brown. Note occasional bare patches with pale pink sand showing through, and laurel and blueberry struggling to gain a roothold. In places, however, runoff from the hills is trapped. For example, north of Kingston there are large areas of waterlogged sand.

The longest of all the Nova Scotia streams must be the Annapolis, a fact which surprised me when I took the trouble to look it up, for this river is so unobtrusive that you often do not notice its presence when you travel through the valley. It is so modest a stream that in slack water a good pole vaulter could probably clear it without wetting his feet, and it is utterly different in character than any of the streams that flow into the Atlantic or the Gulf of St Lawrence. It is a brown river flowing gently through the most fertile land in the whole province.
– Hugh MacLennan, **Rivers of Canada,** 1974

St Mary's Church at Auburn
Northwest of here, at Morden, in 1755–56, a group of Acadian refugees was forced to camp all winter on the exposed Fundy shore, where they subsisted on clams. They left such a heap of shells that the Loyalist settlers who built the church in 1790 finished its walls with plaster made from them.

When postglacial deposits consist of loose soil, they are called loess. *China and the Mississippi valley have large deposits of this yellowish material. Another type of glacial deposit hereabouts is the* kame *(Old English* camb *for ridge). As the ice melted, it plugged parts of the Annapolis and Gaspereau with stagnant ice. Streams running off the North and South mountains flowed over this ice and along its edges. Where it wore holes, conical heaps of sand and gravel piled up on the valley floor. Where it ran along the edges,* kame *terraces formed. Variations of both occur at Wallbrook, Melanson, and south of Berwick. Others can be seen from Hwy 1 or Hwy 101 near Greenwich, Aylesford, and Greenwood. Most of our road-building gravel comes from* kames. *Being usually well-drained and level on the top, they also make good farmland. [See also the* **Trans Canada Highway** *near Folly Lake and the* **Glooscap Trail** *near Parrsboro.]*

VIEW: *Dunes & Kames*

Between Aylesford and Kingston, if you squint and ignore the trees and ground vegetation, you'll notice a few Sahara-style dunes. West of here, some 12,000 years ago, the glacier left a shallow lake. It was milky with suspended sand and rock dust, which settled on the bottom in deep layers. As it had no source but meltwater, it finally dried up, leaving fields of bare sand. Strong westerlies whipped up dust storms that dimmed the sun for weeks. As the sand particles hit each other, they became smaller and lighter—the sands near Wolfville are coarser in texture—building ripples and dunes like drifting snow. The best dunes can be seen from Hwy 101, between Exits 16 and 17W.

Tree Farm

STOP: *Christmas Tree Farm*

After Lunenburg County, Annapolis County is Nova Scotia's leading producer of Christmas trees. For an inside look at this family-based industry, visit Paul Robar's large U-pick, We-cut operation near Aylesford. To arrange a tour call 902-847-9184. [See also the **Trans Canada Highway** near Antigonish and the **Kejimkujik Scenic Drive** near New Germany.]

An interesting place to see native and domestic animals up close is Oaklawn Farm Zoo (Exit 16, Hwy 101).

If you were to hike south with a compass along the base of South Mountain between Wilmot and Lower Middleton, there's a good chance you'd get lost. For the rocks are rich in iron, and iron throws a compass off. The iron occurs as red hematite and magnetite in a strip of steeply tilted shell beds and dark blue slate of Devonian age.

Like the Devonian formations near Londonderry in the Cobequid Mountains [see the **Trans Canada Highway** near Folly Lake] the ore was concentrated by extreme heat and pressure due to continental collision. The rusty deposits occur in surface veins up to 6 m/20 ft wide for about 8 km/5 mi between Torbrook and Nictaux Falls (Mi'kmaq for "fork of a river"). The mine at Torbrook operated from 1890 to 1897. At its peak it averaged close to 20,000 tonnes of ore a year. The smaller Nictaux mine (1855–60) produced only a few thousand tonnes. Most of the ore was smelted at Acadia Mines in Londonderry. At Nictaux Falls Nova Scotia Power operates a hydroelectric plant.

At Lawrencetown on the Annapolis River's south bank is the province's oldest full-time provincial forest nursery, established in 1926. The site was chosen for four main reasons. First, it is flat and stone-free and therefore suitable for the mechanical tilling, sowing, and lifting required in handling thousands of small trees. Second, it's protected from wind. Third, the silty alluvial soil is fertile and well drained, warming up quickly in spring and draining quickly after downpours. Fourth, the soil is deep, making it easy to lift seedlings without damaging their roots.

In the 1930s and 1940s, Scots pine was the forester's darling. You can see this in the many small planted groves throughout the province, especially in the western counties. (Its orange-brown upper bark separates it from the darker red and Austrian pines.) From the late 1920s on, they imported German seed and seedlings, raised them at Lawrencetown, and distributed them in spring to satellite nurseries and to the public.

People soon noticed that these pines grew slowly and often developed a crooked bole. Scientists later learned that in Europe certain soil fungi form partnerships with the roots of this tree, helping it absorb minerals in exchange for nutrients. These fungi are absent from our forests.

Nurserymen turned to native red pine. From the 1970s to the mid-1980s forest managers planted it widely, especially in Cumberland County's Chignecto Game Sanctuary and in Pictou County's Garden of Eden Barrens and the Trafalgar area. Then a fungus disease began to kill young trees. Now reforestation efforts rely mainly on native red and black spruce and the faster-growing Norway spruce.

Faced with such problems, and the need to control competing vegetation in young plantations, forest managers are re-evaluating natural reseeding. It requires no chemicals and no costly nurseries, and in our maritime climate it is usually reliable—though much slower to form a crop. As a result nurseries have been curtailed. For instance, the Lawrencetown facility's chief role in the early 1990s was to supply broad-leaved trees for school programs and provincial parks.

Bridgetown was for years the home of Ernest Buckler, author of The Mountain and the Valley, *an acclaimed 1952 novel set in the Annapolis Valley. Bridgetown sits at the head of tidal navigation on the Annapolis River. Before the bridge was built, New England settlers got by for decades with a ferry. According to Will R. Bird, they were so relieved to finally have a bridge, they named the village after it.*

SIDE TRIP: *Valleyfield Provincial Park*
For an excellent view of the Annapolis Valley and upper Annapolis River, detour to this park. From the nearby fire tower hill you can see how the loops of the river grow steadily larger as they near the basin. The park has picnic tables, toilets, and an interpretive display. Take the road to Hampton north of Bridgetown, drive 4.8 km/3 mi, and watch for the sign.

BACK ON THE HIGHWAY
The Annapolis River from Bridgetown to Granville Centre is a classical mature meandering stream—except that its lower reaches

Fundy's shores are good places to find this rubbery purple alga whose use as food goes back at least to the Vikings. Dulse is sold throughout the Maritimes as a snack and a dietary supplement, and many consider it a delicacy. The plants are about 30 cm/12 in long and grow attached to rocks in the intertidal zone. Commercial dulse is picked or raked by hand at low tide. The best dulse grows in the shade of cliffs; the darker the colour the better. It is dried on the beach or in special ovens. (Five kilograms/11 lb of wet dulse yields about 1 kg/2.2 lb when dry.) It contains most of the minerals and vitamins found in enriched cereals, plus lots of iodine.
"[In] a sort of explosion of the senses, the salty dry seaweed melted on my tongue and triggered a gag reflex."
– First-time dulse eater

have been confined by dykes. Unlike the frisky young mountain brooks that feed it, it runs sedately as befits old age. Its bed is worn nearly to sea level. Meandering from side to side, it travels perhaps 3 km/2 mi to advance 1 km/0.6 mi. The flow is so sluggish it can't even carry sand, so the floodplain consists of fine loam. In the 1970s "tubing"—drifting downstream inside inflated truck inner tubes—became a fad.

SIDE TRIP: *Delaps Cove Wilderness Trail*

Every few kilometres along the highway, you'll see small roads leading north to the Fundy Shore. Most of these roads make their way through narrow valleys lying at right angles to the shore. How did the valleys get there? The answer is that the basalt was fractured north and south, which weakened the rock and allowed streams to erode it.

One of those fractures or faults runs between Port Royal and Delaps Cove. About 2 km/1.2 mi east of Granville Ferry, take Parkers Mountain Road north. Near Mountain Top Cottages you'll see a small roundish lake. Be thankful you're not back in the Jurassic Period when it was a lava vent. From it and other fissures along this ridge came the lava layers that cap the North Mountain.

On the way, you'll pass through a grove of eastern white cedar (*Thuja occidentalis*). Though common from northern New Brunswick west to Manitoba, this native conifer is very rare in Nova Scotia. Natural stands occur at nearby Lawrencetown, near Oxford in Cumberland County, on an island in Silver Lake, Yarmouth County, and at Hectanooga in Digby County. Each appears to be a relic from postglacial times, when the species ranged across a now-submerged coastal plain extending east and south to the Carolinas.

At the cove, pause to examine the zones of marine life displayed on the wharf pilings. In a vertical distance of 6 m/20 ft, they grade from mossy green algae near the top, through rockweed, barnacles (the tiny white cones), snail-like periwinkles, and blue mussels. The reddish growth at low tide mark is Irish moss.

All these marine organisms, unlike those along the Northumberland Strait or the Atlantic coast, must cope with extreme tidal ranges and year-round cold water.

Delaps Cove has a 1.5-km/0.9-mi trail featuring coastal spruce forest, steep basalt cliffs, lava flows, and a waterfall (at Bohaker Cove).

BACK ON THE HIGHWAY

STOP: *Noble Oak*

Granville Ferry boasts a large northern red oak (*Quercus rubra var. borealis*), which was the inspiration for author and local resident H. R. Percy's 1986 novel *Tranter's Tree*—although he made it into an English white oak (*Quercus alba*).

The tree stands opposite the community hall beside the road to

Port Royal. In 1990 its diameter at chest height was 1.4 m /4.6 ft, and it stood 23 m/75 ft tall. Conceivably, British soldiers from Port Royal planted the tree in the 1700s; but it's probably not that old.

STOP: *Annapolis Tidal Generating Station*
As of 1996, this was the Western Hemisphere's only saltwater electrical generation plant. It harnesses the Annapolis River's tidal flow to turn a 20-m/65-ft-diameter turbine, which produces about 20 Mw of electricity.

Inspiration for Tranter's Tree
Granville Ferry

Although France and a few other countries produce ocean tidal power, this is so far the only use of the Bay of Fundy's vast potential. Several major studies have been done. Apart from the high cost (compared to relatively cheap oil), the extreme tidal range, and the likelihood of equipment damage by storms and ice, there are ecological constraints. Among these are possible harm to Fundy fisheries and shorebirds, and the slight possibility of upsetting local weather. There is also the risk of triggering local earthquakes.

Even the Annapolis project has had its critics. Some feel that reducing tidal flow has increased frost damage to local crops. In fact, the reduction was due to building the causeway many years before; the tidal power station has helped to restore the estuary to its natural state by allowing salt water to flow in and out daily.

The brown foam that blows across the causeway comes from the turbine, which churns up froth like an eggbeater. It isn't a pollutant and will not corrode metal. The colour is due to natural tannin in the water, most of which originates in bogs and coniferous forests on the Southern Upland. A powerful underwater acoustic barrier (i.e., noise-maker) deters most fish from entering the turbine. Two fishways allow safe passage for migrating gaspereaux, shad, salmon, smelt, trout, and bass.

Nova Scotia Power, Inc. operates a free interpretive centre, open May 15–October 15.

The Annapolis River was rejected as a Canadian Heritage River because settlement and farming had altered it too much. A local group, the Clean Annapolis River Project (CARP), is determined to change this by raising public awareness, cleaning the river and its tributaries, and monitoring water quality. Since about 1970 shellfish harvesting in the estuary has been banned due to pollution and "red tides." [See also the **Marine Drive** at Ship Harbour.]

The "Tranter's Tree" oak at Granville Ferry has a noonday shadow spanning 25.5 m/84 ft. Although seldom chosen for the purpose, this hardy native species makes a fine ornamental and shade tree. Its handsomely scalloped leaves turn deep crimson in autumn, and the tree holds many leaves all winter. Red oak wood is nearly as strong as white oak, but it is useless for ships' hulls, because it leaks.

LEG-STRETCHER: *Annapolis Royal's Historic Gardens*
This is one of the delights of the whole tour: 4 ha/10 ac of theme gardens and interpretive displays reflecting the area's natural and

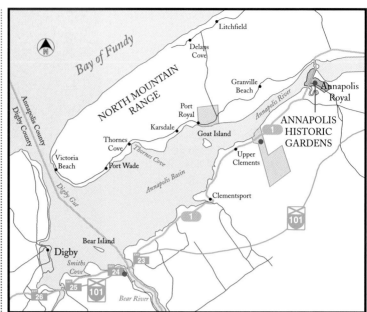

It was on that ground [Port Royal, 1605] was grown the first wheat ever raised in America, and in the rocky suburbs was constructed the first waterwheel to turn a millstone on this Continent ...
— Robert R. McLeod, **Markland, or Nova Scotia,** 1903

human history. Here you can explore an Acadian garden and cottage, smell the Victorians' favourite flowers, see a splendid rose collection, and follow a woodland path featuring native flora in formal settings. It's also a good place to find out about the apple varieties the Acadians brought to Nova Scotia.

The gardens slope down to a freshwater marsh, which Ducks Unlimited has restored to enhance waterfowl habitat. Along the edges in late summer note the 3-m/10-ft reed (*Phragmitis communis*), sometimes called elephant grass. A persistent local myth says it arrived from seed swept from a passing circus train. Actually, the grass is native to western Nova Scotia. Acadians likely used it for thatching roofs.

To reach the gardens, exit Hwy 1 at Route 8 (Upper Saint George Street) and drive a few blocks south. They're open from May to mid-October, 8:00 am to dusk; admission is charged.

Port Royal (11.5 km/7.1 mi west of Granville Ferry) on the basin, the French habitation from 1605 to 1613, was mainland North America's earliest post-Viking European settlement north of Florida.

The first dykes in the New World were constructed along the mouth of the Annapolis River soon after 1605 to reclaim what are now called the Queen Anne and Dentabelle marshes opposite Port Royal National Historic Park.

By 1817 the British had a rough road straight from Halifax to Annapolis Royal. The part from New Ross past West Dalhousie (birthplace of author Ernest Buckler) and Lequille on Rte 8 is still used.

"It is a lovely scenic drive through the valley," wrote Will R. Bird in *This Is Nova Scotia*, "but the highway from Annapolis to Digby is simply thrilling, with a height of land overlooking the water, the basin showing to best advantage, quick corners, tiny villages, ascents and descents, brooks, hedges, fine homes."

Much has changed since that book was published in 1950—yet much remains the same. The sheltered basin that so charmed

Champlain and de Monts in 1605 is still charming, scallop draggers still unload their catches at the Digby wharf, and one can climb the lookoff above Bear River and enjoy the same bold panorama.

Elephant grass at Annapolis Royal Historic Gardens

LEG-STRETCHER: *Wildlife Walk*

Wild creatures are so shy that sometimes the only place to get a good look at them is in a zoo or park. Upper Clements Wildlife Park will show you more native wildlife in an hour than you could see in the woods in a lifetime.

Opened in 1976, this park includes hiking trails, a freshwater marsh (Ryerson Meadow), and a picnic park with washrooms. On its 12 ha/ 30 ac of woodland there are more than 20 exhibits. The trails wend through mixed forest past naturalistic enclosures housing lynx, porcupine, foxes, woodchuck, deer, and moose. (On a slow day the moose will sometimes stroll over to see you.) There is also an English red deer donated by Queen Elizabeth II on her Silver Jubilee in 1978.

One of the most fascinating creatures here is the eastern cougar. In colonial times this very shy greyish lion with the distinctively thick tail and small head was fairly common in eastern Canada. Settlers killed it on sight. For decades it seemed extinct. Since the 1940s, however, numerous sightings and signs, first in New Brunswick and then in Nova Scotia, suggest that it's making a comeback. Its main food is white-tailed deer.

The park is located 5 km/3 mi west of Annapolis Royal and 25 km/15 mi east of Digby. (Watch for the sign on Hwy 1, opposite the Upper Clements Family Vacation Park.)

A few years back, the province passed the park over to the Upper

[For] a full century ... Port Royal ... became famous as the spot where the fierce disputes concentrated in besiegements, assaults, and surrenders, till the town had no rival in that kind of business on the whole Continent. It has been taken by force five times by the English .... It was ... restored to the French four times .... It was unsuccessfully attacked by the English three times ... unsuccessfully attacked by the French and Indians twice .... It was taken, sacked, and abandoned twice—once by pirates in 1690, and once by United States Revolutionary Forces in 1781.
– Robert R. McLeod, **Markland, or Nova Scotia**, 1903

Annapolis Royal

Clements Wildlife Park Society, a non-profit community group. One way they raise funds is through the "Adopt-An-Animal" Program. By donating from $10 to $500, you can house and feed various creatures for a year. [See also the **Fleur-de-lis Trail** for Two Rivers Wildlife Park

Forte Anne

171

Annapolis water gap

near Marion Bridge and the **Halifax-Dartmouth Area Nature Tour** for Shubenacadie Wildlife Park on Hwy 2 just north of Milford.]

VIEW: *Annapolis Basin Lookoff*
If you take Exit 24, pull into the parking lot, climb wooden steps, and walk up the hill, you'll emerge at the edge of an old pasture from which you can survey the whole Annapolis Basin. The town along its west end is Digby. The gap in North Mountain is Digby Gut, through which the Saint John ferry MV *Princess of Acadia* comes and goes. On the near shore to your left is Smiths Cove, and to your right is the mouth of Bear River with Bear Island beyond.

Annapolis River

No wonder Champlain chose this area as the site of his first permanent settlement in New France. Sheltered from Fundy fogs and cold north winds, teeming with marsh birds, shellfish, and finfish, rich in fertile alluvium, ringed with forests of maple, pine, and oak, it was a prize indeed.

The most striking feature is Digby Gut. It was created when a north-flowing ancestor of Bear River cut through North Mountain along an ancient fault. Since the last glaciation, the sea has flooded the basin, forming this perfect harbour.

The grassy lookoff itself is interesting. Clearly, by the kinds of plants along the lane from the parking lot, it was once part of a farm homestead. Besides native sugar maple, ash, and white spruce, there are cultivated cherry, apple, and plum trees. Halfway up on the basin side there's a large clump of ornamental snowberry, a sure sign of habitation.

The farm itself is overrun with native goldenrod and young white spruce. White-tailed deer are attracted by the fruit trees and grass; you may find their trails and bedding places. The brown-barked trees along the managed pasture to the west are native black cherry, likely planted by birds dropping cherry pits from previous meals.

There is an open dug well, 3 m/10 ft deep, in the spruce thicket just west of the lookoff. Though dry in summer, it could cause a nasty fall.

Digby Gut occupies one of several large north/south faults along Digby Neck, stress fractures from the breakup of Pangaea 200 million years ago. At that time earthquakes wracked the North Mountain, shattering rocks and wrenching adjoining parts up to 2 km/1.2 mi out of line. Later these clefts were widened by rivers flowing into Fundy off the Southern Upland, and by glaciation. Valleys too high for the rising sea to reach (e.g., Delaps Cove, Gullivers Cove) became "wind gaps." [See also the **Trans Canada**

Highway at Wentworth.] The deeper ones became "water gaps," of which Digby Gut is the most pronounced. Others are Petite Passage (Digby Neck/Long Island) and Grand Passage (Long Island/Brier Island). These dislocations show clearly on a road map.

VIEW: *Stupendous Squeeze*
Not far downhill from the lookoff, beside the Bear River exit ramp, there's a vivid example of folded bedrock. Rather than drive by it, walk the 100 m/330 ft or so down the curving ramp. High on the west side, in a rock wall dynamited out of solid blue and red slate, there's what looks like an end view of a giant telephone book that was folded almost double. The folding occurred when ancestral North America and Africa collided ever so slowly over 400 million years ago. Gazing at this arch of stone, one can imagine the stupendous forces involved.

Anticline in roadcut

Bear River is the unofficial cherry capital of Nova Scotia. In mid-July, when the trees are extravagantly beautiful, the town stages its annual Cherry Blossom Festival.

NOTE: From Smiths Cove to St Bernard, Hwy 101 merges with Hwy 1. To access the **Digby Neck Scenic Trail**, take Rte 303 into Digby and exit left onto Hwy 217 toward Seabrook and Rossway.

Leaving the Annapolis Basin's rugged shore, the trail runs for five or six minutes through low woodland and alder thickets before emerging on the shore of St Marys Bay. The long dimpled blue line across the bay to the north is Digby Neck.

Geologically, St Marys Bay is an extension of the Annapolis Valley that was flooded by the rising postglacial ocean. It is floored with the same rust-coloured sandstone we saw at Blomidon. You can see this formation at Red Head across the bay and near Plympton on this side. [See also the **Marine Drive** at Chedabucto Bay and the **Glooscap Trail** at West Advocate and at Truro.] So the shoreline is eroding steadily eastward. Within a thousand years it may reach the Annapolis Basin. Long before that, a small rise in sea level could flood most of the land between.

From the head of St Marys Bay to Meteghan, Hwy 101 rides over a low plain of rumpled

Nova Scotia has three native wild cherries: pin cherry (named for its hatpin-like fruit clusters), chokecherry (the fruit "furs" the palate), and black cherry, a tree prized for its dark wood. Like the apple, the cherry was domesticated in ancient times. Its European ancestor is extinct, and the cultivars "gone wild." Like their close relatives the plum, apricot, almond, and peach, cherries belong to the rose family. **Warning:** *The pits, foliage, and twigs of all cherries contain cyanide. Chopped leaves placed in a killing bottle are said to kill insects, and cattle have died from eating the foliage. The fruit is harmless.*

Shallows are ... found [at the] head of St Marys Bay ... [which] is exposed to gales and swells from the southwest. Under such circumstances, rough conditions are found close to the shore between Meteghan and Saulnierville due to shoaling. Beyond Church Point, the waves diminish markedly. The Bay is largely protected to the north and northwest by Digby Neck, Long Island and Brier Island.
— Scotia/Fundy Marine Weather Guide

glacial drift deposited on Meguma quartzites, slate, and greywacke. The landscape plays variations on a theme of small coves with fishing boats and lobster pots, seaside homes with marigolds and potato plots, gnarled, leaning apple trees and narrow pastures running arrow-straight back to dark coniferous forest.

Typically, the coastal forest is mostly stunted white spruce and balsam fir with a sprinkling of birch, poplar, and mountain-ash. Hike a short distance inland, however, away from the windy shore with its cool salt air, and you'll find tall red spruce, maple, and birch.

Much of the land is flat, but at Weymouth the Sissiboo River's curving gorge and drowned valley afford relief. In autumn its steep slopes are brocaded with the reds and yellows of maple, birch, and aspen. Look north while crossing the bridge for a notch in the skyline of Digby Neck where ancestral Sissiboo probably ran before St Marys Bay existed.

South of Weymouth we enter the French Shore proper, a 48-km/ 30-mi corridor of houses, farms, and fishing wharves sometimes called the "Longest Main Street in North America." Its place-names and patois echo old Brittany and Normandy. Property boundaries reflect the old French seigniorial custom of subdividing land within families (also seen in Québec's Eastern Townships). After two centuries, some lots are a mere 200 m/660 ft wide.

The district was settled in 1769 by about 300 Acadian families who walked to Nova Scotia from Massachusetts and beyond, a journey that took several years. Some stayed in New Brunswick (Antonine Maillet's novel Pélagie *vividly recounts what such a trek must have been like). Others continued on to Minas Basin. Some died on the way.*

Finding their lands taken by New Englanders, they continued on to Annapolis Royal. Here they stayed the winter on the promise of land grants along St Marys Bay. In the spring the British allotted each family a strip of beach for mooring boats and drying fish, space for a house, garden, and outbuildings, some pasture, and a woodlot.

Fishing, lumbering, and shipbuilding are the main occupations along this shore. Being wide open to the Atlantic, the coast is often too stormy for small boats to put to sea. But the fishery here has one advantage—there's no drift ice. This means the fishing season is longer than along the Eastern Shore.

You'll see some idle land and run-down barns. As motor power replaced oxen and horses after World War II, growing hay became less important. Hayfields were left unmown and pastures ungrazed. Alders invaded the wetter fields, goldenrod and aster the drier ones. At St Bernard Hwy 101 swings away inland, and the Trail follows Hwy 1 again.

The massive stone church at St Bernard took 32 years to build—one course of granite blocks a year. From this shore the wind gaps of Digby Neck are clearly visible as notches in the skyline. The easternmost notch is Sandy Cove [see also the **Digby Neck Scenic Drive** and the **Trans Canada Highway** at Mahoneys Corner]. Because it lines up with the Sissiboo River, some geologists think it was carved by the ancestral Sissiboo before St Marys Bay existed.

174

STOP: *Belliveau Beach*

Even when the ocean is calm, this short detour just beyond St Bernard gives a strong sense of its power. The cove is tiled with heaps of flattened bluish stones that rattle underfoot. These stones, varying from saucer to platter size, their edges rounded from tumbling in the surf, typify a shingle beach. They are flat because they derive from layered slate cliffs. (Cobble beaches have oval stones derived from rectangular blocks.) [See also the **Lighthouse Route**, the **Marine Drive** near Cape Canso, and the **Cabot Trail** at Green Cove.]

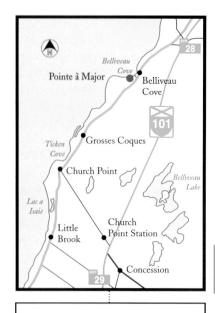

Take the beach road (not the Pointe à Major road) off Hwy 1 just south of Belliveau Cove and follow it 1 km/0.6 mi to the parking lot.

The clams of Grosses Coques (French for "big clams"), about 6 km/4 mi south of Belliveau Cove, are said to be the largest on the Eastern Seaboard.

STOP: *L'Église Sainte Marie*

Pause at Church Point to examine the largest wooden church in North America. It was built between 1903 and 1905 by master carpenter Leo Melanson of nearby Little Brook. Its white Gothic spire soars 56 m/185 ft, a landmark for fishers far out to sea. Knowing well the bay's powerful winds, Melanson ballasted the tower with 36 tonnes of rock. Even so, during autumn gales it sways and creaks like a great tree. Inside you'll see marble-like whiteness rainbowed by stained glass and mellowed by a honey-coloured wooden floor. The pillars are not marble but enormous plastered tree trunks; the arches are of wood as well.

STOP: *Smugglers Cove Provincial Park*

This sea-carved cove with its little shingle beach—supposed haunt of 19th-century privateers and pirates—is a good place to stretch your legs and inhale the salt breeze. Climb the wooden stairs for a good view of the Horse's Rump to the north and of Cape St Marys to the south.

The cliffs are mostly clay that settled and hardened near the South Pole 500 million years ago. During mountain-building epochs that accompanied the formation of the supercontinent Pangaea, immense pressures folded the slates and changed some of them to schist, a rock that sometimes commonly sparkles with blackish mica flakes.

A short walk south of the parking lot, there's a well-kept little park and cemetery with a monument to local pioneers. L'Anse-des-Belliveaux was the first post-Expulsion Acadian settlement in Clare District, and its cemetery is the oldest such in the province (1769).

After British authorities lifted the ban on Acadian settlement in 1763, groups of exiles who had wandered for a decade along the Eastern Seaboard began to trickle back. Folklore says the first group landed at Church Point. Seeing the tree-covered, rocky land, and recalling the fertile Minas and Annapolis meadows, some of the men wept. The story is that when the rowboat touched the beach, Madeleine LeBlanc grabbed an axe, leaped ashore, and felled the first tree in Clare District.

Meteghan is the French Shore's busiest port because it has adapted three traditional mainstays to modern times: shipbuilding, fishing, and lumbering. Local builders craft small pleasure boats and custom-built antique-style vessels. This in turn keeps the sawmills humming. Meteghan also operates a diverse and modern fishing fleet—more work for the boatbuilders. Scallop draggers, trawlers, herring seiners, and cod and lobster boats call this port home.

One of Nova Scotia's largest sawmills, E. M. Comeau Lumber Company, is located here. It saws over three million board feet (531,000,000 m³) of lumber a year. Two even larger mills operate at nearby Meteghan Station. Ask locally about arranging a visit to the shipyard or a mill.

South of Meteghan we leave the shelter of Digby Neck. From here to Salmon River we move due south over a landscape dominated by Meguma slates ground down by glaciers. Slate derives from clay, and clay is slippery. So the glaciers, instead of bulldozing the soil into the sea, slid over it, kneading and moulding beautiful whaleback hills called drumlins. [See also the **Lighthouse Route** at Mahone Bay and the **Marconi Trail** at Mira River.] Clay makes a watertight soil, hence the numerous lakes, ponds, alder swales, and salt marshes here.

STOP: *Seashell Trove*

One of Nova Scotia's best places for collecting seashells is Mavillette Beach Provincial Park between Cape St Marys and Davids Point. Over 100 species have been collected. Storms from a vast fetch of southern ocean pummel this 1.5-km/1-mi sandy beach.

When spring comes to the salt marsh behind the beach, bobolinks bound from tuft to tuft, and large sandpipers called willets nest near several small ponds. There are also savannah sparrows.

The cove was eroded out of a pocket of softer Silurian volcanic tuff and related rocks. Although a human-made wall of great boulders protects the mouth of the brook, battering winter waves continually undermine it. NOTE: A dirt road crosses the tidal inlet on a narrow bridge, but it is rough and could be washed out. According to Dr Albert Roland and others, this shore is sinking about 25 cm/10 in per century. [See also the **Sunrise Trail** and the **Marine Drive.**] Because of this, storm waves behave unusually here. Normally they scoop sand from one place and dump it in another, maintaining the shore's overall level. But on a submerging coast, especially one comprised of glacial deposits over soft bedrock, the sea gains steadily. Davids Point, which supplies most of the material for Mavillette Beach, is visibly undermined. Please use the boardwalks. DNR put them here to protect the fragile marram grasses that anchor the dunes.

To reach the park, exit the trail just north of Mavillette Creek and drive 1 km/0.6 mi along St Marys Bay Marsh to the picnic area beside the beach. Along the way, note how the marsh vegetation grades from freshwater rushes and reeds near the bridge to saltwater plants near the beach's tidal inlet.

Another 2 km/1.2 mi takes you out to the cape. From here there are spectacular views of the coast past Black Point and Cranberry Point south to Yarmouth Bar. Geologists have traced several ice ages in the glacial gravels and shales displayed at the cape.

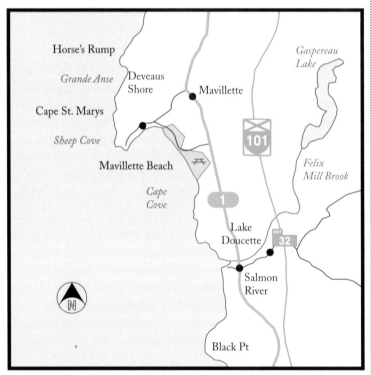

Glaciers flowed in different directions in different parts of the province (e.g., southeast near Halifax, southwest near Glace Bay).

VIEW: *Odd-Shaped Ponds*

Looking south from the highway toward Salmon River, we see a peaceful panorama of salt marsh, drumlin, stream, and ocean. The river, after its short journey from Lake Doucette, has built a marshy estuary with odd U-shaped ponds on either side. As a stream near sea level loops from side to side, some of the loops come so close to each other that sometimes the river takes a short cut between them. The resulting loop is called an oxbow lake (after the wooden neck loop that secures an ox's yoke).

Westward, between the marsh and the coastal spruce forest, water-tolerant alders have invaded old fields.

Between Mavillette and Darlings Lake we leave the slate behind to cross harder Meguma quartzites and greywacke.

VIEW: *Drumlin*

South of the highway at Darlings Lake, near the Short Beach–Sandford exit, sits a classic drumlin. Its streamlined oval rises from the surrounding flats like a whale's back from the sea. The blunt end faced "upstream" to the moving ice, which flowed right to left as part of a major thrust across southern New Brunswick. [See also **Lighthouse Route** near Lunenburg, **Marconi Trail**, etc.]

Like the Mavillette area, the Yarmouth region had a lively volcanic history. There's a lot of basalt and tuff mingled with the soft Silurian sandstone and slate. Evidence of severe Earth stresses are found in northeast/southwest faults, the largest being along the Atlantic shore west of Mahone Bay.

VIEWS: *Lupin Country*

This part of the route has been called "The Lupin Trail." Between Port Maitland and Hebron from mid-June through July, the summer fields are awash in blues, purples, and pinks. Lupins are members of the pea family introduced from the West decades ago, probably in livestock feed. Some may be garden escapees. The two common species abound near Yarmouth. They are said to poison cattle; in farming districts (e.g., Truro, Windsor) they are eradicated wherever possible.

Lupins

Not being a dairy district, this part of Nova Scotia celebrates its lupins. The citizens are also developing a 2.3-km/1.4-mi interpretive trail featuring the area's natural and human history.

SIDE TRIP:

Chebogue Meadows Interpretive Trail

For a leisurely 1.5-hr walk through coastal forest and marsh along the upper Chebogue River, hike this trail a few kilometres east of Hebron. It illustrates 12 wildlife habitats typical of southwest Nova Scotia, including young and old coastal spruce-fir, a black spruce bog, windblown and cutover forest, meadow, a forest thinning, freshwater marsh, and the Chebogue River itself. Each habitat has interpretive signage.

Lupins, like the lichen-derived litmus used in soil-testing kits, indicate soil pH. Redder flowers suggest acidic soil, bluer flowers alkaline.

The walking is fairly easy, but the soil is thin and rocky and sometimes wet. In places there are natural beds of coarse rock crushed by the weight and freezing action of the glacier. You'll see inkberry, a native holly restricted to the Atlantic coast of southern Nova Scotia.

These habitats support a wide variety of wildlife—kinglets in the tops of conifers, white-tailed deer in the swamp, raccoon by the stream, great blue herons and minnows in the marsh. Large nearby lakes (e.g., Lake George to the north) support breeding colonies of great black-backed gulls. The trail is 4.5 km/2.8 mi long, with a loop that crosses the river twice.

To locate the trailhead from Main Street in Yarmouth, drive east on Starrs Road past the Hwy 103 exit to the next set of lights (Hwy

1 or Hardscratch Road). Turn left and drive 8 km/5 mi, passing Brooklyn Road and the Greenville Road lights. Continue about 2 km/1.2 mi until you see Our Lady of Peace Catholic Church on the right; 800 m/0.5 mi farther on, on the same side, there's a parking lot with a large sign.

For an excellent natural history of the Yarmouth region, read C. R. K. Allen's *A Naturalist's Notebook*, found at the Sign of the Whale art and pottery shop and in local bookstores.

When hiking in southwest Nova Scotia from April to July, make a habit of checking for ticks after walking through grassy or brushy areas. (It's best not to bring pets to such areas.) Keep slacks and pants tucked into socks. Before leaving, check yourself, pets, and companions for the tiny, grey spider-like creatures. That way you can dispatch them before they dig in. If they have already done so, grasp the tick's abdomen firmly and pull slowly and steadily until its jaws let go. Should the head come off, tweeze it from the skin as you would a splinter and bathe the spot briskly in clean soapy water. [See also Lighthouse Route.]

In late June–early July check local pools and ditches for yellow iris. Escaped long ago from gardens, this native of Europe has become locally naturalized. [See **Fleur-de-lis Nature Tour** *at Louisbourg.]*

"The Fleet Going Out" (detail) by Fred B. Schell, **Picturesque Canada** (1884)

BACK ON THE HIGHWAY

Yarmouth is an old Loyalist seaport and manufacturing town that is home to Atlantic Canada's largest herring fleet and is the key ferry link to Maine. Here the **Evangeline Trail** ends, and the **Lighthouse Route** begins.

SIDE TRIP: *Forchu*

The breakwater at Cape Forchu is worth a visit just to see the immense boulders and cement slabs that protect it, and in the off-season, the hundreds of lobster pots and colourful buoys. Imagine the sea's power here in a fall hurricane or a February gale!

The local bedrock is unusually diverse, and colourful too. Besides the common dark grey basalt and reddish rhyolite, you may see cement-like lava and ash deposits (smooth where waves have polished it, jagged inland), volcanic tuffs spongy with gas bubbles, and, rarely, spindle-shaped "bombs" flung skyward by ancient volcanoes. [See also the **Fleur-de-lis Trail** near Gabarus.]

Ask locally about The Churn. After a big southeaster, this gully flings geysers many metres in the air.

Exit Hwy 1 at the statue of the Golden Horse in Yarmouth, turn south, drive over the bridge, and continue 0.7 km/0.4 mi. Turn left on Rte 304, with Yarmouth Harbour on your left, and go past Overton and the Churn to Yarmouth Bar. (You may want to walk the magnificent sandbar, or bird-watch here in season.) Forchu's East and West capes lie about 3 km/2 mi beyond, with Outer False Harbour between.

Fleur-de-lis Trail Nature Tour

Canso Causeway to Louisbourg
220 km/137 mi

River Bourgeois

St Peter's Canal

Fleur de lis properly refers to the iris, a close relative of the lily. Our common native species is Blue Flag, Iris versicolor, found in meadows, swamps, wet grazed pastures and along streams. In 2000, the Quebec National Assembly adopted this flower as its floral emblem instead of the non-native white lily.

OVERVIEW

Except for a sheltered stretch between Port Hastings and L'Ardoise, the **Fleur-de-lis Trail** is pure Atlantic coast. Gales lash it, fog often hides the sun, and drift ice sometimes clogs its eastern shores well into June. Yet in smiling weather it is unforgettable.

From the air, the land is a gently furrowed shelf of coniferous woodland, lake, and bog sloping gently south and east from Bras d'Or Lake. Except for the East Bay Hills, the land is low. Spread across it like peanut butter are dollops and swirls of glacial gravels that have made ten small lakes out of one big one and transformed a small stream like the Mira into a broad river. Along the hard-rock volcanic coast the sea has sculpted these gravels into superlative sand beaches and labyrinthine marshes that swarm with wildfowl spring and fall.

The forest along this unprotected shore consists of balsam fir with white and black spruce, their sombre colours relieved in autumn by the golds of tamarack, white birch, and trembling aspen. Here and there on fertile soils a grove of balsam poplar spreads its heart-shaped leaves. Inland, away from wind and salt spray, one finds yellow birch, red maple, white pine, and a scattered elm.

This trail cannot boast the autumn glories of highland Nova Scotia. Sugar maple and beech are rare. The best it can manage is russet and gold with a flash of scarlet here and there. But its peat bogs are beautiful carpets of burgundy, jade, and tan; its barrens glow with the crimson of blueberry; its wind-washed marshes shimmer in old gold and cobalt blue.

River Bourgeois

Along this coast you'll hear echoes of France and Spain in names like Grande Anse ("big bay") and Petit-de-Grat (French/Basque for "place where cod is dried.") Both countries fished cod here 400 years ago.

THE TOUR BEGINS

Port Hawkesbury in the Strait of Canso has now become ... second only to Sydney as a port.
– Robert R. McLeod, **Markland, or Nova Scotia,** *1903*

From Port Hastings we follow Highway 4 southeast along Canso Strait past the Embrees Brook inlet to Port Hawkesbury—known as Ship Harbour in the days when hundreds of sailing ship captains prized its shelter. Just east of town, at the lights, we stay with Hwy 4 toward Cleveland, Grande Anse, and St Peters.

This Coal Age landscape is nearly at sea level because its soft bedrock has been weathering and eroding for 300 million years. As the elm-dotted farmlands of River Inhabitants suggest, the resulting soils are fairly fertile. But most of the country is still woodland, primarily mixtures of maple, birch, and fir. Along the roads one sees a lot of pasture (white) spruce where abandoned fields have been colonized.

A little over 3 km/2 mi east of Cleveland, on Steeles Brook, a tributary of River Inhabitants, there's a picnic area. Here you can rest and get your bearings before tackling the long stretch of rolling woodland and lakes toward Louisdale. This heavily glaciated country wears many rounded, drumlin-like hills of gravel. [See also the **Glooscap Trail** at Old Barns, the **Lighthouse Route** near Lunenburg, and the **Evangeline Trail** near Yarmouth.]

In 1970 the tanker Arrow *foundered near here. Despite vigorous clean-up efforts, traces of oil pollution still taint the salt marshes and mud flats.*

It appears that 10,000 years ago Bras d'Or Lake still had its own glacier, with two more on the coastal plain off Glace Bay and Fourchu. Advancing and retreating, these sheets of ice plucked up bedrock, bulldozed washboard ridges of gravel around Loch Lomond, and dumped whaleback drumlins around St Peter's and Mira. Some of these are 30 m/98 ft thick. A few thousand years later plants, animals, and humans from west and south recolonized the land.

Tombolos at Isle Madame

At Louisdale, instead of driving on toward Grande Anse take a delectable side trip. Double back on Hwy 104 to Exit 46 and take Rte 320 across the long island-causeway to Isle Madame (named for a French queen). From Martinique, drive clockwise around this historic district. Stop at D'Escousse (longtime home of N.S. writer Silver Donald Cameron), Pondville Beach Provincial Park, and Arichat (county seat, seaport since 1700s, pop. c. 900). Spur roads branch off to Petit-de-Grat (the chief fishing centre) and to Little Anse, a mecca for landscape artists.

Like Cheticamp in western Cape Breton and St Marys Bay on the Evangeline Trail, the island fairly breathes Acadian culture. Get a good local map, ask directions, visit its museums and historic sites; above all, talk to people. To see shorebirds and waterfowl, dawdle along Lennox Passage between Isle Madame and the mainland. (Two good places are Lennox Passage bridge and the picnic park at nearby Martinique.) The passage's many islands and tidal marshes act as a magnet to waterfowl and shorebirds, especially during migration.

In late August watch for whimbrel, a long-legged brownish shorebird that is often plentiful then around Petit-de-Grat and Cape Auguet. On migration it hop-scotches from barren to barren down the coast, feeding on crowberries and blueberries. Then it crosses Chedabucto Bay and continues down the Atlantic shore. From Arichat, return by Rte 206 to Hwy 4.

STOP: *St Peter's Canal*

The English dug this waterway between Bras d'Or Lake and Chedabucto Bay between 1854 and 1869, following an ancient Mi'kmaq portage route. The canal saved ships bound for Sydney Harbour a long and dangerous 120-km/ 75-mi voyage out around Scatarie Island or Cape North. Since tide times differ between lake and ocean, to save time a lock has been installed at either end to lift or lower vessels. The lock is 91 m/300 ft long, 15 m/50 ft wide, and 6 m/20 ft deep at low tide. St Peter's

St Peters Canal

Inlet itself is an eroded soft-rock valley drowned by the rising postglacial ocean.

If you'd like an ecological boat tour of this many-fingered inland sea, contact a local tourist visitor centre.

St Peter's pre-dates both Louisbourg and Halifax. The Portuguese who caught and cured cod here in the early 1600s called it San Pedro. In 1713 the French renamed it Port Toulouse. Today there's little to show for its long history save a bronze plaque and a cleared site near a lighthouse.

The first to settle here was French entrepreneur Nicolas Denys. In 1650, after a rival trader drove him from his Chedabucto fishing station, Denys built a fort and trading post just south of where Hwy 4 crosses the canal. Well aware of the site's strategic importance for the Bras d'Or fur trade, he built a stockade. Soon he had cleared 33 ha/80 ac for crops, orchard, and pasture.

Denys also built a timber skidway across the 0.8-km/0.5-mi isthmus for hauling small vessels to and fro. Imagine the surprise of Mi'kmaq travellers on first seeing the mast of a ship moving through the trees.

For millennia the lake had been a Mi'kmaq domain. They liked Nicolas Denys, a just man and devout Roman Catholic, even to making up jokes about him. George F. Clarke in *Return to Acadia* says they characterized the song sparrow as saying, in their language, "Ti-ne-li-am—Nicolai—Nicolai—Denys?—Denys?" ("Where are you going, Nicolas Denys?") Denys' essay *Concerning the Ways of the Indians* is one of the earliest and most astute European accounts of the lifeways of northeastern First Peoples. Eskasoni, Christmas Island, and Chapel Island/Soldier's Cove still have sizeable native communities. [See also the **Bras d'Or Scenic Drive**.]

After St Peter's the trail switches to Rte 247. Watch for the sign 1 km/0.6 mi east of town, by the provincial highways building. Turn south there.

STOP: *L'Ardoise*

This French word, locally pronounced *Lord*ways, means "slate," a reference to Carboniferous cliffs that line the shore and underlie much of Chedabucto Bay. Ask for the best path down to them. These hardened clays end suddenly 1 km/0.6 mi east of the village. Here a major fault marks the beginning of the Precambrian Fourchu Group volcanic rocks that dominate the rest of the trail. You'll see dark grey basalt and tuff, pinkish rhyolite, white granite, and quartz, as well as quartzite and sandstone. This jumbled geology reflects the Cape Breton's complex and violent origins as island fragments came together in Precambrian time.

STOP: *Point Michaud Beach*

Uncrowded beachcombing. Sand between your toes. Boom and swash of surf. This provincial park offers these on 2 km/1.2 mi of ivory-white sand pounded firm by strong waves. Watch for the small, wooden sign just east of L'Ardoise, turn right, and park in the lot overlooking the beach.

Walking down to the strand, observe the succession from white spruce to marram grass to sand dune. Normally a few centuries would reforest such dunes. But since the sea keeps rising (or the land sinking), the process is slow. The speed of dune erosion is demonstrated a few kilometres east at L'Archeveque (near Grand River). Before the breakwater was built, sand accumulated so fast that dredges could barely keep the entrance open for the lobster fleet.

The dark blackish cliff behind the beach is green basalt marbled with white quartz and overlaid with iron-rich glacial drift. Shore plants include crowberry, blueberry, bayberry, foxberry, and sedges. One sees the odd angelica, probably introduced from Louisbourg, where it is colonizing the fields. Lying on the crowberry one may see rock crab skeletons emptied and discarded by gulls or tossed up by waves.

Beachcombing is rewarding here, for the beach is wide open to southeast gales. Washed up on the ribbed sands one finds rockweed (*Fucus* or *Ascophyllum*—also called bladderwrack because of the air-filled nodes that keep it afloat). Sometimes there's a clump of blue mussels attached by silken threads. From deeper water come the rubbery brown fronds of kelp, some over a metre long, wrenched from their root-like holdfasts by the pounding surf.

Other flotsam and jetsam may include the shells of burrowing razor and surf clams, gull feathers and starfish, empty exoskeletons of crabs and sea urchins, broken lobster pots, white, orange, and green lobster buoys, soggy bolts of pulpwood, debarked tree trunks, empty plastic bleach bottles and motor oil containers, green and yellow polypropylene rope, a forlorn glove or boot.

Marine biologists have concluded from a study of dinocysts (microscopic marine fossils) that Bras d'Or Lake was likely salt from 10,000 to 9,000 years ago, before the land had recovered from its load of glacial ice. After that coastal rebound kept the sea out for millenia, making it a freshwater lake. Today it's salty again; but not as salty as the sea.

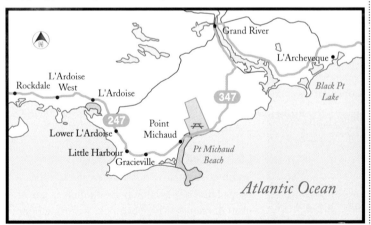

The wooded hump at the beach's south end is Point Michaud, once an island. The beach joining it to the shore is called a tombolo. Tombolos are formed where longshore currents lag and dump suspended silt. Walk 2.5 km/1.5 mi south and you'll discover

... in late spring and early summer fog is frequent, dense and persistent.
– Scotia/Fundy Marine Weather Guide

Grand River Falls
If you'd like to see and hear one of the prettiest waterfalls in these parts, and maybe do some angling for salmon or trout in season, turn north in the village of Grand River onto the Loch Lomond Road. Drive about 9.5 km/ 5.7 mi to a bridge, from which you should see a sign to the left and a road that leads 1.4 km/ .8 mi to the falls. The cataract spills some 10 m/33 ft over a ledge of harder Devonian rock that forms the river valley's west slope. If you plan to fish, ask locally about a guide and be sure to get a licence (corner stores carry them).

another tombolo arching toward Red Point, backed by a marsh and brackish lake. Some of these beaches may have originated offshore and migrated inward as sea level rose.

So much sand! Where did all this come from? Not from the bedrock; most of that is too hard. No, most of it came from glacial gravels, drumlins in particular. As gravel pits reveal, drumlins contain everything from boulders to fine silt—but mostly they're sand. The sandbar across the mouth of Grand River clearly came from the sawed-off drumlin nearby.

In winter these beaches look strangely steep and bare. Storms are much fiercer then. They strip away the sand, leaving coarser stones and pebbles in step-like berms marking the reach of the waves. Against these berms the sea flings cobbles the size of bricks, sucking them back with a grinding roar. In slate areas with rounded coves, this lapidary action produces beautiful blue-grey rocks, some almost oval. [See also the **Evangeline Trail** at Belliveau Beach.]

NOTE: Prepare for a rougher ride between Point Michaud and Framboise. Rte 247 is dirt road north along the Grand River estuary, then pavement to L'Archeveque, then more gravel to Framboise. However, the dirt portions are reasonably well groomed, and traffic is light enough to keep dust within bounds. From Point Michaud to Fourchu the glacial drift is especially deep, forming sea cliffs as high as 10-storey buildings.

VIEWS: *Framboise*

Abundant wild raspberries gave this place its lovely name, and Scottish Highlanders who followed the French in the early 1800s retained it. (Locals pronounce it *Fram-boys.*) Here is one of the best tidal marshes along this coast. The convoluted estuary of half-submerged glacial drift extends nearly 5 km/3 mi to the Atlantic. Sheltered by Framboise Cove's magnificent 4-km/2.5-mi arc of sand beach, it attracts swarms of waterfowl and many uncommon shorebirds.

Unfortunately, in the past, Sydney's appetite for sand to make concrete despoiled parts of Framboise Beach. Contractors were hauling it away faster than the sea could replace it. The Beaches Protection Act of 1976 outlawed the practice, thereby saving this beach.

LEG-STRETCHER: *Bog Walk*

South of Framboise there are excellent slope bogs. These are essentially living mats of sphagnum draped over bare bedrock, with small ponds in the hollows. In a drier climate such bogs could not survive. Here the frequent rains and fogs supply all the moisture they need.

If you're interested in exploring this misty world of sphagnum moss, little pink orchids, yellowlegs, and whimbrels—and your knees

Sphagnum

are up to it—ask at the Framboise general store for directions to Capelin Cove. Woods roads take you to the east end of Marie Joseph Lake (about 7 km/4 mi) and paths go from there to Capelin Cove (another 3 km/2 mi).

If you'd rather explore a bog closer to the road, there are lots to choose from, especially near Gabarus and Louisbourg. This coast gets up to 100 cm/60 in of precipitation a year—the highest in Canada outside of the Cape Breton Plateau, southern Newfoundland and coastal British Columbia. Peat thrives in such places, especially where drainage is blocked by layers of clay, by bedrock, or by the iron-saturated gravel called hard pan.

Gabarus Spit

A Bog Compendium

Sphagnum bogs can be prairie-like, domed, sloped, subdivided into strings by narrow ponds (called string bogs). Most are laced with small ponds stained the colour of tea by tannic acid from slowly decaying vegetation.

The easiest time to walk a bog is when everything is frozen. The most exciting time is in late summer, when water levels are low. Always best to wear rubber boots with inner soles and warm socks; bog water is icy all year. In mid-summer, look for bog orchids such as calopogon, arethusa (dragon mouth), and fringed orchids, all of them pink. You may also find the white, scented vanilla orchis.

Bogs are also good places to find insect-eating (insectivorous) plants. On such sites insects provide the only available nitrogen. One such plant is the tiny sundew, named for the diadem of clear, sweet droplets attached to a rosette of hairs around a spoon-shaped leaf. These hairs bend inward to trap small feeding insects, which the plant digests.

Bladderwort, an equally small insectivorous plant, grows in muddy pools and on moist mud. Its flowers are butter-yellow. The largest insect-trapper here is the pitcher plant. Its red-veined, jug-shaped leaves are lined with downward-pointing hairs and hold enough sweet rainwater to attract beetles, ants, and flies to their doom.

Cloudberry, a relative of raspberry, thrives in cool misty places like this. Also known as bakeapple, it grows along the whole Nova Scotia coast (except for Northumberland Strait), but nowhere better than in Cape Breton. (Inland and farther west, it seldom blooms or sets fruit. Even here, a late June frost sometimes nips the blossoms.)

Most years, however, its white, five-petalled flowers spangle these coastal peat bogs. They look like those of garden strawberries, to which the plant is also related. The multi-globed berries, one to a plant, ripen from creamy white to firm red (don't pick them yet) to amber in late August (the best time).

Like many other northern plants, cloudberries restrict their blooming to a single flower. This conserves energy in a hostile

*Capelin (*Mallotus villosus*) are smelt-like oceanic fish which spawn on sandy beaches from Cape Breton Island to Labrador in June or July near the full moon. Arriving on a flood tide, the females bury their eggs in the wet sand. They hatch in about 3 weeks, in time to ride the next high tide to sea. Capelin are fed open by cod, haddock, flounder, herring, salmon, seals, whales, sea birds, and humans. Canadian fishers sell thousands of tonnes of capelin roe to Asian markets each year.*

environment—but makes for slow picking. Many local people, like their counterparts in Newfoundland, Labrador, Norway, and Finland, make of the bakeapple harvest an annual picnic outing.

They are delectable with cream and make a tasty jam that reminds many of baked apple. (But some find the taste repugnant.) Ripe bakeapples are so juicy you can make delicious jam simply by lightly crushing them in a saucepan, adding sugar (1:3), and simmering for 10 minutes. The Finns make a lovely liqueur from cloudberries; you can find it in Nova Scotia liquor outlets.

Many birds frequent these coastal bogs. In spring, nesting yellowlegs may scold you from above, darting and diving harmlessly with many piercing cries sounding like "Aunt Sarie!" If it's foggy, you may also hear (but not see) low-flying black-backed gulls muttering in startlingly human voices as they fly between inland nests and coastal feeding sites.

[For more on bog types, see the **Marine Drive** near Tor Bay and the **Lighthouse Route** near Shelburne.]

Belfry Lake

The road from Framboise to Gabarus (pronounced Gab-ur-*oos*) swings in behind Cape Fourchu, whose volcanic rocks geologists chose to represent the whole geologic district. North of the cape lies an archipelago of marsh-fringed, wooded coastal hillocks; but we're far enough inland to avoid them. Like Framboise's wetlands they are much hunted for geese and ducks each fall. On the seaward side, one of Nova Scotia's longest series of barrier beaches shelters them from southerly gales. If we include the section from Winging Point (itself a reference to hunting) north to Cape Gabarus, this complex of sandbars stretches over 20 km/12 mi.

Fourchu Harbour seems barren, scraped bare, after all the sand and gravel we've seen. Drumlin material is scarce here. Straight-edged cliffs along the inlet show that it occupies a fault block that sank between nearly parallel fissures eons ago. Look near the lighthouse for bands of purple and red rhyolite that squirted up molten from the Earth's mantle as Cape Breton's various continental fragments were welded together. There is also tuff, so spongy with gas bubbles that it will float like cork. People have also found football-shaped "bombs" blown skyward by violent explosions. [See also the **Evangeline Trail** near Forchu.]

As we head inland along Gabarus Lake, the hummocky sandbox of glacial moraine resumes. But the spruce and fir, sheltered from the sea winds and fogs, are taller. This trough extends north to join the Mira River valley less than 5 km/3 mi away.

After another few kilometres we join Rte 327 coming in from Gabarus, a few minutes to the east.

SIDE TRIP: *Gabarus*

At Gabarus, named for a French officer, is an even rockier harbour. From here around to Louisbourg the waves have scant gravel to play with. And though the bread-like volcanic tuffs erode easily, they make poor sand. The region forms part of the flinty spine of igneous rock that joins Point Michaud to Scatarie Island. Around 650 million years ago, when Cape Breton Island was being welded together, this region seethed with red-hot lava that hissed and smoked by day and glowed by night. Its pinkish rhyolites and dark grey basalts have worn down considerably—but they will last for eons yet. [See also the **Bras d'Or Lake Scenic Drive** at Irish Cove.]

BACK ON THE HIGHWAY

After the old fishing village of Gabarus our trail follows Hwy 327 west for a few kilometres along Gabarus Cove, an exposed rocky shore. One can easily imagine its straggling spruce and fir bent double before howling northeasters and soaked by salt spray from green combers crashing against the rocks nearby.

Battles & Bogs

It was by way of Gabarus Bay, and not by a frontal assault from the sea, that the mighty fortress of Louisbourg was taken in 1745 and again in 1758. Both the New Englanders under William Pepperell and the British under General Wolfe chose this approach—because the French cannon all pointed out to sea.

The French counted on the extensive bogs and marshes behind the Fortress to deter attack from that direction. After all, the attackers would be out in the open and exposed to musket fire from the walls. Moreover, their progress would be slow, as anyone knows who has hiked across waterlogged peat full of hummocks and mud holes. It's like walking on a trampoline in clouds of mosquitoes. After a few hundred metres, knees and thighs cry for relief. But the attackers slogged through and won.

Passing the harbour's twin sandspits, we swing inland for 20 km/12 mi of black spruce thickets, sphagnum bogs and rocky barrens dotted

*The names Bull Hill (on Cape Gabarus) and Bull Rock (just offshore) refer to walrus, which once bred here. Heavily hunted in the 1600s for their ivory tusks (up to 46 cm/18 in long) and oily blubber, they were soon extirpated. [See also the **Marine Drive** at Tor Bay.]*

Iris prismatica or slender blue flag is reported from meadows at Louisbourg and nowhere else in Nova Scotia. Likely introduced from France, it has narrower leaves than do our two native species.

189

with glacial boulders patterned with green, grey, and black map lichens. The higher woodland occupies a landscape shaped by dying glaciers more than 10,000 years ago.

Its main features are hummocky ground moraines, where stagnant ice melted and dumped its debris; and drumlins, elongated gravel hills shaped by moving ice into graceful whalebacks. The Mira valley happens to boast one of the province's principal drumlin fields. [See also the **Lighthouse Route** near Lunenburg.] Curiously, the Mira drumlins are aligned northeast/southwest, not north/south like those in the rest of Nova Scotia. This suggests an independent ice sheet, at least in the later stages.

After 21 km/13 mi we emerge at the village of Marion Bridge, built at the narrowest point between Trout River and the south end of the lake.

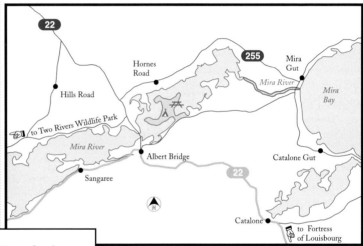

In his haunting *Song for the Mira*, Allister MacGillivary celebrated this unusual river:

*Can you imagine
a piece of the universe
More fit for princes and kings?
I'll trade you ten of your cities
for Marion Bridge
And the pleasures it brings ...*

STOP: *Mira River*

The Mira is broad and sluggish for most of its 55 km/34 mi, more like a shallow lake than a river, especially at this end. It's like something a child would design with a pail and shovel at the seashore, a river not quite sure which way to go. Yet if you drop a wood chip on the current in mid-lake on a windless day, the chip will move toward Mira Bay.

The Mira demonstrates how a melting glacier can divert and disrupt the flow of an established stream by indiscriminate dumping of gravel and sand. Through most of its course it is either backed up in broad lakes as much as 3 km/2 mi wide, or forced to wriggle through a labyrinth of islands and sandy peninsulas.

Therein lies its charm. For its ancient hummocks and sandbars are clothed in windswept marsh grasses beloved of bittern, snipe and heron. Wind and sun play across this gentle filigree of ponds and coves, delighting artist and photographer and luring the Cape Bretoner home. Here, not 10 km/6 mi from the wildest coast in Nova Scotia, are smiling farms and green groves. The effect is magical. Not surprisingly, much of this valley has become cottage country.

Geologically, the valley belongs to a great vanished river. The late Dr Albert Roland speculated in his *Geological Background and Physiography of Nova Scotia* that the river flowed south for eons, then north after gentle tilting a few million years ago. Then for a time at the end of the last Ice Age the sea invaded it, turning Cape Breton County's SE corner into an island. [For other ancient rivers see the **Glooscap Trail** near Parrsboro, the **Trans Canada Highway** near Wentworth, and the **Marine Drive** near Sherbrooke.]

The Mira River supports an isolated natural population of lake whitefish, a member of the trout family. [See also Lighthouse Route at Petite Rivière, which harbours a related species.]

SIDE TRIP: *Two Rivers Wildlife Park*
This free, community-run wildlife park is 10 km/6 mi west of Marion Bridge on the Sandfield Road, overlooking the Mira valley. It offers close-up views of native mammals you would seldom see in the wild, including black bear and cougar, bobcat, lynx, pine marten, and moose, all in natural settings along pleasant walkways. You'll also see Sable Island horses. There are picnic tables and rest rooms.

BACK ON THE HIGHWAY
For a few kilometres south and north of Marion Bridge, the river has cut a narrow channel through the glacial drift. There is a perceptible current. After Trout Brook glacial deposits again obstruct the channel. When we see the river a few kilometres farther on, it is again a shallow lake with numerous low islands.

The hinterland is fairly fertile, with upland pastures and occasional farmsteads.

Albert Bridge is less than 15 m/ 9 ft above sea level. Here the trail links up with Hwy 22 (**Marconi Trail**) between Sydney and Louisbourg.

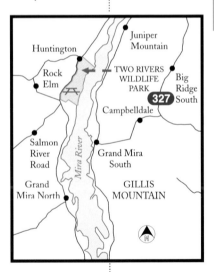

STOP: *Imported Herb?*
In the roadside fields opposite Fortress Louisbourg you'll see a tallish plant with dark, robust, indented leaves and umbels of greenish flowers. Angelica belongs to the carrot family and is represented in Nova Scotia by one native Cape Breton species, namely purple angelica, but the Louisbourg species may be an 18th-century import from France. In Europe the very similar *Angelica sylvestris* is prized as a kitchen herb. In the past it was cultivated for its aromatic odour, its medicinal root and its rhubarb-like stalks, which were candied and used to flavour pastries, cakes, candies, and desserts. In addition, the

Angelica

seeds were substituted for juniper berries in flavouring gin, and its dried roots were powdered to make aromatic sachets to insect-proof and scent stored clothing and linen. Today an oil from its root is used in various liqueurs.

Angelica being so useful, it's reasonable to suppose that French homemakers, both at the fortress and in the town, would have fetched seeds of this hardy herb across the Atlantic. Its also reasonable to expect that during the more than four decades the French held sway here, some garden plants would have escaped and survived.

If so, the plant proved more durable than the original fortress, surviving its destruction by fire and gunpowder over 200 years ago. Some botanists think this angelica is a cross between an import and our native species.

As the botanical debates drags on, angelica continues its slow march north and west along highways and byways. Slow, because although birds eat thousands of the seeds, most get digested. Wind and rain are likely its chief means of spread. Watch along the trail for it, and jot down the farthest occurrence. This National Park is really two parks, the lesser known being the 22 ha/ 55 ac natural area which surrounds the restoration. Ask about it at the visitors centre.

A visiting birder should make two visits—one for the history and one for the natural history.
–Roger Burrows,
Birding in Atlantic Canada, 1988

Shipwrecks

In its day Louisbourg was one of North America's busiest ports. Because the harbour approaches are exposed, ledgy, and often shrouded in fog, it was risky to enter and leave, especially before foghorns, sonar, and radar. Wrecks were inevitable. Moreover, major sea battles were fought here in 1745 and 1758.

Divers find these wrecks and their contents very enticing, so in the 1970s the federal government enacted protective legislation covering wrecks anywhere around Atlantic Canada. Only authorized people may visit them. Meanwhile, Nova Scotia has become a world leader in underwater investigation and interpretation. Professional divers come from all world to explore Louisburg's undersea archives and to take part in workshops and guided tours.

Glooscap Trail Nature Tour

Amherst to Windsor via Fundy Shore
365 km/227 mi

Fundy Bay at low tide

Red cliffs near Advocate

OVERVIEW

From a high-flying plane in autumn, Nova Scotia's second-longest trail looks like a spidery letter Z scrawled along the coast from Amherst to Advocate Harbour, from Advocate Harbour to Truro, and from Truro to Windsor.

We see it slip behind the great meander where the Maccan and Hebert rivers meet, to emerge at Joggins on Chignecto Bay, then head southwest along crumbling grey sandstone cliffs. By degrees the chocolate-brown waters of Cumberland Basin give way to Fundy's jade green and grey. The narrow road now snakes through dense thickets of second-growth red maple, white birch, trembling aspen, red spruce, and hemlock, past walls and vistas of moss green, pale gold, and tomato red. Notched into the low cliffs are the villages of Shulie, Sand River, and then Apple River, the first real harbour on the shore.

Our aircraft banks south across the rolling upland of Cape Chignecto, flinty heel of the Cobequid Mountains. This is high ground. Much cut over, it rises to meet us in billows of yellow aspen and crimson maple cross-stitched with dark spruce and fir. At Advocate Harbour the Bay of Fundy yawns blue and misty beyond a giant sandbar. We zoom east over Cape d'Or and along the southern scarp of the Cobequid Mountains. Toy villages—Fraserville, Wards Brook, Port Greville—scroll by, then Parrsboro and Partridge Island opposite Cape Split. We see tawny hillside pastures and burgundy blueberry fields and dark spiky woodlots. Waterfalls flash from ravines robed in the orange and gold of sugar maple, beech, and yellow birch.

After Two Islands and Five Islands and Economy Mountain, the landscape becomes less muscular, flattening to a bench of land wide enough for dairy farms. The Minas Basin's rust-red cliffs and flower-pot islands swim into view. The water is an unreal pinkish brown. The pilot banks south and west over the satiny mud flats of Cobequid Bay with their thousand winding creeks, to follow the Noel and Kempt shores toward Windsor. The red sandstone fringe is narrower, more gnawed by tides. Past Burntcoat and Tennycape we go, past Walton with its old gypsum quarry, out over the great indraft of the Avon and St Croix with Blomidon's profile rising like a great ship beyond, guarding the Annapolis Valley.

THE TOUR BEGINS

Before leaving the Nova Scotia border, check in at the Welcome Centre at Exit 1 for brochures and maps; also get directions to the Chignecto Bay Wildlife Sanctuary. Exit 4, 10 km/6 mi east on the Trans Canada Highway, puts you on Route 302 at Upper Nappan.

The change from busy highway to quiet byway is abrupt. Pasture and woodlot, farmstead and fenceline, stream and marsh unfold like a green and gold tapestry. Pay attention though, for our stay on Rte 302 is brief. Less than 2 km/1 mi along the winding Nappan River, where it empties into the Maccan (Mi'kmaq for "the fishing place"), we cross the Maccan bridge and bear right onto Rte 242. This road will take us west over the low ridge separating the Maccan River from River Hebert.

These level tidal landscapes are extensions of the great marshes of Tantramar, Amherst, and Minudie, sometimes called the Maritime Prairie. The marshes are the flooded frontage of a worn sandstone plain rich in salt, fossils, and coal. And fish—centuries ago, unbeliev-able numbers of fat, silvery shad ran up these rivers every spring to spawn. So plentiful were they that Mi'kmaq fishers canoed in from distant places to spear and smoke them and to socialize. The shad still come up the rivers, but nowhere near as many as before. Fishing has taken a toll, but so have dykes and dams and sawdust dumps.

> Skirting the sunbright uplands stretches a riband of meadow,
> Shorn of the labouring grass, bulwarked well from the sea,
> Fenced on its seaward border with long clay dikes from the turbid
> Surge and flow of the tides vexing the Westmoreland shores ....
> Miles and miles they extend, level, and grassy, and dim,
> Clear from the long red sweep of flats to the sky in the distance,
> Save for the outlying heights, green-rampiked Cumberland Point;
> Miles on miles outrolled, and the river-channels divide them,—
> Miles on miles of green, barred by the hurtling gusts.
> – Charles G. D. Roberts,
> **Tantramar Revisited**

The Acadians came here from Grand Pré in the 1670s, seeking suitable marshland to dyke and farm. They liked what they saw, and soon Maccan and Minudie and River Hebert grew into major settle-ments. After the 1755

Deportation, English settlers took over the dykelands, cleared the upland, farmed and fished, and mined a little coal.

Despite the rural exodus after the advent of railways and the Dirty Thirties, these fertile haylands were never abandoned. They supplied fodder for horses and cattle throughout Atlantic Canada. Today most of the old Acadian dykes have been incorporated into an extended modern post-World War II system.

Nappan in Mi'kmaq means "good place to get wigwam poles." It's also a good place to get table salt. Only 30 m/100 ft down there are great beds of it. Domtar Chemical's Sifto Salt Division extracts 65 000 tonnes every year. Over 300 million years ago, when ancestral Nova Scotia lay inside the supercontinent Pangaea, an arm of ocean broiled under a tropical sun here. Over millions of years it evaporated, leaving thick beds of the glittering white, soluble mineral that were later buried under sand. [See also the **Sunrise Trail** at Pugwash.]

By injecting hot water, pumping the brine to the surface, and boiling the water away, salt is obtained without digging.

Acadian dyke

Behind the tidal salt marshes lie extensive freshwater peat bogs of unusual origin. These arose when rising postglacial sea levels raised coastal marshes above the level of slower-forming freshwater marshes, thereby blocking their seaward drainage.

SIDE TRIP: *The Chignecto Waterfowl Sanctuary*
From Nappan a short drive takes us west to Amherst Point, site of the province's premier waterfowl marshes. Acquired by the Canadian Wildlife Service (CWS) in 1968, they have been protected and, where necessary, restored to natural habitat. To do so Ducks Unlimited (Canada) and the federal and provincial governments have built dams and gates that control water levels and have blasted potholes to create open water. As a result, thousands of ducks and geese have returned to breed. So have loons, ospreys, and eagles.

The finest marshes in this area are the 600-ha/1,482-ac John Lusby Marsh (opposite Minudie) and the Amherst Point Migratory Bird Sanctuary (between the Maccan and River Hebert estuaries). Besides being excellent examples of co-operative marsh reclamation and preservation, they are superb birding sites. Ask locally about the interpretive trail.

During migration, flocks of up to 1,500 Canada geese alight here. Sometimes one sees a sprinkling of snow geese. Summer migrants include teal, ring-necked duck, gadwall, pied-billed grebe, northern shoveler, ruddy duck, widgeon, coot, and common moorhen. Rare sightings include green-backed herons, snowy egrets, and glossy ibis. In all, 228 species have been recorded. Keen birders may also spot marsh wren, Wilson's phalarope, and black tern.

In summer northern harriers (marsh hawks) nest in the grasslands. (If you spot one flying low, it's likely a male hunting meadow mice for his family nearby.) In winter, cruise the back roads for sightings of rough-legged hawks, snow buntings, and Lapland longspurs. In years when lemmings are scarce up north you may even see a snowy owl.

The sanctuary is about 3 km/2 mi west of Nappan. [See also the **Trans Canada Highway.**]

BACK ON THE HIGHWAY

All summer the fields between Nappan and Maccan are graced with plump cattle and black-faced sheep. They belong to Agriculture Canada's research station 4 km/2.5 mi north of Maccan, which specializes in studies of ruminants (cud-chewers) and pasture management. Visitors are welcome. There is also a marsh, pond, and interpretive trail designed to show farmers how to attract wildlife to idle land.

STOP: *Maccan Tidal Bore*

The Maccan bridge is a good spot to view the river "running backwards." Stand on the bridge facing north. With luck and good timing, you'll see a good six minutes of bore passing under your feet. Full moon and new moon are best.

Maccan resident Gordon Boss likes to talk about the bore. In 1994 he tallied 110 bore-watchers here. He provides local tourist bureaus, hotels, and service stations with June–October timetables. Gordon advises arriving 20 minutes early; wind and weather can hasten or delay the bore.

Another respectable tidal bore runs up the River Hebert estuary. Ask locally about times, and watch it from the bridge. People here say the bore "flattens out" in October and nearly disappears in winter; nobody knows why. From the bridge you can also watch shad in season. The best time is mid-May on a rising tide—when the shadbush, or serviceberry, is blooming.

STOP: *River Hebert*

The village's Heritage Model Centre offers a replica of the community as it looked in the 1800s, and the municipal park has parking space and an interpretive panel suggesting other things to see. One thing is Atlantic Canada's first natural sewage treatment system. It consists of a reclaimed marsh located on land dyked in the 1940s for coal mining and abandoned in the 1970s. Since marshes are nature's kidneys, continually filtering water and trapping suspended solids, they will do the same with sewage and other pollutants. River Hebert's system imitates this process by flooding dykeland to form lagoons. The lagoons are left for a year or two to settle, after which cattails, rushes, and other water plants colonize them. Then wastewater is released into them from settling ponds.

Blueberry fields are blue-green in September, scarlet in October before the leaves fall, and burgundy red all winter.

In the 19th century, Maccan and River Hebert were active coal mining areas. Today the main occupations are dairy farming, forestry, and blueberry growing. Along the Maccan River, blueberry fields are common. The crop is hand-raked with toothed scoops or machine-harvested with a tractor-drawn "Blue Machine," invented by the Bragg family of Oxford. Japan and New England are prime markets; so is the McDonald's fast-food chain. Every two years growers torch their fields with oil-fired burners to stimulate flower bud growth and to discourage native mountain laurel and Labrador tea, and various insects. Blueberry is native to Atlantic Canada and is adapted to wildfire. Blackflies are its principle pollinator.

Natural sewage treatment system at River Hebert

The Saxby Gale of October 5, 1869,
produced a tide of 21.6 m/71 ft at the
head of Chignecto Bay, breaching the
Tantramar dykes and plugging Sackville's
harbour with silt. In the Nappan area, a
tidal surge uprooted barns and haystacks
and drowned cows, sheep, and pigs. By
then almost everyone had fled to high
ground. Next day every cove was strewn
with haystacks and dead animals. It took
days to sort out who owned what
hay. The storm was named after S. M.
Saxby, a civilian instructor in the British
Navy, who in November 1868 had
published a letter in the London press
warning of unspecified cataclysms next
October. He based this prediction on an
unusually precise alignment of Sun,
Moon, and Earth to occur at 7:00 a.m.
on October 5, Greenwich time.

In 1996 the system covered about 1.2 ha/5 ac. High fertility has produced a rich flora and fauna, which in turn extract further nutrients from the wastewater, preventing the algal blooms that cause eutrophication and oxygen depletion.

A sign at the bridge directs visitors to the facility. Berry Shoreline Tours of Amherst operates one-day and half-day geology, nature, and history excursions from June 1 to September 30.

SIDE TRIP: *Massive Marshes, Canada's Grindstone King*
This 20-km/12-mi round trip from River Hebert to Minudie offers superb views of tidal marshes and dykelands on the way to the Amos "King" Seaman School Museum. From the bridge at River Hebert drive 9 km/5.6 mi north past Barronsfield to the Minudie turnoff; Minudie is less than 1 km/0.6 mi beyond.

Minudie's dykes are perfect for long, undisturbed walks under wide skies. The mix of pasture, meadow, wetland, and forest makes for perfect birding. On a map, Minudie Marsh juts like a huge thumb into Cumberland Basin between Maccan River and River Hebert. In fact this is Nova Scotia's biggest meander, and is one of the province's biggest dykelands. It is maintained as a community pasture under Nova Scotia's 1930s Marshland Reclamation Act. For directions and advice about access, inquire locally. Large vehicles may have trouble upon leaving the pavement.

Rocks to Riches
It takes a rare type of gritstone to sharpen metal properly, and Cumberland County happens to have it. It takes a rarer type of individual to see a market for such rock. While still a boy, Amos Seaman left his home near Sackville, paddled over to Minudie, and lived in River Hebert for a time. Later he bought J. F. W. DesBarres' Minudie estate. Seeing local farmers sharpen knives and scythes with local gritstone, he started a quarry.

By 1850, he was annually shipping 30,000 grindstones, mill-

*Four men who went
to Fort Lawrence
creek to secure a
schooner sought
shelter from the wind
in a barn. The tide
rising, they aban-
doned the barn and
took to a fence
[extending] to the
upland, and by
passing along which
they hoped to be safe.
The waves swept
away the fence. Two
... managed to reach
some poles and save
themselves. The others
... were drowned.*
– **Amherst Gazette,**
October 18, 1869

197

stones, and flywheels to companies around the world. Many a New England textile mill depended on Minudie flywheels. Admirers called him the "Grindstone King," or "King" Seaman for short. Seaman also owned quarries at Wallace [see the **Sunrise Trail**]. He had a mansion in Boston and another at Minudie, treated his employees well, and entertained lavishly.

As the quarry grew seaward, some of the best stone was underwater at high tide. So while the tide was out he had the blocks roughhewn to circular shape, holed, and marked with a buoy. At high tide it was a simple matter to hoist the stones off the bottom, row them ashore, and trolley them to the finishing shed. All this and more is documented in the museum which is itself an authentic old rural school house complete with bench-type desks scarred with students' initials.

Minudie once had an important shad fishery. As late as 1950 one or two families still fished a weir, a long net strung on slim poles driven into the mud far out on the marsh. Between mid-May and September, the tides ruled their lives. The weir was tended at low tide in the old way. Twice every 24 hours, in all weathers and at all hours, they drove horse-drawn box wagons several kilometres out on the treacherous flats, where tides rise to 10 metres (30+ feet). Standing in the carts, they plucked the fat silver-blue fish from the nets like apples from a tree, picked the seaweed and debris from the meshes, and scooted back before the next tide.

Shad are bony like all the herring tribe; but the firm sweet flesh is delicious fried or baked.

SIDE TRIP:

From River Hebert village you can opt to drive south on Hwy 2 to Parrsboro, or follow the coast. Hwy 2 passes through the northeast corner of the old Chignecto Game Sanctuary. For nearly 20 km/12 mi it follows a winding gravel ridge that early loggers called the Boar's Back. Mi'kmaq legend says Glooscap built it to reach his home at Blomidon. Geologically it's one of Nova Scotia's longest eskers. An esker is the raised bed of a vanished under-ice meltwater stream. This one probably flowed from a glacier centred on Newville Lake. Along the road you'll see red pine plantations dating back to the mid-1940s, after the government bought the land to restore this fire-ravaged area.

A short drive west from River Hebert puts us on the shore of Chignecto Bay. You might not guess it, but those ordinary-looking sandstone

The United States market is supplied with grindstones from the County of Cumberland [that are] superior to any others ever discovered on the continent of America.
– Abraham Gesner, **The Industrial Resources of Nova Scotia,** 1849

There are records of [Joggins] coal being sold in Boston as early as 1720 and different New England companies tried to operate there before the Expulsion.
– Will R. Bird, **Off-Trail in Nova Scotia,** 1956

A Chignecto view

Looking down a Chignecto beach

cliffs are world famous. They are full of Coal Age fossils. Unlike many fossil cliffs, these are continually being sawed open by fierce tides and churning ice. Among the most spectacular are the 45-m/150-ft cliffs at the old coal-mining village of Joggins.

STOP: *Joggins Fossil Trove*

Go down the wooden stair near Coal Mine Point and imagine yourself in a tropical jungle 300 million years ago, before there were birds or flowering plants or an Atlantic Ocean. Here the roots and trunks of different forests lie buried one above the other in layers. Imprinted in the rocks are ghostly outlines of oversized ferns, horsetails, and club mosses.

These ancient forests were buried under silt by rivers suddenly overflowing in torrential rains. This happened many times during the Carboniferous Period; the Joggins sediments are over 600 m/2,000 ft thick, with over 70 separate coal seams. As the sediments built up, their massive weight compressed the lower layers into rock, the layers of dead plants to coal.

Because this part of Nova Scotia escaped the worst of the mountain-building epoch that closed the Carboniferous, many erect sections of trees survived intact here. After visiting Joggins in August 1852, British geologist Sir Charles Lyell wrote in his landmark *Principles of Geology*: " ... the [tree bark] ... forms a tube of pure bituminous coal, filled with sand, clay and other deposits ... the first tree was fourteen inches at the top and sixteen inches at the bottom. The bark was quarter of an inch thick .... I observed in all at least seventeen of these upright trunks .... "

At Joggins, Lyell and his young Canadian host William Dawson (a graduate of the remarkable Pictou Academy and later a pioneer in mapping and describing Canada's geology, including two books on

I never travelled in any country where my scientific pursuits were better understood or more zealously forwarded than in Nova Scotia....
–Sir Charles Lyell, **Travels in North America,** 1845

Nova Scotia) also found the first-known fossilized Coal Age land reptile. It had fallen into a rotten stump and suffocated. They called the creature *Hylonomus* (Latin for "forest dweller").

To put all this in perspective, visit the Joggins Fossil Centre on Main Street, "the world's largest collection of Coal Age fossils." It includes early land snails, freshwater clams, and a mayfly with an 11-cm/4-in wingspan. Dioramas depict 30-m/100-ft horsetails, 2-m/6-ft sowbugs, crow-sized dragonflies, shiny black trilobites, and giant salamanders.

Guided cliff tours depart the centre on the hour from June through August (by appointment in May and October); children are free. Don Reid also provides May–October beach tours.

Look for coal seams and stones with ridged cylindrical markings or delicate fern prints. Prying rocks from the cliffs is illegal, but you're welcome to whatever falls to the shore. (Please report any animal fossil finds.) Don't stray under the cliffs, since rockfalls are common, especially in spring. It's best to wear a hard hat if you do.

About 3 km/2 mi south of Joggins, watch for a graveyard on the east side. The stones bear the surnames of Irish settlers like Devine (of Donegal), McCarron, Shea, and O'Ryan. There are also Acadian names like Belliveau, Babin, and Melanson, descendants perhaps of exiled Acadians who returned from the Eastern Seaboard when the deportation ban was lifted in 1763. [See also the **Evangeline Trail** near Church Point.] For an engrossing fictional account of their journey, read *Pélagie*, by Antonine Maillet from Buctouche, NB.

In the 1900s, Sand River still had a 6.4-km/4-mi wooden flume that brought lumber from a portable mill down to tidewater. The old Sand River Road along Chignecto Bay is mostly unpeopled now, but its silent creeks and coves have many stories to tell. In the mid-19th century Shulie, Sand River, Apple River, and Eatonville echoed all summer to the chuffing of donkey engines, the wail of sawmills, and the screech of steam whistles as logs were sawed and ships took shape. In winter you would have seen teams of horses yarding great logs to streamside, lake, and flume to await the spring breakup.

During those years, the region's splendid forests suffered from over-cutting and from wildfire. The sandy soils dried out quickly. Settlers' fires often got out of control. Sawmills routinely burned sawdust, and sawdust fires sometimes escaped. The problem worsened after coal-burning locomotives appeared on the Halifax-Montreal Intercolonial Railway in 1876. In 1903, a forest fire burned from Harrison Settlement to beyond Springhill. In 1921, a sawmill fire raged from Shulie almost to Oxford. [See also the **Trans Canada Highway** at Exit 5 and Oxford.]

It was these land uses and abuses that created today's expanses of second-growth aspen, white birch, and cherry. As noted earlier, much of the area has been rehabilitated by government tree-planting.

SIDE TRIP: *Apple River*

Legend has it that this sleepy village, tucked between Cape Capstan and Pudsey Point, with its sandbar, tidal marsh, and lobster boats, got its name when a cargo of apples floated ashore from a foundered ship. Out toward Pudsey Point there used to be a big steam sawmill. Summer kayakers routinely shelter here after rounding Cape Chignecto, bringing stories of seals sunning themselves or diving for fish along the rugged coast, of the basalt sea stacks called Three Sisters near Eatonville, and of Refugee Cove on the Minas Basin side, where a band of Acadians wintered after the Deportation.

Mi'kmaq legend says the Eatonville stacks are three dogs which Glooscap turned to stone when they harassed a moose he was hunting. They say the moose became Isle Haute, a 1-km/ 0.6-mi-long island 20 km/12 mi out in the bay. Isle Haute was the site of ritual Mi'kmaq dog feasts into historical times.

South of Apple River we swing south into a more rugged landscape, the western end of the Cobequid Mountains. [See also the **Trans Canada Highway** near Wentworth.] Rising to over 180 m/590 ft, its resistant reddish cliffs are among the mainland's highest. From West Advocate Harbour to Five Islands we follow the Cobequid Fault, part of the Glooscap Fault system that extends to Cape Canso and beyond. [See also the **Marine Drive** near Guysborough.]

STOP: *Cape Chignecto Provincial Park*

Opened in July 1996, this rugged 4252-ha/10,502-ac wedge of semi-wilderness is our newest and largest provincial park. Although the wilderness character will be preserved, the area will offer camping

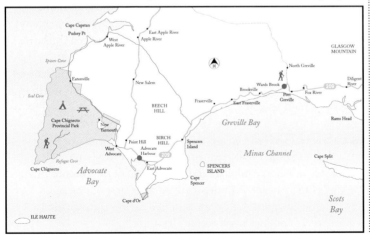

Driftwood on Advocate Beach

Rhyolite cliffs near Advocate

parks, eco-trails, and over 20 km/12 mi of wilderness hiking trails. In addition there will be interpretive centres at New Yarmouth, West Advocate, and Spicers Cove/Eatonville. Much of the area has been logged for masting, lumber, and pulpwood, but pockets of old forest remain in protected ravines, and red spruce and sugar maple is regenerating prolifically.

One of the trails runs from near New Yarmouth across the upland for 12 km/7.5 mi and out to Refugee Cove. On the way, it wends for some 20 minutes through a lovely glade of young sugar maple. Bask in this milky green light that contrasts so dramatically with the sombreness of spruce and fir groves.

The cove itself is a wedge of cobble beach walled in by spectacular pink rhyolite cliffs striped with dark volcanic basalt and topped by windblown conifers. A barrier beach protects a salty pond. From it a brackish stream emerges to disappear into the cobbles and reappear on the outer beach. Offshore, looming like a battleship, is Isle Haute, a mass of basalt columns. The cove is unforgettable, especially when one recalls that a party of Acadian refugees spent the fall and winter of 1755–56 here in misery.

As our highway emerges from the heavily wooded region south of Apple River and descends a hill, the landscape suddenly changes to ocean, headland, and beach. Advocate Harbour, between the horns of Cape Chignecto and Cape d'Or, was the site of an ancient Acadian fishing station. Depending on the tide, the harbour may be an expanse of bare mud laced with freshwater rivulets and smelling of salt and methane, or it may brim with salt water.

LEG-STRETCHER

For a thrilling beach walk, exit Rte 209 at West Advocate (where the road heads north to Amherst) and drive through the community past the end of the pavement to the small parking spot on the right. Walk down the steep gravel road a few hundred metres through alder, white spruce, and mountain-ash to the shore.

On the way, you'll pass Red Rocks, an outcrop of brick-red Triassic sandstone jutting seaward on the left. If there's any wave action, the water near shore will be rust-red from the rapid erosion. This is the first of many such outcrops of this formation you'll see, for it underlies the whole Minas Basin. [See also the **Evangeline Trail** at Blomidon, etc., and the **Marine Drive** at Chedabucto Bay.]

On the left you'll see a few cottages and a battered breakwater of wharf pilings. To the right is a vast curving beach of smooth grey-blue cobble stones broken by spurs and pyramids of eroded black basalt. The beach slopes down to deep water and up to high cliffs of hardened fine-grained rock that gushed molten from the Earth's mantle when the North Atlantic was born. After a kilometre or so, the beach peters out under steep cliffs with large echoing sea caves. Watch for harbour seals sporting in the green surf.

Be careful the incoming tide doesn't cut off your escape, especially during full and new moon. Allow time to retrace your steps. A rocky point you easily walked around on the way out could be submerged on your way back. Always consult local tidetimes before venturing into tidal areas. The little restaurant in East Advocate has a tide-clock.

The village of Advocate Harbour is strung out along one straight street nearly 3 km/2 mi long. At first glance it has a sort of Wild West look—until you see the white and blue and green fishing boats moored behind the high wharf at the eastern end. The village is built on a wide apron of glacial gravel or marine terrace laid down when the land was pressed down under mega-tonnes of ice. A second terrace rises behind the village, with a cemetery spread across it. Beyond the cemetery are windblown spruce.

Red rocks near Advocate

This harbour is exposed to Fundy's full winter fury, with nothing but tiny Isle Haute between it and Cape Cod. But for the massive barrier beach, no boat could live here then. To picture the violence of these storms, walk the beach and contemplate the vast windrow of driftwood: skeletons of whole trees, splintered power poles and wharf timber, broken lobster pots, and miscellaneous lumber; as well as colourful

Isle Haute ("High Island") is a mass of basaltic lava that originated at the same time as Cape d'Or, Cape Sharp, Partridge Island, and Economy Mountain. Along with Two Islands and Five Islands farther east, they are part of a saucer lip or cuesta of Triassic/Jurassic rock. At one time this lip may have divided Minas Basin from the outer Bay of Fundy. Some of the lava flows occurred under and within existing sandstone formations; erosion has since worn the softer rock away.

But for ship worms (Teredo navalis), many of our harbours would be plugged with driftwood. This worm-like marine mollusc riddles any submerged wood with irregular tunnels made by chewing with its modified shells. This weakens the wood and hastens its breakdown. Before wood preservatives such as copper paint and creosote were developed, teredos shortened the life of boats and wharves considerably.

tangles of plastic rope and netting, engine oil jugs, and rubber boots. Another hint of the ocean's power is the steepness of the outer beach.

Advocate's twin spits are continually being built of material brought from the flanking headlands. Igneous rock is hard but full of cracks. Into these water seeps and freezes. The resulting expansion pries off chunks, and gravity delivers them to the grinding action of waves and ice far below. In time, each block is further broken down into cobbles, pebbles, and sand. Meanwhile, longshore currents convey them inward to the harbour, tumbling them as they go, much as a lapidarist polishes stone. The high berms ridges along the beach were tossed up by winter surf. [See also the **Fleur-de-lis Trail** at Point Michaud, the **Sunrise Trail** at Merigomish, etc.]

In Mi'kmaq legend Cape d'Or and Blomidon were once joined to form the dam of a giant Beaver. Glooscap, angry at Beaver for raiding his medicine garden, broke the dam with his axe and flung the pieces behind him to form Partridge Island and the Five Islands. One (not widely held) scientific interpretation is that an earthquake 6,000 years ago fractured the barrier, letting the Atlantic enter. The channel is widening as Blomidon and Cape Split continue to erode.

Advocate Harbour is really a sort of lagoon. The only gap in the beach is on the Cape d'Or side, where McRitchie Brook and two other streams flow out. The entrance is guarded by a concrete breakwater with an automated light. On the west side, sediment from McRitchie Brook has built a small marsh that has been dyked for hay.

One can easily linger here a day or two, hiking the beaches, talking to people, watching the (up to 10-m/33-ft) tides lift brightly painted fishing boats off the mud and set them daintily down again. It's amazing to see the harbour brimming with water in the morning and empty six hours later.

To hike the harbour bar, exit the main street onto the single gravel road a few hundred metres west of the United Church and drive to a little marsh. Park and walk a few hundred metres to the driftwood barricade. (The road is driveable but can be muddy.) On the way, notice short dykes protecting reclaimed hayfields. From the high beach, on a clear day, you'll see spectacular vistas of ocean and headland open before you.

For a good panorama of the village, spit, and harbour, drive up the gravel road to the cemetery. The terrace on which it sits is 35 m/115 ft above current sea level. On the headstones you'll see surnames like Jenks, Turple, Elliott, Morris, Blenkhorn, Rommell, Dewis, Ells, Nuttall, and Spicer, and evidence of deaths at sea.

Aerial view of Cape d'Or

Cape d'Or

SIDE TRIP: *Cape d'Or*

East Advocate occupies a slightly higher marine terrace than the main village. Toward the north, blueberry fields stretch away to the woods. Just before the Harbourlite Restaurant there are two exits south to Cape d'Or; either will do.

Exit Hwy 209 here and drive 6 km/4 mi up a winding gravel road to a lofty parking lot and lookoff. From here a short loop trail, chipped for easy walking, skirts the cliff top. Along the trail you'll see (in season) angelica, mountain-ash, cinquefoil, wild rugosa rose, honeysuckle, blue flag iris, and mountain alder. On the headland itself there are rare arctic-alpine plants like false starry Solomon's seal, *Oxytropis* and *Astragalus* ground

Rip tide at Cape d'Or

juniper. If lucky, you may see a peregrine falcon. The island to the southwest is Isle Haute. From the lot you can look down on the surging Fundy tides, the cape, and the lighthouse facility. In 1995 a citizens' committee saved the facility from being dismantled. They turned the lightkeeper's house into a restaurant (drop in for a snack, they'll appreciate your patronage) and a gift shop that sells local honey, jams, and specimens of copper and amethyst.

Cape d'Or is the geologic twin of Cape Split, whose curving cusp looms 16 km/10 mi to the east. Every 12 hours enough water to fill 40 St Lawrence Rivers pours between the two headlands. You can tell when the tide is coming by a cool, salty breeze followed by a muffled roar as rapids whiten the black basalt reefs below. For decades engineers and politicians have recognized the tremendous hydroelectric potential here. [See the **Evangeline Trail** at Granville Ferry.]

In 1605 Sieur de Monts and Samuel de Champlain, seeking precious metals around what they hopefully named the "Bason des Mines," named this headland Cap d'Or because it glinted in the sun. The metal they saw was not gold, but raw copper. Seams and shelves of it had collected when red hot lava and super-heated steam flowed nearly 200 million years before. The Mi'kmaq sometimes made arrow-heads from it.

Arrow heads

In 1887, Mr J. A. Hanway, president of the Colonial Copper Company of New York, issued five million shares at one dollar each on a proposed mine, saying, "This is no small operation; we anticipate a profit of $1,872,000 in the first year .... "

By 1900 the No. 1 shaft was down 113 m/371 ft, and over 250 m/ 800 ft of tunnels and drifts had been dug; a village of miners' homes had sprung up, and an ore crusher and concentrating plant were working full tilt. To move the ore, a steam locomotive chugged along

Cliffs at Cape d'Or

Eroding basalt at Cape d'Or

2 km/1.2 mi of narrow-gauge railway. A steam power plant, three hoisting engines, boilers, and other machinery completed the facility. Ships loaded the copper from a wharf in nearby Horseshoe Cove.

The assay averaged 20 kg/44 lb of copper per tonne. The mine closed in 1905; the best of the ore was gone. The miners' houses were barged to Parrsboro, Kingsport, Windsor, and Port Greville. One even went around Cape Chignecto to Alma, NB. The narrow-gauge railway was sold to Newfoundland. One can still see two mine shaft openings in the cliff face about 10 m/33 ft above the beach.

The cape's relative isolation and cool, misty habitat have preserved arctic-alpine plants otherwise rare in Nova Scotia. Among these are *Oxytropis* and *Astragalus* of the pea family. You'll also find false Solomon's seal, evening primrose, and seaside goldenrod. The dark-leaved, compact shrubs that clothe the slopes are downy alder, a very hardy member of the birch family. See how wind and fog have dwarfed even these.

Before the onset of heavy pesticide use after World War II, isolated headlands like this were the haunt of peregrine falcons or "duck hawks." In fact, Cape D'Or was the last known Nova Scotia nesting site of these magnificent predators, whose Latin-derived name means "travelling abroad." So it was appropriate that the first-known nesting pair since the fifties was sighted here in 1995.

The peregrine, Falco peregrinus, once prized in the royal sport of falconry, is the world's swiftest bird. It has been clocked at 290 km/h (180 mph) in an attack dive.

Like the bald eagle, the peregrine declined in the 1950s due to thin-shelled eggs and poor nesting success. The 1960s ban on DDT use did not seem to help, and in 1978 Canada put the bird on its endangered list.

Through the late 1980s and early 1990s, biologists with the Canadian Wildlife Service and World Wildlife Fund kept raising and releasing peregrines. They used the "hack box" technique, whereby captive juveniles are fed near the release site without letting them see their caretakers. This eases the transition to the wild. Finally, the young birds are released in suitable habitat. Nova Scotia received 105 such birds from Alberta nests.

For a long time it was like dropping pennies in a well. Hardly any of the birds returned from migration, and none were known to nest. Then, in 1995, six nesting pairs showed up in the Maritimes—and one pair nested on Cape d'Or.

BACK ON THE HIGHWAY

As we head east on Hwy 209, notice how the Minas Basin slowly changes colour. As the basin's silty flow dilutes the ocean waters, the surface goes from greenish blue at Cape d'Or to brownish green at Parrsboro and finally to pinkish brown east of Economy.

Spencers Island is the name of a village as well as an island. Both are named for Lord Spencer, an early official. In Mi'kmaq the name of the dome-like islet just offshore meant "Glooscap's Kettle." Rte 209 cuts behind the community, but we'll follow an old loop past to Spencers Beach.

At the beach, park by the refurbished lighthouse and ask the attendant about the village's shipbuilding past. At low tide one can often see the stumps of old shipyard pilings poking through the vast cobble beach. The wooden ships that slid down these ways are long gone, sold with their cargoes of timber and fish to ports around the world, wrecked on foreign shores, lost at sea.

Beside the lighthouse in Spencers Island is a cairn commemorating the mystery ship Mary Celeste, *reputedly the first built here. Launched in 1861 as* The Amazon, *wrecked at Cow Bay in Cape Breton in 1868, bought and repaired by an American and renamed, the square-rigger left New York in November 1872 for Genoa loaded with casks of pure alcohol. Crew and passengers totaled 10.*

Weeks later, Captain Morehouse of Bear River, bound for Gibraltar, came upon the ship sailing under shortened sail in fair weather. The hatches were open, the compass broken, and the ship's papers and chronometer missing.

Local historian Stanley Spicer maintains that the captain and crew abandoned the vessel as a precaution after storms prevented routine airing of the holds to prevent vapour buildup. Fearing an explosion, he says they opened the hatches, tied their single lifeboat by a long line, and boarded it, intending to reboard after the danger was past. But the line parted, and the unmanned ship sailed away. No trace of them was ever found. The Mary Celeste *was taken to port, a court case was held, and the vessel was sold for salvage.*

In the early 1850s Nova Scotia had the highest per capita volume of home-built shipping in the British Commonwealth. Enormous quantities of pine, spruce, yellow birch, and tamarack (larch) were cut for cradles, scaffolding, keels, ribs, planking, and masts. All this took a toll on our largest trees.

It certainly decimated tamarack stands. Shipbuilders prized the curved lower trunks of this species (which they called "juniper") because the wood made strong and water-durable stem and stern timbers and knees to join ribs to deck. This demand, plus periodic outbreaks of the native larch sawfly (the latest around 1900), helps explain today's scarcity of tamarack.

After Spencers Island we rejoin Rte 209 east of the village. From here to Port Greville our road seldom strays more than half a kilometre from Greville Bay's curving shore. The trail from here to Fox River is a roller coaster of a ride. Fraserville, East Fraserville, Brookville, and Wards Brook are all built on streams. Crossing each entails a long

View from Fraserville

curving swoop, a tight turn, and a hard climb. You'll see dizzying vistas of sky, water, and woods, matchbox villages, hillside pastures, and blueberry fields on glacial outwash plains.

The road builders had to squeeze the highway between salt water and the steep scarp of the Glooscap Fault, which separates the older, harder uplands from the softer lowland sediments. Several fine waterfalls plunge over its rim.

In October these hillsides glow with crimson, orange, and gold as sugar maple, yellow birch, and beech prepare for winter. The scarlet blueberry fields are almost as colourful. (Notice how many fields have windbreaks of planted spruce and pine protecting the tender fruit.)

STOP: *"Age of Sail" Ship Museum*

Nearly every tidal creek along this shore has seen the launch of

Hands-on exhibit in Age of Sail Ship Museum

wooden sailing ships. Wards Brook is one such creek, and the Age of Sail Heritage Centre tells its story and that of the Parrsboro Shore's golden Age of Sail. In the mid- to late 1800s more than 400 wooden ships, from square-rigged barques to coasting schooners, slid down the ways at Spencers Island, Port Greville, and Parrsboro. During the same period, nearly 200 sawmills poured out lumber to build and to load them; Port Greville was a major lumber port.

A kilometre/0.6 mi east of Port Greville the highway crosses Fox River. At its mouth is a good place to see, close up, how a tidal spit forms. Take the second gravel road east of the bridge and drive south just over 1 km/0.6 mi to the end, where there's a small public park. Walk a short distance to the right for a clear view. Use caution; the gravel bank may be unstable.

On a rising or falling tide strong currents swirl through an opening in the spit. Incoming tides meet the river's flow, lose momentum, and dump their suspended sand. Outgoing currents bear sand away.

The spit represents a line of equilibrium. Fox River has just enough energy to keep its channel open.

Across the Minas Channel, less than 10 km/6 mi away, you can see the snaggled teeth of Cape Split. If you decide to explore the shore, ask permission and directions at a nearby farm.

Beyond Fox River the highway hugs the Cobequid Fault for several kilometres, then enters a widening apron of lowland. Inland it is mantled in spruce, fir, red maple, and white birch; toward the shore much of it is cleared for pastures and blueberry fields. For the first time since Apple River, we are riding over soft older sediments laid down under water during the Age of Coal.

Being soft as well as older, the bedrock wore down faster than the resistant Cobequids. A major player in this erosion was and is Diligent River, which rises north of Parrsboro and meanders across the lowland between here and Minas Channel. Its upper course crosses the highway between Wharton and Kirkhill. There are huge blueberry fields on its floodplain.

LEG-STRETCHER: *Wards Falls Hiking Trail*
How long has it been since you gazed into a limpid mountain stream? Too long? This 7-km/4.3-mi (round trip) trail along Diligent River's west branch will let you do so. It begins on the floodplain, passes through alder thickets (a sign of spring flooding), then into second-growth spruce-birch forest, and finally enters an upland forest of sugar maple, beech, and yellow birch. The whole area comprises 61 ha/150 ac of mixed spruce, fir, maple, and birch.

Whoever laid out the trail must have liked bridges. There are 12 in all, each a pleasant excuse to pause and admire the trees, rocks, and crystal-clear water.

But the waterfall itself is disappointing. Perhaps 500 years ago it was higher, but since then the river has cut down through the original 10-m/33-ft cliff, leaving only a 3-m/10-ft overfall. In the process, however, it has created an unusual corkscrew gorge barely 2 m/6 ft wide.

To see this, one climbs the two dozen steps of a sturdy wooden ladder placed against the right-hand cliff and clamber down the far side. For those who want to go inside the corkscrew channel, there's a single log span. From there in summer the venturesome can wade a few metres into the cavern; beyond, there's a 2-m/6-ft hole. (Mid-winter may be the safest time to explore this place.)

As a rule, woodland roads must be cleared every 10 years or they'll revert to forest. The trail honours lumberman Ernie Harrison, founder of C. E. Harrison & Sons Homecare Limited, Halfway River, the firm that donated the land. Over the years branches had grown out over the path, freshets had carved runnels across it, and fallen trees had blocked the way. It was widened in 1993, and some rotting bridges were replaced.

To find this trail, watch for a small white sign on the north side just east of the village of Diligent River. Drive north through the field along a gravel road 0.6 km/0.4 mi to the parking area, where an interpretive sign explains the route. There are rest rooms and picnic tables.

Notice, 2 km/1.2 mi west of the exit to Wards Falls Hiking Trail, high on the hillside to the north, a reddish grey patch of dead conifers. This 1960s plantation of native red pine was killed by Sirococcus shoot blight, a wind-borne fungus that attacks young red pine plantations in foggy coastal areas. By the early 1980s the blight had forced forestry agencies to stop using this species in reforestation. Researchers have since found a resistant strain of red pine and hope to reinstate the tree.

Blueberry fields near Parrsboro

Along the road, windbreaks of jack pine protect blueberry fields.

STOP: *Kirkhill Lookoff*

For a good panorama of the outwash plain and hinterland, take the Kirkhill exit between Wharton and the Department of Natural Resources (DNR) office and drive 1.9 km/1.2 mi uphill until you reach a microwave tower in a blueberry field; park beside it.

From here you can see Parrsboro to the southeast, Partridge Island straight south (with Cape Blomidon across the Basin), and, to the west, the course of Diligent River toward Greville Bay. The steep hill we climbed is part of the Cobequid scarp. The hummocky ground here is typical ground moraine—unsorted rock, pebbles, sand, and clay dumped by a glacier. The flat plain below is sand and silt deposited in a meltwater lake as the ice disappeared.

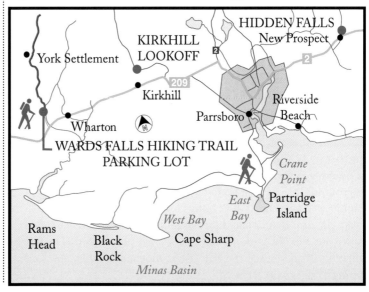

By the time the lowland ice was gone, the sea had nearly regained its normal volume. Gradually it flooded the sunken coastline, cutting new beaches inland. For centuries it covered the land where the highway now runs; at its highest it reached well up this slope. At the land rose, some wave-cut benches were erased and new ones added. Today these marine terraces rise step-like from the plain and follow its contours. They are easiest to spot on cleared land in the slanting light of morning and evening, especially when there is snow.

For half a century there was a DNR fire tower about 4 km/2.5 mi farther north on this road and 1 km/0.6 mi up a side road to the east. (The latter road is best hiked.) In 1996 the tower was slated for removal. Kirkhill is approximately 260 m/850 ft above sea level and on a clear day offers great views of the Cobequid upland and of the Parrsboro valley. This road comes out roughly 10 km/6 mi north at Harrison Settlement.

> *Nova Scotia erected its first steel fire lookout tower in 1936 at Nuttby Mountain north of Truro. By the 1950s every county had one or more, each equipped with an alidade (a large metal 360° circle with a rotating sight for locating fires) and a radio linked to headquarters in Shubenacadie, to local depots, and to truck crews. With the coming of spotter planes, water bombers, infrared detection, and rapid-deployment helicopter crews, towers are being phased out.*

BACK ON THE HIGHWAY

As you approach the DNR office, observe the small quarry to the north. Above its resistant Devonian rock is a thin layer of glacial gravel topped by pasture (white) spruce. The quarry is now a rifle range where DNR conservation officers test the marksmanship of would-be hunters.

Just before we enter Parrsboro, Rte 209 joins Hwy 2 coming down from the famous coal town of Springhill. [See also the **Trans Canada Highway**, Exit 5.] Travellers taking this route to Amherst will pass through what geologists call a wind gap—the abandoned bed of an ancient river. [See also the **Trans Canada Highway** at Folly Lake and the **Evangeline Trail** along St Marys Bay.] The river likely flowed south from the Atlantic Upland through the River Hebert and Avon valleys and south to the continental shelf. (Check your map to see how well they line up.) Another feature of the Parrsboro gap is its abundance of kames, heaps of water-laid gravel along the U-shaped valley walls. [See also the **Evangeline Trail** near Berwick.]

Kames near Parrsboro

Like Wentworth Valley north of Glenholme, the Parrsboro valley was packed with ice during the last glaciation. As the climate warmed, meltwater streams rushed over, beside, and under the glacier, leaving piles of gravel in their wake. Gilbert Lake and Newville Lake are remnants of that glacier.

Springhill has a fine miner's museum. Until the 1930s, Parrsboro shipped Springhill coal; some of the loading piers still remain.

Low tide near Parrsboro

Parrsboro and Area

Approaching Parrsboro from the west, we pass a deep, curving gorge with a sluggish river. The angle of slope and lack of bedrock show the gorge to be carved in solid gravel. Parrsboro itself is built on such gravel. In September the gorge is dotted with people hand-picking the blueberry crop before heavy frost blackens the fruit.

Early in the 19th century, Parrsboro was a major shipbuilding centre. Later it was a busy port and ferry terminus to the Annapolis Valley and Halifax. The ferry ran to Wolfville and Kingsport, directly opposite across Minas Basin. (In fact, Parrsboro town used to be part of Kings County.) The town's red brick Customs House and post office have been boarded up for years. Now Parrsboro relies on manufacturing, blueberries, forestry, and its reputation as a world-class rock-hounding and dinosaur site.

Outwash plains near Parrsboro

Coming into town, Hwy 2 passes a 5-m/16-ft-tall painted statue of Glooscap on the left. Bear right at the bandstand, and you'll be on Main Street. Dinosaur replicas decorate the power poles, storefronts sport paintings of ancient reptiles, and a model sea serpent frolics just east of the harbour bridge.

Less than a kilometre beyond the harbour bridge (turn left off Main Street just past the old brick Customs House) is Fundy Geological Museum on the right. Part of the Nova Scotia Museum, it was opened in 1995 to explain and promote the area's exciting geological history. As you enter, a "time-travel" video whizzes you through half a billion years of Earth history. Ask the way to Wassons Bluff, a world-class dinosaur discovery site.

The Harbour View Restaurant (first street east of the Museum) is a good spot to dine and to watch the Fundy tides. Note that some boats have special cradles to hold them upright at low tide. The restaurant has a "tide clock" and an interpretive display.

LEG-STRETCHER: *Wassons Bluff Walk*

One of North America's most famous dinosaur sites is 8.5 km/5.3 mi east of the museum on Riverside Road. In the late 1970s and early 1980s a National Geographic Society team headed by Dr Paul Olsen of Columbia University and Neil Shubin of Harvard unearthed the most complete assemblage of Triassic/Jurassic dinosaur fossils ever found. It included small and large dinosaurs, lizards, sharks, and the long-legged crocodilian *Otosoum*, which had 46-cm/18-in tracks. Nearly half the Triassic creatures failed to survive a mysterious "extinction event" which some scientists link to a known meteor impact at Manicouagan, Quebec, 730 km/500 mi northwest of Parrsboro. They also found fossils of the 0.3-m/1-ft *Trithelodont*, an ancestral mammal.

In April 1984 local rock collector Eldon George uncovered a set of three-toed fossil footprints only 1.3 cm/0.5 in long. They proved to be the tracks of a robin-sized dinosaur, the smallest ever found. Later findings indicated that most of the Triassic/Jurassic dinosaurs stalking the shore here were turkey- to ostrich-sized, and warm-blooded. The area was then tropical. For eons its lakeshores and streams would be grilled by hot sun; then there would be long periods of monsoon climate.

At the 8-km/5-mi mark heading east toward Greenhill, watch on the right for a dirt road about 1 km/0.6 mi past Swann Creek. Follow the Museum directions, park, and walk down to the beach. You'll find interpretive signage outlining local geological and fossil discoveries. Westward along the shore you'll see chimney rocks (columnar basalt), talus slopes, and lava flows. With luck you'll spot animal fossils, which you can collect if you have a permit.

Check tide times beforehand; people have been caught on the cliffs with no way back or up. It is also a good idea to wear a hard hat to protect against falling rocks.

> *This is the only place where you see, accurately dated, the change in the animal assemblage through that critical time when the dinosaurs began to rule the Earth.*
> – Dr Paul Olsen, Columbia University

Fundy Geological Museum staff taking fossil hunters on a tour

For detailed tour information, see Harry Thurston's *Dawning of the Dinosaurs: The Story of Canada's Oldest Dinosaurs* (Nimbus Publishing/Nova Scotia Museum, 1994).

From the beach you can see Two Islands (The Brothers), remnants of an arc of volcanic rock stretching from Cape Chignecto to Grand Manan, and dating to the initial breakup of the supercontinent Pangaea about 225 million years ago. Two Islands has a heronry. The rugged scenery has attracted cottage development since before the 1950s.

Replica of dinosaur skeleton at Fundy Geological Museum

BACK ON THE HIGHWAY

TO DO: *Parrsboro's Rockhound Roundup*
This annual August event offers walks to collect agates, amethyst, and zeolites around Partridge Island at low tide. The scenery and beach alone are worth a visit. If you haven't time but want souvenirs, visit Eldon George's Parrsboro Rock & Mineral Shop & Museum west of the old post office. It sells gemstones, agates, prospecting supplies, books, and maps.

SIDE TRIP: *Parrsboro Beach, Partridge Island, Black Rock*
Continuing along Main Street past the bridge exit, imagine sighting a large sailing ship stranded high on the river bank to the east. The Saxby Gale and tide of 1869 lifted a large square-rigger right up on dry land here.

To see Parrsboro Beach and remarkable views of Blomidon and Cape Split, drive along the west side of the harbour toward Black Rock. Just before the old coal pier, you'll see a small vessel snugged against the wharf. This is the *Kipawo*, Parrsboro's old-time ferry. These days The Ship's Company Theatre, a local drama group, uses it as a summer stage. In January 1997, a full moon plus three days of powerful westerly winds raised such a tide that the vessel was lifted and tilted against its moorings so that ice pans littered the deck.

If you're a history buff, drop in on Conrad Byers at Time Frame Photo, Main Street. He has a large collection of old photographs and an even larger fund of stories and information about the Parrsboro Shore.

About 3 km/2 mi past the *Kipawo*, you'll see the long dormered roof of Ottawa House; a short, steep gravel road descends to it and the beach.

Ottawa House Museum-by-the-Sea was the summer home of Sir Charles Tupper, a Nova Scotia politician who was Canada's Prime Minister for 10 weeks in 1896. It contains period furniture and many displays concerning local shipbuilding and lumbering. Upstairs you can inspect a timber wall that has been opened to reveal an early method of plastering. Lacking laths to hold the wet plaster, the workers roughened the hewn timbers with parallel hatchet chops.

Along the parking lot and overlooking the basin are interpretive signs explaining local geology. Walking down to the beach, you see the high hump of Partridge Island directly ahead, with Cape Blomidon directly behind it across Minas Gut. Two wide beaches join the 90-m/300-ft-high basalt dome to the mainland, with tidal marsh between. Rockhounds comb the outer cliffs at low tide, looking for amethysts and geodes loosened by ice and tide. Cape Sharp to the west is another basalt remnant.

Parrsboro's first settlers lived on the island for fear of attack. At that time a channel separated it from the mainland except at low tide. The Saxby Gale tossed up so much rock and sand in one night that it all but bridged the channel. Subsequent storms have completed the twin beach or tombolo that now join it to the mainland. [See also the **Fleur-de-lis Trail** at Point Michaud, the **Lighthouse Route** at Rissers Beach, etc.]

Along the beach toward Cape Sharp you can see steeply tilted, beautifully rippled Carboniferous shale cliffs, and ravines filled with fossil-bearing rubble brought here by ancient streams. NOTE: At full and new moon in spring and fall, low points on the beach road may be flooded, but not so deeply as to prevent passage.

About 7 km/4.3 mi west of the Parrsboro Beach exit, where the gravel road crests just past Black Rock, you can see an unusual 1-km/0.6-mi-long, needle-like spit below, fringed with a line of spruce trees. Until about 1910 this spit was called Black Island; then a storm blocked the west passage with sand and gravel, joining it to the shore. Again there are excellent views of Blomidon and Cape Split across the basin. This road is a dead end.

Blueberry fields west of Parrsboro

BACK ON THE HIGHWAY

As you drive east toward New Prospect, watch for step-like marine terraces along the north hillsides. A trained eye can sometimes make out four distinct benches, each representing a different sea level.

Outwash plain

[Partridge Island's] name has probably arisen from the numerous broods of partridges reported to have frequented its surface. These however have long since disappeared ... [It] not only offers a retreat from the fury of the tides, but also in tempestuous weather affords a shelter both on its east and west sides. A fine navigable river at hand, where thousand vessels may lie in safety, opens in the rear; here, during the cold and blustering months of autumn, their masts are seen rising ... like leafless pines ...
– Abraham Gesner, **Remarks on the Geology and Mineralogy of Nova Scotia,** 1836

VIEW: *Meanders of East Parrsboro River*

Along Hwy 2 there's a good example of floodplain development. Like the Diligent River, it meanders over soft Coal Age rock, depositing sediment from the hills. The best view is about 3 km/2 mi east of the road's junction with 2A. Along the valley many blueberry fields have been developed on glacial deposits too stony or infertile to make good pasture. [See also the **Trans Canada Highway** near Folly Lake and the **Evangeline Trail** at the Annapolis Valley.]

A native member of the heath family, blueberry grows best in full light where fire has removed competing vegetation. That's why successful growers mow and lightly burn the fields every two years. This stimulates bud growth and flower production, discourages pests and diseases, and destroys mountain laurel, Labrador tea, and other "weeds."

Cumberland County (see road map) is renowned for its wild blueberry production. There are major production areas south of Amherst and along the glacial outwash plains of the Parrsboro shore. Oxford is known as "The Wild Blueberry Capital of Canada." Its tractor-mounted "Blue Machine" berry-picker was invented by local entrepreneur Doug Bragg.

Watch for windbreaks of spruce and jack pine planted to protect the crop (e.g., near Diligent River, on the waterside).

Blueberries offer many good things: they slow memory loss, improve body coordination and fight cancer. And they taste great! The Japanese adore them. Growing wild blueberries commercially requires large expanses of fairly level, boulder-free land, workable by machinery. Western Cumberland County's extensive glacial gravels on level marine terraces and gentle hills have provided just that combination.

LEG-STRETCHER: *Hidden Falls*

At New Prospect we're again under the shadow of the Cobequids. Numerous streams descend its steep slope, and at the fault line there are falls. One of the easiest to reach is Hidden Falls, 5 km/3 mi east of Parrsboro. It cascades 38 m/125 ft down five ledges into a deep plunge pool.

The lower cascade is an easy 10-minute walk from the highway through old pasture and pleasant mixed forest. The previous land owners provided a railed viewing platform and a brookside bench half-way. There are wildflowers in season.

After New Prospect (a name that reflects the faith of local pioneers), we enter a narrow gorge cut by the Parrsboro River between Devonian granite to the north and Late Carboniferous rock to the south. The granite came from molten magma that welled up here when continental plates collided to form the supercontinent Pangaea. From here to Bass River the trail intersects several short mountain streams, including Moose River (two branches), Harrington Brook, and Economy River. A century ago men herded swarms of bumping logs down these streams each spring with pike poles, dynamite, and colourful cursing. Most of the brooks had dams to control water flow.

Moose River Falls

Where the upper Moose River plunges off the Cobequid upland, there are three waterfalls; one of them is the highest in mainland

Nova Scotia. The first occurs 1 km/0.6 mi upstream from the bridge and is reachable by following the river. A rusty ringbolt in the rock reminds us that until the 1950s, log drivers used this stream. The bolt held one end of a floating log boom that corralled logs after they plunged over the falls. Once the pool was full, the men would release the boom and drive the logs on down to the mill.

To exploit terrain too steep for horses, lumbermen moved portable mills to the timber and brought out lumber instead of logs. This they did by using sluices or flumes. Until the 1930s the Moose River area had a 4-km/2.5-mi-long wooden flume mounted on tall timber trestles and filled with water. Along it, thick deals or planks were floated down from the hills to barges moored off the river mouth.

The flume, about 45 cm/18 in wide, sloped gently and was made of tongue-and-groove lumber with raised sides. To prevent pile-ups, the moving planks were joined end to end by short lengths of chain lightly secured with lumber tacks. Tacks and chain were collected in a pail each evening and toted back to the flume head.

LEG-STRETCHER: *Rainbow Falls*
About 3.5 km/2.2 mi north of Moose River village, on Moose River's main (not west) branch, is one of the tallest cascades on mainland Nova Scotia. Because the woods roads in the vicinity are confusing, the best way to reach the falls is by following the river up. This takes about three-quarters of an hour to the first falls (smaller) and another 15 minutes' climb to the second set (Rainbow). The last 0.5 km is strenuous.

Even before you reach it, the main cascade makes its presence known by a deep rumble, by spray-drenched rocks, and a veil of mist rising beyond a bend in the river. Rounding the bend, you'll see a plume of white-gold water plummeting nearly 18 m/60 ft into a dark plunge pool where patches of white foam move like miniature sailing ships. In summer the glistening cliffs are festooned with saplings and ferns and grasses and violets that sway in the constant downdraft from the falling water. If the sun is out and at your back, you'll see a rainbow—hence the name. In winter the falls are a wall of intricately braided ice with icicle stalactites.

If you climb the east side of the falls and hike 0.5 km/0.3 mi upstream, you'll come to a third falls, not as spectacular but of respectable height.

To find Rainbow Falls, watch for the Moose River sign and bridge at about 8 km/5 mi east of New Prospect. Park in the gravel pit and hike from there.

Until the 1920s loggers commonly drove wood down this river, using gated splash dams to flush the logs along and wooden flumes to bypass wide bends and rocky narrows. Old-timers told retired fisheries officer George Brittain that when the Tuckers of Parrsboro logged here, a Mi'kmaq man accidentally went over the falls— and lived to tell the tale. In fact, when he climbed out of the plunge pool, he celebrated with a whoop. And the late Ronald Roberts of Moose River, when a small boy, used to follow the abandoned sluice upstream to pick mayflowers, and in his teens collected enough old boards to build a camp.

Mayflowers

In the fall of 1995, a few minutes east of the Moose River bridge, a small lake appeared on the south side of the highway. Beavers had dammed Moose Creek. Since then the young fir and aspen on the floodplain have drowned.

Perhaps such a pond—if it does not endanger the highway and have to be drained—will gradually develop its own ecosystem: anaerobic bacteria, algae, mosquitoes, whirligig beetles, dragonflies, pond-lilies, frogs, trout, ducks—perhaps even a mink. [See also the **Trans Canada Highway** near Telford.] Even if the dam is destroyed, nature will take a different tack. Water-logged grasses and ferns will resprout, alders will shoot up, wood rot fungi and bark beetles will invade the dying trees, woodpeckers will jackhammer them out, the trees will fall, and the floodplain will resume its former patterns.

For a few kilometres beyond Moose River, the road follows a western tributary of Harrington River through the same valley, then emerges onto flatter ground.

STOP: *Methodist Cemetery*

To gain a sense of the pioneers along this shore, visit this neatly kept cemetery 3 km/2 mi west of Five Islands Village. It bears surnames like Marsh, Fulmore, Aylward, McLelland, Nickerson, Webb, and Lewis, men and women who settled here from the early 1800s on.

The stones make clear that many women and children died young. For women a great hazard was "childbed fever" caused by unsanitary conditions in the days before the role of germs was understood. For children, in those days before inoculation, it was measles, whooping cough, and scarlet fever. The stones show that old people tended to die in late winter, when resistance was lowest and food often scarce.

SIDE TRIP: *Weir Fishing*

At Lower Five Islands in summer you can see traditional fish weirs—nets strung on tall sharpened spruce poles driven deep into the mud at low tide. Extension poles are added to ensure they reach above high tide mark, when the trap is under water. At low tide the catch of herring and flounder are retrieved with dip nets or picked from the meshes by hand.

Fisherman weaving fish weir off Economy Point

Traditionally, weirs consisted of stakes woven with tree branches. Today, durable (and to the fish almost invisible) nylon twine has replaced the brush. Weir tending is done at low tide, which occurs about 50 minutes later each day, so night trips are necessary.

Watch or ask locally for Philip Fulmore Road, which leads after 1 km/0.6 mi to Harrington Beach. James Webb still uses traditional Mi'kmaq weir techniques. A Bass River tour company called Sandpiper organizes tours to his weir.

BACK ON THE GLOOSCAP TRAIL

VIEW: *Five Islands*
Approaching the village, you'll see spectacular views of the islands. From east to west they are Moose, Diamond, Long, Egg, and Pinnacle, with The Needles beyond. It's no coincidence that the latter look a lot like the stacks off Cape Split. Both were formed by dark basaltic lava squirting up into sandstone fissures and cooling slowly. As the softer sandstone eroded, the basalt stacks were exposed.

The inner islands are made of tilted red Triassic sandstone crusted with the same dark rock. While this rock breaks down readily in the sea, it resists ordinary weathering. That's why the islands and nearby headland haven't eroded away. [See also various places along the **Evangeline Trail.**]

This volcanic activity took place as Pangaea began to pull apart 200 million years ago. The strain cracked weaker parts of the Earth's crust, much as pulling a candy bar apart breaks up the chocolate coating. Sections of crust dropped, creating steep-sided rift valleys like Africa's today. This happened all down the future Eastern Seaboard.

The Fundy trough is the largest of these local rift valleys. As the cracks widened, fiery lava gushed up. The glowing molten rock overflowed the west end of the trough and the land on both sides. Seventeen separate flows have been counted near Brier Island. The future Minas Basin had fewer.

Fundy mud

Long Island used to have a heron nesting site in a fir grove. These birds find a new site once the buildup of guano (dung) kills the trees. The beach road at Five Islands passes a factory where workers shuck local soft-shelled blue clams. Farther on there's a floating wharf where lobster boats tie up. At low tide both wharf and boats are surrounded by mud.

LEG-STRETCHER:
Five Islands Provincial Park
As the highway starts to climb 215-m/700-ft Economy Mountain, watch for a routed pine sign announcing the entrance to this camp-

ing park on the mountain's seaward side. The park offers excellent views of tidal mud flats and of the islands. You can hike (or ski) nature trails through coastal white spruce and upland mixed forest. Lofty cliffs afford excellent views of Cobequid Bay and of the

Economy shore at low tide

Blomidon shore. And if you have something to dig with and a pail, you can go clamming on the mud flats (keeping a watchful eye on the tide), and with luck, cook them on the beach at sunset as the tide comes in. Acadians like to add some apple vinegar to the cooking liquor and drink it; délicieux!)

The grey streaks in the red cliffs here are salt deposits. They reveal alternating periods of monsoon and desert conditions in the Triassic world. Apparently triggered by a slight wobble in the earth, each period lasted about 21,000 years. During the droughty periods, lakes dried up, much as Utah's Great Salt Lake does today, leaving a layer of salt. [See also **Sunrise Trail** at Pugwash and Malagash.]

Driving up Economy Mountain (Mi'kmaq word *kenomee* meaning "long point jutting into the sea"), you can identify the resistant basaltic cap by the steepness of the grade. [See also the **Evangeline Trail** near Port Williams.]

Economy Falls now

The falls in 1997

LEG-STRETCHER: *Economy Falls*

The steepest part of the Cobequids is from Economy west, where intense faulting plus glaciation has produced a scarp. Several rivers coming off the upland tumble over this ledge, each with one or more waterfalls. Economy River has two, and one of them has a trail to it. It's a 1.5-km/0.9-mi uphill walk, with stairs in the steepest parts and benches to get your wind back.

Exit north onto River Philip Road (second road west of Economy River), and if possible get directions at a farmhouse. Failing that, drive past fields 4.7 km/2.9 mi to a junction. Taking the right fork, go another 2.3 km/1.4 mi, where a smaller road to the right runs for 0.5 km/0.3 mi, where you turn right and park. The trail starts at the last turn, heading right. Turn right again after 0.3 km/100 ft and follow the path to a set of steps going to the foot of the falls. Until January 1998 the cascade was almost 30 m/100 ft high. Then a rockfall removed the lip, reducing its height. An estimated 2000 tonnes of rubble fell into the plunge pool, filling the 16-m/53-ft deep hole. An unusually thick ice buildup, plus weakening due to blasting by log drivers around 1923, likely caused the collapse, said local resident Aubrey McBurnie.

STOP: *Cobequid Lookoff*

Like Cape Blomidon, Economy Mountain (Gerrish Mountain on topographic maps) is only here thanks to a crust of hardened lava. Otherwise, most of it would be red mud swishing back and forth in the tides of Cobequid Bay.

From the hilltop lookoff on the north side there's an arresting view of the roof of the Cobequids, here just over 300 m/1,000 ft high. After eons of erosion, it's surprisingly flat. [See also Trans Canada Highway at West Wentworth.] The Cobequids, which were ancient when the Rockies began to rise, were once two to three times higher than this. Thirteen km/8 mi northeast is Simpson Lake, source of Economy River. Inland are dark patches of spruce, fir, and hemlock, cutover areas, and steep ravines. In October the facing slopes flame with vermilion, tangerine, and gold as sugar maple, beech, and yellow birch prepare for winter. There's a year-round spring in the cliff across the highway.

Stack near Economy

You'll need to brake going down the Truro side. The view of Cobequid Bay and Economy Point is spectacular, with farms and woodlots spread over undulating lowlands that grade into level marshlands protected by dykes. The near shore is fringed with crumbling cliffs and flowerpot islands, all made of the same soft red sandstone/siltstone that floors the bay. This accounts for the water's pinkish tint. Twice every 24 hours, the suspended silt is swished to and fro like chocolate powder in a milkshake.

All this sediment has built some of the largest mud flats and tidal marshes in eastern Canada. At extreme low tide they extend several

The January 1997 super-tide removed nearly 30 m/100 ft of cottage frontage near Economy Point.

kilometres out. In fact, from shore level, no salt water can be seen at all then.

These thick flats take up space, forcing the tides still higher. At the narrowest place, between Economy Point and Burncoat Head on the Noel shore, the world's highest tides occur. In 1960 a range of 16 m/52 ft was recorded—eight times that of the open ocean. An estimated 116 billion tonnes of water pours through there twice a day. No wonder both headlands are being rapidly cut back.

As the Economy-Burntcoat gate continues to widen, the flow of water will spread and lose height. Scientists believe Fundy's tides, oscillating in synchrony with Atlantic tides outside, have been increasing for thousands of years and may be near their peak.

STOP: *Cobequid Interpretation Centre*

This new facility about 6 km/3.7 m east of Economy Mountain offers exhibits describing West Colchester's natural history and land use, as well as a computer data bank to help you find local natural attractions. From the tower one can see at least three counties. [See also the **Evangeline Trail** at The Lookoff.]

At first glance the square brown tower resembles a lighthouse. Actually, it's a World War II observation tower. Camp Debert had an airfield where pilots heading overseas practised aerial warfare. The wide mud flats made an ideal target area. From the tower, observers tracked the accuracy of bombing and strafing runs over the bay. Until 1995 the tower, then near the shore, stood closer to Debert. Over the years the tides nibbled away at the bank. In the 1980s the tower began to lean. When it seemed about to topple, community-spirited people planted it here. The view from the top floor is great.

As you pass Carrs Brook, the low land to seaward is part of Economy Point, enclosing the Economy River estuary. Where the highway crosses the brook, on the high west bank, there's an excellent cross-section of local sandstone, its steeply tilted brick-red layers streaked with salt and gypsum.

LEG-STRETCHER: *Thomas Cove*

A few minutes east of Carrs Brook, watch on the right for the sign to this new 81-ha/20-ac coastal reserve. Local people manage the reserve, which has diverse intertidal life, wide vistas of the Noel and Blomidon shores, and 8 km/5 mi of existing and proposed hiking trails.

If you arrive at low tide, take a stroll on the flats—being sure to check tide times first. People seldom sink beyond the ankle; if you're nervous, carry a stick and probe soft spots. On the mud's satiny surface you'll find numerous worm trails, clam holes, and the tiny mud shrimps on which many shorebirds feed. So fertile are these flats that thousands of migrating geese, ducks, and shorebirds use it as a staging area spring and fall.

The hull was built in Portapique in the [early] 1900s and I fished that boat up until the 1970s. We went out on the high water and ran off to our fishing grounds. Once we got there we'd put the net out. We had nothing to do with where the net went; it went with the current and the boat's job was to follow the net.
– Russell Cooke of Portapique "Shad Fishery: Gone but Not Forgotten," **Truro Daily News**, *July 9, 1996*

An island cemetery out on the marsh dates from the area's first settlers in the 1700s. Coastal subsidence since then has lowered it below high tide level. Watch 1 km/0.6 mi east of Economy Village for the dirt road to Economy Point and follow the signs along the access road to parking. There are three trails, one around the headland, one in the cove, and one east of the cove.

STOP: *Bass River Chairs*

For over a century Bass River has been noted for its sturdy chairs and rockers made of rock maple and yellow birch from the Cobequid Hills. Varnish and wood dust are a highly flammable mixture and over the years the Dominion Chair Company has suffered several bad fires. Always it has rebuilt and carried on.

In the mid-1980s a greater problem developed. Good local hardwood became scarce, forcing the firm to import wood from Eastern Canada and the US. Employees at the store will show you the company's product and tell you more. In December 1999 the Bass River Heritage Society acquired a former church, moved it to the factory grounds and began work on the Bass River Interpretation Centre.

Just east of the village is the workshop of stone mason Heather Lawson, who has operated Raspberry Bay Stone since 1992. Using sandstone from Scotsburn or Wallace [See **Sunrise Trail**], she carves garden ornaments, monuments, headstones and architectural pieces.

TO SEE: *Portapique Smelt Run*

This river has cut through deep glacial outwash and built a wide tidal delta clothed in cord grass and other salt-tolerant plants. Each April, spawning smelt (*Osmeris*, a small, silvery member of the salmon tribe), swarm into the estuary. People dip-net them, and children catch them with hook and line. A per-person quota discourages overfishing.

One diatom can produce 100 million descendants in 30 days, alternating between asexual and sexual reproduction.

Near here in 1900 you might have seen a small locomotive puffing down the valley pulling cars loaded with white powder. To the north, at Silica Lake near Castlereagh and at a few other places in the Cobequids, are beds of natural silica. Refined (usually it's found mixed with mud), silica is pure white. It consists of the shells of single-celled, box-like freshwater plankton (diatom: Greek for "cut in two"). Gardeners call it diatomaceous earth and dust it on plants to kill caterpillars. It's also used in detergents and other household products. Other deposits occur on Digby Neck and in Cape Breton.

A century ago this "fossil flour" was sought for making rubber, firebrick and glass, and for refining sugar. Tiny Saints Rest near the mouth of Bass River was the terminus of a narrow-gauge railroad bringing the white substance down from Silica Lake. The deposit covered 1.6 ha/ 4 ac and averaged 1.5 m/5 ft thick. To get at the silica, the lake was drained using a 10-hp pump—no environmental guidelines then! From 1889 to 1923 the Oxford Tripoli Company operated a processing plant there, averaging 40 tonnes per year. Between 1921 and 1955 Nova Scotia exported 11,500 tonnes of dry refined product from this and other deposits.

A 1907 lighthouse at nearby Saints Rest has been renovated for tourists. Ask at the store for directions.

STOP: *Great Village*

In the 19th century, captains and crews from this shore sailed the Seven Seas, bringing back not only curios but new notions of building. These are reflected in Great Village's intriguing older houses and their architectural embellishments. Also, between 1820 and 1885 this immodestly named village built and launched over 40 square-riggers. When a church was to be built, shipbuilders did the job. A good example is the large black-and-white wooden edifice whose soaring spire can be seen where Hwy 2 rounds the cove to cross the bridge. Inside, its rafters and ceiling resemble nothing so much as the hull of a wooden ship. A museum in the basement recounts the community's marine heritage. Next door there's another intriguing museum, housed in a store that's been in the same family for over 125 years.

From Great Village we trim the shore of Cobequid Bay, dipping into the wooded valleys of small creeks, skimming over broad folds with old farmsteads perched on their crests. From the crests you can see out over the mud flats—bald eagles often soar here—and across to Maitland and the mouth of the Shubenacadie River. Most of the farms now belong to Truro commuters.

At Glenholme (Exit 11) Hwy 2 merges with the Trans Canada Highway for about 5 km/3 mi. After crossing the Folly and Debert rivers (note the small dyke on the latter and the strawberry market between), it resumes at Exit 12 to Masstown.

Masstown (formerly Cobequid Village) is so named because in the early 1700s Acadians from surrounding districts congregated near here for Sunday Mass. Until the 1970s the old church foundations were still traceable. Inside that church in 1755 local residents heard with alarm the pronouncement of deportation, soon followed by the burning of their homes and farm buildings. Contrary to popular wisdom which blames England, New England colonists played a key role in this act. They saw Acadia as a threat to their security and France as a competitor for the lucrative cod fishery. Twenty years later they would rebel against England's control to found their own nation.

For decades Masstown has been the unofficial strawberry capital of central Nova Scotia. Check in July at Masstown Market or at local U-pick operations.

Along the bay, you'll catch glimpses of wide dyked haylands. Between Glenholme and Bible Hill on both sides there are roughly 40 km/25 mi of dykes in good repair. The Onslow district on this side was resettled by 30 Massachusetts families in 1761. Other New England settlers soon followed. Lacking the skills to maintain dykes, for a time they let them fall into disrepair. But as cattle and demand for land increased, they restored and extended them.

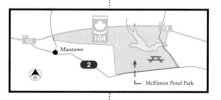

VIEW: *Pine Plantation*

North of the Debert exit are groves of young red pine in neat rows. Planted by DNR in the 1950s, they were thinned in the 1980s by removing alternate rows. As of 1996, the plantation had escaped the Sirococcus fungus, perhaps because sea fogs are uncommon and because the sandy soils are perfect for pines. [See also the **Trans Canada Highway** near Exit 13.]

The provincial Parks Division headquarters and sign shop are located in the angle of Hwy 2 and the exit to the Trans Canada Highway.

SIDE TRIPS: *Debert Area McElmon Pond Wildlife Sanctuary*

Lady's-slipper

Besides being one of the nicest provincial picnic parks in the county, this is an important stop-over for migrating waterfowl. Lakes are scarce in soft sandstone country like this, because streams easily carve channels and seldom become blocked. So this little pond, originally dammed to power a sawmill and grist mill, is all the more important—especially to Canada geese. Here they can rest in safety and forage on nearby corn stubble and rich mud flats. In November, during the peak of fall migration, parts of the pond are alive with shifting brown and white rafts of birds.

Nova Scotia's only sizeable population of breeding American widgeon makes the pond their summer home. A big attraction for this freshwater duck is the floating water plant *Elodea canadensis*. Introduced by DNR biologists years ago, the tiny-leaved nutritious plant now forms thick, yellow-green mats in sheltered coves throughout the area.

If you walk the pondside hiking trail near the south side, you may notice, on the far shore, small wooden boxes nailed to trees. These are wood duck nesting boxes placed by DNR in that cove. To protect these rare and brightly coloured ducks from disturbance, no hiking or boating is permitted in the western arm of the pond. (Hence the floating barrier.) Elsewhere, angling is allowed with a DNR permit.

The picnic area occupies an open field east of the pond. It has tables, fresh drinking water, and toilets. The trail meanders across a footbridge into mixed conifer forest with alder hollows where lady's-slipper orchids grow in early spring (please don't pick them).

To get to the park, take the Debert exit and drive 0.5 km/0.6 mi north of Hwy 2. [See also the **Trans Canada Highway** at Exit 13.]

During World War II the sand plains north of here echoed to the roar of aircraft and the tramp of thousands of soldiers. Camp Debert was one of Canada's largest military bases and a jumping-off point for soldiers and pilots heading to European battlefields. At various times the 78 km²-/30-sq mi base hosted the 3rd, 4th, 5th, and 7th Infantry Divisions. There were bunkers, bomb shelters, a hospital, and two movie theatres. Later, during the Cold War, Camp Debert housed a NATO communications centre and a nuclear fallout shelter. In the same period, hundreds of prefabricated, winterized plywood huts were built here for emergency shelters in the event of nuclear war.

Debert still has an airstrip, and since the 1970s light industries have set up shop along the abandoned roads. However, the rest of this sprawling camp, including its cracked tarmac and crumbling

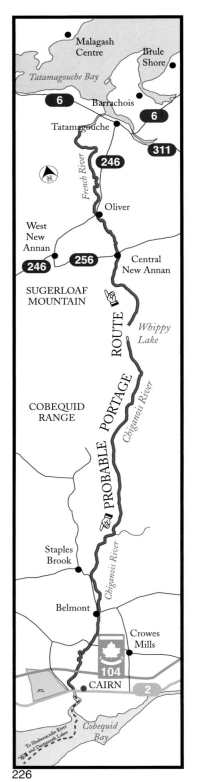

concrete bunkers, is being actively reclaimed by poplar, birch, and conifers. The base was officially closed June 28, 1996.

BACK ON THE HIGHWAY

A little east of the park, Hwy 2 crosses the estuary of the Chiganois River (also called Isgonish), whose dykes protect a wide pasture. The short deciduous trees along the road are red oak. Though more typical of western Nova Scotia, this native species is common enough along local rivers to suggest that migrating geese have transported viable acorns in their digestive tracts.

TO SEE: *Historic Route*

Watch for a National Historic Site cairn on the far side of the Chiganois. The inscription tells us that long ago this river was the main Mi'kmaq and Acadian route across the Cobequids to Northumberland Strait.

The Mi'kmaq would paddle upstream as far as possible, portage their canoes and gear over the Cobequids to the headwaters of the French River, and travel down to Tatamagouche Bay. From there it was only about 32 km/20 mi across the strait to Île St-Jean (Prince Edward Island).

By the 1700s, the Acadians had an oxcart road along the same route, with boat connections to Louisbourg via Canso Strait. This allowed them to sell or barter farm produce and bring back glassware, sugar, tea, and other things they could not make for themselves. [See also the **Sunrise Trail** at Tatamagouche.]

Later, the British used the Chiganois/French River route to get from Halifax via the Shubenacadie River to Charlottetown.

North of Truro, Hwy 2 merges with Hwy 102 to Halifax. Crossing the Salmon River bridge, you'll see broad expanses of dyked hayland opening up toward Lower Truro (downstream) and Onslow (upstream). Parts of these have been farmed since the 1690s. Behind the level marshes are rolling uplands with dairy farms and woodlots of spruce, fir, red maple, and birch. Fertile soils and long experience make the area one of Nova Scotia's chief dairying districts.

The ruined bridge abutments downstream once supported the old Board Landing Bridge. Here in

1761 the New England Planters unloaded the timbers of their dismantled homes and farm buildings. For easy reassembly, each rafter, joist, and sill had been numbered. (This book was written on a desk made from one of those boards, a 71-cm/28-in wide, hand-adzed, white pine plank used in wainscoting a pioneer home at Mingo's Corner in Onslow.)

The Planters came at the invitation of British authorities in Halifax to take up Acadian lands expropriated as a war measure six years earlier.

The trail follows Hwy 102 for about 1 km/0.6 mi, then leaves it at Exit 14. At the bottom of the ramp, turn left onto Hwy 236 and head west along the south side of Cobequid Bay.

STOP: *Tidal Phenomenon*

Here, as in Chignecto Bay, salt water floods every low-lying stream twice daily. In estuaries that narrow gradually, the incoming tide is squeezed into a set of low waves called a tidal bore. These waves travel upstream, making the river "run backwards." Truro's Salmon River has one of the best bores in the province. [See also the **Evangeline Trail** near Avondale and the **Glooscap Trail** at River Hebert.] High tides occur about 50 minutes later each day, with the highest bores (approximately 1 m/3 ft) occurring at new and full moon in spring and fall. For tide times see the local paper (*Daily News*) or listen to CKCL (AM 60). (The Palliser gift shop also has tide tables.)

The best place to watch the bore is from the river bank behind the Palliser Restaurant, which is near the Board Landing Bridge site. To get there, watch on the right as you emerge from the Exit 14 overpass for the sign saying Tidal Bore Road. Turn right and go 0.5 km/0.3 mi to the restaurant parking lot. From this vantage point the bore at its best is a foaming wall of silty water that charges round a bend in the river. Slow but irresistible, it advances between the dykes, pushing a moist breeze before it, smelling of mud and salt. (It smells better since the new sewage treatment plant was built in Lower Truro.) With a hissing roar like surf, it proceeds upstream at walking pace. Behind it the channel fills with impressive speed. Suddenly you realize anew how easily people can get trapped by Fundy tides.

The trees lining the bank north of the Palliser are mostly native red oak.

SIDE TRIP: *Truro*

After viewing the bore, take time to see Truro. Turn left off Tidal Bore Road onto Hwy 236, which becomes Robie Street. "The Hub of Nova Scotia" lies almost halfway between Yarmouth and Sydney

The [Onslow] settlers [endured] great privations, especially the first few years in their new home ... Haliburton says that on [their] arrival ... they 'found the country laid waste to prevent the return of the Acadians, but 570 acres of upland around the ruins of houses were cleared, though partially overgrown ... Remains of French roads were still visible, as also parts of their bridges.'
– Robert R. McLeod, **Markland, or Nova Scotia**, 1903

Truro likely got its name from a town on Cape Cod, Massachusetts, named in turn for a port in Cornwall, England. (The word seems to be a shortened form of "true road.") Before that it was called Cobequid *(Mi'kmaq for "end of flowing water," or tide-head).*

and is therefore an important distribution centre where major roads and railways converge.

The town takes pride in its fine old shade trees, especially its native white or American elm. White elm thrives on river floodplains. During Queen Victoria's Golden (50th) and Diamond (60th) jubilees in 1887 and 1897, dozens of Maritime towns planted thousands of wild saplings. That's why we have so many elm-shaded streets named Prince, Queen, Albert, and Victoria.

But along Prince and Queen streets today, you'll see many fresh elm stumps and severely pruned trees. Since the mid-1980s, the Truro Tree Commission has been curbing an epidemic of Dutch elm disease. [See also the **Trans Canada Highway** at River Denys, the **Lighthouse Route** at Liverpool, and the **Evangeline Trail** at Kentville.] In the 1970s Truro lost over 200 elms to the insect-borne Asian fungus. Since 1999 the town has commissioned local sculptors to carve statues of its noble citizens from dead elm trunks.

Purple loosestrife

The only practical control is sanitation cutting—the prompt removal and destruction of material that is diseased or likely to become so. This material is burned or buried no later than May, thereby denying the elm bark beetle that carries the spores a place to lay its eggs and to rear young. This program saved most of the town's remaining elms, and much of the credit belongs to the late Richard M. Bulmer, a long-time DNR forester, however, the very dry summers later killed many already-stressed trees.

Saving rural elms is much harder. Instead of being in convenient straight lines, in the country they grow singly or in small groups over wide areas, often mixed with other species. To treat or remove a tree here and there is not practicable. In some areas two-thirds of these elms have died.

Amateur gardeners further disseminated [it] by buying supposedly sterile loosestrife nursery stock as an ornamental .... The average loosestrife plant in Nova Scotia each year produces 800,000 seeds ....
– **Rural Delivery,** April 1997

VIEW: *Introduced Plants*

From the day the first Europeans arrived, Old World plants like dandelion, Scotch broom, and pigweed immigrated with them. Most have been naturalized so long that we take them for native.

A recent arrival is purple loosestrife (*Lythrum salicaria*), a native of European wetlands. It showed up in the Annapolis Valley early in the century and has recently has been spreading in central Nova Scotia. Partial drainage of marshes creates perfect habitat, and bulldozing spreads its seeds.

In July watch for its purple-pink flower spikes atop 1–2-m/3–6-ft stems along ditches (not to be confused with native fireweed, which blooms on dry ground in late August). In July the marsh behind

Truro's Kiwanis Park (between Robie and Juniper streets) is awash with its pretty magenta blooms.

Unfortunately, loosestrife has no natural enemies here. No native bird, mammal, or invertebrate is known to consume any part of it. So in time it may fill every shallow marsh and pondside, choking out local plants upon which many wild animals depend.

Scientists at the Nova Scotia Agricultural College in nearby Bible Hill have been seeking a suitable enemy. A few years ago they imported from Europe three kinds of insect that prey on loosestrife: a root weevil with the imposing Latin name of *Hylobius transverovittatus,* and two beetles. They bred them and in 1994 inoculated weevils into loosestrife roots on Belleisle Marsh in Annapolis County. [See the **Evangeline Trail.**] The adults take three years to breed and spread.

Another promising predator is a leaf beetle from central and western Canada. In 1995–96 specimens were acquired from Alberta and Ontario, and by July 1996 1,200 had been raised. Ducks Unlimited (Canada) and DNR are helping to release 50 pairs at a time into key wetlands around Truro, on the Chignecto Isthmus, and in Cape Breton Island. Each female beetle lays about 300 eggs per batch, and the young take a month to mature.

Another plant the summer motorist may see more of is the sunflower. In recent years, farmers in Onslow (just west of Truro) have been harvesting fields of it for bird seed and cooking oil markets.

> *Victoria Park was conceived in 1887 for Queen Victoria's Golden Jubilee. Local lawyer James Ross devoted years to developing the park on land donated by Susan Waddell Stevens (hence Waddell Falls). Sir Adams G. Archibald, Truro's Father of Confederation, chaired the planning committee.*

Truro's Kiwanis Park pond is also a good spot to watch ducks. This reclaimed gravel pit hosts several dozen mallards and black ducks. The birds fend for themselves in summer, but have grown so dependent on winter handouts that many of them no longer migrate. Bird lovers feed them all winter, at great expense to themselves.

Ask at the Colchester Historical Museum on Young Street or at DNR's Bible Hill office for names of members of the Cobequid Naturalists Society who lead local nature walks.

> *Brandy Spring is named for British soldiers who cooled their flasks here during the Fenian troubles of the late 1860s. The clearing above the stairs once had a glebe house or parsonage. In 1885–86 Father Cummaine, an Irish priest, lived here. Bits of his garden remain, including two dying honey locust trees, a snowberry bush and an English hawthorn. ("Haw," like "hip" in "rosehip," is Old English for a small apple-like fruit).*

STOP: *Truro's Jewel*
Victoria Park contains 162 ha/400 ac of old and young forest adjacent to the rugged ravine of Lepper Brook, near the centre of Truro. It offers two waterfalls, nature walks through an ancient hemlock/white pine grove, rustic stairs, and the 2.5-km/1.6-mi Jim

Vibert Trail with exercise stations. It has ample parking, picnic tables, toilets, shelters, barbecue pits, and a swimming and wading pool.

Lepper Brook demonstrates how a stream develops. The level parking lot, playground, pool, and picnic ground occupy the floodplain. It was built up over millennia by sediments eroded from Coal Age deposits. A few hundred metres upstream, the valley narrows abruptly. Here the brook has had to cut through resistant Early Carboniferous shales. The result is a V-shaped gorge some 30 m/98 ft deep. Most of this erosion happened rapidly as torrents of glacial meltwater rushed toward the ocean starting 12,000 years ago.

Enter via Park or Palmer streets off Brunswick (parallel to Prince, south of the railway track). For more information visit the Tourist Information chalet in Victoria Square (opposite the Prince/Willow intersection), or call the Truro Parks Recreation Commission.

One of the nicest walks starts at the footbridge near the swimming pool. It follows along the hillside above the swimming pool, passes Brandy Spring, and climbs a short wooden stair to the right before heading uphill. It passes a small field, then rambles through a forest of 300-year-old hemlock and white pine and a stand of younger red spruce. It ends at a set of stairs above a spectacular waterfall.

In the late 1980s the park's red spruce suffered an outbreak of eastern spruce beetle. These small native insects feed on the inner bark of aging spruce, laying their eggs in distinctively branched tunnels. To the public's dismay, the town had to clearcut several hectares south of the brook in order to save the remaining healthy trees.

VIEW: *Giant River*

Truro straddles a glacial outwash plain created by a river that dwarfed the existing Salmon River. You can detect its ancient channel in the step-like terraces cut into the hills on either side. For a panoramic view, follow Brunswick Street (near sea level) east from Park Street to Wood Street, turn right, and drive uphill past Glenwood Avenue to the microwave tower. On the way you will pass three distinct terraces, each one an ancient river bank. Count them as you drive back down.

These terraces date from different glaciations. The highest water lapped against the foothills of the Cobequids. As the ice melted, the land rose and the river cut narrower channels. The lowest belongs to today's Salmon River.

The original town was laid out on the floodplain. After very heavy rain, or during the spring breakup, the Salmon and North rivers still overflow their banks some years, flooding some basements and adding another layer of silt.

BACK ON THE HIGHWAY

West of Truro on Hwy 236 again, we pass through some of the province's best farmland. Thanks to fertile soils, good markets, and reasonable profits, local farmers have been able to resist suburbanization. Beyond the sewage treatment plant on Savage Island, wide dykelands scored with straight drainage ditches stretch away toward Onslow.

Dykes near Onslow

Dense softwood west of Truro

The embankment paralleling the dykes is the abandoned roadbed of the Dominion Atlantic Railway. It was built through here in 1895, linking Halifax and Yarmouth via Truro and Windsor. Trucking put it out of business and in the mid-1970s the rails were taken up. Now farmers, cross-country skiers, and hikers use the roadbed. The low brown structure on the wooded knoll near the shore is the Truro and area waste treatment facility, opened in 1996–97.

As you go up the first hill into Old Barns the wooded knoll on the right, dwarfed by power pylons, is called Yuill's Island. Like Savage Island it *was* an island before the Lower Truro dykes were built. Later, it was a pasture; still later, it was colonized by white spruce, which are now succumbing to bark beetle and being cut.

From there to the Shubenacadie River, the road rises and falls as it crosses gently rounded hills dotted with dairy barns, silos, and large farmhouses. The bungalows and trailer homes belong to retired farmers and newcomers. These lands were first cleared in the late 18th century and so far have resisted suburbanization.

Old Barns is strung out along the Salmon River estuary. Notice how the road dips and climbs, and how at the bottom of each hollow is the small brook that helped carve it. These rolling fields slope northward down to dykelands and southward to mixed forest. The dividing line between pasture and forest is often marked by cliffs of harder Coal Age shales which made the land too rough to farm. However it grows fine red spruce, yellow birch, red maple, and hemlock. Along the brooks there are ash trees. Small amounts of iron and gypsum were mined here in the 19th century.

> Old Barns
> *This unusual name dates from the Acadian deportation. Local lore states that two Acadian round barns were left unburned to mark safe low-tide fording places for New England Planters arriving to take up the vacated lands. One barn stood on the knoll opposite the United Church.*

LEG-STRETCHER: *Woodlot Tour*

The Loughead Family Demonstration Forest offers guided tours of its silviculture work; watch for the sign on the left, between the octagonal barn and the elementary school, or call the county DNR office. The wood-chipped, 0.8-km/0.5-mi Chesapeake Trail offers a self-guided tour of 14 stops featuring tree identification, a portable sawmill, and examples of wildlife habitat. An extension leads to Irwin Lake. School classes are welcome provided they book ahead.

Toward the north, across the rolling pasture and corn land, you'll glimpse the Cobequid Mountains rising above the Debert sand plains, and notched by the Wentworth wind gap. Far down the bay on clear days one can see Five Islands. (When the islands appear to float above the horizon, it's a sure sign of bad weather.)

Many visitors to Old Barns remark about the many drumlin-like hills, some over 30 m/100 ft high. They consist entirely of sand and pebbles and were formed by moving glaciers and running water. Across the bay you can see where tides have sawed some of them in two.

Until the 1980s one saw few silos here. Then younger farmers, tired of coping with fickle hay-drying weather, switched to storing green hay fermented with molasses. Ensilage not only eliminates the problem of having to dry hay in wet weather, but preserves more nutrients, which produces more milk per tonne. To get even higher milk yields, some farmers began to grow cattle corn and soybeans in rotation. At first these were sown in ploughed ground. Ploughing allows dormant weed seeds to germinate. For weed control, farmers used herbicides like Atrazine and Vision. However, weed-killers also kill essential soil flora, hindering nutrient flow and requiring more fertilizer.

Another problem is that harvested corn and soybean leave the ground more or less bare for half the year. This leads to sheet erosion on sloping land. Freezing and thawing loosens the soil, and wind and water take it away. Wind erosion is worst when sub-zero temperatures dry out the air and the surface layer. Water erosion can occur any time of the year, but is worst from fall through spring. Rivulets running off these rounded hills take grains of topsoil with them, eventually carving deep gullies. To help prevent sheet erosion, farmers are experimenting with no-plough seeding and with leaving stubble to slow the runoff. Even so, there is substantial loss. Contour ploughing and cover crops help, but the only sure cure is to keep hilly land in pasture year-round.

STOP: *Renovated Acadian Dyke*
Between the flashing amber light and the white United Church in Old Barns, a gravel road leads north to Clifton. The marsh on either side has been ditched and "domed" for better drainage. Immediately past the bridge, a tractor lane exits east to a dyke. Mill Brook alongside it has been straightened to prevent flooding. At low tide the brook enters Cobequid Bay through a gated square culvert in the dyke. As the tide rises, a clapper or vertically hinged door swings shut from the outside, preventing salt water from entering and killing the hay. [See also the **Evangeline Trail** near Port Williams, etc.] The gravel pit behind the church contains excellent profiles of layered silt, sand, and cobble deposited as glacial outwash.

Just beyond the cemetery on the right, Black Rock Road loops north around the shore. The first hill it climbs is called Keel Bank Hill locally, a reference to shipbuilders' using the curved larch that once grew here for making the bow and stern timbers that fasten to a vessel's keel.

VIEW: *Beaver Brook*

For a few kilometres beyond Old Barns the trail more or less follows the windings of this alder-fringed stream. Beaver Brook rises near Green Oaks 10 km/6 mi south, dropping about 80 m/260 ft on its route to Cobequid Bay. Like any mature stream flowing over soft rock near sea level, it meanders from side to side along its floodplain. As it undercuts one bank, silt is deposited in the slack water along the other.

Tributaries of the Shubenacadie River

In the 1930s, the Nova Scotia government began to transplant beavers from its well-stocked eastern and northern counties to depleted areas. By the 1960s this program, augmented by closed seasons, strict trapping quotas, and trapper education, had brought the animal back from the brink. The program was so successful in some areas that motorists were complaining of flooded roads.

In the spring, as meltwaters pour from the surrounding forest, snow turns to rain, and the ice begins to break up, it may overtop its banks, submerging the whole floodplain and leaving a new layer of silt. Aerial photos taken of meanders over several years show that these loops migrate slowly downstream like the motion of a snake in sand. As they do so, they cut through older deposits, making a complex pattern and sometimes leaving remnant channels called oxbow lakes. [See also the **Evangeline Trail** at Port Williams and at Belleisle Marsh near Annapolis Royal.]

Streams in the Northern Hemisphere tend to cut into their right banks more than their left; south of the equator they do the opposite. This is due to Earth's west-to-east rotation.

The official Nova Scotia map book lists 10 Beaver Brooks and 40 other place-names containing the word "beaver." Mi'kmaq place-names show the same trend—e.g., the **Evangeline Trail** at Aylesford. In the early years of settlement, this largest of Canada's native rodents was numerous. However, demand for beaver hats and accessories was so brisk that by the late 1920s trapping and hunting had nearly wiped it out in western Nova Scotia.

Beavers help produce some of our best intervale soils. When they have cut all the maple, willow, and alder within easy hauling or floating distance, they seek out new trees up or down the stream, or even on another watershed. In a year or two their abandoned dam collapses, the pond drains, and a new layer of fertile mud becomes available.

About 1 km/0.6 mi beyond the Black Rock Road turnoff (which used to connect with the ferry to Maitland on the road to Windsor and Kentville) you'll see the sign for Stokdijk Greenhouses, the largest such operation east of Montreal. It supplies hydroponic tomatoes and cucumbers to markets throughout Nova Scotia. It began in 1956, expanded in the 1970s, and in the 1990s switched to hydroponic to counter soil disease problems. The plants are fed on liquid nutrients supplied through a mat of rock wool. The greenhouse is heated by a wood-chip furnace and produces nearly 13,000 beefsteak tomatoes per crop.

VIEW: *Tidal River*

Crossing Gosse Bridge over the Shubenacadie River, notice the river's cliffy banks. Fierce tides armed with rafting ice and ranging up to 8 m/26 ft, have cut down through limestone and grey sandstone here. The harder the rocks, the narrower the channel. On a map one sees zigzag bends along the lower river, reflecting its tendency to follow zones of rock weakened by faults. One such bend occurs at Eagle Nest Point, just visible downstream.

The abandoned railway bridge just downstream was part of the Dominion Atlantic Railway connecting Truro to Windsor and Yarmouth. The bridge abutments are pointed at both ends (to resist both incoming and outgoing ice) and encased in hardwood for added protection.

Eagles do nest along this river. A few even overwinter here, feeding on tomcods that arrive in December to spawn. Many of the small fish get stranded on the mud flats at low tide, or are crushed by moving ice.

Some geologists think the Shubenacadie occupies the bed of a very ancient stream that flowed south across the Atlantic Upland through Wentworth Valley, out along Halifax Harbour, and across the continental shelf. Shubenacadie, 35 km/22 mi upstream at tidewater, once had a large Mi'kmaq village.

The river's chocolate colour is due to constant tidal scouring of its bed and soft banks. Most Minas Basin streams (e.g., Avon, St Croix, Salmon) are also brownish—yet above tidewater they run clear. This river is tidal for half its length, but above Shubenacadie it's as clear as any mountain stream. [See also the **Evangeline Trail** at the Windsor causeway.]

Don't stop on the bridge itself; park past either end and walk back.

VIEW: *Water Ballet*

Watching the incoming tide cover the river flats is fascinating. After checking locally for its expected arrival time, pull off the highway on the Maitland side where a gravel road exits just south of the bridge. Walk down this road to the old railbed and thence to the river bank. (You can estimate its arrival time by adding roughly 90 minutes to its arrival time at Truro as listed in your brochure; or ask at the shop just north of the South Maitland intersection.)

Slowly the incoming flood—often preceding by a refreshing breeze—covers the mostly dry bed of the river, creeping first up one sinuous channel, then up another. Soon the bed is braided with skeins of wet and dry. As the water deepens, all the flats submerge. As the brimming flood races inland, standing waves develop—rapids in reverse. The lighter fresh water is on top and the heavier seawater below. Shad, gaspereau, smelt, striped bass, salmon, trout, and tomcod wait off the estuary each spring and travel incoming tides to spawning grounds along the way.

Traditionally, commercial fishermen set drift nets on the rising tide, let it carry the nets upstream, and pull them on the ebb tide.

STOP: *Eagle Watch*
For bald eagle viewing summer or winter, exit Rte 236 onto Rte 289 at Green Oaks (1 km/0.6 mi east of the Gosse Bridge), drive southeast just over 2 km/1 mi. Instead of going on to Brookfield, located on Highway 102, take the gravel road south at Greens Creek and drive 6 km/4 mi to Riverside, where there's a roadside rest stop with an interpretive sign.

From this small picnic area you stand a good chance of seeing bald eagles fishing or resting on nearby trees. Binoculars will help. Nova Scotia boasts the largest breeding population of bald eagles east of Alaska. They frequent Bras d'Or Lake from March through autumn, then drift south to winter here and in the eastern Annapolis Valley [see also the **Evangeline Trail** near Kentville].

TO DO: *Brown-water Rafting*
Some of the roughest water east of British Columbia's Fraser Canyon can be found here when the tide comes in. Scheduled raft tours of the lower Shubenacadie are available. Experienced operators take high-powered rubber rafts out to meet the bore, then ride the fierce tide rips several kilometres upstream before drifting back on the river's normal current.

For times, costs, and reservations see the current *Complete Guide for Doers & Dreamers* or visit the tourist information centre in Maitland or Truro.

BACK ON THE HIGHWAY
Leaving the bridge on the South Maitland side, we cross Five Mile River's small dyked floodplain on a roadbed quarried from the tilted reddish shales off to the right. The trees above the quarry are mostly native red oak.

At South Maitland the trail leaves Hwy 236 and climbs the steep north bank of Five Mile River in a hairpin turn to follow Rte 215 along the Noel and Kempt shores. (Just before the intersection is the country store of Walter and Shirley Collins. Walter is a strong advocate of the area's tourism merits and will be glad to tell you

Ideal eagle habitat consists of large nesting trees in relatively undisturbed habitat near shallow waters with abundant eels and flounder.

about them.) Watch for glimpses of the red Triassic sandstone along Shubenacadie's reddish east bank, with scenes of mixedwood forest and rolling farmland beyond.

SIDE TRIP: *Hayes Bat Cave*

A few kilometres inland along Five Mile River is one of the region's largest bat hibernacula. Bats flock to such hibernation sites, year after year. A 1993 Boy Scout survey tallied an overwintering population of roughly 7,500 little brown bats.

Unlike tropical fruit bats, all northern bats feed on flying insects, consuming vast numbers every summer night. In winter there are no insects, so they must migrate or hibernate. In late fall the little mammals choose dark, undisturbed places such as caves and abandoned mine shafts where temperatures stay just above freezing. Here they congregate, hanging by their hind claws in clusters from the rocky ceiling. In this state their breathing and heartbeats all but cease. Toward spring a few bats wake up, check the weather outside, and if conditions are right, somehow inform the rest and emerge, followed soon by the others.

The Hayes hibernaculum was created by millions of years of mildly acidic rainwater seeping down through soft gypsum beds. The main cavern is about 10 m/33 ft wide by 7 m/22 ft high by 80 m/50 ft long, with a small pond near the entrance. The whole cave complex is over 400 m/0.25 mi long.

To protect the bats, the Department of Natural Resources has sealed the main entrance with a locked steel grid through which the bats can fly. Entry permits are issued only to bona fide researchers or educators.

Gypsum-rich soil is dry and alkaline, and few plants can grow on it. Among the native species that do are bird's-eye primrose (a spring flower), yellow lady's-slipper, round-leafed dogwood, shrubby cinquefoil, and trout-lily. On exposed clifftops and talus slopes fleabane and gypsum ragwort may be found.

Nova Scotia is the world's largest supplier of gypsum, a calcium sulphate rock now used chiefly in plasterboard (gyproc) but also in cement, plaster of Paris, dental work, and as a filler in paints.

Near Hayes Cave

Lawrence House Museum

BACK ON THE HIGHWAY

STOP: *Lawrence House Museum*
In its heyday Maitland launched over 100 wooden vessels, including Canada's largest, the *William D Lawrence*. While honouring those glory days, we do well to recall the vast quantity of old growth trees—pine, spruce, yellow birch, and larch especially—that was cut to make them possible; and the men who toiled with ax and saw and oxen to deliver the wood.

Each September Maitland celebrates that heritage by launching a model ship and holding a parade. Lawrence House, part of the Nova Scotia Museum, captures the era in photographs, period furnishings, memorabilia, shipwright's tools, and carved wooden models.

Immediately west of Lawrence House is a small waterside picnic park offering fine views of the mouth of the Shubenacadie and of upper Cobequid Bay. Until the late 1930s a car ferry plied between Maitland and Black Rock on the far shore. People travelled from there via Old Barns to Truro, New Glasgow, and Halifax.

The brick-red cliff across the river is part of the same formation of Triassic sandstone that underlies the Minas Basin, cropping up on both sides.

On October 27, 1874, the village of Maitland, at the mouth of the Shubenacadie River, launched Canada's largest wooden ship, the 2238-tonne William D Lawrence. *Seventy-two men—carpenters, blacksmiths, ropemakers, sailmakers— had laboured on it for 18 months. The great ship measured 74.4 m/244 ft long, 24.4 m/80 ft wide, and 17 m/55 ft from keel to rail. Its mainmast from keelson to truck was taller than a 20-storey building and could be seen for miles around. Its massive bowsprit overarched the village road, and coaches passed to and fro beneath it. The mighty three-masted square-rigger wore 9 524 m²/8,000 sq. yds. of canvas and could carry twice the normal clipper cargo. When the ship finally slid down the ways that autumn day, part of the Maitland skyline departed. In eight years it earned its builder $140,000—a fortune in those days.*

William D Lawrence

From Maitland the trail follows Rte 215 along the Noel Shore. Rolling farms and large woodlots are interspersed with vistas of mud flats, pinkish water, and the blue Cobequids to the north. Wherever the road touches Minas Basin, we see crumbling red cliffs and flowerpot islets, the handiwork of fierce tides.

The land consists of a series of broad ridges covered with mixed forest and divided by steep valleys. Typically, the streams (e.g., Moose Brook and Tennycape River) follow northeast/southwest-trending faults down to the Basin. There, tidal scouring has helped them scoop small coves from the underlying sandstone or gypsum (e.g., Tennycape, Walton). The surplus silt has formed small tidal marshes.

As you head west, there are fine views of Five Islands and the Parrsboro Shore.

The blackish reefs visible offshore at low tide (e.g., Moose Cove) are hardened lava that oozed up along the Fundy rift valley during the North Atlantic's birth nearly 200 million years ago.

LEG-STRETCHER: *Flower-pot Walk*

Near Selma there's a sandstone stack topped by trees. Property owners gladly direct travellers to a dirt road leading to a lovely 10–15-minute beach walk. The beach is accessible only at low to mid-tide, and currents are swift.

Between Selma and Noel lies Anthony Provincial Park, with easy access to mud flats at low tide. On sunny days the warm mud flats take the chill off the incoming tide, and local people take advantage

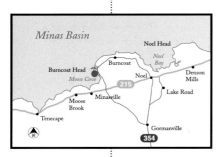

of this to swim. If the tide's in, sight-see from the community wharf. Resident Betty O'Toole knows the park's colourful history, and why it was designated a Natural Heritage Area. As always, check local tide times before venturing onto the flats.

Noel was a common name among the Acadians who moved here from Grand Pré in the late 1600s. During the Expulsion, some Acadian fugitives escaped to the woods and joined the Mi'kmaq in harassing British soldiers and settlers at Piziquid (Windsor) across the Avon. In 1762 their vacant farms were settled by immigrants from Northern Ireland, some of whom (e.g., Densmores and O'Briens) produced notable shipbuilders.

Legend says that the pirate Captain Kidd remasted his ship at nearby Sloop Rock. When he tossed bars of silver to the loggers, they are said to have left them on the reef rather than touch such ill-gotten gains.

STOP: *World's Highest Tides*

At Noel a short paved loop takes you around Burncoat Head, site of the world's highest-known tides. Twice a day, 40 times the volume of the St Lawrence River sluices through the 7.5-km/4.5-mi gap between here and Economy Point. [See also the **Evangeline Trail** at Cape Split.]

Burncoat Head had a lighthouse until the Coast Guard condemned and burnt it in 1913. East Hants Tourist Association has replaced it with a full-scale replica surrounded by a little picnic park with labelled native trees. Displays in the lighthouse explain local history and tidal phenomena. From the tower there are great views of mud flats, red sandstone headlands, tides, and the Cobequids.

Less than a century ago, the small island offshore was joined to the head. The sandstone pillars along the shore mark other eroded points. At low tide you can walk some of the most productive mud flats in the world.

It's best to access the park from the Noel side. Exit Hwy 215 opposite the white United church and drive 5.3 km/3.3 mi north on pavement to the Burncoat Head sign. Here, a new gravel road descends 0.8 km/0.5 mi along the edge of a hayfield. The paved coastal loop rejoins Hwy 215 about 1.5 km/1 mi east of Minasville (intersection unmarked in 1996). The cliffs are steep and continually undercut by tides; respect chain link fences and obey warning signs.

LEG-STRETCHER: *Gypsum Port*
Walton, once called Petite Rainy Cove, pioneered the large-scale export of gypsum in the province. From the late 1700s on, farmers who had gypsum outcrops would cart it to the wharf to sell to the United States for fertilizer. The state of Virginia later bought a form of gypsum to use as a moisture retainer around peanut crops. In 1941 barite, used in oil drilling, was discovered and sold to the West Indies and South America.

Park at the government wharf and walk the shore west to Stubborn Head, 2.5 km/1.5 mi away. On the way you'll see outcrops of gypsum in severely folded formations. These rocks represent three periods of sedimentation separated by two geological upheavals.

West of Walton farms are fewer, and woodlands reassert their dominance. Yet the soils are good, as shown by tall aspen groves on former logging sites.

LEG-STRETCHER: *Rainy Cove Tidal Pools*
Just west of Pembroke there are beautiful tidal pools nestled among folded sandstone and shale formations backed by low cliffs. Tides here recede nearly 2 km/1 mi, exposing sea caves and fossils to the west. Observe that the beaches are sandier than farther east; the bedrock has more sandstone.

During the American Revolution, Yankee privateers would hide their vessels in local creeks to prey on the countryside. Kempt (named for Sir James Kempt, Nova Scotia's Lieutenant Governor from 1820 to 1828) and Walton townships were once referred to as "Man-o'-war's-land," so numerous were local land grants to retired Royal Navy officers.

Local headlands were once nearly level with the North Mountain. Lacking its hard lava crust, they have worn down faster.

Years ago, fishing was the shore's main occupation. Few settled the interior, except on the better limestone soils of the Kennetcook River, which is tidal to beyond Scotch Village. Back of Tennycape there are barrens, but toward Stanley tall groves of red pine flourish on sandy ridges between black spruce bogs. For many years these groves have supplied wharf timbers and hydro poles. The resinous wood is strong and noted for the ease with which it soaks up preservatives.

As we continue westward, the basin not only widens and deepens, but its waters take on a greener ocean look. As we round the bend toward the Avon/St Croix estuary, the water resumes its chocolate tint. Locals call the coast between Walton and the Avon the Kempt Shore.

STOP: *Cheverie Marine Life*

Named for *chevreuil* (French for "buck" or "bull"), this village looks toward Blomidon, whose distinctive dreadnought profile is hidden at this angle.

The coast here is made of picturesque early Carboniferous rocks with bold gypsum outcrops. Sometimes one finds crystals. A few minutes' hike northeast from Cheverie Creek there's a gravel beach, and just beyond that lie shales rich in fossil ferns. Best access is via a road off Hwy 215 east of the creek, just past the general store.

At low tide Cheverie Creek winds through extensive offshore mud flats, which in most places are firm enough to stroll on. Here in mid-summer small sandpipers fuel up on mud shrimp in preparation for their non-stop flight to South America. Ducks, cormorants, black-backed gulls, and herring gulls can be seen here any time of year.

Shallow inshore waters are crucial nurseries for juvenile inshore fish such as flounder. It takes a sharp eye to spot these flat fish, camouflaged to look like mud, in the shallow channels. Other young fish are often stranded in tidal pools among seaweed-covered outcrops offshore. You'll also find periwinkles, dog whelks, barnacles, and other invertebrate life. Striped bass can be hooked with casting rods and lures in season, and fishermen net flounders from boats.

Clamming is great fun too. The Mi'kmaq have done so for untold generations. All you need is a pail, a digging fork, a good eye, and quick reflexes. In half an hour you should be able to harvest a few dozen soft clams. Locate their twin siphon holes in moist mud, insert the fork about 15 cm/6 in away, and quickly—an alarmed clam pulls itself down amazingly fast—heave the mud up and to one side. Clams under 5 cm/2 in long should be put back.

For ultimate flavour, steam your clams in seawater over a driftwood fire and eat with melted butter; some people soak the shellfish overnight in clear water to remove any grit.

Allow ample time to walk back to shore before the returning tide.

South of Lower Burlington, the trail crosses the Cogmagun (Mi'kmaq for "crooked") estuary. The river occupies a shallow syncline, part of an eroded system of northeast/southwest folds running north to the Shubenacadie valley and beyond. (Halfway Brook occupies the same downfold on the Hantsport side.) The next major fold holds the Kennetcook and upper Avon rivers. These small rivers have unusually large estuaries. Tidal scouring of soft sedimentary rock accounts for this.

VIEW: *Acadian Dykes*

Crossing the bridge over the Kennetcook River, you'll see long earthen ridges protecting spacious hay meadows from being inundated.

In their upper reaches these streams are mere fresh-water brooks, but through the lower courses they widen out and are open to the tremendous tides of Minas Basin. When the tide is rising or ebbing, the lower courses of these rivers are deeper and browner than the Missouri, the white foam on the surface like lace, the whole river a seething of liquid salty mud. When the tide is out, only a few runnels of muddy water remain behind the high, slimy, brown banks, and at Windsor, on the estuary of the Avon, ocean-going ships lie high and dry in wooden cradles which are a part of the wharfs. I know of no other rivers in the world quite like these ...
– Hugh MacLennan, **Rivers of Canada,** 1974

SIDE TRIP: *Kennetcook/St Croix Peninsula*

A well-timed detour here offers unmatched tidal bore viewing and a good chance to discover Coal Age fossils. Follow Rte 215 about 6 km/ 4 mi to Brooklyn, turn right past the monument onto Rte 14, and go west along the St Croix flats about 4 km/2.5 mi. When you see the Avondale exit, turn right, cross an iron bridge over the Herbert River, and continue past the dykes and Miller Creek to Poplar Grove.

STOP: *Exciting Bore*

In Poplar Grove ask the way to Elliott Church's Tidal View Farm. The farm is on the right. For years, Mr Church, a retired farmer and trucker, has greeted visitors and shared his knowledge of tides, local lore, and the bald eagles that nest across the river. A short walk to the St Croix River shore will put you in position to see the bore. There's ample parking, and a box for donations. [See also the **Glooscap Trail** at Salmon River, Truro.]

Throughout the 19th century the shores of the Avon River echoed to the sounds of shipbuilding. More than 600 vessels— full rigged ships, barques, brigs, and schooners—were built along its muddy banks.
– Joanne Roy, **The Atlantic Co-operator**, Feb./Mar. 1997

FROM HORTON LANDING – AT THIS PLACE THE ACADIANS EMBARKED. 1755

LEG-STRETCHER: *Fossil Trove*

In a short section of shoreline northeast of the Newport Landing wharf near Avondale, fossils trace the history of a shallow inland sea which stretched from Wolfville south to the Musquodoboit Valley and east to Bras d'Or Lake, 300 million years ago.

It was at nearby Horton Bluff in 1841 that British geologist Sir William Logan discovered the earliest recorded footprints of a four-legged, air-breathing land animal. Here also in the 1980s, a series of 0.3-m/1-ft-long duck-footed tracks were discovered. Some Coal Age amphibian had waddled across the mud flats, perhaps eating blood worms. Nova Scotia Museum staff took hurried plaster imprints before the tides erased them.

(above) Blomidon from Horton Landing, **Frank Leslie's Illustrated Newspaper**, 1882

STOP: *The Avon River Heritage Centre Museum*

This new museum in Newport Landing/Avondale is well worth a visit for insights into shipbuilding and local history.

Avon is Welsh Gaelic for "river."

In 1996 the Avon River Spirit Co-operative financed and built its first wooden vessel, the schooner *Avon Spirit*, which was launched in 1999 and now sails charters out of Mahone Bay. The co-op plans to build one such vessel every year. It welcomes visitors to the shipyard to talk with the shipwrights and to see the work in progress. [See also **Evangeline Trail** near Hantsport.]

BACK ON HIGHWAY

At Brooklyn the trail joins Rte 14 to go west over the St Croix River bridge toward Windsor. After the broadly rolling landscape of the Noel and Kempt shores, these level dykelands and low rumpled hills are restful. The rumpling is karst topography, typical of gypsum areas where rainwater has dissolved caverns and sinkholes. [See also the **Cabot Trail** at Aspy Bay and the **Trans Canada Highway** at Antigonish, Little Narrows.]

This area has been extensively quarried for gypsum since the 1770s. From Sweets Corner to Windsor the road winds among many spoil heaps, some of which the DNR has reforested with spruce. Sinkholes and steep-sided ponds make walking hazardous. At Windsor the **Glooscap Trail** ends, and the **Evangeline Trail** begins.

Halifax-Dartmouth Area Nature Tour

Georges Island in Halifax Harbour

Point Pleasant Park

OVERVIEW

This shortest of our trails isn't really a travelway, but a random swatch of urban and rural landscape embracing parts of Highways 1, 2, 101, 102, 107, and 118 near Halifax-Dartmouth. Its approximate boundary is a line joining Milford, St Margarets Bay, Crystal Crescent Beach, and Cole Harbour. Within this urban hinterland, we'll visit some interesting places and leave the rest for you to explore.

To the nature lover, any urbanized area offers both a challenge and a bonus. The challenge is not only to find pockets of native flora and fauna, but also to visualize the landscape before it was developed. In a sense the parking lots, buildings, neon signs, manicured lawns, planted trees, and artificial ponds block the view. The bonus is that everything is close at hand.

The twin cities, home to one-third of the province's people, face each other across one of the world's finest natural harbours. Within the two cities there are many opportunities for woodland walks, birding, and boating. Within easy driving distance there are also white sand beaches, salt marshes, whale-watching sites, and coastal hiking trails.

The harbour itself is a flooded river valley gouged by glaciers from upended layers of grey-blue slate. During the Coal Age, the slate was part of a mountain chain since worn down. The valley can be traced up through the Dartmouth Lakes, down the Shubenacadie River, and north through the Wentworth gap before it fades into the Northumberland plain. South of Halifax Harbour, its widening gorge can be traced on undersea charts to the rim of the continental shelf.

Halifax's harbour and basin constitute the world's second largest natural harbour after that of Sydney, Australia. It is 21 km/16 mi long, 1.3-2.6 km/1-2 mi wide, with an average depth of 30 m/100 ft.

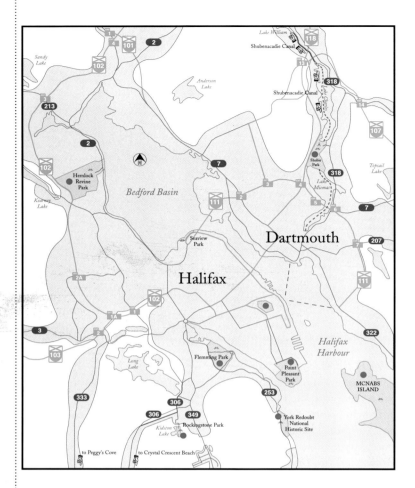

The British established Halifax in 1749 to counter the French military presence at Louisbourg. The harbour was ice-free, sheltered by McNabs Island, and narrow enough to defend with shore-based cannon. Bedford Basin to the north was roomy enough to hide an armada. So, on a ridge overlooking the harbour, they had African labourers reshape a drumlin and dig a star-shaped moat around it. They built a fort walled with 3-m/10-ft blocks of Wallace sandstone. Today their handiwork is called Citadel Hill.

Like lichen on a rock, the garrison town spread outward. Today it encircles Bedford Basin and extends over the ridge to the Northwest Arm and beyond.

Meanwhile, Dartmouth was wild woods, and it remained so for decades. Attempts to settle it were fiercely opposed by Mi'kmaq warriors. For a time the village was a whaling station. At last, guarded by a stockade and soldiers, a colony of settlers took root.

Dartmouth is a city of lovely hills and lakes. In fact, from downtown's Lake Banook one can paddle a string of lakes and human-made locks clear across the peninsula to Maitland on the Bay of

Fundy. The Mi'kmaq canoed and portaged this route millennia before the British came.

For so small an area, our tour covers a diverse landscape. Around Elmsdale we are still in the broad east–west belt of soft Coal Age sandstone and shale that underlies central Nova Scotia and parts of Cape Breton. A characteristic feature is gypsum, of which deep deposits are found near Milford. Because streams cut easily through the soft bedrock, lakes are scarce. Near Milford the skeletons of two Ice Age mastodons have been found.

Since the highways mostly follow valleys, you'll see many farms on these deep-soiled, fertile lowlands. Even before roads were developed, people came up the rivers to harvest the forests and farm the intervales. Today their descendants run dairy farms where plump black-and-white Holstein cattle graze in clover meadows, and concrete silos are stocked each fall with silage made from corn and hay.

From Enfield south we cross a zone of harder, older bedrock. You can see the tilted layers in road cuts, usually planed smooth by glaciers. Pines, attracted by the sandiness, become more common.

An equally dramatic shift occurs south and west of Halifax, where the grey granite floor of the Southern Upland pokes through, and peat bogs become common.

Williams Lake

After more than two centuries of logging, land clearing, and frequent forest fires, the original forest of long-lived, shade-tolerant species—red spruce, eastern hemlock, yellow birch, sugar maple, and beech; the so-called Acadian Forest—has been largely replaced by shorter-lived species like white spruce, red maple, balsam fir, white birch, and aspen. In the 1930s an introduced bark disease decimated beech, the principal broad-leaved component. Since 1969 Dutch elm disease has been making inroads into native bottomland elms.

For convenience the tour is divided into North, East, South, and West sectors, centred on Bedford.

NORTH

First we look at sections of Hwys 102 and 118 between Milford and Dartmouth. Milford is a world-class producer of gypsum used in wallboard. [See the **Evangeline Trail** near Windsor, the **Trans Canada Highway** at Little Narrows, Cape Breton, and the **Glooscap Trail** near Maitland.]

In October 1991, Stanley McMullin was operating an excavator for Milford Gypsum Company in the Shubenacadie valley. Working in dark grey clay under 30 m/98 ft of overburden, his shovel scraped against what looked like pieces of elephant tusk. Broken and yellowed, the tusks were accompanied by several huge teeth. Supervisor Jim McCubbin immediately called the Nova Scotia Museum of Natural History, who sent geologist Bob Grantham and assistant Kelley Kozera from Halifax the same day.

Until then, mastodon bones had been found only three times in the province. In 1833 a femur (thigh bone) was unearthed at Lower Middle River in Cape Breton. In 1895 a tooth turned up near Baddeck. In 1989 a complete tusk was dug up at the Fundy Gypsum Quarry near Windsor.

That winter, working with propane heaters under plastic, museum crews retrieved 60 per cent of the skeleton of a 22-year-old bull mastodon. Nearby they found the bones of a six-year-old calf—a first for Canada, sixth for the world. A pinkish discoloration of the teeth pointed to drowning or suffocation as the cause of death, probably during high water in early spring. The massive animals could have been lured by salt licks and fallen into natural sinkholes. Gypsum areas like Milford's are riddled with holes and caverns caused by naturally acidic rainwater eroding soft alkaline rock.

The fragile bones were quickly sealed for transport and taken to the museum for a four-year process of cleaning, drying, and analysis. Eventually they may be replicated.

After the dig, the museum boxed hundreds of soil samples and sent them to schools. Some 10,000 school children combed the samples and found such things as the skin of a garter snake; beaver, caribou, and mole teeth; a turtle shell; bones of muskrat, birds, frogs, and fish; and thousands of pine cones.

Mastodons (Greek word *mast(os)* for "breast" and *odon* for "tooth," a reference to paired conical cusps on their molars) and woolly mammoths were kin to today's elephants. To cope with Arctic cold, they had smaller ears and coats of coarse reddish hair that hung nearly to the ground. Unlike mammoths, mastodons had domed heads and straightish tusks.

Roaming in herds, both animals inhabited unglaciated areas of North America during the last Ice Age. In Atlantic Canada, mastodons lived along forest edges and stream valleys where pines, alders, and birches grew. We know they ranged far out onto the continental shelf because fishermen have dredged up their teeth. Their main food was conifer foliage, shrubs, and grasses. Mammoths tended to roam the open tundra.

These ancient elephants died out in North America about 11,000 years ago—around the time humans began to trickle east from Asia via the Bering land bridge. Anthropologists suspect human hunting may have caused their extinction, since the animals were superbly adapted to boreal living. They argue that other large Ice Age mammals died out at the same time.

The idea that primitive hunters with flint-tipped spears could even kill these giant beasts seems absurd. However, mastodon and mammoth bones have been found gouged by stone butchering tools. Mastodon hides being tough, the hunters probably used throwing sticks to enhance the thrust and reach of their spears. Ice Age humans had fire, and they likely used it to stampede the herds into cul-de-sacs or bogs or over cliffs (as the Plains Indians did with bison into historic times). Such kills would have been extremely wasteful. Experts also argue that North American herds evolved without knowledge of humans and so were without fear.

Lantz Brick

If you leave Hwy 102 at Elmsdale (Exit 8) and backtrack on Rte 2 to Lantz, you'll notice a dramatic increase in the number of red brick structures. For example, in Lantz they include a large school, a sports arena, and an Anglican church. All are built from an excellent local brown clay, which in places is 12 m/40 ft deep. Toward Shubenacadie an equally fine grey clay occurs within 1 m/3 ft of the surface. Brickmakers prefer Lantz's brown clay, because the iron in it oxidizes during baking and turns a handsome red. Shubenacadie clay fires white.

Lantz has produced bricks since the 19th century. The Miller Brickyard operated here until 1905 and was succeeded by the L. E. Shaw group.

Since 1949 Lantz has also had a name for fine pottery. Alma Lorenzen of Lorenzen Pottery has tried clays from different parts of Nova Scotia and New Brunswick, but prefers the local product. "Lantz clay is far superior to all others, wonderful to work with," she says. The Deichmanns of New Brunswick used Lantz clay too. Aside from normal screening and reworking, it requires only slight additives to improve its firing range. For brick products, Shaw mixes Milford shale with brown clay for their red products and with Shubenacadie clay for buff or grey products.

The Lorenzen studio has been making their famous ceramic replicas of Nova Scotia mushrooms since the early 1950s. To date they have done over 200 species, which are found in collections worldwide. The mushrooms are fired at 920° C (1,600° F) in the bisque (first firing) and are glazed at 1145° C (2,005° F).

Lorenzen mushroom

Back on Hwy 102, heading south, we come down a long hill toward the weighing station and see, east of the exit, a grove of windblown pines. These are white pines and they mark the boundary between the soft-rock lowlands and the hard-rock uplands of the Atlantic Interior. Pines are more plentiful here because they prefer the coarse soils derived from the quartzites (hardened sandstone) of this region. Some of them have dead crowns; this was caused by a wind-borne fungus called white pine blister rust,

247

accidentally imported from Asia via the port of New York on infected seedlings.

Halifax International Airport
The airport site was chosen to be relatively fog-free, but clearing the forest seems to have created more fog. The barren look hereabouts is caused by the removal of soil by glaciers over thousands of years ago.

SIDE TRIP: *Antrim Woodlot*
This 75-ha/186-ac Crown woodlot, under Department of Natural Resource (DNR) care since the late 1950s, is unusual in that several decades of management records have been kept. The documentation covers expenditures on road building and forest inventory, and revenue from harvest and silviculture operations as well as data on growth rates, wood volume by species, and mortality rates.

Although wood has been harvested every few years for most of that time, the woodlot has stayed productive. One reason is that it supports trees of different ages, ranging from over a century to last summer's seedlings. There's always mature wood coming along.

On this Crown lot you can examine harvest sites demonstrating selection cutting, small-scale clearcutting, and other techniques and compare natural regeneration and volumes harvested.

BACK ON HWY 102
For a kilometre or so south of Exit 5A, the road cuts thorough layers of bluish shale. All sedimentary rocks start out horizontal—but these are nearly on end. They got that way in a mountain-building epoch during continental collisions over 400 million years ago, when immense thicknesses of slate and quartzite were folded like a rug to form mountain chains that have since eroded away.

Halifax slate

The ripple marks are "fossil waves" made by gentle wave action on a silty bottom in shallow water. The undulating profile along the cut was caused by glaciers planing harder and softer layers across the folds.

VIEW: *Wildfire Legacy*
Brushland is common on the Bicentennial Highway and along Hwy 118 into Dartmouth, especially 10 km/6 mi east of Exit 5. The cause is frequent forest fires in the 1950s and earlier. This is common outside urban areas. [See also the **Trans Canada Highway** near New Glasgow and Sydney.] Before the advent of helicopter water tankers in the 1970s, such fires often burned for days or weeks.

Why is this forest mostly deciduous? Being resinous, the conifers burnt first, including the seed trees. Conifers cannot sprout from the stump, but deciduous trees can. The scattered stumps of white and wire birch, aspen, and red oak sprouted new growth and later seeded the area. The pin cherry was likely brought by birds dropping cherry seeds from meals eaten elsewhere.

However, repeated burning of topsoil, followed by leaching of nutrients, has stunted the vegetation. Normal white birch and oak are three to four times taller than this. Fire has set them back. It takes about 500 years to build 2.5 cm/1 in of good topsoil. Once bacteria, fungi, and lichens have done their work, shrubs and trees become the main soil builders.

The only sizeable conifers visible from the highway are a few scattered white and red pine and some jack pine. Pines survive because their bark is thick enough to resist fire and their roots delve deep.

Until the 1960s, firefighters had only shovels and water-filled back tanks to work with. The advent of water-bombing aircraft (a technique pioneered in Canada) enabled them to douse fires while they were still manageable, either putting then out or buying time for firefighting crews to arrive. Pranksters have been known to start fires just to see the helitanker do its stuff.

Lightning, the main cause of wildfires in arid and mountainous central and western Canada, causes less than 5 per cent of Nova Scotia's forest fires. Over 95 per cent are human-caused. Spring trash burning is the main culprit, followed by garbage dump fires and arson.

VIEWS: *Conifer Understory and Lake Monster*

Coming south from the airport, where Miller Lake comes into view from the top of a long curving hill, notice on your right the dense growth of young spruce and fir seeding in under old red maple. Within three decades these conifers will overtop the declining maple and shade out all but the tallest. In a sense the maples have been a nurse crop for the spruce. But enough maples will survive to become the next forest, should anything happen to the conifers.

Near the south end of the lake, you may be startled to see what looks like a large serpent rearing its head. For years someone, likely from the Boy Scouts (camp across the water), has decorated a half-submerged piece of driftwood to resemble a monster's head. It went missing in 1996, but has been replaced by a smaller monster.

At the end of the lake, where Miller Lake descends to Lake Thomas on the Shubenacadie Canal through a huge culvert, you can choose to continue toward the Bicentennial Highway, with exits to Hwys 101 and 103, or to take Exit 5 left onto Rte 118.

Incidentally, Miller Lake is the westernmost corner of the Waverley Wildlife Sanctuary, which runs south to Lake Major. This 57 km²/22 sq mi block of Crown land was set aside in September 1974 as a Boy Scout wilderness activity area. In the late 1800s gold pits were common in this district. Large amounts of quartz were shipped out via the Shubenacadie Canal to steam-powered stamping mills (rock crushers) to extract the precious metal. Newfoundland caribou were also penned here in the 1930s during an unsuccessful attempt to reintroduce the animal.

The sanctuary offers good canoeing along Soldier and other lakes.

STOP: *Hwy 118 Lily Pond*

Leaving 102 at Exit 5, we take Route 118 toward Dartmouth. If it's summer, watch for white waterlilies on the right as you come up the long hill south of Miller Lake. Most years these grow in the second pond to the right (not the first, which is marshy in summer).

WEST

STOP: *Sackville Inventor*

Give a thought to an unsung local scientist and inventor who lies buried in Lower Sackville. Until the mid-1800s, the world's paper was made from rags, and demand was rapidly outrunning supply. One day in 1839, a dreamy 18-year-old sat

observing wasps chew and shape wood fibre into a paper nest. It gave him an idea. After five years grinding debarked spruce bolts and playing with grindstones, sieves, and hot irons, Charles Fenerty perfected the groundwood pulping process that most paper mills now use.

In 1844 he sent a sample of his paper to Halifax's *Acadian Recorder*, suggesting they try it. The publishers weren't interested, so Fenerty turned to other projects. That same year a German inventor patented the groundwood process, thereby launching the pulp and paper industry.

By the late 1800s, Nova Scotia had a few small groundwood and chemical mills. With increased demand for paper and cardboard after World War I, the industry grew. By the late 1960s it was consuming more wood than the lumber industry.

Fenerty died at age 71 and was buried in St John's Anglican Cemetery on Old Sackville Road.

[See also the **Marine Drive** at Sheet Harbour, and the **Trans Canada Highway** at Abercrombie.] Old Sackville Road is within 0.5 km/0.3 mi of Hwy 101. Leave Hwy 102 at Exit 4 and drive northwest just over 4 km/2.5 mi, turn right, watch for the sign, and turn right again onto Old Sackville Road. Look for the church and cemetery; ask locally if unsure.

LEG-STRETCHER: *Hemlock Ravine Park*

This complex of woodland trails occupies a slope north of Bedford Basin, halfway between Millview and Birch Cove (Exit 4 off Hwy

102). The estate belonged to Lieutenant Governor John Wentworth, who lent it to Prince Edward, Duke of Kent. Edward, later to become the father of Queen Victoria, commanded the British troops in the Maritimes from 1794 to 1800. He had the estate landscaped for his French mistress and built Prince's Lodge as their music room.

The City of Halifax began acquiring the land in 1970 and started building trails in 1983. Its goal was to preserve the ravine's natural beauty while providing public recreation. With the help of the Nature Conservancy of Canada and the Department of Natural Resources, they have succeeded well. Recent cutting has altered certain parts.

You can reach this park in two ways. From the Bicentennial Highway take Exit 3 onto Kearney Lake Road, turn left onto Castlehill Drive, and take the first left into the Grosvenor Wentworth School parking lot, where the Sir John Wentworth Loop begins.

Or you can come off the Bedford Highway at Kent Avenue (1 km/ 0.6 mi east of Kearney Lake intersection), just west of Prince's Lodge. Drive 0.3 km/0.2 mi along Kent and watch on your left for a lane descending steeply to a parking lot by a heart-shaped concrete lily pond. A map sign will direct you from there.

Although the trails in this 81-ha/200-ac estate are labelled, some are circuitous and confusing. Get a map beforehand from the nearby Econo Lodge Motel (the one with a model lighthouse beside it).

Hemlock Ravine itself is 0.5 km/0.3 mi east of Prince's Lodge, directly behind the Econo Lodge Motel. Park in the motel lot and take the brookside path north past the new construction site.

The path, wending around fallen slabs of bedrock and over roots, takes you along the brook's west side through mossy woods shaded by great hemlocks.

The east slope is mostly yellow birch and beech. After about 550 m/1,800 ft they and the hemlocks become smaller and peter out. The exposed higher ground is occupied by spruce and fir mixed with white birch. Above the ravine the ground is uneven with smallish angular rocks poking through thin soil. Their sharp edges suggest shattering by glacial pressure or frost action. (Water-worked stones are rounded.)

Eastern hemlock (no kin to the poisonous plant that killed Socrates) is a long-lived native evergreen with reddish bark, small cones, and lustrous needles attached by tiny stalks. Although it grows best farther south and west, it is common in mainland Nova Scotia, especially on sheltered hillsides and ravines with percolating groundwater.

There are several fallen trunks, some broken two or three metres above ground. Wind and ice storms weaken aging trees. Fungus spores enter broken branches and rot sets in. The weakened trunk eventually breaks and falls. The logs provide food and shelter for countless invertebrates for upwards of a century. The upright stubs

During the 19th century hemlock throughout the province was heavily cut to plank barns and covered bridges. Its splintery wood was also used in granaries to discourage rats. For a time after the 1920s many trees were felled for the thick, red, tannin-rich bark, which was peeled and dried out and used in making leather. The logs were left to rot.

will last for decades and shelter bark beetles, wood borers, woodpeckers, flying squirrels, and raccoons.

Unlike Point Pleasant Park, this area is lightly used. Hemlocks of every size and age grow here, from giants with 300 or more annual rings to tender seedlings newly germinated. The seedlings tolerate shade until the parent trees fall.

Except that the oldest trees are larger, this forest probably looks much as it did in the mid-1800s. Today its oldest specimens are about 1 m/3.3 ft in diameter and over 30 m/100 ft tall.

Along the trail, human feet have bared many tree roots, weakening some trees until they have fallen. Moreover, traffic and browsing have prevented young trees from germinating.

Other tree species include yellow birch, white birch, and red spruce. Highbush cranberry is common, as are lady's-slipper orchids in June-July.

WEST

STOP: *Spryfield Rocking Stone*

Although glaciers have transported and dumped millions of boulders in temperate and polar latitudes worldwide, few end up so exquisitely balanced that they can be tipped by hand. Such a stone stands near Kidston Lake west of Spryfield—and gave its name to nearby Rockingstone Road.

To reach this huge glacial erratic, follow Herring Cove Road (Rte 349) from the Armdale Rotary to its junction with Old Sambro Road (Rte 306). Turn right and drive past its junction with North West Arm Road. Continue through the four-way stop at Sussex Street and past Leiblin, Dekker, and Ardwell streets, and Elizabeth Sutherland School on the left. At the end, turn right onto Feldspar Crescent and park at the turnaround.

Inside the guard rail, follow the paved utility road through open

About three miles from the North West Arm is a Rocking Stone of very large dimensions. It rests upon a strata of rock ... and moves on a pivot of 12 inches by 6. It is composed of granite, and when set in motion (which may be effected with great ease by means of a short wooden lever) undulates from E.N.E. to W.S.W. It is twenty feet in length, 14 in breadth, 9 in height and ... is supposed to weigh 162 tons."
—Thomas Haliburton, **History of Nova Scotia**, 1829

Kevin McGrath and the Spryfield Rocking Stone

252

conifers to a lakeside clearing with a small cement outbuilding. Scattered around the bare granite pavement, where the melting ice dropped them, are large grey boulders.

The Rocking Stone sits about 137 m/450 ft beyond, beside a wooded path near Kidston Lake. Don't bother trying to move it without the aid of a small log for a lever.

Farther along the path is an interesting geological puzzle. Among the trees lie several thick blocks of grey granite separated by cracks up to a metre wide. Obviously the blocks belong to the bedrock below them. Their shape and arrangement—like pieces of cake on a plate— clearly show they were once part of one slab. What force separated the slab horizontally from its parent rock? What sheared the slab into blocks? What moved or is moving them apart?

Near the south end of Kidston Lake is another interesting glacial formation, called Table Rock. This large flat boulder sits on three smaller boulders forming its legs. The unique thing about it is that one of the legs is made of quartzite, which is not found in the Spryfield area.

Mr Kidston, the owner of the property, says that it used to be possible for him to rock the boulder [by] putting his shoulder to it; but a party from the garrison at Halifax ... moved it so vigorously that it edged along into a position where it is more stable.
— J. W. Goldthwait, **Physiography of Nova Scotia**, 1924

EAST

A lock on the Shubenacadie Canal

STOP: *Inland Waterway*
In its day, the Shubenacadie Canal was North America's largest engineering project. The 90-km/56-mi series of natural lakes and rivers and human-made locks was designed to float small ships overland from Halifax Harbour to the Bay of Fundy. Today it makes a superb two-day canoe trip route.

The idea had been discussed since at least the 1790s, but the impetus to construct it came from Halifax shipping magnate Samuel Cunard and his colleagues. The year was 1826, decades before railroads. Cunard and his colleagues hoped to tap the expanding Fundy Loyalist trade. The canal would shorten the risky voyage from Halifax around Cape Sable to Fundy by roughly four-fifths.

Scottish stonemasons were brought in to construct the canal. Work went well for a time. Then the project ran into labour and money problems, and in 1831 it was abandoned. In 1854 it was revived, with a Nova Scotian engineer in charge. The original locks had been built for small coasting schooners, the dominant trading vessel of the day. He rebuilt most of them for steamships. After 35 years of on-and-off construction, the canal was finally completed in 1861. If you stood beside it in 1865 you might have seen a succession of small ships towing all manner of goods: barges loaded with cordwood, lumber, lime fertilizer, manure, and raw quartz from the Waverley gold mines.

From the start, however, the canal lost money. By 1870 it was abandoned and fell into disrepair, another victim of the Victorian itch for mega-projects. What went wrong? The biggest problem was that it was finished too late. By 1861 the trading axis had shifted from Halifax/Fundy to Halifax/Montreal/Toronto and points west. Railroading had begun in the 1850s and played an important role in bringing about Confederation in 1867. Once railways began to steal freight and move it faster, the canal was doomed. And when the government built two large bridges too low for ships to pass under, its fate was sealed. [For another 19th-century mega-project, see the **Trans Canada Highway** at the Nova Scotia–New Brunswick border and the **Sunrise Trail** at Tidnish.]

Fortunately for canoeists, the locks have been repaired and the bridges are high enough. They can trace this ancient Mi'kmaq canoe route across the whole peninsula. Putting in at Lake Banook in Dartmouth, the route passes through Lakes Charles, William, Thomas, and Fletcher and the locks between, to Grand Lake on the height of land, and then descend the Shubenacadie to Minas Basin. (Check local Fundy tide times; currents at the river's mouth can be dangerous on the rising tide at full moon and new moon.)

In the summer you can drop in at the Shubenacadie Canal Interpretive Centre, 140 Alderney Drive, off Prince Albert Road near Dartmouth Cove on Halifax Harbour for more information about the canal. At the north end of nearby Sullivans Pond is a ramp formerly used to haul ships into Lake Banook. A cairn identifies it as the start of the Shubenacadie Canal.

Sullivans Pond is a favourite stop-over for migrating waterfowl. Some overwinter here, depending on humans to feed them grain all winter.

STOP: *Halifax Public Gardens*
This 7.3-ha/18-ac fenced area between Spring Garden Road and South Park and Sackville streets is a botanical treat, a haven for daytime strollers (open till dusk in summer), and a refuge for ducks and swans.

The gardens grew out of the adjacent Halifax Commons as a traditional English communal pasture and garden. In 1837, Queen Victoria's

Bandstand in the Halifax Public Gardens

coronation year, the Nova Scotia Horticultural Society leased 2.2 ha/5.5 ac "[to demonstrate] the cultivation of choice fruit trees, vegetables, rare plants and flowers."

In 1866 Alderman John McCulloch, inspired by a square in Paris, established a civic garden to the north, bounded by Sackville Street, South Park Street, and Griffin's Pond. Later the city reshaped the pond and added the area west of it.

In 1874 the city combined the two parks. The result has been called one of North America's finest Victorian gardens. Somehow it has survived and resisted modernizing. Besides a period fountain and bandstand, there are statues of goddesses (Ceres, Diana, and Flora for agriculture, the hunt, and flowers, respectively), rock gardens, a tropical bed, and a cactus garden. Numerous beds of perennials and annuals bloom along the winding paths from spring through late summer.

Tree lovers will find labelled specimens of common North American and European trees, and a few rare species. Among the latter are dawn redwood, ginkgo, and American chestnut. Each has a story to tell.

For instance, the redwood is an Oriental cousin of North America's western redwoods. Like them, it flourished worldwide during the Triassic Period 200 million years ago. Botanists considered it extinct until the 1930s, when a few ancient trees were discovered in a Buddhist monastery in central China. Since then cuttings have been propagated widely.

The ginkgo or maidenhair tree, though broad-leaved, has a pedigree so ancient it has affinities to conifers. It has no living relatives and has long since outlived its enemies.

The significance of Dr Swain's efforts is that in the 1930s an Asian blight wiped out the American chestnut throughout its eastern range. Dr Swain's few specimens, plus others raised by interested foresters from Ohio stock, represent some of the largest

The Garden's three American chestnuts were bred by G. S. Swain of Kentville's federal research station in the 1960s. To avoid using diseased US trees, he cross-pollinated a large healthy tree in Bridgewater (since cut) with one at Mount Uniacke Estate. [See the **Evangeline Trail.**] *These trees came from healthy nuts or saplings brought here by Loyalists in the late 1700s.*

American chestnut

healthy trees left in the world. However, imported Chinese and Japanese chestnuts still carry the disease.

In the 1970s Ralph Johnson, forester with Bowater Mersey in Liverpool, tallied all known live American chestnut trees in Nova Scotia, and persuaded his company to raise and plant healthy Ohio stock in pairs across western Nova Scotia. Most of the trees have since died but not, it seems, from the blight.

Public Gardens in winter

In the 1990s retired DNR employee Les Corkum has been breeding NS trees with some success, while the University of New Brunswick is cross-breeding US genotypes with disease-free northern Ontario stock. The goal is to rehabilitate this once magnificent provider of timber, nuts, wildlife habitat and shade for the sake of future generations. [See also **Keji Drive** at Liverpool.]

Near Griffin's Pond on the Sackville Street side there's a fine specimen of European beech. You can identify it even in winter by the smooth, slate-grey bark, so different from that of other trees. Another specimen stands near the fence along Summer Street. For another tragic tree story see the following section on Point Pleasant Park.

One can obtain maps of the gardens from the canteen on the Spring Garden side.

LEG-STRETCHER: *Point Pleasant Park*

The City of Halifax began leasing this 75-ha/186-ac park from the military in 1866 for a shilling a year, and still does. One of its best features is the grove of old white pine and hemlock that graces the northern part. Part of the point was cleared in the late 1700s for purposes of defence. The pines seem to have originated from fire at about that time, with the hemlock germinating in their shade a few years later. The red spruce came in the last century.

See how thin the moss and undergrowth is. This is typical of old pine forests [see the **Evangeline Trail** near Kentville]. The autumn fall of old needles blankets the ground with an acidic undecomposed organic matter called duff. Duff makes a poor seedbed. Here the normal condition is worsened by the heavy off-path foot traffic, which kills any seedlings that germinate. In addition, most of the forest floor has too little sunlight for white pine to regenerate; this species needs at least 40 per cent open sky. But fir and spruce can regenerate in shade, and are doing so in protected gullies and knolls. As the ageing pine and hemlock drop out, the forest composition will shift toward those species unless park managers intervene.

The natural way to prevent this is to fell a few of the oldest trees (they will soon pose a hazard to pedestrians anyway), thereby letting in more light. Then white pine will seed in, as it has already done along the paved roads. If the new growth were then protected by fencing,

Cross-country skiing in Point Pleasant Park

hemlock would follow, and the grove's character could be sustained.

The Martello Tower near the North West Arm has a plant story attached to it. At its base and spreading into the woods are clumps of real Scottish heather (*Calluna vulgaris*). The story is that the plants came as seeds in the bedding of Scottish soldiers who bivouacked here. Not so, said 19th-century botanist George Lawson, who traced the plants to an old garden nearby. Other known heather sites are Pictou (of course) and Cape Breton. [See also the **Lighthouse Route** near Jordan River for imported Scotch broom.]

The park is located at the south ends of Tower Road and South Park Street/Young Avenue. On weekends it's reserved for pedestrians, but cyclists are welcome on weekdays. Bicycle Nova Scotia offers tours of the twin cities.

CRUISE: *McNabs Island*

Directly east of Point Pleasant Park, and separated from the Dartmouth shore by the narrow Eastern Passage, is this 5-km/3-mi-long, 395-ha/ 975-ac ridge of woodland, field, and wetland. A fortress in war, farmed and logged for many years, the island is still rich in fauna and flora. Its landscape is one of slate and quartzite cliffs smeared with glacial till, including several drumlins (e.g., Strawberry Hill). Where the sea can reach them, the drumlins are rapidly eroding. Little Thrumcap (near the southeast end) has almost disappeared. Once a burial ground for cholera victims, its eroding beaches from time to time cough up human bones.

Ospreys, bald eagles, and great blue herons nest on McNabs. The woodland reflects two Nova Scotia climatic zones. On the exposed southern half we find a typical Atlantic Coast forest of white spruce and balsam fir sprinkled with red maple and white birch. The sheltered northern half looks more like a typical Atlantic Interior forest with pockets of beech, yellow birch, and sugar maple, plus wild raisin and mountain maple.

Common ground-cover plants are bunchberry, twinflower, false lily-of-the-valley, star-flower, cinnamon fern, and running club moss (*Lycopodium*). Extensive areas are clothed in club moss and ferns.

Of special interest is the abandoned Perrin Estate, whose extensive gardens of exotic trees, shrubs, and flowers have stood untended since the 1930s.

McNabs Island is jointly managed by the federal and provincial governments and by private citizens. There are daily boat tours, spring to fall, from the Halifax waterfront (check for times).

STOP: *Cole Harbour*

To reach this area, follow Portland Street east; it becomes Cole Harbour Road, Hwy 207. The first section is an uneasy blend of urban and country, bedroom community and suburb. Until the late 19th century, Cole Harbour was a quiet farming and fishing village near a small town, a place where people came on weekends to hunt ducks or to buy clams. Slowly the pressures of weekend recreation, market gardening, dairy farming, and sand and gravel removal for city construction increased. Recently the threats have come from urban sprawl, sewage disposal, and Dartmouth's thirst for clean, fresh water. In 1994 a water shortage led the city to raise the water level in its Lake Major Reservoir, which altered the Cole Harbour estuary and annoyed residents.

Cole Harbour was famous for clams. In the 1920s the flats averaged 227 kg/500 lb a year. Vendors sold the molluscs from door to door in Halifax, ladling them from a bucket at 10 cents a scoop.

They have not been passive. Since the early 1970s, the Cole Harbour Heritage Society has worked hard to balance the conflicting demands on its limited land base. You can learn about their efforts at the Cole Harbour Heritage Farm Museum, 471 Poplar Drive, off Cole Harbour Road (Rte 207) via Otago Drive.

Cole Harbour itself demonstrates glacial smoothing of bedrock, ocean erosion of drumlins, and the dynamics of beaches, bay bars, and tidal marshes. It has other assets too. For a busy suburb, it's surprisingly popular with waterfowl. Migrating ducks and geese congregate here spring and fall, feeding and resting on the tidal marsh and mud flats.

Aerial view of the Cole Harbour marsh

A 1960s travel guide calls it "a good place to shoot geese." Today it's a conservation area. This is because Cole Harbour and vicinity is one of two locations in Nova Scotia where large flocks of geese overwinter. (The other is Port L'Hébert—see the **Lighthouse Route**.) The chief attraction is eel-grass, on which they graze at low tide. When the channels iced up during the harsh winter of 1994, the geese flew to Martinique Beach to graze. Black ducks gather here too.

Farther along Rte 207, across the railway bridge at mid-harbour, on the Lawrencetown side, is a good marsh for observing osprey and herons fishing. In late August people pick huckleberries along the abandoned railroad line west of the harbour. These tall shrubs are related to blueberry and are found in barrens, rocky pastures, and bogs. The fruit is large and bluish purple, a trifle seedy, but much sought by birds and mammals.

To Do: Open a windrow of eel-grass in summer, you'll find it warm and moist with a bracing aroma of iodine and salt. It's a rich little ecosystem. Spiders, beach fleas, and other small land invertebrates will scuttle for cover. With the coming of winter storms, the durable grass blades finally shred into short pieces and form a chocolate brown mulch that sloshes in and out with the waves and coats the bottom. Tiny organisms eat this mulch and in turn feed clams.

Because dead eel-grass insulates well and decays very slowly, people traditionally used it to bank their houses in the fall, using long slotted planks to hold it in place.

In 1930 a disease decimated eel-grass beds along the Eastern Shore. Some blame it on the 1929 undersea quake that inundated southern Newfoundland and broke the transatlantic cable. But this doesn't explain why Britain's eel-grass beds died off that same year. At any rate, Cole Harbour's clam industry disappeared. And of course the geese suffered, especially in 1932 when ice sealed off the remaining beds. In time the eel-grass came back, bringing the geese. But the clam beds, already heavily harvested, never fully recovered.

A century ago, this area of Cole Harbour was once part of a "poorhouse farm" on Bissett Road. The DNR now maintains the barn, and has developed a coastal walking trail over the adjacent drumlin. Farther down Bissett Road, the old railbed is now the Salt Marsh Trail, which goes through woods and marshlands to Lawrencetown. The railroad once carried passengers to City Market in Halifax and freight such as limestone from Musquodoboit Harbour. These trails afford good botanizing and birdwatching—over 275 species of birds have been reported from here—and there are parking areas at both trailheads. From Long Hill on Rte 207 there's a great view of this marsh-and-drumlin landscape.

SOUTH

LEG-STRETCHER: *Coastal Walk*

For an exciting coastal walk along granite cliffs, follow Rte 349 (Herring Cove Road) south from Spryfield past Portuguese Cove. After 2.5 km/1.5 mi, watch for the sign to Duncans Cove. A 2-km/1.2-mi drive takes you to the cove, which is behind Chebucto Head. From here you have over 5 km/3 mi of rocky shore to explore; allow at least two hours. This is granite country, a landscape quite unlike slaty

Near Rainbow Haven Beach Provincial Park (watch for the sign on Bissett Road), an 1870s dyke once linked West Lawrencetown and Cow Bay. The locals had no use for this dyke because it meant no more free salt hay. In 1917 someone dynamited it. The area returned to tidal marsh and mud flats and has been so since.

*Eel-grass (*Zostera marina*) is the only native seed plant that makes its home with marine algae. [See also the **Sunrise Trail** at Fox Harbour and the **Marine Drive** at Martinique Beach.] But you won't find it along wave-pounded shores. Its long flat blades grow in shallow water in sheltered coves along gently sloping sandy beaches with a muddy bottom. By damping the force of waves, eel-grass collects sediment among its roots, slowly building soil and extending the shoreline. Dying, it turns brown and, lapped and rolled by small waves, forms a long windrow at the level of the last high tide. As the tides recede with the waning moon, it sometimes forms a perfect series of windrows, one for each day.*

geology of the Halifax/Dartmouth area. Its signature is a grey, pink, or white boulder composed mostly of small crystals of feldspar. Because granite erodes slowly to sand, soils here are thin. The bedrock shows through in rounded ridges or pavements smoothed by ice and waves. It is as if the bones of Earth were showing through.

Back of the headlands are stunted thickets of white spruce and balsam fir and downy alder. Now and then you'll cross small tea-coloured brooks that trickle out of bogs of sphagnum moss, sedges, bog laurel, and marsh cotton.

Ketch Harbour (so named because it's too narrow for larger vessels)

Aerial view of Herring Cove

is a convenient pick-up point. Or you could hike on around Cape Sambro to Sambro Harbour, or even to Crystal Crescent Beach on the Pennant Peninsula.

The water at Crystal Crescent Beach is cold even in July; but the fine grey sand is wonderful between the toes. A fine coastal hiking trail goes from the parking lot to Pennant Point, a distance of 10 km/6 mi. The headland to the east is Cape Sambro, with its namesake lighthouse island to the south. In foggy weather you may hear the foghorn's doleful song.

City Lights

One of the best birding sites in the area is Hartlen Point, the southeastern extremity of Halifax Harbour. Its blend of salt marsh, mud flat, bog, sand beach, alder, and red maple attracts a wide range of birds. There's another attraction. Migrating birds are often drawn to light. The glow from the twin cities, augmented by the powerful beams of four lighthouses, apparently can be irresistible. Like moths to a porch lamp, many night fliers alter course. As often as not they land around Hartlen Point.

To reach the point, follow Portland Street north to the Pleasant Street lights and turn right. Pleasant becomes Rte 322, which runs past Woodside and CFB Shearwater/Peary to the village of Eastern Passage. Park near the wharf on the right and walk from there. That scrap of land south of the point is Devil's Island.

Lighthouse Route Nature Tour

Yarmouth to Halifax along the South Shore
525 km/326 mi

Coastal barrens in fall

OVERVIEW

Even if you take the newer, straighter Highway 103, the South Shore is a circuitous route—definitely not for anyone in a rush. The whole shore is a filigree of headlands and harbours around which the two highways weave like drunken sailors. As with the Eastern Shore, the sea is never far away, but the climate is milder here. The warm Gulf Stream sweeps to within 50 km/30 mi of the coast before veering toward Britain. Summer fogs are common, however, because northern waters chill its warmth.

This coast is peppered with rocky islands of every size and shape, each edged with pale sand or golden rockweed. The outer ones are treeless, the only greens being those of crowberry, sedges, and mosses, which can survive Atlantic gales and salt spray. Closer to the coast, the islands wear shaggy manes of dark spruce and balsam fir softened by birch, aspen, and red maple. From the coast inland the forest grades into luxuriant groves of tall white pine, red spruce, hemlock, and maple, backbone of an early shipbuilding tradition. Red oak groves—many of fire origin—are more common here than elsewhere in the province.

Scattered through this inland forest lie rocky lakes—Mushpauk, Great Pubnico, Jordan, Rossignol, Mushamush—from which short tea-coloured rivers tumble down the gently sloping Southern Upland to the Atlantic. (The colour derives from tannin in the numerous peat bogs in this glacier-harrowed country.) Indeed, the landscape is fully one-third fresh water.

The western interior, centred on the Tobeatic Wildlife Sanctuary, Kejimkujik National Park, and Lake Rossignol, comprises Nova Scotia's largest remaining wilderness. It was about this area that outdoorsman Albert Bigelow Paine wrote in 1908: "The wilderness will welcome you, and teach you, and take you to its heart. And you will find your own soul there; and the discovery will be worthwhile."

THE TOUR BEGINS

We start in Yarmouth by following Starrs Road to Rte 3. (Often this tour offers the option to leapfrog between Rte 3 and Hwy 103. These options are noted along the way; where possible we follow Hwy 3.)

There could be few better ways to begin this tour than the Utkubok Trail. To find it, follow the Starrs Road extension east past the airport to an intersection with signs for Arcadia (left) and Chebogue (right). Turn left and proceed 0.4 km/0.25 mi until you see, facing each other on a bend, a white Baptist church and the Acadian Consolidated School (right). Pull into the schoolyard and park near the playground on the right. (If school is in session, check at the office first.)

LEG-STRETCHER: *Utkubok Trail*

The only place in Nova Scotia where the rare roseate tern still breeds is on the Brothers (or Twin) Islands off Yarmouth. Elsewhere, human disturbance of nesting sites plus burgeoning populations of herring gulls (themselves a side effect of human activity, they hog nest sites and food) are decimating this lovely world-wandering seabird.

The village of Arcadia, a few kilometres southeast of Yarmouth, has developed a community trail that's a pleasant gateway to our route. In the schoolyard, a large map sign on the right directs you to a self-guided, 1-km/0.6-mi, wheelchair-accessible loop trail. It wends along the Chebogue River, across Arcadia Brook, around a treed drumlin, and back to the playground. It offers boardwalks, lookoffs, a variety of shrubs and trees, and some neat rustic litter bins. Your guide is Ooti the Owl.

Chebogue River at low tide

The stops include an alder swale, old apple trees, pasture (white) spruce, and "the largest salt marsh in Nova Scotia—2,000 ac"(809 ha). Vibrant green in spring, tawny gold in autumn, the marsh is a rippling prairie of salt-tolerant cord grass embroidered with tidal streams, inlets and small treed islands. Migrant waterfowl alight here spring and fall. Great blue herons patrol the shores, and osprey dive-bomb fish.

Great blue heron

Along the route you'll see poplar with distinctive horizontal "rivet holes." The holes are the work of sapsuckers, a kind of woodpecker. Sapsuckers drill horizontal lines of shallow holes in the bark of live broad-leaved trees, which then exude sap to seal the wounds. Sugar in the sap attracts ants, wasps, and flies, which the bird snaps up later.

Leaving the river bank lookoff, the path climbs the slope of a drumlin. Near the top, half hidden in a thicket of pasture spruce, is an old rock wall built of stones that pioneers dragged from the earth when clearing the hill.

East of Arcadia the route curves around Lobster Bay, which separates Wedgeport and the Pubnicos. The bay is a maze of finger-like peninsulas, narrow islands, dangerous ledges, tidal marshes, and winding channels. Geologically it is a washboard of north-south folds in hard greywacke and quartzite, eroded for 500 million years, bulldozed by glaciers, and inundated by the postglacial ocean. [See also the **Marine Drive**, the **Sunrise Trail**, and the **Evangeline Trail** at Mavillette Beach.] "The Pubnicos" were settled by Acadians in 1652, spared during the 1755 deportation and burnt in 1758. The exiles returned in 1766 and stayed. Will R. Bird called it the oldest Acadian settlement in the world.

Lobster Bay

Except for the mild climate—we're almost in the latitude of Boston—the landscape could be southern Labrador. Plants have had a hard time colonizing these scraps of rock, since the ice sheet scraped away most of the soil. Although the vegetation does well where sheltered from sea winds, it has been slow to colonize the islands and capes.

Poor as the land is, the waters are rich. Colliding masses of Fundy and Atlantic waters swirl offshore, drawing mineral-laden bottom waters to the sunlit surface. There it feeds swarms of plankton, which in turn support the whole marine food chain, from microscopic invertebrates to giant whales.

*In the 1970s there was a population explosion of green sea urchins, which feed on kelp. As kelp declined around the islands, many sheep starved. When the surplus sea urchins died off in the 1980s, the sheep recovered. [See also the **Marine Drive**, Port Felix eiders.]*

BOAT TRIP: *Cruise an Archipelago*
The best way to savour the bay is to arrange a boat tour of the Tusket Islands. Call or drive to Wedgeport and book a boat. Guides will outline the natural and human history of these ice-free islands. Two km/1.2 mi east of Arcadia, exit Rte 3 onto Rte 334, drive roughly 15

km/9 mi to Wedgeport, and watch for signs. Tours leave from the end of Tuna Wharf Road. Ask about the International Tuna Cup matches, which made the place famous in the 1950s.

An estimated 2,000 wild sheep live on about 30 islands in Lobster Bay. In summer they find plenty of coarse grass and foliage, but in late fall this withers. Then the resourceful animals eat seaweed, which winter storms toss up in abundance. Kelp, a long-bladed laminarian algae, is especially nutritious.

Although some of the sheep may have survived shipwrecks as did Sable Island's ponies, most were probably ferried there by summer residents fishing lobster and harvesting Irish moss. The animals would have been corralled and sheared each fall, as people do today on the Mud Islands south of Tusket Island. The wool was knit into warm sweaters, socks, and mitts, and the surplus sold to mills like Barrington's. When people abandoned this way of life early in the century, the sheep were left to fend for themselves.

Great Pubnico Lake has a Sheep Island, suggesting that at one time flocks may have summered there too.

At Tusket village we cross the "great forked tidal river" (Mi'kmaq), surely Nova Scotia's most crooked stream. From its headwaters near New Tusket it wanders from lake to lake; but from Kegeshook Lake down it runs southeast, then southwest, then southeast, and it keeps zigzagging until it enters the maze of lakes below Springhaven. Its tributaries follow the same lattice pattern.

There are several reasons for this. First, local Cambrian and Ordovician slates and quartzites are very resistant to erosion. Second, they were severely folded when the continental plates collided to form the super continent Pangaea. Third, erosion has almost flattened the terrain, and no geologic tilting or uplift have occurred for millions of years.

Under such conditions, streams have scant cutting power. Normally they take the most direct route they can find to the sea, carving a tree-like or dendritic pattern. The sluggish Tusket River, unable to cut through the folds, follows the zones of fault-weakened rock. Finally, at least four glaciations have played havoc with ancient drainage patterns. This was a dumping ground for ice sheets that crossed the Bay of Fundy and melted here.

Pubnico is an excellent harbour, from seven to twelve fathoms deep, easy of access, and so situated, that vessels entering the Bay of Fundy in distress, may find shelter and supplies ...
– Thomas C. Haliburton,
History of Nova Scotia, 1829

In fact, western Nova Scotia is a glacial graveyard. The whole region is a rumpled expanse of ground moraine (sand, gravel, boulders) peppered with shallow lakes. The glacial debris blocked the streams, causing the water to back up. As a result, the Tusket zigzags through Gillfillan, Wilsons, Bennetts, Kings, and Gavels lakes before it finally reaches the Atlantic.

Thanks to glaciation, the Tusket's labyrinth of lakes is home to plants found nowhere else in Canada. Their nearest counterparts grow far to the south, separated by hundreds of kilometres of ocean. How then did they get here? The short answer is that they survived on a coastal plain laid bare by melting ice when the sea was much lower.

During warm interludes—some warmer than today's—southern plants ventured northeast. When the sea resumed its old shorelines a few thousand years later, a few species were trapped along the Tusket River valley. Among these are Plymouth gentian (*Sabatia kennedyana*) and pink coreopsis (*Coreopsis rosea*). To preserve such rare plants, residents hope to manage and protect their habitat around Gillfillan Lake and other parts of the lower Tusket as ecological sites under the Special Places Act.

Fishers on Georges Bank have dragged up intact roots of red pine with soil clinging to them.

STOP: *Tusket Falls*
Waterfalls are scarce in western Nova Scotia, but Tusket Falls—actually a set of rapids—is a reasonable substitute, especially during the spring runoff. To view them, Exit 3 at the Tusket Falls sign and drive a bit over 2 km/1.2 mi to the village.

LEG-STRETCHER: *Sam O'Brien Interpretive Trail*
Local legend claims there are 365 islands in Lobster Bay—one for each day of the year. [See also **Mahone Bay**.] You can see a good many from Lower Argyle if it isn't foggy. Glenwood Provincial Park on Rickers Lake opposite Argyle offers a miniature of this island landscape. Its 1.5-km/0.9-mi trail takes us along a boardwalk, across a tidal marsh and onto two drumlins covered with red oaks.

Exit Rte 3 about 1 km/0.6 mi past Eel Brook and turn south just east of the park sign.

After Pubnico, the Lighthouse Route heads south along the east side of Pubnico Harbour before cutting over the peninsula to Woods Harbour. The unusually straight Pubnico shore marks the edge of a band of slates that dips under the harbour; to the east lie harder quartzites and greywacke. "Pubnico" derives from Mi'kmaq for "cleared land," referring perhaps to early Acadian dyking of sea marshes here.

STOP: *Shelburne Dyke*
If you know what to look for, there's an unusual rock formation exposed on the shore not far south of East Pubnico. Look for a band

265

I was born in Woods Harbour. In other words I am a Cockerwitter. My mother told me that when the Indians were canoeing up the pass between Johns Island and the mainland they heard the birds singing "Cock-a-wee! Cock-a-wee!" They so named the pass but later on the white folks changed it to Cockerwitt.
– Erdie Nickerson, **The Antics of a Cock-a-witter**

of dark granular rock, about the width of a four-lane highway, emerging from the harbour and heading in an easterly direction.

A geological dyke happens when molten magma from the Earth's mantle squirts up into a crack in the crust. The unusual thing about this one is its length: it runs from Pubnico Harbour to Cape LaHave Island, 140 km/87 mi away. It formed about the time the super-continent Pangaea was coming apart and the Atlantic Ocean began to open, 200 million years ago. As the magma cooled, it baked the sandstone on either side. The sandstone in turn chilled the magma enough to create a zone of finer-grained rock along each edge.

VIEW: *Harvesting Irish Moss*

In summer at Woods Harbour you may notice people working long-handled rakes in small boats at low tide. They're harvesting Irish moss (*Chondrus crispus*, Latin for "curled cartilage"), a purplish alga that fastens itself to rocky shores. Raking severs the plant but leaves holdfasts to grow new stems. People dry the harvest on fences and rocks along the road and on the old runway at the defunct East Camp military base nearby. Irish moss contains carrageenan, a thickener used in ice cream and pudding mixes. Harvesting it provides jobs and income in the lobster off-season.

In the 1930s Evelyn Richardson and her husband kept the light on Outer Island off Shag Harbour, an experience documented in her moving memoir, We Keep a Light, *which won the Governor General's Award in 1946.*

Petrels are small black open-ocean birds which come ashore only once a year, to breed. They are named for the apostle Peter, described in Matthew 14:29-30 as walking on water. [See also **Marine Drive,** *for another large breeding colony.]*

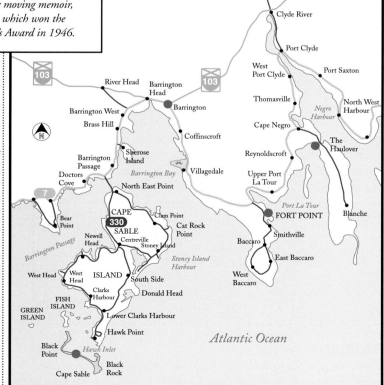

CRUISE: *Bon Portage (Outer) Island*

Even though the island is scarcely 6 m/20 ft above water, people hire boats to visit this scrap of rock 3 km/2 mi out in Shag Harbour. They go not only because Evelyn Richardson immortalized it in a book, but because it's so rich in wildlife.

Shag Harbour itself is named for its abundance of large black fish-eating cormorants. But shags are only incidental to the bird life here. The island lies on the Atlantic flyway, and thousands of migrating seabirds and songbirds use it as a rest stop and stepping stone. It also hosts the province's largest nesting colony of Leach's storm-petrels. An estimated 50,000 breed here. Exotic birds blown off course sometimes show up too.

Fuelling much of this activity is an abundance of seaweeds washed up by frequent storms. There being no sheep or deer to eat all this "sea wrack," it accumulates in fermenting windrows. Inside them live multitudes of shrimp-like amphipods and other invertebrates. Shorebirds feast on these. And what the birds leave, the tiny masked shrew consumes. Gulls, hawks, and owls patrol the beaches, so the shrews survive by staying under cover. Weasels, foxes, and coyotes are absent, because there is never any sea ice to trot out on.

Bon Portage has a few dense thickets of spruce-fir forest and a freshwater marsh or "savannah" in the middle.

Passing from Upper Woods Harbour to Barrington Head, we cross an area of much harder rock where soil is thin or absent. The diorite and gabbro here weather slowly to a quartz sand that makes an acidic soil. Trees are sparse and stunted. However, sphagnum moss does fine, draping itself over the bedrock in carpets of rumpled green and burgundy.

East of Shag Harbour the landscape opens up. There are rock-ringed islands offshore still, but the inlets aren't so narrow, and cobble beaches start to appear. Cool offshore waters produce morning fogs when winds are light. Generally they retreat to the outer headlands in the afternoon and return at night.

Beach on Cape Sable Island

SIDE TRIP: *Cape Sable Island*

Cape Sable (French for "sand"), southernmost tip of Nova Scotia, is part of a flimsy sandbar complex linking several tiny islets like beads on a string. They are a short boat ride from the main island, which is joined to the mainland by a causeway.

This is a birder's paradise. Migrants pass through by the thousands in spring and fall—their last Maritime stop. Winters are so mild that many shorebirds and seabirds stay year-round and strays tumble in during storms.

She said she was never lonely on the island for she could see the mainland all day, and at night there were the lights—Seal Island's to the west; Cape Sable's to the southeast; West Head's to the east; Emerald Isle's only two miles away, and Wood Harbour's to the north. Sometimes the big storms were a bit scary when they made the lighthouse rock and the big metal lantern vibrate, and there was the whistle-buoy at the reefs, The Groaner, to add to the wind's threat.
– Will R. Bird,
This Is Nova Scotia,
1950

Lighthouse on Cape Sable Island

Birds on Cape Sable Island

The Cape Sable complex consists of three parts: grassy dunes in the northwest, narrowing southward to a 0.8-km/0.5-mi sea wall (walkable at high tide) which widens into a swampy meadow and a saltwater pond.

Even in winter, says the Nova Scotia Bird Society, you're almost sure to spot eider, scoter, merganser, goldeneye, bufflehead, and oldsquaw, plus Iceland gulls, murres, dovekies, horned grebes, and guillemot. Smaller birds include snow buntings, horned larks, and Lapland longspurs. Mice abound, so don't be surprised if a northern harrier or even a snowy owl sweeps by.

Sometimes walrus stray this far south. Three have been sighted in this century, including one in the 1970s. (The startled fisherman who saw the long-fanged beast looming in the fog mistook it for a sea monster.)

These huge seal-like mammals used to be called sea cows (hence the Cow Bays near Halifax and Sydney). In fact, they were bigger than cows—the bulls up to 3.7 m/12 ft long and weighing up to 1 400 kg/3,000 lb. Aboriginal peoples hunted them for meat and oil. But after Basque hunters began to slaughter them in the 1500s, their numbers declined rapidly. Europeans needed the oil for light and to lubricate machinery. Walrus tusks grow to 1 m/3.3 ft long; the animal uses them to root shellfish from the sea bottom, for climbing onto ice, and to fight with. The ivory was later used to make piano keys, fancy letter openers, combs, and the like.

By the 1750s Cape Sable Island's sea cows were gone. The Magdalen Islands' breeding population was wiped out at about the same time.

The best time for birding here is June through September. The grassy dunes and sand flats attract hundreds of shorebirds, including dowitchers, piping plovers, and sandpipers. Common and arctic terns dive for small fish, their bounding flight a joy to watch. Bank swallows riddle old dunes with nest holes. In fact all four native swallows—the others being the cliff, tree, and barn swallow—come to Cape Sable to feast on kelp flies. Sometimes a turkey vulture, western grebe, or golden eagle shows up.

The wet pasture hosts American bittern, night heron, glossy ibis, and occasional egrets. Near the light station expert birders have tallied over 30 species of warbler. The rockier eastern shore offers sightings of red knots, willets, and ruddy turnstones.

You can drive onto Cape Sable Island; but to reach the cape itself you'll need a boat. Inquire at the Barrington Passage Post Office

> The yards were full of lobster traps, stacks of them,
> a half-finished Cape Island Boat in a shed
> had the hull of Noah's ark
> in the old picture books.
> At the Baptist church near the sea
> the tombstones stood like boundary markers,
> with lichens on the land side
> and salt on the water side.
> – Bert Almon
> from **"Driving Around Cape Sable Island"**
> Windhorse Broadside: Poets' Choice

... one third part [of Barrington Township] is covered with barrens and bogs. The remaining portion is clothed with spruce and fir, intermingled with maple and birch, and occasionally with [oak]. The soil in general is rocky and stubborn. When first cleared ... it is covered with a deep chocolate coloured turf, which requires to be well manured, before it will produce a crop of potatoes ....
– Thomas C. Haliburton,
History of Nova Scotia, 1829

before you set out, or ask a resident. You'll be dropped at one end of the complex and picked up at the other, with tides dictating arrival and departure times.

From south to north, Cape Sable is a 4.8-km/3-mi walk. Not far—but give yourself lots of time to stop and stare.

The original lighthouse and lightkeeper's cottage are gone, but the automated replacement is impressive, especially at night when its great beam sweeps across the dunes and out to sea. It is the Maritimes' most easterly (not counting Sable Island's).

Leave Rte 3 behind at Barrington Passage (the sign is near the mini-malls), and drive

Tidal wetland at Cape Sable Island

south on Rte 330, keeping right all the way till you reach The Hawk.

STOP: *Home of the Cape Islander*

On the way back, stop a while in Clark's Harbour, a famous fishing village settled in the late 1700s by people from Nantucket and Cape Cod. Here in 1907 Ephraim Atkinson designed and built the first of his unique Cape Island fishing boats. It was 11.5 m/38 ft long and 3.5 m/15.5 ft at the widest point, with high bows to deflect spray. It proved very stable in rough seas, a real asset when hauling or setting lobster pots. Evelyn Richardson compared the innovative hull to a gull's wing. The museum in Centreville has a model; drop in on your

Man, building his greatest and most personal of all tools, has in turn received a boat-shaped mind, and a boat, a man-shaped soul.
– John Steinbeck,
The Log from the Sea of Cortez, 1951

way back. In 1995 the village had several boatbuilding sheds. Traditionally, boats were made of local spruce and larch; now most local builders use fibreglass.

Lobster fishing is important in Clark's Harbour, which has some two dozen live-storage pounds.

If you're not keen on the boat trip or haven't time, there's a splendid beach on the main island that you can comb. Double back to Lower Clark's Harbour and drive toward the village of South Side. Watch on the right for a short dirt road. It leads to a sand beach at Bulls Head over 2 km/1.2 mi away.

Barrington Woolen Mill

BACK ON THE HIGHWAY

STOP: *Woolen Mill*
Because raising sheep on the islands was so convenient—no dogs to contend with, no fences to build and maintain—people often had surplus wool after domestic needs were met, which gave them much-needed cash. This 1884 mill in Barrington was a ready market. Today it's operated by the Nova Scotia Museum. It features original carding and knitting machinery plus exhibits about South Shore sheep raising and wool processing.

River Drive
In the spring of 1983 the last local log drive came down the Barrington River. It was organized by the Scott brothers of Barrington to bring down dozens of large white pines they had cut on the family woodlot the previous winter and hauled to the river bank to await the spring breakup. In late April, when the river was swollen with rain and melting snow, they herded the logs down the normally shallow upstream section. A second drive was run in May and filmed by the National Film Board in cooperation with the Department of Natural Resources. This drive brought the logs to the millpond, where they were sawn into choice lumber.

The stars of the drive were the three Scott brothers, winners of many international log-rolling competitions over the years. They learned the art of "birling" as boys on the family millpond. The film is titled *The Last Log Drive* and may be borrowed from the National Film Board.

TO SEE: *Barrington Kiyak Run*
When the roadside shadbush or Indian pear bloom in late April or early May, check the river on a rising tide for kiyak (pron. *kie*-ak), called gaspereau elsewhere in the province. The proper name for this silvery fish is alewife. They are on their way to upstream lakes to

spawn. Like salmon and trout, this member of the herring tribe is *anadromous*—i.e., it lives in salt water but returns to fresh water to breed, seeking out the very lake in which it was born.

For Mi'kmaq and early settler alike, the arrival of these fish was a welcome relief from winter fare or no fare. Camping near stream mouths, the natives corralled them with brush weirs and scooped up large numbers. Most were smoked for winter use. Settlers sometimes displaced Mi'kmaq fishers from prime sites, causing quarrels and even bloodshed. The pioneers pickled their catch or spaded the fish into their gardens for fertilizer. Later they copied the natives and smoked them. Eels were speared in the Barrington River North in winter, as they lay dormant in the river silt.

From Barrington to Shelburne, Hwy 103 offers short cuts across the Baccaro and Roseway peninsulas, passing through wide expanses of bog or "savannah." Our tour briefly follows Rte 309 around the coast, rejoining Rte 3 at Shelburne.

LEG-STRETCHER: *Port La Tour*

A poignant episode in the vast swirl of 17th-century English and French rivalry in the New World was played out here. Drive 16 km/10 mi down the Baccaro Peninsula past Coffinscroft and Villagedale to Fort Point, about 1 km/0.6 mi past the Barrington/Cape Negro intersection. Here you'll find a small park with parking space on your left.

A pleasant walk of a few hundred metres along a footpath through a grove of coastal white spruce brings you to a grassy knoll and cemetery overlooking the Atlantic. A cairn and plaque explain how Charles de Saint-Étienne de La Tour, defying both the British and his turncoat father, Claude, built Fort Saint-Louis here around 1627. Later his father, now unwelcome at Port Royal, was glad of his son's protection. A few stones remain.

Some 40 years later, Sir Thomas Temple built the first English fort on the coast near here. The French-English struggle over furs and fish was to continue until Louisbourg and Québec fell. Haddock, pollock, and lobster are still caught here.

Port La Tour Bog is one of only four locations in Canada where thread-leaved sundew grows; nearby Baccaro Bog is a second.

Before World War II, bulldozers and graders hadn't been invented and all-season woods roads were rare. Lumbering was mainly a winter occupation. Sawlogs were "snigged" (snaked) from stump to the haul road with oxen or horses and sledded over ice and snow to the nearest lake or sizeable stream. When the ice went out, they were floated or "driven"—the word comes from driving cattle or sheep—down to the mill or to waiting ships.

Spring freshets are fickle, so drivers used gated "splash dams" to hold back the flow until they needed it to flush the wood along. Skilled log drivers were said to be "very light on their feet," or "like a cat on the logs." When a log hung up on a rock or ran ashore at a bend, men wearing spiked (caulked) boots raced over the floating logs to free them. They used a cant hook (an iron-tipped staff with hinged hook) to roll them, and a pike pole to shove them along. If a log jam developed, they would dynamite the "key log." Sometimes drivers rode a big log downstream, rotating it to maintain balance, avoiding spills during collisions by jumping in the air at the moment of impact. Atlantic Canada's last regular log drives took place in the 1950s.

"I'll tow that one alongside for a bit before I bring it aboard." An expression from Barrington Head to express doubt concerning the truth or believability of something someone just said.
– Lewis J. Poteet,
The South Shore Phrase Book

Sand Hills Beach Provincial Park

This wedge of land on the east side of Barrington Bay is blessed with a long white sand beach. The sugary texture is due to quartz grains from local intrusions of granite in the prevailing quartzite and greywacke. This has produced drifting dunes clothed in marram grass. There is also warm-water swimming at low tide.

Lupins bloom here in July [see also the **Evangeline Trail** near Yarmouth and the **Marine Drive** at Lawrencetown], as well as blue-flag iris, beach pea, and other seaside plants. The endangered piping plover nests here, so be careful not to disturb them or to damage the dunes. White spruce, which resists salt spray, is slowly invading the inner sands.

Watch near Villagedale (4.4 km/2.7 mi south of the Hwy 103/Rte 309 intersection) for park signs.

The Haul-Over

Normally a small boat heading from Cape Negro to Port Clyde would have to round Blanche Point—an extra 20 km/12 mi. The Haul-Over—part portage, part canal—shortens this to a few hundred metres. Of the hundreds of ancient Mi'kmaq portages in the province, this is one of the few maintained to this day. [See also the **Halifax-Dartmouth Area Nature Tour**, Shubenacadie Canal.]

You can see the Haul-Over on the road to Blanche, where it crosses the boggy finger of land 0.4 km/0.25 mi south of Cape Negro village. Watch for a ditch-like canal south of the bridge. Tiny Blanche is only minutes farther on and is worth a visit, for it typifies hundreds of small fishing villages that once dotted the South Shore. And if you're in the mood for a beach hike, trek south along the shore 2.5 km/1.6 mi to The Sylvia, a slender sandspit tipped with a teardrop-shaped island.

At Clyde River we join Hwy 103 until 2 km/ 1.2 mi west of Birchtown.

Sand ripples on the South Shore

STOP: Savannah

Being farther inland, Hwy 103 shows better examples of the level expanses of sedges, shrubs, and dwarfed spruce that South Shore residents call "savannah." Monotonous to see from a vehicle, they are fascinating to explore on foot. It is, in fact, the typical bog-and-barren landscape found along the whole glaciated Atlantic Shore, wherever granite prevails and drainage is poor. Another typical feature is glacial erratics (boulders) perched on ice-smoothed rocky knolls. Expect to see them from here to Shelburne.

Walk a short way from the road to experience the spongy, water-logged surface (don't worry; you'll seldom sink to the knee). We recommend rubber boots for the timid, bare feet for the venturesome.

Does the term "savannah" owe its origin to a fancied resemblance to Africa's sparsely treed grasslands? Settlers often used familiar names for New World flora and fauna (e.g., "sycamore" for red maple, "robin" for red-breasted thrush). Perhaps an Afro-American settler or a retired colonel named the savannahs in this way.

Bowers Meadow

British soldier lichens

There's no better way to soothe hot, aching feet. Making headway takes a certain sort of springy stride and a tolerance for mosquitoes and no-see-ums, which breed in the water. The bog's drier edge is ringed with shrubs like leatherleaf and bog laurel mixed with occasional gnarled black spruce and tamarack (larch). Toward the middle it grades into pure sphagnum moss and sedge, with scattered knolls decorated with mini-forests of reindeer lichen and hair-cap moss.

As centuries pass, dead plant material (peat) accumulates in the cold, acidic water. As the humus deepens and dries out, conifers follow the shrubs and envelop the whole area.

Often there are pitcher plants. Except in Cape Breton, these are scarce elsewhere in Nova Scotia. Look for ankle-high rosettes of hollow red-veined green leaves clustered around a tall fleshy flower. They can flourish in soil devoid of nitrogen because they extract it from trapped insects.

Their jug-like leaves contain sweetened rainwater, which attracts insects. Typically a fly or beetle lands on the flared lip, crawls inside, and descends the richly patterned throat. When it tries to climb back up, downward-pointing bristles break its grip. It drowns, sinks to the bottom, and is digested.

Please don't dig up pitcher plants. Except in skilled hands they seldom survive transplanting.

Some granite knolls are truly rock gardens. Crevices sprout clumps of blueberry, crowberry, bayberry, and bearberry. [See also **Trans Canada Highway** near Port Hawkesbury, **Fleur-de-lis Trail** near Framboise, **Evangeline Trail** at Aylesford.] Herbalists use a tea from bearberry (*Arctostaphlos*) to cure urinary tract infections. Scarlet-tipped British soldier lichens brighten beds of mosses, and pale green and grey circles of map lichens spread over bare rock.

Some mosquitoes lay their eggs in pitcher plants. The larvae develop in the water without harm.

Canada's first patented fishway was developed in 1870 by James King of Nova Scotia; he called it the King Fish Ladder.

Spillway on Clyde River

Sawmilling in this area goes back to late 1780s, when incoming Loyalists got government aid to establish mills; 47 were built between 1783 and 1787 on the Roseway and Jordan rivers alone. Laws to protect fish were also on the books very early, but were poorly enforced. By the mid-1800s many south coast rivers had lost their spawning runs. Sawdust from mills and bark from log drives also ruined many streams.

STOP: *Fishway*

Just south of the Clyde River bridge there's an old sawmill and dam. Most old dams completely barred spawning fish, but this one has a wooden fish ladder. It's a simple affair, a series of water-filled, step-like tanks that enable fish to jump the obstacle a little at a time.

Without the fishway they would swim aimlessly below the obstacle, a prey to osprey, herons, otter, and poachers, never reaching their spawning grounds. Sawmill dams did much to destroy salmon spawning runs on East Coast rivers.

If you drove the coast route, you may have noticed an increase in pines near Shelburne, which is somewhat protected. Pines don't tolerate salt spray as well as spruce and fir do, and they like the sandier soils which prevail from here almost to Port Joli.

STOP: *Shelburne*

This Loyalist town is blessed with one of the world's biggest and finest harbours, a drowned river estuary. Settlers chose such deep, sheltered harbours because in those days most traffic was by water. Barrington and Liverpool show the same preference. [See also **Halifax-Dartmouth Area Nature Tour.**]

Many of the free black immigrants moved to the Truro, Halifax and Tracadie areas. In February, 2000 the Nova Scotia Museum honoured their contribution to our life and lore with a major exhibit that will travel to other Nova Scotia venues in the following years.

Newcomers to these coasts often settled on islands, which were closer to the fishery and safer from native attack. Shelburne's first settlers lived on McNutts Island, the low land mass visible outside the harbour. It was named for Alexander McNutt, a visionary land agent who planted his New Jerusalem there in 1764. In a few years it expired.

As the boulder monument at the foot of King Street attests, Shelburne really began in May 1783, when a shipload of aristocrats arrived from New York. Three thousand Loyalists followed, then 7,000 more. Among these were hundreds of black Loyalists. Streets were surveyed, and for a few giddy years Shelburne was the largest town in British North America.

But many of the upper-class immigrants were not fitted for wielding whipsaw, axe, and spade. To make matters worse, a destructive hurricane hit. Most left for greener pastures. But some of those who stayed became world-famous as builders of ships, dories, and yachts. Donald MacKay, the famous builder of clipper ships, though born in nearby Jordan River, learned his trade here.

Echoes of New England remain. In 1994 part of a film based on Nathaniel Hawthorne's *The Scarlet Letter* was shot here.

Ross-Thomson House Museum explains how shipbuilding and fishing built the town from 1784 on. Shelburne once had seven dory shops turning out craft for the Banks fishery. One of these shops, active from 1880 to 1970, has been resurrected as The Dory Shop. It celebrates that heritage and shows how the Banker dory was made.

The Banker dory, workhorse of the East Coast fishery for centuries, is a beautiful blend of form and function. To capsize it is almost impossible. It can lug heavy loads without drawing much water. Its clinker-built construction (overlapping planks) is very strong and seldom leaks. Its sleek lines allow two people to row it at a good clip—as Lunenburg's dory racers prove each summer. It even sails tolerably well.

Traditionally, Lunenburg dory ribs have been fastened to the floor timbers with natural tamarack knees, while Shelburne's are fastened with a locally invented metal clip.

At one point in the late 1800s, Nova Scotia had the highest tonnage of locally built wooden ships per capita in the British Empire. However, this took a tremendous toll on its forests, especially pine, birch, and tamarack.

Canoeing on Shelburne River in the fall

If you enjoy wilderness canoeing, inquire at the local DNR office about the Shelburne River. This candidate for designation as a Canadian Heritage River rises in Digby County, glides past the Tobeatic Wildlife Management Area and Kejimkujik National Park, and links up with the Roseway River, which empties at Shelburne. One could easily spend a week paddling this piney labyrinth of stillwaters, rapids, and lakes.

In the 1920s and 1930 American hunters and anglers considered this part of Nova Scotia untamed wilderness, and came in great numbers. Local guides like Eddie Breck became famous in sporting circles and travelled to trade shows in Boston and New York to promote their homeland. "Nova Scotia was far better known for its game, its fish and its guides during the early part of this century than it is now," said wildlife biologist Dr Donald Dodds—adding that it had more to offer then.

On my first going in shore after traveling five or six hours, returned quite discouraged, and had ... knocked down a brace of Partridges and one Goose .... I tho't Hunger look'd every wretch in the face that could not hit or Shoot for his Subsistance [sic]— Boasted land of Canaan! My stay here shall be very short but I will first look at the fisher; we went off and returned well Satisfied. Providence never was more plenty nor easily come at, as from this place.
– James Courtney, quoted in **"The Shelburne Loyalists,"** *by Mary Archibald,* **Nova Scotia Historical Review**

VIEW: *Pink Sands*

Going down the east side of Shelburne Harbour, near the Sandy Point light, observe the pinkish cast of the white quartz sand along the beach. It's due to crystals of red garnet, a glassy mineral produced when clay is baked at very high heat. The heat came from friction during the faulting and grinding of bedrock when the Appalachian Mountains were rising 380 million years ago. The narrow veins of staurlite and natural glass visible in the bedrock at low tide reflect the same origin.

From here you can either continue around Government Point and up the west side of Jordan Bay, or double back to Shelburne. Rte 3 rejoins Hwy 103 immediately east of town, leaves it at Jordan Falls to follow the coast, and rejoins it just west of Sable River.

VIEW: *Canada Hill Fire*

Near here on May 31, 1992, between the Jordan and Sable rivers, a forest fire razed 192 ha/475 ac of forest and scrubland. Hwy 103 crosses this burn in two places.

The first (pioneer) plants to appear were sheep laurel, blueberry, various ferns (from underground rhizomes), pin cherry and chokecherry (from dormant seed dropped by birds), aspen, red maple, and willow. [See also the **Trans Canada Highway** at the 1967 Telford Fire and the **Cabot Trail** at Cape Smokey.]

Granite Village erratic

Western Nova Scotia's granite areas have been burned over repeatedly, adding to the already extensive rock barrens which glaciers left. Sandy soils lose their moisture quickly in hot dry weather. The region's fairly long growing season makes matters worse, especially inland, where coastal fogs seldom penetrate. A third factor was the deliberate torching of barrens to increase yields of blueberry and deer.

Bernard Fernow's 1912 map shows huge tracts of burnt land back of Shelburne and Liverpool. The late forester Ralph Johnson of Liverpool noted in his *Forests of Nova Scotia* that forest fires raged during the dry summer of 1902. He quoted C. D. Howe, co-author of Fernow's *Forest Conditions of Nova Scotia*, as saying that there were "... over a half million acres of recent burns ... in Nova Scotia proper, on which the re-establishment of timber trees is at a standstill and will be for many years to come, even if future fires are excluded."

There is also evidence that native peoples routinely fired woodland to improve the berry crop, to manage game, and to improve visibility for hunting. But their fires would have been far less destructive, because the large amounts of dead wood and foliage caused by modern harvesting and fire prevention were not present.

VIEW: *Scotch Broom*

Between Shelburne and Birchtown on Rte 3 (and on Hwy 103), especially between Sandy Point and Jordan Bay, you'll see many clumps of this brushy funereal green shrub along roadsides and in pastures and open woods. There is also a colony at nearby Swanburg Lake. In July it surprises people by putting out tiny lemon-yellow pea flowers, proof that it belongs to that family.

Cytisus scoparius is in fact an introduced Old World legume. It now grows in poor sandy soils on both the Pacific and Atlantic coasts, thriving where few other shrubs that robust could live. Although no newcomer to western Nova Scotia—Yarmouth reported it in the mid-1960s—it hasn't spread far inland or northward. The late Dr Albert Roland concluded that the winters were too cold there. However, it has recently shown up in Hants County [See also the **Halifax-Dartmouth Area Nature Tour**.]

In Europe, Scotch broom's flower tips are gathered for medicinal uses before they bloom. They contain sparteine, a volatile compound that causes diuretic, cathartic, and in large doses, emetic (vomiting) reactions. So perhaps Scottish settlers brought it with them for medical reasons. However, American herbalist John Lust warns that large doses can cause fatal poisoning. [For other such introductions, see the **Marine Drive** at Eddy Point.]

At Jordan Falls we leave Hwy 103, which cuts inland across ill-drained flats of barely vegetated and glacially bevelled folds of ancient Meguma rock. Meanwhile Rte 3 loops south to Lockeport. This famous fishing port, pictured on Canada's old $50 bill, was hurt by the mid-1990s collapse of the East Coast fishery. Since then, federal funding from the Atlantic Canada Opportunities Agency (ACOA) has helped citizens build a community centre on Crescent Beach, a classic barrier beach. There are displays interpreting local human and natural history. (Ironically, the building is disrupting dune formation.)

To visit the centre, take Exit 3 halfway between Jordan Falls and Sable River, where the road takes a sharp left; go straight 2.5 km/1.5 mi to Lockeport. From Lockeport we rejoin Hwy 3 to Sable River.

STOP: *Sable River Provincial Park*

This is a good place to rest, to admire the big white pine, to sniff the fragrant *Myrica* bushes (sweet gale), and to explore the small tidal creek where bulrushes grow. This hollow-stemmed, leafless rush grows in shallow water around lakeshores and in tidal marshes. Different types range from knee-high to over 3 m/10 ft tall. [See also the **Ceilidh Trail**, Lake Ainslie side trip.]

Between Sable River and Summerville we're back on Hwy 103. Since the whole area around Port Joli Harbour is surrounded by Devonian

Famed American author Zane Grey (1875-1939, Riders of the Purple Sage, *etc;), caught a blue fin tuna in Jordan Bay. Tuna moved north to Cape Breton and Newfoundland in the 1940's and 50's.*

"Bulrush" to Maritimers commonly means cattail; but cattails belong to the genus Typha. *(One can't trust common names.) Sedges are in the* Carex *genus. To tell them all apart someone wrote this jingle :*

Grasses are jointed Sedges have edges And rushes are round.

granite, not quartzite or slate, expect to see bogs and barrens, glacial erratics, and white sand beaches.

Near the road to well-named Granite Village from Hwy 103 there's a grove of nearly pure birch, likely of fire origin. White birch (*Betula papyrifera*) demands full light and germinates best on bare mineral soil. Unlike yellow birch (*B. allegheniensis*), it's not a long-lived tree (about 80 years). It will only persist until spruce and fir seed in and gradually shade most of them out.

Little Port Joli beach

SIDE TRIP: *Atlantic Coast Close-up: Waterfowl Havens*

Near Port Joli on Hwy 103, watch for small blue signs on the ocean side when passing inlets or estuaries. These are boundary markers for the South Shore Migratory Bird Sanctuary, a complex of four areas administered by the Canadian Wildlife Service (CWS) to protect waterfowl from over-hunting. The areas are Port l'Hebert, Port Joli, Sable River, and Haley Lake.

The Port Joli sanctuary is one of only two sites in Nova Scotia where Canada geese overwinter in large flocks. [See also the **Marine Drive** at Cole Harbour.] The geese feed in sheltered inlets on eel-grass (*Zostera marina*), an unusual flowering plant that thrives in sheltered salt water. It's estimated that 40 per cent of Atlantic Canada's geese use this area.

Locals refer to two waves of fall migrants. "The First Flight" arrives in October/November from Labrador and Québec, and continues on south. "The Second Flight" comes in December and stays all winter. The latter are considered truly "Canadian" birds because they probably hatched in Newfoundland.

For a leg-stretcher, try the 3-km/1.9-mi loop trail through the Port l'Hebert Pocket Wilderness. This is a much-burnt landscape regenerating in aspen, birch, and spruce. Huge, lichen-crusted glacial erratics loom like grey giants in the often foggy woods. The brown water isn't polluted; it's just rich in tannin from all the peat.

The trail is part of a 61-ha/150-ac tract of woodland and coastal habitat owned by Bowater Mersey Paper Company of Liverpool. The CWS manages the tidal marshes as part of its waterfowl sanctuary program [see below].

To reach the trail, exit Hwy 103 9.5 km/5.9 mi east of Sable River (at head of Port Joli Bay) and drive south about 20 km/12 mi. Check first at the corner store located at the junction of the Port L'Hebert/Sandy Bay road and Hwy 103. For more detail on the trail, consult the latest edition of Michael Haynes' *Hiking Trails of Nova Scotia*.

STOP: *Thomas Raddall Provincial Park*

Encircling Sandy Bay on the west shore of Port Joli Harbour, Nova Scotia's newest provincial park honours the late Thomas H. Raddall of Liverpool (d. 1994), writer of Nova Scotia–based histories and historical novels such as *The Nymph and the Lamp*, *Halifax: Warden of the North*, *Roger Sudden,* and *Hangman's Beach*.

The park features pre-Mi'kmaq aboriginal campsites and middens, sand beaches, coastal barrens, and an old cemetery. In May, large numbers of sea ducks raft offshore, notably eiders feeding on sea urchins.

STOP:

Seaside Adjunct Park

Some say the jewel of this shore is Kejimkujik National Park Seaside Adjunct, one of the last unspoiled beach environments on the Eastern Seaboard. It has no fishing villages, no marinas, no cottages, no ATVs, no parking lots—not even roads. The whole beach is a trail, and the only traffic is shanks mare.

The best time to walk, says Michael Haynes, is from September to November. As you hike down to the shore you'll notice a dramatic shift in the vegetation. You go from red maple and red oak forest to coastal barrens carpeted with blueberry and sheep laurel (on the high ground) and sphagnum moss (in the wet hollows). Exposed headlands are mantled with crowberry, creeping juniper, dwarf spruce and fir, and lichens.

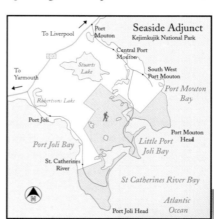

Seaside Adjunct Park

St Catherines River Bay, the southernmost part of the park, has a big barrier beach composed of sands left over from a melted glacier. The beach's flat profile, lack of dunes, and scarcity of plant life suggest that the ocean has destroyed earlier bars. And this one has been breached twice in the last 50 years.

From mid-May to mid-July, piping plovers assemble here. These dainty little shorebirds, called "peeps" locally, lay their eggs on bare sand. So well camouflaged are their eggs and young that people have accidentally stepped on them. Signs are posted during nesting season to warn people off; please be alert for these. Peeps are scarce and need our help. [See also **Marine Drive**.]

Enter Port Joli Park and drive 6.4 km/4 mi down the dirt road past Robertson Lake.

HAZARD: *Wood Ticks*

This small spider-like parasite likely arrived on American hunting dogs in the late 19th century. Since then it has become a nuisance for animals and humans during early summer. To breed, the female must have a blood meal. This enlarges its 3mm/¹/8in greyish body many-fold (up to 12mm/¹/2in, making it easy to spot. Mammals usually pick them up as the ticks cling to tall grass and shrubs. So it's wise when hiking during tick season to wear pants tucked into boots and to keep pets out of tick habitat. [See also **Kejimkujik Scenic Drive** and the **Evangeline Trail** near Yarmouth.]

In the eastern US this tick carries Lyme disease, but no Nova Scotia cases in humans have been reported. However, dogs in Springhill and New Glasgow were found with the bacteria in 1999. It has been speculated that these ticks do not overwinter here, but arrive annually on migrating birds.

> They say the old fishing village of Port Mouton (French for sheep) got its name from a sheep that fell overboard here when Sieur De Monts was exploring the coast in 1604.

Ancient Middens

A curious feature of the Adjunct shorescape is kitchen middens dating from the Ceramic Period 500 to 2,500 years ago. To anthropologists they are windows into the lifeways of early coastal peoples. For instance, the bones of eider and oldsquaw sea ducks have been found, as well as those of thick-billed murre. Eider and oldsquaw still abound, but the murre no longer breeds here. Walrus and caribou bones occur too, as well as extinct species like passenger pigeon and great auk. White-tailed deer, which didn't enter the peninsula until the 1890s, is not represented.

Shell middens are protected under the Special Places Act. If you find one please report it, as ocean waves can easily erase it without human help. To visit a midden, call the Port Joli Conservation Society.

BACK ON THE HIGHWAY

From Summerville to Liverpool we rejoin Rte 3. At Southwest Port Mouton occur some of mainland Nova Scotia's largest "true" dunes—i.e., dunes built by windblown, not wave-thrown, sand. Some reach 15 m/50 ft high. The exposed quartzite coast provides a steady supply. [See also **Sunrise Trail** near Merigomish.]

Perkins House Museum

Rails to Trails

On the west side of Liverpool there's a Rails-to-Trails project, a hiking route that follows an abandoned railway line.

As transport trucks, airlines, and private vehicles have largely replaced locomotives in toting freight and passengers, many rail lines are being abandoned. Being nearly level, these make ideal corridors for hiking, cycling, cross-country skiing, and snowmobiling. Rather than let them grow up in forest and bushes, citizens across the province are clearing rights-of-way, replacing bridges, and promoting hiking. For more information, ask at the tourist information centre or visit the Queens County Municipal Building on West Street.

Inquire also about Meadow Pond, a local park managed for wildlife. The pond has both floating and emergent aquatic plants. The latter include native pickerel weed, which bears spikes of purple flowers in July. Emergents have spongy stems able to pass oxygen directly to their submerged parts; the water lily is a familiar example.

While in Liverpool, be sure to visit Perkins House Museum. This restored 18th-century home recalls the life and times of Simeon Perkins, a local shipbuilder and merchant who arrived from New England in 1762, when the town was only two years old.

Although Perkins' journals from 1766 until his death in 1812 deal mostly with business, they reveal much about how people regarded the environment in his day. For example, he casually remarks that most of the interior between Annapolis and Liverpool had been burnt over. Yet only when forest fires threatened property or lives did they loom large in his thought.

Liverpool has the dubious honour of being the first place in Nova Scotia to report Dutch elm disease, an Asian fungus. In the summer of 1969, two of its elms mysteriously wilted. An alert forester suspected DED; tests proved him right. The next year the disease appeared in Kentville. Both cases occurred near a funeral parlour, likely from caskets crated in Ontario with rough-sawn elm lumber with infected bark left on.

Although the Liverpool elms were promptly cut and destroyed, it was too late. Likewise with a massive elm-removal program in Kentville and the Annapolis Valley, in which several thousand

June 2, 1786: Very warm Day. The fire in the Woods back of Herring Cove Rages very much. We are working on the Floom [log flume or chute]. Most of the Timber is got out....
June 3, 1786: Continues Very Dry and the Fires in the Woods make it very thick & Smoakey. John Hopkins Junr. Lands his Fish to me, about 30 Quintle [1527 kg/3,360 lb].
June 28, 1792: The fire at Herring Cove has raged yesterday, & this day it ran to Beach Meadows. John Miles took the Boards off from his House & carried them into the Creek, but Saved his Frame Standing.
– Quoted in D. A. Benson & D. G. Dodds, **Deer of Nova Scotia**, Dept of Lands & Forests, Halifax (1976)

infected and high-risk trees were destroyed, also failed. Today, dead and dying elms are a common sight throughout rural Nova Scotia. While Chinese and Siberian elms tolerate the disease, they are no substitute for the fountain-shaped native species.

As a native forest species, white elm ranks only 15th in abundance among Nova Scotia's broad-leaved trees. That's because it grows best on river floodplains. Here the soils are rich and stone-free, and its flat floating seeds can colonize new locations in rich silt. In the late 1800s people realized its potential as an urban shade tree and ornamental. Thousands of young trees were transplanted, especially during Queen Victoria's Golden and Diamond Jubilees in 1887 and 1897.

So far no workable cure for the disease has been found, and breeding programs have failed to produce a hybrid with white elm's superior qualities. Prevention is the only option. This means sanitation cutting—regular pruning of dead and dying branches and prompt removal of dying or dead trees. All wood so removed must be burned or buried before May, when the tiny beetles begin to breed (under dead bark) and feed (on new growth).

In this way towns like Truro and Fredericton have saved up to 90 per cent of their elms. However, nobody has had the will or money to do the same for rural trees. The experience with untreated trees, in Europe and Britain in the 1930s, was that a third died outright, a third sickened, and a third survived. Since then more virulent Canadian strains of the fungus have been killing Britain's remaining elms. [See also the **Glooscap Trail** at Truro and the **Cabot Trail** near River Denys.]

The Asian fungus Ceratocyctis ulmi was first identified in Holland—hence the popular name. Eastern Canada's DED was first diagnosed in 1944, when elms in Sorel, Québec, began to die. The spores probably arrived on bark beetles in a shipment of European elm lumber. The disease reached the US in 1930 and Ontario not long after, probably via Ohio.

The Bowater Mersey newsprint mill at Brooklyn, west of Liverpool, was built in 1929 as part of the new Mersey Paper Company owned by Montreal financier Izaak Walton Killam. Power to run the mill comes from the Mersey River, which flows from Lake Rossignol about 25 km/16 mi northwest. Damming has made it the province's largest lake. (Lake Ainslie is the largest natural lake [see the **Ceilidh Trail,** Lake Ainslie side trip].)

Bowater Mersey maintains a number of nature trails and pocket wildernesses, including the Port l'Hebert area.

Trees along Mersey River

From Liverpool to just beyond Mill Village we return to Hwy 103; then we follow Rte 331 to Bridgewater.

The fields of stunted broadleafed trees near the Medway River developed after repeated forest fires, which depleted the humus. Where soils are already thin and sandy, such fires can eventually create barrens. However, light-loving birch, cherry, red oak, and aspen have again greened the landscape. Through leaf fall and root activity, they are slowly rebuilding the soil. [See also the **Trans Canada Highway** at New Glasgow and Sydney; the **Glooscap Trail** near Sand River.]

Soon after crossing the Lunenburg County line near East Port Medway, we enter a less rocky landscape. Swelling hills with trim farms riding on their shoulders come into view, separated by streams and mixed forest. This is drumlin country.

You can tell a drumlin from an ordinary hill by the lack of bedrock along its margins and by its usually whaleback shape. Often it's part of a drumlin swarm, all facing the direction from which the ice came, like minnows in a brook. [See also the **Marine Drive** near Ecum Secum; the **Marconi Trail** near Gabarus.]

The special smoothness of these hills has to do with slate formations that run from here to Chester. Slate is hardened clay, and wet clay is greasy. Moving glaciers normally bulldoze irregular heaps of gravel and rock. Where clay is present they tend to ride over them, sculpting them as they go. Because clay soils are more fertile than granite soils, Lunenburgers had better luck with farming than the settlers farther west and east.

Most of Lunenburg's pioneers came in the 1750s from Germany and Switzerland, where careful land husbandry is traditional. They expected better land, but made the best of what they got. As drumlins offered drier and less stony soil, many chose them. What they couldn't farm they left in woodland. This was the basis for their boatbuilding fame. Within a generation these farmers were making a name for themselves as fishermen. Some woodlots have been in the same family for five generations and are still producing large sawlogs of pine, hemlock, maple, and red spruce.

If you feel like it, trek the rugged 5-km/3.1-mi shore between Broad Cove and Green Bay, arranging for pick-up there. Unlike the granite terrain of Port Joli, this is quartzite and greywacke country. Being softer, the bedrock is more rounded, and there are fewer boulders lying about.

The word drumlin derives from Gaelic druim, *a long narrow hill or ridge.*

Lunenburg drumlins

Each December Bostonians light a massive Christmas tree atop the Prudential Center. Since 1976 Nova Scotia has provided that tree, first from Lunenburg County, then from province-wide.

Why Nova Scotia? Because when a massive man-made explosion flattened the north end of Halifax on December 6, 1917, killing 2200 people and wounding 9000, Massachussetts sent, within hours, a hospital ship and train staffed with 300 doctors, nurses and social workers.

Beach at Broad Cove

You'll find a scalloped shore with numerous pocket beaches of fine sand tucked between small headlands backed by stunted white spruce. These horseshoe coves catch and hold the wave-borne sand. Park at the far end of Green Bay Beach. The hike starts on an old oxcart road. There's good birding here, with occasional coastal warblers in season.

The Shelburne Dyke surfaces on the beach just south of Broad Cove, and on the west side of Medway Harbour.

Boardwalk at Rissers Beach

SIDE TRIP: *Rissers Beach, Crescent Beach, Cape LaHave Island*
Don't miss Rissers Beach Provincial Park, a westerly extension of the magnificent complex of wave-built sands surrounding Green Bay. One striking feature at Rissers is a full natural progression from woodland to ocean: white spruce through marram grass dunes to wet sand. There's also the Salt Marsh Trail. Its 0.5-km/0.3-mi-long, wheelchair-accessible boardwalk takes you into the world of cord grass, salty muck, mosquitoes, and blue heron.

A common "shell" found along this beach is that of the sand dollar. This delicate structure is actually the hollow skeleton of a burrowing type of sea urchin that spends most of its life buried in the sand just below the low tide mark. Some of its many tube feet are greatly lengthened to siphon minute organisms from the seawater and to excrete wastes.

The Petite Rivière near Rissers Beach in Lunenburg County is one of only two places in the world where Acadian whitefish is known to survive. The other is Lake Annis, about 30 km/ 18 mi north of Yarmouth. Whitefish belong to the trout family.

The great curving tombolo of Crescent Beach links the mainland almost to Bush Island, which is reached by a short bridge. [See also the **Fleur-de-lis Trail** at Point Michaud and the **Glooscap Trail** at Parrsboro.] The beach was built by waves and longshore currents eroding and conveying sand from nearby headlands. Just as snow-drifts form in slack air behind hedges and buildings, sand settles where currents lag or meet opposing currents. Unlike most Atlantic coast beaches, Crescent has multiple sand ridges.

With its diversity of habitats Crescent Beach is a birder's paradise from mid-July to late September. In mid-July look for short-billed dowitchers (from "dowager") to arrive, along with sandpipers, greater yellowlegs, and semipalmated plover. A little later there are black-bellied plovers, red knots, and ruddy turnstones. Later still, look for purple sandpipers. Now and then birders spot Wilson's phalarope,

Hudsonian godwit, and stilt sandpiper. One marbled godwit is even on record. The best time to bird watch is at mid-tide. Check locally for tide times, or watch the shore.

In 1905 a violent storm breached Crescent Beach and its dunes. Men plugged the gap with trees, and by 1920 the dunes had recovered. Then, in the dry summer of 1920, a fire killed the restraining marram grass, releasing sand which blew inland and smothered the tidal marsh. It never recovered. In 1938 a long plank barrier was built, but the sea destroyed it. In 1940 old car bodies were dumped in the gaps, trapping enough sand to build steep dunes. Finally, in 1957, a sea wall of big boulders was built, with a surfaced and graded road to relieve dune traffic. So far the defences have held.

SIDE TRIP: *Cape LaHave Island*

Cape LaHave Island—actually two islands bridged by a beach bar—is only 6 km/3.7 mi long by 4 km/2.5 mi wide, but with its cluster of smaller islands it has helped create the beaches around Green Bay. It does this by breaking the force of the waves, much as a windbreak collects snowdrifts.

For a place so close to habitation, the island feels oddly remote. For this reason, generations of residents have picnicked and hunted seabirds there. And for such a small area it's unusually rich in natural history. There are cranberry bogs, tidal marshes, and sand dunes stitched together by marram grass. There are unusual shrubs like ground-juniper (*Juniperus horizontalis*), and hardy mountain-ash brighten the drab spruce thickets with scarlet berries in late August.

Out here one can also find rooted stumps of drowned conifers that grew millennia ago when sea level was lower. On the seaward side there are tilted beds of grey-green, rippled Cambrian quartzites studded with 3-cm/1-in cubes of rusting iron pyrite. Dead seals sometimes wash up here. There's a long central lagoon kayakers can paddle up. And the Shelburne Dyke crosses the island.

Unless you're a kayaker or ocean canoeist, the best way out and back is to hire a fishing boat in West Dublin or Petite Rivière. It's certainly worth the price.

BACK ON THE HIGHWAY

From Crescent Beach the route winds around the LaHave headland and up the drowned estuary of the LaHave River to Bridgewater. A cable ferry links LaHave and East LaHave, with a good chance of seeing ospreys.

Bridgewater, built at tidewater in a time before trains or cars, was the farthest ships could navigate inland. (The river is 2 m/6.5 ft deep at the bridge, and the bottom is sand and mud—easy on a vessel's bottom.) The LaHave River drains seven lakes, and its estuary is 17 km/10.5 mi long and up to 600 m/1,970 ft wide. The average depth is 7 m/23 ft, and mean tidal range is 1.6 m/5.2 ft. Around 1820 the

... in the outer harbour of La Have, there are, as in Chester Bay, very many beautiful Islands affording shelter for vessels, and convenient places for curing and drying fish.
– Thomas C. Haliburton, **History of Nova Scotia,** 1829

river powered 30 mills of various kinds.

The DesBrisay Museum explains how, in 1753, Huguenot turnip farmers from Prussian Hanover and French artisans from

Christmas Tree farm near Bridgewater

Montbeliard, enticed by George II, came and settled here. Realizing there was more future in cod than in turnips or handcrafts, they soon turned to the sea. Before long their sleek schooners were vying with those of New England on the lucrative offshore cod banks.

Others farmed the drumlins, and still do. Drive the back roads north and west of Bridgewater and you'll see these farms. For example, near Bakers Settlement on Rte 210 as it joins 325, there's a sudden detour to get around a big one. [See also the **Evangeline Trail** near Yarmouth, the **Marine Drive** north of Sherbrooke, and the **Fleur-de-lis Trail** near Mira.]

Generations later, as if to honour a tradition begun by the 16th-century German theologian, Martin Luther, they pioneered Christmas tree cultivation in the province. For years, Bridgewater has rightfully called itself the "Balsam Fir Christmas Tree Capital of Canada."

Each fall, when the weather cools enough for the harvested balsam fir to retain their needles outdoors, scores of woodlot owners arrive at wholesale buyers' lots with truckloads of fragrant trees. Conveyer belts trundle them past professional graders who sort them by size, shape, density, and colour, and affix coloured tags. (Nowadays, few uncultivated trees would pass muster. Modern fir Christmas trees, though mostly wild, are far from "natural".) Meanwhile automatic balers bundle trees in plastic netting. This protects branches and twigs during the long truck or train ride to New England, our chief market.

Riverport is near the site of an Acadian settlement founded under Isaac de Razilly, first governor of New France. In the fall of 1632, hoping to impress his sponsors, de Razilly sent home a shipload of the best white pine he could procure. This was the first documented shipment of timber from eastern North America.

Christmas tree farming is a year-round occupation. After removing competing broadleaf vegetation, the trees are spaced and sheared for two or three years in a row to improve density and, if necessary, fertilized to improve colour. Pest and disease control is a continuing task, and thieves have to be guarded against.

These "Lunenburg Dutch" [*Deutsch* = German] still celebrate Oktoberfest, a living reminder of their origins and another thread in Nova Scotia's colourful ethnic tapestry.

White pine has five-needle clusters (W-H-I-T-E or B-L-A-N-C); red pine has paired needles.

After crossing the Main Street bridge, we follow Rte 332 southeast down-river past Dayspring and Riverport and Rose Bay to Lunenburg. Incidentally, the Dayspring Peace Park (4 km/2.5 mi out of town) is worth stopping at just to admire the tall, straight white and red pines.

This is one of the few undeveloped tracts of land along the outer LaHave; much of it has been regenerating to forest for a century.

SIDE TRIP: *Indian Path Ospreys*

On Rte 332 between East LaHave and Lunenburg there's an old Mi'kmaq trail crossing the Rose Bay peninsula, where ospreys nest. Some years ago, finding no nearby tall pines, a pair of these fish-eating hawks built their large nest of sticks on the crosstrees of a power pole. This posed no danger to the birds—an electric shock requires grounding—but it worried the linesmen. And the crews bothered the ospreys. Rather than evict the birds, the men set up separate poles with crosstrees—and the birds adapted.

Indian Path intersects Rte 332 0.7 km/0.4 mi past the East LaHave Ferry wharf. But inquire first in East LaHave on the status of the birds.

Sea caves at Ovens Point

Inuksuk at the Ovens

... gold is found in the sand after a severe storm. Individuals who wash the sands earn $1 to $1.50 a day.
–Ruth Kedzie Wood,
The Tourist's Maritime Provinces,
1915

Sea cave

BACK ON THE HIGHWAY

STOP: *The Ovens Point*

Named for its natural sea caves, this place is worth a visit for its abandoned gold-mining pits and tunnels. The gold came from quartz veins in steeply tilted slates, veins which the ocean exposed. There are three deep caves, one about 20 m/65 ft long. During

The discovery of gold on the beach here in July 1861 unleashed a miniature gold rush. Shore lots sold for up to $4,800. In seven months, $120,000 worth had been washed by hand from the beach sands. Within three years the village was abandoned.

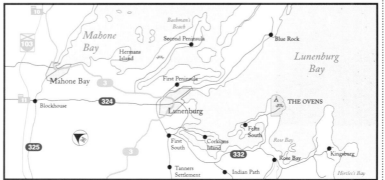

Lava beach and erratics near Ovens

northeasters great waves compress the air in them, causing a booming echo that can be heard a long way. Borrow a sourdough pan and try panning for a nugget.

Watch for the sign to The Ovens Park and turn right onto the gravel road off Rte 332 between the village of Rose Bay and Bayport. Drive 2.7 km/1.7 mi.

The coastal road from Rose Bay to Lunenburg passes some spectacular tidal flats, reachable via two public roads. In summer the flats are bathed in warm shallow water that fosters a diverse marine flora and fauna.

After summer storms, South Shore beaches sometimes cough up oddities from the Gulf Stream. Most are microscopic, but occasionally something exotic, a flying fish or a sea turtle, comes ashore. If you find a stranded purplish jellyfish, don't handle it. It could be a Portuguese man-o'-war, whose tentacles sting painfully even in death. The best time to beachcomb is after a tropical storm in September.

Like ancient Rome, Lunenburg was built on multiple hills—in this case drumlins—but unlike Rome, it encircles a harbour scooped out by glaciers. You'll see its gently rounded earthen domes as you enter on Rte 332, and again when you leave on Rte 3 for Mahone Bay. Visible on their rounded shoulders are old farms, Christmas tree lots, a sewage treatment plant,and numerous other enterprises.

The Theresa E. Connor at the Fisheries Museum of the Atlantic

STOP: *The Fisheries Museum*

The Fisheries Museum of the Atlantic on Lunenburg's waterfront was opened in July 1967 and offers a fascinating look into the fishing tradition of this town. Just down the wharf is where the original *Bluenose* was built, and her namesake *Bluenose II*. After touring three floors of exhibits, board one of the few surviving authentic bankers, the *Theresa E. Connor*. Below deck you can visit the crew's cramped quarters and imagine what it was like to eat and sleep here while trawling for cod in open dories for a living.

They couldn't go ashore with each day's catch, so they gutted and pickled the fish on board to keep it from spoiling. The pickle might have been sea salt made at Big Turk in the Caribbean, or it might have been mined salt from Spain or Portugal. "Cheaper than Malagash or Pugwash salt," explained a local old-timer, "since the skippers were sailing back empty anyway." [See also **Sunrise Trail** at Malagash.]

Back in port, the split and salted cod was sun-cured on airy wooden platforms for a few fine days, longer if it been accidentally uncovered during rainy weather. Once dry, it was packed in wooden barrels made from local fir (fir wood is odourless, spruce isn't) by skilled coopers. Because the barrels need not be watertight, they called this "slack cooperage." To bind them, they used hoops made from split birch saplings secured by notched and overlapped ends. A favourite splitting tool was a Mi'kmaq crooked knife.

Check in the museum entrance for notices of scheduled talks on coopering and many other aspects of the fishery.

Slate at Blue Rocks

From Hwy 3 east of Lunenburg there are good views of the numerous islands of Mahone Bay (likely named for "mahonne," Old French for a low-slung pirate vessel). The bay is said to have an island for each day of the year. Many are submerged drumlins. The outer ones, lacking protective cliffs, are being rapidly undercut by storm waves, especially in winter. But they and the shoals they create protect the inner bay from fierce storms.

Some of the islands are named for families who farmed or fished there. Today only a few such islands (e.g., Big Tancook) have permanent residents. Isolation and lack of doctors and teachers have persuaded the rest to re-locate.

There's a ferry from Chester to Tancook several times a day. Besides giving you a sailor's view of the islands, it offers sightings of seabirds, seals, and whales. Tancook itself has good hiking paths, a cabbage farm, and a fishing village.

A great advantage of drumlin islands was that they made fairly good pastures without the need for fencing. Moreover, gardeners found that with an annual dressing of fish and seaweed, the soil was very fertile. And there was less frost than on the mainland.

During Prohibition, privateers used the islands to elude Coast Guard pursuers in the cat-and-mouse game of rum-running. For a vivid account of this game in the 1930s (off the New Brunswick coast) read Antonine Maillet's *The Devil is Loose!*

At East River on Mahone Bay, the Canexel plant processes wood fibre from low-grade coniferous trees into a fine-grained hardboard panelling for the construction industry.

The process resembles paper-making except that the pulp retains its brownish colour, and natural resin, not glue, bonds the layers under tremendous heat and pressure. The result, popularly called Masonite after its inventor, goes to make wallboard and countertops in

Chester is to the Atlantic shore ... what Digby is to Fundy, though with more aspirations to fashions. For a number of years its invigorating climate and environments have [attracted] a summer colony from the States ...
– Ruth Kedzie Wood,
The Tourist's Maritime Provinces,
1915

East of the La Have, drumlins tend to be reddish. This suggests that they picked up iron-rich Triassic sands while crossing the Bay of Fundy. Most local islands are also of this type.

many printed patterns and designs. (The plant is 9 km/5.6 mi east of Chester, visible on the right after the intersection with Rte 329.)

Chester has an interesting 3-km/1.8-mi walking trail interpreting local woodland, developed by the municipality with help from DNR. It starts next to the Forest Heights Community School.

Pearl Island off Bayswater on Rte 329 near Mahone Bay is an important breeding area for Atlantic puffin, Leach's storm-petrel, razorbill auk (a smaller relative of the extinct great auk), and black guillemot.

From East River Rte 3 cuts across the Aspotogan Peninsula dividing Mahone Bay from St Margarets Bay. The southwest corner is slate, covered with drumlins; the rest is granite. From here to Halifax the bedrock is Devonian granite, part of the great batholith that arches past the Annapolis Valley almost to Yarmouth [see also the **Marine Drive**]. Again we're in a landscape of barrens, boulders, spruce bogs, and countless lakes.

Deep Cove, an unusually narrow and deep inlet just over halfway down the peninsula's west side on Rte 329, is interesting because it occupies a northwest/southeast type of fault that is common on the **Marine Drive** but unusual here. Also, nearby Aspotogan Mountain is

Erratics

a monadnock, a resistant rock dome of slate that rises well above the surrounding land. The rock cuts here are stained red with iron.

"Aspotogan" is Mi'kmaq for "place where you encircle to catch seals."

Queensland Beach just east of Hubbards, like others along this shore (e.g., Cleveland and Black Point), is walled with rounded boulders behind a crescent of clean white sand. The blue-green water never warms up (except in shallow, sheltered coves) even in August—though in photographs it looks almost tropical.

The boulders, of various colours and textures, were dumped here by moving glaciers. Judging by their basalt content, some were dragged from as far away as the Annapolis Valley's North Mountain. Over thousands of years, rain and surf have sifted the gravel and sand from

Coastal barrens in fall

Peggys Cove

the glacial till to form this beach. The windrows of boulders are the work of storms and harbour ice—and sometimes of bulldozers.

But don't let all this talk of ice and cold deter you from an invigorating swim! The bracing water will leave you tingling and refreshed.

The rugged granite hinterland was burnt over in the 1900s and is studded with glacial lakes. With so many upland lakes well above sea level, there's an abundance of potential energy. The French Village hydroelectric power plant at the Head of St Margarets Bay taps this. It's one of nearly three dozen in Nova Scotia. [See also the **Evangeline Trail** at Nictaux.]

As Rte 333 takes us along the east side of the bay toward Peggys Cove, the coast is more and more exposed to open ocean. This exposure, combined with the steep downward slope of the sea bottom here, and the lack of protective islands or shoals, allows tremendous waves to build up. Many people have been drowned on this shore.

Ocean waves come in pulses, which vary with local conditions. On this shore expect a group of three to five small waves followed by three to five big ones, with an average interval of 10 seconds. The smaller waves can fool you. People approach too close, only to be surprised by the big ones. An even greater danger is that after every 7–10 waves the crests are "in phase" and produce a whopper. And there are "rogue waves" that come out of nowhere in fairly calm water. The only sure way is to take no chances and to watch children and the elderly closely. Water weighs a tonne per m^3 and hits *hard*.

For seaside parking, drive east of the Whale Back Restaurant in Cranberry Cove and choose one of several gravel pull-offs, preferably one in sight of Nova Scotia's most photographed and painted inlet, Peggys Cove. This will also be a safer and more sheltered place from which to examine the rocky shore.

Before leaving, take time to explore the tidal pools along the shore. In the upper zone you'll see small blue-green algae, and the periwinkles that feed on them. Farther down, at low tide, there are shrimp-like amphipods, rockweed, more periwinkles, mussels, and barnacles. On the lower shore, which is seldom dry, look for Irish moss and kelp plus shore creatures like rock crabs and sculpin, which can't risk drying out. Seaweed thrives along the whole Atlantic shore because the water is clear and ice floes infrequent.

In spring you might be surprised to see a native toad in a tidal pool. While they don't dare venture into the salty splash zone, they hunt the upper pools for small game, keeping an eye out for marauding gulls.

As at Peggys Cove, the landscape towards Halifax has been heavily glaciated. This shows in the pavement-like smoothness of the bedrock and in the number of big boulders scattered about. Also, the hinterland has been repeatedly burned. Any soil that remained, rain and wind removed. Only in rock crevices can small trees and shrubs eke out a living.

After Peggys Cove the route heads inland past Whites Lake and toward Halifax, passing through Long Lake Provincial Park Reserve (a bit of urban wilderness you may want to explore), Exhibition Park, and so to the city itself. From there you can access the **Marine Drive**, **Halifax-Dartmouth Area**, **Evangeline**, and **Highway 102** nature tours.

Marconi Trail
Nature Tour

Highway 22, Louisbourg to Glace Bay
70 km/43 mi

South Head, Morien Bay

OVERVIEW

The landscape of this short travelway so closely resembles that of the **Fleur-de-lis Trail** that a brief description will suffice. The main difference is that north of Mira Bay we leave the rocky Precambrian landscape and enter a broadly rolling Coal Age lowland.

The latter is formed of nearly horizontal sandstones and shales that have been abraded nearly to sea level. Although its soils are deep and reasonably fertile, exposure stunts the vegetation, especially the spruce, fir, larch, and birch forests. With hardly a hill taller than 30 m/100 ft to shelter behind, they are often lashed by northeasterlies laden with salt spray. In late winter the Labrador Current brings drift ice, and onshore winds may plug the harbours with it for a week or more (hence "Glace" Bay). Sometimes the floes linger offshore until June. This, combined with frequent fogs, makes for a growing season almost a month shorter than the Annapolis Valley's. [See also the **Trans Canada Highway** at North Sydney.]

In the early 1600s this coast was an important centre for Portuguese and French whalers. However, the trail is named for Guglielmo Marconi (1874–1937), Italian inventor of the wireless telegraph. He received the first transatlantic message from Poldhu, Cornwall, to St John's, Newfoundland, in December 1901, and in 1902 he sent the first official west-to-east transatlantic message from Table Head near here.

THE TOUR BEGINS

We begin at Fortress Louisbourg behind Blackrock Point on the south side of Louisbourg Harbour. And we begin with history, for when the Treaty of Utrecht ousted the French from Newfoundland and Acadia in 1713, it left them only St Pierre and Miquelon off southern Newfoundland and Île Royale (Cape Breton Island). A fort was crucial to protect France's interests in the St Lawrence, specifically the fur trade and the immensely profitable cod fishery based at Louisbourg.

Louisbourg

The fortress took 20 years (1717–37) to build [see also the **Ceilidh Trail** at Port Hood, where the principal stone was quarried], and strained the French treasury. But soon its fishing shacks were landing immense quantities of cod—over 14 million kg/30 million lb a year—to sell in Europe and the West Indies. Louisbourg also became a prosperous trading centre, rivalling New England and raising British hackles. In 1745 and again in 1758 they captured it, and in 1760 razed it to the ground.

Since 1963, Parks Canada, using unemployed miners and a staff of researchers, has meticulously restored this 18th-century bastion, as well as part of the town. Each summer the restoration attracts thousands of tourists. A good thing too, because the mainstay of the town, the modern National Sea Products fish plant, is crippled for lack of fish.

A Puzzle

What a poor situation for the costly fortress and city! It had a good harbour ... but it would be difficult to find a more desolate background .... A bleak, rough coast, hidden half the time by fogs, with a soil too poor and thin to cultivate, and surrounded by swamps.

– J. W. Goldthwait, **Physiography of Nova Scotia**, 1924

The sea wall at Fortress Louisbourg has iron ring bolts embedded in cement. When installed in the 1730s, they were 30 cm/12 in above high tide. Now at high tide they are more than 30 cm *under water*. Similarly, sewage outlets and a ramp entrance in the sea wall—which obviously did not flood originally—now flood at high tide. So in the reconstruction they had to be placed higher. Since the North Atlantic's tidal range has not changed since Chabert measured it in 1753 (approximately 2 m/6 ft), the land has sunk or the sea has risen or both.

The conventional explanation is that when massive ice caps depressed the interior of the continent, they warped the coastal areas upward. Then when the ice melted the interior slowly rebounded, forcing the coastal fringe down again. More recent geological evidence suggests that the land is no longer sinking, but that the sea is rising. Whichever is true, Louisbourg's ring bolts give some idea of how much.

Shipwrecks

In its day Louisbourg was one of the busiest ports in the New World. The harbour approaches are exposed, ledgy, and often foggy. In the days before foghorns, sonar and radar, wrecks were inevitable. In addition, major sea battles were fought here in 1745 and 1758. These wrecks and the things they contain have become very attractive to divers.

Since the 1970s, the federal government has forbidden unauthorized tampering with the wrecks here—or for that matter anywhere around Atlantic Canada. However, Nova Scotia is a world leader in diving expertise, and professional divers come to Louisbourg's archive of undersea history for guided tours and workshops.

VIEW: *Louisbourg's Lights*

The low finger of rock jutting from the north side of Louisbourg Harbour is Lighthouse Point. To seafaring people, lighthouses are a matter of life and death. The current light, now automated, was built in 1922 and replaces three others dating back to 1733. The original was constructed of stone—the first fire-proof building in North America—and was 21.3 m/70 ft high. At night a coal fire in a great iron brazier shone as far as six leagues (29 km/18 mi) out to sea. In 1736 the coal was replaced by a vat of cod liver oil, which burned cleaner. This light was shot away by the Royal Navy in the siege of 1758. After 1850, when the Nova Scotian Abraham Gesner demonstrated the use of coal oil for lighting, kerosene became the fuel of choice. Now electricity from Wreck Cove does the job.

From the Lighthouse Point parking lot a walking trail of moderate difficulty traces the coast 5.5 km/3.4 mi through woods, bogs and barrens north to Little Lorraine. Inquire at the fortress.

LEG-STRETCHER: *To Cape Breton's Cape Breton*

The Marconi Trail passes within 5 km/3 mi, as the crow flies, of the cape that gives Cape Breton Island its name. Luckily, a footpath will lead you through bog and barren and stunted conifers almost to that cape. If you're interested, ask in Little Lorraine for directions. Three km/2 mi north of Little Lorraine, take the gravel road to Baleine, Nova Scotia's easternmost village. (In the 1940s the fishing village of Tin Cove on nearby Scatarie Island held that distinction.)

"Baleine" derives from Port aux Baleines (Whale Harbour), a name bestowed on it by Capt Charles Daniel of Dieppe in 1629, when he captured it from Scottish adventurer Sir James Stewart, Lord Ochiltree. [See also the **Trans Canada Highway** *at Englishtown.]*

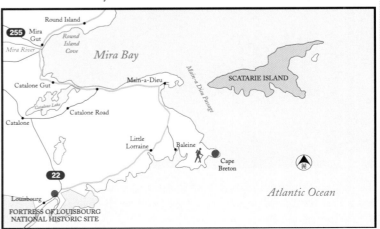

Go south approximately 3 km/2 mi to the village and park near the beach. From Baleine the cape is about 5 km/3 mi east.

Sudden fogs often envelop these barrens. Take prior note of your direction of travel and keep it in mind, or use a compass. If a pea souper does catch you without a compass, the foghorn on Scatarie lies northeast, and Baleine is due west from the cape.

Inquire also about the fascinating 14-km/8.7-mi shore walk from the beach in Baleine.

This French name, "hand-of-God," may refer to a miraculous rescue; others think it derives from an earlier Mi'kmaq word.

STOP: *Main-à-Dieu*

This, the coast's largest fishing village (pop. about 375), actively goes after lobster, clams, and finfish from spring through fall. Sometimes the opening of lobster season in April finds the coast plugged with drift ice held onshore by easterly winds. The occasional conifer skeletons outside the community are from a forest fire that raged here in the 1960s. The village has developed a scenic 15-minute boardwalk along the cobble beach.

For the more venturesome there's an exciting hike around Moque Head. Short of hiring a boat to Scatarie Island, you won't find a richer blend of Atlantic coastal bog, barren, woodland, and rocky shore. Many boreal plants are there—crowberry, cranberry, cloudberry [see the **Fleur-de-lis Trail** at Framboise], Labrador tea, lambkill, leatherleaf, and beach pea. If the day is hot and not too breezy, creeping juniper and crowberry will fill the air with a delicious resiny fragrance. The paths (there are several which coalesce) begin on the hill behind Main-à-Dieu, wend along the shore, cross

Beach pea

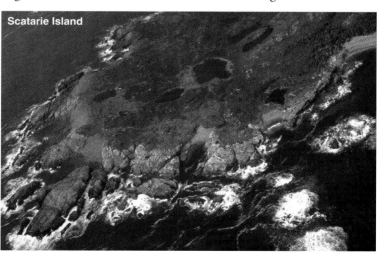

Scatarie Island

Unlike native ruffed and spruce grouse, ptarmigan have feathered feet. They also turn white in winter in response to dwindling sunlight. In the north, this provides excellent protection from predators; but where snow cover is brief or sporadic, as it is here, it makes them more vulnerable.

the shallow outlet of brackish Hall Pond, and so continue to the head. If in doubt, ask locally. From the head you'll have a good view of Scatarie Island, the easternmost point of Cape Breton.

Boaters should be aware that the passage between the island and the mainland is extremely treacherous, with rip tides and instant fog.

Leaving the village, the trail heads left for Bateston and Catalone Gut, a village on the great sandy curve of Mira Bay.

Ptarmigan Transplant

In the 1970s the people of Main-à-Dieu were partners in a biological experiment. The bogs and barrens hereabouts are perfect habitat for willow ptarmigan (silent "p"), a grouse common in Newfoundland and across northern Canada. Hoping to establish it here, in 1969 the Department of Lands and Forests (now Natural Resources—DNR) introduced 60 ptarmigan chicks from Brunette Island off Newfoundland's south coast to the island.

In June of 1969 and 1970, week-old Newfoundland chicks were collected using bird dogs and tape-recorded mother ptarmigan calls. The chicks, comfortably caged with broody bantam hens, were brought by boat on an overnight run. The year was chosen because Newfoundland grouse were then at the peak of their 11-year breeding cycle. Kidnapping chicks would do less harm then, and the transplanted birds, once mature, might continue to produce large clutches of eggs.

To reduce predation, most of Scatarie's foxes were professionally trapped during the winter of 1968–69. That spring the caged chicks were set out on the barrens, with their foster mothers, to feed on insects and berries. The chicks could move freely in and out of the pens, but hens could not escape and predators could not get in.

For several years, spring tallies of mating calls and nesting success showed good numbers. Fishermen tending lobster traps reported seeing the white-patched birds upon the barrens. For some reason, however, the ptarmigan never colonized the nearby mainland as intended. Nor did breeding rates outstrip natural and human predation to produce the desired surplus. Within a decade, no more birds were seen. Perhaps Nova Scotia is a little too far south.

Coming around Mira Bay (named after a French officer), we are suddenly in soft-rock country. The whole district from here to Point Aconi [see the **Trans Canada Highway**] and out under Cabot Strait is floored with nearly horizontal late Carboniferous rock—sandstones, siltstones, conglomerate, and shale. Such rocks weather much faster than the volcanic and igneous rock around Louisbourg. The degree of erosion and glaciation is evident in the bay's deep indraft, in the sandspits on either side of Catalone Point, and in the numerous sandy beaches that fringe the shore all the way to Mira Gut on the Glace Bay side.

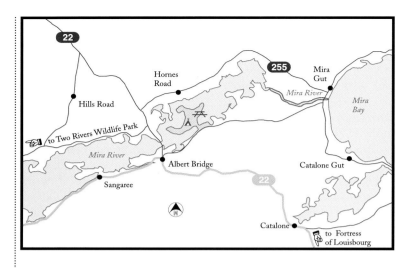

VIEW: *Mira River*

It seems improbable, crossing the Mira River bridge, that such a puny brook could be the same broad stream that flows past Albert Bridge a few kilometres west. But it is. This shows how little flooding it takes in flat country to make a wide expanse of water.

Continuing east, we pass False Bay, which is rocky and uninviting but offers kayakers and ocean canoeists a short cut behind Cape

South Head, Morien Bay

Morien at high tide. After crossing the head of Morien Bay (originally Baie de Mordienne) and veering northeast at Black Brook Meadows, watch on the right for a sandspit over 2 km/1.2 mi long that nearly bars the bay. Actually it is broken in two places, but the near end has a road and makes an interesting walk.

Almost 3 km/2 mi farther along is Port Morien, site of North America's first known coal mine. Here and in other places along the bay, ice and storms continually expose glisten-

The Mi'kmaq called Morien Bay Noolektooch, meaning "place jammed with ice." Their name for Glace Bay was Wosekusegwon which means "Home of Glory", no doubt referring to the sunrise over the ocean.

ing black coal seams. Breton and Portuguese sailors knew about them in the early 1600s. More than likely, they cooked their cod and dried their wet socks over coal fires during the long fishing season.

The first to see commercial possibilities in the coal was Nicolas Denys, a French trader who claimed this area [see also the **Fleur-de-lis Trail** at St Peter's]. "There are mines of coal ... near the sea coast," he wrote in 1672, "of a quality equal to the Scotch ... and [to those of] France, where I have brought them for trial." And Admiral Hovenden Walker of the Royal Navy in 1711 declared that "[Cape Breton] has always, in time of peace, been used in common both by the [New Englanders] and French for loading coals, which are extraordinarily good here, and taken out of the cliffs with iron crowbars only, and no other labour."

One of the coast's thickest seams occurred at Port Morien. During the long years of Fortress Louisbourg's construction, coal from Baie de Mordienne kept its architects, carpenters, soldiers, and their families warm and their cabbage soup hot. By 1720, however, the easy coal was gone. So the soldiers sank a 3.7-m/12-ft wide shaft into the cliff—North America's first coal mine. The coal was carted to a nearby wharf and shipped from there to Louisbourg. Over the years the miners followed the seam back for 0.9 km (0.5 mi).

In 1725 the French fortified the mine. They lost it to the New Englanders in 1745, got it back by treaty, and lost it again. Later it was exploited by the British, by the Highlander Hugh MacDonald in 1852, and finally by the New York–based Belloni family until 1888.

In retrospect, it was the abundance of coal, and not just cod, that prompted France to choose Louisbourg in the first place—for fuelwood is scarce around Louisbourg. Today all that remains of the mine is a deep hollow near the water's edge (more obvious in slanting afternoon or morning light), and some rusty pieces of iron from the Belloni workings nearby.

A short walk past the ball field to the grassy shore of Cow Bay (a reference to walrus, now extinct here) takes you to the site. Ask directions at a local store or service station.

From Port Morien the trail loops out around Schooner Pond Cove past Donkin and Port Caledonia, picking up Route 255 just beyond Glace Bay Bar. The forest out here is markedly coniferous—white and black spruce with balsam fir—with a few hardy white birch and balsam poplar. So it is almost boreal. Sea winds have sloped the trees inland and sheared their seaward sides like a hedge.

Like most coal districts, the Sydney lowlands are rich in fossils. One good place to find some is at Schooner Pond.

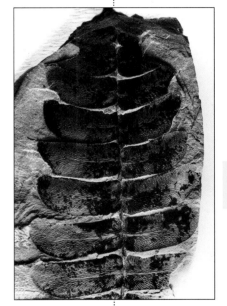

Leaf fossil (Linopterus obliqua) found in Cape Breton

LEG-STRETCHER: *Bird Walk*

Schooner Pond Cove also has a walking trail of about 3 km/2 mi that follows the cliffs east to Wreck Point at the north end of Morien Bay. Uncommon seabirds visit and winter here, and gannets sometimes pause during migration to dive for fish. Other birds you can expect to see are swallow (three species), eastern kingbird, various ducks, American bitterns, and pied-billed grebes. In summer there's a kittiwake colony.

Donkin was also once a coal-mining centre, and the cliffs west of it display intermittent wavy coal seams. Like the bedrock between which they are sandwiched, they slant imperceptibly under the sea. As you travel toward Glace Bay, reflect on the pattern of gentle folds you've been riding over since Mira Bay. Not unlike large swells at sea, they run northeast/southwest, with headlands jutting out from the ridges and coves and lakes filling in the troughs. Like Morien Bay, Big Glace Bay and the lake that lies behind the long sandbar at its mouth occupy such a trough.

As you cross MacAskills Brook at its head, you may be able to see radio towers ("Marconi Towers"). They embody this young inventor's eventual gift to the planet: global communications. Without it, global awareness of environmental issues would not have come about. A museum on Timmerman Street at Table Head in Glace Bay honours his achievement.

Three km/2 mi upstream, the brook has been dammed to create a sizeable reservoir for the needs of Glace Bay and nearby communities.

Like the other spits along this shore, Glace Bay Bar was built by wind- and tide-driven longshore currents bearing suspended sediments eroded from nearby headlands. [For more detail see the **Fleur-de-lis Trail** at Point Michaud and the **Sunrise Trail** near Merigomish, etc.]

LEG-STRETCHER: *Waterfowl Sanctuary*
From late fall to early spring, Glace Bay Harbour is a staging area for gulls; besides the ubiquitous herring gull, look for the glaucous, Iceland, ring-billed and black-headed species. In fact, Big Glace Bay Lake inside the sandbar is a waterfowl sanctuary. The tidal marsh provides nesting habitat for many birds, and northeasters sometimes blow rare visitors ashore. In spring most of Cape Breton's common duck species congregate here, as well as the uncommon pintail and American widgeon.

The sanctuary has three self-guided trails. To reach it, follow Glace Bay's South Street toward the Marconi Trail and ask directions to the old dirt road out to Glace Bay Bar.

STOP: *The Miner's World*
As noted above, the name Glace Bay refers to the Arctic ice that sometimes jams the shore on this exposed coast during easterly winds in spring. It's a far cry from the steamy jungles of ancient Pangaea, where Glace Bay's famous coal measures came into being.

Don't leave here without visiting the Coal Miners' Museum at Quarry Point (off South

At Baie des Espagnols [Spanish Bay, now Glace Bay] there is a mountain of very good coal, four leagues up the river.
— Nicolas Denys, 1672

We are the miners from Cape Breton Isle We don't make much money but manage to smile Workin' hard for a livin' a-mining the coal The dust and sweat seep into our souls.
— Ray Holland of The Men of the Deeps

Street at 42 Birkley). The Miner's Museum and Miner's Village will give you a vivid sense of how generations of men toiled in these fossilized jungle swamps to help fuel the trains, ships, and factories of Canada's Industrial Revolution. Then, unless you're claustrophobic, let a retired miner guide you down into the Ocean Deeps Colliery. Learn how it feels to be hundreds of metres underground (and undersea) in a warm, black, dripping vault supported by pillars of coal and cribworks of wooden pitprops.

From the high-ceilinged, well-lit entrance cavern, your guide leads you into lower and dimmer sections. Suddenly your hard hat and head lamp become very important. At last the ceiling is so low you have to bend nearly double not to bump your head. At this point some people get a strong urge to bolt! Remember, however, that hundreds of men and boys and pit ponies learned to conquer and reconquer that same fear, not to mention putting up with bad air. At mid-slope there's a miniature flower garden under the artificial lights.

Try local bookstores for a short story collection containing Sheldon Currie's "The Glace Bay Miners' Museum." It inspired the award-winning film *Margaret's Museum* (1995).

STOP: *Dominion Beach Provincial Park*

Good environmental news is rare, so pause here to see a successful dune restoration project. For years local residents and contractors scooped so much sand and gravel from the barrier beach that it was in danger of being washed away. The currents and supply of sediment here are such that they form a spit to the south but little or nothing to the north.

Sand quarrying ceased with the Beaches Protection Act of 1976. However, uncontrolled foot traffic still threatened the dunes. To prevent this, local DNR crews installed boardwalks and snow fences and banned ATVs. The fences caught drifting sand and helped local marram grass anchor and rebuild the dunes.

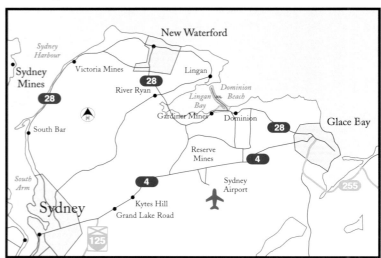

Observe how the road along the spit divides the high seaward dunes from the discontinuous lower dune ridge at the rear. And notice how the highest dunes at the beach's north end are eroding seaward, while those behind the spit are building wide flats to landward. [See also the **Lighthouse Route** at Crescent Beach, **Marine Drive** at Lawrencetown, the **Sunrise Trail** at Pomquet Beach, and "A Note on Sable Island".]

To reach the park, follow Main Street and Kings Road across town to Commercial Street, turn right on Atlantic Drive, and watch for signs or ask the way.

The **Trans Canada Highway Nature Trail** starts from North Sydney (Highway 105), reachable via Hwy 4 from Glace Bay and via Hwy 125 from Sydney, Exit 20.

Marine Drive Nature Tour

Dartmouth to Canso Causeway via Eastern Shore
400 km/240 mi

Coastal granite

Beached fishing
vessel on Eastern Shore

OVERVIEW

From a plane at high altitude, the Eastern Shore is one long arabesque of island, cape, and inlet, of dark rumpled coniferous woodlands, bright lakes, tawny bogs, blueberry barrens, splashes of broadleaf forest, swatches of scant farmland. It resembles the South Shore because it is part of the same rock formation, a folded and faulted slab of ancestral North Africa that stuck to North America when the North Atlantic began to open nearly 200 million years ago.

Indeed, the Atlantic is the single most striking element of this tour. Even in fair weather, the air has a tingling saltness, a hint of kelp and fog and lichen-bearded forest. The sky, too, often has a pearly glow, a moist opalescence born of sea spray and familiar to any seaside dweller.

As one might expect, the coastal road meanders like an old river. This turning can be tiresome in bad weather or when one is in a hurry. Don't be in a hurry on this road; come prepared to dally. Allow a good two days. Stop often. Follow footpaths down through mossy woods to secluded pocket beaches. Poke about in tidal pools for barnacles, limpets, sticklebacks, and baby flounder. Explore salt marshes where blue herons stand as still as statues, waiting for unwary minnows. Tramp a blanket bog to admire pink arethusa orchids and to hear the cry of the yellowlegs. Pick mountain cranberries, blueberries and crowberries five minutes from your vehicle.

Compared to the South Shore, which is by no means overdeveloped, the most obvious difference here is the lack of large towns. Highway 7 was the last main artery to be built on mainland Nova Scotia. It was, quipped Will R. Bird, "paved with a long series of petitions," for the people had long felt neglected by Halifax. Even today it's unusual to see a village of more than 500 people. Eastbound truckers and everyone in a hurry take the Trans Canada. Good roads into the hinterland are few. Except for logging, guiding sportsmen, and a spurt of gold-mining long ago, people here have mostly looked to the coast and sea for a living or moved away. All these things combine to create a sense of stepping back in time. Another obvious difference is the cooler weather. Up here the lukewarm Gulf Stream is farther from shore, the chill Labrador Current closer. So spring comes two or three weeks later than in Yarmouth, and it brings more fog. In summer, overnight fogs are common. Usually they retreat to the headlands by afternoon, returning as the wind drops at sunset. The sea breeze generally starts out southerly, veering southwest across the harbour mouths by mid-afternoon. Snowfall is fairly light.

This coast has fewer sandbars and spits than the South Shore. That's because it has less glacial gravel. Good harbours abound, but east of Liscomb most of them are too exposed for comfort. There are a lot of submerged rocks and shoals as well. Experienced sailors stay outside the 40-fathom line. Kayakers, on the other hand, rejoice in the labyrinth of islands.

Coastal vegetation

The coastal forest has a wind-pruned look, but improves dramatically a surprisingly short distance inland. Along exposed shores you'll see white spruce and balsam fir on higher ground, and black spruce and tamarack on wet sites, with a sprinkling of white birch, trembling aspen, and red maple. Unlike western Nova Scotia, this region has few pine, though scattered jack pine eke out a living in sandy pockets on the fire barrens near Dartmouth and Canso. Red spruce is the dominant conifer throughout. Despite the seeming lack of soil, it thrives among rocks and ledges, seeding prolifically after cutting or fire. Yellow birch does well here too, but only where hills block sea breezes. Like hemlock and red oak, it is scarcer as we move east.

Most headlands above the splash zone wear a distinctive moss-green mantle of crowberry, ground juniper, and mountain laurel. Toward Canso the landscape becomes more like that of Peggys Cove, with bare rock and many granite boulders.

The first recorded Old World visitors were French fishermen

seeking cod. After the Expulsion of 1755, Britain encouraged English-speaking settlers, mostly American Loyalists and Ulster Irish, to put down roots. The Scots never took to this coast.

Starting in the 1860s the shore had several minor gold rushes. In 1885 a pulp mill created some temporary jobs. But the mainstays have been fishing, shipbuilding, lumbering, and subsistence farming. Fishing is still important—but not cod fishing. Since the collapse of that fishery, forestry has become even more important.

Hay fever sufferers will be glad to know that from Halifax east the common ragweed is uncommon.

West River Sheet Harbour

THE TOUR BEGINS

On the Eastern Shore there were never any large urban areas like the South Shore's—only Musquodoboit Harbour and Sheet Harbour. The people were completely dependent on what they could get from the land then and there...small holdings with a few cows, hay for the cows, some veggies and of course the fish.

Typically the road between Jeddore and Moser River was dotted with postage stamp farms cleared around a house. And every inlet was full of boats and little fish houses, with piles of lobster traps or buoys in the bays in season.

You didn't get far without seeing this scene. Now you can drive for miles and not see a boat and if you do, you have to look hard to see if it's a fishing boat or a pleasure boat. People now commute to larger urban centres to work and do not have to drag a living out of the hard, inhospitable land as they used to.

The changes relate to the War, improvements, increased mobility on the all-weather road, the spread of a consolidated school system and the increased scale of the fishery.

—Gerald McCarthy, longtime resident,
  in conversation with Sue Browne, 1995

Properly speaking, the Marine Drive starts in Dartmouth at Exit 15, Hwy 7, passing by Lake Major and through the communities of Preston, Lake Echo, and Porters Lake. Because the shore route offers more diversity, we'll opt for Route 207 as far as Head of Chezzetcook.

Lake Echo is an access waterway into the Waverley Game Sanctuary, a 5 698-ha/14,075-ac candidate for protected status. The sanctuary, which runs from Lake Major northwest to Miller Lake (on Highway 102) and east to Salmon River Long Lake, offers excellent semi-wilderness canoeing (minimum two-day stay). Spring is best for high water; October is best for colour. Jack-pine barrens studded with glacial boulders mingle with lakes of all sizes. The once-logged forest is a rich tapestry of white pine, hemlock, red spruce, red maple, and white birch.

To join Rte 207 we head east on Portland Street toward Cole Harbour and Lawrencetown. From Hwys 118, take Exit 7E (Circumferential Highway.)

Soon suburbs give way to the typical Eastern Shore medley of spruce-fir forest, cove, and headland, small farms on dumpling hills, grey sand beaches, tantalizing ocean vistas. After Cole Harbour [see the **Halifax-Dartmouth Area Nature Tour**], Rte 207 swings southeast toward Lawrencetown and begins its convoluted way up the coast.

Wherever good soil could be found, the settlers pushed back the dark coastal forest. Inland the road cuts reveal much greywacke, a dark, cement-like blend of feldspar and rock fragments. Headlands are mostly slates and siltstone. All are at least 500 million years old.

Since neither slate nor siltstone is very hard, weathering plus the endless fret of waves have smoothed any ruggedness away. Ribbons of sand from that erosion join headland to headland, creating shallow tidal ponds where cord grass and minnows flourish.

About 10 km/6 mi east of the Bissett Road turnoff, between West Lawrencetown and Lawrencetown, an interesting marsh opens up to the right, flanked by a drumlin and some houses. Watch for the Conrad's Road sign 0.5 km/0.3 mi farther on.

SIDE TRIP: *Conrads Beach Piping Plover*

Between West Lawrencetown and Lawrencetown proper, at Conrads Beach, is one of only three or four breeding populations of piping plovers along the whole Eastern Shore. These dainty little shorebirds—locally called "peeps" because they sound like baby chicks—eat tiny beach invertebrates and breed sparsely from Newfoundland to North Carolina and west to the prairies. To learn more, watch for the beachmarker and drive down to the shore, where you'll find interpretive signs.

During breeding season DNR conservation officers post signs urging people to keep to the boardwalks. Please do so.

For some reason piping plovers prefer white (quartz) sand beaches. Not only that; they don't bother to build nests. They also seem to cope better with natural disasters than with human-made ones. For example, in 1959 a storm cut a channel in to West Lawrencetown Marsh, raising fears that the birds would nest here no more. However, they stayed. In 1989 another gale closed the gap.

Peeps lay and hatch their eggs on bare sand. Unfortunately, humans also prefer white sand beaches. In recent years all-terrain vehicles and careless foot traffic have destroyed dune grasses and crushed eggs and chicks. The brownish green eggs easily pass for beach pebbles, and the motionless chicks are almost impossible to see. Until the Beaches Protection Act was made law in 1976, metro contractors routinely scooped sand from here.

The shoal stretching out from Fox Point (south end of the beach) was a fishing station until the last shack was removed in 1980. Long before that, it was a drumlin called Egg Island, where people went to pick berries.

Spruce and low coastal vegetation

BACK ON THE MARINE DRIVE

STOP: *Lawrencetown Beach Provincial Park*
This clearly marked coastal beach offers safe swimming, unlike the shoreline to the west, where there are dangerous undertows. Though crowded on sunny weekends, the park is also an excellent place to study the sea at work.

For instance, where did all the sand come from to create such a long beach? It had to come from somewhere. The beach itself provides a clue. Walk westward and you'll see the pebbles and sand gradually become smaller and finer. So, since small particles travel farthest in water, the geological trail leads in the opposite direction. In fact, the material came via storm waves from a drumlin near Terminal Beach. Longshore currents brought it here. [See also the **Sunrise Trail** at Melmerby Beach, the **Lighthouse Route** at Crescent Beach, and the **Fleur-de-lis Trail** at Point Michaud.]

As one would expect, the largest cobbles and boulders stayed put. These form a "footprint" of the drumlin's former seaward slope called a drumlin retreat shoal. Such shoals are common along this part of the shore. They are the main reason why this area has 10 km/6 mi of some of the best surfing beach in the province.

For good views along the beach and out to sea, it's hard to beat MacDonald Hill at the west end of Lawrencetown Beach. July brings lupins, an introduced western perennial of the pea family, which brighten the flats with purple, blue, and pink.

The farthest speck of land is Shut-In Island, alias Pirates Island. It was a drumlin until the sea sawed it down to a grassy flat where cormorants nest. At one time people kept horses, gardened, cut hay, and pastured sheep there.

Early Nova Scotia tourist guidebooks mentioned little beyond Lawrencetown Beach. Ruth Kedzie Wood's *Tourist's Maritime Provinces* (1915) says, "Dartmouth is the gateway to popular Cow Bay, Cole

A strong sea breeze of 20 to 25 knots blows at Lawrencetown Beach due to the local topography and to the marshy flat inland. This cool breeze is a delight for windsurfers but is not so popular with sunbathers. Large seas also come ashore here and further west, at Cow Bay.
—**Scotia/Fundy Marine Weather Guide**

Eroding Graham Head

Harbour and Lawrencetown, all of which afford, within pleasant driving distance, superior sea bathing." In other words, why go farther, even if the road does?

SIDE TRIP: *Three Fathom Harbour*
Leaving Lawrencetown Beach, watch 4.3 km/2.7 mi east of Porters Lake for a gravel road to Three Fathom Harbour. This road branches to Graham Head and loops back to Hwy 7 within 5 km/3 mi. Along the road, watch for a causeway that traps great quantities of seaweed and eel-grass. Built after World War II to reach the fishing station, it has since become a favourite place for gathering garden mulch. Residents also collect eel-grass for house insulation.

> *Fishing once thrived here. You could buy salt herring for a cent a pound. Eels were speared in the fall as they left the freshwater lakes to spawn far away in the Sargasso Sea.*
>
> *Government land grants were set aside for commercial saltwater fishing and included land for salting and drying fish. Three Fathom Harbour's reserve is part of one established in 1752 that ran from eastern Cole Harbour to West Chezzetcook.*

Look at the size of the boulders flanking the causeway. They express better than words the power of the sea here. Storm waves also batter marine algae (seaweed), which must stay anchored or die. The commonest types are rockweed (*Fucus*) and kelp (*Laminaria*). [See also the **Lighthouse Route** at Cranberry Cove and the **Digby Neck Scenic Drive**.] To avoid being swept away, these rubbery brown, red, and green algae grasp cliffs and rocks with strong root-like holdfasts. Unable to tolerate much dry air, they must brave the surf. But violent fall and winter storms tear many loose and fling great heaps on the beaches.

From this wharf one can see how the harbour has silted up since the causeway was built. One old wharf is half buried. Only regular dredging keeps the channel open. In summer, this is a also a good place to observe great blue herons.

BACK ON THE HIGHWAY
On a map, the upper part of Porters Lake slants northwest/southeast. That's because it occupies a valley formed along faults in the Earth's crust. The rocks were cracked and slid past each other during the continental collision that raised the Appalachians. Thus weakened, they were more easily deepened and widened by erosion and glaciation; later they were invaded by the rising ocean. Most major harbours from here to Canso Strait—and perhaps the strait itself—follow faults with a similar slant.

In 1995 the village of Porters Lake opened its Marine Drive Wilderness Heritage Centre. Residents aim to develop interpretive hiking trails describing the area's natural and cultural history and its recreational resources.

Driving the Atlantic Shore is a constant reminder that nature never stands still. At Gaetz Head (2.8 km/1.7 mi east of the causeway) watch for a unusually symmetrical drumlin with a house on top. Because of the dramatic way the drumlin is being eroded by the sea, this drumlin was featured in the video *Ice Ages,* produced by the Atlantic Geoscience Society. A century from now this hill may be just a memory.

Sometimes people hasten such natural processes. A good example is Grand Desert Beach, a few minutes beyond Gaetz Head. Aerial photographs show that in 1954 the tidal marsh here was a pond. By 1979 the pond had filled in. These changes were brought about by dyking and by sand drifting inland.

In 1754 the inlet had 10 families of Acadians. To harvest the abundant cord grass near the head of the bay, they channeled and drained the flats. (Some of the channels are still visible at low tide.) To collect the hay they used big flat-bottomed boats called gundalows. These boats were also used to ferry cattle out to island pastures for the summer and to bring them home in the fall. (The Maritime Museum of the Atlantic in Halifax has a gundalow on exhibit.) Island pastures were very convenient because they required no fences, and bears and wolves could not get at the animals. [See also the **Lighthouse Route** at Lobster Bay.] In the 1780s Loyalist settlers pressured the government to evict post-exile Acadians from Chezzetcook. Many moved to Larrys River near Canso.

This area is excellent for mountain biking or walking. Until the 1920s, people picnicked on the cleared offshore islands. Now the hard-won pastures are hidden under thickets of spruce and fir.

Just after the church in West Chezzetcook, the **Marine Drive** departs Rte 207 and follows the Shore Road to the head of the inlet. Then, crossing Hwy 107 at Exit 21, it follows Hwy 7 past Gaetz Brook village and Petpeswick Lake toward Musquodoboit Harbour. (Hwy 107 merges with Rte 7 just west of Musquodoboit Harbour.)

Most of the lakes along here are river mouths dammed by glacial gravel. Acadians first settled the area in 1692, followed after the Expulsion by Ulster Irish and New England Loyalists.

TO DO: *Canoe Trip*

Consider a canoe trip along the lower Musquodoboit River (Mi'kmaq for "rolling out in foam"). Except for some challenging rapids near its mouth, it's a gentle paddle. There's a good access point, with parking, at Elderbank on Rte 357, 29 km/18 mi north of Musquodoboit Harbour.

The lower Musquodoboit offers a dramatic mood change. Above Meaghers (pron. "myers") Grant it runs southwesterly through wide marshes cradled in Coal Age rock. Below that village, it angles sharply to the south to fight its way through hard Devonian granite

*Drumlins are heaps of gravel and stones pushed up and smoothed off by moving glaciers. Because clay allows the ice to ride over the heap, drumlins occur mostly where slate is common. [See also **Marconi Trail, Lighthouse Route** near Lunenburg; **Evangeline Trail** near Yarmouth.]*

Scientists tell us that until the sea began to rise 6,000 years ago, Chezzetcook Inlet was a freshwater bog.

The name Chezzetcook derives either from a Mi'kmaq word for "flowing fast in many channels" or from the French phrase chez les coques which means "place of clams."

to the Atlantic shore.

After the tranquil vistas of marsh and farmland, the sensation of slipping in silence down long dim stretches of overarching woods is a rare treat, especially in October when the maples and birches blaze with colour.

Towards Bayers Lake the river again widens into marshes. Finally, below the lake it plunges in foam over dark blue slate ledges, slipping under Hwy 7 and into the long harbour.

Some geologists think the ancestral Musquodoboit flowed north across an ancient, northward-tilting Cretaceous plain into what is now Northumberland Strait. They say a change in tilt, perhaps aided by a barrier of glacial ice, forced it to turn south and to cut its present channel.

The coming of railroads did much to alter our landscapes, especially the forests. Trains ignited forest fires. They also lured people off the land and into towns and cities. For an intriguing look at the province's colourful railroading history, visit the museum in Musquodoboit Harbour. It is housed in the old (c. 1918) Canadian National Railway station and in three railway cars.

East of the Jeddore inlet we first glimpse the granite topography that stretches from Lower Sackville to Sheet Harbour and resurfaces near Canso. It's a thin-soiled landscape of rocky uplands sparsely clothed in spruce, jack pine, tamarack, yellow birch, and red maple. Blueberry barrens and black spruce bogs abound. Consisting of hardened magma [see also the **Lighthouse Route** at Port Joli, the **Halifax-Dartmouth Area Nature Tour** at Kidston Lake, and the **Evangeline Trail** in the western Annapolis Valley], this slab of Southern Upland, being resistant to erosion, and therefore higher, defines the northern extremity of each of the inlets of Petpeswick, Chezzetcook, Jeddore, and Ship Harbour.

Salmon River ridge

Bernard Fernow's 1912 provincial forest survey, Forest Conditions of Nova Scotia, *the province's first, described this country as regenerating with young conifers after logging and wildfire. In the 1920s and 1930s large areas were again cut over, this time for pitprops to hold up the roofs of British mines. The wood went down a log flume to storage booms—corrals of long floating logs chained together—whence they were loaded on ships.*

STOP: *Salmon River Bridge*

Salmon River House, open year-round, is a good base from which to explore. For example, rent a canoe and paddle the inlet above the bridge. If you want to rough it, portage to one or more of the hinterland lakes: Admiral, Salmon River, Moose Cove, Logging. You'll see lots of beavers and other wildlife. For the less venturesome, interpretive trails are being developed all the time.

On the east side of the bridge, watch for a bed of folded slate in the cliff face. Exposed by road building in 1962, it's one of the best places to examine folded Southern Upland rocks. [See also the **Evangeline Trail** at Exit 24.]

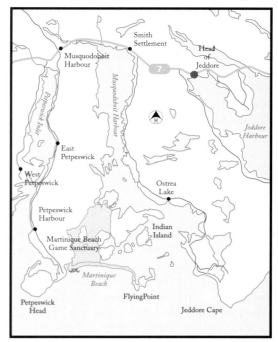

Martinique Beach

SIDE TRIP: *Martinique Beach*

If you liked Lawrencetown Beach but craved more privacy, this narrow arch of sand 20 minutes south of Musquodoboit Harbour is for you. You'll have 5 km/3 mi of firm sand to walk on with nothing between you and Africa but salt sea.

The beach runs east to Flying Point, once a favourite gunning spot for goose hunters. Today the marshes are part of the Martinique Beach Sanctuary, home to the province's most northerly flock of overwintering Canada geese. As at Cole Harbour [see the **Halifax-Dartmouth Tour**], the attraction is eel-grass. Floating green meadows of this seed plant tint shallow muddy coves mossy-green, and the birds graze on them all winter.

Follow the beach road from Musquodoboit Harbour; anyone can tell you the way. The Trans Canada Trail Foundation is developing a trail joining Upper Musquodoboit, Musquodoboit Harbour, and Dartmouth.

BACK ON THE HIGHWAY

STOP: *Fisherman's Life Museum*

At Jeddore Oyster Pond on the east side of Jeddore Bay, take a while to tour a typical 1900s inshore fisherman's home. James Myers built the small home in 1857. It housed his family and then his son's 13 chil-

The further we drove the more we became impressed with the feeling that we were "away from it all." Salmon River Bridge was simply a bridge over an outlet to the sea, and there was but an ordinary-looking inn beside it, yet there was such a hint of vast hinterland to be reached by waterways ... that we stopped and had lunch.
—Will R. Bird,
This Is Nova Scotia,
1950

Fisherman's Life Museum

dren. Though remodeled more than once, it still reflects its humble origins and the rooms whisper of bygone days.

Talk to the guides. Learn about the men who put to sea in small boats after herring, mackerel, lobster, and cod; about their skill in using black spruce for lobster pots and boat keels, of casting cod jiggers in wooden molds from lead saved from tea-chest liners, and so on. No less ingenious and hard-working were the women who tended children, gardens, and aging parents, kept the wood stove going, dried the cod, hooked beautiful rugs from worn-out clothes, and sometimes played the parlour organ. A jewel of a museum.

The land between Jeddore and Ship Harbour is clothed with wood of superior growth: birch, beech, maples, spruce, hemlock, ash and pine. The latter frequently measure 12 feet 6 inches [3.8 m] in circumference, and the spruce and hemlock are equally large.
—Thomas Haliburton, **History of Nova Scotia,** 1829

Until Jeddore Harbour (Mi'kmaq for "place of sea duck"), we at least caught glimpses of the ocean while passing the heads of deep inlets on our shortcuts across one peninsula after another. Between here and Ship Harbour we veer away from the ocean.

The forest reflects the change. Now the seaside pattern—windblown white spruce/balsam on dry ground, black spruce/larch on wet ground—gives way to thrifty mixed forest such as Haliburton described. The same species are still here, but they are taller. Not as tall as those he saw, of course. Remember that the former giants took a century and more to reach that size. Few of today's trees get the chance to grow that big. Now we harvest at younger ages. Today's big trees are confined to parks, private woodlots, and wilderness areas such as the Tobeatic Wildlife Management Area. [See **Kejimkujik Scenic Drive.**]

Bernard Fernow reported heavy cutting all along this shore in 1910–11, not to mention several large burns. He found virgin timber only north of Chezzetcook (mixed conifers and broadleaf trees) and south of Tangier Grand Lake (conifers).

From January to March along this shore, colourful shacks, each covering one or more holes cut in the ice, dot the frozen saltwater inlets. People use them as shelters in which to fish for smelt, a small migratory relative of salmon. The Jeddore inlet is a favourite spot. As the tide comes in, the occupants clear slush ice from holes and lower baited hooks. The silvery smelt, after congregating in the inlets, spawn in shallow coves and brooks in early spring. [See also the **Sunrise Trail** at River John and the **Glooscap Trail** at Portapique.]

STOP: *Lake Charlotte*
That big sheet of fresh water a few minutes east of Salmon River Bridge is Lake Charlotte. Like Porters Lake, it is long and narrow and occupies an ancient fault. It extends 20 km/12 mi into the

wilderness and is a canoeist's delight. Observant paddlers will see the landscape change twice as they go north. In the outer greywacke area, islands are few and the forest cover looks almost lush. Then, about 5 km/3 mi north, the shores suddenly widen into granite country. Now we have scores of islets, the shore is lined with great grey boulders, and the forest is sparse and spindly. Five km/3 mi farther in, the scenery reverts to greywacke.

During the last glaciation Lake Charlotte was a river—hence the immensely deep deposits of gravel near the village. For decades local contractors and road builders have relied on this gravel. In the 1950s it was as deep as a 16-storey building; now it's all but gone.

Stop at Webber's Store and ask about the Lake Charlotte Heritage Society. If founding member Ford Webber is there, you'll learn much about the area's history and folklore.

SIDE TRIP: *Lake Charlotte/Ship Harbour Scenic Drive*
If you've time, drive the 20-km/12-mi loop out around Clam Harbour and Owls Head Harbour. You'll see fascinating variations on the theme of woodland, beach, cove, headland, island, and ocean. The white sand beach at Clam Harbour Provincial Park (4 km/2.5 mi east of Clam Bay; watch for the sign) is one of Nova Scotia's finest. There's access for wheelchair users, a beach boardwalk, and a canteen.

On a sunny summer day the water is bracing, but reasonably warm at half-tide. At low tide you can dig clams or follow the 4-km/ 2.5-mi footpath east along the shore to Little Clam Harbour. Here there are intimate beaches and mossy cliffs bright with blue flag iris, beach pea, and wild violets.

As we round Owls Head Harbour, a flotilla of islands comes into view: Cable, Wolfes, Borgles, and many smaller ones. (Owls Head Bay is also known as Bay of Islands.) Farther up the coast there are Baltee, Phoenix, Stoney, and scores of others in all sizes. Most are so low, big seas break over them. Those represent outcrops of slightly harder greywacke surrounded by eroded slates and faulted rock submerged by the postglacial ocean. Islands are scarce from Dartmouth to Jeddore because the floor of soft slate and siltstone makes poor island-building material.

Clam Harbour Beach

BACK ON THE HIGHWAY
At Ship Harbour, as at Head of Jeddore, the sea laps pale granite boulders, not dark greywacke or slate. Granite is why Ship Harbour's eastern shore was never settled; the place was too rugged and inhospitable for boats and sheds.

On April 12, 1936, up-country from here, a cave-in at the abandoned Moose River Gold Mine trapped three Toronto men at the 43-m/141-ft level. Six days later, rescuers heard faint signals and sank a diamond drill hole. On April 23, two of the men were rescued alive; the third died. Round-the-clock commentary on the progress of the rescue effort was broadcast live on hundreds of radio stations in Canada and the US.

A small provincial park commemorates the rescue. Exit north 2.5 km/1.6 mi east of Tangier and drive 35 km /22 mi; the first 19 km/12 mi are paved. There's also a dirt road branching to Caribou Gold Mines.

STOP: *Aqua Prime Mussel Ranch*

"You can walk across the harbour on the mussel floats," boasted a resident, referring to the scores of buoys that pepper Ship Harbour's east side at low tide. Each line of floats carries up to 122 m/ 400 ft of line with "mussel socks" attached at intervals. The socks are 3-m/10-ft-long fabric tubes that dangle toward the bottom with clusters of growing mussels attached. The harbour may carry 100 mussel lines.

Blue mussel and horse (Old English for "big") mussel do well around our coast. One sees their empty spoon-shaped twin shells (hence "bi-valve") on all rocky beaches. Storm waves often fling them up with kelp attached. They are bluish (young ones) to purple-black (older ones) on the outside and mother-of-pearl on the inside. Sometimes wading children cut their feet on the broken edges.

Wild mussels are marine molluscs that live submerged on rocks, cliffs, and wharves, where they settle after a brief nomadic larval stage. Each mussel is attached by strong silken threads, which dissolve when the creature needs to relocate. Like all molluscs they are filter-feeders. That is, they draw water in through one tube, strain out microscopic animals through sieve-like tissues, and expel the used water, including body wastes, through the other tube.

Mussel farmers collect larvae in July, raise them to "seed mussel" size, and plant them in the underwater socks that autumn. The baby bivalves crawl out through the plastic mesh and fasten themselves to the outside. Here, bathed by the same harbour currents that nourish their wild counterparts, they feed and grow. By harvest time 18 months later, each sock is a blue-black tree of densely packed shellfish.

Most farms stagger their crops in order to get two harvests a year. Aqua Prime is one of over 50 mussel farms around the province.

Wild mussels can become poisonous to humans. When that happens, shellfish areas are closed for a time. The toxins can come from untreated sewage, but more often the cause is natural, the result of a buildup of algal dinoflagellates (e.g., *Gonyaulax polyedra*), which contain natural nerve poisons or neurotoxins. Occasionally these organisms bloom so densely in shallow waters in summer that the ocean turns reddish—a "red tide." Though molluscs are themselves thought to be immune to the toxins, they can concentrate them to levels sufficient to kill invertebrates, fish, and birds. They may also paralyse or kill humans. Shellfish also concentrate chemicals from pesticides, industrial waste, and sewage. For these reasons, government biologists monitor local waters closely and inspect mussel farms regularly.

Aqua Prime will gladly demonstrate, using videos and live mussels in tanks, how they farm these delicious molluscs. The plant is open daily 9 am–3 pm.

The coast from Ship Harbour to Liscomb Harbour is a panorama of small coves and brooks, shores fringed with swaying golden rockweed, misty islands and islets, and fishing and lumbering villages. There are fewer tidal marshes, long beaches, and sandbars, and they are smaller. That's because drumlins are scarce in this hard-rock district. Instead we see pocket beaches of white quartzite, often with offshore shoals.

VIEW: *Seaweed Heaven*

This is a good shore for marine algae, commonly (and unfairly) called seaweeds. The tides are moderate, and the fissured greywacke cliffs provide good anchorage, in marked contrast to Fundy's wide mud flats or Northumberland Strait's flat, crumbling cliffs. [See also the **Lighthouse Route** and the **Digby Neck Scenic Drive**.]

TO DO: *Kayak Cruising*

If you've ever hankered to cruise the coast by kayak, Tangier Bay is the ticket. Kayaks are very safe in skilled hands and less tippy in rough weather than canoes. Because of shoals and narrow passages, many local islands can be reached in no other way.

On the rockier islands, expect to see bird colonies (cormorant, tern, eider, two species of gull), seals, and perhaps an abandoned community with a house or two still standing. For kayak and canoe adventures elsewhere on this drive, see current tourist guide listings.

Tangier is also the home of Eastern Canada's best Danish-style, wood-smoked salmon, mackerel, and eel. Ask for Willie Krauch & Sons; open year-round. Tours are sometimes possible.

The earliest [known] discovery of gold in the Province ... occurred during summer of 1860, at a spot about twelve miles north from the head of Tangier Harbour. The discoverer, John Pulsiver of Musquodoboit, was induced from what he had heard of the gold-bearing quartz of California to search [on] the Tangier River; and ... found several pieces of gold in quartz in a brook, at a place known as Mooseland Diggings.
—Samuel Creelman, Chief Gold Commissioner for Nova Scotia, annual report, 1862

Kayaking is popular around this rocky coast

The Eastern Shore did well by gold in the late 19th century. Besides the Moose River and Tangier finds, minor gold rushes took place at Gold River, Wine Harbour, Clam Harbour, Beaver Dam, Killag, Fifteen Mile Stream, Goldenville, Sherbrooke, Liscomb Mills, and Ecum Secum.

Local gold generally occurs in quartz seams extruded near the eroded crests (anticlines) of giant folds in slate-quartzite layers. These run down the spine of the peninsula. The quartz started out as silica dissolved in superheated water and steam, with gold and other minerals dissolved in it. Forced up into cracks during mountain building, the cooled silica was precipitated as crystalline quartz sometimes laced with gold.

There was more gold east of Halifax because folding was more intense there. Early prospectors had no aerial photos and few geological maps, so they found the yellow metal by shrewd guessing, a knowledge of plants (some species indicate the presence of gold), and sheer luck. It helped that the local gravels had shifted little since the glaciers dumped them so their contents reflected that of the bedrock beneath.

But gold mining was a fickle business. After the rush, all there was to show for it were heaps of sand and rock, a few jagged holes, and some rusting machinery. To encourage a more responsible type of settler, the government offered free land, free log houses, and provisions for a year. In his book *An Icelandic Boy's Adventure in Nova Scotia*, Erikson Hannson tells how in 1875 a group of 17 Icelandic families were persuaded to move from Middle Musquodoboit and settle not far north of here. By 1882 Markland (Old Norse for "woodland") housed some 200 men, women, and children. After a few years of fighting the rocky soils and the isolation, however, the disgruntled pioneers moved on.

After Spry Bay the road swings north and inland to avoid Mushaboom Harbour, and crosses the neck of Taylor Head peninsula on its way to Sheet Harbour. For nearly 10 km/6 mi the scenery is a monotony of dark coastal woodland festooned in old man's beard, rock barrens with stunted larch, and boggy hollows with tea-coloured ponds.

Just as wind, fog, and salt spray have shaped the coastal forest, so fire has shaped the inland forest. Dr Fernow's 1912 forest map reveals that a fire had recently burned a 3-km/2-mi-wide swath of woodland running from the east side of Spry Bay inland 16 km/10 mi past Taylor Bay Grand Lake.

Such blazes, mostly ignited accidentally by a fisherman's lunch fire or a burning sawdust dump, were common, and there was no organized way to combat them. Sometimes they burned all summer. Indeed, in rocky country with deep peat, they could smoulder all winter and flare up again in the spring. Organized forest fire detection and control did not commence until after World War II, when the provincial Department of Lands and Forests expanded its lookout tower network and equipped spotters with portable radios.

Let Will R. Bird describe this stretch of road as it was in 1949: Sign posts told us where we were at intervals—Ship Harbour Lake, Murphy Cove, Pleasant Harbour, Tangier, Popes Harbour and Spry Harbour. Untouched by railways, this shore stretches for 200 miles, completely unspoiled, scarcely tamed by man. There are lighthouses looming above the tree tops in the most unexpected places. Long lagoons where blue heron gaze haughtily at passersby. There are rocky little inlets with deep water close to shore, scarcely changed since they were used as pirate havens.
— Will R. Bird, **This Is Nova Scotia,** 1950

Coastal fog

VIEW: *Lily Pond*

Just east of Tangier Cove on the north side there's a wide marsh where beautiful jasmine-scented white water-lilies as big as teacups bloom in August. [See also **Halifax-Dartmouth Area Nature Tour** on Hwy 118.] The marsh they adorn for a fortnight each summer is also home to muskrats, frogs, waterfowl, and the invertebrates on which they feed.

Jutting into the Atlantic south of Sheet Harbour is a narrow finger of quartzite/slate/schist that in many ways epitomizes the Eastern Shore. In the 1970s residents hotly debated whether Taylor Head should be part of a national park extending west to Clam Harbour. They didn't want it, so the idea was dropped in favour of a coastal reserve. In 1976 the Eastern Shore Islands Wildlife Management Area was set up as a protected breeding zone for colonial seabirds. It's also a Natural Heritage Area. Taylor Head did in time become a provincial park.

STOP: *Taylor Head Provincial Park*

Climb headlands draped with moss-green crowberry. Hike dune-framed white sand beaches smelling of kelp and salt and fog. Wander woodland glades carpeted with wildflowers and bogs where small pink orchids blow. Explore lichen-bearded thickets of gnomish conifers threaded with snowshoe hare paths. Hike lime-green and burgundy sphagnum bogs where snipe and yellowlegs nest. Picnic by the North Atlantic.

A few steps into any black spruce thicket in summer reveals a garden of twinflower, goldthread, creeping teaberry, laurel, and wood sarsaparilla. Tree seedlings are rare. Few fir can germinate on the spongy hummocks of feather

Taylor Head

moss, but black spruce manage to root their lower branches in damp sphagnum and to start new trees by layering. The wispy jade green and brown stuff that festoons the old trees is old man's beard, or usnea lichen.

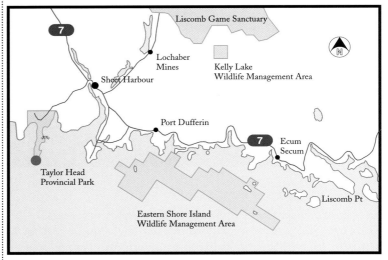

To savour all this, exit Hwy 7 at the sign and drive about 1 km/ 0.6 mi down the ridge to the farthest parking area. On your right is Spry Bay, on your left Mushaboom Harbour. The gravel access road passes through typical coastal black spruce, ancient but barely 10 m/ 33 ft tall. We also cross a small barren where sheep laurel, Labrador tea, and blueberry have seeded in after wildfire. Wet depressions are lush with sedges, sphagnum moss, cranberry, and pitcher plants. Occasionally you'll see pink arethusa orchid and, in mudholes, yellow bladderwort.

Sheep laurel

You could hardly find a better place than Taylor Head to observe seacoast dynamics. Beaches are being built before your eyes, sandspits creep across harbours, dunes advance and retreat, ponds are transformed into marshes. Some of these processes take decades, others a single stormy night. The parking lot has interpretive signs outlining this and more. One is surprised to learn that farms once flourished at Psyche Cove to the east.

At the parking lot you have a choice of hikes ranging from a short beach walk to an 18-km/ 11-mi hike around the whole peninsula.

To protect the head's thin soils and delicate dunes, please stick to the paths.

From Taylor Head the **Marine Drive** cuts north toward Sheet Harbour. The landscape is a repetition of dry ridges and wet swales smeared with glacial sands and clays and clothed with mixed woods where fire and axe have been.

About 7 km/4 mi north of Sheet Harbour on Rte 374 lies the Liscomb Game Sanctuary, a 500-km²/200-sq mi tract of land, set aside in 1928 by the newly formed Department of Lands and Forests. The prevailing wisdom was that this would save game from over-hunting and serve as a reservoir to restock surrounding areas. The department also created the Tobeatic (1927), Waverley (1929), and Chignecto (1938) sanctuaries. Today biologists tell us that habitat protection is at least as important as regulating hunting and trapping.

The quiet little lumbering/fishing community of Sheet Harbour is one of the drive's few population centres. Its name comes from a large sail-like exposure of whitish limestone visible as one sails into the harbour. The inlet is a classic drowned glacial river estuary aligned along a fault. In fact, this fault, which also forms the valley of West River, runs straight as an arrow almost to Upper Musquodoboit.

STOP: *Picnic Park*
Just west of the West River bridge a sign informs us that greenbelts are maintained along this river to protect the salmon and trout. Park here and stroll ferny paths through mixed forest along the river. The sandy soils used to grow white pine. Most of the pine is gone, as are the red spruce that followed it, but there is lush spruce and fir regeneration.

Notice below the highway bridge how an island divides the river. In summer when the water is low one can wade to it and enjoy the sensation of sitting in mid-stream. The concrete fragments nearby came from a dam that supplied water to a groundwood pulp mill from 1925 to 1971. The groundwood process was invented (or co-invented) by Charles Fenerty of Lower Sackville in 1839 [see the **Halifax Dartmouth Area Nature Tour**], but patented in Germany in 1844, and pioneered commercially at Valleyfield, Quebec, in 1869. Short, debarked bolts of wood were pressed against wet whirling gritstones to produce a slurry, which was dried and shipped to mills to make cardboard and brown kraft paper. In 1971 the swollen West River breached the dam, destroying the mill and much property downstream.

The Eastern Shore Islands Wildlife Management Area is an archi-pelago stretching from Sheet Harbour to Ecum Secum. It has one of Nova Scotia's largest breeding populations of Leach's storm-petrel, a small, soot-black bird which comes to land only once a year to breed.

("Seabird" properly applies only to such pelagic or open-ocean species that come ashore only to breed.) Accompanied by hundreds of other petrels—one site in Newfoundland had 12,000 birds—it lays a single egg in a burrow or under a boulder. As the nursery fills with chicks, an eerie underground peeping can be heard day and night, like birds singing in a cellar.

Other birds that breed here are common eider (which feeds on sea urchins) and black guillemot or sea pigeon (a diver which ferrets fish and molluscs from under rocks and seaweed). Like cormorants, guillemots seem to "fly" under water, working their wings almost as they would in air.

Without such cliffy, undisturbed places those birds could not reproduce. Some islands have lost their tree cover due to overfertilization with bird dung or guano.

SIDE TRIP: *Sober Island*

Sober Island, just east of Sheet Harbour, is really two islands joined by barrier beaches with a pond between. Birders love it, especially after spring and fall westerlies. It is said to have been named by a group of thirsty surveyors who ran out of booze and found, to their chagrin, that the islanders were staunch teetotallers.

Migrating birds drop in here because of the diversity of habitat, which includes long beaches and a lagoon. One could easily spend a day here.

The petrel is named for its habit of "walking on water" as the apostle Peter is said to have done in Matthew 14:29-30. Sometimes it's called Mother Carey's chicken, a reference to the sailor's superstition that the bird brought fog and storms at the behest of an evil spirit.

There's a causeway from the mainland.

Exit Hwy 7 about 2.5 km/1.6 mi east of the East River Sheet Harbour bridge onto a dirt road near a small brook. Head south along the harbour about 10 km/6 mi to the causeway. From there the road loops east to the village. Ask about lookouts, birding sites and beaches.

To avoid backtracking to regain Hwy 7, turn right after the causeway. That takes you through the community of Sheet Harbour Passage and up the east side of the peninsula to Beaver Harbour—also part of the Eastern Shore Wildlife Management Area and a good place to watch Arctic terns feeding.

Watch the bounding flight of these graceful terns for several minutes and you're likely to see one suddenly flutter, fold its slender wings, and drop like a stone. A modest splash, a quick tussle while the meal is positioned head-on for easy gulping and the hunter is airborne again. Like ospreys and gannets, terns dive-bomb unsuspecting fish. Gannets do it in deep water with great force; ospreys and terns keep to shallow water where their prey can't dive to safety.

Unlike cormorants and guillemots, terns can't swim under water. [See also the **Cabot** and **Fleur-de-lis** trails].

BACK ON THE HIGHWAY
Between Port Dufferin and Ecum Secum we enter a drumlin zone. Here white spruce occupies the quartzite soils and black spruce and larch the wet hollows. C. D. Howe, working on the 1912 forest survey, remarked on the abundance of yellow and white birch on the drumlin hills. You mightn't know it today, but around 1900 a forest fire razed the east bank of Salmon River.

STOP: *Birding the Ecum Secum River*
After so much boreal ruggedness, these green river flats are restful to the eye. The upstream area is noted for great blue heron, common snipe, and American bittern. (To get there, backtrack 1 km/0.6 mi and take the Pace Settlement exit.) Little blue heron, egrets, and common moorhens have also been seen. This small brownish heron often escapes notice in tall grass by pointing its bill skyward and swaying slightly. Its voice is surprisingly loud; it sounds like someone driving a post with a mallet.

There are more freshwater marshes at Fleet Settlement (exit just south of Pace Settlement), and there's a riverside picnic site at New Chester, 8–10 minutes inland.

Coast near Ecum Secum

The name Ecum Secum derives from a Mi'kmaq word for "red bank," a reference to the iron-rich drumlin soils.

After Marie Joseph, the harbours penetrate farther inland, forcing the highway to loop around their narrow drowned valleys. Your last chance to see the open ocean for a while is the small picnic site on Oxford Point.

One of these jogs takes us across the Liscomb peninsula and east along Liscomb Harbour. This inlet trends east/west, not north/south like the rest. That's because it follows a band of soft slates running that way. This slate also crops up along the north side of Liscomb Island.

LEG-STRETCHER: *Liscomb*
Pause at Liscombe Lodge to walk the 5-km/3-mi interpretive trail that wanders along the wooded river with signs identifying flora and fauna. This is a good chance to see a working fish ladder. A series of water-filled steps allows salmon and trout to get over the cliff to the next pool. In the days before fish ladders, when grist and lumber mills ran off water power, many streams lost their salmon runs when dams blocked the way.

Liscomb estuary

*Canada's first patented fishway was developed in Nova Scotia by James King in 1870; he called it the King Fish Ladder [see also the **Lighthouse Route** at Clyde River].*

As late as 1900 caribou herds roamed this area. There were also herds in the western Cobequids, around Kejimkujik Lake in western Nova Scotia, and in the Cape Breton Highlands. After 1903 no more were seen. Hunting, forest fires, land clearing, and the introduction of white-tailed deer were factors in its demise. [See also the **Cabot Trail** near French River.]

On April 11, 1939, near Trafalgar in the sanctuary, the government released eight Newfoundland woodland caribou (six does, possibly pregnant, and two others, presumably male). By today's standards the release was "violent"—i.e., they were simply let go in a strange environment. Today we would pen and feed them for a time until the trauma of capture and transport wore off.

In any case the introduction was doomed. Caribou are communal creatures that need the stimulation of numbers. Moreover, though this was unknown at the time, the native white-tailed deer harboured a hair-like brain worm that is harmless to them but often fatal to caribou and moose. Like the animals released earlier in the Waverley Sanctuary, they died out. A 1968 release near Cape Smokey suffered a similar fate.

Now the **Marine Drive** swings inland to avoid the deep indrafts of Gegogan Harbour and the outer St Mary's River. About 10 km/6 mi south of Sherbrooke, it passes a side road to Goldenville, another 19th-century gold-mining boom town.

St Mary's River

This famous salmon stream is one of the province's longest. The northern (main) branch tracks the great Chedabucto fault from the village of East River St Mary's to Eden Lake. The west (and longer) branch follows a parallel fault in resistant early Carboniferous rock from Glenelg to Trafalgar, over 40 km/25 mi. (The same fault defines Indian Harbour.) [See also the **Trans Canada Highway** at Londonderry and the **Glooscap Trail** along the Parrsboro Shore.]

The west branch, eroding steadily headward for millions of years, has "captured" many smaller streams along the Southern Upland and greatly eroded the watershed. [See also the **Evangeline Trail** at White Rock.]

Since the lower St Mary's is directly in line with Indian Harbour, logically it should empty there. But just below Stillwater it bends sharply south to exit at Sherbrooke instead. This dogleg is due to a dam of glacial gravel. The same dam created the narrow lake that gives Stillwater its name. Judging by the string of lakes along the Indian Harbour trough, it seems the original St Mary's *did* flow that way. [See also the **Cabot Trail** at Lake O'Law.]

Geologically the river is very old. This is shown by its many well developed tributaries and by its frequent meandering and braiding—multiple channels among gravel islands—in the middle reaches. Also, its valley is one of only three that cross the resistant Southern Upland. The others are Country Harbour's and the lower Musquodoboit's. Postglacial ocean flooding has rendered the St Mary's tidal for the first 14 km/9 mi, allowing large ships to reach Sherbrooke.

The St Mary's is world-renowned for salmon angling. It has 5 km/3 mi of salmon pools below Stillwater and another 5 km/3 mi from there to Glenelg. [See also the **Cabot Trail** at Northeast Margaree.] The key to its success is good policing and good fish habitat, especially in the small upstream spawning tributaries. Achieving the latter hasn't been easy. For over 30 years its watershed has supplied pulpwood to two major pulp and paper companies, namely Scott Paper International (Kimberly-Clark since 1995) and Stora-Enso at Point Tupper. [See the **Sunrise Trail** at Pictou and the **Trans Canada Highway** at Canso Strait.] Many local sawmills likewise depend on the watershed for timber.

Two side effects of logging are siltation and accelerated runoff, both of which can be minimized. The chief culprit is not so much the cutting method, as careless use of road-building equipment and skidders. The worst times are spring and fall, when heavy machines working too close to streams can gouge deep ruts in wet soils. The ruts fill with muddy water which ends up in the nearest brook.

Salmon spawn in surprisingly small streams. In those streams a few centimetres of silt will suffocate both the eggs and the minute hatchlings (called fry). Silt also kills the bottom-dwelling insect larvae (e.g., caddis fly, mayfly) on which they feed. Another hazard is that rapid spring runoff caused by clearcutting encourages incoming fish to start upstream too soon, leaving them stranded in warm pools as river levels fall.

In the 1970s a group of anglers, woodlot owners, industry representatives, and concerned citizens launched the St Mary's River Project. Its goal was and is to preserve and improve river habitat and to resolve user conflicts by co-operation and education. In this they have been quite successful.

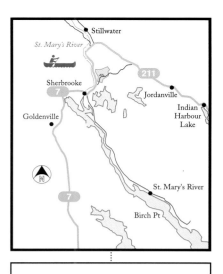

May 16th, 1801—Continued course 10 miles to St Mary's River. At end of one mile passed brook large enough for a mill ...
May 16—Rain.
May 17th—Went 5 or 6 miles down the river ... Spent a lot of time [in] fruitless attempts to ford it ... as it was so rapid and crooked that we could not safely cross it on a raft ...
May 20—Ten miles down, course E 15 S ... Last 5 miles very heavily timbered with sugar maple, beech, yellow birch and some elm.
May 21—Course E 20 S to entrance of other branch which was nearly equal in size to the S. branch. No settlers along and no game, almost no partridges ... saw a multitude of old [Indian] winter camps, and had not the luck to see a bear, though several times we came to where they have been 5 minute before. Resolved to go to Country Harbour, for we had not above 2 days provisions.
—Titus Smith, Jr,
The Eastern Tour, (1801)

Since the closure of the commercial ocean salmon fishery in the 1980s, most salmon you see in stores come from fish farms—aquaculture. The only legal harvests are by licensed freshwater anglers or by certified First Nation fishing. Stocking streams with smolt (juvenile salmon) has been discontinued because few hatchery fish survive for long in the wild. Today hatcheries supply aquaculture stations instead. [See also **Trans Canada Highway** at Whycocomagh, and **Kejimkujik Drive** at McGowan Lake.]

Sherbrooke Village

STOP: *Sherbrooke Village*
Sherbrooke was built on timber and gold between 1860 and 1880. To celebrate that colourful past, the Nova Scotia Museum has preserved and restored more than 30 buildings since 1970. One can easily spend an enjoyable half-day here, visiting the emporium, jail, and post office, talking with well-informed tour guides, watching blacksmiths working red-hot iron, coopers making barrels, and carpenters making wooden implements.

To tour the village and Salmon Museum (seasonal), turn right at the stop sign on Main Street and park as directed.

Don't leave Sherbrooke Village without visiting its water-powered sawmill, among the few still operating in Atlantic Canada. It's like being inside a giant Swiss clock with every moving part made of wood. The air is fragrant with wet logs, resin, and sawdust. You realize how *quiet* sawmilling was before steam engines arrived in the late 1840s. The only sounds are the splash of falling water, the creaky conversation of wooden cogs and wheels, and, like a bass drum accompaniment, the throbbing rumble of the great waterwheel outside. The sawing itself

Here in 1861, so the story goes, a woman gathering wildflowers brought home a pretty piece of quartz that sparkled with yellow granules. A canny traveller who saw it asked her to show him the spot. She did and he secretly mined it until word leaked out. A gold rush ensued. Some claims were worked as late as World War II. An old Department of Mines report states that from 1862 to 1900 the Sherbrooke area was the province's largest single gold producer. Its stamping mills crushed over 226,000 tonnes of rock to extract 3924 kg/138,406 oz of gold. Valued at $19/oz, it sold for $2.63 million.

is barely audible—just a rhythmic *rip*, *rip*, *rip*, like cardboard being torn, as the up-and-down saw makes its slow way down each log.

To reach the mill, turn left at the stop sign on Main Street and follow the signs.

At the end of Wharf Road there's a wetland that should be a salt marsh but isn't. Normally saltwater plants would dominate here, but so great is the St Marys' flow, especially in spring, that it overwhelms the salty tides.

For untold centuries the Mi'kmaq fished salmon on the St Mary's, curing them in bark smokehouses for winter food. In 1655 the French built Fort Sainte-Marie, choosing this spot because it was the farthest upriver a ship could navigate at high tide. For 14 years they fished and farmed and traded furs, until an English force destroyed the fort. After that, the salmon and Mi'kmaq came and went in peace for over a century.

Then around 1800 a few dozen settlers came from Pictou and Truro and struck root. They realized the watershed was rich in great white pine, red spruce, yellow birch, and tamarack, all prime ship-building material. Moreover, streams abounded for driving the wood to tidewater mills. With Napoleon blockading the Baltic ports to starve Britain's Royal Navy of timber, in 1806, the market suddenly mushroomed.

In 1815 they named the village Sherbrooke, after Sir John Coape Sherbrooke, Nova Scotia's lieutenant governor (1811 to 1816). By the mid-1800s, it had become the most important shipbuilding and lumbering centre in eastern Nova Scotia.

The winter's cut would be hauled by oxen or horses and browed, or piled, on a river bank or frozen lake. After the spring breakup, skilled river drivers would shepherd the logs down to tidewater. Here floating booms kept them from drifting out to sea. Most of the lumber was sawn into thick deals or planks for resawing elsewhere. Sailing ships, piloted up and down the river by local mariners, took the lumber to market. The bigger square-riggers had special bow hatches for loading from rafts.

Although the 1860s gold bonanza brought some money to Sherbrooke, it was shipbuilding and lumber that sustained it. Fishing villages up and down the Eastern Shore relied on its craftsmen for vessels. Families like the Cummingers and MacDonalds grew wealthy and built mansions that still stand. In the 1920s, American sports-men discovered the fishing and hunting. Tourism continues to thrive.

Just east of Sherbrooke on Hwy 7 is the St Mary's River Associa-tion Interpretive Centre. During fishing season (June 1–August 1), it offers information on water and fishing conditions and on canoeing. For advice about renting canoes or kayaks, contact the Sherbrooke Tourist Centre. The provincial picnic park is a pleasant rest stop.

Before resuming the **Marine Drive**, check at the Tourist Centre to see whether the Country Harbour ferry is operating.

"Nowhere else in the whole province is there a river [the St Mary's] which has retained so much of its original course."
— J. W. Goldthwait, **The Physiography of Nova Scotia,** 1924

Fiddleheads

For a few weeks in June, anyone can easily tell these species apart by the way they present their spores to the wind. Cinnamon fern sends up a dusty brown spike. Interrupted fern devotes a few pairs of mid-stalk fronds to the purpose. Fiddlehead greens are the curled juvenile fronds of ostrich fern, which bears its spores on the undersides of fronds.

Atlantic Canada has several distinct types of peatland: domed, plateau, slope, basin, blanket, string, ribbed fen, slope fen, and ladder fen. Fens are less acidic than true bogs.

STOP: *Mystery Walls*

Opposite the provincial park is an area with many low stone walls of unknown origin. They enclosed a community pasture in the 1920s, but some think they date back to 17th-century Fort Sainte-Marie.

Nearby is a fine growth of ferns, namely interrupted and cinnamon fern. Just think: their ancestors were the first tall green plants to colonize the continents over 400 million years ago. Before that, only fungi, lichens and mosses existed. Ferns reproduce by spores, pollen-like dots of life that drift on the air to start new plants.

One can still see where old-time log drivers dynamited a channel near the little cascade.

After Stillwater, Hwy 7 proceeds north to Antigonish, passing a string of lakes—Lochiel, Boggs— occupying the valley of a long-vanished river that likely connected with Indian Harbour. At Goshen near South Lochaber, the province's Christmas tree industry had its beginnings in the early 1930s. [See also **Trans Canada Highway** at Antigonish.] The Garden of Eden area on the main St Mary's has extensive DNR red pine plantations covering old fire barrens.

Now **Marine Drive** follows Route 211 along Upper Indian Harbour Lakes to Port Hilford, linking up with Rte 316 near Isaac's Harbour North. Fernow describes recent burns along the whole east slope of this valley—another indication of how little of the original forest escaped fire.

The big lake opposite Port Hilford was created by a glacier. The narrow strip of woodland and fields that separate it from Indian Harbour is a dam of glacial gravel dumped here 12,000 years ago.

After Port Bickerton, we cut north across a wedge of resistant greywacke that separates Fishermans Harbour (scooped from a band of soft slate) from Country Harbour. The dark coniferous woodlands, buffeted by salt air and storms from three directions, again wear their now-familiar coastal look.

On the flat upland, trees give way to open bog. And under the green film of living plants lies a sodden mass of dark brown humus. Peat, the chief fuel of rural Ireland, so beloved by gardeners, is the accumulated dead moss and twigs of thousands of summers. It thrives on thin, sour, rocky soils in cool, wet, foggy regions like this. Even in the hottest summer, its watertight pavement of bedrock and clay ensures against drought.

These peatlands started around barren postglacial ponds on bare rock softened by bacteria, algae, and lichens. Gradually sphagnum moss invaded the pond edges. As generations of moss died, they sank to the bottom in a layer of muck. In time the moss filled the ponds

Country Harbour

and joined with other colonies. Sphagnum's wick-like ability to sponge up water—as much as 90 per cent of its mass—kept raising the water table. This allowed yet more moss to grow. Those same conditions inhibited sedges and trees. As the patches spread, they coalesced to form large raised bogs like these.

The biggest local peatland covers 170 ha/420 ac. The deposits are between three and four metres (10–13 ft) thick—though in one place road builders had to dig down 7 m/23 ft to reach bedrock. If you see a big tractor with huge balloon tires, it's probably cutting drainage ditches. Once the surface is dry and the green vegetation skimmed off, the peat is vacuumed layer by layer into mobile metal bins. Below the water table it grades from brown to black, which is classed as fuel grade. [See also the **Evangeline Trail** at Aylesford.]

The bleak landscape between Port Bickerton and Country Harbour is unpeopled, but the road is well travelled, thanks to the Country Harbour ferry. The ferry allows people from Larrys River to work in the Port Bickerton fish plant without detouring 80 km/50 mi around this fjord-like inlet. The crossing takes only seven minutes.

The ferry departs on the hour from the east side and on the half-hour from the west side.

Country Harbour itself is a classic drowned river estuary carved by ice along an ancient fault. It stretches 25 km/15 mi to the open Atlantic, widening as it goes. Despite some islands and shoals at the entrance, it's one of the best natural harbours in the world, with 20 m/65 ft of water at its head. For this reason and its proximity to Canso Strait, it is the terminus for Sable Island gas. The gas will be processed at the strait and sold in New England.

Small-boat mariners should bear in mind that this steep-sided valley forms a natural wind tunnel.

As we found we had missed the Head of Country Harbour ... we are now resolved to strike Manchester ... The last 6 miles half swamps and thickets of fir. The beech not so large and considerable fir mixed with it.
—Titus Smith, Jr,
The Eastern Tour,
1801

Ask the ferry operator about "Mount Misery" and other Country Harbour tales. The district was settled by Loyalist soldiers disbanded after the American War of Independence.

Between Isaac's Harbour and Tor Bay we cross the Maritime-Northeast Pipeline that carries Sable Island natural gas to the NB border and beyond. The buried conduit emerges from a pumping facility near Goldboro, and snakes westward, marked at crossings by red-and-white signs. Laid mostly in 1999, it supplies markets in the Maritimes and northern New England. Natural gas comes from the buried remains of ancient animal life. [See also Sable Island.]

Leaving the ferry, we follow Rte 211 about 3 km/2 mi to its intersection with Rte 316.

LEG-STRETCHER: *Isaac's Harbour Falls*
It may not be a real waterfall, but this series of 2-m/6-ft cascades is a delight—and anyway it's time for a walk. To reach it, stop where Hwy 316 makes a sharp left turn, then a right to the bridge over the river. Leave the vehicle at the bridge, safely parked, and find the footpath that follows the river's west bank up to the falls. The distance is about 1 km/.6 mi, one way.

Here we turn east. As you travel from Isaac's Harbour past Goldboro (named for an 1861 gold rush), Drumhead, and Coddles Harbour, notice how few salt marshes, beaches, and bay bars there are. All these require soft rock and gravel along the coast, both of which are rare here. What little sand there is gets quickly washed away, leaving rough cobbles.

One of the few deposits of glacial drift lies along the lakeshore above New Harbour Cove. In fact, Rte 316 crosses the lake on the outermost of two glacial dams [see also Indian Harbour].

SIDE TRIP: *Tor Bay Provincial Park*
Take this 3.4-km/2-mi detour just to experience a decent beach again! The cove is nice and cosy too, protected as it is from all but southwest gales. Although rock barrens ring the village, the starkness is softened by rounded hills of outwash gravel. (A gravel pit near the cemetery provides a cross-section.)

At this park you can explore sand dunes and salt marsh, and learn about local ecology from interpretive displays. Walk the coastal barrens and see if you can identify Labrador tea, huckleberry, bracken fern, and sheep laurel (lambkill). Fog is frequent here, so keep a mental picture of where your vehicle is.

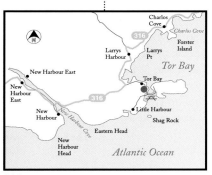

BACK ON THE HIGHWAY

A few kilometres beyond Tor Bay the road takes a sudden turn west and surprises you with Larrys River. This tiny cove opening onto the broad sweep of Tor Bay was settled in the 1780s by displaced Chezzetcook Acadians, whose descendants still live here.

The whole of Tor Bay (Spanish for "bull," a reference to the bull walruses hunted here in the late 1500s for their ivory tusks) has an underlay of slate. Along its eastern shore the slates have been baked into schist (Greek for "splittable") by heat from intruding granite. Schist glistens with small sequin-like crystals of mica and is easy to spot. Schist subjected to further heat and pressure becomes a very hard blackish rock called gneiss (pronounced "nice").

Toward Canso the trees get smaller and barrens begin to dominate. Signs of commercial fishing become more common.

As Rte 316 arcs around the bay toward Port Felix, domes and ridges of whitish granite shoulder through the sparse alder and Labrador tea—bones of the old Earth. Scattered like giant's toys across this rockyard are glacial boulders of all sizes from loaves to cottages, lying wherever the melting ice sheet dropped them—hence the term glacial erratic. Some perch on ridge tops, others lie half-buried in bogs.

STOP: *Sea Wind Landing*

At Charlos Cove (just over 5 km/3 mi east of Larrys River) live Jim and Lorraine Colvin, good people for a nature lover to know. They run a comfortable inn and have produced a booklet titled *The Nature of Sea Wind*, which describes what lives near and under the sea hereabouts. It also contains a comprehensive birding list. You can book a boat tour or guided walk by calling 1-800-563-INNS. Ask also about canoeing the waterways around nearby Cole Harbour.

Port Felix Harbour's Sugar Islands are a year-round haunt of eiders, locally called "sea-duck" or "diving duck." They find the wooded islands and rocky reefs ideal for nesting because their chief food, the sea urchin, is plentiful. In spring, flotillas of these largest of North American ducks raft offshore. You can identify them by the male's black-and-white plumage and greenish cheeks and bill; females are a richly barred brown. Males of the larger king eider species have an enlarged orange bill.

After Port Felix, we cut north along Northwest Branch Arm through rocky barrens and scrub spruce and fir to Philips Harbour on the Atlantic Coast's largest indraft, Chedabucto Bay (Mi'kmaq for "running far back"). Like the Bay of Fundy, it originated as a rift valley during the turbulent Triassic/Jurassic time when the supercontinent Pangaea broke up and dinosaurs came into their own. Both troughs filled with reddish sand that hardened into sandstone. Subsequent erosion and glaciation removed all but a few bits along the shore, and ocean flooding completed the picture. [See also the **Glooscap Trail**.]

SIDE TRIP: *Canso Town*

This 32-km/20-mi round trip brings you as close to Europe and the Grand Banks as one can be on mainland Nova Scotia. Canso was the first part of Nova Scotia definitely known to have been visited by Europeans. Like generations of Mi'kmaq people, they came for whales, seals, and walrus. Above all, they came for cod to feed their protein-starved homelands.

By the early 1500s, Portugeuse and Spanish and French routinely fished out of "Canseau." The French trader Nicolas Denys moved here from Port Rossignol (Liverpool) in 1636 and later established a trading post at St Peter's across the Bay.

Later, New Englanders had a lucrative summer cod fishery out of Canso—and used it as an excuse to trade with Louisbourg. French troops burned Canso in 1744; in 1745 New Englanders assembled in this harbour before taking Fortress Louisbourg. Canso town was mainland North America's terminus for the first transatlantic cable, which created a communications revolution comparable to today's computer revolution.

Canso barrens

The drive east from where routes 316 and 16 meet is starkly beautiful, almost Arctic in its severity. Glistening barrens rise like white whales from tawny peatlands dotted with tea-coloured ponds and flecked with snowy marsh cotton. You'll see long rolling vistas of laurel, Labrador tea, and tamarack studded with glacial boulders.

In many ways it resembles Peggys Cove on the **Lighthouse Route**, and for the same reasons (see below).

To see these landscapes as an artist does, consider joining a Fox Island summer painting workshop. Be sure to visit the Canso Museum and Grassy Island National Historic Site.

BACK ON THE HIGHWAY

From Queensport west past Dorts Cove, Rte 16 follows the scarp of the Chedabucto Fault, which marks the northern edge of the Southern Upland and defines the south shore of Chedabucto Bay. [See also the **Glooscap Trail** near Spencers Island and Economy and the **Cabot Trail** near Aspy Bay.]

STOP: *Halfway Cove Lookoff*

There are excellent views of the bay along here. The land to the northeast is Isle Madame, with Sporting Mountain beyond. If you're up to a short climb, the best of all is from Halfway Cove (halfway, that is, between Queensport and Dorts Cove). A granite dome rises 155-m/500-ft. here a kilometre south of the road. If you're unsure of the way, ask locally.

Many villages along the bay once depended on lobster fishing.

The Canso Causeway may have changed all that. According to *American Scientist* (Jan./Feb. 1997), "between 1955 and 1975, lobster catches in Chedabucto Bay declined by 95 per cent ..." with an estimated loss to the provincial economy of up to $100 million. Since the causeway, finished in 1955, blocked the deepest part of the strait, it is logical to suspect that it interrupted an important lobster migration route to and from St Georges Bay and Chedabucto Bay.

Keep an eye out for whales. Fin whales (the world's second largest) feed on herring here in late winter and early spring.

This coast is wide open to northeasters. After a big blow, huge waves crash ashore here because there are no shoals or islands to break their force. Beachcombers should stay well back! [See also **Lighthouse Route** at Peggys Cove.]

A good place to view the Cobequid/Chedabucto fault escarpment receding westward is at the bridge near the mouth of the Salmon River, just west of Dorts Cove. The river itself follows this zone of fractured, weaker rock for most of its course.

SIDE TRIP: *Lundy Lookoff*

For one of the best views in the province [see also the **Trans Canada Highway** at New Glasgow], climb Lundy Fire Tower hill on a clear day. It's not all that high—only a little over 215 m/700 ft—but its 360° viewplane is magnificent. You can see Guysborough Harbour, Chedabucto Bay, southeast Cape Breton, the Canso Barrens, Tor Bay's broad curve, and the Chedabucto escarpment.

The tower visible on the western horizon is at Middle Country Harbour. To the southwest is Donahue Lake, dotted with summer cottages. It has been dammed at the south end to supply water to Dicky Brook Power Plant. So has Tom Lake, which you passed on the way up.

Here is a landscape barely recovered from the last Ice Age. Granite domes, being harder, stand up like knots in an old softwood floor. Glacial boulders, some as large as cottages, look like pebbles from this height.

Where did all the granite come from? About 350 million years ago, during the formation of Pangaea, red-hot, porridge-like magma oozed under and into thick folds of quartzite and slate, which it baked in varying degrees. Cooling slowly, the magma formed large crystals of feldspar, orthoclase, and other silicate minerals. Eons of erosion and glaciation gradually removed the veneer of softer rock.

Had you been here in an aircraft 15,000 years ago, you would have seen a groaning ice sheet that completely covered the land and stretched far out to sea. The moving ice plucked great blocks of quartzite and slate from the bedrock, scraped the hilltops bare, and filled the hollows with gravel and rock flour. It dammed valleys and forced old streams into new channels.

Forest fires also played a role in creating their barrens. Unless or until government cutbacks remove the fire tower, on fine days the

*The 700-km/430-mi Cobequid-Chedabucto Fault, a long-healed fracture in the Earth's crust, slices across mainland Nova Scotia from Cape Chignecto to Cape Canso. [See also the **Glooscap Trail** near Advocate Harbour, Fraserville, etc.; and the **Trans Canada Highway** near Londonderry.] From there it links up with the Cabot Fault in western Newfoundland. Scotland's Great Glen, with fabled Loch Ness, is part of the same giant fracture. During the welding of Nova Scotia onto the North American plate, the southern and northern parts of the future peninsula slid along that fault. Had the southern portion slid 40 km/25 mi farther west, Chedabucto Bay would not exist.*

operator is in and welcomes visitors. Climbing it (at your own risk) will extend your view by another 16 km/10 mi.

To reach Lundy Hill, coming west on Rte 16, continue beyond Cooks Cove to the "Roachdale/West Cooks Brook/Lundy" turnoff. Go south over the bridge for about 7 km/4.3 mi to the DNR sign. Since much of the road up is unfriendly to low-slung or large vehicles, park and walk the remaining 3 km/2 mi. Mountain Road (left fork just past Dorts Cove) is shorter, but too rough for most vehicles.

On the way you'll pass a manicured pine and fir Christmas tree plantation.

BACK ON THE HIGHWAY

From Cooks Cove to Guysborough you'll see reddish soils. Like those around Minas Basin to the west, they derive from Triassic sandstones underlying the Bay. [See also the **Glooscap** and **Evangeline** trails.]

Guysborough Harbour owes its lumpy north shore to the presence of glacial drumlins. We're in soft-rock country again. From here to Canso Causeway the bedrock consists of soft Devonian/Carboniferous sediments. Here ocean waves and strong currents have moulded these deposits into a barrier beach. So thick are they that heavy breakers near the harbour mouth sometimes make entering impossible. Only regular dredging keeps it open.

TO DO: *Whale Watching/Diving*

Chedabucto Bay near Guysborough

From Guysborough, Captain John Morgan can take you to see humpback, fin, pilot, and minke whales. On a very lucky day you may spot Wilma, the friendly beluga or white whale that's been hanging around this coast since about 1990. Belugas normally stay in the Gulf of St Lawrence, where, unfortunately, industrial pollution is a serious threat. Wilma left in 1999—but locals hope she will return with a mate.

If you want to go diving, contact Jim Johnson; he'll show you not only local marine fauna, but how marine invertebrates and fish colonize shipwrecks.

In shape and size Guysborough Harbour and its Milford Haven extension (named after a harbour in west Wales) are almost a twin of Country Harbour. But this landscape has a gentler look. Rivers and glaciers deepened the sedimentary rock more easily than at Country Harbour, building lots of drumlins, kames, and sandbars.

If you'd like a break from driving, Boylston Provincial Park on the south side of the harbour (just over 1 km/0.6 mi south of the bridge) offers campsites, woodland, and pasture. A short bridge links the picnic area to a small island.

As you cross the harbour bridge to Boylston, the shoreline curves westward to follow an ancient fault.

TO DO: *Eagle Watching*
In recent years the upper inlet has become a summer haven for bald eagles. A leisurely half-hour drive up the south shore to Guysborough Intervale and back should reward you with several sightings. Look for large dead trees overhanging the shore, which make favourite fishing perches. Even if you see no eagles, the scenery makes this drive worthwhile.

Approximately 1.5 km/1 mi east of Boylston, Rte 16 branches north toward Monastery and the Trans Canada Highway, but we take Rte 344 to Mulgrave.

Trans Canada Trail
The first Nova Scotia section of this proposed national hiking trail was opened near here on June 1, 1995. This 3.7-km/2.3-mi (one-way) trail starts 3 km/2 mi south of Guysborough at the intersection of Rte 16, "Larrys River Road," and the road west to Ogden. One can park at the site of an abandoned Irving garage nearby. A sign in the nearby woods labels it the Guysborough Nature Trail; locals call it the Front Country Trail. In 1996 it stopped at the Salmon River bridge, but it has been steadily extended and upgraded.

The trail follows part of the abandoned bed of a 100-km/60-mi railway intended to link Guysborough with Ferrona Junction, Pictou County. Worked on from 1929 to 1931, it was never completed.

The Trans Canada Trail Foundation is creating a coast-to-coast-to-coast hiking trail. By linking sections of old railway roadbeds and other corridors the Nova Scotia portion will connect Inverness, Port Hood, and the Canso Causeway with Boylston, Cross Roads Country Harbour, Pictou, River John, Tatamagouche, Wallace Bridge, Oxford, and so to the Nova Scotia–New Brunswick border.

On the trail

The north shore of Chedabucto Bay presents a landscape of low woodlands checkered with small farms sloping gently down to quiet coves and barrier beaches. The longest of these is at Port Shoreham on Clam Harbour Bay, a crescent 2 km/1.2 mi long. It's part of a provincial park.

Will R. Bird remarked on the number of lighthouses along this shore. In 1950 hundreds of fishing boats plied these waters, and such beacons were crucial. Since then most of the great towers and their outbuildings have been replaced by automated stations designed mainly for coastal shipping.

Guysborough is very old. In 1682 Bergier, an early French adventurer, noting the good earth there, planted wheat and barley and rye. On September 21st he reaped the harvest and took the produce to France for exhibition, having beans and peas in his garden as well. His report of the wonderful New World caused quite a stir in Paris .... There is a sense of dreaminess hard to describe ... a beauty that reaches under the most hardened exterior.
—Will R. Bird, **This Is Nova Scotia**, 1950

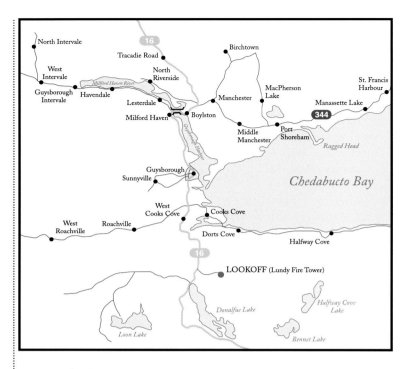

One of Atlantic Canada's busiest waterways is Canso Strait. Its southern entrance is guarded by a modern light station near Sand Point village. As you go down the hill to the village, watch on the water side for a gravel road. Approximately one kilometre down this road is Eddy Point, where there are picnic tables (but no rest rooms or drinking water).

STOP: *Eddy Point Lighthouse*
This automated station sits where two 0.5-km/0.3-mi cobble beaches enclose a salt marsh and pond. The beaches consist of sediments eroded by ocean waves from the tilted blue Carboniferous shales along the shore. Observe where strong currents and winter southeasterlies are still undercutting the soft cliffs. The jumble of concrete and rusting iron is what's left of the old tower.

In clear weather Eddy Point affords a sweeping view of Canso Strait and southeast Cape Breton. North past Melford Point, the strait tapers to a river-like channel that recedes in a broad curve in the blue distance. The tiny white plume comes from the Stora-Enso Forest Industries paper mill at Point Tupper.

The strait is just over 1 km/0.6 mi wide throughout its 21-km/13-mi length. It is remarkably deep—65 m/213 ft in one place. Because Ship Harbour (behind Point Tupper) and some local streams trend northwest, some geologists believe a great river once ran *north* through here and that later its channel was deepened by glaciers and flooded by the rising Atlantic. [See also the **Trans Canada Highway** at the Canso Causeway.]

Eddy Point is a good place to check out coastal flora. Besides cord grass (in the brackish marsh), you'll find beach pea, seaside goldenrod, and orach. The latter grows along the mainland side of the strait and in very few other locations in the province. Botanists suspect it arrived from Europe in ships' ballast. Empty ships coming here for fish or timber would come "in ballast"—weighted with iron slag, beach rocks or sand for stability. Before loading, they would dump this ballast overboard. Old World seeds and roots in the ballast often survived and reproduced. [See also **Sunrise Trail** at Fox Harbour.]

Golden rod

Pirate Harbour

In the 17th and 18th centuries, pirates lurked in this secluded pocket cove across the Strait from Point Tupper. With their ships hidden close to shore, they would lie in wait until a vessel came by with a suitable cargo. Then, with cannons blazing and sabres flashing, they would overtake the ship, clamber over its rails and, if not driven off, steal what they wanted.

From Goose Harbour Lake, a lake behind Mulgrave, fresh water is piped under the strait to Point Tupper to service the Stora-Enso paper mill.

Mulgrave used to be the train ferry terminus for Cape Breton before the causeway was built. Many a Cape Bretoner and Newfoundlander, seeking a new life in Toronto or Boston, first set foot on the mainland here. The huge ice-free artificial harbour is much used by tankers and bulk carriers of ore and paper.

VIEW: *Cape Porcupine*

Coming down the long hill toward Aulds Cove and the Trans Canada Highway, we have a grand view of the causeway on the far right (and of the frowning igneous face of Cape Porcupine above it), of St Georges Bay, and Cape Breton's Inverness shore.

In 1952 construction crews began blasting Cape Porcupine's eastern flank to supply rock and fill for the proposed link to Cape

There are a number of fine farms along the sides of the Milford Haven. The interval ... is settled for about 4 miles above the salt water. It produces very fine crops of English hay ... the inhabitants ... complain of having their Indian corn and potatoes frequently cut off by frosts in the month of August.
—Titus Smith, Jr, **The Eastern Tour**, 1801

335

Breton Island. For over a century people had said nothing could withstand the strong tides and grinding ice floes. Month after month, 40-tonne trucks dumped their loads into the dark waters. Three years and 9100 tonnes later, the world's deepest causeway opened for traffic.

Here the **Marine Drive** ends and connections can be made to the **Trans Canada Highway** and the **Ceilidh, Cabot, Fleur-de-lis,** and **Marconi** trails. If you are travelling the **Marine Drive** from the causeway west beyond Country Harbour, check first at the Port Hastings tourist information centre (or call the Goldboro operator) to ensure the ferry there is running.

Lighthouse on Rock Island near Queensport

Sunrise Trail Nature Tour

Amherst to Canso Causeway
via Northumberland Shore
316 km/196 mi

Common Loons

Melmerby Beach

OVERVIEW

From the air this trail along the Gulf Shore looks like a winding footpath along a very wide, slow river. Southward lies the rumpled Northumberland Plain with its patchwork of woodlots and farms sloping gently up the low wall of the Cobequid Mountains. The wall is notched with ravines where streams like River Philip, French River, and River John tumble off the plateau and meander to broad estuaries on the Northumberland Strait.

Even from the air, this shore looks inviting. Crumbling brick-red headlands shelter quiet coves where the warmest salt water north of the Carolinas laps beaches of sugary pink sand. It has no fierce Atlantic combers, no intimidating heights. Only once, at Cape George north of Antigonish, does the land exceed the height of a 12-storey building. In fact, its lowest parts are being reclaimed by the sea, inexorably, at 30 cm/12 in a century on average.

From Amherst the trail runs north along the level grasslands of the narrow Chignecto Isthmus. At Tidnish it veers east, touching the inlets of Pugwash, Wallace Bay, and Tatamagouche before dipping south to New Glasgow's birdfoot-shaped harbour. From there it heads northeast along the Melmerby and Merigomish sandspits, around the toe of the rugged Antigonish Highlands, and across the Antigonish Lowland to the Strait of Canso.

Cape George Point offers spectacular views of the Gulf of St Lawrence, Cape Breton Island and, on a clear day, the east end of Prince Edward Island. In October this "Mini-Cabot Trail" is embroidered with tangerine and gold as sugar maple, yellow birch, and beech prepare for winter.

The Gulf Shore is renowned for lobster and waterfowl. The strait is shallow and sunlit and fertilized by many rivers. This nurtures a diversity of plankton, which in turn feeds a complex food chain that includes lobster and birds. Its coves are full of eel-grass, clams, and other bird delicacies. Great blue herons stand stock-still in cove after cove, rising on heavy wings when disturbed to hunt minnows elsewhere. Rare short-eared owls nest at Fox Harbour. In spring and autumn the lush tidal marshes come alive with the rushing wings and cries of migrating geese, ducks, and shorebirds. Harbour and grey seals frequent the offshore islands. Sometimes whales come ashore; and sometimes people discover traces of ancient monsters.

All side roads southward from Hwy 6 sooner or later cross the buried pipeline carrying Sable Island gas from Goldboro at Country Harbour [See **Marine Drive**] to the New Brunswick border.

THE TOUR BEGINS

We start at Amherst by taking Exit 3 from Highway 104 onto Victoria Street, then east through the downtown area and suburbs until it merges with Route 366. This road parallels the Amherst Marsh, a northerly extension of the Tantramar system. At 207 km²/ 80 sq mi, it is said to be the largest such marshland in the world. [See also the **Trans Canada Highway**/Hwy 104 at Missaguash River.]

Soon we swing right to join Rte 366, which runs northeast through rolling farm and woodlot country toward Tidnish. The various small streams we cross are feeders of the La Planche River (French for "the plank," named for an Acadian footbridge near

Monument at Tidnish

Tidnish shore where the old railbed ended

Amherst). It empties into Cumberland Basin after meandering through the Lusby Marsh. These lowlands never exceed 30 m/100 ft above sea level.

STOP: *Tidnish Dock Provincial Park*
This picnic area beside Baie Verte (4 km/2.5 mi off Rte 336 on Jackson Point Road) preserves relics of a visionary 19th-century engineering scheme that rivaled that of the earlier Shubenacadie Canal [see the **Halifax-Dartmouth Area Nature Tour**], and ended as badly. All that remains today are crumbling stonework, an old railbed, and rotted wharf pilings.

Henry Ketchum, a New Brunswick–born engineer, saw no reason why two steam locomotives on separate tracks could not tow ships on flatcars over the 27-km/17-mi stretch of level marsh from Fundy to the Northumberland Strait. Doing so, he argued, would shorten the Boston-Montreal sea route by over 800 km/500 mi and work better than Joseph Howe's earlier idea of a ship canal.

With federal government backing, he began work in August 1887. But Halifax shipping interests, worried about losing revenues from shorter voyages, successfully lobbied Ottawa to withdraw Ketchum's funds. Four years into the project, Ottawa pulled out. He continued to seek backers until his death in 1896. Prime Minister Sir Wilfrid Laurier, faced with yet another petition, said in 1911, "I thought the Chignecto business was dead." It took World War I to finally lay the scheme to rest.

The Tidnish Visitor Information Centre has photographs and can direct you to the park. The Corner Store at Tidnish Cross Roads is another source of local information. Tidnish is Mi'kmaq for "paddle."

North Shore sand is visibly coarser than Atlantic Shore sand because of the sandstone's flaky nature and the subdued wave action in these shallow, sheltered waters.

Across Baie Verte and hidden behind Cape Tormentine, the world's longest multispan bridge links Tormentine, NB, and Borden, PEI. Construction of the 14-km/8.7-mi long "Fixed Link" began in 1994. The last concrete span was dropped into place November 19, 1996, just before winter set in.

Most of the aggregate came from the diorite quarry at Folly Lake [see the **Trans Canada Highway** at Wentworth Valley]. Environmentalists and purists protested the project, but builders say the design is the least disruptive to marine organisms and will withstand the strait's churning ice floes.

From Tidnish Cross Roads to Tatamagouche, many small roads branch off to summer cottages on or near the shore. The water here heats up to nearly 21° C/70° F. By contrast, Fundy waters rarely get above 13° C/55° F in summer, and the Eastern Shore waters can be even chillier.

STOP: *Northport Beach Provincial Park*
Test the water's warmth here at the mouth of the Shinimicas River (Mi'kmaq for "shining"). Walk the beach at low tide and observe the ripple marks. They form along sheltered shores where wave action is too slight to erase them. Similar "fossil wave prints" often occur in exposed ancient strata. Small ripples denote light breezes, larger ripples strong winds. Sometimes there are fossil rain prints as well.

Northport Beach

Sheltered shores along here have shallow muddy pools where burrowing clams and polychaete worms live. Look for the twin siphon holes of clams and the sinuous tracks of worms on the bottom. Mud worms in turn attract sandpipers, which also feed on tiny shrimp-like amphipods. [See also the **Glooscap Trail** near Economy and Cheverie.] Here and there you'll see the empty pale grey spiral shells of dead moon snails. This predator bores through a clam's shell, inserts its stomach, and digests the insides.

If you see clam diggers at work with pails and forks, notice how fast they dig. Speed is crucial. Clams anchor themselves below with a long tubular "foot." If alarmed they contract it, yanking themselves down with amazing speed.

Canadian Salt Company

At Port Howe, where River Philip runs into the strait, the trail joins Hwy 6 from Amherst. Port Howe is one of several places along the shore that maintain pounds (saltwater cages) where one can buy fresh lobster during May and June. Fishers haul their traps in the morning, and you can usually find them selling at the wharf by early afternoon.

To produce a layer of rock-salt one metre deep requires the evaporation of about 50 m/165 ft of salt water.

Aerial view of Pugwash

As we cross the Pugwash Causeway (from *Pagweak*, Mi'kmaq for "shallow water"), notice on your right the Canadian Salt Company's 30-m/100-ft tower and plant. The harbour sits over a massive deposit of rock salt (sodium chloride). About 250–300 m/825–990 ft down, it's a world of dry, brightly lit caverns and galleries where large machines trundle about with loads that glisten like ice. The deposit is up to 460 m/ 1,500 ft thick and extends east to Malagash and west almost to Springhill. Another deposit crosses under Nappan. [See also **Glooscap Trail**.] On average the company extracts 900,000 tonnes of salt a year here.

Malagash and Pugwash salt was once used to cure salt cod for Caribbean and Mediterranean markets. Today it is used to make chlorine, tan hides, cure green hay and ensilage, and of course to flavour food. (Road salt is normally calcium chloride.)

Just as a hard white film will form inside a kettle in which "hard" water is repeatedly boiled, salt crystals form when shallow seas evaporate under a tropical sun. When the drifting earth-plates closed to form the supercontinent Pangaea during the early Carboniferous, about 320 million years ago, narrow arms of the ancient Iapetus ocean were cut off and dried up. One of these extended across the future Nova Scotia. A similar process occurs today around Utah's Great Salt Lake and in Israel's Dead Sea. Salts of sodium (including table salt), potassium (potash), and boron (borax) and of the calcium sulphates (gypsum, anhydrite, soda) are called evaporites.

After Pugwash the road veers inland through low mixed coniferous and deciduous woods. Most North Shore woodlands have been repeatedly harvested, cleared, or burned. This accounts for the abundance of light-demanding species like white spruce, trembling aspen, red maple, and white birch.

SIDE TRIP: *Gulf Shore*

Dunes on Northumberland Strait

If you'd rather hug the coast as much as possible and have the time, turn left beyond the causeway onto Gulf Shore Road and do the loop around to Wallace. After 1 km/0.6 mi, watch for a sign indicating McLeans Point and Gulf Shore Provincial Park. Set on a low hill, it offers good views of the strait. There's an excellent beach with broad sandbars at low tide.

In school we were taught there are two high tides and two low tides a day—a semi-diurnal rhythm. But this part of the Northumberland Strait usually gets only one of each a day. This is because Prince Edward Island splits the tides of the Gulf of St Lawrence and the Atlantic tides. So if a strong incoming tide meets a weak ebb tide, the former will prevail, prolonging the high tide. The reverse situation will prolong an ebb tide.

Leaving Lower Gulf Shore, the road runs past the turnoff to the village of Fox Harbour (left) and crosses Fox Creek. About 1.5 km/ 0.9 mi beyond the creek, a dirt road runs east roughly 8 km/5 mi to Fox Harbour Provincial Park—well worth a visit.

STOP: *Eel-grass, Pipefish & Owls*

This park welcomes you with picnic tables, rest rooms, a boardwalk under birches, a broadloom of velvety lawn, a pink sand beach, and warm water, in that order.

On the beach you'll notice mats of bleached brown stuff—last year's washed-up eel-grass. In the sunlit shallows offshore, this year's living green eel-grass undulates in the waves. Did you think it was seaweed? Actually, it's one of the very few seed-bearing land plants able to survive in salt water. (Cord grass is another, but it has to withstand salt only twice a day [see also the **Marine Drive** near Cole Harbour].) *Zostera marina* occurs in sheltered waters from Greenland to North Carolina, around Sable Island, and on the Pacific coast. It is a vital winter food for geese.

If you happen to come here after a northeaster, the windrows of dead grass can be considerable. Each row marks a tidal contour, from lowest (half-moon) to highest (full or new moon). Dig into a windrow. Inside is a moist chocolate-brown world smelling of sea salt and iodine. Don't be alarmed if dozens of "sand fleas" hop away. These tiny crustaceans hide here during the day and feed along the beach at night.

As eel-grass decomposes, the waves slowly shred it into a rich black soup that stinks of methane at low tide. In the cove east of the park, tides and moving ice have built nearly a metre of this muck into new land on which marsh grasses are thriving.

Eel-grass, lacking the strong tubular stems of its land-based relatives, survives by being buoyant and flexible.

TO DO: *Find a Pipefish*
Wade out among the live eel-grass and look for the little northern pipe fish. Like its southern relative the sea-horse, it is well camouflaged. It's green and brown and looks more like a twig than a fish.

Another unusual local creature of the shore is the short-eared owl, a rare hawk-like bird that hunts by day. With luck you'll see one skimming over the marsh, hunting mice. Its large ears tell us that it hunts as much by sound as by sight. Like other owls, it swallows prey whole. Later it spits up neat grey pellets of indigestible fur and bones.

Fox Harbour is one of only two known nesting sites of the short-eared owl in Nova Scotia, the other being the Amherst marshes.

Short-ears nest in open marshland, trusting to sticky mud and excellent camouflage to foil predators. In early spring the male performs a curious courtship display, diving steeply over the nest site, then pulling out with rapid wing beats. Please stay off the marsh until the end of June, when the young will have flown.

Watch too along this shore for great blue herons standing in the shallows, fierce golden eyes scanning the water for minnows or flounder. Wait patiently and you'll see one plunge its spear-shaped beak into the water, yank up a wriggling fish, and swallow it in one convulsive gulp.

Why are marine algae (seaweed) so scarce on the North Shore? There are four reasons: (a) the sandstone is too crumbly for them to fasten securely to; (b) drift ice scrapes the shallow bottom clean each winter; (c) the bedrock is nearly horizontal, which means that water of sufficient depth is far from shore; and (d) on such a level shore, low tide exposes them to sun and wind for too long.

If you find a knobby, roundish chunk of iron half buried in the sand, it's probably a bit of ship's ballast, not a meteorite. Ballast, usually stone, was used to stabilize empty ships until they were loaded; then the material was dumped. Today ships use water for ballast. [See also the **Marine Drive** at Eddy Point; **Trans Canada Hwy** at Baddeck.]

If you don't mind a short walk through scratchy coastal white spruce, trek to Mullins Point about 4 km/2.5 mi farther east. There's

Eastern Meadowlark

American Robin

a good chance of spotting seals. The Crown-owned shore has two key elements for good seal habitat: abundant fish and a boulder-strewn beach.

In summer, harbour seals sun themselves on the rocks and fish the nearby waters. In September grey seals come to breed; the males are first to arrive, then the females a fortnight later. The Point is also a good bird-watching site.

To find it from the park, continue east to Dougherty Point, take the 90° right turn, and head south until you see a footpath heading east to Mullins Point (also called North Wallace Point because it bounds Wallace Harbour).

To get to Fox Harbour Provincial Park if you didn't follow the Gulf Shore loop, take the first road north after Wallace Bridge, cross the bridge, take the first right, and continue to the end of the road.

BACK ON THE HIGHWAY

LEG-STRETCHER: *Wallace Bay National Wildlife Area*
This 585-ha/1,445-ac sanctuary is a bird and frog heaven. It has tidal and freshwater wetlands, and grain fields, and forest. During spring and fall migration the marshes are alive with waterfowl. From October till Christmas as many as 5,000 Canada geese graze the stubble fields, pastures, and wetlands. Brant, an uncommon small goose, come here too. Bald eagles hang out in nearby trees, watching for unwary ducks and fish. Willets, dowitchers, and plovers probe the rich muds with long sensitive beaks. Hudsonian godwits have been spotted in July and August. In late summer Bonaparte's gulls and Caspian terns appear, followed by sea ducks like the greater scaup and inland ducks like the goldeneye.

Hunting season opens here October 1 for some waterfowl. After that, confine your birding to Sundays.

To help you get close to all this bird life, the Wallace Bay Development Association has developed a 4-km/2.5-mi walking trail. To access it, exit Rte 6 approximately 2.5 km/1.6 mi east of the Rte 368 intersection and drive north toward the village of Wallace Bay. Just before the North Wallace River bridge, to the left, there's a parking lot. The Wallace Bay Nature-Wildlife Trail takes you into coastal white spruce, fir, and aspen, across overgrown fields, and through a swamp before returning to the dyke.

Another great way to observe local waterfowl is to paddle the Wallace or Waughs rivers by canoe or kayak. The Wallace is the North Shore's longest stream. Rising in the Cobequids at Folly Lake, it meets the Trans Canada Highway near Wentworth Centre, where it's shallow and rocky, and reaches Wallace Harbour through a convoluted marshy estuary. The last 7 km/4.3 mi are tidal. This is where the birds are. Put in at the Wallace Bay Bridge near the head of the estuary and paddle up or down. Wind can be a problem in the wider outer reaches.

Curious about landscaping for wildlife? Then Wallace Bicentennial Museum on Hwy 6 (2.5 km/1.5 mi west of Wallace) is for you. In 1995 its staff catalogued 28 species of butterflies and 128 species of birds on the property. Interpretive trails are being developed. The museum is open from July 1 to Labour Day. From the picnic grounds you can see a tern nesting site on an island in the estuary; visit it with binoculars.

Near the mouth of Wallace Harbour is the village of Wallace (named for a former provincial treasurer, not for the Scottish freedom fighter). At one time its superb beige sandstone was famous throughout eastern Canada.

Wallace was settled in 1784 by United Empire Loyalists—British sympathizers during the American War of Independence—from New York State. Astronomer and mathematician Simon Newcomb, renowned for his work on planetary orbits, was born here in 1835. Inquire at the Fraser Cultural Centre in Tatamagouche about his centenary monument and the tree under which he reputedly studied as a teen.

LEG-STRETCHER: *Wallace Quarry*

The stone pit is at the end of Quarry Hill Drive, a 0.5-km/0.3-mi uphill walk south from Main Street Park. Near the entrance, on the right, is the office of Stanley J. Flynn Trucking. Before entering the quarry ask permission. The entrance is framed by two massive sandstone blocks with unused dynamite holes. Inside you'll see an oval lake about 300 m/1,000 ft across with steep rocky walls and rubbled shores. From this crater hole came the stone for Canada's Parliament buildings, for Ottawa's Victoria Museum, and for Halifax's Province House and Citadel. Aside from its evenness of texture and soft beige colour, Wallace stone was prized for its freedom from cracks. This meant that large blocks could be removed intact. The stones at Citadel Hill are nearly 3 m/9 ft to a side. [See also the **Halifax-Dartmouth Area Nature Tour**.]

At Tatamagouche are several kinds of Timber Trees for Ship Building, such as Yellow Oak, & Black Birch (both of which have been found equal if not superior to any other wood in the Colonies for making Planks, for Ships Bottoms, because the Worm, will not penetrate them), some white & yellow Pine, Spruce, Hemlock &ca; a good Harbour, Three fathom water...some few Inhabitants.
— Charles Morris, Surveyor General of Nova Scotia (1783)

SIDE TRIP: *Emu Farm*

Allan Rhendress of Wallace raises Australian emus. He and Austin Hiltz saw emus on Prince Edward Island and decided to try raising them commercially. The meat is red, and with a flavour and texture somewhere between wild meat and beef. Females lay big green eggs early in December.

Emus belong to a group of mostly extinct large, flightless birds that evolved in places where predators were originally absent. Most, like the dodo and great auk, were extirpated by human interference or hunting. Ask directions locally and drive by to see the world's second largest (after the ostrich) living bird. Emus live wild in Australia and stand 1.5 m/5 ft tall.

The strait's warmest summer waters lie west of Tatamagouche Bay. Between 8,000 and 4,000 years ago they were warmer still, which encouraged southern molluscs like quahog (pronounced *ko*-hog) and dwarf surf clam to colonize. Today they survive as isolated populations, cut off from their southern kin by the chilly Atlantic.

Grapes do well here. Wines from nearby Malagash's Jost Vineyards have won international prizes since the 1980s. Jost welcomes visitors.

STOP: *Malagash Salt Mines*
In 1994 the Malagash Heritage Museum was opened and a monument unveiled to commemorate Canada's first salt mine. The salt was discovered in 1912 on Peter Murray's land, the first shaft was sunk on July 1, 1918, and the first salt was produced two months later. In the next 35 years, 1.5 million tonnes were mined here.

After crossing the low sandstone peninsula separating Wallace and Tatamagouche bays, the trail continues southeast toward Tatamagouche.

Beaver pond

Beaver lodge

Beaver toothmarks

SIDE TRIP: *Teed Bog*
Some bogs were once lakes. One of the shore's finest examples of such bog succession can be seen southwest of Bayhead on Millard Creek.

To reach Teed Bog, drive to Millard Creek approximately 1 km/ 0.6 mi east of Bayhead (5.6 km/3.5 mi west of Tatamagouche Centre if heading west). You'll see a beaver lodge on the creek. Just east of the creek watch on the south side for the sign for Slade Road. Drive inland 1 km/0.6 mi, take the first right, and keep on for 2.5 km/1.6 mi. Park and follow an old woods road up Millard Creek 1.3 km/0.8 mi to the bog. On the way, watch for birds in season.

A small pond downstream attracts breeding ducks, wood turtles, and salamanders. Nearby spruce thickets shelter warblers and kinglets. In winter there are chickadees, snowshoe hares, voles, and the occasional grey jay.[See also the **Evangeline Trail** at Aylesford, the **Marine Drive** near Tor Bay, the **Fleur-de-lis Trail** at Framboise, and the **Lighthouse Route** near Shelburne.]

Lowland streams tend to converge near the sea (see also Pictou Harbour). Upland streams, being swifter, tend to pirate each other's upstream channels until only one larger river dominates the rest (e.g., Margaree, LaHave).

BACK ON THE HIGHWAY

The Tatamagouche area spreads left and right like the wings of a duck whose eye is Amet Island, in Amet Sound. Tatamagouche is an altered Mi'kmaq word meaning either "where two rivers meet," or "bay enclosed by a sandbar." The bay does receive two sizable rivers, the French and Waughs, which share one estuary.

Tatamagouche was a busy place long before Europeans arrived. Apart from its mild climate and largesse of game, it lay on the ancient canoe route between the Bay of Fundy and Abeqweit, which is now Prince Edward Island. From the Chiganois River on Cobequid Bay the Mi'kmaq portaged over the Cobequids and descended the French River to this bay. [See also the **Glooscap Trail**.] A large native burial ground was located at Tatamagouche.

To learn more about local Mi'kmaq and Acadian history and the town's important shipbuilding past, visit the Sunrise Trail Museum on Main Street. Ask about the Trans Canada Trail as well.

One of the North Shore's best birding sites during fall migration is Sand Point, east of the Waughs River estuary. Exit Hwy 6 just beyond the Waughs River bridge, take the first left to Sandville, and drive about 5 km/3 mi until you see tidal and freshwater marshes. The papery bluish flowers visible from late July to September belong to sea-lavender.

Before leaving the area, visit the Tatamagouche Centre (also known as Atlantic Christian Training Centre). This 6-ha/15-ac facility occupies the site of the old Acadian village. It offers retreats, spiritual and cultural workshops, natural history tours and Elderhostel programs. Its tranquillity is conducive to contemplation, and you're welcome to explore the grounds.

A "walkabout" tour folder guides visitors through five stops, including tidal marshes, red sandstone cliffs, the Alexander Campbell shipyard site, Campbell House (the oldest frame house on the North Shore), and large native red oak and planted black locust trees. Locust, a relative of the garden pea and bean, is an Appalachian species but does well here thanks to the mild winters. (It's common in the sheltered Annapolis Valley.)

An Acadian home

Around 1710, Acadians from the Minas Basin came and settled along the French River 1 km/0.6 mi west of today's village. For purposes of trade between their possessions at Fort Anne (now Annapolis Royal), Île St-Jean (Prince Edward Island), and Île Royale (Cape Breton Island), they built an oxcart road along the Mi'kmaq portage. In June 1745, on the eve of the first capture of Fortress Louisbourg, Capt David Donahew of New England intercepted and confiscated a shipload of Acadian produce which was bound for Louisbourg.

Besides farming and fishing and trading, the Acadians dug and smelted copper from the Mine Hole beside Waughs River. The mine was revived after Confederation in 1867, but ran out by 1909. [See also the **Glooscap Trail** at Cape d'Or.]

In August 1755, with England and France again at war, Tatamagouche's Acadians became the first to be deported. Another New Englander, Captain Willard, torched every building and boat and confiscated two schooners bound for Louisbourg. [See also the **Glooscap Trail** at Masstown.]

To reach the centre, drive west on Main Street past the exit to Rte 246, cross a small bridge, and watch on your right for the sign.

The Trans Canada Trail Foundation is creating a coast-to-coast-to-coast hiking trail, by linking sections of old railway roadbeds and other corridors. The northern Nova Scotia section will pass through Pictou, River John, Tatamagouche, Wallace Bridge, Oxford, and so to the Nova Scotia–New Brunswick border. Ask at the centre for details, or contact the foundation.

From Tatamagouche our route meanders along Brule Shore to River John, settled in 1785 by Huguenots from Tatamagouche.

Amet Island is a speck of rock barely visible in clear weather northwest of Cape John Point. Though buffeted by wind and scoured by ice and tides, to seals and seabirds it's a special place. In 1995 it was *very* popular with cormorants and gulls, because a dead 13-m/40-ft sperm whale lay rotting on the beach.

The whale had drifted ashore near River John two years earlier. With summer coming on, and tourists expected, residents grew alarmed. They tried to haul the carcass away by flatbed truck, but the backhoe operator couldn't lift it. They towed it out into the strait, but winds and currents fetched it back. A whale's thick coat of blubber is naturally buoyant, and this one was further bloated by the gases of decay.

That winter the corpse lay frozen in the ice west of River John. The blunt black head and upraised tail fluke made it look like a small submarine. With the 1995 breakup it was once more on the move, and smelling worse each day. Finally Pictou County's bylaw enforcement officer Mike McKenzie had it towed with steel cables at high tide to Amet Island. Normally Amet's large cormorant colony dines on fish. But when the whale's tough rubbery hide was sliced open for them, the big black birds dug in.

That same year the county had to deal with another dead whale, four beached seals, and a dead porpoise.

This section of coast has long been noted for its unusual bird sightings. In 1969 a flamingo turned up near River John.

Sometimes two or three dozen healthy pilot whales come ashore and die. No one understands exactly why. It may be to save a sick member of the pod, or to follow a senile leader. It may have to do with atmospheric disturbances that disable their delicate navigational apparatus.

SIDE TRIP: *Brule Shore*

In French the word means "burnt," a reference perhaps to a major forest fire which the first settlers witnessed. Most of the farms here have been abandoned and colonized by spruce, alders, and aspen. Others have been bought up for summer cottages, which in choice shore locations stand three or four deep.

Decades ago the provincial government, seeing the rate at which Gulf Shore properties were being snapped up, bought Rushtons Beach near Angel Point for a provincial park. It's a good place to observe the transition from field to low tide zone. A relocated access road takes you through an old pasture restocked by 50-year-old white spruce. See how this species retains its branches nearly to the ground, shading out the grasses that once sheltered its seedlings.

A manicured lawn of fescue, timothy, and clover surrounds the parking lot, from which a long boardwalk leads you past native grasses and a border of alder, willow, and bayberry to a tidal cord grass marsh. Here you cross a sturdy footbridge over a brackish stream whose bottom is furred with green algae, home to minnows and eels. The boardwalk ends at a low dune where marram grass strives to hold the sand in place.

The park is about 5 km/3 mi east of the Hwy 6/Rte 326 intersection; watch for the routed pine sign.

In the summer of 1995, Howard van Allen and his brother Corey, walking the shore near here at low tide, came upon fossilized tracks and tree parts in reddish siltstone. They found "at least a city block" of this, uncovered by the previous winter's ice and tides. The tracks ranged from 1 cm/0.3 in long to the size of child's hand. Experts said they belonged to 290 million-year-old amphibians and reptiles travelling in a forest swamp. [See also the **Evangeline Trail** at Hortons Landing and the **Glooscap Trail** near Parrsboro and Avonport.]

Mr van Allen, a professional renovator living in Dartmouth, was anxious to obtain a record before tides erased his find, so he quickly made plaster casts and collected petrified stumps, logs, and foliage.

SIDE TRIP: *Balmoral Grist Mill*

You can reach this restored 1874 mill from Hwy 6 by travelling south on Rte 326 from Brule or southeast on Rte 311 from Tatamagouche. The mill site is both a beauty spot and a lesson in pioneer ingenuity. Mirrored in its millpond above the dam on Matheson Brook, the red and white mill with its slowly turning waterwheel is postcard perfect.

Inside is a different kind of perfection. Here a clockwork of moving wooden and metal parts turns a millstone to transform tough, unhusked kernels of grain to edible flour. Mornings and afternoons the staff demonstrates how our forebears did this with milled oats and other grains.

Matheson Brook

You can buy samples of oatmeal, whole wheat flour and sometimes buckwheat flour. Try some buckwheat if you've never had it; it makes wonderful pancakes. There's also an authentic Scottish oatdrying kiln.

Ask master miller John Taylor or an assistant about their new stone. The stationary bottom or *nether* stone normally lasts a century or more, but by 1995 Balmoral's was getting thin. The museum advertised for a replacement across Nova Scotia. Donald MacDonnell of Mabou, Cape Breton, had one. It was 23 cm/9 in thick, nearly 2 m/6 ft in diameter and weighed over a tonne. In March 1995 a truck delivered it and a front-end loader hoisted it off to be installed later. (Seeing it gives new meaning to Jesus's saying about being cast into the sea with a millstone around one's neck.)

The milling of grain is so ancient that its terminology has seeped into many languages. The surnames Miller, Millar, and Mueller (Ger.) derive from it. In English we say "It's grist for the mill," meaning "Everything proves useful in the end." *Grist* (meaning grain) comes from Old English *grindan*, "to grind." In England's West Country, in Newfoundland, and in parts of Nova Scotia, a moth is still called a *miller* because of its powdery wings.

When Balmoral Mill was new, Nova Scotian farmers grew wheat, rye, barley, oats, and buckwheat, all needing to be ground. Matheson Brook alone had five mills. The 1861 census for Cape Breton's Inverness County listed 54 such mills, with six in the Mabou area serviced by nine professional millers. By 1891 the county had only 21 grist mills.

Balmoral Grist Mill

To reach the mill from Tatamagouche, head south on Rte 311 for 10 km/6.2 mi to The Falls, turn left at the blue Nova Scotia Museum "key" sign, drive 2.5 km/1.6 mi, turn right onto Peter MacDonald Road, and stop at the mill parking lot. If coming from Brule, take Rte 326 south to East Earltown, travel west 5.5 km/3.4 mi to the sign, then turn left onto Peter MacDonald Road.

Balmoral Grist Mill is operated by the Nova Scotia Museum.

SIDE-SIDE TRIP:

Sutherland Steam Sawmill Museum

This is Nova Scotia's last working steam-powered sawmill/woodworking shop. Alexander Sutherland (1866–1953) of West Branch, Pictou County, built it in 1894. For the next 64 years this family-owned business made sash and door assemblies for homes. They also made horse-drawn carriages, sleighs, and sleds, and turned out "gingerbread" decorations for houses.

Steam-driven mills appeared in Nova Scotia in the 1840s and by the 1880s waterwheels were becoming obsolete. First the side-wheel type (overshot or undershot) went, and then the more modern vertical water-turbine rigs.

Unlike the waterfalls, steam mills like this had muscle enough to run several circular saws and a frame of gang saws at the same time.

Those old water-driven sawmills were quiet. You could live beside one and hear nothing much louder than the morning start-up bell. The only sounds, apart from human voices, were the swish-swish of up-and-down saws, the music of the sawfiler, the rumble of the wheel with its flock of moving pulleys and belts, and the splash and gurgle of water passing underneath. A big log could take more than an hour to saw. Sometimes the sawyer dozed as he waited for the saw to reach the log's end.

The larger ones could turn out far more lumber, shingles, and laths in a day than the old mills could manage in a week, and with fewer men.

All this came at a price. The new mills chuffed like locomotives, and their swift saws wailed. The firemen had hungry boilers to stoke, and the mill stack belched acrid black smoke. There was the loss of craftsmanship and lore. Finally, it was common for wood-fired boilers to overheat and burn down the mill and half the lumber yard. (Alexander's first mill burned.) And if a mill stood near coniferous forest and the weather had been droughty, there was a good chance the woods would burn, too. [See the **Trans Canada Highway** at the Springhill exit and the **Glooscap Trail** at Shulie.] And of course the new mills had much bigger appetites.

To reach the sawmill from Balmoral, drive east about 8 km/5 mi to East Earltown on Rte 326 and north about 10 km/6 mi to Denmark. Coming from Brule, drive south to Denmark.

Several times from July through October the Sutherland mill is fired up to saw a truckload of logs. This event, which draws hundreds of spectators, is more vivid than any printed description in a book.

Along the abandoned railroad west of the mill, beavers have built a lodge against an embankment. The lodge was occupied in recent years. Ask directions locally, and whether it is still active.

The Cobequid Mountains are maple sugar country. In March–April clouds of sweet steam billow from local sugar woods as sap is boiled to make syrup, maple cream, maple butter and maple candy. Maple Ridge Farm (6 km/3.7 mi from the pavement near New Annan) is one of several operations that welcome visitors who call ahead.

Nearly every year in December and January, North Shore newspapers carry stories of "lost seals" being found. As drift ice moves south with the Labrador Current, thousands of harp seals migrate through the Strait of Belle Isle into the Gulf of St Lawrence. A few travel as far as the Northumberland Strait. When the ice is hard-packed, seals will come ashore, startling motorists and farmers as they flop around on roads and fields. With help, most find their way back to salt water.

BACK ON THE HIGHWAY

East of Brule we enter a more rolling landscape of farmland and woodlots. Again, soft underlying sandstones and shale have produced fine beaches, some with extensive dunes. Private cottages crowd every available beach, threatening some dunes with too much ATV and foot traffic. The tidal marshes and meandering streams between low, crumbling brick-red headlands abound with great blue heron, ducks, and geese.

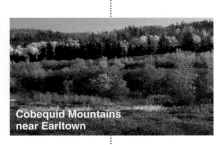

Cobequid Mountains near Earltown

Canoe River John

This stream, which rises in the Cobequid Mountains near North Earltown, is short but interesting for it offers two distinct landscapes. From East Branch to Welsford, it's a frisky mountain stream that tumbles in white foam through secluded woodland and an imposing gorge. Below Welsford, it's a tame lowland river meandering through a soft-rock tidal estuary past the village of River John to the strait.

The upper section is usually navigable in spring or fall by skillful paddlers. The only real hazard from Welsford down is contrary winds. For the gorge section, put in at East Branch River John bridge. (Drive up from Welsford about 10 km/6 mi, turn left at the sign, and continue about 1 km/0.6 mi to the river.) For the lower section, you can either paddle upstream from the small park near River John bridge or drift down from near the Welsford bridge.

In spring look for eagles fishing from tall trees near an old railway bridge about 3 km/2 mi down from Welsford. In the fall, fly-anglers sometimes catch a salmon. In winter smelt are netted and handlined through the ice of River John Harbour.

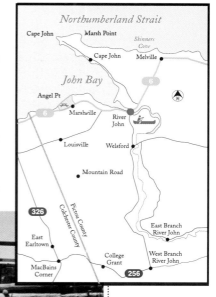

Bridge at Toney River

Between Seafoam and Caribou River one can see on a clear day the southeast corner of Prince Edward Island, 22 km/14 mi away. Often there's a car ferry in view as well, coming or going between Caribou and Wood Islands, PEI.

Just over 5 km/3 mi east of Seafoam is the village of Toney River. In the early 1800s the area was renowned for white pine, with large sawmills shipping lumber to England. One early settler is said to have filled three large sailing vessels with pine lumber as he cleared his land. It was said that every tree for miles around would yield squared timbers 36 cm/14 in or wider.

Less than1 km/0.6 mi west of Caribou River, a 6-km/3.7-mi dirt road detour takes you to Caribou Provincial Park on the Gulf Shore. From the picnic area you can drive onto the island. It's actually a series of low sandstone ridges joined by brown sand beaches and sandbars. There are open fields, white spruce thickets, and a tidal marsh. Much of it is private property, so ask permission beforehand.

SIDE TRIP: *Munroes Island*

To see undisturbed Gulf shore, exit Hwy 6 at the Pictou Rotary and drive abut 7 km/4 mi north to the Caribou Ferry terminus. Ask there for directions and perhaps a brochure. You can reach the island on foot near Widow Point, just over 4 km/2.5 mi east of the terminal on the Braeshore Road. (For some years the island has been connected to the mainland at its south end by a sandbar. There's a human-made channel to let fishing boats move in and out without using the ferry side of the harbour.)

"Undisturbed" is not quite accurate for this island. Before 1992, people raced recreational vehicles along its beaches, and developers had big plans. That year the Nature Conservancy of Canada, which solicits donations to purchase endangered special places, acquired it after negotiating with the province and two private owners. In 1997 the island became part of Caribou Provincial Park. Now the ecosystem is reverting to its natural state. Please help keep it so.

Munroes Island sits 1 km/0.6 mi offshore and consists of 110 ha/ 270 ac of white spruce and fir forest, tidal and freshwater marshes, and sand beaches spread over two larger and five smaller islands linked by sandbars. It is reached on foot by a sandspit that points south from its eastern end.

This wildlife preserve is a great place for watching birds in late summer and early fall. Besides northern harrier, osprey, and bald eagle, people have seen Bonaparte's and ring-billed gulls, teal, sandpipers, plovers, snow buntings, eiders, and greater and lesser yellowlegs. Occasionally our largest seabird, the gannet, shows up.

For many, however, the chief attraction is the teeming invertebrate life—voracious salt-marsh mosquitoes excepted. Walk the marshy shores. Observe how salt-resistant cord grass grows above the low tide mark and eel-grass below it. In the mucky shallows you'll see mud snails, ribbed mussels, blue mussels, moon snails, oysters, and sand shrimp. Tidal pools harbour hermit crabs, starfish, and amphipods (small shrimp-like crustaceans on which small sandpipers feed [see also the **Glooscap Trail** at Evangeline Beach]).

At low tide you may notice small holes in the lower layers of the sandstone cliffs. They are the work of the great piddock, a bivalve equipped with a bulky toothed "drill." Piddocks live for years at the bottom of these burrows, which are exposed at low tide. This mollusc abandons its hole only when surface erosion threatens to expose it. Then it crawls to a new spot, anchors itself to the cliff, and, waggling its two toothed shells against it, drills a new hole. (Unlike regular bivalves, whose shells have a door-type hinge, piddock shells have a special ball-and-socket joint.)

A piddock can bore 30 cm/12 in into a submerged soft cliff. Once there, it extrudes the usual two-holed siphon tube from its rear. One hole draws in seawater, from which it filters tiny food organisms; the other expels filtered water and body wastes.

Caribou and Munroe islands demonstrate two important differences between the Gulf Shore and the Atlantic/Fundy shores. The first is that the bedrock is so soft it crumbles between the fingers.

The second is that the waves are gentle, so gentle that ripple marks linger on the bottom for days.

These differences affect local marine life. For example, blue-green algae—and the periwinkles that feed on them—are scarcer in the splash zone here than at the same level on the Atlantic Coast. So are barnacles; the cliffs are too unstable. There's no kelp for the same reasons. To withstand the storms of fall and winter, these large marine algae need firm anchorage for their holdfasts. They also need deep water. Here the bottom is too sandy and the slopes too gentle. Another factor is ice scour in the winter.

Understandably, the Gulf Shore attracts more of the small, many-branched sort of marine algae (e.g., rockweed and Irish moss) than do the Fundy and Atlantic shores.

Marine algae like rockweed (Fucus) *float upright when the tide is in, and lie flat when it is out. Air-filled bladders buoy them up, and swaying with the waves prevents breakage. The tall kelps* (Laminaria) *grow in deeper water where wave action is slight.*

BOAT TRIP: *Pictou Island*
Less than an hour by boat north of Caribou lies Pictou Island. This oblong mass of sedimentary rock, 10 km/6 mi by 3 km/2 mi wide, once had thriving settlements. It still possesses farmland and forest, good drinking water, and good lobster fishing. In the mid-1800s the island supported 400 people. Today only a few brave the isolation and lack of services. In winter, drift ice prevents boat travel for weeks on end.

But a summer visit by ferry or hired boat from Caribou is pleasant. You can cycle or hike its single gravel road, enjoy its rocky northern coast and white sand beaches, and visit its heronry (hold your nose). An automated lighthouse at either end keeps vessels off the cliffs. There are no shops or hotels.

Pictou Island reminds us of the many conveniences we take for granted: low-cost electricity (windmills once supplied power for island telephones), daily mail service, prompt medical care, shopping malls. For more information, ask at the ferry terminal or in Pictou.

Backtracking down Hwy 106, we rejoin the trail at the Pictou Rotary.

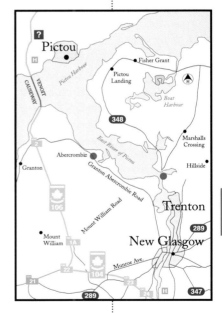

BACK ON THE HIGHWAY
At the rotary, exit onto the main road leading into town.

STOP: *Hector Heritage Quay, Pictou*
Here Pictou's first group of white settlers, six families from Pennsylvania and Maryland, came ashore from the Brig *Betsey* on June 10, 1767.

The settlement languished until 1773, when the decrepit sloop *Hector* limped into the harbour bringing 189 Highlanders—33

353

families and 25 single males—mostly from Loch Broom, Scotland. Scots came in droves to this province in the late 18th and early 19th centuries. Evicted from ancestral Highland crofts by local lairds in the pay of English sheep farmers, they were lured to the New World by land costing pennies an acre.

At the quay, visit a replica of the *Hector*, where a voice reenactment of the captain's log recounts their terrible crossing. The settlers' first act on landing was to bury a woman who had just died. Their next was to build log cabins before winter. With help from the large Mi'kmaq village nearby, they procured game and survived the winter. Thus Pictou became the "Birthplace of New Scotland." The name Pictou is Mi'kmaq for "big harbour," or perhaps "bubbling forth." Some think the latter refers to a natural tar spring which existed in historical times.

A monument in Pictou's Market Square honours these pioneers. Their steadfast belief in the value of education and good government improved the lot of citizens across Canada. A replica of their first church, built of peeled logs, stands across the harbour at Loch Broom; Sunday services are held there from time to time.

Pictou is central to a major lobster fishing zone that stretches from Malagash Point to Cape George. You can buy fresh lobsters from May to June. A July lobster festival has been held here since 1934.

STOP: *Landscape Art*

At Crombie House (the family home of businessman Frank Sobey in Abercrombie), there's a small but fine collection of Group of Seven paintings. In the 1920s this group of young Canadian artists, inspired by the work of Tom Thomson, broke with European tradition and painted Canada's rugged North as none had ever done. Their bold, colourful work provoked ridicule at home but was admired in Britain, Europe, and the US. Today it is eagerly sought by collectors.

The Sobey collection also contains work by Cornelius Kreighoff, whose paintings depict habitant life in early Québec. It is open on Wednesdays in July and August with hourly tours from 9:30 am. Ask for directions at the Pictou tourist information centre or at the Hector Centre just west of the rotary.

From the rotary, Hwy 106 takes you across Pictou Harbour on the Veniot Causeway. The harbour's trident shape is due to the convergence of the West, Middle, and East rivers as they cut their way through late Coal Age sediments to join the ancient river that became the strait. Postglacial rise in sea level has flooded these river valleys. The causeway lands at Abercrombie Point, between the middle and eastern arms. We leave Hwy 106 at Exit 2, cut across the peninsula on the Abercrombie Road to the East River, and thence to New Glasgow.

VIEW: *Kraft Mill*

One doesn't travel far in Pictou County without seeing truckloads of pulpwood, mostly low-grade spruce and fir. If it's tree-length, it's likely heading for the Kimberly-Clark mill (Scott Worldwide until 1995) to your left at Abercrombie Point. The company buys most of its wood from contractors and private woodlots, harvesting the rest on company lands scattered through central and western Nova Scotia.

If the mill's plume of steam is pointing your way, you may get a whiff of rotten egg (sulphur dioxide), a side effect of the kraft or sulphate process. (The sulphite process smells pungently resinous). Although this mill's stack emissions of SO_2 are within the 40 ppm federal standards, they can be detected over 50 km/30 mi downwind.

In the chemical pulping process, digester vats cook debarked and chipped wood chemically to break down lignin, the glue that binds wood fibres together. After waste products are removed, the resulting porridge is washed, dried, pressed into thick sheets of unbleached grey kraft, and baled for shipment to the US for remanufacture into toilet tissue, paper towels, and sanitary products.

While the mill provides hundreds of jobs to mill workers, forest workers, truckers, and service industries, it has been criticized for its clearcutting policy and its waste disposal. In the early 1990s, in response to public criticism and the high cost of protecting conifer plantations with herbicides, Scott began recycling more of its spent black liquor (waste lignin), put in a new effluent treatment facility [see Boat Harbour below], and began testing harvest methods that foster natural regeneration.

VIEW: *Cormorant Colony*

One of the best places in the Maritimes for viewing double-crested cormorants (shags) is from the causeway. Normally cormorants nest on cliffy offshore islands. These birds were drawn to the bridge pilings left when the causeway was built. When the supports rotted away in the late 1970s, DNR replaced them. The colony, undeterred by traffic and bird watchers, still thrives.

Cormorant Colony next to the causeway to Pictou

In the Orient, cormorants are trained to dive for fish; they are prevented from swallowing their catch by a neck-ring that is removed to feed them.

From April until mid-summer you can watch these big glossy black birds incubating eggs, feeding their young with fish they have caught under water, and drying their outstretched wings in the sun. Shags mainly eat coarse, non-commercial fish such as sculpin, cunners, and eels.

The secret of the cormorant's great underwater speed is in the feathers. Unlike those of other seabirds, they aren't waterproof or fluffy. This allows them to lie flat. But after each hunt the birds must stand for long periods with wings outstretched to air-dry them, thus restoring insulation.

VIEW: *Boat Harbour Lagoon*

*Nova Scotians depend on steam-driven (thermal, coal, and oil) generating plants for most of their electricity. Nova Scotia Power has plants at Point Tupper, Lingan, Glace Bay, Maccan, and Halifax-Dartmouth. It also has over 30 hydro-electric plants (of which Wreck Cove is the largest [see the **Cabot Trail**]), a few gas turbine plants (e.g., Tusket [see the **Lighthouse Route**]), one tidal facility [see the **Evangeline Trail** at Annapolis Royal], and one wind installation (Wreck Cove).*

To see what happens when black liquor from a pulp mill spills into an ocean inlet for over 25 years with inadequate treatment, visit Boat Harbour. From 1967 to 1994, the Scott mill legally piped its liquor under the East River to Boat Harbour, where the Nova Scotia Department of the Environment mixed it with air before discharging it into the strait.

During the latter years, the aerators often broke down. Often the air stank. Foam flecked the brown water and blew to and fro like toy sailboats. The outfall kept the water from freezing. Except for the algal slime that coated every submerged rock, the pond became virtually lifeless. Today, little has changed, though alders and a few white birch grow along the shore. In 1995, after years of protests by three nearby Mi'kmaq reserves and from the public, a self-contained disposal system was built.

Take Hwy 348 north from Trenton. Just beyond the exit to Marshalls Crossing you'll pass a small inlet with a sign saying "Dalmanie Christmas Trees." After 1.7 km/1 mi, watch on the right for a sign saying "Boat Harbour Treatment Facility." The lagoon is just over 2.5 km/1.5 mi along this gravel road. The new treatment facility is nearby, about 0.5 km/0.3 mi south of the harbour. There were plans to dredge and restore the old lagoon.

Electricity and Waterfowl

While retracing your way south on Rte 348 from Boat Harbour, stop opposite the Trenton Coal Generation & Car Works (near the mouth of the East River) to consider an unexpected wildlife bonus. This coal-fired electrical generation plant, one of several in Nova Scotia, has become a favourite winter rendezvous for birds and bird watchers. Before the plant started, this estuary froze over each winter. Now warm water from the plant's cooling system keeps the river open, attracting waterfowl.

Stand on the East River bridge any time between December and March and you may see mergansers (all three species), goldeneyes (two), greater scaup, bufflehead, widgeon (American and European), mallards, black ducks, and Canada geese. You will also see herring gulls and possibly black-backed, Iceland, and glaucous gulls.

If approaching from New Glasgow, cross the East River at George Street and turn left onto Rte 348. Drive north along the river for just over 3 km/2 mi until you see the plant on your right. (The road left leads about 1 km/0.6 mi to the outermost bridge on the East River to link up via Exit 2 with Hwy 106 to Pictou.)

And if you prefer to go directly to Melmerby Beach Provincial Park, our next stop, travel north via Marshalls Crossing to the strait and head east past Chance Harbour to Little Harbour. Or you can head north on Rte 289 via Almont Street and Little Mountain Road in New Glasgow.

BACK ON THE HIGHWAY

Entering New Glasgow from Hwy 106 and Abercrombie Road, we cross the East River on the George Street bridge. Turn right onto Provost Street and follow it until it merges with Archimedes, left onto Marsh Street, and thence left onto Merigomish Road (Rte 4).

You may prefer to stay on Hwy 106 to the Trans Canada Highway, where a left turn allows you to pick up Rte 4 via Exit 25 onto East Mountain Road (Rte 348) and Marsh Street. Another route from the Pictou Rotary is Rte 376 to the Trans Canada Highway via West River. This allows you to visit Green Hill Provincial Park with its 800-m/500-ft lookoff at the eastern extremity of the Cobequid Mountains. It overlooks a grand sweep of farm, forest, river, and strait. To the west rises Dalhousie Mountain, Westville and Stellarton are to the east, and Pictou Harbour lies to the north. Hang-gliders take advantage of Greenhill's steep western precipice for its brisk updraughts.

The forest around New Glasgow wears the scars of decades of brush fires. You'll see a lot of stunted aspen, white birch and pin cherry. All are pioneer species that follow disturbance, the birch and aspen arriving by windborne seed, the cherry by seeds dropped in birds' excrement. The original forest was a mix of conifers and broadleaf species, with considerable white and red pine.

What wasn't cut for masting and lumber the early fires destroyed, leaving spruce and fir, then considered less valuable. Once conifers are burned or cut and their seed source gone, broadleaf trees and shrubs take over the site. Conifers can't sprout from stumps or roots as can many deciduous trees.

Until DNR established a reliable fire control system after World War II, every spell of hot dry summer weather brought many fires that burned out of control.

"Merigomish" is Mi'kmaq for "place of merry-making." Long before the modern Olympics, natives held their "Summer Games" here, with contests of running, leaping, throwing, and wrestling. Abundant clams provided a ready source of food. At Big Island they had a burial ground.

Saltmarsh near Merigomish

Some maintain that Prince Henry Sinclair, Earl of Orkney, saw the strait from this lookoff in the summer of 1398, then followed his Mi'kmaq guides along the strait to Baie Verte, NB, and thence overland to present-day Parrsboro and Cape d'Or, where they say he overwintered.

Like Pictou, New Glasgow was built on the site of a large Mi'kmaq village.

A Note on Fire Weather

Hot, dry May days make firefighters edgy. That's when people rake up their yards and burn trash. On such days, untended fires can race through dead grass to nearby woods in minutes. Other common forest fire sources are campers, smokers, and anglers, land-clearing crews who lack proper equipment, and town dumps. Besides these fires there are always some arson and lightning fires. DNR issues free burning permits and instructions to any who ask.

The New Glasgow basin is almost a metaphor for the 19th-century Maritime economy, which went from a boom in lumbering and shipbuilding and agriculture to a boom in manufacturing, followed by a slow decline after the 1880s.

Blessed with ample coal, the "Five Towns" (Pictou, Trenton, Westville, Stellarton, and New Glasgow) became a major manufacturing centre after the mid-1800s. North America's first all-metal rails were cast here, and its first stationery steam engine operated here. (One of the earliest locomotives, the *Albion* (1854) is displayed in Stellarton's park.) There were iron and steel foundries, machine shops, forges, and brick and tile works. Hundreds of Nova Scotians left their farms and fishing boats to work here.

Over 300 million years ago, the New Glasgow basin was part of a steamy jungle near the equator, probably a river estuary. Large amphibians and invertebrates roamed through swamps of huge club mosses, fern trees, and horsetails. As many as 70 times, floods of sand and clay buried all life, after which the region would sink and a new jungle would grow. In time, the layers were pressed into rock. The Foord seam, one of the world's thickest, is 12 m/39 ft through.

But soft coal is gassy. A series of mine explosions or "bumps," coupled with worldwide economic depression in the 1930s, crippled the industry. The 1950s shift to oil finished the area as an industrial centre. The tragic loss of 26 men at the Westray Mine in Plymouth in May 1992 was a further blow. In recent years, the sifting of waste heaps has recovered much useable coal. Today the area's largest employer is the Sobey's grocery chain, based in Stellarton. [See also the **Trans Canada Highway** at Stellarton for the Nova Scotia Museum of Industry, opened in 1994.]

Cinnabar vs Ragwort!

Every summer in this area a biological battle is waged. Tansy ragwort (stinking willy), a yellow-flowered composite plant that can poison cattle, is very common in ditches, pastures, and burnt ground from here to northern Cape Breton. To control its spread, government weed specialists introduced the cinnabar moth. Its larvae eat only ragwort and in some areas can keep it in check.

This is an example of biological control, which uses parasites or predators to attack pest species. Dr Pickett of the Kentville agricultural research station pioneered the method in Canada, using it to control oystershell scale in Annapolis Valley apple orchards in the 1920s. Dr Douglas Embree of Forestry Canada likewise defused a winter moth epidemic on deciduous trees in Nova Scotia in the 1950s.

The convoluted coast from Caribou Harbour to Lower Barneys River contrasts sharply with Pictou Harbour's regular shoreline. We see coves within coves, curving sandspits and sandbars, and numerous islands with irregular shapes. All point to flooding of coastal lowlands underlain by soft rock. [See also the **Lighthouse Route**, Mahone Bay.]

East of Pine Tree, Rte 4 merges with the Trans Canada Highway for a few kilometres, then exits east onto Rte 245 for the 55-km/ 34-mi trip around Cape George.

Sandbar (Melmerby Beach)

Melmerby Beach

SIDE TRIP: *Drive a Tombolo*

The long line of sand visible off Lower Barneys River is Melmerby Beach, the Gulf Shore's longest sandbar and one of the province's finest bathing spots. The bar links Merigomish Big Island to the mainland and therefore is called a tombolo. [See also the **Fleur-de-lis Trail** at Point Michaud and the **Lighthouse Route** at Crescent Beach.] It was built from eroded sandstone and glacial gravel transported by longshore currents. Driven by northeast winds sweeping down from Cape Breton Island, waves pick up sand from the exposed shore, draw it into deeper water, and deposit it farther along.

Besides being a good place to observe dune and salt-marsh ecology, it's a favourite birding site during migration. Birders have seen not only winter wren, grey catbird and various warblers, but flycatchers (there are lots of blackfly, mosquito, horsefly and deerfly to catch), grey jay, pine siskin, two kinds of crossbills, and the ruby-throated hummingbird.

Drive out on the bar and note the boulder wall that keeps storm waves from breaching the dunes. From here to the island, drifted

Ruby-throated hummingbird

sand rises in high, multiple ridges that are continually sculpted by wind. The broken ridges along the backshore (landward side) are old dunes that the sea is slowly submerging. In winter smelt are fished through the ice in the harbour.

About 2 km/1.2 mi east of Lower Barneys River, watch for DNR signs to Merigomish. Take the dirt road north to Paterson Point. Just over 5 km/3 mi west, near the village of Kings Head on Little Harbour, is Melmerby Beach Provincial Park—also located on a tombolo.

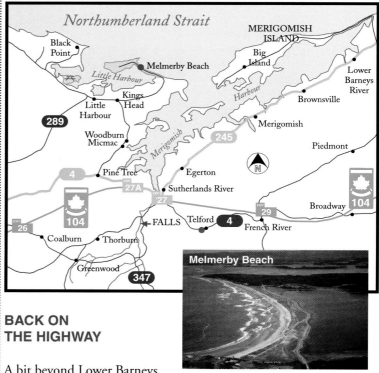

Melmerby Beach

BACK ON THE HIGHWAY

A bit beyond Lower Barneys River is the village of Ponds. It was named for local bodies of water (e.g., Galt Pond) enclosed by creeping sand spits many years ago. This is how longshore currents "even out" coastlines.

After Knoydart we leave the soft bedrock behind to follow the so-called Hollow Fault escarpment northeast. The hard Silurian formations here erode too slowly to produce sandbars or dunes. The only decent harbour, Malignant Cove (named for a wrecked ship), sits in a zone of softer Carboniferous rock hemmed in by Precambrian volcanics. [See also the **Fleur-de-lis Trail** at Fourchu.]

From here the Sunrise Trail follows Rte 337 around Cape George. The cape is the point of the triangle called the Pictou-Antigonish Highlands. Like the Cobequid Mountains, they are flattish on top, but generally older and less high, with more evidence of volcanic action.

Within 2 miles after we struck the [Antigonish-Pictou] road we passed one stream running N. which we were told empties into Marigamish [sic].... We were informed at Pictou that there is a large tract of barren land S. and S.E. of this place.
—Titus Smith Jr, **The Eastern Tour,** 1801

LEG-STRETCHER: *Arisaig Provincial Park*

Along the beach at Arisaig you can collect fern-like fossils uncovered by wave action in tilted blue Silurian shales. Turn left at the church and park at the wharf. At low tide you can hike west along the shore past an old wharf and across McDougalls Brook (wadeable except in spring). Check tide times; the beach is narrow and the cliffs steep. Please confine your fossil picking to fallen material; prying material from the cliffs is illegal.

This park has a 565-m/1,850-ft hiking trail. It starts at the picnic park's northwest corner (i.e., uphill from the entrance) and descends through old white spruce and alder thickets to a railed wooden lookoff. Here McDougalls Brook has carved a steep ravine in deep glacial gravel. About 2 m/6 ft above the present beach there's a distinct bench or ancient marine terrace cut by waves when the land was pressed down under glacial ice. [See also the **Cabot Trail** at Chimney Corner and Aspy Bay, and the **Glooscap Trail** at Parrsboro.]

Near the park entrance there's a fine view of the strait and a helpful interpretive centre.

From Arisaig and other points, challenging hiking trails cross the Pictou-Antigonish Highlands. Consult a tourist information centre or Michael Haynes' *Hiking Trails of Nova Scotia*.

All along the flanks of these highlands one sees many abandoned farms, especially at Livingstone Cove. They are being colonized from the rear by alders (wet clay soils) and by white or pasture spruce (sandy soils).

Like much of eastern Nova Scotia, this district was settled by Scots. Clearing sugar maple and beech from the slopes and spruce and pine from the flats was hard work for untrained axemen. The coast is exposed and windy, the intervales prone to frost. By the late 1890s most of the settlers had emigrated to New England or gone West. But some stayed; their descendants still farm and log and fish here.

In clear weather from the lookoff just east of Doctors Brook you can see the long, low profile of Prince Edward Island. Geologists say the strait, which is only 20–30 fathoms (37–55 m/121–180 ft) deep, was once dry land, a shallow valley watered by one or more major rivers.

STOP: *Livingstone Cove Terrace*

If you go down the 1-km/0.6-mi dirt road to the government wharf and look southwest, you should be able to see a sort of bench above the present beach. Unlike the fairly recent terrace at Arisaig, this one was cut into reddish sedimentary bedrock some 600 million years ago. The cliffs immediately above this marine terrace are 200 million years younger (Middle Devonian); the intervening material is missing. The gravel along the bench was deposited during the last Ice Age.

SIDE TRIP: *Cape George Light*

For a dramatic view of eastern Prince Edward Island, western Cape Breton's highlands, and St Georges Bay, exit Rte 245 approximately

20 km/12 mi east of Exit 27 onto Lighthouse Road and drive 0.7 km/0.4 mi on the good gravel road to the end. Like most Canadian lighthouses today, the Cape George facility is automated and modest in size. The cape itself is a much-faulted knob of hard igneous and metamorphic rock dating roughly from the formation of the supercontinent Pangaea. Birders consider the cape a good place to look for ocean (pelagic) birds.

Ballantynes Cove

There's another lookoff above the fishing village of Ballantynes Cove that covers St Georges Bay and much of the Antigonish basin. A nearby lighthouse was erected around 1895. Go down on the wharf and talk to a white-haired fisherman about life in this old fishing village.

At a lookoff 1.6 km/1 mi farther south, where Marsh Road meets Rte 337, there's an sign interpreting local geology.

BACK ON THE HIGHWAY

The drive south along St Georges Bay toward Antigonish is full of hills and dips and curves and resembles the **Glooscap Trail** near Cape d'Or. Glimpses of the bay alternate with rock faces and lush intervales. South of MacIsaac Point, look for lumpy karst topography characterized by sinkholes and small ponds where rain has dissolved the gypsum bedrock.

STOP: *Peppermint Cliffs*

At Crystal Cliffs, one km/0.6 mi south of MacIsaac Point, is a beautiful 65-m/200-ft vertical outcrop of pink crystalline gypsum striped with white limestone. These rocks mark the northern rim of the Antigonish Basin, an eroded Carboniferous trough bounded by highlands to the north and west. It extends inland to James River and Lochaber, and northeast to Havre Boucher. [See also the **Trans Canada Highway** at South Gut St Anns and the **Glooscap Trail** near Windsor.]

Like the New Glasgow and Pugwash basins, this area contains salt—hence the name Salt Springs near Antigonish and Greenhill.

Roger Burrow's *Where to Find Birds in Canada* lists a colony of great cormorants near here, accessible via Jimtown Road about 1 km/ 0.6 mi south of Antigonish Harbour. Ask locally for precise directions if interested.

From here to Antigonish (Mi'kmaq, possibly "five-forked rivers of fish"; for another translation see **Trans Canada Highway**), the low coast assumes the typical soft-rock pattern of beaches, dunes, bay bars, and low convoluted shoreline that we saw around Merigomish and Caribou. The deep inlets of Pomquet and Tracadie Harbour likewise reveal coastal flooding since the last Ice Age.

Antigonish Harbour

From Mahoney Beach to Monks Head a massive barrier beach extends for some 10 km/6 mi, with a smaller arc toward Pomquet Point. Fresh water flowing from the basin's several creeks and rivers maintains a gap in the western sector that is wide enough for boat traffic. You can walk to this beach from the Mahoney Beach parking lot (about 2 km/1.2 mi).

This system of dunes and tidal marshes is managed as a Provincial Wildlife Area. And near the edge of town, where big ships used to dock, is the Antigonish Landing Wildlife Sanctuary. A loop walking/ jogging trail explores the estuary system. Eagles and ospreys are common around here in summer. For directions ask locally or at the Visitor Information Centre (Exits 31, 32, **Trans Canada Highway**).

...[at] Crystal Cliffs... colonies of great cormorant and black guillemot share the limelight with feeding bald eagle and osprey.
– Roger Burrows, **Birding in Atlantic Canada**, 1988

STOP: *Pomquet Beach*

This provincial park (named for the nearby village, which was settled in 1761 by Acadians from St Malo, France) contains Nova Scotia's largest mainland dune system and one of its finest examples of dune

Greenhill

Piping plover or "peeps" breed on Pomquet Beach in early summer. Be careful not to walk near their nest sites. [For a fuller treatment of this endangered species, see the **Marine Drive** *near Cole Harbour and the* **Evangeline Trail** *at Evangeline Beach.] Peeps also nest on both sides of Antigonish Harbour and there is an island colony of common and Arctic tern. Goodly numbers of great black-backed gulls also occur year-round.*

succession. Unlike most dune systems, it has been spreading seaward and growing higher since the 1980s. This is because of the shore's unusual abundance of sediment.

Typically the fore-dunes rise more than 4 m/ 13 ft above high tide. Behind them, more than a dozen dunes march landward like ocean waves, each older than the last, into the scattered pines and oaks. To the rear, tidal flooding has led to marsh development.

The dunes are so high and stable that at least 39 plant species find a home in the sheltered hollows. One of these is poison ivy; perhaps it protects the local vegetation?

On entering Antigonish, Rte 337 merges with Main Street, crosses the bridge over Wrights River, and exits east onto Hwy 4 to join the **Trans Canada Highway** (Hwy 104) 3 km/2 mi west of Lower South River. About 4 km/2.5 mi east of Pomquet Forks, our route leaves the 104 for Tracadie and Havre Boucher.

South of St. Georges Bay, the **Sunrise Trail** continues across an undulating lowland of farms and woodlots intercut by occasional small streams. Sheltered on three sides, its climate tempered by the bay, this basin enjoys weather almost as warm as Tatamagouche's. The fertile soils derive from shale, reddish sandstones, and conglomerates. The latter consist of cemented pebbles and sand and are sometimes called pudding stone.

Toward Havre Boucher, harder and older inland rocks crowd toward the coast, making the landscape more rugged.

Beyond Tracadie Harbour the supply of coastal sediment again dwindles, and we see no more big barrier beaches. The spits and bars at Linwood Harbour, Cape Jack, and Havre Boucher are much more modest.

As Hwy 4 curves southward toward the Strait of Canso to rejoin the **Trans Canada Highway**, we see across the water Cape Breton's Creignish Hills to the northeast. To the south is the thin S-curve of the world's deepest causeway and the frowning precipice of Cape Porcupine, from which the fill was quarried. Just before the causeway, the **Marine Drive** Rte 344 exits to the right. On the Cape Breton side you can access the **Trans Canada Highway**, and the **Ceilidh**, **Fleur-de-lis** and **Marconi** trails.

Dune at Antigonish Harbour

Bras d'Or Scenic Nature Drive

Sydney River counter-clockwise to Ben Eoin,
St Peters, Grand Narrows, and return
250 km/155 mi

Middle River Delta at Nyanza

OVERVIEW

This route circumnavigates most of Cape Breton's gentle inland sea. It's a good way to unwind from busier roads. Almost anywhere you stop, it's quiet. The cry of birds and chirp of crickets may be the loudest sounds. You can sit on a bone-white driftwood log in early morning and watch the rising sun unwrap distant Iona from skeins of white mist. Small waves lap the cobbled shore with a sound like kittens drinking. You can admire tapestries of orange and gold reflected in the lake on a still October afternoon. Perhaps you'll find a purple-flowered sea-rocket. Or you may see a red fox, backlit by the sun, trotting in a coat of flame.

Looping around the long inlets of St Peter's, West Bay, and East Bay, we have a water backdrop all the way. Though the lake is cradled among hard-rock uplands 400–600 million years old—North Mountain, Marble Mountain, Sporting Mountain, and the Boisdale and East Bay hills—the shore itself is seldom rugged. From a submerged lowland, the land rises gently up to old farms colonized by spruce and fir. At the rear of this rise, the Carboniferous lowlands meet the older uplands, which pose as muscular slopes and ravines mantled in sugar maple, yellow birch, and beech.

Geologically, the basin is part of a vanished Coal Age sea floorbed with limestone, sandstone, and gypsum, with a fringe of Precambrian volcanics along East Bay. Its topography runs like a series of accordion pleats oriented northeast/southwest, with the grooves deepened by glaciers and flooded by the postglacial sea. Since the lake is almost landlocked, the result is a cottager's dream, a sailor's delight. North Atlantic storms cannot get in, tides are slight, and reefs are rare.

THE TOUR BEGINS

From Exit 6 on the Trans Canada Highway we join Highway 4 and head southeast over rolling farmland along Sydney River. The river lies in the same faulted valley as East Bay. Near Coxheath it was partly dammed by glacial drift, which makes it sluggish and wide until at Blacketts Lake it fills the valley. [See also the **Fleur-de-lis Trail** at Albert Bridge.]

VIEW: *East Bay*

A few minutes beyond the village of Portage (on the old boat carry between Blacketts Lake and Bras d'Or Lake), East Bay opens before us. To the southwest, far down the lake, are Sporting and Marble mountains. To the north are the burly Boisdale Hills; ahead and to the left are the low East Bay Hills. It's a picture to remember, especially in October.

Observe how remarkably straight the near shore is. It marks one of the island's dramatic geological folds. The water offshore is as deep as an ocean. Yet with only two natural openings to the Atlantic, the tidal range of these bays is only 0.5 m/20 in—a fourth that of the open sea. Another difference is the scarcity of sandspits and bay bars around the lake. The waves are too small, and in most places sedimentary rock is scarce. A few spits occur where soft rocks abut the shore, but even there they are small. On the Atlantic and eastern gulf shores things are quite different. There, great breakers continually grind bedrock into sand, scoop it off the bottom, dump it near shore, and sculpt it as wind and currents dictate.

Eagles

STOP: *Ben Eoin Provincial Park*

This secluded park and Natural Heritage Area (pronounced Ben-*yon*, after *Eoin*, Gaelic for Jonathan, a local pioneer) occupies an old farm fronting on deciduous slopes. It's a good place to spot bald eagles all summer and Bonaparte's gulls in the fall. The eagles feed on flounder, eels, and sculpin; the gulls come to fatten on Atlantic silversides, a minnow. For great views and a closer look at upland forest, climb the short steep trail at the back.

VIEW: *Bald Eagles*

This shore is one of the best places east of Alaska to see eagles; another is River Denys Basin on the far shore. The likeliest places are brook ravines opening onto shallow coves. If you see none flying, check the tallest lakeside trees for telltale white heads. They prefer a tall white pine with a dead top.

Although eagles can spot a mouse from a kilometre high, most of their time is spent scanning the shoreline and shallows for dead fish, their chief food. They also eat road kills and farm refuse—but will take live fish, ducks (on the wing), and other small prey.

As early as February, in time for spring breakup and open water, mated pairs—bald eagles mate for life—sail in from the Annapolis Valley and the Eastern Seaboard to prepare a nest. Instead of building a new one, they repair an existing one with dry sticks, which they fetch in their talons. Over the years these flat-topped nests may swell to 2.5 m/8 ft across and nearly 3 m/10 feet deep. (Osprey nests attain about half that size.) It takes a sturdy tree to hold an old eagle nest.

In this nest the female lays one to three eggs, dull white and about 7.5 cm/3 in long. Incubation takes about five weeks. Since the eggs hatch a day or two apart, the eldest eaglet gains a size advantage and may starve out its sibling(s). Both adults take turns feeding the ravenous young until they can fly. By September the nest is again empty.

Between Ben Eoin and Middle Cape, watch to the north for four fine sandspits enclosing small coves. They were fashioned from the only available soft shoreline rock, a sliver of late Coal Age rock centred on Big Pond. The sandspit off Big Pond Centre, untied from the shore at both ends, bends like a giant boomerang across Lochmore Harbour.

STOP: *Big Pond*

Home of Cape Breton singer Rita MacNeil, Big Pond offers daily eagle-watching tours and nature hikes. If you feel like a hike, visit the 7-m/23-ft waterfall on a branch of Breac Brook, total walking distance about 2 km/1.2 mi one way.

SIDE TRIP: *Lake Country*

Sheltered between the volcanic East Bay Hills and the granitic Mira Hills is a broad, eroded trough of younger sedimentary rock with

The names of the two largest lakes, Loch Lomond and Lake Uist (pronounced Yoo-ist)—echo the settlers' Scottish origins.

good soils and irregular lakes. To this country in 1827 came many Highland Scots. Tackling the dense forests of spruce, hemlock, yellow birch, fir, and maple with characteristic energy, within two generations they had cleared wide tracts of cropland and pasture. After the 1880s exodus to industrialized cities, most of the land returned to woodland [see also the **Sunrise Trail** near Knoydart and the **Trans Canada Highway** near Glen Bard]. This "second-growth forest" was dominated by balsam fir and white spruce, aggressive species noted for colonizing vacant lands. In the 1980s an epidemic of spruce budworm devastated these stands. A woman from the area described the hills as grey. Today natural regeneration of young fir is greening the hills once more. [See also the **Cabot Trail** east of Pleasant Bay and the **Trans Canada Highway** near Barneys River.]

To access this area, take the Loch Lomond Road from Big Pond after asking for directions. Ask about a marsh where ducks, rails, and bitterns can be found near Enon at the Mira end of the lakes. Along the way, check the lakes and ponds for loons. Many nest here. Pause now and then to explore roadside fir and spruce thickets, especially in the first 10 km/6 mi. Summer or winter, there's a good chance you'll see two of its characteristic birds, the reclusive spruce grouse and the grey jay. The spruce grouse, dark brown with a red eyebrow patch, is a tree-dwelling version of ruffed grouse, and lives on conifer shoots. The grey jay or whiskey-jack, a cousin of the blue jay, lives on insects, seeds, and carrion.

From Enon, explore the Glengarry Valley, whose numerous woods roads offer owl and hawk sightings during migration. Again, inquire locally for the best spots.

At Loch Lomond village one can exit southeast either to Grand River or Framboise, both on the **Fleur-de-lis Trail.** One can also canoe from Loch Lomond to Grand River (portaging the falls), a distance of roughly 18 km/11 mi.

All these roads are gravel with minimal signage. To avoid getting lost (any more than you want), consult the Nova Scotia map book, which shows all gravel roads, including many forest access roads.

BACK ON THE HIGHWAY

STOP: *Irish Cove*
Watch for the routed wooden sign and picnic tables of this pleasant provincial park. The cove is here because a wedge of soft limestone allowed wave action to carve a nook in resistant volcanic basalt. After an onshore gale the cobble beach can exhibit distinct wave-built berms (benches). The olive-grey cliff jutting from the bluish cobble stones is 300 million years older than the limestone. It consists of lava from the Earth's mantle and has a bread-like texture from bubbles of trapped gases that expanded as the molten rock pushed toward the surface. There's a limestone quarry just inland. Cobble beaches form where the bedrock breaks down in angular chunks;

shingle beaches come from layered rock. [See also the **Evangeline Trail** at Belliveau Cove and the **Cabot Trail** at Broad Cove.]

Nearing Johnstown, we leave the lumpy volcanic terrain and enter a Coal Age landscape flooded since the last Ice Age. This is signalled by the twin Red Islands off Johnstown and by the archipelago of low headlands, islands, and coves from here to St Peter's. Cormorants, gulls, and mergansers nest on the Red Islands.

Another way to access the Lake Lomond district is via the Mount Auburn road, which exits east between the communities of Johnstown Harbour and Hay Cove.

VIEW: *Mi'kmaq Religious Centre*
Off Soldiers Cove in the mouth of St Peter's Inlet lies Chapel Island, where there is a sizable First Nations community. In 1792, Mi'kmaq converts to Catholicism built a chapel here after two chiefs, Francis Bask and Michael Tomma, petitioned the military. The island is still a revered site for powwows and religious gatherings, some lasting nearly a week, which draw Mi'kmaq from all over Nova Scotia.

Less than 1 km/0.6 mi west of the St Peter's Canal [for more detail see the **Fleur-de-lis Trail**], we head out around the Sporting Mountain peninsula. (Watch for the sign to French Cove and Cape George Harbour.) Along the shore there are glimpses of the East Bay and Boisdale hills to the north, and of North Mountain with the villages of Marble Mountain and Malagawatch near its northern tip. This is a spectacular drive in sunny October weather when the fall colour is at its peak and the lake is cobalt blue.

As noted above, the shores of West Bay are prime bald eagle country, especially near the head. The land is not only well wooded with many coves and shallows, but sparsely populated, since most of its farms were abandoned in the late 1800s. The drive along the winding west shore road is largely variations on a theme of spruce and white birch ridges, aspen hollows, and glimpses of lake and islands, as if you were leaving civilization behind.

STOP: *Limestone Town*
Marble Mountain is another town that boomed and went bust. [See also the **Trans Canada Highway** at Londonderry; the **Glooscap** Trail at Cape d'Or; and the **Evangeline Trail** at Ellershouse.]

Quarrying began after Nicholas Brown, a geologist from Prince Edward Island, found a seam of superior marble in 1868. Soon the stone was in great demand in Halifax and elsewhere. By 1910 the quarry employed over a thousand people, more than 700 of them miners. They blasted the slabs loose and sent them to the cutting mill for custom shaping and polishing.

Meanwhile, Dominion Steel of Sydney leased local quarries for limestone to flux impurities from iron. For a time the village echoed to the roar of steam rock crushers and the clank of conveyers loading ships for Sydney. But demand for marble fell, Dominion didn't renew its lease, and the industry all but expired. Today, only rusting scraps of machinery remain. In recent years L. E. Shaw of Shubenacadie has quarried agricultural limestone here.

Visit the village's small museum, which recounts its glory days.

It seems ironic that when we want durability and grace in a building, a monument, or a grave marker, we turn to rock made from the bodies of the most fragile of sea creatures. Marble is hardened limestone. Limestone consists of the cemented shells of microscopic zooplankton, which swarm in the sunlit upper layers of all oceans. When these organisms die, their ornate calcium cases fall, twinkling like frost crystals, to the dark ocean floor perhaps a kilometre below. There they form a grey ooze that thickens and hardens into chalk or limestone or, if pressed and heated enough, into marble. The face of Marble Mountain is at least 600 million years old and was many thousands of centuries old when it was lifted into the air.

To reach the quarry, continue east through the village to the picnic area on the right. Opposite the park, a gated path leads to a point overlooking the great bite in the mountainside. Be careful; the path is steep in places. If you don't feel like climbing, there's another striking view of the mountain from the beach below the park.

From Marble Mountain our tour continues past Malagawatch and around the rugged North Mountain promontory past Valley Mills to Orangedale on sheltered Denys Basin. Unlike North Mountain, this is soft-rock country, a landscape of low hills and convoluted waterways. It is also one of North America's prime bald eagle sites.

If you want to stay on pavement, detour from Orangedale (but first check out its interesting 19th-century train museum) through the village of Iron Mines to Hwy 105 (Trans Canada Highway), proceed east past Whycocomagh, and take Exit 6 to Little Narrows. From there Rte 223 takes you via Iona to Grand Narrows.

For a short cut to Little Narrows, follow the West Alba road east from Orangedale along the CNR line to Estmere. It saves more than 15 km/9 mi — but after 2 km/1.2 mi the pavement peters out.

STOP: *Little Narrows Quarry*
Most people know that interior walls in North American homes are usually sheathed in "gyproc"—powdered gypsum pressed between

The settlers decided to leave the Indian name [Malagawatch] as ... it was easier to pronounce it than translate it to "the triangular piece of land formed by a river on two sides and a lake or larger body of water on the third side."
– **Truro Daily News**
July 17, 1980

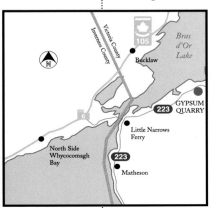

thick grey kraft paper. Fewer know that Nova Scotia has long been the world's largest supplier of raw gypsum. Gypsum, like rock salt, is an evaporite. Ours was deposited during ancestral Nova Scotia's long tropical sojourn in the belly of the supercontinent Pangaea. [See also the **Glooscap Trail** near Windsor and the **Halifax-Dartmouth Area Nature Tour** at Milford.]

Canadian Gypsum Company Limited operates three quarries at Little Narrows on the Barra Strait. All are open-pit operations. The quarry wall is drilled and dynamited, and the loose rock trucked in giant off-road vehicles to conveyer belts that feed it to the top of a tower. Inside the tower it descends through a crusher and sorting screens to emerge as a coarse white powder. Another conveyer moves the gypsum over the highway to a warehouse and wharf for shipment. During the three months when the strait is frozen, the quarry is shut down.

Take Exit 6 off Hwy 105, cross on the ferry, turn left, and drive 3.5 km/ 2 mi on Rte 223 to the Little Narrows Gypsum Company operation. For a panoramic view, follow the public road past the plant (under the conveyer) and park at the top of the next hill, a spoil heap. A short climb gives a view of a quarry big enough to hold several football fields. The dumpling-shaped ridges to the east consist of unwanted rubble. Over the years, frost and rain have gullied them badly. To counter erosion, the company has seeded the slopes with grass and legumes. Today, all rock debris is returned to the quarry. To explore further, return to the quarry office near the crusher and ask permission. The company has literature.

Backtracking to Little Narrows, we return to Rte 223 and head south past Estmere to Iona. Unlike North Mountain, this landscape is one of low hills.

STOP: *Highland Village*

Twelve kilometres/7.5 mi west of Iona on Route 223, overlooking beautiful Barra Strait, is a place that will make you think you're in Scotland. This restoration shows the lifeways and accommodations of a 19th-century community of crofters. It also demonstrates how they adapted to life in New Scotland.

A logical place to begin your tour of this 17-ha/ 43-ac village is the traditional Hebridean "black house," a windowless, thatch-roofed hut of undressed stone. From there you can progress to a New World log house, then to frame (sawn lumber) houses of 1830, 1865, and 1900. There's also a wool carding mill, a blacksmith's forge, a general store, and a 1920s schoolhouse. Along the footpaths, gentle long-horned Highland cattle with

Highland Village

Long-horned Highland cattle

Black House at Highland Village

flowing red coats gaze from behind split rail fences. A small garden displays traditional herbs.

These New World Scots toiled from dawn to dusk, but they made time for fun. Highland Village Day celebrates this heritage in August with traditional Cape Breton music.

Iona's first settlers were Barra-born soldiers from Scotland who fought at Louisbourg in 1758. When Donald Og MacNeil, Donald MacNeil, and Finlay Glas MacKenzie sailed through these narrows, they were so impressed that after Louisbourg fell they staked out land here and later fetched their kin from Scotland. They called the place Caolas nam Barrach *(the Barra Men's Strait).*

STOP: *Soft Forestry*

While in the area, look in on a kinder brand of forestry. Route 223 Forest Management Co-op at Iona manages local woodlots under contract for their owners. To explain good forest stewardship, it has developed a self-guided interpretive trail system through 567 ha/1,400 ac of Acadian upland mixed forest. The hikes range from 2.5 to 9 km (1.6 mi to 5.6 mi) and explain local history and land use. Signs identify spruce and pine plantations and describe thinnings, shelterwood harvesting sites, and wildlife habitat projects. Ask about the Highland Hill view that takes in all four Cape Breton counties.

There are signs at McKinnons Harbour and at Jamesville West directing motorists to Barra Glen Road. Follow them 3 km/1.9 mi to the trails.

White spruce

From Iona, before crossing the Grand Narrows bridge, detour north 2.8 km/1.7 mi on Rte 223 to see the striking exposures of gypsum along the shore, including a flowerpot island. Then backtrack and cross the bridge to head east around the heel of the Boisdale Hills. If you'd like a break, just across the bridge on the north side is MacCormack Picnic Park, a spruce-shaded field overlooking the lake.

The East Bay road takes us around the broad sweep of Pipers Cove with its miniature bay bar and pond, past the drowned valley of Benacadie Brook, and around the corner past Castle Bay (with one of the best sandspits we've seen) and Christmas Island to Eskasoni.

STOP: *Mi'kmaq Community*

The name of this reserve, *Eskasoni*, may mean either "still water" or "green boughs." Housing over 2,000 people, it is Nova Scotia's largest native community. It is centred on the mouth of Indian Brook, a traditional source of fresh water and of fish and a natural entry to hunting and trapping areas in the rugged Boisdale Hills. In the words of long-time resident Rita Joe:

> *A winding bay embraces the land*
> *With spirited hills a protection.*
> *The giving seas and the prize*
> *My hunger ease, lifegiving.*
> — Rita Joe, LL.D., O.C.
> "Eskasoni," **Songs of Rita Joe,** 1996

The reserve runs from Castle Bay along the rugged shoreline almost to Island View, and inland about 4 km/2.5 mi. Low islands—among them Christmas Island—shelter the shore; sandbars cradle quiet ponds, which draw geese and ducks. The big-leaved common shrubs along the road are Japanese knotweed (two kinds), perennial plants of the buckwheat family. [See also the **Evangeline Trail** near Harbourville.]

Stop at the local craft shops to talk with the people and perhaps purchase a gift for someone back home.

LEG-STRETCHER:

About 4 km/2.5 mi east of Island View there's a fine gorge here and, about 1 km/0.6 mi up, a pretty waterfall. The easiest way to it is along (and in) the brook. Sneakers are best for good traction, plus they dry fast. Wool socks are an asset, since wet wool keeps you warm. The cascade has a deep plunge pool, so don't leave children unattended.

Back on the road, we continue up the narrowing shore past the rugged hills of Northside East Bay (opposite Ben Eoin) and along the forested flats. Now the bay is less than a kilometre wide. About 1 km/0.6 mi from its head, a gravel road cuts across to the other shore on a sandbar. Exit here to Hwy 4, which gives you a view out the bay and saves a few kilometres.

At Sydney River the tour ends.

To access the **Trans Canada Highway** (Hwy 105), take Exit 4 west to Coxheath, turn left onto Hwy 125, and follow it past North Sydney to the Trans Canada Highway, Exit 20. To reach the **Marconi** and **Fleur-de-lis** trails, follow Hwy 4 through Sydney to Glace Bay (Hwy 125 is shorter, but misses downtown Sydney). For more information about the town and its steelmaking history, see the **Trans Canada Highway Nature Tour.**

Digby Neck Scenic Nature Drive

Digby to Brier Island
73 km/45 mi, one way

Digby Neck from the mainland

OVERVIEW

Digby Neck from the air is a curving, nicked blade with two breaks—one at the tip, the other a third in from the tip—with the pieces slightly offset. Geologically the neck is a western extension of North Mountain that slopes gradually down from Digby Gut until it reaches sea level at Brier Island. It is bounded on the north by the outer Bay of Fundy and on the south by St Marys Bay, which is a flooded extension of the Annapolis Valley.

The peninsula and its two islands comprise up to 17 layers of dark grey basaltic lava. The lava, which welled out of fissures along the Fundy rift valley as the North Atlantic opened 200 million years ago, also covers the floor of Fundy. As the lava cooled on contact with air, it developed polygonal columns, which the sea and glaciation later exposed, at Brier Island in particular. At intervals the peninsula is scored across by narrow valleys that follow ancient faults.

With ocean on both sides, the neck is more truly marine than any other part of Nova Scotia. While this isn't obvious near Digby, it becomes more so as you travel west. Even though the road follows a sheltering central groove (where softer rock has been eroded from between harder layers), the stunted spruce, fir, and alders obviously suffer from exposure.

It's interesting to observe how inland tree species like maple, yellow birch, and red spruce drop out as you travel west. You'll see far more white spruce, white birch, and aspen here. Toward Brier Island these give way. In place, alder, willow, and sheep laurel occupy

375

Digby Gut from Bear River Lookoff

the high ground, while sphagnum moss and sedges dominate wet hollows.

This tour entails two ferry crossings—one at Petit Passage to Long Island, the second at Grand Passage to Brier Island. Though annoying to anyone in a hurry, they are part of the charm. The ferry service was established in 1822 and runs daily on the hour (and nights if need be). The charge is refreshingly low.

THE TOUR BEGINS

After Smiths Cove on the **Evangeline Trail**, where Hwy 1 merges with Hwy 101, take Exit 26 north, go almost 1 km/0.6 mi, then bear right onto Route 303. If you want to bypass Digby, go another 2 km/1.2 mi, turn north onto Victoria Street, and follow it about 1 km/0.6 mi to Rte 217, which takes you west toward Rossway, East Ferry, and Westport. If you want to soak up Digby's pleasant seaport atmosphere, continue past Victoria Street and follow Warwick down to Water Street. This again puts you on Rte 217. For local history be sure to take in the Admiral Digby Museum.

Like many fishing communities built around rocky harbours, part of Digby's downtown stands on stilts out over the harbour. Roam the wharves and talk to fishermen and other mariners. Herring is important here, but scallops are more important. In fact, Digby is home port to the world's largest scallop fleet. Scallops, bivalved molluscs with ribbed pink spoon-shaped shells (see Shell Oil's logo), abound from here to Annapolis. If you hanker to fish, guides and boats can be hired in the town for either fresh or saltwater excursions; ask at the Welcome Centre.

If the day is fine, drive up the microwave site on Beamans Mountain for a view of Annapolis Basin and Digby Gut with its fierce, 6-knot tides [see also the **Evangeline Trail** at Exit 24]. To reach it, cut south to Victoria, follow it to Lighthouse Road (not Culloden Road) just north of town, and drive about 3 km/2 mi to the tower. With luck you may see the Saint John ferry, MV *Princess of Acadia*, heading out or in. Along the shore road below, there are always cormorants and gulls fishing, and occasionally a great blue heron.

The first leg of our journey runs straight as a survey line across wooded flats to Roxville and from there along a ridge to Rossway. Here we touch the head of St Marys Bay. The exposed shore is buffeted by wind and waves and is eroding rapidly despite the sea wall. Pull off by the beach 1 km/0.6 mi west of the road to Gullivers Cove and look back. See how the brick-red headland (Red Head) contrasts sharply with the surrounding dark volcanic basalt. Like Cape Blomidon and the Annapolis Valley floor, it's made of iron-rich sandstone. [See the **Evangeline Trail** at Windsor.]

The expression "Digby Chicken" (i.e., herring) comes from the fact that the first Loyalist settlers of 1783 practically lived on this fish for a year. The name took root all along the Fundy shore.

Rossway was settled in 1785 by military officers from Annapolis Royal. Gullivers Cove is said to have been named for Cut-Throat Gulliver, a pirate who preyed on Fundy shipping.

According to measurements made on the Admiralty chart, over 21,000,000,000 cubic feet of water run in and out of Annapolis basin through [Digby Gut] on each tide ... on the coast chart [there is] a ... hole, in the middle of the passage ... over 180 feet deep ....
– J. W. Goldthwait,
Physiography of
Nova Scotia,
1924

The sandstone is Triassic in age, older than the basalt, which dates from the early dinosaurs less than 200 million years ago.

Running north from this beach to Gullivers Cove on the Fundy Shore is one of the neck's several cross-faults. On a road map one can see that the east and west sides of this valley have been wrenched almost a kilometre out of line.

After Centreville, Rte 217 mostly follows the eroded groove down the middle of the neck, skirting first Lake Midway and then a series of peat bogs. Originally this road followed the shore. In the 1930s, it was rerouted north of the lake to take advantage of the more sheltered central valley. Parts of the old road are now a walking trail that explores beaches, tidal pools, cliffs, and plant life. One access point is the provincial picnic park at Lake Midway, where you can amble through deciduous trees to the shore. Ask locally about other points and about safety precautions. Lake Midway is said to offer good trout fishing "at the right time of year."

VIEW: *Sad House*

Rossway

Between Waterford and Sandy Cove we see many abandoned farms, sad reminders of uprooted lives. Where fat dairy cattle once grazed, deer now wander, foxes bark, and owls hoot. One such farm lies 6.5 km/4 mi east of Sandy Cove. The weathered farmhouse looks as if a giant fist has smashed the roof. Wild mustard has taken over the kitchen garden, and alders and white spruce are reclaiming the hard-won pastures. Through the tall grass wander walls built of stones laboriously hauled from the fields. Near the highway is a stand of young beech that invaded a pasture. Unlike the beech in most parts of Nova Scotia, which suffer from an imported bark canker [see the **Halifax-Dartmouth Area Nature Tour**, Public Gardens] they seem healthy. White-tailed deer, attracted by the nuts in autumn and the twigs in winter, regularly browse here.

A few kilometres farther on, the road plunges down a steep hill and the village of Sandy Cove opens before us. It has all the elements of picturesqueness: wooded hills brooding over a peaceful harbour lined with homes, fishing boats swinging at moorings, lobster pots on the wharves, the smell of salt air and seaweed.

The cove is the south end of a flooded and glacier-deepened crack in the Earth's crust. To explore the valley's glacial past, turn right at the Kwik Way store at the base of the hill. Driving north, notice, behind the homes and gardens, mounds and ramps of gravel. They were built by meltwater streams running over and alongside the melting ice. Soon you'll come to delightful Lily Lake. It occupies a hollow, likely imprinted by a lingering ice block. [See also the **Trans Canada Highway** at Folly Lake.]

Whatever the causes of its present appearance, Sandy Cove is more like something a poet or a painter might dream of ....
– Sir William Dawson, renowned 19th-century Nova Scotian geologist

VIEW: *Sea and Sky*

Drive a kilometre or so farther and you'll emerge at West Sandy Cove, a small Fundy fishing village. Going down toward the government wharf, the road winds past small fenced gardens and (in the off-season) between walls of lobster pots hung with colourful floats and loops of nylon rope. Find someone to talk to on the wharf; learn what the people do here and what the place is like in other seasons. To the west, a wide cobble beach curves out to a rugged basalt headland crowned with windblown spruce and fir.

If there's no fog and you want a loftier view, backtrack to Sandy Cove. Watch on the west side above the village for a gravel road to the right. This road climbs through a border of dense pasture spruce to an old field. From the field edge you can view not only the cove but a wide sweep of the outer Bay of Fundy. (Don't camp here without permission.)

In summer fishing craft come and go; offshore there may be a curved weir or two. To your left is the Gulf of Maine; ahead, just under the horizon, is Grand Manan Island and the New Brunswick shore. Eastward lies the inner Bay of Fundy, framed by rugged blackish rocks and golden rockweed, receding into the distance. Across the valley the rugged promontory of Mount Shubley rises invitingly above a patchwork of mixedwood forest and pale green pasture.

LEG-STRETCHER: *Mount Shubley*

Now that you've seen the Fundy panorama, how about an eagle's view of St Marys Bay. This hill (locally called Mount Shubal) is only 100 m/330 ft high, but it offers a spectacular panorama as your reward for the stiff climb. It also gives a clue to local geology.

Sandy Cove

At the Kwik Mart, backtrack on Hwy 217 for 0.4 km/0.25 mi and park off the shoulder opposite the gravel road. (If in doubt, ask for directions at the store or a nearby home.) The trailhead is 175 m/575 ft in, half hidden by alders and marked only with a small weathered board. About 160 m/525 ft in from the road you'll come to a tiny turnaround on the left. The sign is 15 m/50 ft beyond. (If you pass it you'll soon come to a camp.)

From the sign a winding footpath, sparsely flagged with pink plastic surveyor's tape, runs about 300 m/1,000 ft to the top. Toward the end there's a dense thicket of white spruce and mountain-ash carpeted with feather moss; then you'll break out into an open grove of large old white spruce. The length of their lower branches reveals that they began life in an open pasture. Some have been toppled by recent storms.

A few steps to the left is a bare ledge overlooking Sandy Cove, now resembling a matchbox village with toy boats and a toy wharf.

In front of you, stretching out of sight toward Digby and opening into the Gulf of Maine beyond, is the Acadians' Baie Sainte-Marie.

The dark rock at your feet has a curious honeycomb pattern. You're looking down on the eroded tops of lava plumes. When hot lava hits air of a certain temperature, each cooling plume forms a polygonal border with its neighbour. [See also the **Evangeline Trail** at Scots Bay wharf.] On the cliff face itself are matching vertical columns—but don't climb down to inspect them unless you have proper gear and training. The columns on Brier Island are superior and easier to reach.

VIEW: *Exotic Deer*

About 4 km/2.5 mi west of Mink Cove is a high-fenced field where British fallow deer and Japanese Sika deer sometimes show themselves to motorists. Owners Marlene and Gary   Trask don't mind your stopping to watch or photograph them, so long as nobody feeds or teases the animals. In Westport the Grahams keep New Zealand red deer.

Boars Head light, Petit Passage

At Tiddville near East Ferry, south of the highway, there's a marshy pond where ducks, grebes, and an occasional egret come in late summer. Also, brant (a small goose) overwinter in Freeport Harbour.

The ferry ride across Petit Passage to Long Island takes only a few minutes, but you're almost sure to see small, swallow-like terns, several kinds of gulls, and cormorants or shags. The latter is a long-necked black fish-eater that flies swiftly at wave-top level.

For a glimpse of Long Island's history and culture, visit the museum and tourist bureau just west of Tiverton.

LEG-STRETCHER: *Seaweed Gardens, Tidal Pools*

Halfway down Long Island is Central Grove Provincial Park, a pretty picnic park by a little pond. Watch for the wooden parks sign and pull in. From the park a 1-km/0.6-mi trail leads north to the rocky Fundy shore. At low tide the cliffs contain tidal pools—a wonderful place to explore the bay's rich flora and fauna.

Tidal pools, unlike the brackish ponds behind sand bars, are truly salt water—miniature seas that last only from high tide to high tide. Some have sandy bottoms, others are cliffy, still others are pebbly. Some reveal their contents plainly; others are draped in yellowish rockweed, a marine alga which shades the bottom, concealing who knows what?

Roll up your sleeves and poke around. Overturn rocks. (Don't worry; although white sharks sometimes enter Fundy, nothing bigger than a rock crab or sculpin is likely to grab you.) Besides the usual barnacles and periwinkles you should find sea urchins, sticklebacks, a starfish or two, maybe scuds (a sowbug relative), shrimp, and some-times a small eel. Lobsters and small flounders have been known to get trapped in such pools as well.

Approaching Brier Island, observe how the vegetation becomes more stunted. Trees huddle in hollows, alders and laurel hug the ground. Like desert scenery, the landscape is subdued but arresting.

At East Ferry one can sometimes spot a great blue heron fishing for sticklebacks beside the cliffs. Without the usual backdrop of a grassy marsh, it seems out of place.

You cross Grand Passage from Freeport to Westport on the *Joshua Slocum* or the *Joe Casey*.

Brier Island, the province's westernmost point, is named for the bramble fields on its western side. Like the rest of the Neck, it's made of basaltic lava. The boggy central valley we saw on Long Island continues down through Brier. Gardens are rare, yet one time almost every family here grew a plot of vegetables fertilized with seaweed and fish.

Take time to see the columnar cliffs on the east side. A century ago, Canadian geologist Sir William Dawson wrote, "... [the cliffs] were adorned with buttresses, outlying towers, and pinnacles, such as basaltic cliffs alone can produce in their full perfection." The sea stacks of Cape Split, Cape d'Or, and Cape Chignecto all arose in the same way, though Brier Island's are the most symmetrical. The resemblance of Brier Island's cliffs to the Devil's Causeway in Ireland is no coincidence; both were formed by waves eroding basaltic lava that cooled in air.

Brier Island is a special place. It has the mildest January temperatures in the Maritimes, the greatest concentration of migratory birds, and some of the best whale-watching in North America. In addition, its shoreline bogs contain

Columnar basalt on Brier Island

Mountain avens opens one blossom at a time. In a harsh environment where insects are scarce, this strategy conserves energy and, by prolonging the display, improves its chances of being pollinated.

arctic-alpine plants unique in Atlantic Canada. These include dwarf arctic birch, curly grass fern, and a basalt-loving primrose.

At least one Brier Island species is found nowhere else in Canada. Eastern mountain avens, *Geum Peckii*, a member of the rose family, grows on burned areas between Westport and Big Cove and on one roadside bog. Otherwise this plant is reported only from Maine and the mountains of New Hampshire and North Carolina.

To preserve this plant and other rare local plant communities, the Nature Conservancy of Canada, in co-operation with the Nova Scotia Department of Natural Resources (DNR) and other agencies, has bought 485 ha/1,200 ac on the southwest third of the island, including 10 km/6 mi of coastline.

Austere as Brier Island looks, it teems with life in May and August through September. One reason is that the island is the right distance from certain bird sanctuaries along the Bay of Fundy and the Gulf of Maine. Another is that for thousands of land birds it's the first and last landfall between Nova Scotia and the Eastern Seaboard. So from late August through September, scores of species of land birds, including various hawks, funnel down to the western tip. Here, like aircraft lined up for takeoff, they await good weather before making the sea crossing to the United States mainland or to South America.

For shorebirds its marshes and ponds become staging areas. For ocean species it's a vital feeding stop. Nutrient-loaded waters from both Fundy and the Atlantic meet and mingle here, breeding multitudes of plankton, shrimp, and fish.

Altogether bird watchers have noted over 150 species, more than for any other coastal island except Cape Sable. [See the **Lighthouse Route** near Barrington.] Among the rarer ones are Hudsonian godwit; stilt, buff-breasted and Baird's sandpipers; and glossy ibis. From the ferry you're almost sure to spot black guillemots, cormorants, and eiders; you may see phalaropes and kittiwakes (a kind of gull) too. A choice viewing location is the Pond Cove area; ask locally about others.

Recently several turkey vultures have been spotted feeding on dead porpoises and seals. Local birders suspect they may nest on Long Island.

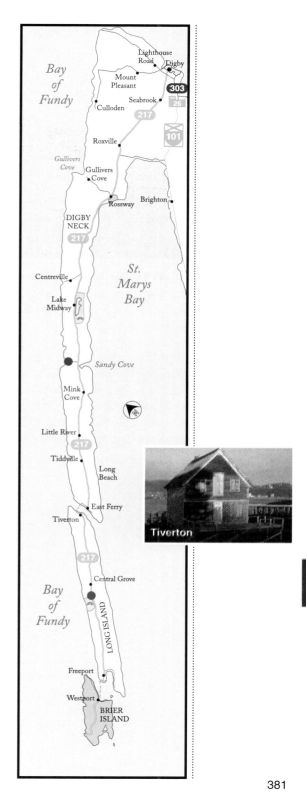

Tiverton

The Gulf of Maine, which includes the Bay of Fundy and Georges Bank, has been called one of the most productive marine ecosystems on the planet. Largely cut off from the rest of the Atlantic by an underwater sandbar that arches from Nova Scotia to Massachusetts, it has its own fish populations and tidal circulation. (One large school of herring winters off Boston and spends the summer feeding in the Fundy waters.) Because of the rising levels of PCBs and other pollutants, a Maritime/New England team met in June, 2000, to develop joint management strategies to conserve this vital ecosystem.

BOAT TOUR: *Whale-watching*

Any place that is so rich in fish is likely to attract whales, porpoises and seals. Whales fatten here before departing for less fertile southern waters to calve and spend the winter. One very important visitor is the threatened North Atlantic right whale.

For a day that is sure to fascinate, book a boat tour out of Tiverton, Freeport, Tiddville, or Westport between June and September. You're almost certain to see porpoises and the gentle and demonstrative humpback. Even if no whales show themselves, you're sure to see kittiwakes, shearwaters, Atlantic puffin, murres, petrels, and our largest seabird, the power-diving gannet.

Flintstone Scenic Nature Drive

Shelburne to Carleton via Rte 203
74 km/46 mi

Jordan River

OVERVIEW

To experience a vivid sense of the immense power of ancient glaciers, drive this mostly unpopulated route arching across the western interior. In the central part, between Shelburne and Carleton, you'll see the combined effects of massive ice movement and repeated wildfire on terrain that would otherwise be forested. You'll also experience a shifting spectrum of vegetation, from tall forest to stunted mixed conifers and broad-leaved trees to brushfields to bog and barren—and the same sequence in reverse at the Carleton end. We halt at Carleton because the landscape from there to Yarmouth is typical of terrain described elsewhere.

THE TOUR BEGINS

Minutes after leaving Highway 103 at Exit 26 and turning north onto Route 203, the road enters open glades of tall white pine growing on deep sandy soils over granite bedrock. Here the road is never far from the Roseway River. If you pull over and listen you may hear it off to westward through the woods, as it tumbles over several ledges before passing through Nova Scotia Power's hydroelectric station above Shelburne.

STOP: *Shelterwood Site*

Here, 9 km/5.6 mi north of Exit 26, is a different way to harvest conifers. Instead of clearcutting and planting this white pine stand, the owners are harvesting it gradually over a decade or more. The phased increase in light and warmth encourages pine seedlings to germinate. After 10 or 15 years, when restocking is sufficient, the remaining overstorey will be carefully felled so as not to damage the young trees.

Pine seeds fall every year (with a heavy crop every few years), but in the dim light and cool temperatures under a full canopy almost none germinate, and of those that do, few survive. In nature, wildfire is the usual thinning agent. But since this wastes a lot of wood, forest managers prefer to imitate the process by removing one-third to one-half of the overstorey in two or more stages. The resulting influx of

sunlight and warmth encourages more pine seeds to germinate and more seedlings to survive. Where this method is not used, most white pine stands are replaced over time by fir or spruce that can thrive in shade.

This shelterwood harvest was done around 1992. By 1994 new seedlings could be seen, especially on the east side where the highway let in more light. Between 1982 and 1988 the Shelburne office of the Department of Natural Resources (DNR) had set up seven white pine shelterwood trials in Shelburne County at Purdy Hill (three), Middle Ohio (one), and Middle Clyde (three). After only five years natural pine seedlings exceeded 50 per cent of all regeneration.

Watch for a large green and white "Managed Forest" sign on the west side. These woods are private land, so leave nothing but tracks.

After Lower Ohio, we leave the granite zone and enter a soft-rock area of slate and schist. As the deep sands and gravels thin out, the tall pine groves also fall behind.

Between here and Upper Ohio, a distance of over 25 km/15 mi, we trace the shores of rocky lakes with such names as Deception, McKay, Jones, Philip, and Back Lake, each 2–4 km/1–2.5 mi long. These lovely lakes keep the Roseway flowing. We pass stretches of river shadowed by occasional pine and hemlock, then rock-studded sheets of water and stillwater coves fringed with tall grasses.

At Upper Ohio we enter a less fertile region underlain by resistant quartzite and greywacke. The mixed forests take on a gaunter look. There are many dead and dying old trees festooned with the lichen called old man's beard—a sure sign of clean air.

STOP: *Altered Forest*
Selecting a typical patch of forest, park by the road and walk a short distance in the woods. Notice the diversity of trees; besides balsam fir and black spruce there are white and grey birch, red maple, and red oak.

Several of these species point to ecological disturbance—in this case fire. For years each spring, people regularly torched the woods around the barrens, believing it would create more blueberry land and boost moose and deer herds.

At first it worked. However, some fires got out into the better woodland, where they burned for weeks or months. Over the years the barrens spread as intended, but the remaining woodland changed from pine, hemlock, and beech to the mixture you see today.

Observe the flat-topped look of most of the fir. This is the work of an aphid-like insect which drills into their bark and sucks the sap. This causes the young shoots to swell, interferes with sap circulation, introduces wood rotting fungi, and eventually brings growth almost to a standstill.

The woolly adelgid was accidentally introduced into North America from Europe before 1900. It is widespread on fir in Atlantic Canada [see also the **Cabot Trail** east of Pleasant Bay, and the **Kejiimkujik Drive**], but does especially well in this mild, moist climate. Despite its white woolly coat, extreme cold kills it.

As we continue north and west beyond Back Lake, the forest gradually thins and recedes, shrubs begin to dominate and the number of boulders increases.

VIEW: *Glacial Rock Yard*

A few kilometres east of East Kemptville we emerge into a landscape of Arctic severity. It is a place scarred by ice and fire, a land of granite barrens, peat bogs, and lakes the colour of weak tea. With so much granite bedrock, one might expect to see deep sandy soils and tall pines. But the soil is almost gone, scraped off by glaciers and scorched by fire.

The most striking feature is the abundance of glacial boulders. Each hectare of barren, bog, or lake is studded with grey boulders, some as large as small cottages. They lie singly and in heaps, some half-buried in bogs, others perched atop low hills. All are patterned with black, grey, and pale green lichens.

At first the land looks barren. But look again. You'll see bearberry and mountain cranberry on the barrens; sheep laurel, Labrador tea, and blueberry on the slopes; and rhodora, sedges, and sphagnum in

Lichen.

A lichen is part alga, part fungus. The two cooperate in what biologists called a symbiotic relationship, the alga providing photosynthesis and the fungus a primitive root system. Map lichens such as grow on these boulders start as windborne spores and expand outward. The largest are a century old.

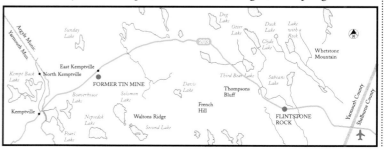

the wet hollows. And scattered across the low hills are islands of remnant pine and tamarack.

The weather is mild here winter and summer. On a misty April or October day, the air feels as if we were next door to the sea. But in fact we are in the very centre of western Nova Scotia, the very heart of the Southern Upland, the western extremity of that great belt of granite arching from Yarmouth to Halifax. The wind seems incessant.

For most of the year the colours are muted. Summer brings a palette of green foliage and inky blue lakes; winter is all burgundy, tan, grey, and white. For two brief weeks in October, the huckleberry bushes drench these barrens with a scarlet almost as vivid as the flames that once rampaged here, while rhodora bushes flush the hollows with delicate pink and puce.

STOP: *Flintstone Rock*

Here is the heart of the glacial graveyard. Pull over and feel its power. Through this giant rock garden ran the original gravel road, sometimes near, sometimes screened by birch and poplar. Just east of the old road stands a 3-m/10 ft-high boulder, cloven from top to bottom like a split loaf. In the 1960s it had a thick slab across the top, but freezing rain has long since split it, causing it to fall.

Soon after "The Flintstones" appeared in comics and on television, the boulder acquired its nickname. People spray-painted it on the rock, adding their names and those of friends and lovers. The immediate area became Flintstone Theatre.

Kaolin, a fine white natural clay used in coating magazine and book papers for optimal colour rendition, has been discovered here. A test pit dug in 2000 demolished part of the Theatre area, but similar portions of the old road remain.

In 1994 the author found a black locust sapling here, complete with seed pods. How it got here is a mystery, since it isn't a native plant. However, it is common in the Annapolis Valley. Perhaps a jay or crow brought an undigested seed. On good soil this member of the pea family grows to be a large tree.

Most of these rocks came from farther north. The ice sheet, grinding over the bedrock with immense weight, fractured it into great slabs, which were carried several kilometres "downstream." Some were embedded in the ice, others lay directly on the bedrock. Acting like coarse sandpaper on wood, they scratched and smoothed the surface while they themselves became rounded and flattened. At last, as the ice melted, they were dumped randomly (hence the term erratics). [See also the **Marine Drive** at Canso Barrens and Lundy Hill.] When a moving rock was particularly hard, it scored the bedrock with straight scratches or striaie.

There have been no forest fires here for some time. There's almost nothing to burn. Slowly, bacteria, algae, and lichens are building new soil. Almost as slowly, blueberry, bearberry, pin cherry, aspen, and birch are starting the long march back to forest. One hazard is the increasing number of ATV drivers bouncing over the barrens, apparently thrilled by the desolate landscape. As the many well-worn footpaths show, the barrens are also popular with berry pickers and hikers.

The old winding gravel roadway, still traceable in places, makes a nice botanical walk. You'll find such typical heathland flora as teaberry, crowberry, bearberry, mountain laurel, and huckleberry. There are also young white birch, red maple, red oak, white spruce, and white pine.

Off the road, the higher ground is fairly good walking, especially on the paths. But in the hollows you'll struggle through chest-high thickets of huckleberry, steeplebush, and downy alder.

Despite rough treatment by ice and fire, scattered groves of white pine, oak, and aspen still hang on. Typically, the pines fling their long graceful branches downwind, dancing with the prevailing southwesterlies.

A word of advice for those who decide to hike the barrens. Leave your vehicle on a rise where you can see it, especially in overcast or foggy weather. These barrens look very much alike when you're out in them.

To the north, in the Tobeatic Wildlife Management Area, there are numerous canoeing possibilities. [See also the **Lighthouse Route** at Shelburne, and **Kejimkujik Drive**.]

After crossing the utmost headwaters of the Clyde River a couple of times, a few kilometres east of East Kemptville we leave the granite country and re-enter the greywacke and quartzite zone. The boulders are still with us, but mostly screened now by spruce and white birch. Groves of red maple and red oak also appear, tentatively at first, then more abundantly.

STOP: *Abandoned Mine*

About 14 km/8.7 mi west of the Clyde River, partly screened by tall spruce on the west side of the highway, watch for a high, sulphur-yellow dome beside a huddle of dark grey metal towers. Here until the 1980s Rio Kemptville extracted tin from the rocks. The mining process involved quarrying bedrock with dynamite, trucking the rock to a central crusher, and extracting the heavy silvery metal.

To get rid of the powdery waste, electric fans blew it over the surrounding landscape through large pipes. As the midden of green sand grew, new sections of pipe were added, and the lines shifted in different directions.

Today the surface resembles that of sand dunes in a chartreuse desert. Wind makes herringbone ripples across the loose surface. Snow fences keep it from drifting across to the highway. Lengths of abandoned pipe lie half buried. It is doubtful whether anything will grow on such an unstable surface. Chemically the sand seems harmless. North of the plant, a steep ridge of it has enveloped part of a black spruce bog. The trees seem healthy. On the low ground to the west there's a shallow pond the colour of lime soda—but no fish or frogs. Signs warn visitors to keep out.

A few kilometres west of East Kemptville, the gaunt interior forests give way to healthy woodland. Homes, some of them new, appear among the trees, then bits of farmland, then bigger farms, then older houses. The upper Tusket River appears, and we are in Kemptville. It is a delightful village, straddling the river between little Travis Lake above and Pearl Lake below. Pearl Lake is a sheltered sheet of water, marshy at its west end, with a wooded ridge to the south.

From here to Yarmouth the landscape is one of low, forested ridges of deeply eroded and glaciated greywacke and quartzite peppered with irregular lakes. This is where the western ice sheet, after several advances and retreats, finally melted. It left its muddy tracks in the form of a vast end moraine of gravel hummocks and scattered boulders. The gravel blocked established streams and sent them running elsewhere to find alternative routes down the long gentle slope to the Atlantic. Some followed weakened fault zones until blocked, then zigzagged across to a parallel fault. The Tusket is a classic example of this lattice pattern.

The Tusket valley is also home to some rare plants that are found nowhere else in Atlantic Canada but which are native to New England. They migrated here thousands of years ago over a land bridge that existed late in the last Ice Age. When the ice melted, the ocean rose and they were cut off. [See also the **Lighthouse Route** near Tusket Falls.]

At Carleton our tour ends. From there, Rte 340 takes you south past Ohio to Exit 34 on Hwy 101, and to Hwy 1 (the **Evangeline Trail**) at Hebron.

Kejimkujik Scenic Nature Drive

Annapolis Royal to Liverpool
115 km/71 mi

Canoeing in Kejimkujik National Park

OVERVIEW

This is a drive unlike any other in the province. It gives a true cross-section of the western interior—that great wooded whaleback of granite and greywacke sloping gently south and west to the Atlantic. Despite millennia of native use, and more than two centuries of settlement, it is still sparsely populated and little developed. The population has, if anything, dwindled since the glory days of white pine lumbering and gold mining in the 19th century.

The traveller still gets a whiff of wilderness here, the sense that a canoe-load of Mi'kmaq hunters could appear out of the Kejimkujik mist, or that a party of off-duty British soldiers from the Citadel in Halifax might troop by, lugging a trophy moose head.

Above all, it is a forest drive. If you don't know a pine from a spruce, a beech from a birch, this tour should teach you. Except for some farmland around Caledonia and Pleasantfield, it's wooded all the way.

Historically the route spans two key periods in Nova Scotia's post-settlement story, namely the Acadian occupation of the Annapolis Basin in 1604, and the Loyalist influx to Liverpool after the American War of Independence.

Geologically the route is intriguing too. For one thing, it crosses a slab of ancient North Africa that stuck to North America when the North Atlantic Ocean opened 200 million years ago—our oldest rocks outside of northern Cape Breton. For another, it demonstrates how profoundly Earth history shapes human endeavour.

Sawmill on the same site as first mill

When the Annapolis area was settled in 1605, all grain had to be hand-ground with stone wheels—hard work indeed. After six men died from over-exertion, a watermill was built, the first in Canada.

No sooner have we left the pastoral loveliness of the lower Annapolis Valley than we climb into a landscape strewn with granite boulders and shadowed by white pines, oak, and beech. Since it is unfarmable, hunting, angling, and logging have long been its bread and butter. Then, halfway across this Southern Upland, we enter a slate region. Once the bottom of an ancient sea, its soils are deep and fertile enough to grow apples, livestock, and hay. From there to Liverpool we cross a belt of mostly greywacke, a gritty rock from the same seabed, yielding soils—midway in fertility between granite and slate—perfect for growing Christmas trees.

Don't expect startling vistas. Though there are hills and valleys, the skyline is nearly level. Though this area once had lofty mountains, today Highway 8 seldom exceeds 180 m/600 ft above sea level.

Do expect to see signs of forestry: pulp trucks heading for the Bowater Mersey newsprint mill near Liverpool, a woodlot owner driving home on a green tractor after a long day winching sawlogs, workers pruning pine Christmas trees in June.

THE TOUR BEGINS

LEG-STRETCHER: *Annapolis Royal Historic Gardens*

America's first sawmill, a waterpowered pit saw or whip sawmill, [was] built at Lequille in 1612. It used a large ... flat steel blade toothed along one edge for sawing logs lengthwise into lumber. In such mills the saw was fastened in a heavy wooden frame or gate that moved up and down in wooden slides fastened to heavy posts. Power was conveyed from a waterwheel to the saw by a long pitman or rod connected with the shaft in the waterwheel.
– Ralph S. Johnson, **Forests of Nova Scotia***, 1986*

Two blocks south of Hwy 1 on Hwy 8 (upper St George Street) there are 4 ha/10 ac of wonderful theme gardens. For a small fee you can amble among the flowers of Queen Victoria's day, including a collection of old roses. You can explore an Acadian kitchen garden and cottage and examine native wildflowers under native conifers.

The gardens slope down to a freshwater marsh restored and maintained by Ducks Unlimited to attract ducks and geese. The gardens are open from May to mid-October, 8 am till dusk.

From the lower garden, note the tall, tasselled grass towering above the other vegetation. It's called elephant grass, and local legend has it that it came from seed dropped by a train carrying a circus troupe. However, elephant grass, though uncommon, *is* native to Nova Scotia.

The sturdy, rough-barked trees beside the iron garden fence are imported white oak. Unlike native red oak, these have fat acorns and smallish, round-lobed leaves with U-shaped clefts. If you come in October, look for new-fallen acorns on the pavement. It's possible to raise your own oaks. Collect a pocketful, sow them 2.5 cm/1 in deep in good soil under mulch outdoors, and in spring you may be rewarded with a few seedlings. (Testing the acorns beforehand by putting them in water will better your chances; unsound nuts float, sound nuts sink.)

Leaving Annapolis Royal, our route parallels the dyked east bank of the Allain River. It flows from a small lake on the Southern Upland, named, with typical Nova Scotian hyperbole, Grand Lake. Upstream, a dam has created a second lake on the height of land. From there a pipeline conveys the water down a drop of 142 m/465 ft to a power station housed in a replica of an Acadian grist mill.

TO SEE: *Lequille Mill*

Lequille Mill

This mill at Lequille represents the oldest water-powered grist mill in North America. Until Cape Breton's Wreck Cove power project came on line in the 1980s, it was also the highest harnessed water in Nova Scotia.

The mill is worth a visit just to examine the construction. Watch for the sign a few minutes south of town on the left.

Most roads heading south from the Valley floor face a fairly steep climb up South Mountain. Hwy 8 avoids this by following the Allain River valley. On the way up, just beyond Lequille (French for the small eels that once swarmed here), you'll see outcrops of the exposed granite batholith that arches from Yarmouth to Halifax. [See also the **Flintstone Scenic Drive**, the **Lighthouse Route**, and the **Evangeline Trail** near Halifax.]

This crystalline, domed pavement welled up from the earth's interior as liquid magma into the roots of ancient mountains nearly 400 million years ago. As the mountains wore down, the resistant granite was exposed. It dominates the landscape from here to Maitland Bridge with a montage of rocky lakes, bogs, hardwood ridges, and, scattered everywhere, glacial boulders.

From here the Upland slopes down imperceptibly to the Atlantic shore, some 96 km/60 mi away as the crow flies.

VIEW: *Lady of the Forest*

About 3 km/2 mi north of Annapolis Royal the road runs through a lovely grove of tall white birch extending for half a kilometre on both sides. Although white birch is common throughout Nova Scotia on cutover lands, it's unusual to see almost pure stands like this. [See also the **Trans Canada Highway** near Exit 5 to Springhill.] That's mainly because we don't get as many large forest fires as we once did. White birch seeds have trouble germinating in moss and grass. They need fire to bare the mineral soil. If they do germinate, they must have full sunlight or they wither.

Yet even among the densest conifers, a few survive by outgrowing the competition. Their chalky white trunks add contrast and variety to the sombre evergreens. But they seldom constitute a grove.

Fire makes a grove possible by removing all competition. Any

You can tell the origin of birches by their appearance: clumps develop from stump sprouts, single trees from seed.

isolated mature birches that escaped the fire now have the whole place to themselves. For decades they have been dropping seeds in vain; now they begin to restock the burned area. (They'll also restock a newly bulldozed roadside, a log landing, or a nature trail.)

Should fire kill the seed trees, they can sprout from the stump. This survival tactic is shared by many broad-leaved trees, but not by conifers.

Between Lac La Rose and Mickey Hill, the height of land is roughly 150 m/500 ft above sea level. Temperatures up here are cooler than on the Valley floor. Spring frosts continue longer and autumn frosts hit earlier. This shorter growing season, plus acidic soils, makes mainstream agriculture unprofitable and forestry more important. However, you will see many small farms raising vegetables and beef cattle.

LEG-STRETCHER:
Mickey Hill Pocket Wilderness

Only 1 km/0.6 mi long, this self-guided nature trail 4.2 km/2.6 mi from Annapolis Royal is nonetheless a jewel. Snaking among a jumble of massive glacial erratics (boulders dumped by a melting ice sheet), it gives a strong impression of the Upland landscape. There are hoary old white pine over 25 m/80 ft tall, white birch, large-toothed aspen. There's a marsh, a pond (Lamb's Lake), and a stream (Ten-Mile River). Stops and signage, aided by a cartoon saw-whet owl, explain each feature. Some carry false information, such as: "Poplar leaves grow facing the prevailing wind." (They flutter in the least breeze thanks to their flattened stems.) There are well-placed stairways and viewing points and a rope suspension bridge that sways as you cross a ravine.

The trail is marked with small white signs, which are easily missed in the dim green light of a dark day.

The overall effect is that of a wild Japanese garden, with a small surprise at every turn. One of these surprises occurs near the end—a big white pine trunk riddled with woodpecker holes.

At Graywood, 13 km/8 mi from Annapolis Royal, we begin to see more white pine. This pine grows so fast (shooting up 1 m/3 ft a year on good sites) and lives so long (over 300 years) that it towers above the shorter-lived white birch, red maple, balsam fir, and white and red spruce here. This sandy-soiled, well-watered habitat is its natural element.

SIDE TRIP: *Milford: Canoeist's Heaven*
From the Milford area one can reach more than a dozen lakes, as well as the Mersey River and Thomas, Flanders, and East Branch brooks.

For more information, ask at the Visitor Centre in Maitland Bridge or Caledonia.

TO SEE: *Forest Takeover*

South of Lake Munro, observe the lush growth of young white pine crowding the roadsides. They seeded in from nearby mature pines after the right-of-way was last cleared. If left to grow, they will soon block the views on either side, and in time overshadow the road. This demonstrates how quickly our native trees restock cleared land here. The secret is our moist maritime climate. From Ontario west to the Rockies drier air greatly hampers natural regeneration.

TO SEE: *Beech Bark Disease*

About half-way between Milford and Munro Lake the road swings close to the upper Mersey River and we pass through a broadleaf forest consisting of mostly beech. Beech is normally smooth-barked, even in old age. But these have cankered bark, and their trunks are contorted and short. The cause is beech bark disease, an introduced fungus carried from tree to tree by sap-sucking aphids. [See also the **Halifax-Dartmouth Area Nature Tour**, Halifax Public Gardens.]

A few kilometres north of Maitland Bridge we leave the granite country with its bony ridges, shallow valleys, rounded knobs, thin soils, and numerous boulders and enter a gentler landscape of deeper soils.

From here to Liverpool the land is relatively flat. It wasn't always flat. Four hundred million years ago, Alp-like mountains of layered slates and sandstone raked the clouds here. Countless eons of erosion and glaciation planed them down to the almost-level skyline you see today. The two major rock types, slate and greywacke, are mantled in deep drifts of gravel, sand, and soil. Collectively the formation is called the Meguma Group, after a Mi'kmaq word.

Hwy 8 crosses these planed-down ridges of slate and greywacke at right angles. It's as if one took a telephone book, soaked it in glue, folded it several times lengthwise, let it

Beech bark disease

Experts agree that beech bark disease was accidentally introduced into America via Halifax, most likely on European beech saplings that Queen Victoria donated to the Public Gardens on her Diamond Jubilee in 1897. (European beech harbour the Asian fungus but have built up immunity.) By 1910 forest workers were seeing the symptoms—bark lesions, spore clusters, cottony masses of aphids—in central Nova Scotia. Like ink on a blotter, the disease spread into New Brunswick and Maine. By the 1930s it was killing and deforming beech throughout New England. It is spreading westward still!.

The loss to Nova Scotia was immeasurable. Until 1900, beech was the province's principal broadleaf tree, outnumbering maple or birch or oak on uplands from Yarmouth to Cape North. Carpenters prized its durable brown wood for furniture and flooring. As fuelwood it was ideal. Beechnuts were a crucial autumn food for bear, deer, and grouse preparing for winter, and for the now extinct passenger pigeon. Over time red maple took its place, but the ecological damage had been done. Our only other native nut sources are hazelnut (a small shrub) and red oak (whose acorns are bitter with tannin and must be soaked for human use).

The Meguma sediments were laid down in vast thicknesses by rivers running into an ancient sea and later compressed. The continental collision that thrust up the Appalachian chain 400 million years ago folded these rocks into lofty ranges that today survive as low ridges, about 5 km/3 mi apart, running parallel to the Atlantic shore.

harden, and planed the hardened folds level. The stubs of white, yellow, and blue pages would represent bands of slate, greywacke, and quartzite.

From Maitland Bridge to South Brookfield we're in slate country. Topographically, it's more interesting than the granite or greywacke areas. The bedrock being softer, there's more glacial drift. For the first time we begin to see drumlins, whaleback ridges pushed up by moving ice. The stream valleys are deeper. White pine and hemlock are more common, and beech and sugar maple scarcer.

TO DO: *Find a Drumlin*

In this heavily glaciated country, drumlins often provided the only fairly stone-free soil for agriculture. Compared to nearby Lunenburg County, they are scarcer here because there is less slate. Slate is a key factor in drumlin formation because of its clay content. A glacier moving across granite or greywacke acts like a rock crusher and bulldozer combined, grinding up rocks and dumping them as it goes. In slate areas, however, pulverized rock and meltwater combine to make slippery clay. This acts as a lubricant to carry the ice sheet up and over its bed of gravel, creating a school of beautifully rounded hills. [For more detail, see the **Lighthouse Route** near Mahone Bay; also see the **Marine Drive** near Ecum Secum and the **Marconi Trail** near Gabarus.] Often these hills face upstream to the direction of ice flow, like trout in a brook. Near Lunenburg, there are "drumlin swarms."

The Cambrian/Ordovician epoch marked the end of the Earth's first great flowering of marine life, as evidenced by fossils worldwide. Oddly, southern Nova Scotia's rocks from this period are nearly devoid of fossils. This suggests that these sediments were laid down in deep water near the South Pole. Continental drift then rafted them here.

See if you can spot a drumlin farm, and think how difficult it was to choose a good farm site when Mary and William Burke trekked through the dense woods here over 200 years ago.

TO DO: *Rock-Hunt*

Since road cuts and rock outcrops are rare in soft-rock areas like this, the best place to see the bedrock is in stream beds and on lakeshores. (Ignore loose rock, however, which could have been dragged several kilometres by a glacier.)

Slate (compressed shale) is fine-grained and layered like the leaves of a book. The colour is normally dark greenish or bluish grey, but sometimes iron pyrites stain it rusty red. (Then it's called ironstone.) [See also **Highway 102 Nature Trail** near Halifax.] The layers here are tilted, sometimes steeply. With luck you may see schist or gneiss (pronounced "shist," "nice"). These are sedimentary rocks deformed by heat and pressure into marbled patterns, often with glistening mica flakes.

As prospectors know, mountain building sometimes results in deposits of gold and other minerals along the crests and troughs of the folds.

TO SEE: *Maitland Bridge*

Here you're in the heartland of old-time outdoorsmen who guided "sports" from Boston and New York to trophy moose and bear in the '20s and '30s. The village lies a few kilometres north of the upper Mersey River (named after the English river on which the original Liverpool sits), a few kilometres upstream from where the river plunges down two falls on its way to Kejimkujik Lake.

Like Milford, this is a canoeist's heaven; but with even more connections. Besides numerous local lakes to paddle, Kejimkujik

> At Maitland Bridge in 1861 was born Margaret Marshall Saunders, author of *Beautiful Joe*, a dog story that won the hearts of animal lovers in America and Britain and earned her a "Companion of the British Empire" citation.

Roseway River

> Ked-ge puts a spell over you before the first hour has ended. There is the sheer beauty of the place, the lake like a mirror, the trees, the birds, and the forest stillness. You are away from everything ....
> – Will R. Bird, **Off-Trail in Nova Scotia**, 1956

("Keji") Lake offers access to the Mersey system, whence one can canoe and portage to Liverpool. In fact, it is claimed that with ingenuity one can link up from here with the Bear, Clyde, Jordan, Roseway, Sissiboo, and Tusket systems.

STOP: *Kejimkujik National Park*

This unique park, 1 km/0.6 mi south of the Mersey River in one of Canada's best wilderness destinations, was created in 1968. Its name is generally agreed to mean "swollen parts" in Mi'kmaq—but why? Does it refer to the discomfort of paddling the tortuous shoreline for days in a cramped canoe? No one knows. We do know that this area was important to the Mi'kmaq as a source of trout, caribou, beaver, birch bark, and many other essentials of their nomadic life.

Kejimkujik National Park

Canoeing at Kejimkujik

The park itself occupies an oval of undeveloped woodland about 25 km/15 mi across and embracing 381 km²/147 sq mi of woodland. More than a third of this is fresh water, notably Keji Lake itself.

Watch for the sign (and the nice new pavement), turn west, and drive 1 km/0.6 mi to the Visitor Centre just beyond the entrance. To enhance your visit the centre has brochures, exhibits, and audio-visual programs. You can choose among numerous camping sites and 14 woodland hiking trails ranging from 3 to 6 km/1.8 to 3.6 mi long. Canoe and bicycle rentals are available. The park offers boat ramps, designated back-woods camping and, in winter, cross-country skiing.

Things to Know at Keji:
• The pictographs are protected.
• Should you come upon a beautiful turtle with a dappled dark blue-grey shell, count yourself lucky. It belongs to an isolated population of rare Blanding's turtle, which inhabits certain grassy coves and bogs in and around Kejimkujik and Grafton lakes and nowhere else in Nova Scotia. The nearest population of this species lives in eastern Massachusetts, separated from them by the Gulf of Maine. How did ours get here? Most likely it migrated north over the boggy coastal plain that joined New England to Nova Scotia during the retreat of the last ice sheet.
• Open fires are allowed only in designated places, and not even there during times of high hazard. Wood is provided but you'll need an axe to split it.
• Woods travel is arduous. Glacial boulders lie everywhere, some as big as cottages. Often they're hidden under moss, ready to break an ankle. Lakes too are strewn with them, and the peaty, tea-coloured waters can make them hard to see beyond a metre's depth. Paddle slowly in rough water or fog.
• Poison ivy occurs in several areas. If you don't know what it looks like, check the fenced plot of it on the Mersey Meadow Trail by the Visitor Centre. And remember: "Leaves three, let it be."

The dog tick (Dermacentor spp.*) likely reached Nova Scotia via New France, Digby County between 1895 and 1899 (R. Johnson, 1986). At first they spread slowly. Until 1935, they were largely confined to Digby County and northern Yarmouth County. A dozen years later, they had reached the Lake Rossignol country. By 1985, they were east of LaHave River. Dog ticks can stand cold weather, so will probably spread through-out the province. Ours are known to carry tularemia ("rabbit fever"), which, if untreated, can be fatal to humans. No cases of Rocky Mountain spotted fever have appeared, but in 1999 Lyme disease (a disabling, recurrent arthritis) was found in dogs from Springhill and New Glasgow, the result of being bitten by a different pin-head-sized wood tick. Dogs can be inoculated against the latter.*

Canoeing at Kejimkujik

• The American dog tick, a small grey relative of the spider, is common in the park in May and June and sometimes through to September. Like other ticks it needs a blood meal to develop, but our Nova Scotia strain isn't known to carry any dangerous diseases. As a precaution when hiking through grassy or brushy areas, wear trousers cuffs tucked into heavy socks. Before leaving, check your person carefully and pick off any you find. A tick attached to the skin can usually be pulled off (gently); if the tick's head stays attached, treat is as you would a splinter. A feeding tick injects a nerve toxin, so you may not feel it. [See also the **Evangeline Trail** at Chebogue Meadows.]

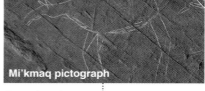

Mi'kmaq pictograph

TO SEE: *Pictographs*

Etched in smooth slate ledges around the lake are many Mi'kmaq pictographs executed with quartz chisels or beaver teeth centuries ago. They depict reptiles, birds, mammals, humans—and what look like Viking ships. Some are decorative, some are symbolic, a few depict battles (the Mi'kmaq claim they won a great battle here against Mohawk invaders) and hunting scenes. The inscriptions occur in an area 11 km/7 mi across and range in size from a few cm to 60 cm/24 in.

As they are near water level, the best way to view them is from a boat. Since 1930, dams to supply hydro power for the Bowater mill have submerged many pictographs. Fortunately, since the 1880s many researchers, including the Smithsonian Institute, have recorded these works of art.

From Maitland Bridge to Caledonia we trace a section of 19th-century stagecoach track that linked Liverpool with Annapolis Royal. As you glide along over smooth pavement, imagine that overnight journey by lantern glare or moonlight.

Like other coach roads of that era, it was little more than a rutted forest trail over stumps and rickety bridges. Dreading swamps, road builders generally stuck to high ground. This meant exhausting climbs and bone-jarring descents. There were frequent stops to extricate the wheels from axle-deep mud while mosquitoes and blackflies tormented man and beast. To ease the horses, teamsters often had passengers walk—or even push. Every few kilometres the teams had to be watered, and every few hours fresh horses had to be hitched up. The journey was so rough that even the veteran traveller and journalist Joseph Howe complained publicly about it in 1840.

SIDE TRIP: *McGowan Lake Trout Hatchery*

South of the village of Kempt, watch to the east for the sign to this facility, operated by the provincial Department of Fisheries and Aquaculture. Located 2.5 km/1.5 mi east of the highway and 7 km/4.2 mi north of Caledonia, it was opened in 1987. It raises speckled (brook) trout to stock selected waters in the western counties.

Wild trout populations can decline from over-fishing, logging silt, predation [see also **Highway 102 Nature Tour** at Shortts Lake], and acid precipitation. This last is a particularly severe problem in western Nova Scotia, where the granitic soils are naturally acidic and air pollution from the Eastern Seaboard is more intense.

In fact, for most of the year McGowan Lake is so acidic (pH less than 5.0) that many young trout would die if the hatchery's incoming water wasn't limed. This is done by running it over a bed of limestone. The treatment shed handles 22 000 litres/4,400 gallons of gravity-fed water per minute. Workers flush the limestone now and then to keep it clean.

Another hazard for hatchery trout is low oxygen in hot summer weather (warm water holds less oxygen). This is corrected by an oxygen generator and injector. When the system was installed in 1993, hatchery output tripled to over a million fish a year.

Each November 1.5 to 2.0 million eggs are delivered from the Frasers Mills Hatchery in Antigonish County and placed in troughs of cool, oxygen-rich water. By February their eyes are visible and they are called fry. Volunteers working on the Stream Side Incubation Program "seed" suitable streams with these eyed fry.

By mid-April the fry have absorbed their protein-rich yolk sac and have begun to swim in search of real food. Again, some of these fish are stocked in selected streams. In mid-May workers place the remaining fry, now 3–4 cm/1.2–1.6 in long, in the hatchery's 10 concrete raceways or man-made brooks. Each raceway measures 30 x 2.5 m /98 x 7.2 ft and 1.2 m/4.9 ft deep and holds some 70,000 fish.

Come October, the fish have grown into fingerlings 18–22 cm/7.2–8.8 in long and are ready for the real world. All but 150,000 of these are trucked in tanks to carefully chosen lakes in southwest Nova Scotia. The rest are kept over winter to be stocked as yearlings. The hatchery operation is partly funded by anglers' license fees; volunteers help with stream stocking.

Visitors are welcome seven days a week from 9 am to 4 pm. The Visitor Centre in the hatchery building is open during working hours and features videos and displays. A highlight is its two aquaria: one shows speckled trout, the other insects that wild trout eat.

BACK ON HIGHWAY

VIEW: *White Pine*

A striking feature of the Caledonia area is the grove of white pines that tower around it like ancient sentinels, dwarfing the houses. They recall the district's colourful 19th-century pine lumbering era, when trainloads of lumberjacks, cooks, teamsters, and horses fanned out from here to remote woods camps, and when log drivers herded the winter's cut down white-water streams to Liverpool.

Most of the big white pine are gone, their places taken by smaller spruce and fir; but forestry is still important here. After 1929 the Bowater Mersey newsprint mill in Liverpool needed a steady flow of pulpwood—and still does. Another market is the Irving mill in Saint John, NB. And local sawmills always need large spruce sawlogs.

Notice the many run-down apple orchards. Caledonia used to export thousands of bushels of apples each year to Europe and the US. Farming is still important here, for the climate is warmer and sunnier than anywhere in most of western Nova Scotia outside the Annapolis Valley, and the clayey soils are deep and rich. Dairy farming with Holstein cows is a mainstay.

TO DO: *Caledonia Museum*
To learn about the era when this quiet village boasted a railway and bustled with gold miners and woodsmen, visit Heritage House Museum on West Caledonia Road. You'll find a library, clippings from the 1880s, an archive, and a forestry exhibit. The house itself was the home of the Douglas family, who arrived around 1850.

Tobeatic Wilderness
Not far west of here, adjoining Keji Park, is the Tobeatic Wildlife Management Area. About the size of Keji, it embraces the headwaters of the Tobeatic, Mersey, Jordan, Roseway, Clyde, and Tusket rivers. There are three large lakes (Tobeatic, Jordan, Roseway) and numerous smaller ones. It abounds in beaver, deer, and other game.

The secretive and protected fisher, a large tree-going weasel with glossy black fur, was reintroduced into western Nova Scotia in 1947

Tobeatic area

and again in the 1960s after being nearly wiped out by trapping in the 1920s and 1930s. One of the few predators of porcupine (the others being bobcat and great horned owl), it seems to be doing well.

Our route from Caledonia to Pleasantfield lies over greywacke bedrock rich in white pines, hemlock and forest trees in general. A few kilometres to the north is Molega (Mi'kmaq, possibly "fretful water") Lake, site of a famous annual guides' competition entailing canoe-racing, fly-casting, shooting, axe-throwing and the like.

Less than 10 km/6 mi to the southwest is Lake Rossignol. It's named for a 17th-century French furrier, the first white man to paddle up the Mersey River. It is said that rather than pay income tax to the King of France, he hid out for years with the natives, and died near the lake that bears his name. It is doubtful if Monsieur Rossignol would recognize the lake today. Since the 1930s it has grown to become the province's largest body of fresh water, thanks to a series of power dams that have joined several lakes, drowning large tracts of woodland in the process. Our largest *natural* freshwater body is Lake Ainslie in western Cape Breton. [See the **Ceilidh Trail** near Inverness.]

One kilometre/0.6 mi or so beyond South Brookfield, we leave the slate area and enter a greywacke/quartzite belt extending almost to Pleasantfield. This type of bedrock, more resistant to erosion, makes for a monotonously flat topography with poor drainage. Walk any distance in the woods here and you'll come upon moss-grown slabs and chunks of greywacke strewn about. Glaciers plucked these from bedrock ledges, dragged them along, and dumped them as the ice melted. We're back in forest country: long stretches of red and black spruce, level peat bogs, and sluggish streams overhung with alders.

TO SEE: *Cradle Hills*

Another thing you may notice in older woods here is how hum-mocky the ground is. In places it looks like the surface of a frozen ocean, so regular are the waves beneath the trees. At first you might suspect the presence of rocks under the moss. Sometimes there are, but more often the undulations are ridges of soil.

These "cradle hills" are the work of gales. Nova Scotia, and particu-larly southwest Nova Scotia, lies in the path of autumn hurricanes. Every few decades a windstorm will topple large tracts of aging spruce and fir, as hurricanes Edna and Carol did in the mid-1950s and as the Saxby Gale did in October 1869. [See also the **Glooscap Trail** near Nappan.]

Where the soil is shallow or rain-soaked, whole trees are uprooted—soil, rocks, and all. As these masses of earth fall, they form a series of hillocks. In spring the intervening hollows fill with snow water and rain. The only place softwood seedlings can germinate and grow is on the drier hummocks. In time each supports a new clump of trees. But when the next big blow hits, these trees topple. More soil is dumped, more seedlings take root, and so on until the forest floor looks like this.

LEG-STRETCHER: *Picnic Park*
About 5 km/3 mi from South Brookfield there's a pleasant little wayside park. It's between First Christopher Lake on the west and an arm of Ponhook Lake to the east. Ponhook (Mi'kmaq for "first lake you meet as you ascend a river"; also pronounced *banook* [see **Halifax-Dartmouth Area Nature Tour**]) is a splendid canoeing lake, an archipelago of bays and islands. The Medway River, which flows out of it, isn't so hospitable to canoeists, for it tumbles over numerous waterfalls (those resistant greywacke ridges again) on its way past Greenfield, Riversdale, and Mill Village to meet the Atlantic at Medway. However, the Medway is a respectable salmon and trout stream. Guides can be hired locally.

TO SEE: *Fir Parasite*
Have you noticed the flat-topped conifers? These are fir that have been attacked by the balsam fir adelgid, alias fir bark louse, a tiny aphid-like Old World insect that sucks sap (not resin) through its straw-shaped proboscis, weakening or killing mature trees and stunting the growth of saplings. The flat crowns are due to gradually declining shoot growth.

The adelgids cluster under blankets of white fluff which they secrete. Even so, they cannot survive extreme cold unless protected by deep snow. For this reason the insect, which arrived via Europe decades ago, has done more damage in the milder western counties than farther east. You'll see lots of thrifty young fir, but few healthy full-grown ones.

Christmas tree growers fear this pest because its feeding raises unsightly lumps where the twigs join the stem, thereby reducing market value. [See also the **Flintstone Scenic Drive**, and the **Cabot Trail** near Pleasant Bay.]

By its name, Pleasantfield expresses the fond hopes of the Loyalists who ventured up from the newly independent United States to make a new life here in the 1780s. To Liverpool's burghers it was the Northern District, "Britain's woodlot behind Liverpool," a trackless wilderness patrolled by hostile Indians and good only for securing fresh meat and timber for the Royal Navy.

As time went on, however, the merchants and sea captains soon realized that to build more ships and bolster the cod fishery, forest workers would be needed. It was a time of mass migration from

Britain and Europe, with many immigrants seeking land. The thin coastal soils could not feed many more.

The first couple to tackle this roadless wilderness were William and Mary Burke. In 1799 they took their few belongings plus axe, saw, and hoe, and trekked northwest some 48 km/30 mi into the forest. The good land at Milton was already taken, so they journeyed on to the next slate area and the next. At last they chose a whaleback ridge with good brown soil between Lakes Rossignol and Ponhook, with a high conical hill to the southwest for a landmark. They chopped down trees, hewed a cabin for themselves and hovels for livestock, and piled firewood for the winter. Come spring they planted crops in the clearing. What they couldn't grow, collect, hunt, or make meant a trip to Liverpool. Mary also travelled to Liverpool to birth their four children. Year by year, Pleasantfield became more pleasant and drew more pioneers.

After Pleasantfield, Hwy 8 again runs through fairly level mixed woodland. The forest here, being closer to the coast, which was settled first, has a longer history of land clearing, logging, and fire. Also, gold was mined near here in the late 1800s. These disturbances echo down to our day in the prevalence of short-lived pioneer species like white birch, grey birch, and aspen on the drier knolls, and of larch and red maple on the wetter flats.

A few minutes beyond Middlefield (another 19th-century gold district), watch for an inviting provincial picnic park by the shore of Ten Mile Lake. The lake itself is only 5 km/3 mi long; its name refers to the approximate distance of its southern end from tidewater. It connects through Great Brook Meadows to the lower Mersey River.

> **Milton**
> *This village, a few kilometres upstream from Liverpool, once had several waterwheel-driven grist mills and sawmills, hence the name. It's said that Milton once boasted a 6-km/4-mi plank road that was a marvel to walk and cycle on—not a bump or a puddle. But after five years it rotted away underneath and was never renewed.*
>
> *Milton was the likely entry point for the introduction to Canada of the European winter moth, a voracious defoliator of broad-leaved trees. Apparently it arrived on apple tree nursery stock in the 1930s. By 1953, the infestation covered mainland Nova Scotia and part of New Brunswick, worrying farmers and foresters alike. In 1954 and 1959, federal entomologists released winter moth parasites. By 1966, with the help of a virus raised by the Canadian Forestry Service in Fredericton, NB, the insect had been reined in—one of Canada's most remarkable success stories in biological insect control. [See also the Evangeline Trail at Kentville.]*

TO SEE: *Christmas Tree Lots*

From time to time you'll see orderly rows of young pines, or a field of balsam fir carefully spaced and pruned. Christmas tree cultivation is an important source of off-season income hereabouts.

Raising natural fir for market entails several steps: weeding out competing vegetation to release natural regeneration, spacing the remaining crop trees, pruning to increase foliage density, and perhaps fertilizing with nitrogen to improve colour. To ensure that only the right trees are cut for market, current crop trees are commonly colour-coded. Baling is usually done at a central yard. Ask locally for the name and location of a grower who gives tours.

Just above Milton the highway comes within a few hundred metres of the Mersey River. Narrower here than upstream, its last several kilometres are punctuated by falls and dams. No fewer than six hydro generating stations operate along this stretch. They power the huge newsprint mill in nearby Brooklyn, with enough voltage left over for the town and environs.

STOP: *Liverpool*
For information on this Loyalist seaport and on how the forests and fisheries shaped its life and character, visit the Perkins House Museum, open June 1 to October 15. [See also the **Lighthouse Route** at Liverpool.]

If you tour the mill, stop at the main gate to see the planted American chestnut trees. They are part of the company's 1960s effort to rehabilitate this northeastern species, which was wiped out in the 1930s and 40s here by an Asian fungus. Thanks to tree-loving Loyalist settlers who brought the nuts with them, Nova Scotia has some of the few large healthy Castanea dentata *specimens left in the East. These Bowater trees, however, are from Ohio stock. [See also **Halifax-Dartmouth Area Nature Tour** and **Evangeline Trail** at Mount Uniacke.]*

The summer of 1930 was the driest in Nova Scotia for a century ... Western Nova Scotia suffered the worst damage with 163 fires destroying 25,961 acres [10 506 ha].... On May 7 the most destructive forest fire started near Milton, Queens County about 2:30 p.m. and before 3:30 p.m. it had reached the shore of Liverpool Harbour between Liverpool and Brooklyn, more than three miles from where it started. The blaze destroyed 37 homes ....
– Ralph S. Johnson, **Forests of Nova Scotia**, 1986

LEG-STRETCHER: *Pine Grove Hiking Trail*
This self-guided, 1.6-km/1-mi trail in a community park offers an easy hike through open mixed woods along the famous Mersey River. The trail starts in a marked parking lot on the west side of Hwy 8, approximately 200 m/220 yd north of Exit 19 on Hwy 103. Once

on the trail, turn left at 100 m/110 yd and left again at 200 m/ 220 yd, then follow the river up the bank. In season you'll see various ferns and wildflowers; please love 'em and leave 'em.

Notice how brown the river water is. This isn't pollution. Most streams along the South Shore are naturally tea-coloured, especially in late summer when water levels are low. It's due to tannin leached from peat bogs upstream.

For current information on other trails in the area, see the current *Nova Scotia Complete Guide for Doers & Dreamers.*

At Liverpool Hwy 8 joins Hwy 103, the **Lighthouse Route.**

Near Caledonia

A Note On Sable Island

*No other bit of land on the coast is so fully exposed to the fury of north
Atlantic storms. It stands near the outer edge of the banks, with 100
fathoms [183 m/600 ft] of water close to its eastern end. Rich in
romance as well as tragedy—on its shores and hidden reefs countless
vessels have been wrecked during the last three centuries—inhabited
by a flora which curiously resembles that of New Jersey rather than
Nova Scotia, and by birds which are not known to breed elsewhere ...
it is at once the loneliest and the strangest spot in the Maritime
Provinces.*

– J. W. Goldthwait
Physiography of Nova Scotia, 1924

Few road maps show Sable Island (French for
"sand"), yet it is part of Nova Scotia. Although
inaccessible without a boat or an aircraft (plus a
government permit), geologically and ecologi-
cally it is interesting for several reasons. Lying
160 km/100 mi off Canso Head, it marks the
edge of the vast Ice Age coastal plain that
bordered the Eastern Seaboard when sea levels
dropped as much as 150 m/500 ft. (Long Island
in New York State is another such remnant.)

**Ships wrecked
off Sable Island**

Curving like a bow about to shoot an arrow
south, Sable consists of two nearly parallel sand
dunes up to 30 m/98 ft high that meet at either
end, cradling rainwater lakes and salt marshes
between. The sand is whitish quartz with traces of garnet and
magnesium.

*Some geologists think
Sable Island may
have formed fairly
recently, perhaps only
6000 years ago.*

The island proper is about 50 km/21 mi long; adding the west
and east bar brings it to roughly 80 km/50 mi. At its widest it's about
3 km/2 mi across—and getting narrower. These dimensions change
continually as wind and waves recycle sand, but the fear that it is
migrating eastward into the abyss seems unfounded.

The ancient land bridge explains why Sable Island's vegetation
resembles that of coastal New Jersey more than that of the Eastern
Shore. As well, long isolation has altered some of its indigenous
animals. For example, the Savannah sparrow breeds here in a paler,
sand-coloured version called the Ipswich sparrow (after the Massachusetts town where it was first identified). Fossil sods and shells
indicate that 5,000 years ago warm-water scallops and oysters

Half a century ago, Nova Scotian author Thomas Raddall kept the Sable light for a time. His novel The Nymph and the Lamp *is based on that experience.*

Many schemes to control Sable's drifting dunes have been tried. In 1901 the following plantings were carried out by the federal government: 69,000 evergreens, 1,000 willow cuttings, 600 fruit trees and shrubs, 12,500 deciduous plants, and many rhubarb roots. As well, 2.5 kg/55 lb of native pine seed was sown. By 1913 only 13 plants survived; by 1927 only one was left.
—NS Conservation, Vol. 12, No. 2 (Summer 1988)

flourished here. A temporary westward shift of the Gulf Stream perhaps explains this.

Sable Island has earned, with is notorious shoals and fogs, the title "Graveyard of the North Atlantic". In the days before wireless communication and the provision of a lighthouse at either end, scores of ships met their doom here. More than 300 years of human contact have changed the face of this giant sandbar. Of Sable's 200-plus plant species, some 70 have been introduced. Many, like tussock grass from the Falkland Islands, were planted to control drifting sand. Ever since the lifesaving station was built in 1901, dunes have been less stable.

Sable's famous wild horses may be one reason. They derive from shipwrecked stock brought from France about 1632 by Isaac de Razilly, who settled at the mouth of the LaHave River. [See also the **Lighthouse Route** at Riverport.] A herd of several hundred wild horses galloping about cannot be good for the dunes; yet the herd seems in balance with its environment. The only other large mammals are grey seals, which come to the shores to breed in autumn.

From time to time, fences of wood or wire have been set up to corral drifting sand and to shelter and encourage marram plantings. In one failed attempt, Christmas trees—7,400 in all—were brought from the mainland and stuck into the sand.

The current threat comes from industrial development. In the 1980s, Mobil Oil discovered quantities of oil and gas around the island. Low oil prices made development unprofitable then, but the potential of natural gas has changed that.

In 1999, the first Maritime-Northeast pipeline was being laid between Country Harbour [see **Marine Drive**] and the New Brunswick border, ready to carry gas from five wells south and east of Sable. Natural gas comes from decomposed remains of ancient animal organisms.

Renewed concern for the island's ecosystems has led to closer studies of its flora and fauna and more attempts at dune control. Since 1987, plantings have focused on native colonizing species like marram, sandwort, and beach pea. Results have been promising. Nowadays road building and even the making of footpaths are curtailed. Dykes have been built to stop sea flooding.

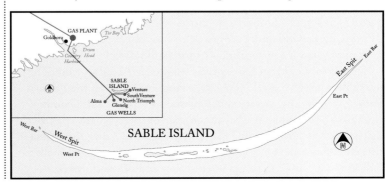

There is concern that oil and gas drilling and exploration, plus increased marine traffic (one ship a day, on average) is harming the ecology of The Gully, a recently discovered marine canyon east of Sable. Roughly the size of Bras d'Or Lake and up to 1 000 m/ 3,300 ft deep, it seasonally shelters several kinds of whales (including the rare blue and sperm), three kinds of dolphins, plus seals, tuna, sharks and the endangered leatherback turtle, which follows clouds of lion's mane jellyfish north each year. The endangered northern bottle-nose whale lives here year-round.

Atlantic Leatherback Turtle

GLOSSARY

aboiteaux - a sluice gate in Acadian dykes allowing runoff to drain, but blocking tidal waters from flooding fields (French for "water box").

anticline- folded layers of rock formed by upheaval of the earth's crust. In anticlines, the rocks fold upward with the oldest layers nearest the centre of the fold. Synclines are basin-shaped folds with the youngest rocks at the centre.

barachois- spit enclosing triangular beach, formed by meeting currents. Brackish body of water landward of barachois is called a barachois pond.

barrens- unproductive habitat of heath plants, shrubs, and stunted trees that results from soil depletion after repeated burning of the coastal forest.

barrier beach- sand or cobble beach protecting an estuary or coastal body of water from the open ocean.

batholith- scientific name for a large intrusion of igneous rock, typically granite, with an exposed surface area exceeeding 100 square kilometres.

berms- low, landward sloping area or side of beach made from sand deposited by wave action.

bog- wetland characterised by production of peat, an organic substance formed from partial decomposition of mosses, heath plants and sedges.

braiding- pattern of meandering in a mature river delta. From above, river channels interweave as though plaited.

carrying capacity- the volume and diversity of life that can live sustainably in a given habitat.

climax forest- a forest whose species composition is more or less stable and self-sustaining.

cobble beach- beaches composed of water-worn blocks of rock eroded from nearby landforms.

columnar basalt- symmetrical formations of basaltic lava that cooled in air to form conjoined columns.

conglomerate- coarse-grained sedimentary rock that looks like a natural cement or concrete.

continental drift- the movement of the continental plates of the earth's crust over time.

continental shelf- the submerged coastal plain stretching from the Atlantic coast approximately 100mi/160km offshore to present-day Sable Island; southwestern portions once (when seas were lower) formed a land bridge to Massachusetts.

deals- large planks rough-sawn in the woods and floated via flumes or sluices to sawmills for further processing.

deciduous- having leaves which die and drop each growing season.

delta- a large, roughly triangular deposit of clay, silt or sand at the mouth of a river (see braiding, meander).

dendritic- tree-like drainage pattern of rivers or streams.

dinoflagellates- microscopic one-celled algae propelled in water by a hair-like whip; "blooms" of some dinoflagellates are associated with "red tides" and paralytic shellfish poisoning (PSP).

diorite- a salt-and-pepper coloured igneous rock formed by intrusion into existing rock.

drumlin- a smooth hill of glacial till formed over slate bedrock, often found in "swarms", like fish facing "upstream" to the direction of the glacier's movement.

drumlinoids- drumlin-like formations found in non-slate areas.

dyke- 1. levee with a wall to hold back water and a ditch, used to drain intertidal wetlands; 2. a table-like body of igneous rock that cuts across adjacent rocks.

end moraine- ridge of glacial till from the leading edge of an ice sheet, left behind after melting.

erratic- large rock or boulder that has been transported some distance from its source, typically by a glacier.

esker- long, winding ridge of sand and gravel which originated within or beneath glacial ice.

estuary- bay at a river mouth formed by subsiding land and/or rising sea level. Fresh river water mixes with salty ocean water to form brackish, or low-salt conditions.

eutrophication- increased nutrient production in fresh water. Occurs naturally, but is greatly accelerated by organic pollution.

evaporite- rock formed by the evaporation of mineral-laden water, like rock salt or gypsum.

exotics- species which do not naturally occur in a given area.

fault- a fracture in the earth's crust along which movement has occurred.

feldspar- group of abundant rock-forming minerals that are the principal components of igneous rocks.

floodplain- land bordering a stream, built up by sediments deposited when the stream floods.

glacial dam- a ridge of till deposited by a glacier and damming or diverting a watercourse.

glacial drift- unsorted sediments (till) deposited as outwash by streams within or beneath glaciers.

gneiss- (pronounced "nice") course-grained metamorphic rock with a layered structure.

granite- course-grained igneous rock composed mainly of alkali feldspars and quartz.

greywacke- sandstone which carries rock fragments and grains of quartz and feldsspar.

ground moraine- rolling plain with gently sloping swells, sags, or basins made of till.

gypsum- commonest suplhate mineral; found with halite and anhydrite in evaporitedeposits; processed for use as wallboard.

habitat- the natural home or environment of a plant or animal.

hard pan- a layer of cemented material occuring in sediments that have not been consolidated into rock.

hardwood- deciduous, broad-leaved trees such as oak or maple and the forests they form.

hibernaculum- communal hibernation chamber to which bats return year after year; usually caves.

highgrading- tallest trees are removed from a stand.

holdfasts- structure of certain algaes (seaweeds) anchoring them underwater, for instance to rocks.

igneous- one of three main groups of rocks, formed by the crystallization of magma.

intervale- low-lying topography between ridges, hills or formations.

kame- steep-sided mounds formed like sand in an hourglass by material falling out of a glacier.

kaolin- a valuable, fine clay used in papermaking and other industrial applications.

karst topography- typical landscaape of gypsum and limestone areas, where rainwater has dissolved rocks to form sinkholes, separated by narrow, crumbling ridges.

krummholz- stunted, deformed tree growth from exposure to extremes, like high winds and salt spray.

limestone- bed deposit of sediment, chiefly composed of calcium carbonate.

longshore currents- ocean currents running parrallel to a coastline, critical to beach formation in certain areas.

magma- molten rock material generated within the earth, intruded or extruded as igneous rocks.

marine terrace- nearly level surface or bench bordering a steep slope, the remnant of a former sea level.

meander- loop-like bend in a stream, eroded from the floodplain by waterflow over level land.

Meguma- slate formation underlying the slope of Nova Scotia's Atlantic coast; regarded as a slab of ancestral north Africa, welded to North America when the Atlantic Ocean opened 200 million years ago.

metamorphic- one of three main groups of rocks. Properties in rocks are altered by temperature and pressure to form other rock types.

midden- garbage dump of shells and discarded bone, stone, and pottery fragments deposited in prehistoric times by aboriginal peoples.

mixed forest- a mixture of softwood and hardwood species.

monoculture- forest characterised by single species; frequently planted for later commercial harvest.

neap tide- tide near the time of the moon's quarters, and running typically 10-30% less than the mean tidal range.

outwash plain- level area of sediment layers deposited by glacial meltwater.

oxbow lake- a lake formed when a river meander is cut off from the main channel.

Pangaea- a supercontinent of all earth's landmasses squeezed together by continental drift, formed c. 400 million years ago, brokeup c.200 million years ago.

parent material- the original source formation for a deposit of rock or sediment.

parr- the post-larval stage of the salmon, when the feely swimming fish first feeds for itself.

pelagic- oceanic, referring to lifeforms which make landfall rarely, or live in the open ocean.

peneplain- a smooth, rolling surface, formed after sustained erosion.

planation surface- a peneplain associated with a particular geologic era, as in Cretaceous planation surface.

quartz- very hard, glassy mineral (silicon dioxide crystal) found in all acidic igneous rocks, some metamorphic rocks, and sandstone.

quartzite- a metamorphic rock made mostly of quartz.

rift valley- valley formed by the faulting of the earth's crust.

rip tide- churning torrent of crests and eddies formed by the convergence of tidal currents.

river capture- diversion of stream flow when a stronger-flowing stream erodes across a weaker stream, capturing " its flow.

sandstone- a sedimentary rock composed of sands-sized quartz grains.

sanitation cutting- removal of diseased or broken tree limbs to prevent disease spread.

scarp- a steep slope schist-a medium-to coarse-grained metamorphic rock containing platy minerals like mica.

scions- reproductive shoots of deciduous plants.

sea stacks- offshore pillars formed when a coastal landform erodes from around an intrusion of basalt.

sedimentary- one of three main groups of rocks; formed from sediments consolidated into rock by pressure.

semi-diurnal- tide in which high water occurs twice daily (roughly 12.4 hours apart).

shingle beach- beach composed of water-worn slabs eroded from layered rock along shore.

sinkhole- a depression caused by the erosion of evaporites by rainwater and runoff.

slate- a fine-grained metamorphic rock easily split into flat, smooth plates.

slope bog- a bog spread over sloping bedrock by layering of mosses and heath plants - each generation rooting not in ground but in the previous generation.

smolt - third stage in the salmon life cycle, after fry and parr, and before yearling.

softwood- coniferous evergreen trees like spruce and fir and the forests they form.

spring tide- tide at full or new moon; exceeds the mean tidal range by more than any other tides.

striae- small grooves on a rock surface formed by glacial action.

taiga- transition zone between boreal and tundra conditions, featuring dwarf vegetation.

talus- rock fragments from "mechanical" weathering, like glacial grinding.

tidal bore- the leading edge of a tidal current, in confined channels forming a "moving wall" of water on the incoming tide.

tombolo- a beach formed in the sheltered lee of an island, often connecting the island to mainland.

tuff- rocks consolidated from volcanic material, with fragments not greater than 2cm in diameter.

wind gap- a low depression or notch in a ridge where streams used to flow.

REFERENCES

Allen, C.R.K., 1981. "Muskegooakade", Journal of Education, Vol. 7, No. 1, NS Dept of Education, Halifax
      1987. Yarmouth County: A Naturalist's Notebook, Nimbus Publishing Ltd, Halifax

Anderson, A.R., 1990. Diatomaceous Earth Occurrences in Nova Scotia (Economic Geology Series 90-1), NS Dept of Mines & Energy, Halifax

Archibald, Mary, 1983. "The Shelburne Loyalists," Nova Scotia Historical Review, Vol. 3, No. 1, Halifax

Attenborough, David, 1979. Life on Earth, Little, Brown & Co., Boston

Beardmore, R.M., 1985 Atlantic Canada's Natural Heritage Areas, Canadian Government Publishing Centre, Ottawa.

Benson, D.A. & Dodds, D.G., 1976. Deer of Nova Scotia, NS Dept of Lands & Forests (NSDLF), Halifax

Bird, Will R., 1950. This is Nova Scotia, The Ryerson Press, Toronto
      1956. Off-Trail in Nova Scotia, Ryerson

Blomidon Naturalists Society, 1992. A Natural History of Kings County, Acadia University, Wolfville, NS

Brown, R.G., 1976. Blood on the Coal, Lancelot Press Ltd., Windsor, NS

Burzynski, M. & Marceau, Anne, 1984. Fundy: Bay of the Giant Tides, The Fundy Guild, Inc., Alma, NB

Coady, Howard, 1988. Sheet Harbour History: From the Notes of An Old Woodsman, Lancelot Press, Hantsport, NS

Cohrs, Shirley (Ed.), 1991. Birding Nova Scotia, Nova Scotia Bird Society, Halifax

Comfort, Judith, 1995. Rediscover The Lighthouse Route, Nimbus, Halifax
      Country Roads of the Maritimes, Nimbus, 1994

Creighton, Helen & Senior, Doreen; 1950. Traditional Songs from Nova Scotia, McGraw Hill Ryerson, Toronto

Creighton, Wilfrid, 1988. Forestkeeping: A History of the Department of Lands and Forests in Nova Scotia, 1926-1969, NSDLF, Halifax

Cunningham, Scott, 1996. Sea Kayaking in Nova Scotia: A Guide to Paddling Routes Along the Coast of Nova Scotia, Nimbus Publishing, Halifax

Davidson, A.G. & Prentice, R.M., 1967. Important Forest Insects and Diseases of Mutual Concern to Canada, the United States and Mexico, Queen's Printer, Ottawa

Davis, Derek S., 1993. Official Nova Scotia Nature Map, Land Registration & Information Service, Amherst/Province of Nova Scotia

DeGraaf, Richard M. & Rudis, Deborah D., 1986. New England Wildlife: Habitat, Natural History and Distribution, Gen. Tech. Rpt No. NE-108, U.S. Forest Service; Broomall, PA

Denys, Nicolas, 1672. Concerning the Ways of the Indians: Their Customs, Dress, Methods of Hunting and Fishing, and Their Amusements (Reprint, Nova Scotia Museum, Halifax , 1972)

Dodds, Donald, 1993. Challenge & Response: A History of Wildlife and

Wildlife Management in Nova Scotia, Nova Scotia Dept. of Natural Resources [NSDNR], Halifax

Donohoe, H.V. Jr & Grantham, R.G., 1989. Geological Highway Map of Nova Scotia, 2nd ed., Atlantic Geoscience Society, Halifax.

Dunn, Charles W., 1953. Highland Settler: A Portrait of the Scottish Gael in Nova Scotia, University of Toronto Press, Toronto

Ecotour of the Trans-Canada Highway: Nova Scotia, 1973. Environment Canada, Ottawa

Erskine, Anthony J., 1992. Atlas of Breeding Birds of the Maritime Provinces, Nova Scotia Museum/Nimbus, Halifax

Ferguson, Laing, 1988. The Fossil Cliffs of Joggins, Nova Scotia Museum, Halifax

Fernow, B.E., 1912. Forest Conditions of Nova Scotia, Commission of Conservation, Ottawa

Forest Resources of Nova Scotia, The; 1958. Eds. Bulmer, Richard M.; Hawboldt, Lloyd S.; Dept of Lands & Forests, Halifax, NS

Fundy Shore Eco-Guide: A Traveller's Companion to the Fundy Shore, 1995. Central Nova Tourist Association, Truro

Gilhen, John, 1974. The Fishes of Nova Scotia's Lakes and Streams, Nova Scotia Museum, Halifax

Goldthwait, J.W., 1924. Physiography of Nova Scotia, Dept. of Mines, Ottawa

Gordon, Joleen, 1993. "The Woven Weirs of Minas." Curatorial Report No. 73, Nova Scotia Museum, Halifax

Harris, R.C., Warkentin, J., 1974. Canada Before Confederation, Oxford University Press, London, New York.

Haliburton, Thomas C., 1829. An Historical and Statistical Account of Nova Scotia (Reprinted by Mika Publishing, Belleville, ON, 1973)

Haynes, Michael, 1995. Hiking Trails of Nova Scotia (7th ed.), Goose Lane Editions, Fredericton, NB

Hicklin, Peter & Smith, Allan D., 1988. "Naming and Protecting Wildlife Habitats: Hemispheric Shorebird Reserves and Ramsar Sites," NS Conservation, Vol. 12, No. 2 (Summer), NSDNR

History of Advocate and Area, Super Seniors, 1994. Lancelot Press

Hockney, Helen, 1996. "The Shelburne River," in NS Conservation, Vol. 20, No. 3 (Fall), NSDNR, Halifax

Hosie, R.C., 1979. Native Trees of Canada (8th edition), Fitzhenry & Whiteside Ltd/Environment Canada, Ottawa

Hruszowy, Susan, 1996. "Canoeing the St Marys River," in NS Conservation, Vol. 20, No. 1 (Spring), NSDNR, Halifax

Hutten, Anne, 1991. Valley Gold: The Story of the Apple Industry in Nova Scotia, Petheric Press, Halifax

Industrial Minerals of Nova Scotia, (undated). Information Circular No. 24, Mines Branch, NSDNR, Halifax.

Israel Longworth's History of Colchester County, Nova Scotia, 1989. Ed. Sandra Creighton, 1989. Book Nook, Truro, NS

Joe, Rita, 1996. <u>Song of Rita Joe: Autobiography of a Mi'Kmaq Poet</u>, Ragweed Press, Charlottetown, PEI

Johnson, Ralph, 1986. <u>Forests of Nova Scotia</u>, Four East Publications, Tantallon, NS

Kinsman, Brian, 1994. <u>McNabs Island, Halifax County, Nova Scotia: An Historical Review</u>, NSDNR, Halifax

Lacey, Laurie, 1993. <u>Micmac Medicines: Remedies and Recollections</u>, Nimbus, Halifax

Lawley, David, 1994. <u>A Nature and Hiking Guide to Cape Breton's Cabot Trail</u>, Nimbus, Halifax

Light, Joanne, 1993. <u>Coastal Nova Scotia: Outdoor Adventure Guide</u>, Nimbus, Halifax
       1995. <u>Hiking Nova Scotia: Thirty of Nova Scotia's Best Hiking Trails</u>, Nimbus, Halifax

Lucas, Zoe, 1988. "Vegetation and Terrain Management on Sable Island," <u>NS Conservation</u>, Vol.12, No. 2 (Summer), NSDNR, Truro

Maass, Oliver, 1992. <u>Reading the Earth: Opportunities and Options for Interpreting Geology at the Proposed Cape Chignecto Provincial Park</u>, NSDNR, Halifax

MacLeod, Robert R., 1903. <u>Markland or Nova Scotia: Its History, Natural Resources and Native Beauties</u>, Markland Publishing Company, Toronto

MacNeil, Neil, 1948. <u>The Highland Heart in Nova Scotia</u>, Charles Scribner's Sons, New York.

<u>Map of the Province of Nova Scotia, Canada</u> (4th edition), 1992. Formac Publishing/Province of Nova Scotia, Halifax

<u>Maritime Dykelands: The 350-Year Struggle</u>, 1987. Dept of Agriculture & Marketing, Halifax

Mintz, Patty, 1996. <u>Rediscover The Evangeline Trail</u>, Nimbus, Halifax

Mitcham, Allison, 1984. <u>Offshore Islands</u>, Lancelot Press
       1989. <u>Island Keepers</u>, Lancelot Press
       1995. <u>The Best of Abraham Gesner</u>, Lancelot Press
       1995. <u>Prophet of the Wilderness: Abraham Gesner</u>, Lancelot Press

Moores, Ted, 1983. <u>Woods and Water: A Common-Sense Guide Book of Canoeing</u>, Camden House, Camden East, ON

Moser, Edith, 1984. <u>Old Time Travel in Nova Scotia</u>, Lancelot Press

Municipality of Colchester, 1996. "Planning for the Future," <u>News Letter</u>, Truro, NS

<u>Natural History of Nova Scotia</u>, Eds. Davis, D; Browne, Sue, 1997. (Two volumes), Province of Nova Scotia, Halifax

Nickerson, Erdie <u>The Antics of a Cock-a-witter</u>, [Self-published, undated], Shelburne, NS

<u>Nova Scotia By Bicycle</u>, 1995. Bicycle Nova Scotia, Halifax

<u>Nova Scotia Resource Atlas</u> [undated]. Dept of Development, Halifax

<u>Nova Scotia: The Doer's and Dreamer's Complete Guide</u>, (annual). NS Dept of Tourism & Culture, Halifax

Nova Scotia CHRS Background Study: St Marys River System, 1968. N.S. Dept of Lands & Forests, Halifax.

Nova Scotia Tour Book, 1973. Department of Tourism, Halifax.

Ogden III, J.G., Harvey, M.J., 1975. Environmental Change in the Maritimes, Nova Scotian Institute of Science, Halifax

O'Neil, Pat, 1994. Explore Cape Breton: a Field Guide to Adventure, Nimbus, Halifax

Poole, Stephen, 1996. Nova Scotia: A Colour Guidebook, Formac Publishing Co Ltd, Halifax

Poteet, Lewis J., 1983. The South Shore Phrase Book Lancelot Press, Hantsport

Robertson, Barbara R., 1986. Sawpower: Making Lumber in the Sawmills of Nova Scotia, Nimbus/Nova Scotia Museum, Halifax

Robertson, Marion, 1991. The Chestnut Pipe: Folklore of Shelburne County, Nimbus, Halifax

Roland, A.E. & Smith, E.C., 1969. The Flora of Nova Scotia, Nova Scotia Museum, Halifax

Roland, A.E., 1982. Geological Background and Physiography of Nova Scotia, Nova Scotian Institute of Science, Halifax

Rowe, J.S., 1972. Forest Regions of Canada, Information Canada, Ottawa

Saunders, Gary L., 1996. Trees of Nova Scotia: A Guide to the Native and Exotic Species, Nimbus/NSDNR, Halifax

Scotia/Fundy Marine Weather Guide, Environment Canada (Atlantic Region), 1992

Sherwood, Roland H., 1973. Pictou Pioneers, Lancelot Press

Smith, Dale & Scrutton, Ted, 1995. "Rails to Trails in Nova Scotia," in NS Conservation, Vol. 19, No. 2 (Summer), NSDNR, Halifax

Smith Jr, Titus, 1955. A Natural Resources Survey of Nova Scotia, 1801-1802, NSDNR, Halifax [Compiled by Lloyd S. Hawboldt]

Stehelin, Paul H., 1983. The Electric City: The Stehelins of New France, Lancelot Press

Swartz, Hill, 1992. "Saving Munroe's Island," in NS Conservation, Vol. 16, No. 4 (Winter), NS Dept of Lands & Forests, Halifax.

Thurston, Harry, 1994. Dawning of the Dinosaurs: The Story of Canada's Oldest Dinosaurs, Nimbus/Nova Scotia Museum, Halifax
        1990. Tidal Life: A Natural History of the Bay of Fundy, Camden House, Camden East, ON

The Maritimes: Tradition, Challenge & Change, 1987. Eds. Peabody, George; MacGregor, Carolyn, Thorne, Richard; Maritext Ltd, Halifax

Towers, Julie, 1995. Wildlife of Nova Scotia, Nimbus/NSDNR, Halifax.

Trans Canada Trail, 1996. Trans Canada Trail Foundation, Montreal, QC

Tufts, R.W., 1973. The Birds of Nova Scotia, Nimbus/Nova Scotia Museum, Halifax

Wetlands of Canada, 1988. Ecological Land Classification Series No. 24, Environment Canada, Ottawa

Young, Tom, Fundy Shore Eco-Guide, 1995. Central Nova Tourist Association, Truro

INDEX

419

424

PHOTO CREDITS: